# THE STEPHEN KING COMPANION

## FORTY YEARS OF FEAR
### FROM THE
## MASTER OF HORROR

## GEORGE BEAHM

illustrated by Michael Whelan
and Glenn Chadbourne

Thomas Dunne Books/St. Martin's Griffin

NEW YORK

# TABLE OF CONTENTS

## PART FIVE: SCRIBNER: BUILDING BRIDGES

# A Note

## to the

## Reader

This book is the third iteration of *The Stephen King Companion*. The first edition was published in 1989; the second, in 1995; and this third, in 2015, owing to King's prolific output during the past twenty years.

In 1989, as reported to *Time* magazine, King's publishers celebrated the fact that King had published "20-odd books" that sold 60 million copies earning him $20 million. But by the end of 2015, King will have published, according to his Web site, 74 books (56 novels, 7 nonfiction, and 11 story collections) that have sold an estimated 350 million copies (biography.com).

But his real life is not about the fame or the fortune; it's all about storytelling.

This book celebrates his storytelling, from the early days when he was self-publishing in a few dozen copies in rural Maine, to *Revival*, which reached millions of readers worldwide.

My approach to the book is clearly pop culture, not academic; in other words, a college professor, I ain't. I've arranged the contents chronologically and in context, so you'll get a sense of his life and times; the text herein is spiced with interviews, anecdotes, factoids, and commentary by important figures in the King community. For a retrospective book like this, a wide range of voices is essential.

Because King's early years in Durham and in college are critical to understanding him and his work, I've devoted considerable space to both, to lay the necessary groundwork for the discussions of the books that follow. Consider both skeleton keys to unlocking King's fiction.

This book is an overview covering four decades, written with King's new fans in mind, especially younger readers who watched *Under the Dome* on TV or picked up his latest novel and wondered, Who is this guy, and what *else* has this guy written?

This book answers that question. But despite its length, it could have been far longer had space not been a consideration: Writing about Stephen's career requires king-size books: Stephen Spignesi's 1991 *The Complete Stephen King Encyclopedia* is 780 letter-sized pages, and Robin Furth's *Stephen King's* The Dark Tower: *The Complete Concordance* (revised and updated in 2012) runs 688 pages.

Given his popularity and visibility, King will assuredly be the subject of many more books in the years to come.

The text to this book is supplemented by artwork by Michael Whelan and Glenn Chadbourne, and by photos from my files taken since 1988. Both the art and photos herein give a dimension to this book that text alone cannot achieve.

By the way, there is some unavoidable duplication of text in this book because this is a companion book with both original and reprinted material.

One final note: Just as I finished up this book, Rocky Wood—a well-regarded and highly respected King critic—passed on. Unlike some others, Rocky always gave credit when due, and his sudden departure is an immeasurable loss. As Stephen King wrote, Rocky, you rock.

Rock on.

George Beahm

Writers are exorcists of their own demons.

—MARIO VARGAS LLOSA

Now the simple fact of horror fiction in whatever medium you choose . . . the *bedrock* of horror fiction, we might say, is simply this: you gotta scare the audience. Sooner or later you gotta put on the gruesome mask and go booga-booga.

—STEPHEN KING, *Danse Macabre*

GLENN
CHADBOURNE

# THE LEARN'D ASTRONOMER

*STEPHEN J. SPIGNESI*

This introduction is dedicated to
the memory of Rocky Wood

In order for the light to shine so brightly,
the darkness must be present.

—FRANCIS BACON

It was the possibility of darkness that made
the day seem so bright.

—STEPHEN KING, *WOLVES OF THE CALLA*

Is writing nature or nurture?
　　　Is the ability to write brilliantly inherent? Is it in the genes? Or is it just a craft that one gets better at with hard work?
　　　Lately, whenever I speak about Stephen King in different venues, I read aloud a brief

*King reading from "The Revenge of
Lard Ass Hogan" for an event with
JK Rowling and John Irving in NYC,
August 1-2, 2006.*

excerpt from the writings of Joe Hill, Stephen King's eldest son. I then ask the audience
if they believe that Stephen King wrote what they just heard.

The majority of times, they say yes.

King himself was once asked what would happen to his unfinished works if he
unexpectedly, y'know, took a ride on a pale horse. His response was revealing, and boiled
down to "Joe could finish them."

Is it a coincidence that the writers Stephen King and Tabitha King gave birth to a
son who ended up being a writer and, more important, a writer whose work reads like
that of his father's?

I don't think so.

And let us not overlook the fact that their other children are also writers. Owen is a
novelist; Naomi writes essays and sermons.

I teach composition at the university level, and I ceaselessly emphasize to my students
that writing is, indeed, a craft that can be learned. We wouldn't attempt to wire a house
without learning the skills of an electrician. Language skills and rules; syntax and diction
guidelines; and, of course, a voluminous vocabulary need to be learned and fully absorbed
before we can use these tools effectively. This is sadly proved by reading the writings
of people who may have a terrific imagination, but who never troubled to acquire the
fundamentals of grammar and writing. As Irving Berlin said, "Talent is only a starting

point." And King himself weighs in on this in *Danse Macabre*: "Talent is a dreadfully cheap commodity, cheaper than table salt. What separates the talented individual from the successful one is a lot of hard work."

That said, I also tell my students that no teacher can teach imagination. Creativity cannot be learned from a book, but—and this is key—if you have it, it can be cultivated.

In *Breaking Bad*, Gale Boetticher, probably without intent, made this exact point when he recited the Walt Whitman poem "When I Heard the Learn'd Astronomer" to Walter White:

> When I heard the learn'd astronomer;
> When the proofs, the figures, were ranged in columns before me;
> When I was shown the charts and the diagrams, to add, divide, and measure them;
> When I, sitting, heard the astronomer, where he lectured with much applause in the
>     lecture-room,
> How soon, unaccountable, I became tired and sick;
> Till rising and gliding out, I wander'd off by myself,
> In the mystical moist night-air, and from time to time,
> Look'd up in perfect silence at the stars.

Knowledge of the empirical world is one thing; an understanding of the human heart is quite another.

The creative among us can see beyond the "proofs," the "charts" and "diagrams"; some can see *truth*. And then they can create.

And that brings me to Stephen King. Aside from his prolificness (his output amazes and makes most writers' eyes turn green), his ability to take the classic and timeworn writer's cliché What if? and create compelling characters and narratives is, oftentimes, a beautiful and wondrous melding of inspiration and creativity, as well as an obvious master's-level proficiency of the English language.

The first Stephen King book I ever read was *The Shining*. I finished it, and then rhetorically asked myself, Did I really just read what might be one of the all-time greatest American novels, written while the author was still in his mid to late twenties? Who the hell is Stephen King? (And, yes, I can be prolix when I'm talking to myself rhetorically, truth be told.)

After *The Shining*, I went back and read *Carrie* and *'Salem's Lot*. And in 1981, I read *Danse Macabre*, in which King talks about the three levels of fear: terror, horror, gross-out.

As you can tell, I was hooked, and I have continued to be hooked going on forty years now.

A U.K. review of *Revival* nailed the King appeal:

> Despite the fact that he could comfortably rest on his laurels as the world's most successful writer of horror fiction, Stephen King continues to demonstrate that his compulsion to entertain remains firmly in place—a fact for which his legion of admirers is extremely grateful. Once more . . . King is not content simply to

repeat himself, and he still possesses the ability to conjure up utterly original scenarios dedicated to his primary purpose: chilling the blood of the reader.

Chilled blood? Where do I sign up? (We should have jackets made.)

The three elements of fear are deep in King's wheelhouse.

One of the most terrifying scenes King ever wrote was the Lincoln Tunnel scene in *The Stand.* Just describing it can bring chills: The Lincoln Tunnel is filled with cars containing the corpses of the victims of Captain Trips. Larry Underwood enters this black-as-pitch realm of the dead . . . and suddenly hears a car door open. Oh, yes.

And can there be a more horrifying scene than little Gage Creed getting pureed by a tractor-trailer after wandering into the middle of the road in *Pet Sematary?* Oh, no.

And when we talk gross-out, there are a couple that make the grade, so to speak. The cockroach scene in "They're Creeping Up on You," from *Creepshow,* and the "suicide by garbage disposal" scene in *Firestarter.* (The ax/blowtorch scene in *Misery* is a seriously close runner-up.) Oh, gag.

This profound ability to frighten is why King has long worn (sometimes uneasily) the mantle of "Master of the Macabre," "King of Horror," or "America's Bogeyman."

But the truth is that King is much more than just a horror writer. In an October 2013 article in *The New Yorker* titled "What Stephen King Isn't," Joshua Rothman lays out the truth we serious fans and Constant Readers (including George Beahm, the author of this tome) have known for decades: What Stephen King isn't is just a horror writer.

My good friend George Beahm and I have now come full circle. I was working on my *Complete Stephen King Encyclopedia*[1] in the mid-eighties when George was writing the first *Stephen King Companion,* and they came out around the same time.

George and I were pioneers. We both recognized very early on that Stephen King was a writer for the ages, and that he was, as *The New Yorker* seemed to discover twenty-five years later, more than just a horror writer.

I recently spoke about Stephen King at the university where I teach, and there was a very big turnout. The university librarian, in her thank-you note to me, commented on the many hands that went up for the Q&A session at the end of my talk. There were people of all ages at the talk, but most were students (18–21 years of age), and they were the ones asking the questions. Here's a funny incident: a young man asked me "Where does Stephen King get his ideas?" to which I replied, "Congratulations! You win the prize for asking the question King gets, and hates, the most!" We all laughed, but it's true. So I said that King, when asked the question, often replies, "Utica," but then I explained seriously that King is a master at the writer's classic What if? question. And then I said,

---

1 Editor's note: Stephen Spignesi's *The Complete Stephen King Encyclopedia* was published in two editions. The first, from Popular Culture Ink, was titled *The Shape Under the Sheet: The Complete Stephen King Encyclopedia;* the second, from Contemporary Books, was simply titled *The Complete Stephen King Encyclopedia.* Both were published in 1991. Throughout this book, I refer to Spignesi's with its simplified title.

"For example, what if Annie Wilkes from *Misery* suddenly burst through that library door swinging an ax?" King is able to take that What if? scenario and run with it. (And more than a few heads turned to look uneasily at the library door. That was when I knew I had achieved my mission.)

I think an important point to keep in mind is that George and I, as well as all our colleagues who write books about Stephen King and his work, are writing because King's Constant Readers want to know more. This is not up for debate. They want insights, explications, details, discussions, and other info they don't possess about King, his writings, and, now, the other published writers in his family. They want expert opinion on the film adaptations; they want conversations and debates; they want to stay in the Stephen King universe just a little bit longer.

Books like *The Stephen King Companion* and other King-focused volumes remind me somewhat of the special features on DVDs for TV shows and movies. We watch an episode (or 10!), and when we're done, we want to know more; we want to experience more. This is why the "behind the scenes" features and "making of" features on DVDs are incredibly popular.

Frankly, there are not many popular writers whose work warrants this kind of attention, whose audience wants more. If there were, there would be companion books, encyclopedias, "lost works" books, quiz books, and all other manner of tomes about these writers. For the most part, people read a novel, and then they either put it on the shelf, give it away, or donate it. People rarely do this with Stephen King books. In fact, with King, it's the exact opposite: If you ask a roomful of King fans, "How many of you have more than one copy of many of your King books?" a multitude of hands would go up.

This is amazing, and mostly unique to King.

Will King's work survive? It's a fair question. And the answer is, the best of it, most certainly. Will readers still be reading King fifty years from now? Again, certainly. Books like *The Stand, It, Misery, The Shining, 'Salem's Lot, Revival,* and many others do not simply go away. They become part of the culture of new generations. Just like the Beatles. (I have eighteen-year-old students who are Beatles authorities.)

And how do these young people get exposed to King and the Fab Four?

Their parents.

Many college-age students today grew up in homes with Stephen King books and Beatles CDs.

And thus the word is spread to younger generations, and the torch is passed.

A book like the one you're holding contributes to spreading the word that Stephen King rocks. As did the Beatles, and as did Walt Whitman.

The road goes ever on.

*Cover to Sunday supplement,* USA Weekend, *with King cover story,*
*"35 Scary Years with Stephen King."*

# INTRODUCTION

---

# THE GOLDEN YEARS

## GEORGE BEAHM

I'm closing in on sixty-two. I might have ten productive years
left, twenty if I'm lucky and don't get hit by any more minivans.

—STEPHEN KING, FROM HIS COLUMN, "THE POP OF KING,"
*ENTERTAINMENT WEEKLY*, JULY 24, 2009

## TIME ON MY SIDE

Although King planned to take a break in 2014, he changed his mind and hit the road
to promote *Revival* in November. At an age when most people are retired and enjoying
their golden years, King is still hammering down the highway, pedal flat down to the
metal. In recent years, he's settled in on publishing two books annually.

King turned sixty-eight on September 21, 2015. He shows no signs of slowing down,
much less retiring, which is good news for his millions of fans, whose worst nightmare
is that in his golden years he's going to put down the pen, or turn off the computer, and
tend to his garden as did Sherlock Holmes.

King's forty-year-long writing career—encompassing poetry, screenplays, nonfiction,
short fiction, and book-length fiction—staggers the imagination. From his body of work,
bibliographies and concordances of his oeuvre have been compiled, as have critical studies
of his fiction and nonfiction, and even entire books on single aspects of his output.

Though his life had nearly been cut short by a reckless driver who hit him with a minivan, King miraculously survived, endured a painful recovery, and slowly picked up where he left off. As King realized, nothing can protect you from the randomness of the universe—in his case, a fool behind a wheel who drove on the shoulder of the road where King had gone for an afternoon walk.

King's near-death experience shook him up. As King vividly recounted in his most personal and poignant essay, in *On Writing*, he came close to crossing over:

> I don't want to die. I love my wife, my kids, my afternoon walks by the lake. I also love to write; I have a book on writing that's sitting back home on my desk, half-finished. I don't want to die, and as I lie in the helicopter looking out at the bright blue summer sky, I realize that I am actually lying in death's doorway. Someone is going to pull me one way or the other pretty soon; it's mostly out of my hands.

King fortuitously survived, but his sobering experience understandably affected him deeply, and in his subsequent fiction, he increasingly ponders the greatest mystery of all: What lies beyond this world? What happens when you shuck your mortal coil and cross over?

We cannot know for certain, but what we *do* know, and what we plan our lives around, is the undeniable fact that time is an irreplaceable resource: We only have a finite amount of it. As Gandalf reminded Frodo in *The Fellowship of the Ring*, "All we have to decide is what to do with the time that is given us."

King, by choice and inclination, has spent his lifetime writing. It is his way of passing his time productively, of keeping his imagination active, of making sense of the universe in an attempt to understand it; writing also provided a one-way ticket out of the misery he suffered in the wake of the accident. In pain and on pain-killers, King wrote his way out of his bleak situation.

In *On Writing*, he concluded:

> Writing isn't about making money, getting famous, getting dates, getting laid, or making friends. In the end, it's about enriching the lives of those who will read your work, and enriching your own life, as well. It's about getting up, getting well, and getting over. Getting happy, okay?

Okay.

Let us hope that King's optimistic appraisal of his remaining years of productivity is realized. And let us realize, too, that there will come a point when—by choice or circumstance—he will put down his pen and write "The End" to his stellar writing career, and know that he gave it his all. He writes like a man possessed because he wants as many stories as possible to take flight and soar out of his imagination, because he wants to create.

Also, isn't it high time that we dispense with the hoary stereotype that he is just a horror writer? For various reasons—including his self-deprecating comments about being the "literary equivalent of a Big Mac and fries"—King's been tarred as a genre writer who writes only about spooks and monsters and things that go bump in the night. Make no mistake: He *does* write about monsters, but more often, especially these days, the monsters walk among us unnoticed; to paraphrase Walt Kelly's Pogo, we have met the monsters and they are us. (Read "A Good Marriage" in *Full Dark, No Stars* and you'll see what I mean.)

King will never shed, as he put it, his reputation as America's best-loved bogeyman, but we know better. The man who wrote "The Body," "Rita Hayworth and Shawshank Redemption," "The Reach," and "The Man in the Black Suit" is no mere genre writer, and it's a disservice to him to even think so, despite the assertions of the literati who consider him little more than a bestselling outsider in the world of fiction.

## The Outsider and Others

When Stephen King and his best friend, Chris Chesley, went to the Ritz Theater in Lewiston for Saturday matinees, King explained in interviews that he carried his birth certificate to prove that he shouldn't be charged an adult fare just because he was adult-size: He then stood six feet, two inches.

Stephen was ungainly, according to his brother, Dave, who told Spignesi in an interview for *The Complete Stephen King Encyclopedia* that "Stevie was husky, and he wasn't too well-coordinated. He looked like Vern in the film *Stand by Me*."

Abandoned by his father, and physically distanced from his peers because of his height and lack of coordination, it was his passion for writing that proved to be his ticket to gaining social acceptance—especially when he lampooned authority figures, in a parody of the high school newspaper. Hilarity ensued among his admiring classmates when he self-published *The Village Vomit,* but his fledgling career as a satirist came to an abrupt halt: He earned a trip to the principal's office because his "newspaper" took personal digs at teachers and staffers.

*The Village Vomit* earned King a three-day suspension. Moreover, his teachers were not amused, least of all the draconian Miss "Maggot" Margitan, who, as King wrote in *On Writing,* "commanded both respect and fear." She obviously didn't share Steve King's adolescent sense of humor; she was the one who had pressed for his suspension. She followed up with a veto when King was nominated for entry into the National Honor Society. She never forgot the sting of his juvenile jibes, and it came back to haunt him. King quickly learned that making fun of people at their expense would kick him in the ass.

The next time he published his perceptions about high school, it would be *Carrie,* a novel about high school hell that drew on his position as an outsider. King saw high school as socially stratified, a caste system with reigning prom queens, cheerleaders, and jocks on top as part of the "in crowd" and everyone else far below, including Steve King, as part of the "out crowd."

In the professional world of fiction writing, King was also an outsider. Perceived as a horror writer early on, he got no respect. Fuming, King, as a sign of protest, spent twelve thousand dollars to buy tables at a National Book Award ceremony; he invited his friend John Grisham and others, to make their presence known. If he couldn't get in through the front door, he was storming the gates from the back. He seemed to be saying, "We're here; we're writing; and you can't ignore us, because *we aren't going away*." (Years later, when King received the National Book Award for "distinguished contributions to American letters," some of the literati howled in protest.)

Writing about people whom we'd recognize—our family, our friends, our neighbors—who get caught up in extraordinary situations, Stephen King's body of work reflects our times to such an extent and in such vivid and memorable prose that in the future historians will look to him to show what it was like to live in the twentieth and early twenty-first centuries.

As King explained to *The Paris Review*, "If you go back over the books from *Carrie* on up, what you see is an observation of ordinary middle-class American life as it's lived at the time that particular book was written." He has captured American middle-class hopes and fears, brand names and subtle nuances, with remarkable fidelity. He is, simply, America's storyteller, though he's most often perceived and categorized as a horror writer.

## In the Beginning Was the Word

Although the book industry is going through a sea change, with the growing popularity of e-books and multiple devices, what hasn't changed is, as King puts it, the primacy of the written word. As he explained in a Facebook posting ("Official Stephen King," September 28, 2014), "Books have been around for three, four centuries . . . There's a deeply implanted desire and understanding and wanting of [a] book that isn't there with music. It's a deeper well of human experience."

King, in drawing from that well, has drawn unique and memorable portraits of people whom we remember, some drawn with fondness, some with love, and others with well-earned revulsion. From the put-upon, victimized Carrie White (*Carrie*, 1974) to a fallen-away minister named Charles Jacobs (*Revival*, 2014), we see an endless parade of the good and the bad reflected in the mirror King holds up to the world—and in the end, we see, with startling clarity, ourselves.

# THE
# STEPHEN
# KING
# COMPANION

# PART ONE

# MAINE ROOTS

Durham at that time was a different place than it is now. The old small farm ethic—which had been the rule for many generations past—was just on its way out; and what we had was a community where people got up in the morning and went to work in the factories in the surrounding towns. It was a working class rural town.

—Chris Chesley, interviewed in
*The Complete Stephen King Encyclopedia*

*A screenshot of King in his summer home in Florida with Dr. Gates, from PBS's televison show, "Finding Your Roots."*

# Family Roots

## Donald Edwin Pollock

At his winter home in Florida, Stephen King sat down with Dr. Henry Louis Gates Jr. for an appearance on the PBS television show *Finding Your Roots*. Combing genealogical and military records, Gates's research team turned up a wealth of information about King's father, Donald.

The compiled information, assembled scrapbook-style for King's perusal, was an eye-opener for King, who understandably wanted to know more about the father who abandoned his family in 1949, when Stephen was two years old. According to what he remembers his mom said, his dad went out for a pack of cigarettes and never returned.

Leafing through the leather-bound scrapbook, Stephen King turned the page and saw a black-and-white photograph of a six-foot-tall man with glasses.

Gates asks, "Now you know who that is."

*A military file photo of Donald Edwin Pollock (Stephen King's father), from PBS's television show, "Finding Your Roots" with Dr. Henry Louis Gates.*

Stephen King replies, "Not right offhand." He pauses. "Is that my dad?" In a shock of late recognition, Stephen exclaims, "He looks like me! . . . a little bit." He shakes his head, and has a wistful expression on his face.

"No kidding," says Gates.

It was Stephen King's father. But his birth name isn't Donald Edwin King. As Gates pointed out, a record of birth and military records show that his name was Donald Edwin Pollock.

Twenty-five at the time of his marriage to Nellie Ruth Pillsbury, Donald listed his occupation as "seaman" in the merchant marine. On David King's birth record, his father's occupation is listed as "master mariner." And on Stephen King's birth certificate, he's listed as "captain, merchant marine."

From there, Gates takes Stephen King on a genealogical trip into the past, showing that his roots go all the way back to Ireland on his father's side.

Despite the considerable passage of time, there are still unresolved issues and anger that fester in Stephen King, who is upset at the circumstances and consequences of his dad's unexplained departure.

Stephen King tells Gates, "I can remember as a kid, thinking of myself, well, if I ever meet my dad, I'm going to sock him in the mouth for leaving my mother. And as I got older, I would think, well, I want to find out why he left and what he did, and *then* I'll sock him."

King and Gates have a good laugh over that, but the question that's haunted Stephen King for all those years will forever remain unanswered: Who was Donald E. Pollock?

Stephen King's father died at age sixty-six in Wind Gap, Pennsylvania, but as to which cemetery, I couldn't determine. The largest, though, is Fairview Cemetery, near a town called . . . Bangor.

As to his public records, they show that he remarried, and genealogical records online indicate five children by that marriage.

As to what he left behind in the wreckage of his first marriage: What we *do* know is that Nellie Ruth Pillsbury King picked up the shattered pieces of her family's lives and heroically moved on. Scrambling to make ends meet in her new, and unexpected, role as the family's breadwinner, survival became an extended family affair, with her four sisters helping out.

David King recalls moving all over the map, until they finally dropped anchor and settled in for the long haul in Durham. Aided financially by her siblings, Nellie Ruth was a single mother who not only raised two young boys but also her aging parents in a small, two-story house in Durham, Maine, that lacked a shower. It'd be difficult enough to be a caregiver even with a spouse to share the burden, but to do it essentially alone was an act of quiet courage and iron resolve: She was not going to abandon her family as her husband did.

## A Child's Worst Nightmare

The emotions of fear and horror are inextricable in King's fiction, and justifiably so. There was, as Chesley pointed out, no respite for Stephen King's powerful imagination, which conjured up awful possibilities.

*A road sign showing the way to Freeport, Pownal, and Bradbury Mountain in southern Maine.*

But the fear began early on in King's life when he was abandoned by his father—a small child's worst nightmare. Parents, after all, are supposed to be a bedrock, a solid platform on which children build their lives. But when one parent leaves for whatever reasons, children often blame themselves ("Was it something I did?"); they endlessly torture themselves asking a question that can't be answered: "Why?"

Conjecture is no replacement for knowledge, and understandably the fear of abandonment prefigures largely in King's early fiction: Carietta White (*Carrie*), whose mother is a fundamentalist Christian, raising her alone; Danny Torrance (*The Shining*), whose dysfunctional father is slowly spiraling out of control; Charlene "Charlie" McGee (*Firestarter*), whose mother dies at the hands of the nefarious federal agents at "The Shop"; and others. The repercussions of parental abandonment reverberate in King's fiction, as they clearly do for Stephen King himself, who was never able to take out his long-simmering anger on his dad and punch him out. He can only live with the knowledge that, as Dick Hallorann tells Danny Torrance in the epilogue to *The Shining*,

> The world's a hard place, Danny. It don't care. It don't hate you and me, but it don't love us, either. Terrible things happen in the world, and they're things no one can explain. . . . But see that you get on. That's your job in this hard world, to keep your love alive and see that you get on, no matter what. Pull your act together and just go on.

With his mother as his shining example, Stephen King went on to do just that: He went on.

## FLOTSAM AND JETSAM

The expression around the King family was that "Daddy done gone," and what he left behind, the physical artifacts from his past, had been boxed and stored at a relative's house down the street. Aunt Ethelyn and her husband, Oren, kept the flotsam and jetsam of Donald King's life in their attic, where one day Stephen went to see what he could find, the only physical remains of what once was presumed to be a good marriage.

In Spignesi's *The Complete Stephen King Encyclopedia*, David King was asked, "What do you remember about your father?"

David King replied:

Nothing. I don't remember the man personally at all. I do remember that at one point—I guess when we got back to Durham, Maine—Stevie and I found a trunk up in Aunt Ethelyn's garage that contained a lot of books on seamanship and that sort of thing, and in fact, there was even one of his Merchant Marine uniforms in it.

We also had several still pictures of him and one sixteen-millimeter film that he had taken. One scene from that film that I can remember was of the ship he was on going through a storm. There were waves crashing over the bow and everything. And surprisingly (since this was the mid-1940s), there were also some shots on that reel in color—footage of both Stevie and I as little kids running around.

In *Danse Macabre*, Stephen King wrote that he found in their attic boxes of his father's past, now gathering dust and long abandoned: merchant marine manuals and scrapbooks of his travels worldwide, including an 8mm movie reel, sans sound, which he shared with David; they saw, for the first time, their father waving to them in absentia. From *Danse Macabre*:

He raises his hand; smiles; unknowingly waves to sons who were then not even conceived. We rewound it, watched it, rewound it, watched it again. And again. Hi, Dad; wonder where you are now.

Their dad, as it turned out, left Maine permanently and headed to Pennsylvania, where he would settle down permanently. But the boys had no way of knowing that. All they knew was that their father had left.

One thing Donald did leave behind, a blessing in disguise, was a box of cheap paperbacks, science fiction and horror, which Ruth said were his main interests, the kind of fiction he enjoyed reading. An aspiring writer, Donald King had tried his hand at writing fiction, even submitting items for publications, collecting a few rejection slips.

In time, if Donald King had applied himself to the craft of writing fiction, he might have produced a salable manuscript. But that never happened, possibly because, as Stephen, in *Danse Macabre*, recalls Ruth explaining, "Your father didn't have a great deal of stick-to-it in his nature."

That afternoon in the dusty attic was a defining moment for a young Stephen King, who in *Danse Macabre* recalls what happened afterward: "The compass needle swung emphatically toward some mental true north" when he found a "treasure trove" of horror novels published by Avon. It was his first fictional encounter with the bogeyman of Providence, Rhode Island, a tall, saturnine-looking man named Howard Phillips Lovecraft, better known as H. P. Lovecraft.

A Lovecraft collection was, recalled King, "the pick of the litter." Lovecraft, "courtesy of my father . . . opened the way for me, as he had done for others before me: Robert Bloch, Clark Ashton Smith, Frank Belknap Long, Fritz Leiber, and Ray Bradbury among them."

Had Stephen King not found the box of horror books, would he have eventually turned to horror fiction? Or would he had turned in another direction, perhaps the books he'd eventually write under the Richard Bachman pen name?

It's a moot point because King found himself comfortably at home with the horror writers, the fantasists, the dark dreamers. Stephen, as a fledgling writer, would ironically follow in his father's footsteps, but where his father ultimately failed, Stephen would eventually succeed, and brilliantly so, because unlike his father, Stephen had, as his mother termed it, a "stick-to-it" nature, which must have come from his mother.

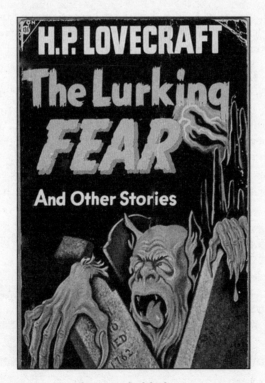

*Avon paperback book cover*

## 2

# DURHAM, MAINE

### STAND BY ME

The King family, particularly David and Stephen, bounced around like pinballs among relatives on both sides of the family all over the map. As David King recalled in an interview with Spignesi in *The Complete Stephen King Encyclopedia*:

> When we were very small, I heard that we lived in Scarborough for a while, and then we lived in a place called Croton-on-Hudson, New York. That part is just hearsay, of course, because I really don't remember that. And then there was a period of time when Stevie stayed with Ethelyn, my mother's sister, and Oren Flaws, in Durham, and I stayed with Molly, another of her sisters, down in Malden, Massachusetts. Mother was working. I don't remember too much of that. I do remember one thing, though. Mom came to visit me at Molly's once,

*A sign welcoming drivers to Lisbon Falls, Maine.*

*An open field in Durham, Maine, taken in front of the two-story King home.*

*A fall in Lisbon Falls, Maine.*

and I remember at breakfast time Molly always used to put wheat germ on our cereal, and I told my mother that my aunt was feeding us germs.

After that we went to live with my grandmother on my father's side in Chicago for a period. I was in kindergarten at the time. I can remember at one time seeing a picture of me in my kindergarten class. All of us in the class had made Easter bonnets out of paper and whatnot. I don't know if that picture is still in existence or not.

I can vaguely remember that we had a dog, and that the dog was kept in the front yard, and so you had to be very careful where you walked.

After Wisconsin, we then went to live with my father's sister Betty, and a lady she stayed with named Rudy. We have a picture of that somewhere, too—Stevie and I sitting on a lawn in front of a house. That was in the Fort Wayne, Indiana, area. Aunt Betty was a schoolteacher, as was Rudy, and I skipped second grade because she thought that I should.

After that we lived in an apartment of our own in Fort Wayne. I can remember some of that. We shared the apartment with a number of cockroaches. It was an apartment house, but I'm not sure if it was a single-family dwelling or if there were a couple of apartments in it.

They finally planted geographic roots in Durham, Maine, in 1958. For the next eight years, it would be the place they called home.

The Kings' small home was a stone's throw from Methodist's Corner (named after a local church). It housed Ruth, her two sons, and also her parents, then in their eighties, and in declining health.

Like most towns in Maine, Durham is rural. Chris Chesley, who was a young teenager living there in the late fifties, recalled that most people in town commuted to bigger, nearby towns to make a living. Chris's recollection was that they were all "poor." Or, at least, not well off.

In 1962, noted Stephen King in *On Writing*, Durham's population was approximately 900. Its population according to the 2000 census was only 1,496 households (3,381 people).

Unlike most writers who grew up in comfortable surroundings, whether in urban or

*Runaround Pond in Durham, Maine.*

*Lisbon Falls High School, which King attended.*

suburban environments, Stephen King and his family had a hardscrabble life. There were no luxuries. Understandably, his early fiction reflected a desire to escape, and he did it through his rich imagination, which transported him away from the rural dreariness of Durham.

It was the only world he knew, though in later years he made more frequent trips to nearby Lisbon Falls, where he saw life unfold in small-town Maine. A working-class town, with the Worumbo Mill as its primary employer, it was surrounded by small-town stores, shops, and businesses. (The mill burned down in 1987.)

Durham is mostly open fields, farmland, inexpensive single-family homes strung out on remote roads, and churches that formed its social hub. Its principal landmark is a large lake called Runaround Pond.

In later years, Stephen King's references to himself as a "hick" can be seen as self-deprecation. Clearly, he was never a stereotyped Mainer, parodied in *Creepshow*, in which he played a hayseed farmer named Jordy Verrill.

Back then, in the late fifties and early sixties, Stephen King knew that financially his family wasn't well off, but he did not consider them poor. Grounded in the reality of living in rural Maine, King's early values—hard work, honoring the family, self-sustainment, and lack of pretense—would later be reflected in the naturalism of his fiction. King wasn't the literary equivalent of John Updike writing about the solidly middle-class folks who come "from away" (a Maine term for non-Mainers). King didn't write about the affluent tourists who come to Bar Harbor or other scenic destinations; instead, he wrote about the blue-collar working class because that was what he saw growing up in Durham.

Without the distractions of big-city life, or even small-city life on the scale of nearby Lisbon Falls, Durham was simple and unglamorous. His friends back then accepted him for who and what he was: a big, goofy kid who found self-worth in writing. He wore thick, black glasses and spent most of his time inside a cramped upstairs bedroom that he shared with his older brother David, who, along with an old, battered manual typewriter and his overactive imagination, were Stephen's constant companions.

King's life and times as a teenager were captured with fidelity in his story "The Body," set in rural Maine and fictionalized as Castle Rock (the film version was shot in Oregon). In "The Body," King wrote: "I never had any friends later on like the ones I had when I was twelve. Jesus, did you?"

Adapted by director Rob Reiner as *Stand by Me*, "The Body" perfectly encapsulates the life and times of a young Stephen King growing up in rural Maine: the first-person narrator, in fact, is King as Gordie LaChance, who finds validation in himself through his storytelling.

Gordie's great fear, even as a young teen, is that he, like many of the others, would be trapped in Castle Rock and never realize his dreams. At one point Gordie's best friend Chris asks him, "I'm never gonna get out of this town am I, Gordie?"

Gordie replies, "You can do anything you want, man."

In the end, it is not Gordie who becomes a permanent resident of Castle Rock: that would be John "Ace" Merrill, who bullied him when they were younger and has become a fixture in the small town. As an adult, Gordon sees Ace leaving work from his job at the local mill and heading into a bar called the Mellow Tiger; Ace is now a thirty-two-year-old man, no longer lean and mean as he was in his teens, but overweight and resigned to his mundane life. Gordie looks on and thinks, "So that's what Ace is now."

Their world has moved on, and when life's cards have been dealt, it's Ace who holds the losing hand: He's the joker. The winning hand is held by Gordie, who grew up, matured, and finally escaped the confines of rural Maine:

> I'm a writer now, like I said. A lot of critics think what I write is shit. A lot of the time I think they are right . . . but it still freaks me out to put . . . those words, "Freelance Writer," down in the *Occupation* blank of the forms you have to fill out at credit desks and in doctors' offices.

But time is a river, and like the rushing waters of the Androscoggin River that runs through Lisbon Falls, past the abandoned Worumbo Mill where Stephen King once worked, life, too, moves on.

*Worumbo Mills and Weaving*

## Seduction of the Innocent

I think Hitler was a beginner compared to the comic-book
industry.

—Dr. Fredric Wertham,
ON AN INDUSTRY HE RAILED AGAINST

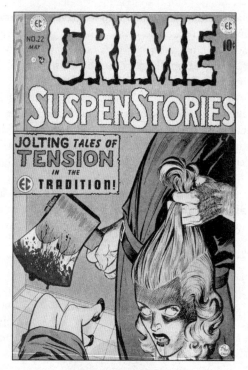

Crime SuspenStories
*(April/May 1954)*

The infamous cover to *Crime SuspensStories*, an EC Comics book, showed a man with a bloody ax in one hand . . . and a severed woman's head in the other. Just so the readers get the point, her lifeless body lays on the floor.

The message, the psychiatrist Fredric Wertham pointed out to a Senate subcommittee on juvenile delinquency, was that comics—all comics, not just the grisly fare EC Comics published—were in effect a seduction of the innocent: children had to be protected from the insidious scourge of comic books. In his 1954 *Seduction of the Innocent: The Influence of Comic Books on Today's Youth,* he writes about Batman:

> Several years ago a California psychiatrist pointed out that the Batman stories are psychologically homosexual. Our research confirms this entirely. Only someone ignorant of the fundamentals of psychiatry and of the psychopathology of sex can fail to realize a subtle atmosphere of homoerotism which pervades the adventures of the mature "Batman" and his young friend "Robin."

Wonder Woman and Black Cat get no better treatment. "The Lesbian counterpart of Batman may be found in the stories of Wonder Woman and Black Cat. The homosexual connotation of the Wonder Woman type of story is psychologically unmistakable."

To which any sane person should reply: horse pucky, as did Michael Chabon, who, in *The New York Times* (February 19, 2013), said: "You read the book, it just smells wrong. It's clear he got completely carried away with his obsession, in an almost Ahab-like way."

Now thoroughly discredited, most significantly by Carol L. Tilley, from the University of Illinois's Graduate School of Library and Information Science, Wertham's "findings" were twisted to serve his purposes. As Tilley told Dave Itzkoff, a writer for *The New York Times*, Wertham "manipulated, overstated, compromised and fabricated evidence," leading her to conclude that he was "carried away with his own preconceptions, his own agenda, that became perhaps disconnected from the kids that he was treating and observing" ("Scholar Finds Flaws in Archenemy of Comics," February 19, 2013). Wertham's book was a sign of the times. It was the era of Senator Joseph McCarthy, who saw communists under every bed. For good reason, cartoonist Walt Kelly, in his strip *Pogo*, depicted the senator as a bobcat named Simple J. Malarkey.

The fifties was a time of national fear. The bogeyman didn't lurk in the closet to come out under cover of darkness; he lived in radioactive clouds and communism, and in an atmosphere of suspicion and censure that bracketed the baby boomers' lives, including a young, impressionable Stephen King.

Back then, pop culture, especially movies, reflected the fear of atomic attack such as Japanese movies that proclaimed their public fear of nuclear annihilation, and for just cause: In 1945, two atomic bombs spread radioactive death on Hiroshima and Nagasaki.

Back in the day, in the fright-filled fifties, popular culture—including movies, comic books, cheap horror and science fiction paperbacks, and television shows—was the fountain from which impressionable youth drank. Among them: youngsters named George Lucas (three years older than King) and Steven Spielberg (one year older than King), who wholeheartedly embraced popular culture, adamantly rejecting Wertham's thesis that comics—and by extension, popular movies and television—constituted a wholesale "seduction of the innocent."

If comics were a seduction, then Stephen King was willingly seduced . . . and so were millions of other kids who found pop culture theirs to embrace. It was, in short, their preferred literature.

It was also the final years of radio dramatizations as a form of mass entertainment. As King pointed out in *Danse Macabre*, "I am of the last quarter of the last generation that remembers radio drama as an active force—a dramatic art form with its own set of reality."

In 1947, for instance, there were 40 million radios in American homes, but only 44,000 television sets. In the fifties, when King was growing up, TV displaced radio, and by 1958 television was the undisputed king. Back then, viewers used antennas on top of televisions ("rabbit ears") to get reception and could choose among only three networks: ABC, CBS, and NBC, and programs were broadcast in black-and-white.

## Classics Illustrated

Ruth King clearly had a mind of her own, and did not share the views of Dr. Fredric Worthless—er, Wertham. She enjoyed reading comics aloud to her sons, who loved

Classics Illustrated *comic book (no. 118).*

listening to her. From the time Stephen was six years old until he was ten, Ruth read comics to her sons. Celebrated for her dramatic skills in high school, Ruth was an excellent reader and chose her reading material well. She read from the Classics Illustrated line (Classic Comics until 1947), which issued adaptations of classics in the public domain, among them: *Ivanhoe, The Count of Monte Cristo, Moby Dick, A Tale of Two Cities,* and *Robin Hood.* The comics were well drawn and, clearly, wholesome fare, though Wertham's book specifically cited their unwholesome and corrupting adaptions of *Uncle Tom's Cabin* and *Dr. Jekyll and Mr. Hyde.* The comic books, accessible and bought at local drugstores or other retailers, were pathways to "real" books. Classics Illustrated enjoyed a long run and went on to produce 169 issues.

Comic books were King's constant companions as a child, when he suffered an extended illness and thus missed much of first grade. Bedridden for the better part of a year, he found entertainment in "six tons of comic books" (*On Writing*). As he explained, "At some point I began to write my own stories. Imitation proceeds creation; I would copy *Combat Casey* comics word for word in my Blue Horse tablet, sometimes adding my own descriptions where they seemed appropriate."

Comics—an artful blend of art and text—rely heavily on the visual, which contributed to how King saw the world, through the lens of four-color comics.

King initially came to writing not from the classics in prose form but through comic book adaptations of the same. At an early age, inspired by movies and comics, he began to write visually, which became one of his trademarks.

As King pointed out in *On Writing*, his mother was impressed with his early, imitative efforts, but thought little of the physical violence in *Combat Casey*. She also felt that, if he was going to write, he should do it his way. "I bet you could do better," she told him. "Write one of your own."

He would do just that.

## AN HONEST BUCK

As Stephen King recounted in *On Writing*, he was mindful of his mother's admonition when he penned a four-page story about a character named Mr. Rabbit Trick who was the leader of "magic animals who rode around in an old car, helping out little kids."

After confirming that this was an original story, Ruth praised it. "She said it was good enough to be in a book. Nothing anyone has said to me since has made me feel any happier," Stephen asserted in *On Writing*.

He immediately sat down and pulled four more rabbit stories out of his hat, for which his mother gave him four quarters, and distributed the stories to her four sisters. It was an honest buck earned, and his mother's encouragement and approval was like manna from heaven for the seven-year-old eager to please his mother and prove himself. No doubt his aunts were bemused by his fledgling literary effort. It was a good start, but not King's milieu. Bunny rabbit stories, like Trix cereal, are for kids. He was destined for more gruesome fare. (Rabbit stew, anyone?)

In time, the needle swung, hovering over the true north of his fictional interests. In *The Art of Darkness*, King recalls the first horror/science fiction story he ever wrote, at age seven: "I wrote about this big dinosaur that was really ripping ass all over everything. . . ."

Though low on scientific plausibility, the dinosaur is eventually dispatched by leather clothing and boots thrown at it. It was a start. His patented stories would get better over time, but given King's lack of interest and aptitude with science in general, storytelling, not science, would always carry the day, if not the tale.

## KING SUBMITS FICTION PROFESSIONALLY

In terms of his interests in writing, the turning point came when King was twelve, when he got his first typewriter, a heavy-duty Underwood, which allowed him to produce professional-looking manuscripts, which was critical because magazine publishers didn't accept handwritten manuscripts.

But King's typewriter couldn't bear up under his constant key pounding, which eventually broke off the ends of some type bars, which meant he had to fill in missing letters by hand.

Douglas E. Winter, in *The Art of Darkness*, explains that King submitted to *Fantastic*, edited by Cele Goldsmith. She was also its slush-pile reader and would have been the one who read King's early submissions and would likely have been surprised to learn that he was a young teenager.

We don't know what short fiction he submitted to Goldsmith. We only know that his stories were rejected with preprinted rejection slips, with variations of "thank you but no thanks." In Sam Barry and Kathi Kamen Goldmark's book, *Write That Book Already!*, King recalled of this time:

> When I was sixteen, I pounded a spike into my bedroom wall and started spiking rejection slips. The spike tore out of the wall four years later. I was home on semester break from college when it went. I counted, and there were over 150 rejection slips on it (which didn't count the slips that came to my college dorm). After that I just piled them up. I sold my first story about eight months later.

Among them, King submitted to the most prestigious publication in the field, *The Magazine of Fantasy and Science Fiction*. As with *Fantastic*, *Fantasy and Science Fiction* initially rejected King's work with form rejection slips that were like stretch socks—one size fit all.

Like *Fantastic*, *Fantasy and Science Fiction* didn't pay fantastic word rates; they paid only a few pennies per word. But, unlike *Fantastic*, *Fantasy and Science Fiction* encouraged King. The editor at that time was a well-known fantasy writer named Avram Davidson, an award-winning writer who was at the helm of the magazine from 1962, when King was only fifteen, to 1964.

In *Art of Darkness*, Winter noted that Davidson had rejected a story on the grounds that it was more horror than science fiction, which was true: King was no Peter Parker in the lab. In fact, in King's fiction, the science is not rigorous.

Science fiction—especially hard science fiction, the kind written by Robert A. Heinlein, Arthur C. Clarke, and Isaac Asimov—was not King's "thing." King's "thing" was anything that slithered, oozed, and went bump in the night: monsters, not handsome, rock-jawed spacemen in shining uniforms dispatching bug-eyed monsters slavering after shapely, buxom blond women in tight-fitting clothes.

No wonder, then, that King instead found his interest in the dark side of human nature, including teenage killer Charles "Charlie" Starkweather, a figure of fascination to a young, impressionable Stephen King. Using a .11 rifle, a .410 shotgun, a handgun, and a knife, Starkweather dispatched his eleven victims in a one-month period between 1957 and 1958, accompanied by his fourteen-year-old girlfriend.

When Stephen constructed a scrapbook of Starkweather's rampage across Nebraska and Wyoming, it gave Ruth King pause. As Stephen King told Winter in an interview for *The Art of Darkness*, "My mother was ready to have me placed in analysis."

## No *FLOWERS IN THE ATTIC*

The Avon paperbacks, digest-size anthologies termed "samplers," were intended to provide a cross-section of storytellers who wrote in the same vein, with the hope of tapping into new blood: first-time readers who would come back for more. Recalling with great fondness one Avon book, an H. P. Lovecraft anthology with a lurid cover that depicts a cemetery with a creature emerging from beneath a tombstone, King noted in *Danse Macabre* that it "remains the one which best sums up H.P.L.'s work for me." Stephen's "first encounter with serious fantasy-horror fiction" showed him that more than two decades earlier, supernatural fiction, regarded by many as escapist trash, was written with serious intent. Lovecraft, he realized, wasn't screwing around. "He *meant* it, and it was his seriousness as much as anything else which that interior dowsing rod responded to," King wrote in *Danse Macabre*.

Reading in the horror field meant discovering other writers, and it wasn't long before King encountered the work of a California writer named Richard Matheson who wrote about horror in a contemporary vein: The monsters weren't in moldering graveyards and decrepit castles in Europe but in American cities.

His best-known novel, *I Am Legend,* published in 1945, single-handedly popularized the vampire genre and the disease-borne apocalypse, both major themes that would show up later in King's novels for Doubleday, *'Salem's Lot* and *The Stand*.

In *Dark Dreamers,* Matheson told Stanley Wiater, "King said that because of reading *I Am Legend,* he realized it was not necessary to write everything like H. P. Lovecraft; that you could have a contemporary shopping mall, housing-tract setting and still do a horror story. So that was very crucial in his decision as to what he was going to write."

King, in an interview with Winter, in *Art of Darkness,* elaborated:

> I realized then that horror didn't have to happen in a haunted castle; it could happen in the suburbs, on your street, maybe next door.

In other words, it could happen anywhere—even in your own home.

It was time to drive a stake through the heart of horror fiction set in cobwebbed Europe. It was time to bring the horror to small-town America, and King would do just that.

King embarked on a path that would make him the King of Horror, the darkest of the dark dreamers.

## Silver Screams at the Ritz and "Poepictures"

It's no coincidence that King's writing is cinematic. During his impressionable youth, King haunted the the Ritz theater in nearby Lewistown. In *On Writing,* he explained:

> I wanted monsters that ate whole cities, radioactive corpses that came out of the ocean and ate surfers, and girls in black bras who looked like trailer trash.

King and his friend Chris Chesley enjoyed what they termed "Poepictures." It was a reference to Roger Corman's movies, such as *The Pit and the Pendulum, The Premature Burial, Tales of Terror, The Raven, The Masque of the Red Death,* and *The Tomb of Ligeia,* which were loosely inspired by Edgar Allan Poe's fiction.

Back then, kids didn't sit sedately in their seats; the matinees were participatory theaters, with kids shouting out warnings to the actors on screen when danger lurked. For most kids, the matinee was just a good time, but for King, the experience of seeing movies was a lot more valuable. In *The Complete Stephen King Encyclopedia,* Chesley observed that:

*A bridge over the Androscoggin River in Lisbon Falls, Maine.*

Steve was very influenced by the movies. He would write up sequences for these stories. For instance, he did one called "The Pit and the Pendulum," but he didn't use Edgar Allan Poe's story. Instead of telling the story from the book, he would write the movie scenes down in words. And so even though he read a lot when he was young, and he learned from what he read, he also learned as much or more from the way scenes are written for television and the movies. And, of course, as I said, it's no secret that his writing is like that now. His writing is extremely cinematic, extremely visual. It's almost like you're watching a movie when you read it.

It's not traditionally literary prose at all, which I think is one of his greatest gifts. When people talk about Stephen King, they don't talk about that aspect of his writing enough. I think one of the most powerful aspects of his writing is that he doesn't write prose like anybody else does. He writes cinematically.

## "THE KILLER"

When King was fourteen years old and in the eighth grade, he submitted a short story titled "The Killer" to Forrest J. Ackerman, the editor of *Spacemen* magazine. In his cover letter, King explained that he was fourteen years old, and a subscriber to the magazine. King wrote that he had been writing "as far back as I can remember, and submitting manuscripts for the last couple of years."

Ackerman was likely amused and charmed by the notion that the fledgling writer sent him a story for publication, just as he had to admire the young boy's determination to get in print; after all, didn't he say he had been at it for the previous two years? Nonetheless, Ackerman rejected the story because he didn't publish fiction written by children.

Ackerman kept all submissions that came over the transom, the slush pile, and true to form he kept King's. (The original cover letter was sold at auction in 1988 for $440.) We do not know if Ackerman sent the young writer a rejection slip, but the story *was* eventually published in 1994, thirty-three years later, in Ackerman's mainstay magazine, *Famous Monsters of Filmland*, issue 202. In an article accompanying the one-page, single-spaced story, Ackerman wrote:

> Stephen King was in my home sometime in the early '80s, and I surreptitiously produced this manuscript. "Steve," I said, "I'd like to try a little experiment with you. I'd like to read you a portion of a story and see if you can identify its author. Is it an obscure tale told by Poe? An unknown work by H. P. Lovecraft? Something written by Robert Bloch?"

It was "The Killer," by Steve King, who recognized it as his own work and then inscribed it "For FJA—with all best wishes, Stephen King." Ackerman concluded his humorous piece on the little-known story behind King's early submission thus:

> In the meantime, Stevie, here's your check for $25. Don't spent it all on comics. Or perhaps you'll want to frame it. If you have any more stories suitable for *Famous Monsters*, we'll welcome them with open arms. And a similarly generous check.
>
> I won't even edit your manuscript.

King finally published his fiction in 1965, when he was eighteen years old, but not in a professional magazine—in a fanzine, *Comics Review*, which paid in copies only. The story was luridly titled "I Was a Teenage Grave Robber."

Famous Monsters of Filmland *202 (Spring 1994), publishing King's first professionally submitted story, "The Killer."*

In *The Complete Stephen King Encyclopedia,* Chesley recalled that "the story . . . is amateurish and very derivative, specifically of B monster movies—but the narrative power is overwhelming."

*Comics Review* was an amateur publication produced on a Ditto machine (named after its manufacturer). Creating a Ditto involved typing on a two-ply "master." The front sheet was white paper, and could be typed, written, or drawn upon; the second sheet was the "master" itself, a waxy sheet that came in different colors, which was used to run off printed copies.

Popular with schools and civic groups, the Ditto machine allowed inexpensive printing in-house. It wasn't possible to print photos, though; moreover, text corrections involved using a razor blade to scrape off the mistakes and retyping, which was so tedious that typists strived to get it right the first time.

Edited and published by Mike Garrett, whom King credits in *Danse Macabre* as being his first editor, *Comics Review* was one of many small-press publications produced by and for comic book, science fiction, and fantasy fans.

Fanzine publications earned their amateur writers "egoboo" (an ego boost) from getting into print and seeing letters of comment in subsequent issues; they offered showcases for aspiring writers, some of whom, like King, would go on to more professional publications.

In 1963, when King was sixteen, he completed his first book-length work of fiction. Though it was clearly juvenilia, it was long—approximately fifty thousand words. A science fiction story, it posed a question: "Are the evils of government any worse than the evils of anarchy?" (Not surprisingly, King's later fiction also exhibits a distinct lack of trust with the government at large.)

Composed of three parts, the postapocalyptic novel begins on August 14, 1967, with a teenager named Larry Talman, who infiltrates and attempts to destroy a dubious paramilitary organization called Sun Corps: Talman's suspicions are realized when the organization turns out be a front for an alien invasion by the Denebians.

Despite its derivative nature and soapbox lecturing, the story showcased King's natural ability to spin a yarn. It was pure pulp fiction. As Chris Chesley pointed out in *The Complete Stephen King Encyclopedia,* when King was "twelve years old . . . he already had a way with words. . . . The essential ability to write was there in the first thing I ever read by him."

The kid always was one hell of a storyteller.

## A Young Journalist

I was as a teenager haunted by newspapers.

—Stephen King, *On Writing*

Though King could clearly write nonfiction, he preferred fiction because telling stories was all fun. Writing nonfiction, though, was less challenging and more mundane, because it felt more like work. King did, though, write fiction for *Dave's Rag,* a home-brewed paper run by his brother, or at least such fiction was announced in its pages. ("Land of 1,000,000 Years Ago" was one such offering.) But, on the whole, journalism wasn't Stephen's thing, though he was listed as a "reporter" for it.

The first issue of *Dave's Rag* circulated only as two individually typed copies. Dave graduated to printing multiple copies with a hectograph, known as a gelatin duplicator. The process, though, was maddeningly slow, and David soon increased his output with a secondhand mimeograph machine, which used a wax stencil that could be typed or drawn on. It was a substantial improvement over the prehistoric hectograph. Equipped with a hand crank, the mimeo allowed multiple copies to be printed rapidly, at least until the crank broke and the printing drum had to be rotated by hand.

As King explained in *On Writing*, his interest in contributing to *Dave's Rag* ran a distant second to his consuming interest: sitting in a darkened theater watching Saturday matinees.

*Dave's Rag*, like a favorite toy that had outlasted its appeal, eventually ceased publication when Dave King moved on to other interests. Smart but restless and impatient, Dave indulged his varied interests instead of focusing on one area, unlike Stephen, who was always either reading, writing, or watching Saturday matinees in nearby Lewiston.

Later, when word got out in high school that Stephen had previously worked as a reporter on a newspaper—no matter its modest origins—he was drafted for the editorship of *The Drum*.

Stephen King recounted in *On Writing* that he was game, albeit reluctant, and gave it his best shot—in fact, only one shot, since the students only saw one monster-size issue published during his stint as editor, in his sophomore year. To King, nonfiction was more

*Lisbon Falls High School.*

work, and no play, which dulled his interest. He much preferred having fun writing the aforementioned parody newspaper *The Village Vomit*. Eventually, King's writing talents were put to productive use as a sports journalist for a local newspaper.

"I was a journalist for a while," King told *The Maryland Coast Dispatch* in 1986. "The first thing I was ever paid for was a sports column . . . I protested that I didn't know anything about sports and the guy says, 'Do you know how to write?' I said I thought I did. He said, 'We're going to find out.' He said if I could write, then I could learn about sports. So I wrote about bowling leagues and basketball games and stuff like that."

## GETTING IT ON: RAGE

At the end of his senior year in high school, King realized he had learned a lot about the stratified social structure in high school, which he would later put to good use in his fiction. King always stored away his experiences to later mine for use in fiction.

As King told Winter in *The Art of Darkness*, his public face was different from his private one. "Inside," King said, "I felt different and unhappy a lot of times. I felt *violent* a lot of times. But I kept that part of myself to myself. I never wanted to let anybody get at it. . . . It wasn't the same as being embarrassed about it, so much as wanting to keep it and sort of work it out for myself."

King worked out his frustrations by sublimating them in his fiction.

In grammar school, for instance, King had written a story that he passed around, which his fellow classmates loved reading, in part because they were the stars of the story. As Chesley recounted in *The Complete Stephen King Encyclopedia*, it was a pass-along story:

> But anyway, it was a mini-novel, and in the story he had us real kids—including him—take over the school. We stole our parents' guns, and everything else we could get, and we holed ourselves up in the elementary school. The whole story was basically like an Alamo kind of thing, where first the local cops, and then the National Guard come and try to get us out of the school; and in the end we all died. . . . The story went from hand to hand—everybody read it, and Steve was lionized. That was the beginning of his mythology. People were just floored by that. We all loved it.

During the summer of 1966, after graduating from high school and before heading off for college, King revisited the story he passed around in grammar school and wrote what would clearly his first mature work, *Getting It On*, a psychologically intense short novel. It was not horror or science fiction; it was naturalist fiction.

King finished the novel in 1971, and drew its title from a popular song at the time, T. Rex's "Bang a Gong (Get It On)." It eventually saw publication in 1977 as *Rage* (published by NAL).

# 3

# EC COMICS

In the old EC Comics, the guilty were always punished. That
was the traditional American view of morality.

—STEPHEN KING, *STEPHEN KING AT THE MOVIES*

In the opening scene of *Creepshow*, an homage to the horror comics of the fifties, an
enraged father snatches a comic book out of his son's hands and throws it in the trash.

The message is clear: Comic books are thought by the older generation to be the
lowest form of trash literature, unfit for human consumption, and sure to pollute the
minds of the youth.

The EC line included *Weird Science, Weird Fantasy, Frontline Combat, Two-Fisted
Tales, Vault of Horror, Tales from the Crypt, Haunt of Fear, Crime SuspenStories, Shock
SuspenStories*. They were works of comic book art, well written and drawn, and highly
moral.

King has repeatedly said that horror stories must have a sense of morality. It's
not enough, he argues, to throw in shock effects to surprise or stun the reader into
submission. The writer's job is to show the truth, and that means the bad guys get their
comeuppance—their seeds of destruction lie within.

That sense of morality was the cornerstone of EC Comics. Despite the admittedly
gruesome fare between the lurid covers—shown out of context by Frederic Wertham to a
concerned nation of parents who thought, "I don't have to *read* trash to *know* it's trash"—
the bad guys reaped what they sowed in an EC story.

King's *Creepshow*, published in 1982, was a loving homage to those comics. Both
King and George Romero (who directed the film) love the EC line, and it shows. In both
the film and comic book adaptation, the look and feel of the horror comics of the fifties

Courtesy of William Gaines

*EC publisher, William Gaines.*

are deliberately evoked. The comic book adaptation is replete with direct and indirect EC references. The cover was drawn by Jack Kamen, an EC artist; the framing device of a ghoulish figure introducing each story was the technique EC Comics employed; the theme of revenge is incorporated in the stories; and Bernie Wrightson, who illustrated the book, would have felt right at home in the stable of EC artists in the fifties, whom he studied and admired.

# 4

# "Three Durham Lads Publishing Bright Hometown Newspaper"

### by Don Hansen
### *Brunswick Record,* April 23, 1959

*GETTING OUT THE PAPER,
Dave King (left) and Donald Flaws
get together on an issue of* Dave's
Rag, *a semi-monthly, individually
typed newspaper circulated in
Durham. At the moment the paper is
circulated primarily to friends, but the
editors are planning to include wider
coverage of the West Durham area.
The editorial and printing offices are
in Dave's bedroom at the moment. The
circulation is now 20.*
—original caption for photo taken
  by Mr. Downing.

*What follows is an article on Dave King's newspaper* Dave's Rag. *The newspaper is defunct, and this story is now part of King history. General reporter Don Hansen was probably bemused at three kids writing and publishing a newspaper, but he took it seriously, took them seriously, and wrote about it accordingly.*

*David had printer's ink in his veins, but not for long. Innately curious and obviously intelligent, his wide-ranging mind was always moving on in search of new worlds to conquer. (As an adult, David became a high school math teacher and a town selectman. He and his wife are evangelical Christians.)*

Newspapers throughout this area have stepped up their coverage recently as the result of a new semimonthly newspaper now being published by three Durham lads.

The paper, called *Dave's Rag*, is published by 13-year-old David V. King, the editor, publisher and photographer; his 11-year-old brother Stephen, and Donald Flaws, 15, the sports editor.

Boasting an all paid circulation of 20 copies, the typewritten newspaper thus far has had a good reception with readers.

While the paper is supposed to "hit the streets" every two weeks editor Dave noted that "I think you had better not expect your paper every other Tuesday. Until I get a mimeograph machine things are going to be rather rushed."

At present each copy is individually typed.

Six issues have been published since the paper first appeared with a circulation of two in January.

In the manner of all good newspapers, *Dave's Rag* probes deeply into the lives of its readers for news. One news story, for example, covered a fire in detail:

"A few weeks ago, Doris' house, in Scarborough, caught on fire. It leveled the barn, the shop, and the out-buildings. Doris was in Boston, but when she heard about it, she came home. The only fatality was the cat, Confucius. Oren is fixing it back up, at least the house. The cause is not known."

Local news of interest is also covered in detail. In a February issue the following item appeared:

"Today the Pillsburys and Kings were surprised by the arrival of Francis and Phil. They also brought Aunt Gert. They arrived about 2:00 Sunday afternoon, and left at about 4:30. Dave took a picture of them which will probably be in next week's pictures. Aunt Gert put her hands over her face when Dave took it, but you can still tell who it is."

And in a later issue:

"Aunt Gert recently appeared in movies! While attending a Stanley Party at Jane's, moving pictures were taken at the refreshment table. Aunt G. is seen juggling her coffee with one hand while she covers her face with the other."

The sports stories also cover every aspect of the games. The following story, written before the New England high school basketball tournament, ended on this note of doom:

"On Feb. 25, Donald and Dave went to the basketball tournament in Lewiston. Brunswick kept up the pace in the first half, but in the second their best player broke his glasses. He cannot shoot without them. The final score was 59-50."

A weather story contained this interesting sidelight:

"Friday the snow drifted something awful on Route No. 9. There were three cars stuck. A truck, and two cars. A road commissioner was stuck for about 2 hours, and I imagine he got plenty mad."

Or again:

"On Donald's birthday the three Kings were invited down to the Flaws estate for supper, at about 6:00 P.M. Dave was all dolled up in a tie, sports shirt and all the works. Everybody thought that he looked very funny."

The classified advertising department seems to be thriving. In one issue the following advertisements appeared:

## CAT WANTED!!!

Do you have a baby or half-grown cat that you do not have room for?
All we need is one! If so, contact Dave King.

## WATCH FOR THE NEW [STEPHEN] KING STORY!!!!

### *Land of 1,000,000 Years Ago*

Exciting story of 21 people prisoners on an island that should have been extinct 1,000,000 years ago. Order through this newspaper.

Editor Dave takes his responsibility seriously. He points out strongly that "anonymous letters go into the waste-basket."

Dave and Stephen are the sons of Mrs. Ruth King of Durham. Sports Editor Donald is the son of Mr. and Mrs. George Flaws of Durham.

Dave and Donald are freshmen and sophomore students, respectively, of Brunswick High School. Stephen attends the West Durham school.

Although Dave is probably the nation's youngest newspaper editor, he doubts that he will make newspapering a career. Sports editor Donald thinks he'll go into the field of mathematics as a teacher.

What will be the fate of *Dave's Rag*? Dave plans to continue publishing just as long as time allows. If he should cease publication to enter some other field, however, we're certain that at least 20 subscribers (all paid) will be sorry to see it die.

So will we.

Chris Chesley in front of Runaround Pond.

The United Methodist Church (Durham), which the Kings attended.

Harmony Grove Cemetery in Durham

The country road that runs past the Kings' home

Runaround Pond

David King holding a ceramic dog named Cujo.

Courtesy of Dave Lowell

# 5

# A Special Occasion:

## Chris Chesley's Friendship with Stephen King

I never had any friends later like the ones
I had when I was 12.

Jesus, does anyone?

—Gordie LaChance, "The Body," from *Different Seasons*

To put things in proper perspective: Imagine collaborating with an eighteen-year-old named Elvis Presley *before* he walked into the Memphis Recording Service at the Sun Record Company, on July 18, 1953, and paid $3.98 to cut an acetate with two songs: "My Happiness" and "That's When Your Heartaches Begin." Or, perhaps, jamming on a regular basis with a baby-faced teenager named Paul McCartney who lived in the Allerton district of Liverpool, *before* he met a fellow guitarist and songwriter named John Lennon, on July 6, 1957.

Likewise, Chris Chesley met Stephen King in 1958–59, when the King family—Ruth, David, and Stephen—made a permanent move to rural Maine, to Durham. Stephen, eleven years old, entered the same grammar school that Chris attended, and it didn't take long for Chris to realize he had met a kindred spirit, someone who'd become a fast friend and shared many common interests. Chris and Stephen had a mutual love of rock and roll, movies, science fiction, and paperback horror books. They also collaborated on self-published "books." Even at that young age, Chris saw exceptional promise in his friend's writing, which would in time range far beyond the confines of rural Maine to encompass the world.

Lifelong Mainers are by nature wary of outsiders who come knocking at the front door, and Chris is no exception. After Chris and I spent a long day together, we ended up at Harmony Grove Cemetery, and he turned to me as the sun set behind us and said that he had been checking me out to see if I was "genuine." Once I earned his trust, and he was convinced that I wasn't a phony, he lowered his shield and opened up. He was kind and warm and generous. We had hit it off. It wasn't a sit-down, formal interview; instead, we drove around Durham, parked the car, got out and walked around, and just talked. To ensure I got the quotes right, instead of relying on a notebook, I carried a portable tape recorder.

Chris has only given two interviews about King. The first was in Spignesi's *The Complete Stephen King Encyclopedia* (published in 1991), and the second was in the last issue of *Phantasmagoria* (2001), a King fanzine with a circulation of only three hundred copies.

Covering a lot of ground, this interview limns the background and sets the stage for discussing King's family, the remoteness of rural Maine, and the significant influence of pop culture on his writing, all of which combined to shape his worldview: his main, and Maine, roots.

A talented writer, Chris has imagination and passion, but for unknown reasons never pursued writing professionally. That's unfortunate, because he could have gone on to a successful writing career in fiction or nonfiction had he—like his friend Steve King— persisted.

The interview was conducted in the spring of 1990.

### GB: When did you first meet King?

**Chris Chesley:** [Pointing to a building] That was the schoolhouse where he and I went to school. I had been going to another one-room schoolhouse on the other end of town, but my parents switched me over to this one, mainly because it was closer to the house. That's where I first met him. It was his first year in Durham, around 1958 or 1959.

He wore old-fashioned, black-rimmed "fifties" glasses. His hair was kind of messy. He was kind of slow. He was chunky but he wasn't fat. But, interestingly enough, he did have an ability to really talk, which he got from his mother. When I went to his house, it was so interesting because he and his brother and mother talked like no one you ever heard.

### GB: What was the schoolhouse like?

**Chris Chesley:** It was a one-room schoolhouse with twenty-five or thirty kids, grades one through eight. It had a wood stove in the back of the building. Beyond that, there was a two-hole outhouse. There was one teacher, Miss Heisler. She wasn't married. She pretty much devoted her life to teaching. She was very good. She was strict and had a lot of respect for learning. When you did well, she let you know she appreciated it. That was very important encouragement for people like Steve, who did well on pretty much everything.

*The one-room schoolhouse Stephen King attended in Durham.*

**GB: In *Danse Macabre*, King cites a turning point in his life. It's when he discovers a box of old, forgotten paperbacks that belonged to his father. Since you were there at the time, what do you remember?**

**Chris Chesley:** The books that he got from his aunt and uncle's attic included an Avon paperback by [Abraham] Merritt, and an H. P. Lovecraft book—the first Lovecraft story he and I had read. There was also an anthology of Lovecraft stories that were completed by August Derleth.

But I swear what I remember is that there was *another* gift of books beyond that first box. This other was much larger, nearly two hundred books. A friend of one of his aunts was a teacher who had a big collection of fantasy and science fiction. When she died, they got this big collection. So Steve, who didn't have bookcases in his room, put them all the way around the baseboard.

There were a few more Lovecraft books, including *The Color Out of Space*. But most of the books were science fiction, and it was there we began a literary parting of the ways.

Although I liked Lovecraft more than he did, what Steve learned from him was the possibility of taking the New England atmosphere and realizing that one could use that as a springboard, a place to tell your stories, as he did with *'Salem's Lot*, in which Dracula was basically moved to Durham.

Forget Lovecraft's prolix language; he showed Steve that there was definitely a

New England horror, a milieu. Steve didn't keep reading Lovecraft, but in terms of his development, he took that kind of European horror and set it here.

**GB: King credits Richard Matheson for that.**

**Chris Chesley:** I think stylistically he learned more from Matheson, who was innovative in working the aspect of daylight horror, finding it in everywhere U.S.A. Steve got a degree of inspiration from that.

**GB: I think too much has been made of it. King was also influenced by other writers, to varying degrees.**

**Chris Chesley:** Well, in his twenties, Steve read Evan Hunter's novels and, of course, Ed McBain. In fact, that's where he got some of the stylistic devices he uses, putting thoughts into italics and writing snappy dialogue, which is why he really liked McBain.

**GB: Did he read a lot of science fiction?**

**Chris Chesley:** He read a lot of science fiction mainly because he had this big collection. The person who had gotten that collection of fifties' science fiction had great taste. She had the best that was published back then.

Steve liked Ray Bradbury, but not his science fiction. Steve liked the Bradbury that wrote *Something Wicked This Way Comes.*

There was also an anthology by William Tenn, *Children of Wonder,* a great collection. It dealt with children and the supernatural. We read those stories together, which I think were very important in his seeing the possibilities of working with children in fiction. One of them was called "The Idol of the [Flies]," which is one of the oddest stories I've ever read. It's about a kid who likes to pull the wings off flies. It's a fascinating story, but extremely weird and very offbeat.

I found one of the best science fiction novels of all time in that collection, *A Canticle for Leibowitz,* by Walter M. Miller, Jr.

**GB: What was your relationship with King like? How did you see him grow as a fledgling writer?**

**Chris Chesley:** When we were in grammar school, we saw each other quite a bit, but when we got into high school, I would see him only on weekends, and during vacations I'd see him in the evenings.

Sometimes he'd show me things he had written, and sometimes he wouldn't.

What I remember seeing was a progression: When we started hanging out together, he was writing short stories. Then they got longer and turned into novellas. Finally, the novellas turned into novels. It was a very gradual progress.

The full-fledged novel he showed me was the high school novel about a race riot, *Sword in the Darkness.* I read that and thought, He finally broke through the short-story length and had the ability to create something novel-sized.

**GB: Tell me about his writing process.**

**Chris Chesley:** We were speaking earlier of the fact that he writes intuitively. He'd say, "I'm going to write a story about *this*," and that would be the inspiration. He would sit down, put paper in the typewriter, and write. It sounds rather obvious to say, but that first page would lead to the next. He wouldn't know where the story was going. He'd have ideas that he would be tossing and turning around in his mind, but beyond that he wrote what simply came to him.

**GB: What about his famous rejections?**

**Chris Chesley:** Steve got a lot of rejections. He used to put them up on the wall, on a nail. In an odd way, they were trophies. He was paying his dues, and he wanted to see that with each rejected story, he could see beyond it. He submitted to science fiction magazines and also mainstream magazines. The rejections depressed him, but he still had the sense that with each form rejection slip, he was moving forward.

**GB: What did his teachers think of him as a writer?**

**Chris Chesley:** I don't know if they ever saw that he was going to be a writer, but they certainly knew that he had a talent for writing. We could all see that.

In the last years of grammar school, in the seventh or eighth grade, he wrote what was his first novel-type story, twenty pages long, in which he used real kids—he used us— in which we had taken over the grammar school. Because of things like that, Steve was lionized.

He could take real people and set them into a novelistic setting in which we were heroes who died fighting the National Guard. And the people he liked best died last. We all wondered when we were going to "die."

**GB: What about his visual style of writing?**

**Chris Chesley:** People talk about his cinematic style, which he learned from going to the movies. For example, after seeing *The Pit and the Pendulum*, he novelized it. It wasn't merely a takeoff on that story. He learned to write from what he saw on the screen at the Ritz theater.

It was like what Shakespeare plays must have been during the Elizabethan times: the audience did not sit quietly; they interacted with what they saw.

We were all between two and fifteen years old, so if you didn't like something, you'd shout at the screen. If there was a suspenseful scene when the heroine was walking up the dark stairs, everybody would holler, "No, no, don't go up there!" It's just what those B-movie makers would have wanted their audiences to do.

We saw some pretty good movies there, including *Dementia 13,* by Francis Ford Coppola. We thought that was great.

**GB: You mentioned David King in passing but didn't elaborate. As you know, David's the "invisible" King. What are your thoughts about David and his relationship with his little brother?**

**Chris Chesley:** I didn't see much of David. He was older and had his own friends. He was more mature, in a way, and a very self-sufficient kid. Very smart. He did a lot of reading; he read a lot of science fiction. He ran a newspaper that he put out for a while. He was a kid with a lot of ideas.

I think David and Stephen probably had, in a way, a similar relationship to each other and to their mother like William and Henry James had. Henry always felt slighted when he was growing up because William was thought to be the heir apparent.

You felt that David was the heir apparent. I think of "The Body" when I think of that, because there's the older brother who was looked up to . . . but in the story, he dies. There's the same sense that David was the one from whom they expected great things to come.

As for Steve, we have to go back thirty years, relative to the time, to think of what people thought of him.

Everybody thought, considering how much he read and wrote, that his behavior was not normal. He was thought to have spent way too much time in his room, in his imagination, and it was generally thought to be unhealthy.

I think he felt that and was sensitive to it. It was very difficult for him to be who he was and also be accepted for it. In that respect, I think Steve felt more alone; he felt a sense of isolation, but I think it went with the territory. Given who Steve was, the isolation was necessary to make him who he eventually became.

He is aware of what he needs to do to preserve himself, aware of the time and space and distance that allows him to write. That's pretty much what he is, and that's pretty much the way he always was. He was certainly not a recluse. He had friends like the rest of us, but when he was done with them, he would always return to the typewriter. And watching him with his writing, well, you knew that was where he belonged.

I liked to go see him. To me, it was important to have a friend like Steve because of what he was doing.

**GB: What's the connection between Runaround Pond and "The Body"?**

**Chris Chesley:** A friend of mine came over to where Steve and I were and asked, "Do you want to see a dead body?" We said, "Sure!"

They had dragged the body up. It was lying on this muddy stretch, and they had lights shining on it. They had not covered up the corpse yet because he had just drowned an hour ago. He was out in a boat, drinking with some friends, and fell overboard. He couldn't swim. It used to happen once a year or so. They fished him out and had gotten him up on the bank. It was summertime, and it wasn't a pleasant sight.

We used to come down here. Some of the other stuff in "The Body" comes from here: The bloodsucker incident probably had its origins here. On hot summer days when you went swimming, we learned early on that you couldn't swim near the shore because the bloodsuckers would be in the warm, shallow water. If you walked around on the mud on this side of the rocks, you'd come out covered with bloodsuckers.

It was an educational experience for all of us. We were in high school. I might have been fifteen, maybe sixteen.

**GB: What's it been like for you, an aspiring writer, to be a writing buddy with the young boy who seemed destined to be the bestselling author Stephen King?**

**Chris Chesley:** It's been a very fortunate experience to have known Stephen King, but it's very inhibiting for me. I know this guy. I was in the position of watching him develop as a kid. I could see the kind of talent he had. I'm the first to admit that I'd been doing other things, but at the same time, having known someone who is that good, why aren't you? What are the probabilities?

Steve showed some concern and said, "Don't worry about that. You can't think like that. You have to do your own stuff."

**GB: Give me a sense of what it was like to be around him when he turned on his powerful, imaginative storytelling machine.**

**Chris Chesley:** Last night I was trying to think of a way to describe what it was like—his intense use of imagination—and I came up with the only way I can describe it, by trying to find something in your experience. So I say to you: You've been in a position where somebody you really care about, like your wife, hasn't showed up at the right time; it's dark and your imagination begins to work overtime, suggesting possibilities. You can see them vividly in your mind.

Well, take that intensity of imagination and make it a constant in your life. Imagine having that ability, not just in times of stress or joy, of constant imagination, and you have a picture as to what Steve was like as a kid.

A literary example: One of my favorite ghost stories is *The Turn of the Screw*. Is there a ghost? Is there *not* a ghost? The governess is out there on a big place with the kids, but do the kids see the ghost?

My own opinion is that the governess's imaginative function is so Stephen Kingish, so intense, that she is able to create for the children a sense of the actual existence of the ghost, which winds up destroying them. *That's* what it was like to go to Stephen King's house and write stories with him.

There was a sense that these things weren't just things in a book. When you walked inside, there was a sense of palpability, almost as if the characters in the books, the stories, and the atmosphere had real weight.

Imagination made it real, not only for him but also for me. To go inside his house was like being pulled into a different world than Durham with its cowsheds and its lack of imagination, and that's why trying to describe it to people is so difficult. It's what drew me to go see him. He had that ability. If you went inside his house and were susceptible, you'd be drawn into that. And when you read stories with him, they took on weight. His was almost a world unto itself, which I was privileged to enter.

Even as a kid, a teenager—remember, this wasn't an adult creating a world—Stephen had the power to do that. It was an amazing thing. He'd be working on *The Long Walk* or another story, and when I got there I'd ask, "What have you done? What's happened with this character?"

Basically, you had a kid who, from the time I knew him, wrote between two and four hours, or maybe more, a day. It was like someone who has a talent for the piano: You sit down and just do it.

**GB: What about the fabled Underwood typewriter with missing keys?**

**Chris Chesley:** I tend to think it was a Smith Corona. It wasn't the world's best typewriter. It was missing letters, like the *o*. Then the *e* broke off, and I remember typing a page and then filling in the letters; he did that, too, because we weren't content in leaving the space blank.

**GB: What did you do out here in the sticks to entertain yourselves?**

**Chris Chesley:** That's one of the interesting things about Durham back then: There weren't any social activities. It's unimaginable for someone who came from an urban or suburban environment. In fact, it wasn't until we became teenagers that they had dances down at the local hall. At one point there were Boy Scout activities, but that was in Pownal, the next town over. Here in Durham, you were pretty much on your own. School was really the only institution that affected us.

You did what you would do in any small little town. It was like Mayberry, where people are walking down a road, kicking up dirt: You did that. You went fishing. You went over to see your friends. You hung around. You rode your bikes. And that was it. You made your own fun, and with not many people around to do it with.

That situation contributed to Steve's ability to create fictional worlds. A definite lack of outside stimulation allowed his own creative abilities to come to the forefront.

*A manual Underwood typewriter similar to what King's mother bought him.*

**GB: Any local haunts?**

**Chris Chesley:** There used to be a house that Dave mentioned in *The Shape Under the Sheet* [*The Complete Stephen King Encyclopedia*]. Steve and I got a hold of a movie camera. We weren't seriously trying to make a movie; we were trying to figure out by taking shots how you designed it to make it scary. We were trying to figure out how you got the person up and down the stairs, and how to get the shadows.

It was a deserted house, the kind of place that had enough vibes so that you didn't want to spend the night there. I don't think we ever got enough nerve to do that. It had enough of a feeling of previous occupancy so that you didn't want to hang around too long.

Inside those little rooms, it was different. It had the staircase that Steve mentions in *'Salem's Lot*, where they went upstairs and found a hanged man, Hubie Marsten.

**GB: Were there any television shows Steve particularly liked?**

**Chris Chesley:** Sure. *The Fugitive. Thriller.* Steve especially liked *The Outer Limits*, which didn't stay on the air that long. He was crazy about that show. *Twilight Zone.* Those shows were on during the heyday of television, which sucks now. Back then, they used to have shows that were entertainment-oriented, and not so market- and issue-oriented.

In those days, television had no competition, and that made a difference.

**GB: Did any of the shows affect Steve as a writer?**

**Chris Chesley:** Earlier today, you were speaking about the kinds of shows that were on: *Father Knows Best, Leave It to Beaver, My Three Sons.*

We were taught that there were certain ideals that TV represented, and that's what we learned—the ideals of what Americans lived like.

I think what Steve does in his books, in *Pet Sematary*, for example, he's got an ideal family that's moved to Maine. The happy family is living in a rural setting. Steve sets

*An abandoned building where Chesley and King shot a movie.*

it up beautifully, so that when [their young son] Gage dies, you are heartbroken, just devastated. It's the setup for the whole book.

This ideal can be destroyed. Steve not only had a sense of the ideal that he got from living here, he also had a sense of the fragility of that ideal, because a lot of what he saw around here couldn't live up to it, so there's tension.

*Carrie* has got some of that, too, with the ideal high schoolers—the difference between those wonderful, golden youths—and Carrie. The tension of *Carrie* derives from that. Steve felt like that idea existed, and he wanted to believe it was valuable, and it was the right thing. But of course, coming from where he did—this community and his own life—this idea was distant from it. I think that makes a lot of difference in *Carrie*.

**GB: Do you think there's a lot of pent-up anger in *Carrie*?**

**Chris Chesley:** Steve never talked about that. I saw him periodically on the weekends. He never talked very much about his high school years. It was understood that we got together to talk about movies, books, and things like that. I've always assumed since then that he didn't have a wonderful high school experience; it wasn't that great a time for him.

**GB: What was it like in the days when he was actually writing *Carrie*?**

**Chris Chesley:** Steve and Tabby lived in a double-wide mobile home. When I went to the University of Maine at Orono, I moved in with them at their house on Stone Street in Bangor. The year after that, he moved to Hermon, and I moved in with them because I wanted to live off-campus. I used to hitchhike to and from school every day. It was about fifteen miles from his home to Orono. It was on top of a windswept hill with snowplows buzzing back and forth during the winter.

I would hitchhike home from school around 2:00 P.M. I had to go from Orono, through Bangor, and out to where Route 2 connects to the turnpike, and down Route 2 to Hermon. I wound up home around 3:30 P.M.

Steve would get home around then, too. He was driving a big, old, midnight-blue gas guzzler, which was on its last legs when he bought it. It was a piece of junk. Sometimes, I'd meet him at the exit ramp on Route 2, where he'd pick me up, if it was just the right time, and I'd ride the rest of the way up to the house.

**GB: Where was Tabitha at the time? Working or at home?**

**Chris Chesley:** She was home with the kids. It was an extremely difficult time for both of them. They were in a bind. Joe was a baby at the time, so Tabby was in a position where she couldn't get out of the house that much. She was taking care of the kids during the day while Steve taught. Plus, in the evenings, he graded papers and wrote. This was long before the days of day care and support systems.

**GB: Tabitha is a very private person. We know a lot about Steve but very little about her.**

**Chris Chesley:** One of her qualities is that she gets impatient a lot sooner than Steve. She's got a much more critical eye toward people than Steve does. Her eye was much more measuring of the world than Steve's. She had that degree of impatience with what she saw around her, so she might be impatient with the problems that would arise with interviews, where she might be misquoted, or the wrong impression would be led.

**GB: Tabitha's obviously had a big influence on Stephen's thinking.**

**Chris Chesley:** I would say that's true. That's pretty much been the way it was since they were married.

Steve also trusts her opinion. He knows that she can give an accurate opinion of his work. When I knew them back on Stone Street or in Hermon, she didn't skew what she said. Because she cared for him, she told him the truth. She does not pussyfoot around. It's one of her more endearing qualities. She knows who she is, and she's got her own opinions of the world and the people in it.

**GB: In the Durham days, would the King family be considered working-class? And to what extent did his family and the rural environment that he had grown up in play a part in him becoming a writer?**

**Chris Chesley:** Right around here was farming, but the majority of towners went out of town to Lewiston, Auburn, or Brunswick. Durham's farming days had been over after the war, but there was the last breath of that then.

The community's complexion had changed. When we moved here, the town was basically a working-class town; in a sense, a hard-luck town.

When we talked about Steve's situation, we have to put it in perspective. A lot of kids we knew, and a lot of people we knew, had the same kinds of problems that he did, or worse.

I'm very careful not to want to attribute his writerliness to his family background. Other kids didn't become writers, and they had situations that were just as bad, so we have to be careful about how we view the contribution of his family background.

We were all poor. Nobody had any money. Two dollars was a lot of money for us back then. To be able to go to the drive-in every two weeks was a real big deal. Not to sound like an old mossback, but I think that contributed to the way we valued things. We didn't buy very much, but when we bought books or something else, we got deals. It wasn't just for the sake of buying something; we had a sense of value about them. Mainly, we weren't consumers. We didn't have the money to *be* consumers.

You also have to be careful when you say, Well, Steve was a poor boy, so he wanted to become rich. There were a lot of people down here who didn't have any money, whose houses didn't have central heating or bathtubs. And, again, a lot of those people didn't become writers either, so I wouldn't want to say that Steve's financial circumstances when he was growing up had that great of a role to do with why he became a writer.

**GB: If you had to sum up your friendship with Steve, how would you describe it?**

**Chris Chesley:** It was a special occasion.

Road sign: "Welcome to Orono: (home of the University of Maine).

A statue of a Black Bear, the UMO mascot.

Burton Hatlen, friend and mentor, and college professor who taught King.

The Penobscot River that runs past the University of Maine at Orono.

"Ted" Holmes, a college professor who taught King.

The Old Town public library, which Tabitha King frequented.

Road sign: "Welcome to the city of Old Town," where Tabitha King was born.

Carroll E. Terrell, a college professor who taught King.

# 6

# STEPHEN KING AT THE UNIVERSITY OF MAINE

## A WRITER IN THE MAKING

BY SANFORD PHIPPEN

UNIVERSITY OF MAINE AT ORONO, CLASS OF '64

FALL 1989

*"University of Maine" sign on campus.*

*King inside at a protest rally against the Vietnam war.*

*King outside at a protest rally against the Vietnam war.*

He is certainly the University of Maine's most famous graduate. (Can you name another who has made the cover of *Time*?) What F. Scott Fitzgerald is to Princeton, what Nathaniel Hawthorne is to Bowdoin, and what Thomas Wolfe is to Chapel Hill, Stephen King is to Maine.

People tend to fall in love with authors more than with engineering programs, forestry schools—maybe even athletic teams. Look at the people who come to the state because of E. B. White, Robert McCloskey, even Helen and Scott Nearing. On a recent literary tour of the Bangor-Brewer area, Mary Lou Colbath (a Maine Public Broadcasting Network staffer) and I had to cut short part of a planned itinerary because so many of the librarians and teachers, mostly from Ohio, wanted to be sure they reached Stephen King's house to have their pictures taken before it got too dark. Students are now enrolling at Maine because of King's influence. And in the creative writing department, where I taught for a year (1987–88), his presence is strongly felt. One of my former colleagues says, "I don't mind Stephen King, but I wished he lived in Arizona. So many students try to imitate him—and badly. They think writing like this is an easy way to make money."

The influence of King on the university seems natural enough. The fact is that U Maine is where Stephen King started to become STEPHEN KING. Orono is where he first began to publish his work, both in his regular columns for *The Maine Campus* and the college literary magazine, and in national magazines like *Cavalier*. Orono is where he impressed his professors as a good student and was encouraged by them in his writing. Orono is where he received an important forum and feedback for his early work. Orono is where he made lasting friendships. And Orono is where he met his wife, Tabitha Spruce ('71), from Old Town.

Of course, the era he attended the university was also an important factor in the development of Stephen King. It didn't hurt to be a writer in the making on a college campus during one of the most turbulent times of the twentieth century. Steve was a student from 1966 to 1970, and while no race riots or antiwar demonstrations got wildly out of hand at Maine, there were demonstrations and protests, there was a Students for Democratic Society group on campus, and there was a three-day unofficial moratorium after the Kent State University tragedy in the spring of 1970. And Maine, like other U.S. colleges at the time, was undergoing many changes, especially in the areas of students' rights and residential life.

King's popular column "Garbage Truck," which appeared in *The Maine Campus* from February 20, 1969, through May 21, 1970, reflects much of what was going on at the time. While mostly he reviewed movies, TV shows, and rock music (just as he still does in his work), he did call for a general student strike on April 24, 1969. And he wrote in one column about what it was like to be called dirty names and have eggs thrown at you during a relatively peaceful End the War protest march on campus in May 1969. He attacked such establishment organizations as the All Maine Women, Senior Skulls, Sophomore Owls, and Eagles, calling them irrelevant and elitist. In reaction to such groups, he invented his own organization, which he called the Nitty Gritty Up Tight Society for a Campus with More Cools, and he handed out "gritties," or awards, to those people at Maine who, in his opinion, did cool things. His columns also attacked Pope Paul and supported the California grape pickers' strike in October 1969. On the other hand, he wrote in support of police officers and against those at the time who called cops "pigs."

In a March 3, 1970, column, he suggests that the university would be a better place if it got rid of all required courses and abolished requirements for all branches of the school. In one of his final columns (April 1970), he writes about how he changed from being a conservative who voted for Nixon in 1968 to becoming what he termed a "scummy radical bastard." The radical image of Stephen King was featured in a photo by Frank Kadi ('69) on the *Campus* cover of January 15, 1969. King looked as wild as one of his evil characters, sporting long hair, a beard, a deranged look in his eyes; grinning a buck-toothed grin; and pointing a double-barreled shotgun at the reader. Underneath the picture, in "coming-of-Christ" headline print, is the exclamation: "STUDY, DAMMIT!!"

In a May 1, 1969, column, King wrote about being part of the first "special seminar" created at the university during the fall semester of 1968. This was Contemporary Poetry, taught by Burt Hatlen ('65) and Jim Bishop ('61), two of King's favorite instructors, to whom, along with fellow English professor Edward M. "Ted" Holmes[1] (M.A., '54), he dedicated *The Long Walk*, one of the four novels written under King's pseudonym, Richard Bachman.

According to Hatlen, the special seminar courses were created to allow faculty members and students to plan classes outside the curriculum. And students needed to apply for admission. The Contemporary Poetry seminar was limited to twelve students and involved a "very intense discussion about poetics, how you write poetry, and so on." Hatlen says that Steve "wasn't very theoretical, but on the fringes." Tabby King, who was then a sophomore, says she'll never forgive Hatlen for not letting her in.

As a sophomore, King had taken Hatlen for Modern American Literature, and Hatlen feels that this course had a long-term influence on King, for it's where he came into contact with Steinbeck and Faulkner (King now collects first editions of Faulkner).

Before the contemporary poetry seminar, Jim Bishop had King as a student in 1966 in freshman English, and he remembers "Steve's big physical presence" and how King was "religious about writing." He also remembers that King always had a paperback in his pocket and knew all these authors that nobody else ever heard of. "Steve was a nice kid, a good student, but never had a lot of social confidence," Bishop says. "Even then, though, he saw himself as a famous writer and he thought he could make money at it. Steve was writing continuously, industriously, and diligently. He was amiable, resilient, and created his own world."

In his introduction to *Moth*, a student literary magazine published in 1970, Jim Bishop wrote about that extraordinary poetry seminar: "From that seminar, which supposedly terminated in January 1969, came a half dozen or so energetic and highly individual young poets who have been rapping in hallways, in coffee shops, in front of Stevens Hall, or wherever any two of them chance to meet, ever since, and that original group has

---

1 Edward M. "Ted" Holmes was the long-time creative writing professor at the University of Maine where he also taught American literature. He was the first to declare Stephen King "a writer." Ted himself was the author of two short story collections: *Driftwood* and *A Part of the Main*, and one novel, *Two If By Sea*. He was an expert in the works of William Faulkner whose first editions are collected by King. Holmes also wrote *Harriet Beecher Stowe: Woman and Artist*. He lived to be 99 years old.

grown this year to a dozen, sometimes as many as twenty, who meet every other Friday in an informal workshop to read their poetry, alternatively to read and reassemble one another, and hopefully to emerge with a better understanding of themselves, their world, and their work. This anthology brings together selected works of that amazing group and marks perhaps the climax of an extraordinary phenomenon."

Besides Stephen King, whose poems "The Dark Man," "Donovan's Brain," and "Silence" were included in *Moth,* the anthology includes six poems by Tabby Spruce, as well as poems by Michael Alpert ('72), a Bangor publisher, who has since collaborated with King on a fancy edition of *The Eyes of the Dragon;* by three of King's best friends from college, Jim Smith ('72), Dave Lyon ('70), and Bruce Holsapple ('73); by Diane McPherson (who designed the *Moth* cover); and by George MacLeod ('72), King's former roommate. The others who have work in *Moth* are Susan Lienhard ('71), Stephen Black ('70), Mike Gilleland ('72), Sherry Dresser, and Jean Stewart.

The poetry workshop met frequently at the Maine Christian Association House on College Avenue, among other places, throughout King's senior year. Jim Bishop was on leave from teaching that year and living at Pemaquid Point. But he still commuted to Orono for the meetings. Tom Bailey and Graham Adams of the English faculty presided, and it was Adams who allowed King to teach a course as a senior undergraduate. Adams served as the front person, because the university wouldn't allow a student to teach a course. But King was, in reality, the teacher, and the course, naturally enough, was called Popular Literature in America.

King's own thoughts about the poetry workshops and creative writing courses at Maine were recorded in interviews with the University of Southern Maine's *Presumscot* in 1977, and with UM's *Ubris II* in 1984. "I realized that what I had for those years I was involved with the writing seminar was a big blank," King told *Ubris II.* "There were about forty to fifty poems, and two of them I've still got around. So for me, there was this tremendously exciting experience and nothing came of it. It was like being on a long drunk. But, on the other hand, I wasn't typical. For a lot of people, good did come of it."

When asked if he learned the craft of writing in college courses, King replied: "No, no, but I don't think it was bad. The creative writing courses at the college level are very important, but I don't think they're necessary. It's a supportive experience. . . . The best thing about it was that the art of writing was taken seriously, and that's an awfully good thing."

In 1969–70, students from the workshop were involved with much more than poetry. George MacLeod, for instance, was one of the leaders of the student strike. Members of the group would often meet at the coffee shop that was part of the old bookstore in the Memorial Union.

Diane McPherson, who has a Ph.D. from Cornell, and who was a member of both the seminar and the workshop, shared tutorial writing sessions with King under Ted Holmes. "We wrote independently but then got together once a week, and it was great fun, often hilarious. I was the ideal audience for Steve's wildly inventive fantasies. My thing then was to cut all the extraneous adverbs and adjectives. Steve was pretty pop. He was writing exciting stories, but with no control."

McPherson also remembers King singing. "There was this coffeehouse on campus—

the Ram's Horn—and there would be these open sings, or open hoots. People brought their instruments, and Steve would always sing country and western songs about this terrible loser who never had any luck. I remember thinking at that time that Steve was singing about a version of himself that rang true."

King is also remembered hanging out at the back booth of the Bear's Den with fellow students Jim Tierney ('69—later, Maine's attorney general) and Steve Williams ('70). And he was known to frequent the old Shamrock Bar across from Pat's Pizza, where he would join friends and members of the more radical campus groups for folk music and beer.

At the end of the tutorial time with Professor Holmes, Ted sent McPherson's and King's stories to his agent, and soon after King had a story accepted by *Cavalier*. "He decided early what kind of writer he wanted to be, and he went and did it," McPherson says. "He used to say, 'I'm hoping to have my own career.' Now and then I think how funny it is that I went to college with Stephen King."

Everyone agrees that the first person to officially declare King a writer was Ted Holmes. In *Stephen King: The Art of Darkness*, Winter writes that King, as a sophomore, showed Burt Hatlen the manuscript of a novel he had written his freshman year. Hatlen in turn handed the manuscript to Holmes, who, after reading it, said ecstatically, "I think we've got a writer." "When Steve was a junior and senior," Holmes says, "we had a lot of conferences over his work. He was a natural storyteller, of course, and his craftsmanship was always pretty good."

One of King's stories, "Night Surf," eventually became *The Stand*. Other stories completed at UMaine were "Here There Be Tygers," "Cain Rose Up," "The Blue Air Compressor," and "Heavy Metal."

For most of the decade of the sixties, Ted Holmes was the sole creative writing teacher at Maine. Winthrop C. Libby, then president of the university, remembers a talk he once had with Holmes about King's prospects as an important professional writer. "Ted was not especially complimentary on that point. He said, as I recall, that while Steve certainly had a knack for storytelling, he wished that Steve would write more than horror stories."

Today, Holmes says of King's career, "I'm very glad that he's so successful. I respect his craftsmanship, but I haven't read all his books."

For his part, Libby remembers King as "essentially a very gentle person who acted the part of being a very wild man." Libby said that he'd see King "hovering around in the background" of student affairs committee meetings (King was elected to the Student Senate by the largest vote ever cast up to that time). "I'd always stop and chat with him; and my wife and I went to his wedding in Old Town, which was rather strange, because the ceremony was at the Catholic church and the reception at the Methodist" (Steve was the Methodist; Tabitha the Catholic).

As a freshman, King lived at 203 Gannett Hall. But after that first year, he moved off campus. In his senior year, he remembers living alone in a "scuzzy riverside cabin not far from the university." In his junior year, King lived on North Main Street in Orono in a house that has since burned down. One of his roommates was George MacLeod, who now operates MacLeod's Restaurant in Bucksport. There were two apartments for ten people, and MacLeod remembers King had a "whole regiment" of open beer bottles around his bed. He also remembers the future novelist's avid reading habits. "Steve read like his life depended on it," MacLeod says. "He was writing and reading all the time. Basically, he was an insecure kid who hid in books." MacLeod remembers that a lot of energy from the poetry workshop went into politics, but he says that while King would make a lot of noise and contribute to the chaos of the times, he was not an effective leader for causes.

"He's a loose cannon as far as politics go," MacLeod says. "He was a noisy radical opposed to Vietnam, and he did lead a group of students one night to President Libby's house. He was kind of an odd person: on one hand very private and yet public in a loud way."

Some of the political gains that resulted from what MacLeod terms a coalition of splinter groups from the SDS and other activist organizations were a program for independent study and having a pass/fail option instead of grades for students. "Steve was a figurehead for some radical efforts," claims MacLeod, "but basically he was middle-of-the-road in most areas. However, he was always there with his pitchfork and torch when you needed him."

MacLeod, who was a member of both the poetry seminar and workshop groups with King, also offered some insights into the popular novelist's personality. "Steve is uncomfortable with certain people and with large groups," he says. "He's erratic because he's nervous. He's a figurehead with feet of clay, and essentially he hasn't changed."

Emily Woodcock Templeton ('70), who audited the poetry workshop that Steve was in, has some clear memories of the late sixties at Maine. "You felt like you were part of a school that was on the vanguard of great change, a time of building," she says. "People were working hard. Reading was something everyone was doing then. In contrast to today's atmosphere, a lot of people were at college to just read and learn. It shouldn't be forgotten that at Maine no one was looking down on the soldiers fighting in Vietnam, but we were against the war. The University of Maine was the only university in the U.S. at the time that held a blood drive for the soldiers. As for Steve King, he was one of the more committed people on campus, not a rabble-rouser, but he spoke out about what he thought."

David Bright ('70) was the editor of *The Maine Campus* when King began his Garbage Truck column in 1969. He remembers King coming to him and saying he'd like to write a column. "Steve named it Garbage Truck because you never know what you're going to find in a garbage truck."

Bright was amazed at how King would stroll in just before deadline, put the paper in the typewriter, crank out his column, and hand it to the editor. It would be "letter-perfect copy," Bright remembers, that would fit the space to the inch. "This is a guy who has at least seven stories going on in his head at the same time," Bright says.

Even after he graduated from Maine, when there was a summer *Maine Campus* edited by Bob Haskell, King wrote "Slade," the story of a western gunfighter—the seed for King's novel *The Dark Tower* (book 1).

In the afterword to *The Dark Tower,* King writes about how the conception for the story began to take shape in March 1970:

During that spring semester, a sort of hush fell over my previously busy creative life—not a writer's block, but a sense that it was time to stop goofing around with a pick and shovel and get behind the controls of one big great God almighty steam shovel, a sense that it was time to try and dig something big out of the sand, even if the effort turned out to be an abysmal failure.

This statement indicates that King developed confidence in himself and his talent at quite an early age. David Bright attributes some of that development to the University of Maine.

"The University of Maine is a good place," Bright says. "You can be just about anything you want to be here." He added that he thought the times, the atmosphere, and the type of campus that Win Libby created all contributed to the development of Stephen King.

"The university served King well," Bright wrote in an article in the *Portland Monthly*, "taking a rather shy but brilliant Maine boy and turning him into an outgoing, productive asset to the state, yet leaving intact his wit, character, and eye for observing the people around him."

Bright claims that Steve would like to provide more opportunity for other potential writers to do what he did at the university. "King sees a need for a program to help new writers develop," Bright says. "He envisions some sort of a foundation—supported artists' guild, which would help writers move their families to Maine, pay their expenses, and find an environment in which to write."[2]

Bright agrees with King that the university could do more for young writers. "The university did for King what it's supposed to do for its citizens," he says. "But the university has got to remember that some kids aren't as motivated as Steve King was."

A few years ago, King did want to endow a creative writing chair in the English department, but there were some disagreements over how the gift was to be used and the matter fell through.

King's former teachers at Maine disagree somewhat on his stature as a writer, but all seem to think highly of him as both a student and a person. Robert Hunting was chairman of the English department and had King as a student in an English drama course. "Steve and I are good friends but I don't really read much of him," Hunting says. "I've read a couple of his books, but I like him better as a person than a writer. He's a very successful pop cult figure, and I'm a square. I have to remind myself, though, that Mozart also was a pop cult figure. Some of them become classics and some are forgotten. "Steve was in my class as a senior," Hunting continued. "I was brand new here then. He was a very good student and helped me with the class. And I read his column with interest. Actually, I got to know him better when he was coming back after graduation. He was

---

2  Ed. note: This idea never reached fruition, though the Kings did establish the Haven Foundation to help "freelance writers and artists experiencing career-threatening illness, accident, natural disaster or other emergency or personal catastrophe." (King's official Web site)

always very generous with his time. He talked to the students in many classes. Then for one year, he was my colleague."

Hunting is referring to 1978, when King taught creative writing at Maine. Ulrich Wicks, the man who hired him, remembers King as a popular and effective teacher.

"Steve was very much liked and very good with students," agrees Hunting. "He had all of these creative types. He was true and candid with them, but very kind also. I remember his saying to some very noisy young fellow that he'd have more of a chance with editors if he'd pay more attention to the nuts and bolts. He said they'd like it better if he'd spell better and if he'd write grammatical sentences. The student left happy."

Hunting says he has always been fond of Steve as a person and in later years as a public-spirited citizen. "I like the positions he takes, even if I'm not his most admiring reader. I don't think he'd mind me saying that, for I do admire him in so many ways."

One of the students Steve had in 1978 in his creative writing course was the novelist Margaret Dickson, who admits she didn't even know who he was. She says he was a good teacher because he was interested in all of his students and cared about them. "I found Steve a very generous, widely read, and interesting teacher," she says.

King helped start Dickson on her way as a novelist, as he had done with Michael Kimball and Rick Hautala.

Although Robert Hunting has not read many of King's books, other veterans of the English department do keep up with their most famous student's works.

Burt Hatlen thinks King is one of the most serious writers working today. And creative writing teacher Connie Hunting brushes off the criticism that King's works are shallow. "They're always saying that Steve doesn't say anything," she says, "but *The Stand* says something."

Professor Carroll Terrell says he quit the Maine Council of English and Language Arts a couple of years ago over King. "I stopped going there because they had such awful opinions of him," he says. "And these opinions were based on not having read anything of his at all."

There does seem to be a group of people who refuse to read King—probably the same folks who make a big thing out of not watching TV or not listening to popular music.

Christopher Spruce, King's brother-in-law and the former manager of King's WZON radio station in Bangor, says this argument over whether King is an artist or just a good, entertaining storyteller is never-ending:

> I can tell you that people should read his work seriously, because I believe he is a serious writer. He's not just out for a fast buck—why should he be at this point? There's a deep investment in his being the best writer he can be.

Connie Hunting says that although Stephen King has great influence on current writing students, they often pick up his tricks but not his deeper philosophical stances. "A novel like *The Stand* is not just a collection of horror—it's saying something very clearly. But the students only pick up on the exaggerated style and write stuff like 'the road regurgitated in front of us.' What they get is only the glitz."

Talking about her own friendship with Stephen King, Connie Hunting says, "People have very warm feelings about Steve—it's not just that he's the world's best-selling novelist. It's because he's Steve and we know him, okay? It's not that we've got a stake in him. He's the neighborhood. He's the Maine neighborhood."

It is clear that King's four years at the University of Maine were a time of tremendous growth. No, UM didn't make Stephen King into the world's bestselling author—it didn't create that horrific and prolific imagination. But it did give him a solid foundation in literature and it did provide him with an environment where writing—most especially his own writing—was taken seriously. And more important, it gave him the freedom to explore, to be accepted for who he was, and to "act the part of a wild man," as Winthrop Libby said. By his own account, as well as that of friends and faculty members, Stephen King left Maine with self-confidence and craftsmanship. Not a bad accomplishment for any college graduate.

*Sanford Phippen at the UMO bookstore.*

# King Graduates: A Blessed Event?

When King graduated from high school, his yearbook photo showed a conservative young man with neatly trimmed hair and large glasses, straight out of a fifties or sixties' television sitcom, recalling *Leave It to Beaver* or *My Three Sons*. But on the cover of the school newspaper, *The Maine Campus* (January 15, 1970), it depicted a maniacal-looking Stephen King brandishing a shotgun.

As Tabitha King wrote in *Murderess Ink,* "There is a striking resemblance to Charles Manson, and the picture trades on it. It is the very face that made my parents less than enthusiastic when I first brought him home."

We also find, in *Prism,* the yearbook from the University of Maine at Orono, a photo of King at an antiwar rally. He's sporting long hair, a thick beard, and brandishing papers in his upright hand. Standing six feet three and weighing over two hundred pounds, King stood out on campus: He was indeed a big man on campus, in stature and in reputation. In four turbulent years, he had grown from an apprehensive freshman wearing the requisite beanie to a world-and-war-weary senior. It's little wonder, then, that he wrote about graduation as a "BLESSED (?) EVENT" in his final "King's Garbage Truck" column dated May 21, 1970:

> This boy has shown evidences of some talent, although at this point it is impossible to tell if he is just a flash in the pan or if he has real possibilities. It seems obvious that he has learned a great deal at the University of Maine at Orono, although a great deal has contributed to a lessening of idealistic fervor than a heightening of that characteristic. If a speaker at his birth into the real world mentions "changing the world with the bright-eyed vigor of youth" this young man is apt to flip him the bird and walk out, as he does not feel very bright-eyed by this time: in fact, he feels about two thousand years old.

Lisbon Falls High School yearbook

*King's senior picture from high school.*

Frank Kadi

*King on the cover of the* Maine Campus.

# 7

## RICK HAUTALA

### MAINE'S *OTHER* HORROR WRITER

A lot of interviews try to turn me into 'Steve King Jr.' I'm sure
Steve blurbed my books because he genuinely liked them, not
because we are friends and he wanted to get me started. Now
and again he's offered advice that's been right on target, and
again, I'd be a fool not to listen. He's had a helluva lot more
experience with publishing than I have!

—RICK HAUTALA, *CASTLE ROCK*

When you think of Maine writers, Stephen King comes first to mind, but standing in King's long shadow in Maine was another horror writer who also attended the University of Maine at Orono: Rick Hautala (1949–2013), a self-effacing
man who was too shy in college to introduce himself to Stephen King.

Riding the shock wave created by King's popularity, Rick was able to sell horror
novels, until the bottom dropped out of the market.

I first contacted Rick back in 1988 when I was working on the first edition of this
book, to solicit an interview. He happily gave one, but pulled it at the eleventh hour for
private reasons. Here, for the first time, the original interview finally sees publication.

I'd spent time with Rick on two occasions, both in Portland, in the company of two
Maineiacs, the writer David Lowell and illustrator Glenn Chadbourne. I look back at
both times with fond memories.

*Portrait of Rick Hautala by Glenn Chadbourne.*

What I want to write about is an act of kindness by King that helped Rick launch his career. It's a good example of how King's star power and connections opened doors for another talented Maine writer, and speaks well of King's unpublicized efforts to help other writers less fortunate than himself.

The small community of horror and fantasy writers comes together annually at the World Fantasy Convention and the World Horror Convention, where King's name is justly celebrated: His work transcended the horror genre, making it more legitimate and main-stream, and his support of the field's small presses has kept them afloat, by allowing them to make a profit on his books without risk. Today, a signed Stephen King limited edition always sells out its entire print run in a matter of hours, months before its publication.

Rick Hautala had gotten not one but two blurbs from King, emblazoned on the covers of his mass market paperback novels: *Moondeath* and *Moonbog*.

In his posthumous autobiography, *The Horror . . . The Horror,* Hautala tells of working as a clerk at a Waldenbooks in 1975 in Portland, Maine. King walks in, and they talk. When Rick tells King that he's writing a horror novel, King offers to read it, but there's one problem: Rick hasn't finished the novel. Two years later, it's finally done. Rick ships it off to King, who reads it, writes an enthusiastic cover letter to accompany it, and sends the package on to his literary agent, Kirby McCauley.

What Rick didn't know was that King went the extra mile and furnished an unsolicited blurb.

No first-time novelist could wish for more from anyone, much less King.

McCauley eventually sells *Moondeath* (1981) to Zebra, and it's published as a mass market paperback emblazoned with King's blurb on the top. You can't miss it: "One of the best horror novels I've read in the last two years!"

Rick published a second novel, *Moonbog* (1982), with a King blurb on its front cover: "Hautala's new book is an impressive novel of suspense and dark horror."

Rick's bestseller was *Night Stone* (1986), the first book to have a hologram on the cover, which helped goose sales to over a million copies in mass market paperback. (I think, though, that the writing had a lot more to do with it than Rick admits.)

In 2012, the year before he died, Hautala received a Lifetime Achievement Award from the Horror Writers Association. It meant the world to him, to be recognized by his peers. It also speaks volumes about just how good a writer he was, especially since he was his own worst critic, and suffered from self-esteem problems, which he took no pains to conceal.

*Book cover to Rick Hautala's* Moondeath, *with a cover blurb by King.*

# RICK HAUTALA:
# AN INTERVIEW
# 1988

Sure a blurb from Steve helps sell a book, but even better, I like knowing that he's read my books and liked them. Steve's been a tremendous inspiration for me in my career because he was the first "flesh and blood" writer I ever knew, and that gave a reality to the possibility of me getting my own work published. I don't think I would have had that if I hadn't known him before he or I got a book under contract.

—Rick Hautala, interviewed by David M. Lowell
(*Castle Rock,* March 1989)

**GB: What was King's role in the horror boom in the eighties?**

**Rick Hautala:** King took what began with *The Exorcist* and gave it another boost of legitimacy as a viable form of fiction. Until that time, any kind of writing with supernatural overtones, or straight-out horror novel, was under the umbrella of science fiction.

**GB: What were your impressions of King's ambitious novel *'Salem's Lot*?**

**Rick Hautala:** The first thing that hit me was that King used small-town Maine stuff, settings, and characters I knew and experienced. I felt an incredible amount of identification with the characters and settings, and *'Salem's Lot* scared me. I've read a lot of horror fiction and seen a lot of horror movies, and it freaked me out: I wasn't ready for it. I remember it was the first, and only, time I had to sleep with the lights on.

**GB: What do you feel is King's best book?**

**Rick Hautala:** I view *The Dead Zone* as his best book because I saw it as a culmination of that phase of his career. I know a lot of people who also think that it is his best book.

**GB: How would you describe your relationship with King vis-à-vis asking for a helping hand?**

**Rick Hautala:** I have made it a personal point of honor that I won't beg Steve for help. I won't do it. But when he offered help, I wasn't stupid enough to reject it. When he offered to read *Moondeath* and liked it, he sent it around to some people he knew, and turned it over to his agent, Kirby McCauley, and that got my career going. Kirby made it clear that he wasn't handling me as a client; he was doing it as a favor for Steve.

**GB: You were a contemporary of King's at the University of Maine at Orono. How was he perceived on campus?**

**Rick Hautala:** There was a group of writers, English majors, who were also publishing in the literary magazine and the newspaper, and of those writers he was the one whose stuff stood out. There were a lot of poseurs and sensitive poets, but his was the only stuff I consistently read because it delivered. He was the most talented of the English majors. I didn't dare show my writing. I didn't hobnob with the students who were writing.

**GB: In terms of success and other writers in the horror field, how would you describe King's success?**

**Rick Hautala:** I think people are beginning to realize that there isn't going to be another person in the field who writes like King does; no one else is getting $40 million for three or four books like King.

**GB: What accounts for his success, and his growing audience?**

**Rick Hautala:** He always delivers a story, and he proves himself with every successive book. I'm convinced that if he released a book under another name that nobody knew about, it would disappear without a trace. The Bachman books didn't set any bestseller records when nobody knew it was Steve.

**GB: So, is King going to retire anytime soon?**

**Rick Hautala:** When he "retired" a few years back, as soon as I read that, I laughed. Steve not write? It just isn't in his makeup. He said in print that he writes to keep himself from going crazy. He needs that outlet.

# 8

---

# Burton Hatlen:

## An Interview

### 1988

On the one hand, there have been a lot of people who are regarded as major writers who were very popular—Mark Twain, Charles Dickens, William Shakespeare. I think that there's another issue here, and that is that Steve's work really in some ways grows out of a conscious critique of that cultural split itself, and his critique of it is that what the split does is automatically write off everything that's on the popular culture side as mere commodity, trash, a contribution to the debased tastes of an illiterate mob. . . . We have a massive rethinking of the whole issue of canonicity and canonization; Steve's work is one of the forces that has initiated this rethinking of that issue.

—Burton Hatlen, *Stephen King's America*

T
he late Burton Hatlen was King's professor, mentor, and close friend. In a postscript to *Lisey's Story,* a novel published in 2006, King wrote:

> Finally, great thanks to Burton Hatlen, of the University of Maine. Burt was the greatest English teacher I ever had. It was he who first showed me the way to the pool, which he called "the language-pool, the myth-pool, where we all go down to drink." That was in 1968. I have trod the path that leads there often in the years since, and I can think of no better place to spend one's days; the water is still sweet, and the fish still swim.

It was Hatlen who wrote the first major review of *Carrie.* A well-respected scholar who published dozens of essays in journals, he wrote several pieces on King. Hatlen also worked with Carroll Terrell to build the National Poetry Foundation and became its director in 1991.

Though Hatlen never collected his critical writings in book form, his wife, Virginia Nees Hatlen, told me that she's currently working on a collection.

When Stephen and Tabitha King made a generous donation to their alma mater of $4 million, they gave the first installment of one million dollars to Hatlen to hire more arts and humanities professors.

When Hatlen died at age seventy-one, King, contacted by the local paper for a comment, said that Hatlen "was more than a teacher to me. He was also a mentor and a father figure. He made people—and not just me—feel welcome in the company of writers and scholars, and let us know there was a place for us at the table."

King paid homage to Hatlen in "Rita Hayworth and the Shawshank Redemption" (in *Different Seasons*) by naming one of its characters after him: a prison librarian named Brooks Hatlen.

This interview was conducted in the summer of 1988 at Hatlen's book-filled home in Bangor.

**GB: When did you first encounter Stephen King?**

**Burton Hatlen:** During my first year here, which was his sophomore year, he took a course from me on modern American literature. He did read some stuff in that course that I think had an influence on him, including John Steinbeck. We read Steinbeck's *In Dubious Battle,* and I remember him being very struck by that. He got very interested in Steinbeck, and is still a Steinbeck fan.

Within the last four years, Steve, as a way of giving his kids jobs to do, paid them to tape-record novels. They recorded Steinbeck's short stories and *East of Eden.* When he was traveling, he would listen to the tapes.

In a recent conversation, he and I were talking about various things, and I mentioned that I hadn't read *East of Eden,* and he was surprised. So I immediately ran off and read it; he's always been able to do that to me. It's a good book, and I liked it. It's regional stuff, and that's one of the things he got from Steinbeck, a sense of place that he could make his own.

We also read Faulkner's *Light in August* in that class, and he was very excited by it. He was very taken with William Carlos Williams's *Paterson,* and when we did a hundredth anniversary conference at Orono in 1983 on Williams, Steve did a reading from it.

So several of the things that he read in that course have had an impact on him, though I don't think Faulkner has been as strong a force as Steinbeck on him.

He's still interested in Faulkner, and in recent visits to his house he showed me a first edition of *The Town,* one of the middle-period Faulkner novels. He was excited he had found it.

During that year—the fall semester of his sophomore year—Jim Bishop and I came up with the idea that we wanted to do a course on contemporary American poetry, the first special seminar offered at the university.

We had a very exciting class composed of twelve students. It included Stephen King, George MacLeod, and Bruce Holsapple, who went to Portland and started a magazine called *Contraband,* in which there were some early King poems in the first couple of issues.

The course was a very dynamic experience for a lot of people. Many of them started writing poetry as a result of it, and then a poetry workshop grew out of that, which lasted for the rest of King's college career. As a poet, I thought Steve was very good.

**GB: Who influenced him at the University of Maine at Orono?**

**Burton Hatlen:** Jim Bishop, one of Steve's teachers, had *The Long Walk* dedicated to him. Ted Holmes was also one of the most affirmative of his work when Steve was a student.

**GB: King is best known, or at least pigeonholed, as a horror writer. Do you read much in that genre?**

**Burton Hatlen:** I read a lot, but I didn't read horror fiction then, and in fact I don't read it now. It's not a major interest. That's not the dimension of his work that interests me.

I've written about him as a writer who happens to use the conventions of the genre but is interested in some very serious issues, including American society. He has basically a counterculture, New Left perspective. Although our politics are pretty similar in some respects, he was radicalized to some extent by the experiences of the sixties, of which I was very much a part of that process, very involved in the antiwar protests. He was listening to me. I felt I really had an impact on him. He's testified to this on many occasions.

**GB: What about the question, attributed to you in *Rolling Stone,* that Douglas Winter alluded to in *The Art of Darkness*: "Is there such a thing as white soul? Is there a suburban soul?"**

**Burton Hatlen:** Steve attributes that to me, but it's my distinct memory that it was he who came to me and said, "Well, here I've been reading all this stuff about black soul, and what I'm interested in is whether there's such a thing as white soul."

I was struck by it. That's why I remembered it, which is why I can envision the conversation, because we were walking somewhere and he's talking about his own writing; he wants to make his writing an expression of white soul.

It also has a racist overtone to it that I don't like. It's not the kind of thing I would say.

**GB: As you know, King said that he couldn't see why popular culture—particularly in literature—was held in such low regard. What are your recollections of his position?**

**Burton Hatlen:** I want to elaborate a little bit about that business of popular culture and traditional or high culture.

Steve took his courses, read everything, and was actually a very good student, but he was also quite critical of the faculty.

I remember a meeting in which the students and faculty were supposed to get together and talk about the curriculum of the English department. Several people have a memory of Steve standing up and denouncing the department, because he had never been able to read a Shirley Jackson novel in any of the courses he had taken. So he criticized the curriculum and constantly insisted on the value and importance of popular culture and mass culture.

What I'm trying to circle toward here is the fact that either during his junior or senior year, he proposed a course on popular American fiction. He wanted to do a special seminar, which produced a crisis because here was an undergraduate proposing to teach a course. Graham Adams agreed to be a front person for the course, but I didn't participate. Nobody seems to have tuned in to Graham as somebody who had an important part in Stephen's life.

**GB: Why is Shirley Jackson not relegated to the horror genre?**

**Burton Hatlen:** What's worth remembering about Shirley Jackson is that she was married to one of the most influential literary critics at that time. Not only was there the connection with Stanley Edgar Hyman, who taught at Bennington College, but Kenneth Burke, a high-powered, erudite critic who was also teaching there, and he was writing about Shirley Jackson early on. She had entrée into the literary world.

**GB: After King graduated from the university, he returned to teach as a writer in residence. How did that come about?**

**Burton Hatlen:** Ted Holmes was forced to retire at sixty-five, so we then had the question of what to do with a creative writing position. Ted also had the Lloyd Elliot chair. So what the department decided, instead of bringing in a permanent creative writing teacher, was to bring in writers for relatively short periods. Steve was invited, and he accepted the offer.

The understanding was that it was for one year, although we tried to talk him into extending it, but he didn't want to. I think he wanted to come back and be in the university in the English department in a different role than previously. Perhaps it was a curiosity: What would teaching be like?

When he was a student, he was never really quite a student, but he was never really a faculty member, either. Now, he had a position as a member of the faculty. He was so different from most students. He had such a clearly defined identity and a sense of purpose. I think that's quite unusual—for a student to know so clearly and decisively what he wanted to do, and [to be] on the way to doing it as an undergraduate.

**GB: He had a real sense of purpose as a writer.**

**Burton Hatlen:** Yes. Remember, he started writing *Rage* before he came [to the university], between his high school graduation and his first year of college. *Rage* does not seem to me to be a fully successful book. I still think *The Long Walk* is a first-rate book. I think it's a better book than *Carrie*. I think it was the best thing he wrote as an undergraduate, and the best thing he wrote until *'Salem's Lot*.

**GB: I believe that the mechanics of writing can be taught, unlike the art of storytelling, which is innate.**

**Burton Hatlen:** I agree with that. That was what was most striking about *The Long Walk*. Steve had a fully developed sense of narrative and pace. One day I happened to have brought it home and laid it on the dining room table. My wife picked it up, started reading it, and couldn't stop. That was also my experience. The narrative grabbed and carried you forward. The narrative sense was fully developed. It was like it was all there already. It was really quite amazing to see that.

**GB: What about the Bachman pen name? Was it an open secret at the university?**

**Burton Hatlen:** A few of us knew. I obviously knew, but I was sworn to secrecy and preserved it.

**GB: Did you ever have Tabitha King as a student?**

**Burton Hatlen:** She was never a student of mine. I came to know her through the poetry workshop because there was another special seminar that's important to this story: We had a great success with it in the spring semester of 1968, so in the fall of 1969, the seminar was repeated.

*The Kittery Bridge connecting New Hampshire and Maine.*

*"Welcome to Maine" road sign after crossing the Kittery Bridge.*

Courtesy of Dave Lowell

# 9

# CROSSING THE KITTERY BRIDGE[1] INTO MAINE'S HEART OF DARKNESS

I have been asked time and again why I want to live here. Of course we fell in love with the house we live in. [West Broadway] attracted us, with its graceful Victorian homes, its lovely trees, and its feeling of being a peaceful sort of inlet very close to the bustle of downtown.

—STEPHEN KING, FROM *A NOVELIST'S PERSPECTIVE ON BANGOR*, BANGOR HISTORICAL SOCIETY, 1983

*The Sarah Long Bridge connecting Portsmouth, NH to Kittery, Maine,*

*The Kings' main home in Bangor, Maine.*

1 The bridge that connects New Hampshire to Maine is called the Piscataqua River Bridge, but because it's a mouthful to say, locals call it the Kittery Bridge. (It connects Portsmouth, New Hampshire to Kittery, Maine.)

## It's Wicked Cold in Maine

Burton Hatlen wrote eloquently about Stephen King's "myth of Maine." His thesis was that King *chose* Maine, and has made it his own, just as Steinbeck claimed California's Salinas Valley and Faulkner claimed Mississippi's Yoknapatawpha County.

Today, King could buy a home anywhere in the world. But before he bought a home in Florida in 2001, and a second Florida home down the road for visiting family in 2007, the Kings called Maine home on a year-round basis. Unlike the "summah folk from away" who only come up when the weather is good, in the spring and summer, Stephen King has spent most of his life in Maine.

One wag on his Web site suggested "Maine is for Maniacs," which suggests you'd have to be crazy to live in a state with record-setting cold winters.

Let's face it: If you live in Maine, you've got to be of hardy stock. The winters aren't so much experienced as they are endured; and as they say about old age, which is also true for Maine winters: It ain't for sissies.

Ayuh, it's wicked cold in the winter months.

Stephen King's main haunts in Maine include: Durham (as a youth), Orono (as a college student), Bangor and environs (pre-*Carrie*), Bridgton (where he bought his first home, which he has since sold), Center Lovell, and, finally, back to Bangor, on West Broadway, part of the historic district, where lumber barons in the nineteenth century built their palatial homes.

The Kings' main home in Bangor is the most distinctive on West Broadway, and fans who come from around the world to see it and take photos will have no difficulty finding it. With its high, cast iron fence decorated with bats and a three-headed creature right out of "The Mist," the red-colored house is a standout.

The other folks who live on West Broadway don't miss any meals, either, but their houses, and the nearby streets, contrast sharply with those near the Penobscot River, where blue-collar folks live. The Kings would recognize that neighborhood because they used to live on Stone Street, in a walk-up apartment.

If you want to see the "summah" folk, you can start in southern Maine, in York, or in Freeport, which are havens for bargain-hunting shoppers at outlet stores that have sprung up like mushrooms after a warm spring shower.

Further north is Maine's capital city, Portland, which is trendy and upscale. The Kings considered moving there—Tabitha preferred Portland; Stephen preferred Bangor —but chose Bangor partly because Stephen needed to research a novel titled *It*, which was set in Bangor, fictionalized as Derry.

Still further north, hugging the coastline, is Bar Harbor. It's a favorite tourist spot, but the prices for lodging at the best resorts in town are surprisingly affordable, especially when contrasted to a big city like Boston. That's one of the beauties of Maine: prices are reasonable for practically everything.

## Hidden Maine

The Maine that tourists don't see, much less visit, are its small towns. Maine is 85.6 percent wooded, and it's properly characterized more by its small towns than by its two biggest cities, Portland and Bangor. As of 2013, Portland had an estimated population of 66,318, and Bangor's is about half that, at 32,673, but they're small potatoes to other New England cities, notably Boston, with 645,966 people.

But small-town Maine is what King knows best; thus, it's the backdrop for most of his fiction. King knows the texture and distinctive "feel" of rural Maine because he's lived there. For example, in Durham, when the Kings' well went dry, so did their toilet. They had to go out back to the outhouse, which stank to high heaven in the summer and was wicked cold in the winter.

Air-conditioning? Out of the question. Television? It was years after they moved to Durham that a used television found its way into the house. Their neighbors—some better off, some worse—worked blue-collar jobs in nearby towns. There's no town in Durham named Easy Street.

When Stephen King was a college student living in the dorms in Orono, he was, as Tabitha recalled, as poor as only a college student could be; he had no money, and didn't care, she wrote. He was only interested in perfecting his craft, learning how to write, and getting out of college to pursue his writing career.

Living in Hermon, in a trailer from which they were unceremoniously evicted, the Kings saw snow-covered fields and heard snowmobiles buzzing across the landscape. The fields were alive with the sound of gunshots, and one day a trigger-happy hunter shot the Kings' family dog; Stephen carried it back home on his back, with one leg nearly shot off. He has no good memories of Hermon and has said so to the media, to the town's discomfort. (No wonder they canceled Stephen King Day, about which he never gave a tinker's fart.)

King sees a view of Maine filled with rented trailers, backyards littered with used cars, and modest one-story homes where the working class live. It's rural Maine where woodstoves heat the house in the winter and where it's thirty-year mortgages because people can't afford a shorter-term loan. It's used cars, not new ones; dinners in, not dinners out; and "staycations" instead of real vacations, which are what folks with money can enjoy.

When the tourists in their Mercedes and Audis go home, heading south to cross the Kittery Bridge when the weather turns cold, away from the heart of darkness, they leave behind the lifelong Mainers who have to stick it out during the harsh winters and the even harder times.

In one of his essays on Stephen King, Burton Hatlen, who came from California to finally settle down in Maine, quoted a longtime resident: "The only people who stay here are the ones who can't scrape together enough money to leave."

They leave like the Joads did from Oklahoma, on their trek to California, the promised land, chronicled in John Steinbeck's *The Grapes of Wrath*. Hatlen, similarly, writes of an exodus of the poor from Maine:

And as you watch the fleet of cars heading south over the Kittery Bridge in the last week of August, you'll see a few Maine cars mixed in, towing trailers loaded not with camping gear but with faded mattresses and chrome and Formica kitchen sets, headed south for Connecticut or wherever, hoping to leave behind that darkness back among the fir trees—although, as Stephen King also likes to remind us, you always carry that dark spot in your heart with you, wherever you go.

They can escape and get away, but as King reminds us, you can take the man out of Maine, but you can't take Maine out of the man.

That "dark spot" is Maine's *real* heart of darkness.

## OUTSIDERS

The conventional perception is that Mainers are naturally suspicious of outsiders, and there's some truth in that. In "The Mist," a big-city lawyer named Brenton Norton refuses to accept reality, even when the evidence is incontrovertible; he stubbornly resists going to the back area of the supermarket to see the physical remains of a monster's tentacle. He figures it's just another example of how he, the outsider, will be the butt of the townsfolk's jokes.

As he told the Mainers:

It's a banana skin and I'm the guy that's supposed to slip on it. None of you people are exactly crazy about out-of-towners, am I right? You all pretty much stick together. The way it happened when I hauled you into court to get what was rightfully mine. You won that one, all right. Why not? Your father was the famous artist, and it's your town. I only pay my taxes and spend my money here!

"Keep Maine Green, Bring Money" is a slogan on a sign mentioned in King's short story, "The Road Virus Heads North." Those Mainers readily accept the cash but won't easily accept the tourists into their compartmentalized lives.

But sometimes they are accepted, as in *The Colorado Kid*, which features a pretty twenty-two-year-old recent college graduate nicknamed Steff, who is an intern writing for *The Weekly Islander*. She's "from away," a Maine expression for out-of-towners, but her mentors, well-seasoned Maine old-timers (Dave is sixty-five, and Vince is ninety), like and respect her—although they do like to "shock her young bones."

Steff earns her mentors' respect and is accepted by them, but that's not usually the case. Mainers look askance at strangers, and are bemused by rich tourists who come with their airs and preconceived notions of how to fit in. They're usually city folk who only see the veneer of Maine; they never see its true, dark nature.

Burton Hatlen called them the "Summer People" and characterized them as

lean and quietly polite and carefully casual when you meet them in the corner store, copies of the *Maine Times* tucked under their arms. They're headed for a cedar-shingled cottage ("been in the family for three generations") nestled among the pines, a few yards up from a piece of rock-rimmed shoreline . . . and with a neat, white sailboat ("just a thirty-footer") bobbling picturesquely, discreetly, a dozen yards or so offshore.

Hatlen explains that they are the "middle class folks with their trailers or their campers or, occasionally, their huge, rectangular motor homes, and the rich folks with their shore estates and their yachts—make the trek north to Maine every summer" because they want to get away from the stress of the people-choked cities and suburbs.

## BUT IF . . .

If King had been born into a solidly middle-class family, his fiction would reflect that world, and perhaps focus on the angst of modern-day life in the cities and suburbs. The stories would be mainstream fiction and reflect a world in which many of King's current readers live in.

But King doesn't write those kinds of stories. He writes best about the underprivileged, the put-upon, the unfortunate, the dispossessed: an outsider named Carrie whose monstrous treatment at the hands of her peers causes her to vent her destructive fury; Ben Mears, a one-time successful novelist whose career had stalled, perhaps forever; Jack Torrance, an alcoholic whose writing career, and life, is slowly but inexorably spiraling downward; Johnny Smith, a schoolteacher whose spin on the wheel of (mis)fortune takes a bad turn; Dolores Claiborne from Little Tall Island—the list grows long.

They aren't the scions of high society, the captains of industry, the powerful and elite. They are ordinary people caught up in extraordinary circumstances and indelibly captured with the "camera" lens of King's imagination in word pictures that linger in our mind's eye.

*Moose Crossing: a replica of a frequently seen road sign in Maine.*

# 10

# From Student to Teacher

## Stephen King and Carroll Terrell

In 1989, when I was writing the first edition of *The Stephen King Companion,* I sought out Carroll Terrell, who, as a member of the English faculty at the University of Maine at Orono, served not only as a teacher but a mentor, like Burton Hatlen, to Stephen King.

In 1988, I spent a pleasant summer afternoon in Orono with Terrell, known to his friends as Terry. He spoke about himself and his connection to Stephen King. That he would turn his critical attention to King spoke of his high regard for his former student, who sought publishing advice.

On that day I recorded a lengthy interview with Terrell, which I've misplaced, but I vividly remember what he wanted to emphasize: the time when King asked him to read and provide feedback on a manuscript (then titled *Getting It On* and eventually published by NAL in 1977 as a mass market paperback titled *Rage*).

What Terrell told me is exactly what he later wrote in chapter 2 of *Stephen King: Man and Artist,* which I read in manuscript form. Publishing it at the University of Maine at Orono's Northern Lights Press, Terrell solicited, and got, blurbs for the book from Stephen King ("I am very pleased and proud to have been the subject of your incisive mind and careful thought"), Dr. Michael R. Collings, and me.

Professor Terrell, best known as an Ezra Pound scholar, passed away on November 29, 2003. He had also published several volumes of criticism on other poets, including Louis Zukofsky, Basil Bunting, William Carlos Williams, and Robert Creeley. Fittingly, in *Paideuma,* a journal of poetry, it was Burton Hatlen who wrote Terrell's obituary.

I didn't know Terrell well, but I knew how much he cherished the memory of that first encounter with King, as well as how carefully he recounted it to me and, subsequently, put it on paper in *Stephen King: Man and Artist.*

Long out of print, the first edition of Terrell's book was published in hardback, in December 1990 (a revised edition, a trade paperback with a print run of 325 copies, was published in 1991).

I remember giving Terrell advice on how to publish a limited edition for the collector's market and introduced him to Kenny Ray Linkous, the mercurial artist who illustrated the Philtrum Press edition of *The Eyes of the Dragon*. Linkous, flattered that Terrell would ask him to illustrate one of his books, drew all the art at no charge and gave the originals to Terrell as a gift. I also wrote a two-page letter praising the book, which he sent out to booksellers with the finished book.

Of the book, Collings—writing as a scholar evaluating the work of another scholar—said:

> *Stephen King: Man and Artist* provides an invaluable next step in the critical transformation of our assumptions about King, elevating him from mere *shock-meister* to acknowledged voice of an age. Terrell is to be congratulated as much for his courage in accepting such a task as for the wealth of knowledge and perception he marshalls in fulfilling it.

Terrell, an early reader of *The Long Walk,* found himself in an awkward position. He knew King wanted feedback, and was hopeful that the book was publishable, but Terrell wasn't optimistic. As he wrote in *Stephen King: Man and Artist,*

> My dilemma can be posed as a question. How could I talk to him about his book and do three things at the same time: (1) Tell him how remarkable it was, but (2) tell him there wasn't a nickel's worth of chance that anyone would publish it; and (3) because of these two things encourage him to keep working; that is, to hold out hope but not false hope. At this distance in time I remember only a few things about our discussion, but even so I remember a whole lot more than I do of talks with anyone else twenty years ago. After praising the book as a whole, I told him it posed certain technical problems which would require more practice for him to solve. The design of the book made the action repetitive and got him into a kind of "another Indian bit the dust" trap. The solution to that might be a more extensive use of flashback to flesh out the characters.
>
> I am conscious now that I thought *The Long Walk* was a first novel. But I should have known that it could have been no such thing: No one could have written such a balanced and designed book without a lot of practice; not just aimless practice, but conscious and designed practice. It wasn't until some years later that I knew about the several books he had written in high school. They have the same problem: certainly no one could write *Rage* or *The Running Man* without a lot of practice. The evidence we have before us shows that he must have started writing as early as the sixth grade. Both of these books showed a conscious knowledge of unities and form, as well as a deep understanding of the causes of slowly maturing emotional states. . . .

Buoyed by the enthusiasm of his college professors, King submitted the fledgling novel, hoping for a quick sale, but Terrell felt that wasn't a likely possibility. As he explained to King: "I thought the book was potentially marketable, but not something in 1969 that a publisher would give an advance on. So I told him they'd read it, tell him it showed great promise, and invite him to send the completed version, but they wouldn't give an unknown either an advance or a contract. A few weeks later, he handed me a letter from a publisher and said something like: 'At least you hit this nail on the head.'"

# PART TWO:

# PRE-*CARRIE*: A HARDSCRABBLE LIFE

*Reimagining of the Kings' rented trailer in Hermon, Maine by Glenn Chadbourne.*

Glenn Chadbourne

# II

# A Writer's Nightmare, a Writer's Dream

> All the claustrophobic fears would squeeze in on me then, and
> I'd wonder if it hadn't already all passed by me, if I weren't just
> chasing a fool's dream, and I'd say to myself, "Shit, King, face it;
> you're going to be teaching fuckin' high school kids for the rest
> of your life."
>
> —Stephen King, *Playboy*, 1983

## A Minimum Wage Earner

After graduating from college, Stephen King moved out of a cabin by the river and into an apartment in Orono. Encouraged by Chris Chesley's enthusiastic comments, King picked up pages he had written about what would become one of his most famous characters, a gunslinger named Roland, and continued to write. He was on the long road of chronicling the epic tale of Roland and his journey to the Dark Tower.

Like others armed with recently minted teaching certificates, King discovered that having a diploma didn't automatically open doors. Teaching positions were scarce, and he was unable to find gainful employment in his field in the surrounding school systems. Had he chosen to range afar and look in other cities or move to a larger city in another state, the odds of finding a teaching job would have been significantly enhanced, but he chose not to do that. Being geographically dislocated from Tabitha Spruce was the major consideration; she was in her senior year and carrying a full load, not only academically but personally: she was visibly pregnant with Naomi.

With no professional employment in the works, King took work where he could find it, pumping gas for $1.25 an hour at a station in nearby Brewer. Later, when an opportunity arose to improve his income, he grabbed it: His wages leaped up to $1.60 an hour at the New Franklin Laundry in Bangor, where he handled industrial loads.

In June 1970, "Slade," the humorous Western story, began serialization in the University of Maine at Orono campus newspaper; it ran through August. It was free exposure for King's writing, but also free of charge to the newspaper.

From Stephen King's perspective, the American dream of earning a college diploma, with its implicit promise of a good-paying job, more closely resembled a Kafkaesque nightmare.

## STARTING A FAMILY

On December 29, 1970, a marriage license was issued to Stephen and Tabitha; they lived on North Main Street in Orono. Between Stephen's poor-paying job at the laundry for which he earned $60 a week, and Tabitha's rapidly depleting savings account and student loans, they made ends meet as best they could. Their situation, though, became more acute when Naomi Rachel King was born, because it meant another mouth to feed and more bills.

On January 2, 1971, the Kings were married in a church in nearby Old Town.

In March, Stephen King sold his second story to *Cavalier*: "I Am the Doorway," which, despite its science fiction trappings, was a horror story. He was on his way, but not fast enough to relieve him of his financial straits.

In May, Tabitha graduated with a B.A. degree in history. But, like Stephen, she was unable to find gainful employment and waitressed the second shift at a Dunkin' Donuts in downtown Bangor. "Nice aroma at first," Stephen King told *Playboy* in an interview. "All fresh and sugary, but it got pretty goddamned cloying after a while—I haven't been able to look a doughnut in the face ever since."

In an interview with Douglas Winter, for *Stephen King: The Art of Darkness*, Tabitha recalled, "I was devastated to get out of college and find that no one wanted to hire me. I had managed to work all of the way through college and make money, only to discover suddenly that my B.A. was worth absolutely nothing."

Meanwhile, Stephen spent his nights finishing *Getting It On*, a novel for which he had high hopes. A sale meant welcome money, more than he'd ever earned as a laborer. After reading a suspense novel he borrowed from the library—Loren Singer's

*The New Franklin Laundry in Bangor where King worked during college and the summer after graduation.*

*The Parallax View*—King said that "it reminded me of my own work" and wrote a query letter to Singer's editor at Doubleday. But it didn't go to that editor, who was out sick at the time; it went instead to another Doubleday editor, William G. Thompson, who asked to see the manuscript.

As King recalled in an essay, "On Becoming a Brand Name":

> I sent him the book. He liked it a great deal, and tried to get Doubleday to publish it. Doubleday declined, a painful blow for me, because I had been allowed to entertain some hope for an extraordinarily long time, and had rewritten the book a third time, trying to bring it in line with what Doubleday's publishing board would accept.

Thompson delivered the blow as kindly as possible, but it was still a blow.

With both Kings underemployed and their impoverished incomes supplemented with an occasional fiction sale, money was very tight; when a position as an English teacher became available in nearby Hampden, Stephen grabbed the lifeline.

Because Hampden is southwest of Bangor and the Kings lived north of Bangor, it made little sense to stay in the college town. To save on commuting costs—after all, gas cost twenty-five cents a gallon—the Kings moved to downtown Bangor's Stone Street and defrayed costs by taking on a boarder, Chris Chesley, who was in his first year at the University of Maine at Orono.

### "Hope Is a Good Thing"

Teaching is historically a woman's profession, and as such does not pay well in comparison to other professional jobs. Even today, according to the U.S. Bureau of Labor

*Hampden Academy.*

*A sign on the grounds of Hampden Academy, where King taught high school English.*

*A statue of the Hampden Academy mascot, a bronco.*

*King reading an issue of* Mad *magazine in the teacher's lounge at Hampden Academy.*

*King in the teacher's lounge at Hampden Academy.*

Statistics report (February 2013), 82 percent of elementary and middle school teachers are women. The same report states that women, on the whole, earn 82 percent of what men earn.

In other words, King had chosen a profession that traditionally doesn't pay well. King's salary as an English teacher at Hampden Academy was $6,400. His fear in taking the job was that he'd find himself stuck like a fly caught on flypaper; he'd spend the rest of his life teaching instead of doing what he loved, and what he believed he was born to do: write fiction. If that happened, it would be King's worst fears realized. But with no prospect of any book sales on the horizon, and no other professional job in the offing, Stephen King took the teaching job. He was gainfully employed, but he knew it came at a cost: it'd take precious time away from writing.

A natural teacher—like his mother, he had a dramatic flair and enjoyed public speaking—Stephen King nonetheless found the teaching experience draining; he described it metaphorically: It was as if he was a car battery and the students were constantly draining him by attaching jumper cables. Moreover, taking papers home to grade and preparing for classes took up precious time in the evenings and weekends. Psychically drained, King forced himself to carve out precious time in the evenings to write fiction. He did so under difficult circumstances, typing on his wife's portable Olivetti with its square-lettered typeface, hammering away so hard at it that his fingerprints were eventually embedded in its keys.

Because of his low salary, King supplemented his income in the summers by working at the New Franklin Laundry in Bangor for $60 a week. His wife still worked at the doughnut shop, "stealing" her own tips because sharing them, as per the restaurant's policy, meant she'd take home even less, and they needed every thin dime.

Between their combined incomes, they simply couldn't get ahead financially. Things had to change. *Had* to. It meant Stephen would have to keep pursuing his dream as a writer, because his failure meant that they were condemned to live the lives of the working poor, like other people they knew. They'd be living their hardscrabble existence for the foreseeable future—a grim slog.

The following year proved to be no different financially; if anything, it was worse because of more child-related bills: They had their second child, Joseph Hillstrom King, who was born on June 4, 1972. Still a teacher at Hampden Academy, and writing on the side, Stephen at least was able to sell four more stories to *Cavalier* that year, but once again he had pinned hopes on a "hail Mary" pass, hoping to sell a book to Doubleday written mostly over a Christmas vacation; the novel, *Running Man,* was science fiction. But the manuscript shot back within a week, albeit with an invitation for King to try again.

Living in a trailer park in Hermon, Maine, money was so tight that they had the phone taken out. In "On Becoming a Brand Name," King recalled those times as the lowest point in his life. "If anyone should ever ask you, Hermon, Maine, is not Paris, France. It is not even Twin Forks, Idaho. If it is not the pits, it is very close." But in a *Playboy* interview, he was less polite, saying that if it wasn't the asshole of the universe, it was within farting distance of it, which raised a big stink with the town's officials.

In December, with a slowly dying Buick in their driveway and writer's block brought on by King's anxieties about money, King, lacking any fresh ideas, decided to rewrite a story he had begun a previous summer about an outsider named Carrie White. When pushed beyond her breaking point by her high school peers, she used her latent psychic talent to push back hard, laying waste to the town.

To Stephen King, time was money; in other words, he couldn't afford to spend what little free time he had in writing a story that wasn't going to sell immediately to his editor at *Cavalier.* Frustrated with the beginning of the short story, set in a girl's locker room, he balled up the first few pages and tossed them in the trash. But Tabitha retrieved them, smoothed the wrinkled paper, and began reading. She liked what she read and encouraged Stephen to carry on. He protested that he didn't know anything about what went on in a girl's locker room in high school. She countered, saying that she'd help him, and she did. Stephen carried on.

The problem, though, was that King had hoped to sell it to *Cavalier,* but the short story had morphed into a novella of twenty-five-thousand words, which was far too long for the magazine. Lacking any other story ideas, though, King figured that he was in for a penny, in for a pound, and began rewriting and adding bogus documentation to boost the wordage to fifty thousand words.

*Cavalier* as a potential market was out of the question, but perhaps Bill Thompson at Doubleday might possibly be interested in a short novel, since they had asked for another submission.

In "On Becoming a Brand Name," King wrote, "My considered opinion was that I had written the world's all-time loser. The only thing I could say about *Carrie* was that it had a beginning, a middle and an end, and that for some crazy reason my wife liked it better than anything I'd written before."

## 12

# "A Good Angel":

## *Cavalier* Editor Nye Willden

The mechanics of writing fiction back in the days before word processors and computers was no simple matter; from start to finish, it was tedious work. And if the editor who received the manuscript decided changes were warranted, it meant retyping the manuscript again.

Back in the early to mid-seventies when King was submitting to *Cavalier,* the best typewriter on the market was the IBM Selectric, so named because you could select different typefaces by changing the type element, commonly called a "golf ball." An electric, state-of-the-art typewriter, the Selectric was the preferred machine of its day found mostly in the offices of Fortune 500 companies that could afford it.

Though King, a two-finger typist, would have loved to have one, he could not afford it. He had instead hammered out stories on his wife's inexpensive electric typewriter, a Smith Corona.

When King broke in with his first sale at *Cavalier,* it opened the door to further submissions, to the point where King became a regular, and developed a working relationship with an associate editor, Nye Willden.

But getting paid was no easy matter. Magazines like *Cavalier* paid on publication, not on acceptance, so it meant waiting months. In contrast, *Playboy* paid up to two thousand dollars on acceptance, which made it a popular market for professional writers.

Though *Cavalier* sold principally on its sexy contents, King never submitted any erotic fiction because he couldn't write it without cracking up. When he was at the University of Maine at Orono and money was very tight, he attempted to write erotica to pay the bills and began a short story about a pair of sexy twin girls in a birdbath, but he did not complete it. He'd leave erotica to other writers who were more bound to please.

In his essay, "On Becoming a Brand Name," Stephen King characterized Willden

77

as "a good angel." It was Willden at *Cavalier* who read, encouraged, and bought Stephen King's short fiction pieces, most of which were subsequently collected in *Night Shift*.

King finally broke in at *Cavalier* in its October 1970 issue with his story "Graveyard Shift," which appeared under the byline of "Steve King." This in-your-face story, with artwork accompanying the piece, made no bones about its subject matter. The artwork depicted an extreme close-up of a rat's face. It recalls Winston Smith's nightmare in George Orwell's *1984*, when Smith, his head immobilized, sees a rat in a cage staring him in the face, separated only by a thin wire gate. (In 2014, in an interview on *People TV*, with actress Joan Allen of *A Good Marriage*, King cited *1984* as the scariest book he had ever read precisely because of that scene.)

In "The Glass Floor," his first professional publication, in *Startling Mystery Stories*, King's name was cover worthy for the October 1970 edition of *Cavalier*. What *did* help sell copies was the sexy photo on the cover, which featured a color photo of a naked redhead seductively smiling at the reader. When King finally saw his story in print, it was sandwiched in between photos of naked women and ads for marital aids and X-rated movies and photos. Anyone interested in fiction would not think of *Cavalier* as a place to find it, unlike Hef's *Playboy*, which had a deserved reputation for literary excellence.

In *Stephen King: The Art of Darkness*, Winter writes that he expressed surprise when he encountered King's fiction for the first time in *Cavalier*. While waiting to get his shoes shined at an old-fashioned shoeshine parlor, he turned to the reading material at hand, a random selection of men's magazines. "The magazine covers," he wrote, "and most of the revealing photographs had been torn away, leaving the customer with the even more dubious textual content."

But there was a diamond in the rough: He pulled out an issue of *Cavalier* with a King story and was struck by its excellence:

> [I]t captured me, there in a decaying (and now long-ago demolished) shoeshine parlor in downtown St. Louis, taking me away to a strawberry spring in New England where horror walked in every shadow.

It was his first encounter with King, and it changed his life. The story he had read was "Strawberry Spring," and he immediately became a King fan.

King's sale to *Cavalier* was no accident. Lacking a literary agent to do the legwork, King did what every other smart writer does: He did his own homework.

In "The Horror Market Writer and the Ten Bears," published in *Writer's Digest* in 1973, and reprinted in *Secret Windows*, King lays out the nuts and bolts of submitting professionally, a process he dutifully followed when submitting "Graveyard Shift" to Willden: He didn't add gratuitous sex just because it was for a men's magazine; he studied the market by reading what the magazine published; he took a critical eye to his own work, to improve it; he admonished against being influenced by Edgar Allan Poe and H. P. Lovecraft because both were "rococo stylists"; he pointed out that a story's word length should fall within the published guidelines; and he said that rewriting, though painful, was necessary.

Even though another editor, Robert Lowdnes, was first to publish King professionally in *Startling Mystery Stories, Cavalier* gave King a more mainstream showcase and went on to publish numerous short stories by King—enough to help him fill a book (*Night Shift*, published in 1978).

As King pointed out over the years, those checks from *Cavalier* often appeared just in time to help stave off the wolves at the door, at a time when every dollar counted. Breaking editorial policy just for King, Willden, upon request, would send King a check on acceptance. That's what guardian angels do, and that's what he did for the Kings, who have never forgotten his kindness.

What follows, from the 1989 edition of *The Stephen King Companion*, is Nye Willden's view of a young, talented, twentysomething writer whom he knew was destined for bigger and better things.

## AN EDITOR'S REMINISCENCE

"Graveyard Shift" was King's first story published by us, and "I Am the Doorway" was the second. As an editor for a men's magazine which dealt primarily in sexually or erotically oriented fiction, Stephen's story was an exception; and had it been written by someone less talented, it probably wouldn't have made it. But to be honest, I was very impressed, sensing that there was something very out of the ordinary about this writing. I was so excited that I called our "freelance" fiction editor, Mr. Maurice DeWalt, on the phone— he read a lot of the slush material for us, and still does—and read him the story. He had the same feeling that I did, that here was a major talent in the making. I was not at all surprised by Stephen's subsequent success and still am not, although the scope of it is a bit mind-boggling.

We never did much editing of his work. I recall one time we didn't like the ending of a story, or there was something that had to be eliminated because it didn't fit somehow, and I called him; he asked that he be allowed to make the change, which he did.

*Cavalier* pays on publication, but on occasion Stephen would call and ask if we could pay in advance, and we always did. He was having a difficult time financially.

Stephen was always a very friendly, easygoing, grateful, and accommodating young man who came down to New York fairly frequently, and he'd come to my office. We got to know each other fairly well and had lunch occasionally. He was a big, warm teddy-bear with a very boyish, impish grin and absolutely serious and dedicated to his writing. From the very beginning he struck me as someone with a purpose, and he was never deterred from that.

My last direct contact with Stephen was when he called me here in Florida and asked me if I knew of some out-of-the-way place where he and Tabitha and the kids could go just to get away. I called Sanibel Island on the west coast of Florida and found them a house to rent for a week. The island was, at that time, very private and somewhat sparsely populated, and they had a wonderful time walking the beach and looking for shells. Sanibel's called the shell capital of the world because there are literally millions of shells on the beaches.

He came back through Miami and came up to see me. Still the same, friendly guy.

Fiction editor DeWalt was invited to one of his editor's parties. I think it was for

*Dead Zone* and was at the Tavern on the Green. DeWalt had never met Stephen and reported that he was gracious and funny and expressed how grateful he was to me and Doug Allen, the publisher, for our kindness to him in the early days.

We did pay him a bit more than our usual rate after his first few stories, because we knew he was special. I think that was about $250 or maybe even $300 a story.

By 1977 Stephen King was world famous, but was still the same, gentle, nice, kind man he'd always been; and although I have lost touch with him, I'm sure he'd respond immediately if I wrote him.

I think his lack of egomania is what still makes his books so wonderfully believable for his public. I find it a bit amusing—no, charming—that he still expresses gratitude to us for giving him his chance at publication. My attitude is one of gratitude for having the opportunity to have rubbed shoulders with genius—and there's sure as hell no argument that that is what he possesses in his genre—and to have my name included in some of his forewords and acknowledgments.

We've never tried to exploit our association with Stephen, and never would: the mentions have all come from him. We also signed over all rights to his stories immediately upon request.

But it's great to pick up a book by or about him and see my name mentioned. It was, and is, a pleasure to know him, not just because of his fame but because he is a genuinely nice human being.

*A cake in the shape of a rat, a refreshment for the world premiere of* Graveyard Shift *at a Bangor, Maine theater, where King held a press conference.*

*The Kings: Naomi, Joe, Owen, Tabitha, and Stephen*

13

# The Bones of the Family Business:

## Writing

Of course, it is the family business.

—Owen King on writing
(*Maine Sunday Telegram*, July 24, 2005)

We've always been a family that cares very passionately
about books. Our dinner conversation was literary
conversation . . . And after dinners, often we would have a
family book we'd go and read together, we would pass the book
around. Our framework for thought was built around writers
and stories and literary content and scene-creation—so in
that sense the [book] *trade*, not so much the art, but the trade,
was constant conversation.

—Joe Hill, on the King family (*Vulture*, May 2013)

*One of two bats flanking the main gate to the Kings' Bangor home.*

## We Are Family

The "typical" American, according to one source, reads five books a year.

The Kings aren't typical Americans: They're biblioholics and consume books like the typical American gobbles down a Big Mac with fries. If there's one thing that defines them, it's their love of storytelling, so it's no surprise when a major profile, "Stephen King's Family Business," in *The New York Times* magazine, focused on that theme.

Consider the published novelists in the family: Stephen King, who in recent years has published two books annually; Tabitha King, who has published eight novels, the last a posthumous collaboration with Michael McDowell, whose family approached her to complete his novel, *Candles Burning*; Joseph Hillstrom King (who uses the pseudonym Joe Hill, following that used by Joel Emmanuel Hägglund, a Swedish-American labor activist), who has published one collection of fiction, numerous comics (notably the long-running series, *Locke and Key*, with illustrator Gabriel Rodriguez), and three novels, with more in the pipeline; Owen King, who published a collection of short fiction, edited an anthology, and published a novel; and Owen's wife, Kelly Braffet, who has published three novels. (Naomi King is the exception, and does not write fiction.)

The fiction-writing gene, apparently, has now extended to the third generation of the King family tree: In Susan Dominus's profile "Stephen King's Family Business," in *The New York Times*, Joe Hill's youngest of three sons, only ten years old, is working on two stories: "Scrap" and "The Bad Thing," a title both his father and grandfather admire. (Stephen King, upon hearing it, said, "I'm sorry. I might have to use that." Echoing his father, Joe replied, "I know. I had the same thought myself.") Whether the family's talent is due to nature or nurture (genes or upbringing) is immaterial; I believe it's both.

In terms of book sales, Stephen is the king whose book sales overshadow everyone else's, but Joe Hill, who taps the same vein, is the rising dark prince. As Joe told *Vulture* in 2013:

> Our dad is a really unique figure in the history of American letters. With *NOS4A2* [I will have published] four books in nine years, which feels like it is pretty prolific but isn't in our comparison to our dad. I think compared to most working, professional writers, Owen and I are both about as prolific as any of 'em.

Numbers, though, are only a small part of the picture; the American landscape writ large can be found in their various fictions. As much a family business as it is a family passion, they celebrate what John D. MacDonald said about their patriarch's fiction in his introduction to *Night Shift*:

> Diligence, word-lust, empathy [and] equal growing objectivity and then what? Story. Story. Dammit, story! Story is something happening to someone you have been led to care about.

That is the secret sauce in the Kings' fiction: It's all about people.

In his acceptance of the National Book Foundation's Medal for Distinguished

Contribution to American Letters in 2003, Stephen properly credits Tabitha as his inspirational force; in his heartfelt acceptance speech, Stephen made it a point to go out of his way to praise Tabitha, even asking her to stand up so people could see her:

> The only person who understands how much this award means to me is my wife, Tabitha. . . . When I gave up on *Carrie*, it was Tabby who rescued the first few pages of single-spaced manuscript from the wastebasket, told me it was good, said I ought to go on. . . . My point is that Tabby always knew what I was supposed to be doing and she believed that I would succeed at it.

She was there during the early years when he wasn't Stephen King the bestselling writer—when he was just an aspiring, hardworking teacher/writer named Steve King who earned $6,400 a year teaching, when he was perceived by locals as just another working Joe.

## TABITHA KING

Just as Stephen had staked out Jerusalem's Lot, Tabitha has staked her claim to Nodd's Ridge, Maine. Depressingly, the sales of her novels compared with those of her husband's are, as she put it, a faucet to his river. It's an apt metaphor, which is not surprising given that Tabitha was trained as a poet.

As Stephen has pointed out, Tabitha took her study of poetry seriously. He recalled sitting with her in a poetry class at the University of Maine at Orono listening to the sophomoric scribbling of wannabe Sylvia Plaths whose work reeked of pretension. But when it was Tabitha's turn, his attention perked up because she read a poem titled "The Bear" that was so good it immediately earned his respect. She wasn't screwing around; she was serious about her work, and it showed. Not surprisingly, her first book was a collection of poetry, *Grimoire*.

Likewise, Stephen King's serious interest in writing was one of the things that attracted her to him: They were of like minds. He was, as she recalled in Winter's *Art of Darkness*, interested in "getting everything he could out of school and writing his head off." And as Stephen recalled in *On Writing*, aside from her interest in writing, he was attracted to her; he appreciated her comeliness and down-to-earth qualities. Tabitha was "a trim girl with a raucous laugh, red-tinted hair, and the prettiest legs I had ever seen, well-displayed beneath a short yellow skirt. She was carrying a copy of *Soul on Ice*, by Eldridge Cleaver. . . . Also, heavy reading or no heavy reading, she swore like a millworker instead of a coed."

In other words, she was Stephen's kind of girl; she wasn't Betty Coed looking for a MRS degree. As King explained in an interview for *Faces of Fear*, he had no truck with snooty coeds whose lives revolved around superficialities:

> [T]hese little dollies were bopping into their eight o'clock classes with nine pounds of makeup on and their hair processed to perfection, and the high heels and everything, because they wanted husbands, and they wanted jobs, and they

wanted all the things their mothers wanted, and they wanted to get into a big sorority. Big deal.

Tabitha King's novels include: *Small World* (1981), *Caretakers* (1983), *The Trap* (1985), *Pearl* (1988), *One on One* (1993), *The Book of Reuben* (1994), *Survivor* (1997), and a posthumous collaboration with the late Michael McDowell, *Candles Burning* (2006).

Sports fans will want to check out Tabitha's self-published book in magazine format, *Playing Like a Girl: Cindy Blodgett and the Lawrence Bulldogs Season of 93–94* (1994).

Inevitably, the subject of Stephen's sales when contrasted to Tabitha's provokes an understandable reaction in the family. As she told *People* magazine in 1981, "I put 10 years into helping his career," she reasons, "so if his name helps me with mine, I think it's legitimate." But Tabby scoffs at the notion of ever being a rival for his readers. "I'd be nuts to compete with him."

## On Tabitha King

Harlan Ellison:

> There is a quality of kindness in [her work] that is missing from Stephen's work. There are a number of women writers I read specifically because there is a quality of humanity, a kindness in their work. Tabby's stuff is quite different from Stephen's, and in some way is far more mature.

Douglas E. Winter:

> There is an aspect of her work in which she is a very strong regional writer, and I say that in a complimentary sense. We're talking about Faulkner, O'Connor, or a Steinbeck. There is regional power in her books. In other words, part of the power of her fiction is its setting, its people. It is a peculiar kind of setting. Now, on the other hand, I don't think that limits her powers, as it does some regional writers. I think that she's also very capable of communicating the peculiarities of that region to outsiders like me. I've read, for example, some other Maine writers who make the society so alien that essentially it *becomes* an alien society, and you don't feel that you understand that much about it.

## JOE HILL AND THE BONES OF THE BUSINESS

On June 4, 1972, around the time when Stephen King began writing a short story called "Carrie," his first son, Joe Hillstrom King, was born. Joe, now divorced, has three sons, one of whom shows signs that the third generation of Kings may take up storytelling, the family business.

In a competitive field like writing in which every advantage is used by first-time writers to get ahead, Joe King adamantly refused to play the trump card: Hey, I'm

STEPHEN KING's son! That got him in print as a teenager when writing a nonfiction piece that was published in the hometown newspaper, the *Bangor Daily News*, but it proved to be an object lesson when he realized it was published *because* he was King's son. Either he could ride in on his famous father's coattails, or he would be judged by his own work's merits and demerits. To his credit, he chose the latter.

Early on, he asked his parents about what was required to legally change his name, which he eventually decided not to do. But he did submit under his real name, without the famous last name appended: Joe Hill, not Joe King.

Securing a literary agent, Joe Hill kept his identity carefully hidden, but when he began giving interviews, people noticed the uncanny resemblance between him and Stephen King at the same age, and tongues wagged. And, just like his father who eventually came clean and admitted he wrote the Richard Bachman books, Joe Hill got to the point where denial was neither plausible nor possible: He admitted it after *Variety* broke his cover.

For Joe Hill, in the beginning, writing fiction wasn't a bed of roses; it was a bed of thorns. A writer for *Wired* explained:

> Much of Hill's early work was rejected by publishers, including several novels and dozens of stories, which he sees as the pseudonym doing its job. He did eventually break through with the short story collection *20th-Century Ghosts* and the novels *Heart-Shaped Box* and *Horns*, and is now widely acknowledged as a leading horror author. He's also come to accept that people will inevitably compare him to his dad. His latest novel *NOS4A2* is peppered with Stephen King references.

Working in the same field and being related to a famous parent may open doors, but in the end it's the work that's important; his fiction has garnered multiple awards, attesting to the quality of his work: a Ray Bradbury Fellowship, a World Fantasy Award, the A. E. Coppard Long Fiction Prize, a Bradbury Fellowship, three Bram Stoker Awards, five British Fantasy Awards (including two for comic books, with Gabriel Rodriguez, and a newcomer award), an International Horror Guild Award, and the International Thriller Writers Award.

In terms of his fiction, his work—in tone and style—closely resembles his father's, to such an extent that their collaborations are seamless.[1] If Stephen King suddenly stopped writing for some reason (perish the thought), he has said that Joe could pick up his unfinished manuscript and complete it.

In another parallel, Joe Hill's fiction has also seen adaptation to the silver screen: *Horns*, starring *Harry Potter* actor Daniel Radcliffe, was released as a major motion picture—appropriately, on Halloween day 2014. Critics gave it a 50 percent rating on *Rotten Tomatoes*, but fans took a shine to it, and gave it a 94 percent rating.

For critics who opine that Joe Hill capitalized on his father's commercial writing

---

[1] Their collaborations include "In the Tall Grass" (short story), "Throttle" (novella), and "But Only Darkness Loves Me" (unpublished short story).

style, I would respectfully disagree. Hill's literary leanings recall the observations made by his father in *Night Shift*:

> Writing is a catch-as-catch-can sort of occupation. All of us seem to come equipped with filters on the floors of our minds, and all the filters have differing sizes and meshes. What catches in my filter may run right through yours. . . . So each day I sift through the sludge anew, going through the cast-off bits and pieces of observation, of memory, of speculation, trying to make something out of the stuff that didn't go through the filter and down the drain into the subconscious. . . . Louis L'Amour's "obsession" centers on the history of the American West; I tend more toward things that slither by starlight. He writes Westerns; I write fearsomes.

Joe Hill also writes fearsomes. And, like his father, he's much in demand by collectors, who snap up his signed, limited editions from Subterranean Press, which has also issued some of Stephen King's limited editions. There's obviously cross-over between collectors of the two writers, but Hill's audience understandably skews younger.

### On Joe Hill

Stephen King, when his son was nine years old:

> The kid can write a story—he's really got the bones of the business.

Stephen King, on the movie *Horns*:

> I liked *Horns* for the crisp, bright cinematography, but what I loved about it is the fearless way it mixes humor and horror, creating an all new taste treat. Daniel Radcliffe's performance encompasses both the laughs and screams effortlessly. I go to the movies to be entertained. *Horns* was big entertainment. (*Vulture*, October 2014)

Owen King:

> Joe's focused; he's got a good work ethic—he's everything that I'm not. There's a lot more forward motion coming from Joe's office than from mine, I think. We both work at it every day, like it's a job, but he's more confident. (*Vulture*, May 2014)

## OWEN KING:
## WE'RE ALL IN THIS TOGETHER

Well, the thinking goes, Stephen King writes horror, Joe Hill writes horror, so why wouldn't Owen King write horror?

Because he doesn't.

Owen, born on February 21, 1977, attended Vassar College, like his brother, then went on to get a M.F.A. at Columbia University. His first book, *We're All in This Together*, was a collection of short fiction, published in 2005 by Bloomsbury USA; his second, a novel, *Double Feature*, was published in 2013 by Scribner, which also publishes his father's fiction.

In interviews Owen makes it a point to inform readers that anyone looking for a horror fix in his work are bound to be disappointed. As he told Christian A. Larsen (thehorrorzine.com):

> I've said this before and I'll say it again: because I have the greatest affection for my father's work, and the greatest appreciation for the readers who have read it so enthusiastically—whose money put clothes on my back and paid for my education—I do not want to give a false impression about the kind of things that I write about. This isn't because I'm embarrassed by my father's career or subject matter; it's because the last thing I want to do is to leave anybody feeling cheated.

Author David Thomson, writing in *The New York Times*, called *Double Feature*

> a novel that is epic, ambitious and dedicated to the uncontainable. . . . The novel is maybe a third too long, chiefly because as he wanders around King can hardly see a place, a face or a chair without embarking on a wordy, if not literary, description of it. This might have been cut by someone (why not King?) who can see that brevity is his best quality. But he may be a tricky man to edit or organize. He should persevere, for when he is good—and that is often enough to make a page turner of this book—he has a captivating energy, a precision and a fondness for people that are rare and that make the reader doubly impatient for him to do what he does best.

Thomson's perceptive review suggests that Owen's fledgling novel shows great promise, and that he is a writer to watch.

### On Owen King

Joe Hill:

> I sometimes think Owen is more architectural about his work. The pieces fit together and there's an almost perfect stitching there. (*Vulture*, May 2013)

Kelly Braffet (a novelist, and Owen's wife):

> I can't even come close to approximating how wild and cool his ideas are, so I'm going to stop trying. But his finished work combines that wild, sparkling inspiration with true, heartfelt emotion that's always right on key. (*Litpark*, August 2006)

## Kelly Braffet

I'm a writer. I swear a lot, and I write dark, creepy books about
people who also swear a lot. Trying to succeed in the publishing
industry while navigating the fairly choppy waters created by all of
these factors swirling around me has been, and continues to be, an
experience that swings from exhilarating to infuriating from one
split second to the next.

—Kelly Braffet

Kelly Braffet, a relative newcomer to the King family, has published three novels: *Fabulous Things* (2005), which was retitled and republished as *Josie and Jack* (2005), *Last Seen Leaving* (2006), and *Save Yourself* (2013). Kelly is painfully aware that life is too short to waste time reading books that can't hold her attention. "I already probably own more books than I can ever reasonably finish before I die," she told *My Bookish Ways* in August 2013. "If a book feels too familiar to me and the prose isn't blowing me away, I might put it down. If I have to force myself to pick it up, I might put it down."

She never had that problem with Stephen King's fiction, though, which she first encountered in high school. "In 1990," wrote Susan Dominus of *The New York Times*, "when Kelly Braffet was a high-school freshman in Western Pennsylvania, her parents gave her, for Christmas, a Stephen King book-of-the-month subscription. . . . It was just what she wanted. She was in her 'Stephen King completist' phase, and she was trying to track down hardcover copies of his more obscure books."

By now it's a certainty that she's got them all, even the obscure ones, since she has access to the original source: Stephen King is her father-in-law, and, because he values her opinion, she's one of his early readers, who gets a copy of his latest manuscript for which he solicits feedback before sending it off to the publisher.

She talks easily and openly with her in-law, but it wasn't always that way. *The New York Times* noted that

> Braffet was nervous about meeting her future in-laws, nervous even at the sound of Stephen King's voice on Owen's answering machine. "It took me two years before I could actually speak in front of Steve and Tabby." . . . Her first visit to the King family home, which is in Bangor, was unnerving: all those endless rooms and hallways, like a real-life version of the hotel in *The Shining*, and that crazy, famous fence around their home, with its wrought-iron bat and cobwebs. "Their underground library . . . was bigger than the entire library in the town I grew up in. It was . . . a lot."

Between the two of them—Tabitha and Stephen King—there's a lifetime of reading and writing; both are now accessible resources to Braffet, so for her latest novel, *Save Yourself*, when "she was worried that she lost her way," the two gave her time-tested feedback. "Tabitha provided structural advice; Stephen, some notes on language. Mostly they told her to keep going."

She's kept going, and never stops.

## On Kelly Braffet

Owen King:

> She understands that writing requires constant fuel—sugar, Triscuits, hugs. At unpredictable times, Kelly often pops into my office with these things. She's an incredibly insightful critic. She's sympathetic to the primary difficulties of the job, rejection and uncertainty. (*Litpark*, August 2006)

*Booklist*, on *Save Yourself*:

> Braffet's excruciatingly rendered characters and locomotive plotting make her a writer's writer, though this novel shows all the signs of a popular breakthrough. . . . Sex is the driving force here—as power, as weapon, and as shield—and the sweaty mechanics of a few characters recall Tennessee Williams . . . Perceptive, nervy, and with broad cross-genre appeal.

# PART THREE

# DOUBLEDAY BOOKS

## MAGIC TIME—THE MAKING OF THE MASTER OF HORROR

# 14

# KING'S CLASSIC BOOKS:

## AN OVERVIEW

B usiness is all about relationships with people. This is especially true in book publishing, which is a close-knit community: everyone knows everybody else, because editors frequently change publishing houses. Though authors occasionally gripe about their publishers, the marketing department, the advertising department, and others, they rarely complain about their editors, with whom fast friendships and lasting bonds are formed.

King, who found a friend in Bill Thompson, had gotten a country music calendar from him in December 1972. In an essay, "A Girl Named Carrie," Thompson wrote, "Country wasn't trendy then, but he and I were both buffs and I thought he'd enjoy knowing Earl Scruggs' birthday. But I also wanted to hear from this talented writer whose letters I enjoyed and who was going to make it as a published author."

Thompson sent the calendar off, along with a note: "What have you been up to lately?" King responded with a thank-you and a query, asking if he'd like to see a new manuscript.

Because King could barely afford to buy paper to feed into the typewriter, he was typing his manuscripts single-spaced, which editors hate because they want room to make editorial comments and corrections. But the single-spaced manuscript went off to Thompson, and the Kings crossed their fingers. Maybe *this* time . . .

### MAGIC TIME: THE FUTURE LIES AHEAD

"The script was *Carrie,* and it was magic time," Thompson wrote.

In an interview conducted by Stanley Wiater and Peter Straub at the 1979 World

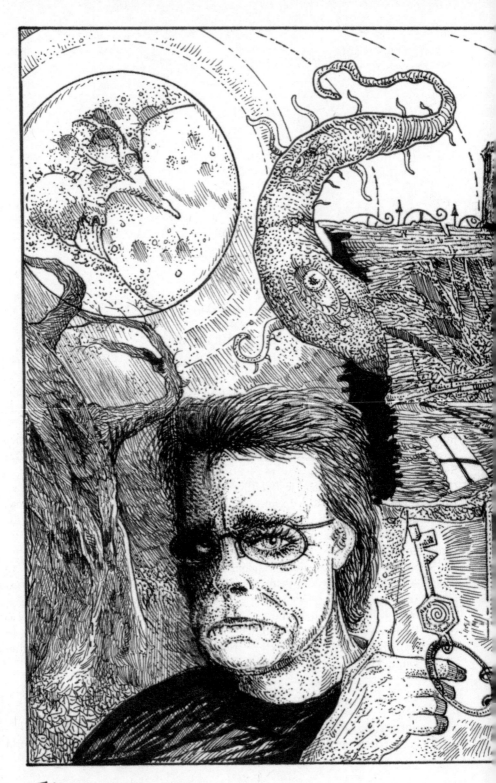

GLENN CHADBOURNE 2007

Fantasy Convention (held in H. P. Lovecraft's haunting grounds: Providence, Rhode Island), King explained:

> But, in a way, with those early novels I felt like a guy who was plugging quarters in the machine with the big jackpot. And yanking it down. And at first they were coming up all wrong. Then with the book before *Carrie,* I felt I got two bars and a lemon; then with *Carrie,* bars across the board—and the money poured out. But the thing is, I was never convinced that I was going to run out of quarters to plug into the machine. My feeling was, I could stand there forever until it hit. There was never really any doubt in my own mind. A couple of time I felt like I was pursuing a fool's dream or something like that, but they were rare.

After reading the manuscript, Thompson requested a rewrite on the last quarter of the book, which King admitted, in "On Becoming a Brand Name," didn't work. "I knew what he was talking about: tired and anxious to finish, the last fifty pages of the original draft bore a strong resemblance to a best-forgotten John Agar horror picture called *The Brain from Planet Arous.*"

King dutifully complied. Thompson's suggestions were right on the mark, as King wrote in "On Becoming a Brand Name": "It was as if he had seen the corner of a treasure chest protruding from the sand and had unerringly driven stakes at the probable boundaries of the buried mass."

In other words, Thompson could see the direction in which King was going with *Carrie,* and his editorial suggestions helped King get back on track. The result was a manuscript that was ready to present to the editorial board, which had the final say.

In February 1973, the rewritten manuscript went back to Thompson, who recommended it for publication. Then King took a bus from Hermon, Maine, to New York City to meet Thompson.

The country mouse went to meet the city mouse, and with only ten bucks in his pocket and a return bus ticket home, the country mouse, who wanted to put his best foot forward, bought new leather shoes to make a good impression. He couldn't afford taxi fare, and walked from the Port Authority Bus Terminal near Times Square in New York City, to Doubleday's offices at 277 Park Avenue, a long walk—a mile away.

When King arrived at the skyscraper housing Doubleday, Thompson took the impressionable young author to lunch, along with his secretary, and King had the first of what would be many publisher's lunches. King's recollection is that, among other topics, they discussed the possibility of *Carrie's* selling.

In "On Becoming a Brand Name," King recalled, "I asked Bill . . . to estimate the chances that *Carrie* would be published by Doubleday. He told me he thought they were 60-40 in favor."

The editorial board was the final hurdle. If he cleared that, King knew, he was home free—and a first-time published novelist. But if they passed on it, as they had his earlier submissions, he was back where he started: living in a writer's nightmare with 1,500 pages of unpublished manuscripts, his hopes dashed, and his prayers unanswered.

King took the bus back to Maine. It was an eleven-hour ride to Bangor and, from there, a half-hour ride to Hermon. All he could do was go home and wait for the word. It was out of his hands.

As Thompson wrote in an essay, "A Girl Named Carrie," published in *Kingdom of Fear*, "I was determined to see *Carrie* published, but this time I downplayed reactions from editorial colleagues in favor of the profit-center types—sales, publicity, subsidiary rights."

When the editorial board met to discuss buying *Carrie*, Thompson knew the book had gotten a thumbs-up when the advertising manager called it a "cooker." King was home free. His talent, persistence, and bridge building with editors would finally pay off.

Knowing the Kings had no phone in their trailer on Klatt Road, Thompson sent a telegram in March or April. Addressed to Stephen King at RFD #2, Box 499D, in Carmel, Maine, 04419, it read: "Bingo. Carrie officially a Doubleday book. $2500 against royalties. Call for glorious details. Congratulations. Love. The future lies ahead."

Stephen King recalled, in "On Becoming a Brand Name," that

> Tabby called me during my free period at school. I went up to the office to take the call, aware that it was necessary for her to go next door to make the call, and quite sure that one of two things had happened: Either Doubleday had decided to publish *Carrie* or one of the kids had fallen down the front steps of the trailer and fractured his or her skull.

*Kevin Quigley below a road sign,*
*"Welcome to Hermon" Maine.*

In an interview in *The Complete Stephen King Encyclopedia,* Chris Chesley vividly recalls the day that changed the Kings' lives forever:

> Steve was living in Hermon then, and I was again boarding with him. I would hitchhike from Hermon to Orono and back again at the end of my school day. So one day I hitchhiked home, and I came down this little dirt road that his house was on, and I had just gotten in the yard, when Tabby ran out the front door . . . and she was waving a telegram. "Look, look at this!"
>
> She handed me the telegram—it was just a few words—and I read it.
>
> And Tabby jumped and shouted, and I jumped and shouted, and when Steve got home, I got out of the way. They just hugged each other and cried. I could hear them from the next room; not that I was eavesdropping, but you just couldn't avoid it. It was one of the best days that I have ever spent.

Chris Chesley recalled that night when Stephen King got home, which Chris discussed in an interview published in a King zine, *Phantasmagoria.* He went over the contract with King.

> He stroked the neck of his beer and grinned like a pimp as I kept poking my finger at one pretty clause after another: percentage for foreign sales, percentage for film deal, percentage for T-shirts.
>
> Stephen King sat and grinned like a man capable of high and fancy rolling.
>
> I remember looking up from the contract and watching him finish his beer. He started talking about the second draft of *Second Coming.* Soon he had got up and went to work on it, down the hall in the little room with space enough only for him, his typewriter, the loud furnace, and the louder radio. The kids came in while he banged the keys.
>
> As it got dark, in the kitchen Tabby sang along with Steve's radio.
>
> I remember the carton of cigarettes still gracing the living room table, the packs fanned out, gleaming luxuriously under the ceiling light.

They moved out of Hermon and moved into an apartment in Bangor.

## "Ch-Ch-Changes"

Tabitha King's recollection of the move from Hermon was a little more grim. In a collector's edition of *Carrie,* she wrote that "it was the end of a cycle for us, though we didn't know it. . . . We got evicted from the trailer in Hermon and moved back to Bangor."

They moved into a second-floor walk-up apartment with four rooms in a modest house at 14 Sanford Street, which rented for $90 a month, but at least they could afford a phone now. (The house has since been torn down.)

Despite the book sale, Stephen King couldn't afford to simply quit teaching. The $2,500 was an advance against royalties; and once the book was published, the publisher would wait a half year to gauge and report sales and then give him a royalty check *if* the book's advance earned out. (The original advance was only $1,500, but Thompson got it goosed to $2,500.)

Now nearing the end of his second year of teaching, King had two more months left on his contract to finish out the school year. King hoped he would be leaving the teaching profession behind him, just as he permanently left behind what he termed "shit work," the low-paying, menial work that paid the bills when he was in high school and college, as well as after college: janitor, bagger, dyer and sewer in a textile mill, gas station attendant, and laundry worker—the kind of poorly paid work his mother had also stoically endured after being abandoned. Therefore, that summer, he planned to write and hoped to make another book sale or more sales to *Cavalier*, because the Kings always needed the money: The book advance could only stretch so far.

In a cover letter dated April 20, 1973, King returned the contract for *Carrie* and wrote that he could "see himself in a big yella Cadillac" and hoped Doubleday could "sell the rights forty different ways." They weren't sold forty different ways, but there was one significant sale, and it would make all the difference in the world: It would change his life forever.

As it had turned out, NAL (New American Library) made a preemptive bid for *Carrie*, to keep it from going up for auction, fearing it'd set off a bidding frenzy. The bid shut the auction down even before it started, and soon King would get the good news.

On Mother's Day, May 13, 1973, King got a phone call from Thompson. The news was that the paperback rights to *Carrie* had sold to NAL for $400,000. King, by contract, would get half. King had suddenly and unexpectedly been catapulted to instant success.

Flabbergasted by the news, King felt he had to somehow mark the moment, and decided to buy Tabitha a gift. He walked to LaVerdiere's Super Drug on Main Street and bought her a hair dryer for $16.95. When she returned home and asked what it was for, as King recalled in *On Writing*, "She didn't appear to understand. I told her again. Tabby looked over my shoulder at our shitty little four-room apartment, just as I had, and began to cry."

*Sanford Street, to where the Kings moved after* Carrie *sold; they rented a walk-up, four-room apartment in a house.*

David Bright, who was King's editor at *The Maine Campus* when they were both students at the University of Maine at Orono, was now a reporter with the local paper, the *Bangor Daily News*, in which he reported the news of King's breakthrough sale:

> Steve King can't quite make up his mind whether or not he should retire. For King, the book marks his first hit after three strikeouts in trying to break into the novel business. That the book is about Maine high school life is no coincidence, for King wrote his first book while in high school himself. His first rejection, along with a letter that perhaps he should try another field of endeavor, came that same year. King says teaching often takes up time he'd rather spend at writing. . . . Five of his students at Hampden Academy have asked his advice on novels they are writing and he is encouraging them as best he can, which is one of the reasons he hasn't decided to quit teaching despite his new-found fortune.

## "A GOOD STORY"
### 1974

In a letter sent to reviewers of *Carrie*, Doubleday wrote:

> Doubleday is pleased to present you with this special edition of *Carrie*, by Stephen King. We feel it may be the novel of the year—a headlong narrative with the drive and the relentless power of *The Exorcist*, with the high voltage shock of *Rosemary's Baby*. More than that, it is part of a rare breed in today's fiction market—a good story. Don't start it unless the evening in front of you is free of appointments; this one is a cooker.
>
> *Carrie* is the story of a girl who has been the odd one all her life, the misfit, the born loser. Torn between her fanatic mother who sees sin everywhere—in the nudity of a girl's shower room, in any friendship Carrie might develop with girls her own age, and especially in dating—and her own pathetic wish to become part of the world that shuns and attracts her, Carrie becomes the butt of every cruel joke, the object of any malicious prank. But Carrie is different, more than a victim of forces she cannot understand, she possesses a strange and frightening power which she can hardly control. And when one final prank is played, the unleashing of Carrie's power proves as spellbinding as it is devastating.
>
> We hope that *Carrie* will excite you as much as it has us. A tremendously readable ESP novel, it is also a quietly brilliant character sketch of a young and unusual girl trying to find her way out of a very personal hell. We think *Carrie* and Stephen King have a bright future, and we welcome this chance to share both of them with you.

## 15

# WILLIAM G. THOMPSON:

## ANOTHER GOOD ANGEL

Most of the books I liked seemed to carry the Doubleday
imprint. I particularly liked one of their novels, *The Parallax
View* by Loren Singer, so when I finally had a manuscript ready,
I addressed it to 'The Editor of the Parallax View' and sent it
off to Doubleday.

—STEPHEN KING, 1981

Acquisition editors serve as reconnaissance scouts for their publishers, ranging far ahead of the main body to find new writing talent. Sometimes, the talent comes to them; sometimes, they search authors out. The stakes are high. Finding, nurturing, and publishing the right author can be a windfall for the publisher. As the saying goes: publishers make books, but authors make publishers.

King is certainly right in saying that, in the midseventies, Doubleday was a book-publishing powerhouse. By his estimate, Doubleday was issuing five hundred books annually, and had its own book club as well. King's initial thinking was that their sheer volume meant they were always on the prowl for new writers; he was right in thinking so. In fact, publishers are always on the lookout for fresh, new talent: They can't get enough to suit them, and regrettably settle for less: It's a seller's market if you've got the goods, as King does.

In King's case, he was fortunate to get William G. Thompson for his editor, if only by default: The editor of *The Parallax View* was out sick for the day. Just the flu. King's query letter was passed on to Thompson, who responded to King.

101

After a long and stellar career, Thompson no longer hangs his shingle at a publishing house; he's an independent editorial consultant helping authors with their book-length manuscripts. For writers of commercial fiction, that's good news. What are the odds that the same editor would discover not one but *two* of the bestselling authors of our time? Thompson discovered Stephen King, of course, and also John Grisham. It was hardly luck: A good editor recognizes great talent when he sees it.

A lifetime in the book trade, as an editor, has served him well. On his Web site, Thompson gives two pieces of advice, to whet an aspiring writer's appetite for his editorial services. On premature submissions, he writes:

> A lot of new writers make the mistake of sending a manuscript to an agent or publisher before it's actually ready. You may have an interesting story line, but it doesn't translate into potential sales until it's wrapped up in a full-size, polished, marketable manuscript. Then you have something to offer.

In other words, you don't get a second chance to make a first impression, so make it count by making your manuscript as good as possible.

In King's case, Thompson asked for a rewrite on the last quarter of *Carrie*, which King was happy to do. That the book sold to Doubleday and went on to command a record sale to a paperback house is testimony to the validity of Thompson's acumen. On stories, Thompson offers the following:

> If a fiction author knows how to tell a story, I can help him nail down what the story is—help him flesh it out and give dimension to the characters without losing track of the story. With many manuscripts, I also try to bring a cinematic sense, thinking of how it would play as a movie.

Thompson started out at the bottom rung of the ladder, selling to independent booksellers. "Carrying the bag," as it was called, meant carrying an overstuffed, big bag of advance copies, promo sheets, and other sales literature to pitch books individually, and as quickly as possible, to booksellers. His "beat" was New Orleans and Memphis.

He then moved to New York City to begin his career as an editor, where he is properly credited for discovering and nurturing Stephen King. He went on to serve as editor for Everest House, which published King's major nonfiction work, *Danse Macabre,* and also worked as editor for G. P. Putnam and Arbor House. He finished his editing career at Wynwood Press, where he served as editor in chief. Though the company is now defunct, it published John Grisham's first novel, *A Time to Kill.* (Grisham's second, more commercial novel, *The Firm,* catapulted him to fame and fortune.)

Writers who've been privileged to work with Thompson and have their manuscripts sharpened and honed to a razor's edge sing his praises. Novelist Kate Wright wrote on his Web site, "Bill is the perfect kind of editor who can be critical, discerning, precise and, most important of all, encouraging. You can trust him to know what needs to be done to get your manuscript in the best possible shape."

Rev. Canon John H. Taylor, wrote, "No one knows writing—the arc of a story, the texture of a description, the heartbeat of character—and nobody knows the publishing industry like Bill Thompson. If you have a book in you, he's the one to help you bring it to life."

In "A Girl Named Carrie," an essay Thompson wrote for *Kingdom of Fear: The World of Stephen King,* he boiled it all down to this: "Basically the editorial process means understanding what the author wants to do and helping him get there."

He realizes that authors, for all sorts of reasons, can lose sight of the story's objective by getting caught up in the details and failing to see the big picture or the flaws inherent in the structure. Even Stephen King, whose submitted manuscripts usually require little editing, acknowledged that, for *Carrie,* Thompson's editorial input was invaluable. In "On Becoming a Brand Name," King wrote:

> Thompson's ideas worked so well that it was almost dreamlike. . . . That was my first experience with what editors are supposed to do. I think that on subsequent occasions, Thompson's advice has been good or better, but in that particular case, it was inspired.

The book industry is replete with good editors, but Bill is a rara avis, a black swan among white ones. As King and Grisham would tell you, Bill is, simply, the best.

# 16

# NELLIE RUTH PILLSBURY KING:

## THE FUTURE QUEEN OF DURHAM

### THE POWER TO DREAM

Parents are supposed to be safety nets for their children; the ideal 1950s nuclear family included a set of parents—a father and mother—who functioned as just such a safety net, but Stephen King's mother, Ruth, had to take up all the slack because the other "safety net" had a king-sized hole in it.

Back in the 1950s, the local, state, and federal governments didn't have an interlocking system of support for single mothers. The support system, instead, was the extended family, which comprised siblings and grandparents—the more, the merrier.

Everything we know about Ruth King we know through Stephen King's interviews, autobiographical pieces in *Danse Macabre,* and afterwords to his stories (notably, "The Woman in the Room"), as well as through one interview with Stephen's brother, David.

From Ruth's high school yearbook we learn that she excelled in public speaking, which "won distinction for her in numerous plays and honor for the school in every contest she has entered." Trained as a pianist, she also played the organ on a radio show that was broadcast on the NBC network, recalled Stephen.

Lacking a college education, and, after her husband left the family, saddled with the responsibility of looking after two children and her own parents, Ruth could never afford the luxury of pursuing her own dreams. She lived and sacrificed for her boys to ensure that they, unlike her, would go on to realize their dreams. She wanted them to have a better chance of succeeding in life by going to college and earning a diploma: a one-way ticket out of Durham, Maine, which held her captive from a better life.

Stephen King once observed that dreams often die before the dreamer, which unfortunately was true in his mother's case. As King told Mel Allen in an interview published in *Bare Bones: Conversations on Terror with Stephen King*:

> She was a very hardheaded person when it came to success. She knew what it was like to be on her own without an education, and she was determined that David and I would go to college. "You're not going to punch a time clock all your life," she told us. She always told us that dreams and ambitions can cause bitterness if they're not realized, and she encouraged me to submit my writings.

It was all Ruth King could do to make ends meet by working a series of low-paying, blue-collar jobs. In fact, over a nine-year period, Stephen recalled his mother worked as a "presser in a laundry, doughnut-maker on the night shift at a bakery, store clerk, housekeeper." (From the bakery, she brought home broken cookies for dessert.)

Like his mother, Stephen shared a talent for public speaking and a love of drama activities, which may help explain why Stephen King can speak with ease extemporaneously at public events.

Early on, when Ruth saw Stephen's love of writing, she not only encouraged him but also gave him money for postage to send the manuscripts off to publishers. And for both her sons, when they were in college, she scrimped up five dollars for each on a regular basis so they'd have pocket money. It would only be later that Stephen discovered she skipped meals to come up with the "money we so casually accepted. It was very unsettling," he recalled in an interview reprinted in *Bare Bones*.

As for reading material, Ruth enjoyed reading *Fate* magazine, which purported to publish "true stories of the strange unknown," according to its cover. It focused on the paranormal field, which the magazine's current-day Web site defines as embracing "vanished civilizations, communication with spirits, synchronicity, exotic religions, monsters and giants, out-of-place artifacts, and phenomena too bizarre for categorization." Science fiction, horror, and the paranormal were all subjects of intense interest to Stephen King, too.

When Stephen King was a teenager growing up in Durham, his neighbors thought of him as weird for preferring the company of his imagination instead of playing with his friends outside. But it was a good weird. Ruth encouraged him to dream and write, and, as he continued reading and writing popular fiction, he inevitably turned his attention to professional publication.

It wasn't clear where Stephen King's writing talent would take him, but it was clear that he had the goods. The big question was what he would do with it.

## No More Broken Cookies

As children, we need to have our dreams encouraged and nurtured.
My mother did that for me.

—STEPHEN KING, DEDICATING THE MILTON ACADEMY'S RUTH KING THEATRE

In a perfect world, people would get their just desserts, not broken cookies.

The Kings didn't live in a perfect world; they lived in a hardscrabble world. "For ten years," he told *Playboy*, "we lived a virtual barter existence, practically never seeing any hard cash. If we needed food, relatives would bring a bag of groceries; if we needed clothes, there'd always be hand-me-downs. . . . So, yeah, I guess in many ways it was a hard-scrabble existence but not an impoverished one in the most important sense of the word. Thanks to my mother, the one thing that was never in short supply, corny as it may sound to say it, was love."

In early 1973, King had just sold his first book, *Carrie*: He was on his way to becoming a professional writer. King, finally, had broken through in a life-changing way. That was when Ruth King knew everything would turn out just fine for her son; it was, she knew, only a matter of time because he'd keep at it until he reached the level of success he'd strived for. Sadly, Ruth King's days were numbered: the cancer that riddled her body would soon take its inevitable toll. Upon learning this, Stephen and his family moved from Bangor to North Windham, Maine, to be near her.

Stephen made sure she got an advance copy of *Carrie*; in a short chapter in *Lord John Signatures* (1991), he explained that

> I signed my first autograph in late 1973. . . . That autograph read: *For Ruth King—Thanks for letting me wonder. I love you, mom—Stephen King.* . . . I haven't the slightest idea what happened to the proof copy. It would be worth a small fortune, I suppose, in the mad atmosphere of today's collector's market, where the autographs of some writers command sums of money which seem—to me, at least—surreal.

In *On Writing*, Stephen King recalled her last moments. "My boys," she said. A shadow of her former self, Ruth was 90 pounds, down from her normal weight of 160. On December 18, 1973, at 7:15 A.M., Nellie Ruth Pillsbury King passed away. She was only sixty years old.

"She was a wonderful lady," Stephen recalled to *Playboy*, "a very brave lady in that old-fashioned sense, and went to work to support us, generally at menial jobs because of her lack of any professional training. After my father did his moonlight flit, she became a rolling stone, following the jobs around the country. . . . She worked as a laundry presser and a doughnut maker—like my wife, twenty years later—as a housekeeper, a store clerk; you name it, she did it."

Stephen King later told Mel Allen in an interview, "Ah, if my mother had lived, she'd have been the Queen of Durham by now."

If only.

## Ruth P. King Obituary

*The Lewiston Daily Sun,*
December 19, 1973

Durham—Mrs. Ruth P. King, 60, a resident of Methodist Corner, died Tuesday at the home of her son [David] in Mexico [Maine]. She was born in Scarborough, Feb. 3, 1913, the daughter of Guy H. and Nellie Fogg Pillsbury. She was educated in schools of Scarborough and the New England Conservatory of Boston, Mass. She was a retired worker from the housekeeping department at the Pineland Hospital. She was a member of the First Congregational Church of Durham. Surviving are two sons, Davie V. of Mexico and Stephen E. of North Windham; three sisters, Mrs. Mary Donahue, Durham, Mrs. Lois Story, Scituate, Mass., and Mrs. Ethelyn P. Flaws, Durham.

### PAYING IT FORWARD

After King became successful, he told David Pettus during an interview in *Fan Plus* that he had no love for his father but loved his mother. When asked, "Do you ever wish they could see you now?" King responded,

> Sure. I mean, my father I could care less about. But I wish my mother could see me now. It would be great. She worked very hard all her life for us, and I'd like to give her all the nice things I could give her now. I *always* think of her when something good happens to me. I think, gee I gotta call my mother and tell her—and then I say, shit, she's dead. It's really a nasty trick for things to have turned out that way. But it leaves me, as her son, in a position of not being able to pay back—*anything*.

Stephen and Tabitha King do what others in their position have done: They pay it *forward*. Their generosity, through foundations they've established, and especially to the Bangor community, speaks volumes about their character. The Kings know what it's like to not have money, so they donate money to pay for critically needed heating oil for indigent families and donate to other worthy causes. That's how the Kings were raised. Their parents taught them well.

*The Doubleday dust jacket for* Carrie.

*The "Carrie" cover to* Cinefantastique *(1977).*

# 17

CARRIE

## 1974

I remember once years ago seeing the author of *The Third World
War* on a TV chat show in England. And when the interviewer
asked John Hackett about his book, the first thing he said was,
"Oh yes, it's just some old trash I put together." I do think of
*Carrie* that way.

—STEPHEN KING, *PUBLISHERS WEEKLY*, JANUARY 24, 1991

H arlan Ellison, looking back at some of the big mistakes in his life, pondered why
he had committed them and came up with an explanation: It seemed like a good
idea at the time.

It explains why Stephen King signed a one-sided contract, without the benefit of
agent representation. One of the clauses, involving subsidiary rights, gave the publisher
fifty percent of the proceeds on a paperback sale. Never having had that much money
in their lives, the Kings welcomed the $200,000. But back in those days, when a literary
agent sold the writer's work, he or she got 10 percent of the proceeds. So why should the
publisher, doing the same job for the author, get paid *five* times as much? At the time, did
it even cross King's mind? Agency representation would have been the wisest move he
could have made. King could have asked his editor for a recommended literary agent or

found one himself. And with a contract in hand from Doubleday ready to be negotiated, King would have had no problem finding a reputable agent to take him on as a client.

At the time, it was a nonissue because King had other concerns. He was writing and publishing his short fiction and writing more novels; simultaneously, his publisher became actively involved in promoting and positioning him, building and billing him as the King of Horror, a title King realized was good for marketing but not so good for his literary reputation: Once a bogeyman, always a bogeyman . . .

In the five years spanning 1973 to 1978, King's main novels—*Carrie, 'Salem's Lot, The Shining,* and *The Stand*—and a collection of short fiction, *Night Shift,* firmly cemented him as a horror writer. Had King never published anything else in his life, his fortune and reputation would forever be secure: Those four novels became classics, and all four would be adapted into movies for the silver screen or for television. (*Carrie* saw multiple adaptations; and *The Shining* would also see King's own version, after the famous Kubrick version, which he disavowed.) Even *Night Shift,* a collection of stories from *Cavalier,* shined: Many of the stories were adapted for motion pictures, including "Trucks," which was a major motion picture titled *Maximum Overdrive,* directed by King himself. As King pointed out in numerous interviews over the years, when signing copies of the book for fans, he'd write, "I hope you enjoy these one-reel movies."

Had King begun publishing the nonhorror novels first—the books later published under the pen name of Richard Bachman—his career may have gone down a different path. But, as he pointed out in a foreword to *Night Shift,* eventually the monsters would have come out.

Whether King is writing about monsters—the human or the inhuman kind—he's always focused on the people. As readers, once we're invested with the people in the story, we're interested and concerned about their fictional lives. It's all about story, as John D. MacDonald wrote in his introduction to *Night Shift*; and King, also in *Night Shift,* reaffirms it:

> All my life as a writer I have been committed to the idea that in fiction the story value holds dominance over every other facet of the writer's craft; characterization, theme, mood, none of those things is anything if the story is dull. And if the story does hold you, all else can be forgiven.

## PAPERBACK WRITER

*Carrie* is a straightforward story about Carrie White, a high school student who's the butt of everyone's jokes. She reaches her breaking point after she's set up for a final humiliation that triggers her latent telekinetic power, with devastating consequences: 409 people in Chamberlain are killed, and 49 are missing in the wake of her destructive path.

At its dark heart, *Carrie* is a horror story, but there's more to the novel than simply being a frightening tale. The book is really about high school hell, about the outsider who stands inside a glass dome through which she can see the rest of the world—one in which she will never be accepted. It's the horror of loneliness, of not being accepted, of being *different,* and the hell of not being able to do anything about it. High school is four years of misery for the ones who, for whatever reasons, don't fit in, like Carrie: "Graffiti scratched on a desk of the Barker Street Grammar School in Chamberlain: *Carrie White eats shit.*"

In "Harlan Ellison's Watching," a film-review column for *The Magazine of Fantasy and Science Fiction,* he wrote about *Carrie,* explaining its popularity and enduring appeal:

> That first scene bit hard. It was the essence of the secret of Stephen King's phe-nomenal success: the everyday experience raised to the mythic level by the ap-plication of fantasy to a potent cultural trope. It was Jungian archetype goosed with ten million volts of emotional power. It was the commonly-shared horrible memory of half the population, reinterpreted. It was the flash of recognition, the miracle of that rare instant in which readers dulled by years of reading artful lies felt their skin stretched tight by an encounter with artful truth.

Stephen King, in one apocryphal image, had taken control of his destiny.

The movie *Carrie,* directed by Brian De Palma, was released two years after the hardback book was published. Starring Sissy Spacek in the title role and Piper Laurie as her religion-obsessed mother, both were nominated but neither won Academy Awards for their stellar performances. Grossing more than $33.8 million domestically at the box office, *Carrie* helped carry King's name to monstrous heights. As King himself observed, "I made *Carrie,* and *Carrie* made me."

*Carrie,* a $5.95 hardback, sold a modest 13,000 copies. But New American Library's $1.50 paperback edition, published in April 1975, blew out of the stores with over a million copies sold. As King explained in "On Becoming a Brand Name," the publishers must orchestrate book releases so that they work in tandem: "[T]he writer produces a series of books which ricochet back and forth between hardcover and softcover at an ever-increasing speed." When the kinetic energy reaches critical mass, then boom! The writer becomes a brand name, which is what happened to King.

*Carrie* the movie, released on November 3, 1976, helped bring a large, mainstream audience into King's camp. These were not book readers but moviegoers, teenage boys with their dates, who would scream their heads off and clutch their boyfriends in dark theaters—the perfect date movie, insofar as boys were concerned.

The iconic image of a bucket filled with pig's blood is now an indelible part of the pop culture landscape, just like Carrie. Mention her name, and anyone will make the connection: *Yeah, she's the girl in the Stephen King movie who had pig's blood dumped on her. Glad it wasn't me.*

For millions of young girls who feel victimized like Carrie, the book and the movie struck deep, responsive chords. They may not have been set up as she had been, or had pig's blood dumped on them, but they had been dumped on in other ways in junior high school or high school and empathized with Carrie's tragic situation, which triggered her cataclysmic rage and claimed hundreds of lives, including hers.

A timeless story of bullying, *Carrie* will forever live on. There was a film sequel in 1999 (*The Rage: Carrie 2*); a made-for-TV film in 2002; an ill-fated musical on Broadway, on which the critics dumped the equivalent of pig's blood in their reviews; and yet another theatrical release in 2013 starring Chloë Grace Moretz in the title role. But none of those could hold a candle to the original movie, and fans and purists who want to see a faithful adaptation of the book are advised to seek the 1976 film, though its grave (heh heh) ending was to my mind a bit of an overreach. (But then, you gotta hand it to De Palma; he knew *exactly* what he was doing.)

Michael Collings, the first major critic who wrote about King's work in a book series for Starmont House, observed in *The Films of Stephen King* that

> As a film translation of King's prose, *Carrie* ranks among the best. Since the novel was itself spare and concise, the film comes closer to the major narrative threads. The documentary sense of the novel helps the film in determining and developing characters, while the casting led to strong and believable characters. Sissy Spacek [as Carrie] and Piper Laurie [as Carrie's mother] do not physically resemble King's Carrie and Margaret White but bring an intensity to their roles that penetrates beneath the physical and re-creates the psychological. . . . As the first film of a King novel, *Carrie* brought King to public awareness. De Palma made the film, King once commented, and the film made him. After the appearance of *Carrie*, Stephen King was well on his way to becoming a household name in horror.

Years later, in a book review for *Stephen King Companion* (1995)[1], Collings wrote:

> Rereading it after twenty years, and with the experience of the intervening forty-odd novels and collections, dozens of short stories, decades of film versions, and constant streams of imitators and parodists, it may be rather surprising to see how well the novel holds up, particularly since it's a "first novel." *Carrie* is a precise, focused, controlled exercise in narrative, as compelling for its story as for its brutal images of death and wholesale destruction and its examination of wild-card psychic talents as metaphors and symbols for things deeply wrong with American society and life. In its stark portrayal of the bleakness, the terror, the emptiness of the life of an adolescent outsider, it is difficult to surpass. And given the fact that one of King's primary audiences consists of precisely that age group that the novel anatomizes and in part pillories (that is, high school students), it is almost perfect in its ambitions and its effects. It presents the world of its characters—and of a large group of its readers—with clarity, skill, and appropriate brutality.
>
> Against the crispness of a "real" world, he juxtaposes the dark places that lie beneath the intellect, beneath reason and logic, beneath coherence and motivation and probability—these are the areas King has taken for his own and begins to map in *Carrie*.

---

1  Ed. note: Throughout this edition of *The Stephen King Companion* (2015), I've quoted at length from Michael Collings's reviews of King's books published in 1995, in the second edition of *The Stephen King Companion*.

*King's first professional sale, to* Startling Mystery Stories *(Spring 1967), was a short story, "The Glass Floor." (Note that King's name was not listed on the cover, because he was not then a brand name.)*

# 18

# Campus Columnist Publishes Novel

## by Burton Hatlen

*The logo to King's campus newspaper column (the editor's title), "Garbage Truck."*

*The first major, serious review of Carrie appeared in Alumnus (Spring 1974), a publication of the University of Maine at Orono. Written by one of King's college professors, the review takes King and his work seriously.*

*C*arrie is the first published novel by Stephen King, a 1970 UMO graduate. Steve will be remembered by some readers of the *Campus* as the author of a notorious column called "The Garbage Truck." During the hectic years of campus radicalism, Steve was one of the most radical of them all—in hair length and in life-style at least. Even then he was committed to a career as a writer, and in the quiet moments between the strikes and demonstrations, he worked at developing his skills as a novelist. When I met him as a sophomore, he had completed two novels. By my count, *Carrie* is not his first novel, but his sixth. So if the $200,000 he has received for paperback rights to *Carrie* looks like easy money, remember this guy developed his talents by sheer hard work. . . .

However, when we turn from Steve's life to his book, we find not the American Dream but the American nightmare. Steve seems to have learned early what it feels like to be the outsider at the orgy of American affluence. His sympathies are always with Lazarus, crouched at the rich man's gate. He knows, too, how many Lazaruses there are in America—not only the Blacks and the Indians and the Chicanos, but also the poor white living on the back roads of rural Maine. These people—the mill workers, the pulpwood cutters, the service station attendants—are Steve's people. Like them, he dreams of wealth. ("The first thing I'll do when I sell a novel," he once told me, "is buy a purple Cadillac convertible with a tape deck and quadraphonic sound.") But he also knows the desolation of rural Maine—the dreams gone sour, the bodies and souls twisted by lives of deprivation. And he knows the emotion which rules these lives is neither envy nor longing, but hate—a hate which, if it is ever unleashed, will bring down all the dream castles crashing down on our heads.

Carrie, the central character, is a classic outsider. She is "a chunky girl with pimples on her neck and back and buttocks," a "frog among swans." The symbolic pattern emerges in the first two pages of the novel. Carrie is the "sacrificial goat." She has been appointed by the community to serve as the scapegoat, the one that "everyone picks on." As we watch this born loser, we gain a horrifying vision of how our society demands losers, victims, and outsiders—scapegoats. If there were no losers, how could there be any winners? . . .

Few of our writers have such a clear sense of the demons that lurk within the American psyche. And if Steve's ability to project this vision continues to develop, he has every promise of becoming a major American writer.

## Stephen King: American Gothic

It also seems to me important to recognize that Steve is writing within a distinctly New England literary tradition. There is some deep affinity between our dark woods and the Gothic mode in fiction. As a student, Steve was addicted to the *Dark Shadows* television series, a Gothic soap opera set in a crumbling mansion on the Maine coast. One of his favorite writers, even in his student days, was Shirley Jackson, who lived and wrote in Vermont and whose *The Haunting of Hill House* remains to my mind the most chilling of all American Gothic novels. Another favorite of his student days was H. P. Lovecraft, who was based in Providence, Rhode Island, and who evoked a haunted landscape of rural New England. And then there's the Gothic granddaddy of them all, Nathaniel Hawthorne.

—Burton Hatlen, from joshuamaine.com

## 19

# 'SALEM'S LOT

### 1975; ORIGINAL TITLE: *SECOND COMING*

The town knew about darkness. . . . The town cares for devil's
work no more than it cares for God's or man's. It knew
darkness. And darkness was enough.

—STEPHEN KING, *'SALEM'S LOT*

*The Marsten House from* 'Salem's Lot, *by Glenn Chadbourne.*

## SECOND COMING

In *Different Seasons,* a collection of four novellas that by consensus is Stephen King's best, King's afterword sheds light on what he would publish after *Carrie*. He had submitted two novels. The first was a suspense novel titled *Blaze,* which he described as "a melodrama about a huge, almost retarded criminal who kidnaps a baby, planning to ransom it back to the child's rich parents...and then falls in love with the child instead." The second, titled *Second Coming,* which he described as "a melodrama about vampires taking over a small town in Maine."

As King tells it, he and Bill Thompson were standing on a street corner in New York, and Bill had to decide which book to publish. Bill voted for *Second Coming,* which was also King's choice. But the discussion brought up a growing concern of Bill's that King was going to be "typed" as a horror writer.

"I don't want there to be a time when I think that Steve King should be exclusively a horror writer," King told *The New York Times* (September 1981). "The temptation is great, though. You say to yourself, if I don't produce horror stories, I won't have any more Number Ones—and it's very satisfying to have Number Ones."

Years later, though, King's horror affiliation would come back to haunt him when he sought to cross the bridge over from popular fiction to literature. Critics of his work made no bones about their contempt for King's body of work. Insofar as they were concerned, he was simply a popular novelist with literary pretensions, whose work was summarily dismissed.

Nonetheless, Thompson and King made the right call. *Second Coming,* which would be published as *'Salem's Lot,* was the better choice because it's an imaginative retelling of the vampire myth in a small Maine town where the Old World vampire could draw new blood without arousing suspicion—until it was too late: By then, a goodly number of the townsfolk would be infected, becoming vampires themselves, looking for more victims to feed upon, the vicious cycle continuing.

## BLAZE

*Blaze,* on the other hand, was a crime suspense novel, and at odds with *Carrie,* which if published second would have had horror fans scratching their heads and wondering why he didn't write another horror novel, which was what they wanted and expected.

*Blaze* eventually saw publication under King's pen name, Richard Bachman, in 2007. In its foreword, King wrote that when he went looking for the manuscript, with an eye toward republishing it with Hard Case Books, he couldn't find it and had no idea where the original manuscript was. I'm surprised he didn't make a phone call to the special collections department at the University of Maine at Orono's library, which would have cleared up the mystery, because it's been listed in their card catalog since 1988, which I consulted before sitting down and reading the manuscript of *Blaze* along with "The Aftermath" and "Sword in the Darkness." (I wrote about all three in the 1989 edition of *The Stephen King Companion.*)

The manuscript of *Blaze* is 173 double-spaced pages, with twenty chapters, totaling approximately fifty thousand words. There was also a partial rewrite of 106 double-spaced pages. The first draft, it should be noted, had editorial suggestions; I’m of the mind that the suggestions were by Thompson, who read the manuscript with an eye toward publishing it, as discussed in King’s afterword to *Different Seasons*.

The manuscript’s dedication page read: “This is for my mother, Ruth Pillsbury King.” When eventually published in 2007, the book’s dedication was “For Tommy and Lori Spruce / And thinking of James T. Farrell.” (The Spruces are part of Tabitha’s family tree, and James Thomas Farrell was a novelist best known for his Studs Lonigan trilogy.)

## ’SALEM’S LOT

King’s fans who enjoyed *Carrie* may have been surprised when they saw the mature writing in *’Salem’s Lot*, but they shouldn’t have been—not if they had known about King’s history. As Burton Hatlen pointed out in his review of *Carrie*, by his count it was preceded by five other novels. Excluding the juvenilia (“The Aftermath”), King’s then unpublished novels included “Sword in the Darkness” (still unpublished, and likely to remain so), and four novels eventually published under the Richard Bachman pen name: *Getting It On* (published as *Rage*, in 1977), *The Long Walk* (published in 1979), *The Running Man* (published in 1982), and *Blaze* (published in 2007).

If *Carrie* can be considered a simple meal, then *’Salem’s Lot* is a Thanksgiving feast with all the trimmings.

The story behind the story, recalled King, goes back to a conversation he, Tabitha, and Chris Chesley discussed at the kitchen table in their trailer at Hermon, Maine.

King writes about it in detail in his essay, “On Becoming a Brand Name.” As he explained:

> There are so many small towns in Maine, towns which remain so isolated that almost anything could happen there. People could drop out of sight, disappear, perhaps even come back as the living dead.
>
> I began to turn the idea over in my mind, and it began to coalesce into a possible novel. I thought it would make a good one, if I could create a fictional town with enough prosaic reality about it to offset the comic-book menace of a bunch of vampires.

The key, King thought, was to follow Bram Stoker’s device of keeping the vampire off-stage. “Stoker,” wrote King in his nonfiction examination of the field, in *Danse Macabre*, “creates his fearsome, immortal monster much the way a child can create the shadow of a giant rabbit on the wall simply by wiggling his fingers in front of a light.”

King is correct in thinking that, in the wrong hands, vampires can be cartoony caricatures, but in the right hands, their malevolent evil will strike fear—as it should—in any reader’s heart.

Though numerous horror films over the years have featured Dracula, and the vampire himself has become a staple in pop culture—the breakfast cereal Count Chocula and his pal Franken Berry come to mind—Stoker’s Dracula inspired Anne Rice’s seminal novel about Lestat, *Interview with the Vampire* (1976), with its many sequels, including 2014’s

*Prince Lestat*; it also inspired George R. R. Martin to write *Fevre Dream* (1982), a darkly erotic, atmospheric novel set in the Louisiana bayou and redolent of decadence and the ennui of near-immortal vampires that live only to feed upon humans, whom they term "cattle."

Just as Richard Matheson brought horror home in *I Am Legend*, King transplanted vampires to rural Maine to great effect. Clearly more in tune with a Grimms' fairy tale instead of one reimagined by Disney, King's vampire story bites deep. There is hidden evil among some of the small town's residents, who harbor their own dark secrets; and there is external evil in the form of the vampire, Barlow, and his faithful servant, R. T. Straker, with long fingers, sunken eye sockets, and a bald pate.

In an introduction to the Stephen King Collectors Edition of *'Salem's Lot* (1991), Clive Barker explains that "[t]he story of *'Salem's Lot* and its battle to survive the evil that comes to nest in its midst is, it seems to me, one of the finest examples of Mr. King's extraordinary story-telling talents, and is likely to remain both popular and persuasive for many years to come."

Clive called that one right.

Whether or not the vampire is drawn to Jerusalem's Lot, or whether the town drew the vampire, is immaterial. The fact is, the classic vampire has come to small-town Maine to feed, though the town is already sickened from within. As Barker explains,

> It is not, finally, the vampires that kill 'Salem's Lot, but rather a corruption in the town itself, or more correctly, in its people; a number of little sins that allow the greater villainy it holds upon the town's soul. Perhaps it's this, more than any other element, which so distinguishes the book for me: the sense that 'Salem's Lot is complicit, by dint of its apathy and obtuseness, in its own destruction. The novel, after all, is not named after the vampire, but after the meat upon which the vampire feasts.

The evil, Barker suggests, and King reaffirms in interviews about the book, is free-floating and will find residence elsewhere:

> There can be no blithely happy ending. Though there is a purifying conflagra-tion, it too is a devourer, and in the act of cleansing the town it will also destroy it. 'Salem's Lot is eradicated, along with Barlow, but while the town will never be recreated, the legendary evil *will* reappear—if not in the next town, then in the next state: if not this year, then the one after—and the form it takes will be much like the form that perished in the Marsten House.

*'Salem's Lot* was adapted for the visual medium as a television movie in 1979, and again in 2004. The first version was directed by Tobe Hooper, who hewed closely to the original novel. It is regarded as far superior to the second, directed by Mikael Salomon, which is based on a screenplay that took far too many liberties with major plot points and characters. Given that Hollywood periodically revisits King's major books with new versions, we may yet see a major motion picture of King's classic vampire tale. But in the

interim, Hooper's TV version still satisfies; it is a solid, honest piece of work, even with the limitations inherent in bringing the novel to television.

Of Hooper's version, King has said, in an interview conducted by Paul Gagné in 1980, in *Famous Monsters of Filmland*:

> Let me sum up by saying that when I first learned the book was being done for television, rather than as a theatrical release, I was very disappointed. Television does tend to take quite a bit out of a story to avoid the risk of offending the "average" viewer. But that initial disappointment did not extend to the finished product. It was done for television, but it was done *well* for television. It's funny because most of the reviewers I've talked to since the thing was shown on TV seem to be expecting me to really come out against it, but I just didn't feel that way. Sure, it probably would have been better if it wasn't done for television, but I'm certainly not gonna run around screaming, "They wrecked my fuckin' book!" I have a lot of respect for Richard Kobritz [producer], Tobe Hooper [director], and the *'Salem's Lot* production crew, because they made what is definitely one of the best horror films that has ever been made for television.

As with *Carrie*, *'Salem's Lot* sold to New American Library for a princely sum—$500,000, of which King got (again) half the proceeds. With two supernatural novels attached to his name, King knew that he was a brand name in the making, a realization shared by his publishers, who were happy to find a convenient marketing hook on which to hang his work. "Horror was big in those days," King recalled (in "On Becoming a Brand Name"), "and I showed no signs with my second book of exchanging my fright wig and Lon Chaney makeup for a pipe and tweed jacket and writing something Deep and Meaningful."

In *Horror: 100 Best Books* (1988), novelist Al Sarrantonio was clearly bitten, if not smitten, by *'Salem's Lot*:

> While *Rosemary's Baby* and *The Exorcist* mined supernatural niches in the bestseller list, I would argue that *'Salem's Lot*, because of its genuineness, its verve, its originality, its willingness to reflect, expand and *celebrate* its sources, and, most importantly, its establishment of Stephen King, after the sincere but *un*seminal *Carrie*, not as an interloper but as a pioneer in a field ripe for reinvention, was *germinal* and *originative* of the entire boom in horror fiction we find ourselves in the middle of—with no culmination in sight.

Of course, a bust always follows a boom, which is what inevitably happened.

Michael Collings, writing in *The Stephen King Companion* (1995), observed that

> *'Salem's Lot* stands today as one of the finest treatments of the traditional vampire since Bram Stoker's *Dracula* (1897) and one of the last serious treatments of the mythos surrounding the vampire that has developed over the course of the preceding century. In a period when vampire lore was already moving from

a source of horror to fodder for parody, and when most conventional vampire stories looked to the past not only for inspiration but also for settings and characters, *'Salem's Lot* infuses vitality into a tired tradition while simultaneously attempting to re-create in a contemporary American idiom the atmosphere of evil that characterizes Stoker's *Dracula*. Just as Stoker's tale of the walking undead was set in then-contemporary late Victorian England, so King's tale unfolds in a small New England American community, at once typical and unique.

. . . *'Salem's Lot* (which remains one of King's favorites among his works) demonstrates his ability to write complex, multileveled narratives; to create extraordinary but ultimately believable, memorable characters; to make full use of his increasingly symbolic landscape, eventually building from the rough blueprints for the Lot his own private landscape for horror in Castle Rock and its haunted environs; and to write fictions that, while making full use of horror motifs, nonetheless touch readers on levels transcending mere horror.

## On *'Salem's Lot* as the Great American Novel

Oh, man—I hope it would be the Great American Novel. But, you know what this is—the idea of the Great American Novel— it's like when you're driving on the interstate, and it's a hot summer day and on the horizon you see this quicksilver—it looks like a puddle; and you get up to where it was, but you can just see it farther on. Nobody's ever going to write the Great American Novel.

What you do is stand out there, or you try to maintain integrity, whatever that is. You try not to say the cheap thing and the easy thing. You have to ask yourself, do you have the intellect—and if you have the intellect, do you have the talent to support an idea for the Great American Novel? You can't answer it. All you can do is do the best you can.

—Stephen King, *Penobscot Review,* 1977

*Kurt Barlow, the vampire, from* 'Salem's Lot

Glenn Chadbourne

## Stephen King and Frank Darabont on Limited Edition Books

*2007*

Courtesy Doubleday

*The signed, limited edition of* The Stand.

Stephen King, in an interview with Hans-Åke Lilja, from *Lilja's Library: The World of Stephen King* (2009):

Frank Darabont is really high on the idea of doing a limited edition of "The Mist." I don't like them, I don't like them. I think they are books for rich people and they're elitist and the whole idea of limiteds . . . there's something wrong with it, you know. The idea that people want a book that they can kind of drool over or masturbate on . . . I don't know what it is they want with these things, but it's like they get this book and it's this beautiful thing and they go like, "Don't touch it, don't . . . oh God it's worth a thousand dollars, he signed it" and all this, and my idea of a book that I like is when someone comes up to me at an autographing, and you got this old beat-to-shit copy of *The Stand* and they say, "I'm sorry it looks this way" and I say, "I'm not." It means a lot of people have read it and enjoyed it.

Frank Darabont, in an interview with Hans-Åke Lilja, from *Lilja's Library: The World of Stephen King* (2009):

When I read your interview with Stephen King, I had to laugh when I read his comments about limited edition books. I laughed because he and I have had this debate many times. It is a loving debate, as only friends can have. After I read the interview, I sent him an email that said: "Steve, contrary to your notion that people who buy limiteds never read them, I've read every single one of mine, some of them more than once. I had the gigantic *'Salem's Lot* limited from Centipede Press, all twenty pounds of it, resting on my stomach for three nights in a row as I lay in bed. Not only did I enjoy every word of it, but it also strengthened my stomach muscles. And last year I reread that gorgeous *The Stand* limited edition published some fifteen years ago that looked like the Bible and came in a wooden box." (That *The Stand* limited was actually a gift to me from Steve was incredibly generous of him!)

I went on to tell him: "I agree it's absurd to put a book on a shelf and never touch it, as if it were some holy relic instead of a book. That's like being afraid to open a bottle of wine because it's too expensive and rare, or afraid to drive a classic car for the same reason. Wine is meant to be drunk, books are meant to be read, classic cars are meant to be driven—and I do all three!" (He responded by suggesting that I refrain from doing all three at the same time.)

As I've told Steve in the past, I really feel that presenting a beloved book as a limited edition is a way to honor that literary work and the author responsible for it. The people who create these limiteds do so because they love the book; it shows in the care and quality and effort they put into creating them. I feel it's a huge compliment to the book and its author. I became email friends with Jared Walters (who runs Centipede Press) because I was so knocked out by that awesome huge *'Salem's Lot* he published. So I got in touch to compliment him on it; I sent him a fan letter. And it was very clear to me as we emailed back and forth that he published that limited for one very compelling reason: Jared read *'Salem's Lot* when he was younger, and it changed his life. He loves that book so much that he wanted to honor it, make something special of it, like putting a painting in a perfect frame and hanging it on a wall with just the right lighting.

As for people who buy these books, like me, they do so for the same reason: we love the book. I certainly wouldn't buy a limited of a book I didn't care for just as an investment, or some other silly reason—but for a book I love, how wonderful to have a special edition of it! I've told Steve that as long as the books are also available in low-cost trade editions ("books for the people," as Steve admirably calls them), then what harm is there in doing a small number of special editions for loony, hardcore book lovers like me? It is the difference between buying a gorgeous custom-made chair lovingly handmade by an artisan who withholds no effort in crafting it, and buying a cheap mass-produced chair at Ikea. You can sit on both, they serve the same function, but the aesthetic of the hand-crafted chair makes it a piece of art in itself.

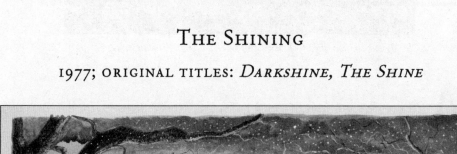

# 20

# The Shining

## 1977; ORIGINAL TITLES: *Darkshine, The Shine*

The Overlook Hotel by Glenn Chadbourne.

Glenn Chadbourne

*The signed, limited edition of* The Shining *from Subterranean Press.*

After twenty-seven years of seeing little of the United States except the confines of Maine, Stephen King decided it was time for a change of scenery. Randomly pointing a finger at a map, his finger landed on Colorado, and the family packed up to move to Boulder, a town northwest of Denver, located at the eastern foothills of the Rocky Mountains.

Living in a rented house at 330 South 42nd Street, King began work on a novel with the working title of "The House on Value Street," which proved to have no value. After six weeks of attacking it and getting nowhere, King reluctantly abandoned it. Instead, he picked up another idea, inspired by a Ray Bradbury story, "The Veldt" (originally published as "The World the Children Made"), which had been published in *The Saturday Evening Post* (1950).

A cautionary tale about how immersion in a telepathically controlled virtual reality can replace the real world, two children become fixated on a scene of the African veldt that overrides everything else, to the point that the family psychologist suggests weaning the kids away by shutting it down, but the addicted kids lure their parents to the veldt, where they're devoured by lions.

King liked the idea of a child's mind acting as a psychic receptor. "I wanted to take a little kid with his family and put them someplace, cut off, where spooky things would happen," he told attendees at a talk in Pasadena, California. *Darkshine*, set in an amusement park, proved to be unworkable. "The thing is," King told the audience, "you can't really cut a family off in an amusement park; they'll go next door and say, 'We've got some problems here.'"

King, though, liked the idea, but knew it required more thinking, and decided a vacation might be the answer.

On the advisement of locals who suggested a resort hotel located in Estes Park, an hour's drive away to the north, Stephen and Tabitha King found themselves checking in at the Stanley Hotel just as its other guests were checking out, because the hotel was shutting down for the winter season.

After checking in, and after Tabitha went to bed, King roamed the halls and went down to the hotel bar, where drinks were served by a bartender named Grady. As he returned to his room, numbered 217, his imagination was fired up by the hotel's remote location, its grand size, and its eerie desolation. And when King went into the bathroom and pulled back the pink curtain for the tub, which had claw feet, he thought, "What if somebody died here? At that moment, I knew that I had a book."

Salvaging the best parts of *Darkshine*, King began writing *The Shine*, a reference to the paranormal powers of Danny Torrance, whose father would become the winter caretaker of the Overlook Hotel, with disastrous results. Deliberately structured like a five-act play, the novel was a modern-day Shakespearean tragedy. It even had a lengthy prologue ("Before the Play"), which was cut from the novel, due to length considerations, though it saw print in a special Stephen King issue of *Whispers*, a semipro magazine published and edited by Stuart David Schiff. It was subsequently reprinted in *TV Guide* (1997), with illustrations commissioned by horror artist Bernie Wrightson. The original epilogue was also reworked and incorporated into the last chapter.

With the passage of thirty-seven years, *The Shining* has lost none of its considerable power as a narrative. Considered by college professors as King's best and most teachable novel because of its psychological complexity, Michael Collings explains,

> *The Shining* also represents one of King's few narrative excursions beyond New England. To this extent, his story of greed, moral corruption, and haunting fear represents a transfer of the darker elements of King's New England—and Hawthorne's, and Poe's, and Lovecraft's—to the newly opened West. King amplifies this sense of transplanted literary heritage with multiple allusions to mainstream writers (Frank Norris, Shirley Jackson, and others), horror writers (it is almost impossible to read the novel without recalling again and again Poe's "The Mask of the Red Death," or missing offhand allusions to Ray Bradbury), modern dramatists (the novel is structured like a five-act play, with its own prologue in the separately published original introduction, "Before the Play"), and others. In fact, *The Shining* is one of King's most teachable novels simply because in it he consciously incorporates so much of his own reading background, while at the same time using those references to create unique sequences of symbolic images. *The Shining* functions throughout on several levels—literal, symbolic, metaphorical—often with characters themselves pointing out the connections the readers should be making, as in Jack Torrance's elaborate meditations on the meaning of wasps. The novel provides a casebook example of literary nurturing, owing much of its power to King's articulate manipulation of others' words and images in the process of creating his own. This is not to suggest that *The Shining* is limited by its literary connections; on the contrary, here King demonstrates an unusual skill in controlling outside references, in matching his style to meet the needs both of his story and of his literary texture.

*The Shining* is the second of King's "Big Three"—three novels completed during his first decade as a published novelist that to this day still largely define his role in American letters and that provide an internal standard against which almost all of his subsequent books have been judged: *'Salem's Lot, The Shining,* and *The Stand.*

In other words, *The Shining* is an enduring classic. King friend and literary collaborator Peter Straub, in *Horror: 100 Best Books,* wrote, "I can't think of another book in the field of horror that affected me as strongly, and of only very few outside it. In its uniting of an almost bruising literary power, a deep sensitivity to individual experience, and its operatic convictions, it is a very significant work of art."

In the hands of a hack novelist, *The Shining* would have been an eminently forgettable book, but King realized that in order to terrify—to fulfill the highest level of art in a horror novel—he would have to create fully rounded characters that aroused the reader's empathy.

Jack Torrance, the protagonist of the novel, rings true because he's a down-on-his-luck guy at the end of his fraying rope, which is already unraveling. In an essay, "On *The Shining,*" King wrote, "I saw a face that hypnotized me because it was, to a large extent, my own. . . . The book became a ritual burning of hate and pain, and in the actual writing, done in a quiet, rented room overlooking the Flatiron Mountains, I found myself mesmerized by the story."

Recalling the days not too long before that when King also found himself at the end of his fraying rope, he was able to transmute those experiences and channel them into the character Jack Torrance, a novelist who was clearly out of control and nearly driven mad by frustration in the process. King only had to look within himself to tap into Torrance's well of despair:

> During those years before *Carrie* allowed me to write full-time, I felt like a man caught in a malign funhouse, blundering his way around with increasing desperation, looking for the way out. I had my dark nights when I saw myself at fifty, my hair a salt-and-pepper color that was more salt than pepper, my nose full of those burst veins that are known in the services as "drinkers' tattoos," my trunk full of unpublished stories and novels.

*The Shining* remains (to date) the only novel to which King's written a sequel (*Doctor Sleep,* 2013), and it spawned a movie adaptation so divergent from the book that King himself stepped in to write a screenplay for a made-for-TV movie (ABC-TV, 1997).

Stanley Kubrick's reimagined version of the book is best termed "Stanley Kubrick's *The Shining,*" to differentiate it from King's made-for-TV movie.

## STANLEY KUBRICK'S *THE SHINING*

In numerous interviews over the years, King has stated that he considers a book as a separate entity from the movie adapted from it. Nonetheless, he still harbors strong feelings when a director forcibly imposes his or her vision onto one of his own books, especially if the adaptation omits key points. King's book *The Shining* was "kubricked"—that is to say, bent, folded, spindled, and mutilated to accommodate Kubrick's vision, instead of giving us King's.

*The Shining* is in many ways a brilliant, disturbing, and admittedly unnerving film, despite its tonal divergence from the novel. Moreover, as King has pointed out on numerous occasions, the casting of Jack Nicholson was the triumph of box office bankability over proper casting. Coming off the success of his role as R. P. McMurphy in *One Flew Over the Cuckoo's Nest*, Nicholson, said King, comes off as a loony from the beginning of the movie, which significantly undermines our sympathy for him.

What's lost in translation, King says, is the heart of the film: the love Jack Torrance has for his family, which becomes imperiled when the insidious effects of the Overlook Hotel's haunted history take a cumulative, psychic toll on Jack: He finally snaps and loses his tenuous grasp on reality.

## A Rope with Which to Hang Oneself

After King vocally criticized the movie at length in multiple venues, Stanley Kubrick had had enough, and one of the conditions of allowing King to remake the movie was that he stop the endless kvetching to the media. King dutifully complied.

At a press conference to promote the remake, King said, "In order to get this project off the ground, a deal was made between me, Warner Brothers, and Stanley Kubrick. One of his stipulations was that I would not talk about his version of the film, so I don't . . . because I can't. If you ask me about it, I'll say 'No comment.'"

Directed by King's friend Mick Garris, based on King's own screenplay, with Steven Weber in the title role of Jack Torrance, and Rebecca De Mornay as his wife, Wendy, we finally see *The Shining* through a new and sympathetic lens: It's *all* about family; it's specifically about how the Torrances are afflicted with major fissures in the family structure that threaten to break it asunder.

At a press conference held in Pasadena on January 9, 1997, Stephen King, who also doubled as an executive producer for the $23 million, six-hour movie, shed light on why he felt impelled to go back to the drawing board and remake the film, even though Kubrick's was well-regarded by the general public, critics, and Kubrick fans. As King told the media, "Doing *The Shining* was like a dream to me, to be able to do it, to have it put together, to have ABC be as welcoming and supportive of the project as they were, and to get a chance to work with Mick Garris again, after working with him on *The Stand*, and having that turn out the way that it did, to get a chance to work with the cast that I did."

Filming at the Stanley proved to be a challenge. Shooting on location always presents its own host of problems, but who would have thought the cast and crew would have to endure ghostly sightings? From *TV Guide* (April 26, 1997):

> Tonight, even as crew members sweep away the confetti from the dance floor, the Stanley looks like a train wreck. The hotel, built in 1909 as a getaway for the rich, has been transformed into a studio set, with all 92 rooms occupied by cast

## The Stanley Hotel Shines On

As I write this, it's Halloween and, appropriately, IKEA released a horror-themed commercial showing a young boy named Danny pedaling around in an IKEA retail store, replete with cobwebbed skeletons and other macabre touches, that culminates on a happy note: the frightening-looking pair who urge him to "come play with us" are in fact his parents.

It's an imaginative, timely ad, and if nothing else, it shows the enduring power of Stanley Kubrick's vision of *The Shining*. No one needed to be told about the ad's inspiration because it's long since become a part of our popular culture, just like *Carrie* has become a symbol of a put-upon girl who is perceived as an ugly duckling.

In a disclaimer to *The Shining,* King writes: "Some of the most beautiful resort hotels in the world are located in Colorado, but the hotel in these pages is based on none of them. The Overlook and the people associated with it exist wholly within the author's imagination." But in the real world, the Stanley Hotel does have its own ghost stories, as Lindsey Galloway of BBC Travel pointed out in a story online in March 2014:

> Though King called the hotel in his book The Overlook, the fictional Overlook and the real-life Stanley not only look alike, with sprawling front porches and crisp Georgian architecture, but both were completed in 1909. . . . The Stanley's original MacGregor Ballroom, with its raised stage and large windows showcasing expansive mountain views, was reincarnated in the pages of *The Shining*. . . .
>
> Long before King's stay, room [217] had a history. In 1917, the chief housekeeper Elizabeth Wilson was lighting the hotel's acetylene lanterns during a storm in case the electricity went out. When she went to light the one in what is now room 217, the lantern exploded, blasting out the floor beneath her feet and sending her falling down to the story below.

and crew. Everything that's tough about making a movie has been crammed into the first three weeks of shooting: makeup effects, snow, no snow, cold, night shooting, a child actor who can only work half days, explosions—everything. And then there are the *real* ghosts. Doorknobs turn. Mysterious thumping disrupts shooting. "One of our costume people went to bed one night," says director Garris (*The Stand*). "Five minutes after he hit the sack something sat down on the bed next to him." Weber has heard the stories, too. "When you have big, beefy grips come down to breakfast and say, 'Man, something walked *through* me last night!', you know they are not kidding."

She survived (albeit with two broken ankles). Even so, guests of 217 report her spirit stops by on occasion—usually to tidy things up, sometimes putting stray items away or unpacking a suitcase. The hauntings, both the fictional and the ostensibly real, hardly deter guests. In fact, room 217 is usually booked months in advance.

Not surprisingly, the hotel capitalizes on the Stephen King tie-in: In its gift store, you can buy a coffee mug or T-shirt labeled REDRUM year-round, but when it's Halloween, the Stanley celebrates in style with *The Shining*–themed events.

There's a masquerade party, and *The Shining* ball, a danse macabre, but for those who aren't in the spirits to dress up, drink and dance, there's spirits of a different kind available on the hotel's ghost tour, which runs year-round to satisfy demand: the tour will teach you everything you want to learn about the paranormal activity of the Stanley Hotel. The tour "begins with an introduction into what paranormal activity is and an explanation of the different types of paranormal phenomenon and experiences that we have at The Stanley Hotel. From there we will venture to some of the most paranormal areas of the Stanley Hotel property," says its Web site.

*Two bottles of beer with art inspired by* The Shining, *bottled for the Stanley Hotel in Estes Park, Colorado.*

# 21

# Night Shift

## 1978; ORIGINAL TITLE: *Night Moves*

*A press conference for* Graveyard Shift *at a Bangor theater; screenwriter, John Esposito; director, Ralph S. Singleton, and Stephen King.*

A collection of short stories titled after the Bob Seger song, the book's title was subsequently changed to *Night Shift*, commonly known in the workaday world as the "graveyard shift."

Actually, it's a little-known fact that early promo material went out with the book titled *Night Moves*, but Rick Hautala, in a conversation with King, kept hammering away at him, saying *Night Shift* was a better title. King agreed, and the title was changed in midstream.

These short stories, culled from their original appearances in *Cavalier*, *Maine*, *Penthouse*, *Cosmopolitan*, and *Gallery*, make for a remarkable collection. All but one, an epistolary story titled "Jerusalem's Lot," were optioned for the movies, and the collection as a whole shows King's skill at writing science fiction, horror, suspense, and mainstream fiction. As novelist John D. MacDonald wrote in his introduction,

> Now at the risk of being an iconoclast I will say that I do not give a diddly-whoop what Stephen King chooses as an area in which to write. The fact that he presently enjoys writing in the field of spooks and spells and slitherings in the cellar is to me the least important and useful fact about the man anyone can relate. . . . One of the most resonant and affecting stories in this book is "The Last Rung on the Ladder." A gem. Nary a rustle nor breath of other worlds in it.

Here are some facts about these stories:

"Jerusalem's Lot," an epistolary story, foreshadows *'Salem's Lot*.

"Graveyard Shift" recalls King's days as a dyer at the Worumbo Mill, where he worked during high school and in the summers during college.

"Night Surf" foreshadows *The Stand*, with its A6 virus.

"I Am the Doorway" is the kind of horror story masquerading as science fiction that he submitted to science fiction magazines.

"The Mangler" draws on his experiences working at the New Franklin Laundry in Bangor.

"Trucks" is the basis for the movie *Maximum Overdrive*, directed by King.

"The Lawnmower Man" was made into a movie and also a comic book.

"Children of the Corn" was made into a movie and spawned several forgettable sequels that made me want to tear my eyeballs out of their sockets. (Counting the original adaptation, there are nine in total.)

"One for the Road" ties into "Jerusalem's Lot" and *'Salem's Lot*.

"The Woman in the Room" is a poignant story that draws on King's personal experience of his mother dying of cancer. (It was adapted by Frank Darabont as a "dollar baby" movie, the rights for which were sold for one buck, with the proviso that it wouldn't be shown for profit, and not released without permission as a commercial product.)

"I Know What You Need" is King's first appearance in a mainstream magazine (*Cosmopolitan*, September 1976). The story was sold by his agent at the time, Kirby McCauley, who placed several stories with well-paying magazines to show King he could produce the goods as a literary agent. (McCauley, who edited the groundbreaking horror anthology *Dark Forces*, which included King's "The Mist," subsequently engineered

King's move from Doubleday to New American Library, in a multiple-book deal that earned King his first big advance.)

In a lengthy, informal foreword to *Night Shift*, King writes:

> I didn't write them for money; I wrote them because it occurred to me to write them. I have a marketable obsession. There are madmen and madwomen in padded cells the world over who are not so lucky.
>
> I am not a great artist, but I have always felt impelled to write.

---

## Keep on Trucking: *Maximum Overdrive*

As anyone who lives in North Carolina will tell you, July and August can be unbearably muggy. Now imagine having to spend a summer filming a movie there and being a first-time director. It doesn't get much more challenging than that.

Far from his stomping grounds in Bangor, Maine, Stephen King set up shop at a dummy truck stop ten minutes out of Wilmington, North Carolina. It was such a convincing set that truckers pulled in for chow and gas.

Unfortunately, the movie itself drove viewers away. Based on "Trucks," a short story published in *Cavalier* magazine, *Maximum Overdrive* is a good example of how a story capable of suspending the reader's disbelief is nonetheless difficult to translate for the big screen, even when the screenplay is written by the author.

It also speaks to how difficult it is to make a convincing movie by bringing to life inanimate objects like trucks. Even with the best of intentions, "Trucks" would be a challenge for any director, but it was on-the-job training for King.

Grossing only $7.4 million at the box office domestically, *Maximum Overdrive* is King's first, and last, self-directed movie based on his work. One time, King said, was enough; in the end, he had to chalk it up to a learning experience.

For *Maximum Overdrive,* King took on a production fraught with weather delays, language difficulties (the crew was Italian, and they didn't speak English), and other problems, including an on-site accident during the filming that resulted in a lawsuit settled out of court.

Because of the time, money, and effort required to film a major motion picture, no one deliberately sets out to make a bad movie; the hope is that the movie will be profitable and earn money for everyone. But, as it turned out, *Maximum Overdrive* was a minimal film. Citing a lack of support from the producer Dino De Laurentiis's organization, King told interviewer Gary Wood, for *Cinefantastique,* "I didn't do a very good job of directing it."

There are critics, including John D. MacDonald, who would dispute that King is not a great artist. "The Woman in the Room" and "The Last Rung on the Ladder" are not simplistic fictions. Even at this early stage in his career, King separated himself from his contemporaries by hitting high notes beyond their range. Later, in *Different Seasons* (1982), we see him flex his authorial muscles with longer stories that buttress their arguments: King is no hack writing horror but, instead, a writer who challenges himself and stretches to create complex fiction that resonates.

It takes an honest man to make such an admission. As Clint Eastwood reminds us, "A wise man knows his limitations."

Directing is a craft and an art that, like any such endeavor, requires years to master. King, who had never put in the time, did the best he could, but he was in over his head, and he knew it. In one instance, he was setting up to shoot a scene, and the cameraman told him that he was shooting it cross-axis. King didn't understand what he was doing wrong, until it was pointed out to him.

Nominated for two Golden Raspberry Awards (Worst Director for King, Worst Actor for Emilio Estevez), the campy movie, according to the film Web site Rotten Tomatoes, got a 17 percent approval rating from critics, but fans gave it a 50 percent rating. In other words, it was a movie more for fans than critics, a popcorn movie at which you're best advised to check your brains at the door and go in to have a good time.

When asked by *Cinefantastique*'s Gary Wood if he'd consider directing again, King demurred. "I can't see myself doing anything like this again, at least not until my family has all grown up. I want to be around to enjoy them while I can."

King never sat in the director's chair again, preferring to sit himself down in front of his computer to instead put it into maximum overdrive. (He has since expressed a desire to direct *Lisey's Story*.)

One anecdote that didn't make the news: King, at the time of filming already a household name and recognizable figure in public, had his family down for a visit on the set. They went to a local restaurant for a sit-down meal, and King remarked that he was surprised when no one came up to him with a piece of paper in hand to get an autograph. But when they left the restaurant, they saw why: Dozens of fans had lined up outside for an autograph, waiting for him and his family to finish their meal.

Southerners are nothing if not polite.

# 22

THE STAND

## 1978

On his Web site, King wrote that:

> for a long time—ten years, at least—I had wanted to write a fantasy epic like *The Lord of the Rings,* only with an American setting. . . . Only instead of a hobbit, my hero was a Texan named Stu Redman, and instead of a Dark Lord, my villain was a ruthless drifter and supernatural madman named Randall Flagg. The land of Mordor was played by Las Vegas.

And, like Tolkien's epic fantasy, King's epic American fantasy grew in the telling, until it became, in the view of Doubleday executives, too big to publish as is. Consequently, to keep the cover price down, the decision was made to cut text; the only question was, Who would make the cuts? The publisher's staff or the author?

Accounts of exactly what happened, and how, vary in the retelling. Bill Thompson's recollection differs from King's, but one thing is indisputable: The original manuscript was cut by four hundred manuscript pages, resulting in a final page count of 823 pages.

Published in 1978, *The Stand* reflected the publisher's concerns, not the author's; King had input but not final say in the matter of editorial cuts. Years later, in 1990, King gave his side of the story. As he explained,

> The cuts were made at the behest of the accounting department. They toted up production costs, laid these next to the hardcover sales of my previous four books, and decided that a cover price of $12.95 was about what the market

would bear. . . . I was asked if I would like to make the cuts, or if I would prefer someone in the editorial department to do it. I reluctantly agreed to do the surgery myself.

King, in fact, also wanted to simultaneously publish a limited edition of *The Stand* but was thwarted by contractual concerns; Doubleday's book club edition trumped King's own desires to issue a small run, which would have appealed to his ardent collectors willing to pay a premium price for an elaborate edition; thus, it would have had no impact whatsoever on Doubleday's cheapie edition. Doubleday's intransigence on this issue was one of a number of growing concerns that would eventually lead to an acrimonious divorce between author and publisher.,

King, who appreciates a beautifully printed and bound book, found nothing to like in the physical production values of *The Stand*, which he termed ugly and bricklike in appearance. He knew he had to pick his fights, and this one was a losing battle, so he tactically retreated. Years later, though, he would reenter the battlefield and emerge victorious by holding his ground: He'd eventually see the book published the way he, not the publisher, intended.

## Taking a Stand Against Doubleday

In 1973, when King was anxious to sell a novel to Doubleday, his situation was so dire that he was ecstatic when *Carrie* sold for $2,500. Five years later, the working relationship between author and publisher had frayed to the point of completely unraveling.

In all of this, however, King's relationship with Thompson remained one of mutual respect, personally and professionally. As is often the case, despite problems with the publisher, the editor remained in the good graces of the author.

But King had several concerns with Doubleday's ironclad contracts. Some key points:

**Book advances**: For the five Doubleday books, King got a total advance of $77,500, while the publisher earned millions.

**Limited editions**: Citing contracts with book clubs, Doubleday refused to allow King to publish a limited edition of *The Shining* the first time around. (In truth, a thousand copies of a limited edition has no effect on sales of the trade edition, as King has repeatedly proved.)

**Being taken for granted**: King's perception was that, despite being the goose that lays the golden eggs, his publisher's staff took him for granted, a perception shared by William G. Thompson, his editor, who sided with King. (Thompson was fired by Doubleday when King left.)

**The editorial cuts**: Doubleday's bean counters, who were more concerned about cover price than about what the readers wanted, requested cuts to King's large canvases, first on *The Shining* and then on *The Stand*. So, according to King, both books were arbitrarily cut in length to accommodate the money men in suits, to the books' detriment.

**Yearly allowance**: King had signed a contract that gave him $50,000 a year from his royalty earnings. It was supposed to allow him to defer income and thus save him money on taxes, but it backfired because he earned so much that he couldn't, in his lifetime, ever see the royalties totaling $3 million paid back to him.

**The 50/50 split on paperback sales**: King hated this clause, which was the straw that broke the camel's back. As King recalled it was "non-negotiable" and "finally led to our parting of the ways," he recalled in *Fear Itself*.

King had no agent, little clout, and no ally, but he found support in a young literary agent looking for clients in the science fiction, horror, and fantasy genres. The up-and-coming agent was thirty-four-year-old Kirby McCauley, who first met King at a literary party for James Baldwin in New York City. As McCauley told *Castle Rock,*

I had heard of Steve, but frankly, when I went to the party I had only read one thing by Steve. Before the party, I went out and got a copy of *'Salem's Lot,* and I was blown away by it. I loved it. So I went to the party and said to Steve, "I love that book, but to be honest, I haven't read anything else by you." So we started to talk about writers in general and the field of horror and science fiction. As it turned out, Steve's interests and my interests were very much alike. He was more interested in talking about relatively unknown writers like Frank Belknap Long and Clifford Simak and people whom I knew or represented, than he was in staying in a corner and talking with James Baldwin.

It's a beginner's mistake, and an understandable one, for an author to sell books without agency representation, but for whatever reasons, King remained agentless for all six Doubleday books, to his detriment: When he asked Doubleday for an advance of $3.5 million for a package deal on his proposed new novels after *The Stand,* he was turned down. It was McCauley who engineered a big deal, but not at Doubleday; McCauley struck a deal with New American Library.

"By the time I met Steve," he told *Castle Rock* in 1986, "I had made it over the hump as a literary agent. I was earning a modest income, but I was by no means big time. But I did represent a number of minor, prestigious writers in the science fiction and fantasy field. Steve and Tabby, quite frankly, took a chance. It put me in a whole different league. Not just income, but now that of a major agent."

Kirby McCauley, who died in August 2014, had also represented Roger Zelazny, and George R. R. Martin, best known for his TV miniseries *Game of Thrones*, who wrote at length, and affectionately, in a blog on his Web site:

Kirby was good-looking, fast-talking, charming . . . and he was there with us in the con suite. The established agents of the day never came to cons. Kirby came to all of them. . . . He was One of Us. He was a fan. He knew SF, fantasy, horror. Robert E. Howard, H. P. Lovecraft, Clark Ashton Smith, he knew more about all of them than you did. . . . He was the best agent any writer could hope for. He made amazing deals for me, helped launch my career in 1976, and relaunched me in 1994 when I came back from the dead. . . . I was by no means his biggest success story, either. He did as well or better for a dozen other young writers on his list . . . and one of them, this guy from Maine named Stephen King, did better than all of us together. It is probably an exaggeration to say that Kirby McCauley was entirely responsible for the huge SF boom of the late 1970s and the horror boom of the early 1980s, but he sure as hell helped.

## MICHAEL COLLINGS ON *THE STAND* (1978)[1]

To place *The Stand* in the context of a larger body of interrelated works is not to diminish its impact as a story. Although long, it is one of the three or four best novels to read for an introduction to King's style, techniques, and sheer storytelling ability. Its cast of characters is enormous, as befits a work about the end of things and about new beginnings. Unusual for a King novel, its settings range from New England to Los Angeles, with multiple stops at key places throughout the Midwest, finally focusing on Boulder, Colorado (where King lived for a short time in the mid-1970s), and Las Vegas, Nevada.

Its genre is equally all-inclusive. The story begins as a straightforward science-fictional extrapolation: what if there were a superflu that destroyed almost every human alive (along with most of the larger land mammals)? How would the survivors deal with such pragmatic questions as what to do with the bodies, how to re-create an orderly society, how to bear up under almost unimaginable burdens of guilt, loneliness, and despair? Within a few chapters, however, King adroitly shifts genres, as the survivors begin dreaming true dreams and feeling the call of the Dark or the Light. He moves almost seamlessly from SF into high fantasy, with theological, moral, allegorical, and philosophical overtones that highlight even more the commonplace personalities and actions of his characters as they struggle against nearly insuperable odds. As the dreams and visions intensify, so do biblical allusions—and suddenly the reader discovers that the novel had become an apocalyptic vision dealing with the End of Things and the physical revelation of Evil. Without relying on elevated tone, self-consciously heroic personages, or other traditional elements of epic, *The Stand* nevertheless takes on epic qualities of

---

1 from *The Stephen King Companion* (1995)

breadth and scope, magnitude and significance (again amplified in the restored 1990 edition).

To support such an ambitious undertaking, King builds on the literature of quest-epic, apocalypse, high fantasy, and horror. He amplifies his already expansive vision with specific references to Herman Melville's *Moby-Dick*; H. P. Lovecraft's mythos of the Great Old Ones; John Milton's epic *Paradise Lost* (especially through oxymorons such as "dark life and hideous good cheer"); J. R. R. Tolkien's *The Lord of the Rings*; H. G. Wells's end-of-the-world nightmare, *The Time Machine*; George Orwell's classic tale of the bureaucratic Dark regime, *1984*; Bram Stoker's archetypal conflict between good and evil, *Dracula*; Edgar Allan Poe's "The Raven," as well as his tales of madness and mystery; William Golding's allegorical apocalypse, *The Lord of the Flies*; Richard Adams's equally allegorical beast-fable, *Watership Down*; and others. Along the way King invites into his novel W. B. Yeats, Robert Frost, Ernest Hemingway, William Faulkner, William Shakespeare, Bob Dylan, "The Who," Cary Grant, and *Charlotte's Web*, as well as a handful of his own novels and stories. The result is a richly embroidered tapestry that is simultaneously an extraordinary story on its own merits and a perceptive anatomy of late-twentieth-century, technologically oriented, morally confused American society on the brink of destroying itself.

# CEMETERY DANCE'S
# DELUXE EDITIONS OF THE
# DOUBLEDAY BOOKS

*The traycased "Artist Edition" of* Carrie *published Cemetery Dance.*

To the frustration of King's American fans, some of his hardback books—notably Doubleday—have sported cheapie glue bindings. The printing industry calls this "perfect" binding, but it's not; once the glue dries out, and it eventually will, the book will literally split in two, permanently damaging it.

The interior pages for books are printed in sheets that are folded and then gathered. With "perfect" binding, the pages are gathered and one edge sliced off, producing a pile of loose pages; hot glue is then affixed to the left-hand side and bound into the book. But despite the assurances from the publisher that the binding will hold, it won't. It's a cheap way to save a few pennies per copy at the customer's expense. It means the book will not hold up under repeated readings, because each time it's opened it puts stress on the glue that dries and cracks.

With "sewn" signatures, the F&Gs (folded and gathered sheets) are sewn together with thread and then glued in. This process keeps the book intact, and, with care, it will outlive the original owner and can be handed down to the next generation. It is how books *ought* to be produced, but unfortunately King's early Doubleday books were simply glued together.

Given that publishers tout hardbacks as the preferred edition for gift giving, the fact remains that it's not the hardback boards that make the book itself permanent—it's the *binding* that literally holds the book together. The purchasers of hardback books with "perfect" bindings are thus short-changed: They're paying a premium price for a subpar product in terms of book production.

With the exception of the "Complete and Uncut Edition" of *The Stand* (1990) in trade and limited editions, King's Doubleday books—*Carrie, 'Salem's Lot, The Shining, The Stand* (1978 edition), *Night Shift,* and *Pet Sematary*—were unimaginatively designed, printed on standard interior paper stock, glue-bound, and lacked illustrations.

Here's the difference:

Michael Alpert, who designed all of Philtrum Press's publications, likened a book—its layout, typography, design, and production values—to a "private theater." If you've seen his work, notably for *The Eyes of the Dragon,* you know exactly what he means: It's an oversized volume; printed on heavy, white stock that recalls the texture of napkins; and has generous margins, a beautiful typeface, and appropriate illustrations. Alpert showed us how beautiful a book can be, and how its production values and design aesthetic enhance the reading experience.

Doubleday's King books aren't private theaters; they are small, darkened rooms poorly lit with a naked lightbulb dangling from a frayed wire.

King's classic books deserve a better presentation.

In 2014, we finally get what King and his books deserve from Cemetery Dance, which published *Carrie* in December 2014, the first of six Doubleday books, to be followed by *'Salem's Lot, The Shining, Night Shift, The Stand,* and *Pet Sematary.*

Cemetery Dance calls them "deluxe special editions." Issued in small print runs for collectors willing to pony up for handsome editions, the higher production values come at a correspondingly higher price than their cheaper brethren. (Don't confuse this with Plume's Collectors Edition of *Carrie* in trade paperback; the Cemetery Dance editions are in hardback.)

*Carrie* features newly commissioned art by Tomislav Tikulin. It includes a new introduction by Stephen King on why he wrote the book, and it concludes with a lengthy piece by Tabitha King (from the New American Library Collectors Edition). It is an oversize edition measuring seven by ten inches. It is printed on a heavy, high-grade interior paper, with a better distinctive finish and "feel" than traditional book stock. It has a full-color wraparound jacket. It has high-quality endpapers and a sewn signature; it will hold up under repeated readings. The book is also protected by a slipcase or tray case, depending on the edition you buy, and they have foil stamping.

The limitation page, illustrated by longtime Cemetery Dance artist Glenn Chadbourne, is printed in a tinted rust-red ink for the trade edition; the artist edition prints the art in full color and sports a different dust jacket and illustrated endpapers.

The last color plate is a full-page reproduction of the original Doubleday cover art.

All of this doesn't come cheap, but for fans of King's classic books that consistently rank high among their favorites, it's a small price to pay to finally own them in handsome editions: $85 for the least expensive edition, in hardback, with jacket and in a slipcase, in a run of 3,000 copies; $225 for the numbered and signed "artist edition" in a tray case, in a run of 750 copies; and $1,000 for an oversize lettered edition in a tray case, in a run of 52 copies, with enhanced production values. (Note: The books are *not* signed by Stephen King.) For more information, go to: cemeterydance.com.

## 24

# THE EARLY BACHMAN BOOKS:

## *RAGE* (1977), *THE LONG WALK* (1979), *ROADWORK* (1981), *THE RUNNING MAN* (1982)

No, that's not me. I know who Dick Bachman is, though. I've heard the rumor. They have Bachman's books filed under my name at the Bangor Public Library, and there are a *lot* of people who think I'm Dick Bachman. I went to school with Dicky Bachman and that isn't his real name. He lives over in New Hampshire and *that* boy is crazy! That boy is absolutely crazy. And sooner or later this will get back to him and he'll come to Bangor and he'll kill *me*, that's all.

Several times I've gotten his mail and several times he's gotten mine. He's at Signet because of me and when the editors got shuffled, things might have gotten confused. Maybe that's how it got all screwed up and the rumor started.

But I am not—*not*—Richard Bachman.

—STEPHEN KING, *SHAYOL*, 1982

*R*age (originally titled *Getting It On*) holds three distinctions: It was King's first book published under his Bachman pen name. It's been linked to school shootings, including one that King calls the "Carneal incident." And, as a result of the "incident," it's the only King novel that he deliberately put out of print.

When it was initially released, its publication was not greeted with fanfare because only a handful of people knew *Rage* was in fact written by Stephen King under a pen name. An inexpensive mass market paperback, *Rage* went out to drugstores, supermarkets, and other retailers and stayed on the racks for a few weeks; then they were pulled, their covers torn off and submitted for sales credit and their guts pulped.

King's hope was that he could write under the cover of darkness and avoid detection from his rabid fans, because he wanted to see how successful his novels would be without being attached to a bestselling brand name. It was a forlorn hope kept alive for six years, until the publication of *Thinner* in 1984, which read more like King than any of the other Bachman books.

Keen-eyed booksellers in the fantasy/sci-fi field, notably Robert Weinberg and L. W. Curry, had already put the word out through their newsletters that King and Bachman were one and the same; they listed Bachman books as "Stephen King writing as Richard Bachman," based on an educated guess: There was rampant speculation but no incontrovertible proof.

But the smoking gun came when a bookstore clerk in D.C. checked the copyright paperwork filed by King's agent at the Library of Congress, which requires registration for copyright protection; on the paperwork for *Rage,* Stephen King was listed as the copyright holder.

The *Bangor Daily News* broke the story on February 26, 1985. It was headlined with a photo-reproduced header from King's *Castle Rock: The Stephen King Newsletter,* coverdated March 1985. King's sister-in-law Stephanie Leonard, who doubled as King's main secretary and editor/publisher of *Castle Rock,* spilled the beans:

> Yes, Stephen King is indeed Richard Bachman. One of the toughest things about doing this newsletter has been that I've not been able, until now, to reveal that to the readers. I have known that Stephen was using a pseudonym for years, but I was sworn to secrecy. I am relieved now that I don't have to lie or be evasive anymore. Last month I hinted that a secret would be revealed, and Stephen intended to keep it quiet until March 1st, but a local newspaper decided they would run the story with or without his comment, as they had enough proof, and as Stephen told them, the whole thing was coming apart—he likened it to having a bag of groceries that gets wet and things keep falling out of the bottom until you can't hold it together anymore.

At that point, there was no denying the connection, and the media reported the news, setting off a buying frenzy among King fans, who searched out the mass market paperbacks that originally retailed for $1.50 to $2.50. But fans soon learned that of the four other titles, two were out of print.

In retrospect, it was hard to see how the secret could have been kept much longer, given the visibility accorded *Thinner* by its publisher, who was determined to get Bachman's sales into high gear: At the Book Expo America in the spring of 1984, where advance review copies of the fall list were freely given out, *Thinner* was stacked four feet high on two wooden pallets. Jaded booksellers, though, walked by them to get freebie copies of name-brand authors.

As for *Thinner*'s sales, its first printing was 26,000, but when the news broke about King writing as Bachman, it rocketed up to 280,000. Ironically, a Literary Guild reader wrote the following before the news broke: "This is what King would write like if King could really write."

Bachman, who died a sudden death, went on to posthumously publish *The Regulators* and also a "trunk" novel, *Blaze*, in his introduction ("Full Disclosure") to which he wrote, "During those years [1966–73] I was actually two men. It was Stephen King who wrote (and sold) horror stories to raunchy skin-mags like *Cavalier* and *Adam*, but it was Bachman who wrote a series of novels that didn't sell to anybody."

Whether another Bachman book will be published, only time will tell: King's fabled writer's trunk is probably empty. King's books as Bachman include: *Rage* (1977), *The Long Walk* (1979), *Roadwork* (1981), *The Running Man* (1982), *The Regulators* (1996), and *Blaze* (2007).

## RAGE

*Rage*, wrote Collings in *The Stephen King Companion* (1995)

> is an extended study in adolescent *angst*, beginning with its first-person killer/ protagonist, Charlie Dekker, and spreading like an infection throughout the high school class he holds hostage. The action is direct and brutal: Dekker meets with the principal for disciplinary action after Dekker nearly killed the shop teacher. He is expelled and told to leave school immediately. He stops at his locker, takes out a pistol, returns to class, shoots the teacher and intimidates the students until it is too late for them to escape. For the next several hours, he invites them to "get it on" with him—to examine their own lives and motives, their frustrations and fears. After systematically making fools of school and police officials, Charlie lets the class go and fakes the police into shooting him.
>
> Compared with *It*, *The Stand*, or *The Shining*, *Rage* is certainly a weaker novel and a lesser achievement. On its own terms, however, with its narrowly defined characters, perhaps the most limited time span of any King novel or story, strictly focused themes and development, and idiosyncratic narrative voice, it nevertheless manages to hold its own as a document of a past time and as a novel examining ongoing human crises and resolutions.

## THE LONG WALK

*The Long Walk*, dedicated to three of King's college professors in the English department, was submitted to a Bennett Cerf / Random House first novel competition in 1967, but it was rejected with a form note. As King recalled in "On Becoming a Brand Name", "I was too crushed to show that book to any publisher in New York."

A dystopian novel, and an intense study in psychological horror, written when King was in college, the book was inspired by President Kennedy's popular walkathons, when in 1962 he enjoined the public to take it up: "I would encourage every American to walk as often as possible. It's more than healthy, it's fun."

Not, however, for the young boys in this novel, who give it their best shot.

"I thought of it while hitchhiking home from college one night when I was a freshman," King told Michael Collings in a letter.

The plot: In a totalitarian America, teenage boys take part in an annual event held on May 1 called "The Long Walk," in which they must walk from the Maine/Canada border and head south at a predetermined pace (four miles per hour)—or risk being shot, until there's only one boy standing.

The Long Walk is organized by a mysterious figure known only as "The Major," who bookends the Long Walk: at the start line, he's there to encourage a hundred boys and see them off, and he's also there to congratulate the winner who will receive "The Prize," which is anything he wishes for the remainder of his life.

## ROADWORK

Roadwork is dedicated to the memory of one of King's teachers, Charlotte Littlefield. Billed by its publisher as "a novel of the first energy crisis," set in an unnamed Midwest city circa 1973–74, it's the story of Barton George Dawes, who loses his tenuous grip on reality after his son dies and his marriage disintegrates. On top of that, his house and workplace will literally be demolished when the government makes room for an interstate highway extension.

James Smythe of *The Guardian* explained:

> As with the other early Bachman books, there's no supernatural menace, no ghosts or possessions. Instead there is something more tangible, yet no less horrifying: cancer. King watched his mother die from it only a year or so before he wrote *Roadwork,* and his personal pain is there on every page: in the loss of Fred, the way that Barton can't forget him, can't move on past the pain of seeing him suffer before being stripped away. In the first collected editions of the books, King wrote an introduction in which he said that *Roadwork* was written when he was "grieving and shaken by the apparent senselessness of it." He says the book is the worst of the Bachmans, simply because it's "trying to find some answers to the conundrum of human pain." To my mind, that doesn't make it a bad book; that makes it a book that strives for something other than scares. It's trying to fathom exactly what a person goes through; how low they can go when faced with direct loss, and how painful that loss (and its repercussions) can be.
>
> Over time, though, King had a change of heart: In a later edition of the *The Bachman Books: Four Early Novels by Stephen King,* he wrote an introduction in which he says that *Roadwork* is "(his) favorite of the early Bachman books."

## THE RUNNING MAN

*The Running Man,* set in 2025, is, like *The Long Walk,* a dystopian novel. "Writing it was a fantastic, white-hot experience; this book was written in one month, the bulk of it in the one week of winter vacation," he wrote in "On Becoming a Brand Name."

At the time, King was teaching, and used the time during his Christmas break to write this novel with the hope that he could sell it quickly to earn money. He submitted it to Doubleday's Bill Thompson, who rejected it; he resubmitted it to publisher Donald A. Wollheim at Ace Books, who returned it after three weeks with a terse note: "We are not interested in science fiction which deals with negative utopias."

As he wrote in "On Becoming a Brand Name," "The book, unfortunately, was not fantastic. . . . I was as depressed as I had been over the failure of Book #1. I began to have long talks with myself at night about whether or not I was chasing a fool's dream."

The plot: Big business is calling the shots, and Ben Richards, who lives in Co-Op City with his family, whom he is unable to support, is forced to make a drastic decision: He decides to appear for money as a contestant on a game show in which he's pursued by trained killers, termed "Hunters." The show is witnessed by millions of TV viewers glued to their sets: It's the ultimate reality show.

He becomes a man on the run whose covert goal is to destroy the network's headquarters, to strike a death blow on a pandering organization that feeds on the public's insatiable desire for bloodlust.

There are 101 chapters, the first titled "Minus 100 and Counting," as the clock starts ticking downward to its last chapter, "Minus 000 and Counting."

In 1987, the book was adapted for a motion picture with Arnold Schwarzenegger in the title role.

# PART FOUR

# THE "BESTSELLASAURUS REX" STOMPS OVER TO NEW AMERICAN LIBRARY

I started out as a writer and nothing more. I became a popular writer and have discovered that, in the scale-model landscape of the book business, at least, I have grown into a Bestsellasaurus Rex—a big, stumbling book-beast that is loved when it shits money and hated when it tramples houses. I look back on that sentence and feel an urge to change it because it sounds so self-pitying; I cannot change it because it also conveys my real sense of perplexity and surprise at this absurd turn of events. I started out as a storyteller; along the way I became an economic force, as well.

—Stephen King, "On the Politics of Limiteds,"
*Castle Rock* (June 1985)

---

# 25

# TURNING THE PAGE:

## KING GOES TO NEW AMERICAN LIBRARY

No major author likes to change publishing houses because it's disruptive to everyone in the food chain: the author himself, his publisher, booksellers, distributors, and readers. But sometimes, as King realized, a divorce is the only solution. In hindsight, Doubleday's decision not to retain King was a major strategic blunder. After all, there are only a handful of superwriters, of which King is one, and they deserve special consideration because they've earned it: Their books have built up a ready-made audience over the years that guarantee a profit on every new book. It's risk-free publishing in an industry fraught with financial risk.

Doubleday maintained that it tried mightily to keep King in-house and made a strong bid for his next three books; they came up with big bucks for King, eclipsed their previous advances for his books, showing a new commitment. But New American Library was determined to snag King, and their $2.5 million offer trumped Doubleday's, at which point everyone saw the handwriting on the wall. Also, Kirby McCauley's sale of King's books earned him a commission of $250,000, which immediately put him in the top league of agents representing major talent.

Doubleday, though, would still benefit from King's growing audience for many years to come, because its contracts tied up the books' copyrights for King's lifetime, and then some years afterward. The irony, though, is that had they kept King happy in the first place, they would have been the publisher of his subsequent books, which now total seventy-four.

Doubleday, of course, marketed King as a horror writer, which handicapped book sales (and movie tickets) by stereotyping him, thus limiting his potential to sell to a larger, mainstream market. In an afterword to *Different Seasons*, King recounts a conversation he had with Thompson, who explained that he was in danger of being "typed." As Thompson explained: "*First* the telekinetic girl, *then* the vampires, *now* the haunted hotel and the telepathic kid. You're gonna get typed."

King's response: "That's okay, Bill. I'll be a horror writer if that's what people want. That's just fine."

It was certainly fine when King was at Doubleday, but that perception explained why film director Rob Reiner initially downplayed King's authorship of "The Body," on which *Stand by Me* was based: He was concerned that it would scare away viewers unaccustomed to King's name being attached to what was clearly a nonhorror film.

The problems began when *Time* magazine's cover story on King (October 6, 1986) quoted the characterization of his novels proffered in his *Different Seasons*: "The literary equivalent of a Big Mac and a large fries from McDonald's."

King's comment provided food for thought and also plenty of ammunition for critics who took the opportunity to lock, load, and fire away at him. They took it to mean that King considered his work to be the equivalent of junk food; in other words, King's fiction is dismissable.

Many writers in the literary community—writers whose books sold poorly, and who were envious of King's sales—celebrated his statement with glee. *See, I told you so! Straight from the horse's mouth: King admits he writes junk books! He's admitted to being a hack!*

In *Weekly Reader Writing* (October 2006), King elaborated, "I'm still paying for that remark. What I meant by it is that I'm tasty and I go down smooth, but I don't think that a steady diet of Stephen King would make anybody a healthy human being."

But the damage had been done. Critics, even today, take potshots at King because of that original comment. After all, it's hard for critics to take your work seriously when it appears you are disparaging your work, even though that was never the intention.

# 26

## THE DEAD ZONE

### 1979

King's first book for NAL was, as Collings pointed out in *The Stephen King Companion* (1995), a good entry point for his new readers. "If one is looking for a starting place in 'things King,' *The Dead Zone* is indeed an ideal choice."

In *The Art of Darkness*, Douglas Winter's interview with King sheds light on the genesis of *The Dead Zone*. King explained it came out of difficult circumstances. "I had a bad year in 1976—it was a very depressing time." After two busted attempts at writing new novels, King followed up with "a trial cut on *The Dead Zone*. It was a small-town story about a child-killer."

In *The Dead Zone*, a freak accident suffered by Johnny Smith has a side benefit (or drawback, depending on your thinking): He now has a "wild" talent, precognition: the ability to see into the future. But when he sees what will happen if presidential candidate Greg Stillson gets elected, his hand is forced: He decides his mission in life is to stop Stillson, no matter what the cost.

A first-rate suspense novel that saw a faithful translation to the big screen, Collings points out that

> Throughout, King preserves a sense of balance in treatment. Johnny Smith is a quiet, reserved character who merits a quiet, reserved novel—and for the most part, this is what King provides (this characterization is brilliantly retained in David Cronenberg's film version, with Christopher Walken capturing the essence both of character and of story).

It also marked a major change in how King's books were designed. They now had a more mainstream look, flensed of designs that screamed "horror!" As King explained:

I like books that are nicely made, and with the exception of *'Salem's Lot* and *Night Shift,* none of the Doubleday books were especially well made. They have a ragged, machine-produced look to them, as though they were built to fall apart. *The Stand* [1978 edition] is worse that way: It looks like a brick. It's this little, tiny squatty thing that looks much bigger than it is.

*The Dead Zone* is really nicely put together. It's got a nice cloth binding, and it's just a nice product.

In *The Stephen King Companion* (1995), Michael Collings wrote:

As to where to start if one has never read a King novel, *The Dead Zone* comes almost immediately to mind as one of King's most restrained and controlled, mostly nearly mainstream, and least "horrific" novels, especially among those published during his first decade as a writer.

Although dated by period references to the mid-1970s, *The Dead Zone* nevertheless reads well, even for [today's] audiences. Unlike many of King's other works (and even unlike the Bachman novels), this story of prescience and its devastating consequences on one individual and those nearest to him does not focus on a strong central character, an almost superman "hero" who, like Roland of Gilead, for example, clearly differs from the common run of humanity. King deftly defines his protagonist with his name—Johnny Smith. It is an ordinary name, a literary everyman kind of name that urges readers to see Smith less as exception and more as type. And in almost every respect, Johnny Smith is an ordinary man: he has goals and dreams; he loves and hopes; he must confront problems of both life and death.

The novel's gentle, haunting ghostly conclusion returns Johnny Smith and his treacherous gift to the realm of the private; his final touch is reserved for the woman he loved.

## 27

---

# THE KINGS' MAINE HAUNT IN BANGOR

Bangor, Maine . . . is not a town calculated to make anybody
feel famous. The only claim to fame is a big plastic statue of
Paul Bunyan. You just live there and keep your head down.

—STEPHEN KING, *BARE BONES*

*The bat and spider–designed gate to the Kings'
Bangor home.*

*The Paul Bunyan statue facing
Main Street in Bangor.*

B efore Stephen King hit it big, the big man in town was Paul Bunyan—a towering presence, a statue in Bass Park standing in front of the town's civic center. Dressed in a plaid shirt, wielding an ax in one hand and a peavey in the other, the thirty-one-foot-tall statue harkens back to the city's origins as a major lumber town in the late 1800s, when Bangor was known for its prized white pine, which shipped worldwide. As Abigail Zelz and Marilyn Zoidis explain in *Woodsmen and Whigs: Historic Images of Bangor, Maine*:

> Bangor's lumber exports peaked in 1872, when almost 250 million board feet were shipped from the port. Because of the tremendous volume of lumber that left the city on ships, Bangor became known as the "Lumber capital of the World." The harbor and its surrounding neighborhoods bustled with activity; between 1860 and 1872 an average of more than 2,200 ships entered the harbor each year. Today, Bangor shows little evidence of the once thriving industry. The waterfront is quiet, woodsmen and sailors no longer roam the streets, sawmills are gone, and the boarding houses, hotels, bars, and houses of pleasure have been torn down.
>
> It was back then that, in 1856, one of the city's most distinctive houses went up. An Italianate villa, and the first built on West Broad Street, William Arnold's house cost $6,000 to build.

King and his family bought the villa in 1980. Although the "Queen City," as Mainers call her, is no longer the king of the lumber industry, entire forests still fall to provide printing paper for the new king in town, whose books sell worldwide.

The widow who sold them her house had no idea that, at thirty-three, Stephen King was already a multimillionaire because of the three-book deal with New American Library that McCauley engineered. After watching the Kings walk through the house and hearing Stephen say he wanted to buy it, the widow spoke to the Realtor afterward to express her concerns. He seemed like such a nice young man, she said, but could he *really* afford a house that cost $135,000?

The Realtor assured her that the Kings could afford the house.

For Tabitha King, the house—bought with money earned from books that tapped into people's nightmares—was a dream come true. As reported in the *Bangor Daily News*:

> As a girl she strolled down West Broadway with a friend and dreamed of living in one of the mansions. She leaned toward the red one with towers. She certainly never thought she'd live there one day.
>
> But the wide-eyed girl grew up to be author Tabitha King and married the man who became the most famous horror author of our time, Stephen King. He decided the barn-red Victorian mansion at West Broadway replete with towers, secret passages, and unbeknown to them at the time of purchase, a ghost, was his kind of place.
>
> "I thought it was destiny," said Tabitha.

The twenty-three-room house was certainly big enough for the family of five: Stephen, Tabitha, and their three children. The house would also serve duty as home offices for both writers, and, at least temporarily, house secretaries, too. (Wanting to preserve what little privacy they could, the Kings eventually moved the office out of the house and into a nondescript building near the Bangor airport.)

The major home renovations included a front porch, a carriage port, an indoor pool (forty-seven feet long) with windows, a climate-controlled underground library housing seventeen thousand volumes, and numerous interior modifications.

In the beginning, the Kings were reluctant to put up a fence and had hoped a small placard near the door, explaining that the Kings were working writers and couldn't be disturbed, would be enough to deter the tourists with books they wanted signed. But as they found out, that wasn't enough to deter the curious. The tourists still came up to the door bearing books. *Surely,* they thought, *Stephen King can make an exception this time just for me.* . . .

Stephanie Leonard, King's sister-in-law, wrote in *Castle Rock,* "Why do they come by? To take a picture of the house, hoping to catch a glimpse of its residents coming and going? To get a book signed, or to knock on the door and hope to pass a word with the author of the books they carry? To see the house that is now familiar to them from magazines and calendar covers? All of the above."

## TERRY STEEL ON THE KINGS' FENCE
### FROM *FINE HOMEBUILDING,* OCTOBER/NOVEMBER 1983

*The bat and spider–designed gate to the Kings' Bangor home.*

*The fence to the Kings' Bangor home.*

I brought a lot of magazines showing examples of ironwork to my first conference with the Kings, along with a lot of photographs I'd taken of fence and gate work around Beacon Hill in Boston. The Kings also had books with drawings of ironwork, and we discussed possible designs. It was important for the fence and gates to work with the architecture of the house, to be graceful and attractive, and yet reflect the personalities of the occupants as well. King, a writer of macabre fiction, wanted bats worked into the design. His wife wanted spiders and webs.

We walked the property line, and I recorded the length of the fencing perimeter and the widths of the sidewalks where the gates would go. We got a survey map and found some old photographs of the property. It looked about five feet high, and we decided on the same height for the new fence.

Next I studied the house's architectural details. My eye was caught immediately by the attractive wooden applique on the south sidewall of the house, whose design had been borrowed, I was certain, from classic wrought-iron scroll work. I borrowed it back for the fence design—it shows up in the support sections, and in the side gate design.

The stained-glass windows throughout the house offered another design possibility; their arches and radius lines gave me an idea for the design of the spider webs. The front gate, with its circles and arches, repeat motifs I found over the doors and the back barn's circular windows.

After the initial brainstorming session, I went home and worked up a proposal, including design drawings and cost. Once the Kings approved the picket and fence-section design, I drove back to Bangor to take exact measurements. After consulting with the Bangor Historical Society, we got a building permit.

The commission took a year-and-a-half to finish—270 lineal feet of hand-forged fence, weighing 11,000 pounds, punctuated by two gates composed of spider webs, goat heads, and winged bats. The editor of the local paper called the project a major contribution to the architecture of the city of Bangor. A neighbor comes over to tell me the fence is "just what the house needed," and turns to eye her own front yard.

One thing's for sure: Anyone touring Bangor trying to pick out the house where Stephen King lives will have little trouble finding it.

*A newspaper ad in the* Bangor Daily News *the Kings ran to discourage trick-or-treaters for Halloween.*

*A hotel employee in Bangor dressed up for Halloween.*

*Of course, on Halloween, the house is spook central. In the past, the Kings used to hand out candy, but when thousands of children began showing up every year, and the police cruisers parked on West Broadway to handle the crush of crowds, the Kings realized that even that simple pleasure would be denied to them: They couldn't just blend in with the neighbors—especially not on Halloween.*

*These days, the Kings are either gone on Halloween night or they're home, with the main lights turned off to ward off the trick-or-treaters who are drawn to the house. Understandably, what was perhaps King's favorite holiday quickly became his least favorite, at least in terms of trick-or-treating.*

## "Bats and Spiders"

*A three-headed creature is perched on top of a fence in front of the Kings' Bangor home.*

I had a design flash, a moment of creativity, as the design of the gate emerged. I had the concept and drew it on the chalkboard. Then I started making it, putting it together. I was pretty much done when Tabitha drove down [to my workshop in southern Maine] to take a look.

Steve initially said he wanted creatures like bats and spiders, so the front gates incorporates them, drawn from the fear imagery that we as children had of the creatures of the night. That seemed to me to be where King was coming from in his writing. I wanted the gate to say something about the person behind the door.

Also, on my visits, I noticed a lot of comic books lying around, including *Superman* and *Batman*.

Remember the bat symbol that is flashed on the clouds in *Batman*? That's what I used for the two bats on the fence—superhero, not demonic, characters.

—Terry Steel, in an interview with George Beahm

*An aerial shot of the Kings' Bangor home. (To the left is the other Bangor home the Kings own.)*

# 28

---

## FIRESTARTER

### 1980

#### INCENDIARY NOVELS

In *Art of Darkness,* King remarked to Douglas E. Winter that when he ran into problems writing *The Dead Zone,* he put it aside to work on *Firestarter* instead and realized that it echoed, to a strong degree, his first published novel, *Carrie.* He told Winter, "I had this depressing feeling that I was a thirty-year-old man who had already lapsed into self-imitation."

*Carrie* is the story of a teenage girl with a "wild" talent who unleashes it to devastating effect; and *Firestarter* is the story of a teenage girl who has a "wild" talent that allows her to unleash her power also to devastating effect.

But King, an English major who went back to teach at his alma mater, reconciled himself with the notion that he wasn't simply rewriting *Carrie*; he was "attempting to amplify themes that are intrinsic to his work."

*Firestarter,* however, never became a household word like *Carrie.* As Collings pointed out, in a review published in *The Stephen King Companion* (1995), "With the possible exceptions of *Cujo* and *Christine,* probably no other single King work has attained to such a level of popular culture, mass name recognition."

Now, four decades later, *Carrie* still carries the day: As a movie poster for the 2013 *Carrie* movie proclaimed, "You will know her name."

*Firestarter* is the story of a teenage girl named Charlene "Charlie" McGee, who shares much in common with Carrie. As John Grisham explained in an introduction to the New American Library "Collectors Edition" of the novel, "The bad guys pursue with a

161

vengeance, and the chase is on. The Government wants Charlie in custody, in a cell some-place so she can be drugged and controlled. The Government wants to study Charlie, to watch her make fires, to measure the incredible heat she generates, and to use her as a weapon."

In the end, stated Collings in *The Stephen King Companion* (1995), *Firestarter* is

> a midrange King novel, certainly an interesting read, but representative neither of his strongest nor of his weakest works. It lacks the breadth of plot and setting that elevate earlier novels such as *The Shining* or *The Stand* to the level of mas-terworks and potential classics of contemporary American letters; and it equally lacks the cosmic scope of later works, including *IT, The Talisman,* and *Insomnia,* that expand readers' horizons and expectations to something approaching epic intensity.

## Michael Whelan's Firestarter Painting

As can be seen in *Knowing Darkness: Artists Inspired by Stephen King,* Michael Whelan's art has graced several King books, the first being a cover painting for the Phantasia Press limited edition of *Firestarter,* which was issued in a run of 725 signed copies.

King, though he's no artist himself, has a fine sense of art and design and is an ardent collector of original art based on his fiction.

In October 2014, Whelan's original 24-by-32-inch painting for *Firestarter* went up for sale at Heritage Auctions in Dallas. It had belonged to bookseller John McLaughlin of the Book Sail in California, who had offered it years ago in a book catalog for $35,000.

King admired the painting so much that he chose Whelan to illustrate *The Dark Tower: The Gunslinger* (1982). Whelan was asked to illustrate the second book in the series, *The Drawing of the Three* (1987), but previous commitments to other publishers made that impossible. (Whelan even turned down what he termed two "dream" assignments, illustrating *The Hobbit* and *The Lord of the Rings* for their fiftieth-anniversary editions, citing a too-heavy workload.) As Whelan said in *The Stephen King Companion* (1995), "Both nearly drove me crazy because I tried every way I could to work them into my schedule, but it was impossible."

Whelan's *Firestarter* painting is a high watermark in the fantasy illustration field. Your eye is immediately drawn to the young girl in the wraparound cover art, Charlie McGee, the focal point of the novel and the illustration. Look closer, though, and you'll see in the foreground charred bodies, which graphically display her wild talent, her pyrokinetic power.

But for all of her power, she's an orphaned child, an outsider, though perceived by one of the characters in the book as a "monster." But she's no monster; she's just a scared teenage girl on the run, though she harbors a latent, devastating power.

As Whelan wrote in his coffee table book, *The Art of Michael Whelan*:

> After reading Stephen King's *Firestarter,* there was only one image I could en-vision for the cover: the moment of the supreme realization of the protagonist's

power. . . . A look of trancelike fascination, as if she were enthralled by the experience of her power blossoming into fullness.

To me, Carrie must have had a similar moment of awareness when she, too, realized she had a devastating power that remained hidden until triggered by external forces.

In *Knowing Darkness*, Whelan explained, "In three of my favorite books of his—*'Salem's Lot, The Shining,* and *Firestarter*—it's the sense of love and self-sacrifice between the protagonists that's very convincing to me as a father; I find myself identifying with the main character in these three books."

## PHANTASIA PRESS

In a footnote in *Danse Macabre,* King writes affectionately about Arkham House, a small press well known to aficionados of fantasy, science fiction, and horror. What he says about Arkham House can also be said about all the small presses—of which there are many—that have published King's own limited editions:

> There is probably no dedicated fantasy fan in America who doesn't have at least one of those distinctive black-bound volumes upon his or her shelf . . . and probably in a high place of honor. August Derleth was the founder of this small Wisconsin-based publishing house . . . and an editor of pure genius: Arkham was the first to publish H. P. Lovecraft, Ray Bradbury, Ramsey Campbell, and Robert Bloch in book form . . . and these are only a few of Derleth's legion. He published his books in limited editions ranging from five hundred to twenty-five hundred copies, and some of them—Lovecraft's *Beyond the Wall of Sleep,* and Bradbury's *Dark Carnival,* for instance—are now highly sought-after collectors' items.

It's worth noting that Conan creator Robert E. Howard's first book, *Skull-Face and Others,* was also published by Arkham House. And, yes, Arkham House titles are collectible, some commanding thousands of dollars.

The publisher of the first limited edition of any Stephen King book, Phantasia Press opened the way for the other presses who followed, issuing splendidly illustrated, beautifully bound books in small print runs: Whispers Press; Everest House; Mysterious Press; Donald M. Grant, Publisher; King's own Philtrum Press; The Land of Enchantment; Scream Press; Lord John Press; Alfred A. Knopf; Doubleday; Mark V. Ziesing Books; Cemetery Dance Publications; Centipede Press; Subterranean Press; PS Publishing; and others. (Much of the art from these limited editions can be found in *Knowing Darkness.*)

# 29

DARK FORCES: "THE MIST"

*You're supposed to visualize that entire story in a sort of grainy black-and-white.*

—STEPHEN KING, *TAMPA TRIBUNE*, 1980

This is what happened: Anthony Cheetham, the publisher of Futura Publications Limited, recommended that Kirby McCauley "edit an anthology of new stories of horror and the supernatural for him to publish, which . . . could in turn [be] published elsewhere around the world," as McCauley recalled in the introduction to his anthology *Dark Forces*. Published in 1980, *Dark Forces* had to have a contribution by Stephen King, then one of McCauley's clients. In short order, King contributed "The Mist," which became the lead story in *Dark Forces: New Stories of Suspense and Supernatural Horror*. (It was also the lead story in King's anthology *Skeleton Crew*, for the same reason: The strongest story in the book gets the lead position, to draw in readers.)

The tale grew in the telling, as McCauley recounted in his introduction: seventy pages, then eighty-five pages, then a hundred pages, and finally 145 manuscript pages totaling forty thousand words.

"I expected an ordinary-length story and ended up with a short novel by the most popular author of supernatural horror stories in the world," McCauley wrote.

In his notes to *Skeleton Crew*, King explained that the story was written in the summer of 1976, when he and his family were living in Bridgton, in a house on Long Lake; Stephen King, in the aftermath of a storm, made a run to the supermarket, when

> my muse suddenly shat on my head—this happened as it always does, suddenly, with no warning. I was halfway down the middle aisle, looking for hot-dog

164

buns, when I imagined a big prehistoric bird flapping its way toward the meat counter at the back, knocking over cans of pineapple chunks and bottles of tomato sauce. I was amusing myself with a story about all these people trapped in a supermarket surrounded by prehistoric animals.

The resultant story, pitting ordinary folk in a supermarket besieged by monstrous creatures, is a classic King story—and a classic horror story as well. King, who takes delight in putting ordinary people in extraordinary situations, knows that a pressure-cooker environment is ideal for stripping away the thin veneer of civilization, revealing people's true nature: sometimes good and sometimes not so good. (He revisits this theme in *Storm of the Century* and *Under the Dome*.)

"The Mist" is a full-blown horror story and apocalyptic fiction at its best: Out of seemingly nowhere, for no apparent reason, monsters emerge out of a mist to attack. No one is safe.

As Michael Collings wrote in *The Stephen King Companion* (1995):

The length of a short novel, this story of unknown horrors suddenly descending on an unsuspecting humanity contains in miniature the distilled essence of King's storytelling. It showcases virtually every technique, device, theme, twist of characterization and plotting, landscape, and atmosphere that King's readers respond to so strongly. Its story is simple: one day, out of nowhere, a mist settles over a small town. A number of people, including the narrator and his son, are trapped in a supermarket when the first monsters arrive. From then on, the trapped handful of people battle for survival against the mist and the shadowy horrors it hides . . . and, in some ways more frighteningly, against themselves. Finally, a small group leaves the market to try to drive to safety, or at least to discover if there is an end to the mist. The story concludes with their holing up for the night in the lobby of a Howard Johnson's. The mist is still out there; and so are the monsters. Worse, instead of becoming familiar with continued exposure, the monsters seem to be even more alien, larger, more threatening. But, as the final lines indicate, there is also Hope. Out of darkness and death emerge optimism, a thin thread of hope that keeps the survivors struggling to survive. With its microcosmic scope, its emphasis on human types as well as on individuals, and its constantly transmuting monsters that take on the force of allegories for psychological states, "The Mist" taps into archetypal patterns of fear and strength, horror and hope. It is one of King's most tightly focused stories, presenting the illusion of vast human experience in an unusually compressed format.

A quintessential King story, and one of his finest, it was also adapted as a film by Frank "Don't Send Me Back to Prison!" Darabont, with a reimagined ending that is bound to disappoint some reader-viewers because of its overt optimism and finality, in contrast to the published story's more nebulous ending, which offers only a glimmer of hope.

There are also two splendid audio versions of "The Mist," including an unabridged reading by Frank Muller and also a dramatization, which succeeds brilliantly for the same reason that radio shows like Arch Oboler's *Lights Out* from radio's golden era worked so well: They let the listener create his own special effects in what King calls "skull cinema." As King once told Muller regarding straight readings, "the recording seems a lot closer to the mind of the writer" than any other kind of adaptation.

The dramatized version is recorded in binaural sound, which uses a special microphone to give the illusion of three-dimensional sound. The unsettling effect is substantially enhanced when wearing headphones. Case in point: When I was writing the first edition of this book in 1988, in the basement of a three-level townhouse, it was late at night, and I was listening to the ZBS recording with headphones on. My basement had two doors to storage areas. At one critical point in the recording, a door suddenly slams shut, and I nearly shat my pants. I had thought, for a frightening moment, that someone had come in out of nowhere, perhaps by way of the storage-room door, with a bloody ax in hand—imagining a scene from the kind of illustration Bernie Wrightson delights in drawing. *That's* how convincing the ZBS recording is, and, as for my nearly soiling myself, I think the folks at ZBS would have been proud: They wanted to make the unreal appear real, and succeeded brilliantly. I can't recall a time my heart beat faster than that night. I immediately shut the recording off and went upstairs, leaving the late hour and the darkness behind me.

If you've not heard the dramatization of "The Mist," I recommend reading the story and then reliving it with the 3-D audio recording. I can think of no finer introduction to King, since in this horror story King achieves the most difficult of writing tasks: convincing the reader to suspend disbelief.

As I write this, I'm in the basement of *another* house, which has several doors, and it's late at night. I've got headphones on, and the dramatization of "The Mist" on my desk. But having an aversion to self-soiled clothing, I'll wait until daylight to give it a repeat hearing.

# 30

# FRANK DARABONT ON "THE MIST"

## AN INTERVIEW BY HANS-ÅKE LILJA

### JANUARY 7, 2008

*Entire books have been written about movies based on King's writings. Some have been critical analyses, but most have been pop culture overviews, heavy with stills and anecdotal information, focused on the moviemaking process in front of and behind the camera. To date no book has been published on King's movies that comprehensively puts them all in context and explains why some have worked so well and others are cinematic embarrassments.*

*Similarly, no book of interviews with directors who have filmed King projects has been published, which would make for compelling reading.*

*In looking at the many film interviews that have been published over the years, I wanted to reprint one that most people will not have read, an interview that wasn't published in a general interest fan magazine or film magazine. I also wanted to pick an interview that I thought served the reader instead of being a fluff piece on the director. In other words, I wanted a no-holds-barred, straight-shooting director who doesn't mince words.*

*I chose Frank Darabont.*

*I think you'll agree with me that his insights on the moviemaking process and his discussion of being involved in one of his favorite King stories, "The Mist," are compelling reading.*

**Lilja: Last time we talked you were about to shoot *The Mist*, and now it's done and has had its premiere. Are you happy with the result?**

**Frank Darabont:** Delighted. It was deeply satisfying to put this story I've loved for so long on film. The result is the story I always saw in my head when reading the book—and I'm very happy to say that Stephen King loves the movie. That's our best endorsement, as well as my greatest personal satisfaction: the fact that it pleases him. Also very satisfying for me was the opportunity to try a completely different stylistic approach from anything I'd ever done before as a director, which was very exhilarating and liberating for me. It was a blast, tremendously fun in that regard, and a great learning experience. Mostly I'm very happy that we accomplished what we set out to do, which was to make a movie on a low budget and a very tight schedule—for the record, it was seventeen million dollars and a thirty-seven-day shoot. That's not much money these days when major studios are regularly making genre films in the one-hundred-to-two-hundred-million-dollar-budget range. Our goal was to make an ambitious movie with limited resources, very much in the spirit of the grainy low-budget genre films I grew up watching and loving.

**Lilja: Personally, I really liked *The Mist*. In fact, I think it's the best adaptation of a King story to date. What reaction have you gotten on the film? Does everybody like it as much as I do?**

**Darabont:** Thanks, I'm so glad you like it! Overall, reactions have been very gratifying. A lot of people love it and have blessed us with lavish praise; one critic said it's the best movie of the year and one of the best horror movies ever. I don't know if that's true—time is the only real judge of these things—but I appreciate the opinion. The people who have embraced the movie love it for the raw quality, the intensity, and the uncompromising ending.

Of course, there are some people who hate it, too, and I think for those very same reasons. It's real and harsh in a way they don't expect. I think they went in expecting a "popcorn" monster movie with some thrills and a typical ending—a date-night movie, basically—but that's not what they got. They got a bleak, nasty movie that kicked them in the stomach and said some deeply negative things about humanity they weren't prepared to hear. That's not the sort of thing they expect from "just a horror movie," so it pisses them off.

That's okay. You're allowed to hate my movie as much as you're allowed to love it. I always say there's never been a movie that was loved by everybody. (I can read you a few scathingly bad reviews I got for *The Shawshank Redemption* when it first came out.) But with *The Mist*, I set out to make a horror movie, which by my definition is intended to horrify and disturb you. If the movie did that, I succeeded. Some people love those sensations and admire the result. Some people don't; they'd rather go through the motions of a scary movie but not get kicked in the stomach. They prefer horror that doesn't get too real, and *The Mist* got too real for some people, especially at the end. And that's fair, too. Like I said, there's never been a movie that pleases everybody.

What I love is that the film provokes strong reactions either way, but nobody's walking out unaffected by it. And that delights me, because I don't want to make a movie that leaves you unaffected, which is the worst way a film can fail . . . especially a horror film. The films I've loved most in the genre didn't pull their punches—they wanted to fuck with my head. Mind you, I'm not comparing my movie with anybody else's or claiming similar greatness—that would be arrogant and idiotic of me—but *Night of the Living Dead* leaps to mind. Man, do I love that film. What a subversive piece of filmmaking that was in its day, and it certainly didn't let us off the hook with warm platitudes or a misplaced happy ending; instead, it kicked us in the stomach. So did Carpenter's *The Thing*, another admirably disturbing and subversive film. And Cronenberg's *The Fly*, another masterpiece. Again, I'm not comparing—I'm just bringing these movies up because they've always been genre inspirations for me, iconic high points that took their shit seriously and said something about the human condition. They were made for adults, not the teen-date crowd. They did what horror should do: take chances, say something, risk pissing you off. *The Thing* certainly pissed a lot of people off when it was originally released in 1982, though I thought it was a classic the moment I saw it.

**Lilja: And what an ending! I just loved it. I still have goose bumps from seeing it. I must admit that it's even better than the one King wrote [in the original story]. Did you have to fight to get everyone to agree on having such a dark and sad ending?**

**Darabont:** You can't have an ending as downbeat as this without many people questioning it along the way. Especially on the business end. It certainly scared off a lot of financiers who were otherwise prepared to fund the film. I had a meeting with one producer, very well-known, a guy with his own ministudio. He was prepared to make the movie for thirty million dollars and offered to write me the check before I even left the room. But he insisted I had to change the ending.

It was a tempting offer, but also one of those "do I sell out or not" moments in life. I asked him what he thought the ending should be. He had no idea: all he knew was that he wanted it to be any ending but this one. I told him I had no idea either, that this was the only ending that made sense to me . . . and I'd been thinking about it for twenty years! So we shook hands and parted ways.

I suppose for the sake of the money, I could have come up with some other ending. But the truth is, I didn't want to sell out. I never have before and saw no reason to start now. I think it would have been lame to tack on a conclusion that let the main character and the audience off the hook. What would that even be? Suddenly the mist parts and the National Guard is handing them coffee and doughnuts and putting blankets on their shoulders? How obvious and not real. It makes me cringe.

So I ended up making the movie for Bob Weinstein, the only guy with the balls to say, "Hey, I love this, let's make this movie." Of course, I had to make the movie for almost half the money the other guy had offered me—seventeen million dollars instead of thirty. That involved all the typical things: I didn't take a directing salary up front, everybody was working for reduced fees, we had to very strictly control the spending, etc. But at least I got to make the movie my way. I'm sure some people will think I'm a moron for walking away from all that dough, and others will admire my integrity—and, you know, both opinions are fair. But it's not as if I had a choice, really. I have to make the movie I see in my head. I can't render somebody else's creative vision; I can only render my own, for better or worse. It's not even ego—the path I have to follow is the one that makes sense to me; otherwise, I'd have no idea what the hell I'm doing.

**Lilja: How did you get to think of such a grim ending? I can't even imagine how David feels when he sees the military arriving.**

**Darabont:** It's funny . . . most people assume I came up with that ending entirely on my own. Even Stephen King thought so. And I haven't yet gone on record to dispute that notion, but I will do so now. Here's the truth: The idea for that ending is right out of Stephen King's book, and I told him so when we were in New York together doing the press junket for the movie. He asked me where I'd gotten the idea. I said, "Steve, I got it from you! Look at this line in your story, here in the last chapter . . . we're hearing David's thoughts near the end, and it says: 'There are three bullets in the gun, there are four of us in the car. If worse comes to worse, I'll figure a way out for myself.'" (I'm paraphrasing that line right now, but that's essentially what it says.) Steve got this great look on his face when I told him this, because I think he'd forgotten that he ever wrote it.

So all I did was take King's darkest thought and follow it to its most logical and horrible conclusion. The idea for the movie's ending is right there in the original text; I didn't just come up with an idea out of the blue and tack it onto Steve's story. I did what I always do when adapting King or any other author—look for clues in the story that give me insight into the author's thinking and that I can make dramatic use of. I did the same thing quite a bit when adapting *Shawshank* and *The Green Mile*.

**Lilja: I just couldn't believe what I saw. And even if it sounds harsh, I really like that we didn't get that typical Hollywood ending where all turns out for the best.**

**Darabont:** Thanks, me too. Here's my favorite anecdote about the ending. We did a test screening of the film in Burbank. Two guys came up to me afterward with tears in their eyes and said, "Frank, we love this movie, but we beg you to change the ending. It's too much!" After they were gone, two different guys came up, also with tears in their eyes, and said, "Frank, we love this movie. We beg you not to change the ending. It's perfect!"

As I said, it polarizes audiences. I always figured it would. That's why I was willing to make the movie so cheaply—I always recognized we were taking a risk, but I also knew if we made it cheaply enough, the movie would still earn a profit. As you can imagine, I'm very grateful to Bob Weinstein for taking that risk with me.

**Lilja: Now I guess we just have to wait for the Oscar nominations to see how many *The Mist* gets? Both *The Shawshank Redemption* and *The Green Mile* have been nominated, and even though it's harder for a horror movie to be nominated, there are a lot of actors in *The Mist* who ought to be.**

**Darabont:** I appreciate your kind thought, but there's no way we'll get any nominations. A low-budget horror movie like ours isn't even on the Oscar radar screen. I do agree my actors would be deserving of recognition for the work they've done—perhaps they'd get that recognition if they'd been in another kind of movie—but not this one.

**Lilja: Your next Stephen King movie is *The Long Walk*, right? Where are you with that one now? Is a script written?**

**Darabont:** There isn't a script yet. I plan to write it this year.

**Lilja: I guess that script will demand a lot if you're going to succeed in making it into a feature film. *The Long Walk* is one of my favorite books, but you must admit that it's not the first book you're thinking of when you think of a Stephen King book being turned into a movie. What got you hooked on that particular book, and aren't you worried that it's not doable as a movie?**

**Darabont:** What makes *The Long Walk* a great story is how stripped-down and spare it is. Not much plot—just kids walking, talking, and dying. It's a very existential work; Stephen King meets Eugene Ionesco. And that's what I love about it. It's small and fascinating and weird, and I think the movie should be, too. It's more of an art house movie the way Steve wrote it. I don't want to reinvent it or blow it out of proportion to justify it as a big commercial film, which is how they screwed up *The Running Man*. I'm not sure it's even possible with material like *The Long Walk*. Of course, doing it faithfully means I'd have to do it cheaply—far more cheaply than *The Mist*—but at least I can stay true to what Steve wrote. Perhaps as a cool little film for HBO or Showtime?

**Lilja: Last time you also mentioned "The Monkey." Any news on that one?**

**Darabont:** I'm hoping to write that script this year, too. We'll see how it turns out. It might make a good theatrical feature. We'll see.

**Lilja: Any other King/Darabont collaborations that you can talk about?**

**Darabont:** We're going to have a baby through in-vitro fertilization. No, that's not true. I'm just messing around. I should know better, because that's how rumors get started.

**Lilja: What else are you up to? I guess you might be taking a well-deserved break now that *The Mist* is done.**

**Darabont:** Yes, I need it. I've never made a movie this quickly. We started prepping the film in January, and we finished everything at the end of October—ten months of production from start to finish. (Plus, I did a few months prior to that casting actors with Deb and designing monsters with Greg Nicotero, so maybe twelve months for me in all?) I'm glad I did it, I'm glad I proved I could do it, but I don't want to do it that way often. It kills you. It's intense and exhausting. What I learned making *The Mist* is that it's just as hard making a seventeen-million-dollar movie as it is making a sixty-seven-million-dollar film like *Green Mile*. But with a bigger budget, you at least have the additional advantage of time.

# 31

## CUJO

### 1981

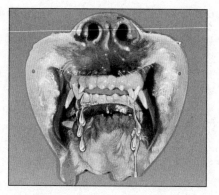

*A "Cujo" mask given out at the American
Booksellers Association convention.*

There is no higher tribute to the effectiveness of a writer of
fiction than when a phrase or title becomes part of the greater
lexicon . . . *Cujo*, as a word-image of the friendly and familiar
suddenly turned monstrous, is another phrase that has entered
our collective consciousness.

—DAN SIMMONS, INTRODUCTION TO *CUJO*, 1994

Over the years readers have asked King the question he most dreads: Where do you get your ideas? Like other writers, he usually makes a humorous joke out of it, because it's a question that doesn't lend itself to a sound bite. In this instance, however, King knows exactly where he got the idea for this novel. He told Winter in *The Art of Darkness* that in the spring of 1977, outside of Bridgton, Maine, he took his ailing motorcycle to a mechanic who had "this huge Saint Bernard" that "came out of the barn, growling." The owner, recalled King, slapped the dog's rump and got it to stop, and the idea of writing about a large, out-of-control dog leaped forward. It's a great doggone story, but critics are divided about the novel's status in King's canon.

Writer Dan Simmons, in an introduction to the 1994 Collectors Edition of *Cujo*, explained that the novel is more than what it seems. It's "a serious horror novel on more levels than one. . . . I am going to suggest that *Cujo* is not really about a rabid dog. I submit that it is about something even more terrifying. It is about a parent's ultimate nightmare—the inability to protect one's child when the universe suddenly grows fangs."

Winter's assessment is that it's "one of King's best novels" and cites its exploration of reality as a strength, its "stripping away . . . of supernaturalism to confront us with the mundane here-and-now" to support its thesis that "reality is an unnatural order."

But others, including Michael Collings, have a bone to pick; specifically, "In *Cujo*, almost every key event seems accidental." As he wrote in *The Stephen King Companion* (1995), "In King's stronger pieces, there is frequently an underlying current of purposefulness approaching tragedy. Characters make important decisions and then must accept the consequences of those actions. . . . Cujo remains a 'tweener,' a novel captured between two opposing states of storytelling, and as a result, is it weakened."

Originally conceived as a Bachman novel, it's the story of a rabid Saint Bernard that attacks and kills both its owner, Joe Camber, and Joe's pal, Gary Pervier, and then lays siege to Donna Trenton and her son, Tad, who are trapped in their Ford Pinto: Though Donna survives, Tad does not; he dies of dehydration, which understandably upset readers, who wanted him to live.

A relentless, grim, in-your-face novel, *Cujo* marks a departure from King's previous novels, which have overt elements of horror or the supernatural. In this novel, though, the horrors of everyday life, told through the Trenton family's efforts to simply stay alive during a difficult time economically, hits closer to home. The economic hardship experienced by the Trentons could happen to any of us, if the wheel of fortune spins and we find ourselves in an unfortunate circumstance.

## RIDING WITH STEPHEN KING

### By Suzi Thayer

One day in 1977 I went with three friends to see the movie, *The Deep*, at a theater in Westbrook, Maine. It had been my idea to take a taxi from Portland, so as we were leaving and realized we were all low on cash, it was up to me to find a ride back to Portland.

I spotted a lone man with a friendly-looking face leaving the theater and asked if he might give four poor women a ride to Portland. He happily obliged and led us to a big, sleek-looking black car. (I wouldn't be so quick to hop in these days.)

I sat in the backseat, behind him, where I could see his eyes in the rear-view mirror. They looked familiar. Then I noticed a metal plaque on the dashboard that read: Stephen & Tabitha King. I said, loudly, "Oh my God guess who's driving this car!"

King laughed. When asked what he was working on, he told us he was just starting a story about a rabid Saint Bernard. Cujo hadn't even been named yet.

## Coming Clean: King's Addiction

Most of King's Constant Readers, who thought they knew everything there was to know about him, were surprised to discover that, as he confessed in *On Writing*, he is a recovered alcoholic and drug user.

It got so bad that, as he explained, "At the end of my adventures I was drinking a case of sixteen-ounce tallboys a night, and there's one novel, *Cujo,* that I barely remember writing at all. I don't say that with pride or shame, only with a vague sense of sorrow and loss. I like that book. I wish I could remember enjoying the good parts as I put them down on the page."

King's choices: Straighten up and fly right or crash and burn. Pilots call it auguring into the ground.

To King's credit, he straightened up and flew straight.

At its worst moments, though, things looked pretty bleak. During an intervention, Tabitha King had gone around the house, collected the detritus of his various addictions, and, as he recounted in *On Writing,* dramatically emptied "a trash bag full of stuff from my office out on the rug: beer cans, cigarette butts, cocaine in gram bottles and cocaine in plastic Baggies, coke spoons caked with snot and blood, Valium, Xanax, bottles of Robitussin cough syrup and NyQuil cold medicine, even bottles of mouthwash."

The reader engaging in pop psychology might speculate that King suffered from self-esteem problems, or that he was clearly running away from reality and seeking escape through substance abuse, but the simple fact is that it takes trained medical professionals to diagnose and treat such addiction, which is a very serious matter. So let's not speculate.

You have to give King credit: He came clean—both in stepping forward to admit it and in taking steps to overcome it—and accepted full responsibility for his actions. In the end, he realized that "[c]reative people probably *do* run a greater risk of alcoholism and addiction than those in some other jobs, but so what? We all look pretty much the same when we're puking in the gutter."

King, finally, conquered his demons.

# 32

## Danse Macabre

### 1981

> I think the most important thing I learned from Stephen King
> I learned as a teenager, reading King's book of essays on horror
> and on writing, *Danse Macabre*. In there he points out that if
> you just write a page a day, just 300 words, at the end of a year
> you'd have a novel. It was immensely reassuring—suddenly
> something huge and impossible became strangely easy. As
> an adult, it's how I've written books I haven't had the time to
> write, like my children's novel *Coraline*.
>
> —Neil Gaiman, "The King and I,"
> *Sunday Times Magazine* (U.K.), April 28, 2012

In the dedication to *Danse Macabre*, King writes, "It's easy enough—perhaps too easy—to memorialize the dead. This book is for six great writers of the macabre who are still alive." He cited Robert Bloch, Jorge Luis Borges, Ray Bradbury, Frank Belknap Long, Donald Wandrei, and Manly Wade Wellman.

When King's book was published in 1979, all six were alive and well; now, with the passage of time, they are all gone, but we are left with a body of work that continues to impress, delight, and entertain; to borrow a phrase from Pixar's *Monsters, Inc.*, they care enough to scare.

I was fortunate enough to see Bradbury at several public events, at which he was always accommodating to fans. He especially loved to attend the San Diego Comic Con, even if it meant having someone transport him in a wheelchair. The last time I saw him was at SDCC, with a big smile, like a kid in a candy store, as he took in the sensory overload and spectacle of the event, in all its splendor and gaudiness. I also met Manly Wade Wellman, a gentleman from North Carolina who attended the one-day Durham minicons, which were held at the home of Edwin and Terry Murray, whose unparalleled collection of pop culture—comic books, science fiction, fantasy, and horror—now resides in the special collections of Duke University, which both men attended.

Like Bradbury and Wellman, Stephen King is a master in the horror field, and, like them, he's a fan at heart. Attendees at the fifth World Fantasy Convention recall seeing him walk around the dealer's room, where stacks of pulp magazines, hardback books, and other collectibles commanded his attention. It was the time for him to round out some holes in his collection and get them signed by other writers in attendance, who shared with him their love of the field. That's what fandom is all about.

What makes *Danse Macabre* unique among King's works is that it is his first nonfiction book. An extended love letter to the genre of fantastic literature—science fiction, fantasy, and supernatural horror—and its practitioners, the book was written at a time when researching the subject meant spending time in the library, calling up people to get information, buying or borrowing publications of interest, and hunting down rare items from rare book dealers.

These days the Internet makes such tasks immensely easier, but what it can't do is take all these disparate elements and bring them together in a whole. That requires a lot of analysis and synthesis, which is what English majors are trained to do, and King, a former English major, did just that in *Danse Macabre*, an accessible text written for a general audience.

The book's genesis, as King points out in his forenote, can be credited to King's former book editor at Doubleday, William G. Thompson. It was Bill who called King, in November 1978, with a suggestion—and a challenge: "Why don't you do a book about the entire horror phenomenon as you see it? Books, movies, radio, TV, the whole thing."

The timing was right. King, who was preparing to teach a class at the University of Maine at Orono, Themes in Supernatural Literature, realized that it was his opportunity to kill two birds with one stone: In doing the homework for the book, he'd be prepping for the class itself, and he'd be able to publish a book that shared his enthusiasm for the field with his readers.

Everest House issued the trade edition, and Otto Penzler's Mysterious Press issued the signed limited edition. The editor at Everest House was—you guessed it—William G. Thompson, who had moved there after being forced to leave Doubleday.

The resultant book is a detailed, informal, and entertaining overview of the horror field. Appropriately, the book's title is referred to in "October 4, 1957, and an Invitation to Dance," the first chapter's title.

I think the *The Milwaukee Journal* nailed it when describing the book: "*Danse Macabre* is a conversation with Stephen King . . . It's comfortable and easygoing. At the same time it's perceptive and knowledgeable, a visit with a craftsman who has honed his skills to an edge that cuts clean and sparkles with brilliance."

The *The Baltimore Sun* stated, it "succeeds on any number of levels, as pure horror memorabilia for longtime ghoulie groupies; as a bibliography for younger addicts weaned on King; and as an insightful non-credit course for would-be writers of the genre."

Michael Collings wrote:

Anyone associating the terms "critical," "academic," and "scholarly" with a book claiming to be the results of university courses or a disquisition on the development of a literary genre will be pleasantly relieved to discover, early in *Danse Macabre,* that just because King is writing nonfiction he has not left behind the distinctive narrative voice that had already become his trademark. Although the book is a cogent and concise study of dark fantasy, it is also clearly from the mind and pen of Stephen King, replete with personal reminiscences that in turn set the stage for conclusions about the functions, nature, and purposes of horror.

Amply illustrated with black-and-white photos, the book covers radio, movies, television, and books; in other words, it thoroughly covers the field. The book is especially useful for its discussion on radio. As King explains, "I am of the last quarter of the last generation that remembers radio drama as an active force—a dramatic art form with its own set of reality."

If you have any interest in the field whatsoever, the book will repay multiple readings. For newcomers, King's list of recommended movies and books is a good starting point: There's plenty of source material here, and it'll take a chunk of time for you to watch the movies and read the books.

Now thirty-five years down the road, it's time for a young writer to assay the field anew, bringing the book's contents current, because so much has happened in the field, notably with films and books.

But King's book still remains the best single source overview of the field that he so obviously loves, and loves to write about when the opportunity arises.

# 33

## STEPHEN KING'S CREEPSHOW

### 1982

It's like the proverbial rollercoaster ride, where you laugh and

you scream, and it doesn't leave a bad taste in your mouth. You

just feel like, "Wow, that was great! Let's go do it again!"

—STEPHEN KING, ON THE MOVIE *CREEPSHOW* (*CREEPSHOWS* BY STEPHEN JONES)

King's graphic novel *Creepshow* consists of five stories drawn in full color by Bernie Wrightson. It's unique among King's books because it's drawn from a movie with a screenplay written by Stephen King.

The 1982 movie, which took $8 million to make and had veteran horror film director George Romero at the helm, grossed—a rather apt word, I must say—$21 million domestically at the box office. (A sequel, *Creepshow 2*, released in 1987, didn't fare as well: It earned only $14 million in domestic box office receipts.)

The film was inspired by editor Bill Gaines's Entertaining Comics (EC Comics) line of horror comic books: *Tales from the Crypt, The Vault of Horror,* and *The Haunt of Fear.* The comics are collector's items, which prompted Russ Cochran to reprint them in sturdy, full-color hardback books, which have a place of honor in Stephen King's book collection.

The movie opens with a scene familiar to all too many comic book fans, whose

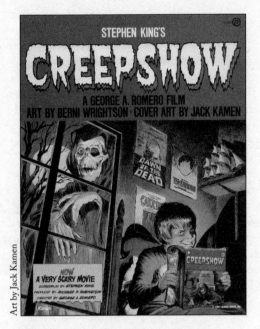

The cover to the graphic novel, Stephen King's
Creepshow, with art by Jack Kamen.

parents—mine included—considered comic books to be trash, to which they were quickly
consigned. The eight-year-old boy in bed, reading his comic at night, looks familiar; he's
Joe Hill King.

Joe Hill makes a brief appearance, but Stephen King is front and center in one of
the five stories, "The Lonesome Death of Jordy Verrill." The short story version, titled
"Weeds," appeared in the May 1976 issue of *Cavalier* magazine. In the film version, King
plays the part of a Maine farmer who discovers that a meteor has landed on his property;
he hopes to cash in by selling it to the local university . . . until it breaks open, spilling its
green-colored goo, causing him to itch insanely.  Like an alien kudzu, the "meteor shit"
slowly covers his house, his yard, and finally him. (For his role, noted Stephen Jones in his
film study *Creepshows*, "To create the plant effect, King wore latex make-up appliances
created by Tom Savini for the early stages of the growth and dyed yak and horse hair was
glued directly onto his face and hands. 'I just wanted to cover him in moss. Make him
itch!' joked Romero.")

The bottom line, according to King, from Ann Lloyd's *The Films of Stephen King*:
"I'm happy with *Creepshow* because I was involved with the entire thing, from beginning
to end, and the writing process was original." It was all in good fun for King, who loved
its connection to the horror comics of the past. "As a kid," wrote King in *Danse Macabre*,
"I cut my teeth on William B. Gaines' horror comics. These horror comics of the fifties
still sum up for me the epitome of horror, that emotion of fear that underlines terror, an
emotion which is slightly less fine, because it is not entirely of the mind."

## THE COMIC BOOK

The original idea the studio pitched was a straightforward novelization, which King rejected because it wasn't in the spirit of the movie. The only way King would allow a tie-in was if it made sense visually, and that meant a comic book adaptation.

King turned to Bernie Wrightson, who cut his teeth illustrating horror comics for Marvel, DC, and Warren Publishing. Working from the movie and King's script, Bernie had a blast illustrating the sixty-four-page comic published as a trade paperback, for which he rendered pencils and finished ink; the coloring was done by his former wife, Michele.

The cover was drawn by EC Comics artist Jack Kamen, showing a boy in bed at night reading a ten-cent comic titled *Creepshow*, with posters decorating his bedroom wall (George Romero's *Dawn of the Dead*, *The Shining*, and *Carrie*). A hooded, skeletal figure peers in through the boy's window, illuminated by a full moon in the background.

Of the five stories, two stand out because of the outstanding artwork: Bernie excels in depicting monsters, and so "The Crate" is memorable, with its werewolflike creature, as is "The Lonesome Death of Jordy Verrill," which recalls the humorous flavor of Wrightson's "Uncle Bill's Barrel" and his work for the DC comic *Swamp Thing*.

34

---

# Drawn to Darkness

## Bernie Wrightson, an Artist Inspired

### by Stephen King

For the privileged few who bought any edition of *'Salem's Lot* from Centipede Press, you own one of the finest examples of specialty publishing in our field. The one-man press, based in Denver, Colorado, is run by a high-energy, enthusiastic guy named Jerad Walters, whose sense of aesthetics in terms of book design is second to none. Like an Arkham House book published when August Derleth was at the helm, a Centipede Press book is singularly distinctive. Jerad also has what I consider to be an essential quality for any man crazy enough to run a one-person small press: He has the capacity to take infinite pains; he's detailed-oriented and sweats the small stuff.

He followed up his gorgeous edition of *'Salem's Lot* with another Stephen King–related title, *Knowing Darkness: Artists Inspired by Stephen King,* which I wrote. That tombstone-sized book is also out-of-print, and it too sported first-class production values. The 1,500-copy slipcase edition cost $395, the 300-copy tray-case edition cost $895, and the 25-copy lettered edition cost $4,995.

In his introduction to the book, film director Frank Darabont shares a telling anecdote about a phone conversation he had with Stephen King years before Jerad independently came up with the same idea. Frank's idea: King "should put all that art together and publish it as a huge book, call it *The Art of Stephen King.*"

King's response: "Jesus—you know how much *art* that is? Or the effort that would go into a book like that? *No way, Jose!* There aren't enough hours in the day, or days in the year! It would take forever! Sober up!"

I'm glad that no one dissuaded Jerad Walters, because he was crazy enough to pursue his mad dream, for which we are all indebted: Almost all the art was shot from the

181

originals or color-adjusted scans of the original art, instead of printed pages overlaid with type. In other words, Jerad went above and beyond, to the point where he commissioned artists to render new pieces just for this project.

Karen Haber of *Locus* (October 2010) sang the book's praises:

> From the first glance at the slipcover of *Knowing Darkness: Artists Inspired by Stephen King,* with its lunatic demon-possessed lawman from *Desperation,* painted by Don Maitz, or the flip side, with its dark portrait of Randall Flagg, arch villain of *The Stand,* as rendered by the late Don Brautigam, you know you are in for a wild ride. What else would you expect from a giant volume filled with art inspired by the master of darkness? The only thing missing is a sound chip implanted in the cover to provide a faint scream or anguished groan as the book is opened.
>
> With this beautiful volume, and its predecessor, *A Lovecraft Retrospective* (2008), Centipede Press has set the bar even higher for fine art book publishing—and for weight training on the part of any readers who hope to read this thirteen-pound book. Centipede's second mammoth tribute volume measures eleven by fifteen inches, with 448 pages and over five hundred illustrations, including thirty double-page foldouts. This definitive collection of art spans King's 35-plus-year career, with newly commissioned artwork and reprinted art.
>
> The lineup reads like a Who's Who of dark fantasy, science fiction, and horror artists, represented by a wide variety of media including collages, scratchboard, oils, acrylics, watercolors, graphite pencil, photographs, and digital art. . . . As if the artwork and essays weren't enough, the sheer quality of the physical materials used to create the book inspires admiration: the heavy matte varnished paper, the sewn-in binding and ribbon bookmarks, and custom-fitted illustrated slipcases.

Like Harlan Ellison, who is an ardent collector of artwork, especially pieces illustrating his book covers and interiors, Stephen King is also a collector and has several fine pieces in his collection, including a Phil Hale piece from the limited edition of *The Talisman,* a Jeffrey Jones painting from the same edition, and a gorgeous Michael Whelan painting from the seventh book in the Dark Tower series, titled *The Dark Tower.* Moreover,

*The Centipede Press edition of* Knowing Darkness: Artists Inspired by Stephen King.

King—like most writers—is very concerned about cover art, for the simple reason that even though you can't judge a book by its cover, it's what the potential customer sees before he opens the book for a sample reading.

As booksellers will tell you, when a potential customer is browsing a book in a retail store, he's halfway to a sale when it's picked up: the cover is not mere decoration but an essential sales tool. It explains why publishers go out and hire the best cover artists—Michael Whelan, Drew Struzan, Bernie Wrightson, and others—because their work helps draw you into the book.

*Knowing Darkness* remains a testament to the many artists who have illustrated King's work, and it'd be impossible to do them all justice in this book, so I'd like to concentrate on Bernie Wrightson, who has illustrated the most diverse selection of King books: *Creepshow, Cycle of the Werewolf, From a Buick 8, The Stand, The Dark Tower: The Wolves of the Calla,* and art for *TV Guide*'s cover story on *The Shining*.

## BERNIE WRIGHTSON
### 2009

*When I was working on* Knowing Darkness: Artists Inspired by Stephen King, *I especially enjoyed interviewing as many artists as possible. Some of them I had not known, but I'm glad to say I've known Bernie since the seventies when he burst on the comic book scene and made everyone sit up and pay attention. One look at his work—the draftsmanship, the humor, the sheer inventiveness of his graphic storytelling skills—was enough to show that he was destined for great things: Early on, he showed considerable promise, and in the years that followed, Bernie delivered.*

*His masterpiece is surely his series of pen-and-ink illustrations for* Frankenstein, *which has seen print by three publishers (so far). The best, in my opinion, is from Dark Horse Books (October 2008), which unfortunately is out of print. Fortunately, it is available on the secondary market, and it is well worth your time to track down a copy to add to your collection.*

*If Franklin Booth, another great pen-and-ink artist, had seen Bernie's work on Mary Shelley's haunting novel, he'd whistle in admiration. Yeah, Bernie's work on* Frankenstein *is that good.*

*Switching gears here: The best interviews are conducted in person at a creator's studio, because that's where he is most comfortable; he's in his element, relaxed, and won't be interrupted as he would in a more public environment, like a convention. Fortunately, I was able to conduct an interview for* Knowing Darkness *with Bernie at his studio. I'm was with veteran Disney artist Tim Kirk in Bernie's studio, a small but cozy apartment crammed with a lifetime of collecting curiosities both mundane and macabre: skeletal models of dinosaurs; a life-sized human figure showing musculature and bones; figurines of Dracula, Frankenstein, the Bride of Frankenstein, and the creature from the Black Lagoon; angelic figurines; a shelf crammed with unabridged audiobooks of fiction by Stephen King and J. K. Rowling; shelves crammed with books on art, anatomy, history, and novels; and, in every nook and cranny, paintbrushes sprouting from tin cans and glass jars.*

Bernie's studio was exactly as I had imagined it: a cross between a young boy's toy shop and a biological-specimen house. Clearly, buried within the adult are the sensibilities of a little boy who delights in artifacts of innocence and experience. His world is suffused with popular culture, fueling his wondrously macabre imagination. (One can say the same about Stephen King, who is one year older than Bernie.)

Growing up in the fifties, in the shadow of the atomic bomb, against the backdrop of the Cold War, both Bernie and Stephen lived at a time when the United States enjoyed a postwar boom, making it the preeminent world power militarily and economically. The two both grew up in blue-collar households where money was tight. They both haunted movie theaters, watching endless B movies showing mutated insects, people, and monsters—all accidental victims of radiation poisoning. The two devoured pop fiction in well-thumbed paperback books and comic books, especially Bill Gaines's lurid line of comics: science fiction, suspense, and horror rendered in exquisite detail and four-color by Frank Frazetta, Wally Wood, Jack Davis, and others.

"We didn't have books in the house," Bernie recalled, "but we had comics. My mom read romance comics, my dad read war comics, and I got Superman and Donald Duck."

But, in a scene reminiscent of *Creepshow*, Bernie's mom threw out his collection of horror comics because she perceived them as being trash, which is where they ended up, to his dismay.

Years later, as adults, both Bernie and Stephen tapped into the latent power of the outsider, a staple in pop culture: Wrightson's Swamp Thing, who reared up out of the wetland, and King's young adults Carietta "Carrie" White (*Carrie*), Arnie Cunningham (*Christine*), and Charlene "Charlie" McGee (*Firestarter*).

Fueled by endless cups of black coffee, chain-smoking cigarettes, and glazed doughnuts, Bernie sat back to relax behind his drawing table. He took a long drag on his cigarette, exhaled slowly as smoke eddied and filled the room, and got down to the business at hand: talking nonstop for the next four hours.

A longtime collector of his work, I have his retrospective collection, *A Look Back*, and his classic *Frankenstein* on my shelf, and I also have many of his art prints. I'd met him through my associations with Vaughn Bode and Jeffrey Jones, two of the finest artists to emerge out of the comics field. (Vaughn passed away in 1975, at age thirty-three, and Jeff in 2011.)

Those were heady days for art collectors. I was at a Phil Seuling Comicon in 1971, talking to Russ Cochran, who had just begun representing Frank Frazetta. Russ had one of Frazetta's paintings for $700. We witnessed one fan complain about the price, saying that no one would ever pay that much money for a painting by him. Flash forward to 2010: a Frazetta painting of Conan the Barbarian sells for $1.5 million.

Who would have guessed that comic books would be four-color treasures the likes of which Smaug would have hoarded? That original art from comics and paperback book covers would be worth a king's ransom? Our parents never knew—they considered it all junk—but we knew better.

What follows are observations from Bernie from my interviews with him over the years, some with explanatory texts by me on some of Bernie's King-related projects.

## STEPHEN KING'S *CREEPSHOW*
### NEW AMERICAN LIBRARY, TRADE EDITION, 1982

"King was in Pittsburgh. I don't know how much time he spent there, but he was filming his segment 'The Lonely Death of Jordy Verrill,' in which he was cast as a country bumpkin. I got a call one night. My wife gets the phone, hands it to me, and tells me it's Stephen King. Yeah, right. I'm thinking it's a prank from one of my friends, like Bruce Jones."

"'Is this Bernie? This is Steve King.'"

"*Wow,* I thought. *It's really him.*"

"'I'm in Pittsburgh, and I'm working on a movie with George Romero. You know George Romero, right?'"

"Sure," I said. *"Night of the Living Dead."*

"'We're working on a movie. It's an anthology movie with several stories from a horror comic. We are working with [EC artist] Jack Kamen, who is also working on the movie. We assumed Jack was doing the comic book version, but when we asked him about it, he said he didn't know what we were talking about.'

"Stephen King said, 'Is there any possibility that you could do the comic book?' And at the time, there was something else I had to put aside to take it on. They wanted the whole thing done in two months, but it took me four months to do it.

"I probably put the most work into 'The Crate' and 'Jordy Verrill.' Those were my two favorite segments from the movie. 'The Crate' because it's a movie within a movie. And 'Jordy Verrill' because it was played for laughs."

The graphic novel was published in July 1982. The cover was by Jack Kamen, but the interiors were by Bernie. The contents included "Father's Day," "The Lonesome Death of Jordy Verrill," "The Crate," "Something to Tide You Over," and "They're Creeping up on You." A homage to the EC Comics line, this movie tie-in edition ran sixty-four pages.

### *CYCLE OF THE WEREWOLF*

### The Land of Enchantment, limited and trade edition, 1983; Signet, trade edition, 1985

[The Land of Enchantment publisher] "Chris Zavisa put that whole thing together. It was his idea for a long time to do a project with Stephen King, with me as the illustrator. Chris wanted to do new material, a small project that he could handle as a specialty publisher. We were talking about it and Chris came up with the idea of doing a calendar. It'd almost have to be a werewolf story because the *only* thing *all* the months have in common is a full moon.

"What I wanted to do would tie in with the dates of the calendar. Whatever year this was coming out we'd time it so that the events were happening on the same day as the calendar with the full moons. After we got this all worked out, Chris approached King, who seemed excited by the whole idea. King started working on it as a calendar project. Each story was to be several paragraphs, a block of copy under the illustration, and under this, the calendar itself. As he was writing, King said the story began to grow on him, and he couldn't contain it to just a few paragraphs per month. Finally, it was becoming obvious that it was not going to be a calendar.

"King sent me the finished book version and I just did the illustrations."

## THE STAND: *THE COMPLETE AND UNCUT EDITION*
### Doubleday, limited and trade edition, 1990

Bernie was commissioned by Stephen King to illustrate the book and did so with twelve pen-and-ink pieces that add a visual cachet to the expanded edition; the original edition, published in 1978, lacked illustrations. With a mixture of pieces rendered in a film noir style and a sweeping landscape recalling his work in *The Cycle of the Werewolf,* the illustrations are among Bernie's best work.

The artwork was subsequently published as a separate portfolio of art from Glimmer Graphics (1,200 sets, out of print). Nakatomi (nakatomiinc.com), which publishes Wrightson's prints, published ten prints in a portfolio: 40 sets ($300) in a regular edition, and 15 sets ($500) in the artist edition, in June 2015.

"I did twelve pen-and-ink interior illustrations. The deal was done with Stephen, who commissioned and paid for them, and not with the publisher.

I worked from both the original and revised versions of the book.

There are two or three drawings that, if you haven't read the excised stuff, you wouldn't know what it's from. In the revised version, there's material involving the Trashcan Man that is really going to change your mind about how you are going to feel about him. And bits and pieces, here and there, that clarify things or add another dimension to it. And some material involving a new character that is just some of the creepiest stuff you'll *ever* read.

## FROM A BUICK 8
### Cemetery Dance, limited and trade edition, 2002

The limited edition is illustrated with color illustrations that draw on Bernie's strengths as an illustrator. Because monsters are his strong suit, his visual interpretation of the alien creature from another world strikes all the right notes; there's three plates of an alien-looking creature who opens a portal in his attempt to transport Ned Wilcox into its world.

The juxtaposition of the real and the unreal—the setting of a state police barracks in western Pennsylvania—is stark: one illustration shows the horrified look of state troopers as they stand outside a garage and stare with incredulity through the garage windows to see lightning crackle inside housing what appears to be—but is clearly not—a Buick Roadmaster.

## THE DARK TOWER: *THE WOLVES OF CALLA*
### Donald M. Grant, Publisher, limited edition, 2003

It's September 21, 1988—Stephen King's fifty-first birthday—and he's on the set of *The Green Mile,* directed by Frank Darabont, with Bernie Wrightson present. As Bernie recalled, "I got to see King in the electric chair and writhe around and make faces."

At that informal gathering, King told Bernie, "Oh, by the way, I was wondering if you'd be interested in illustrating the next Dark Tower book." Bernie immediately agreed, though it had been a while since he had read them and would need to reread them before tackling the art.

Time, though, was not a problem. Bernie told me, "I got jury duty right around that time and I had to be downtown every day for over two weeks. In fact, I had to be on call at the courthouse for almost three weeks because of jury selection for two murder trials. I had nothing to do all day but read the Dark Tower books. It was great. I read them one after the other, and then read the manuscript of *The Wolves of the Calla*." He added, "When I'm illustrating a book, I'll read the whole thing and bookmark the scenes that immediately stand out; then I go back and reread those passages. I considered their spacing throughout the book, because I don't want the illustrations too close to one another or to have too long a stretch without one. With Steve's writing, though, there's a picture on almost every page, so it was very easy to pick out the standout moments."

Bernie recalled, "During that time, Steve sent me a letter, saying he was glad I was on board. He told me: 'If you don't mind, I have a list of suggestions for scenes. I'm not art directing, by any means, but these are scenes that I would like to see illustrated. If you agree, that's fine; and if not, just illustrate the scenes you want.' As it turned out, King's list of twelve scenes were exactly the ones I picked. I wrote back to tell him he had picked the best scenes—the same ones I had picked; they were also spaced exactly right throughout the body of the book."

## *TV Guide: The Shining* issue

## April 26, 1997

For a cover story on King's remake of *The Shining*, starring Steven Weber as Jack and Rebecca De Mornay as Wendy, Bernie Wrightson provided a color painting for the cover of *TV Guide* and an interior illustration for "Before the Play."

As *TV Guide* noted:

Weber knew that King didn't want another psycho Jack [Nicholson]. The story King wanted to tell emphasized a family torn apart by a much more prevalent demon: alcohol. "It's not just about a big star going mad," Weber says. De Mornay agrees: "When I first saw the script I thought, 'Who are they kidding? They're going to do this again?' But this script had nothing to do with the movie. It haunted me. It was a metaphor for the classic American alcoholic dysfunctional family, where the real ghost in the family is rage."

Bernie's painting of a snowy winter's night, with Jack Torrance in the foreground and the Overlook Hotel in the background, grabs your attention, as does his interior illustration for King's "Before the Play," depicting Lottie Kilgallon, who reaches for cigarettes on the floor and has her wrist grabbed by a man under the bed.

## 35

———— ◆ ————

# STEPHEN KING:

## A CHAUTAQUA IN PASADENA, CALIFORNIA

I can't really lecture. I'm not good at that, and I can't speak with
any sense from prepared notes. About the most I can do is
*chautaqua*, a fine old word that means you babble on for a little
while about the things that you do and then you sit down.

—STEPHEN KING IN HIS INTRODUCTORY COMMENTS TO A
PUBLIC TALK IN VIRGINIA BEACH, VIRGINIA, IN 1986

*I was at the Virginia Beach lecture, for which King solicited questions from the au-
dience to be submitted in writing prior to his talk. He pulled out a few at random,
answered them, and decided to take questions from the audience instead, saying he
prefers live interaction. Immediately, hands went up as they always do when he appears in public, because people are curious about him and his work.*

*At the Pasadena talk, King answers a lot of the most commonly asked ques-
tions his readers pose to him. The following quotes are from his Q&A after his
informal talk.*

*On Lobsters*: For a lot of my childhood, I grew up where I live now, which is Maine. We
used to eat a lot of lobster—a poor man's steak. We always used to get seconds, particularly in the summer. Whatever was left over at the end of the day, you could buy for a
dollar a pound.

Some kid told me that if you bought a lobster and cracked open the tail, there's a
nerve dangling down its back; and if you eat that, you'd be paralyzed. I know it's not true,
but I can't bring myself to eat that black thread.

188

*On a fearful imagination*: I relate to the kid who is afraid because he's heard his father talking about the twilight double-header, a monster that he thinks is in his closet.

*On his fan mail*: You'd be surprised at some of the letters I get. There are some strange people out there—present company excepted, of course.

*On symbolism in horror stories and films*: They are unreal symbols of very real fears. I don't think that horror fiction works unless you are talking in two voices: on one level, in a very loud voice, you are screaming at your audience about ghosts, werewolves, and shape-changers; and in another, very low voice, a whisper, you are talking about *real* fears, so that in the best cases, you are trying to achieve that nightmarish feeling we've all had. We know it's not real, but that doesn't matter anymore. When I can get that, I know I've got people right where I want them.

*On why he writes horror fiction*: I like to scare people.

*On whether or not he's ever going to write serious fiction*: I'm serious-minded whenever I sit down, regardless of what I'm writing about.

*On whether evil exists*: I'm haunted by the idea that there's some kind of outside evil—something that almost floats free. I worry about guys like Ted Bundy. Whatever it was that was in him was gone when they put him in the electric chair—they fried a shell. Maybe whatever it was blew away.

*On a ghost*: I have seen a ghost. It's a real ghost story. [He was at a political fund-raiser event in 1984, and went upstairs to retrieve his and Tabitha's coats.] I realize there was a man sitting by the window across the room, so I raised my head slightly to bring him into sight. Through my glasses, I saw a bald seventy-year-old man with round glasses. He was wearing a blue pinstripe suit. I began to feel very strongly that this man thought I was looking through the coats to see what I could steal, and I was feeling more and more uncomfortable. I finally said: "Gee, it sure is hard to find coats when people come in." And as soon as those words came out of my mouth, I realized that the chair was totally empty—nobody was sitting there. My reaction to this was to get our coats and say nothing whatsoever about it.

We got halfway to the restaurant where we were going to eat dinner, and inside my mind I stopped and said to myself: Now wait a minute, the guy was there—you saw him. Why are you pushing this away? You never took your eyes off him.

My guess is that's about as exciting as most psychic phenomena get.

*On his writing speed*: I write very fast.

*On his storytelling process*: I usually know where I'm going, and I usually have an idea about what the end is going to be. I think some of you who have read my books would be surprised to find out how many of them were intended to be much bleaker than they turned out to be. For instance, I expected everybody to die at the end of *'Salem's Lot* and at the end of *The Shining*.

*His favorite story*: "The Body."

*On his reading material*: I read a lot of novels. I have a tendency to enjoy crime novels, suspense novels, and some horror novels, although I don't read as many horror novels as I used to. If I had to name a book that's made an impression on me lately, it would be Larry McMurtry's *Lonesome Dove*, which I liked very much. ... I just got around to reading for the first time *Look Homeward, Angel* by Thomas Wolfe. I loved that book. The guy didn't know how to say quit; he would turn [to] his typewriter and everything would vomit out. I can relate to that.

*On the novel* Misery: It's pretty accurate in terms of emotional feeling. I sometimes don't know what people want. ... People really like what I do, or at least some people do, but some of them are quite crackers. I have not met Annie Wilkes yet, but I've met all sorts of people who call themselves my "number-one fan" and, boy, some of these guys don't have six cans in a six-pack.

*On selling his work to Hollywood*: When you sell something to the movies—and I love the movies; it's immensely flattering to have somebody want to turn your book into a movie—there's two ways to go about it: Get involved all the way, or part of the way, and stand up and take the blame or criticism for everyone else; or to say, I'm going to sell it and take the money. But when you don't get involved, you are in a no-lose situation because if it's good you can say, "It's based on my work." But if it's bad you can say, "I didn't have anything to do with that."

*On being typecast as a horror writer:* All I can say is ... I'm a horror writer if you *want* me to be one. You can call me anything you want to—I don't care.

In America, everybody's got to have a brand name. You've got your generic game-show host; you've got your generic Western writer; you've got your generic bad-guy actor; and you've got your generic horror writer.

I just write stories, but I *tend* to write horror stories.

A few years ago I tried very hard to write a western because it's a form I like. I wrote about 160 pages, but the only scene that really had any power was when the old guy got drunk outside a farmhouse and fell into the pigsty, and the pigs ate him. That one scene had some real drive and punch. That is what turned on my lights, for some reason I don't understand.

*On his writing schedule*: I write two or three hours in the morning. I crank up the music as high as I can: It keeps people away when you turn the music up loud, because it poisons the air.

*On his taking a break from writing*: I'd go crazy. I'm a creature of habit.

*On breaking into print*: I'm not sure what you do about it. I was lucky enough to have a book that was adapted into a successful film [*Carrie*]. I've always wondered what would have happened if *Carrie* the film had been a failure. Would I be anywhere near where I am today? I like to think so, but who knows?

I think it's something of a crapshoot, but I'll tell you one thing I believe: talent almost always finds the light, even today. If you need proof of that, look at Amy Tan, who is a fantastic success story and deserves every bit of it. I just wish as many people as know Amy Tan knew Katherine Dunne, who wrote *Geek Love*.

*On writer's block:* I've had it twice. Shortly after *Carrie,* I went through a writer's block that was about a year long. And after I finished *The Tommyknockers,* I went through a year of hell that I would never wan to go through again. Nothing would seem to come up. I would write and it would fall apart, like wet tissue paper. I don't know how to dscribe it, except to say that it's the most impotent, nasty, awful feeling. You feel like a batter in a slump. Finally, what happened was that I wrote a little story called "Rainy Season" [in *Nightmares & Dreamscapes*] and, all at once, everything opened up and flooded out. I've been writing horror every since.

# 36

---

## DIFFERENT SEASONS

### 1982

The four stories in *Different Seasons* were written for love, not
money, usually in between other writing projects. They have a
pleasant, open-air feel, I think—even at the grimmest moments
… there's something about them, I hope, that says the writer
was having a good time, hanging loose, worrying not about the
storyteller but only about the tale.

—STEPHEN KING, ON *DIFFERENT SEASONS*,
IN A WALDENBOOKS PUBLICATION, *BOOK NOTES*

Stephen King's readers know that he has a penchant for addressing the reader directly in the forewords or afterwords of his short-fiction collections. He began this practice with *Night Shift,* for which he wrote a lengthy piece that dovetailed the introduction by John D. MacDonald, whom he asked to write it.

The practice of commenting on the fiction, so far as I can tell, was popularized by Harlan Ellison, whose prolific output of short fiction gave him ample opportunities to explain the story behind the stories, which he does in an entertaining and illuminating fashion.

Readers, for the most part, like it when the author comes out of the shadows to shed

*From "The Body": Runaround Pond in Durham.*

light on the stories. It's as if you've met the writer at a bar afterward as he explains what happened behind the scenes. It's one reason why King's fans feel connected to him in a personal way, because his forewords and afterwords read as if they are long letters to the reader—and in a way they are.

In collections of short fiction in which there's no explanatory text, the reader comes away with a distancing experience, because the author himself is out of sight. Typically, novels never have any explanatory text, which is a shame because there's much an author can say about a novel—its genesis and its connection to the real world—that readers would find interesting.

In an introduction to a collection of his short fiction, Neil Gaiman, who like Ellison and King is also fond of writing introductions and afterwords, wrote in *Smoke and Mirrors* that "[s]tories are, in one way or another, mirrors. We use them to explain to ourselves how the world works or how it doesn't work. Like mirrors, stories prepare us for the day to come. They distract us from the things in the darkness."

As Gaiman knows, writers hold up mirrors to reality, but they aren't ordinary mirrors, the kind most often used. A writer's mirror reflects different realities, showing us what could be, or what could never be: It makes us see the world in a new, different light, as do the stories in this collection.

In King's afterword to *Different Seasons,* he explicates an oft-asked question: "Is horror all you write?" His short answer is "no," but a simple answer isn't what the audience wants to hear.

An afterword is King's opportunity to have the reader's undivided attention and write the answers to these questions at length, without the pressure of time at a public event.

Although King answers both questions to most readers' satisfaction in this book's afterword, I'd like to add a few thoughts on the second question, because it strikes at the heart of this collection of four novellas.

As King readily admits, usually with a long, deep sigh, Americans—and indeed the world—perceive of him as being, as he put it, America's best-loved bogeyman. It's a convenient label for people who haven't read his work but only know of him as a household name because of his general reputation. They would likely be astonished if they only knew the wide range of his literary output—poems, screenplays, nonfiction of all stripes, short fiction, novella-length fiction, and novels. Certainly the element of fear is a thread that runs through most of his works, but horror takes many forms: both supernatural, of course, and real-world—horror, unfortunately, is an inextricable part of life, the dark side of human existence.

Of the four stories in *Different Seasons,* only one has an element of supernatural horror—the last one, "The Breathing Method," about a very unusual birth. The other stories explore nonsupernatural horror: "Rita Hayworth and Shawshank Redemption" examines the horror of incarceration, of losing one's freedom, sustained by dim hope; "Apt Pupil" examines the parasitic and horrific relationship between a former Nazi concentration camp commandant and his impressionable protégé, whose great interest in the "gooshy stuff" is a whirlpool that sucks both teacher and pupil under; and "The Body," a coming-of-age story that explores two young boys' fears of growing up only to be trapped in dead-end jobs in small towns: a fate almost worse than death.

In other words, when someone asks King if horror is *all* he writes, the questioner is thinking about *'Salem's Lot, The Stand,* "The Mist," *Cycle of the Werewolf,* and other tales in which supernatural horror is obviously an element.

I submit that King's enduring popularity stems in part from his refusal to write only supernatural horror, in which the monsters are external. Those books can be highly entertaining fiction, and popular in their own right—*The Stand,* in fact, is often cited by fans as their favorite King novel—but the stories in which the monsters are mortal are often more frightening because they are *real*: In "Rita Hayworth and Shawshank Redemption," the warden of Shawshank Prison is a sanctimonious yet monstrous man who hides behind his piety and wields the Bible as a weapon while behaving demonically. And in "Apt Pupil," Todd Bowden's abnormal interest in sadism, in the suffering of Jewish concentration camp inmates, is horrific; his wholesome outward appearance contrasts sharply with the moral decay that rotted him from the inside out.

The standout piece in this collection is "The Body," a carefully nuanced tale whose narrator is Gordon LaChance, who grew up in Castle Rock and aspired to break free from the confines of that small Maine town. Gordon's fear is that he, like his friend Chris, will be trapped and never go beyond its restrictive confines, that he will never realize his dreams or fulfill his potential; Gordon's hope is that he *will* break free to realize his dream as a full-time freelance writer.

Taken as a whole, this collection of stories stands among his best books. As Michael Collings wrote in *The Stephen King Companion* (1995), "[T]he stories in *Different Seasons* are among King's most powerful mid-length works. Lacking the depth and breadth of the novels, they nevertheless allow King more scope than the short stories."

Which brings us back to the original question: Is horror all that King writes? As this collection amply illustrates, obviously not.

## MICHAEL COLLINGS ON NOVELLAS FROM *DIFFERENT SEASONS*

"Apt Pupil" is appropriate as a companion piece to *The Shining*. In both stories, innocence is corrupted by pervasive evil. Jack Torrance's alcoholism is as destructive as Todd Bowden's obsession with the "gooshy" parts of Kurt Dussander's Nazi past, and both aberrations lead the characters to insanity and murder, either potential or actual.

"The Breathing Method" is a traditional "winter's tale," a fireside story of single-minded determination (an internal connection among the four stories of *Different Seasons*, by the way) that results in a fracturing of what one assumes to be natural law. In its closing paragraphs, in fact, "The Breathing Method" expands until it comments elliptically, and with more than a touch of horror, on the nature of fiction and storytelling itself.

"Rita Hayworth and Shawshank Redemption." In spite of its horrific setting—Shawshank Prison, with its concrete walls and cruel, sometimes stupid wardens and guards, and its bands of "Sisters" whose lives are devoted to viciousness, rape, and violence—"Rita Hayworth and Shawshank Redemption" paradoxically comes across not as an exercise in gritty realism but almost as an attempt at idealism. As seen through the eyes of a hardened inmate . . . Andy Dufresne brings light to the darkness, a strong gentleness that opposes the stone walls surrounding him. His ultimate escape becomes not only a justified consequence of his patient endurance of a judicial injustice, but also a tribute to the indomitable human spirit.

"The Body." Of the four stories, the most resonant is "The Body," perhaps because it is more familiar to recent readers through Rob Reiner's superlative film adaptation, *Stand by Me*. Again told without any substantiative recourse to supernatural horror, "The Body" is a semiautobiographical story of a young would-be author finding in himself and his experiences the stuff of true storytelling. . . . Restrained, symbolic, even apocalyptic in the etymological sense of "uncovering that which is hidden," "The Body" is a remarkable achievement. With only minimal plotting, it nevertheless provides riveting portraits of boys on the verge of become men, of children confronting adult realities, and of the necessary transition from innocence into experience.

# 37

## THE ROAD TO THE DARK TOWER:

### ROLAND'S QUEST

I'm never done with The Dark Tower. The thing about The Dark
Tower is that those books were never edited, so I look at them
as first drafts. And by the time I got to the fifth or sixth book,
I'm thinking to myself, 'This is really all one novel.' It drives
me crazy. The thing is to try to find the time to rewrite them.
There's a missing element—a big battle at a place called Jericho
Hill. And that whole thing should be written, and I've thought
about it several times, and I don't know how to get into it.

—STEPHEN KING, *ROLLING STONE*, NOVEMBER 6, 2014

### A CHANCE ENCOUNTER

The longest journey begins with the first step.

And so it was that in 1970, when King was a senior in college, he began writing what
would prove to be his magnum opus, a massive work that still occupies his mind. Nearly
five decades later, King is still drawn back to Roland's world and impelled to write about
a big battle at Jericho Hill. Dark Tower fans are already anxiously waiting its eventual
publication.

The Dark Tower story began when King had gotten odd-sized, thick, lime-green
paper that he fed through a battered Underwood typewriter. Then living in a cabin
near the Androscoggin River in Orono, King began the first chapter of what would be

published as *The Dark Tower: The Gunslinger* and showed them to Chris Chesley, who was impressed, and told King so.

Serialized in *The Magazine of Fantasy and Science Fiction,* the novel appeared in five installments, starting with "The Gunslinger," followed by "The Way Station," "The Oracle and the Mountains," "The Slow Mutants," and "The Gunslinger and the Dark Man."

### Donald M. Grant, Publisher

The Director of Publications at Providence College in Rhode Island, Donald M. Grant wore a different hat away from the office: He was the publisher of a small press in the fantasy/horror field. Best known at the time for publishing Robert E. Howard's fiction, Grant got to talking with King at a college dinner and asked him if he had anything suitable for his small press.

The Magazine of Fantasy and Science Fiction *(October 1978), in which "The Gunslinger" appeared—the first publication of King's ambitious story cycle.*

King offered the Dark Tower stories, which he felt were similar to the kind of books Grant had previously published. King also felt that the subject matter of the Dark Tower was sufficiently a departure from his horror novels that a small press and its correspondingly small audience was the only way to go: The Dark Tower, King felt, wouldn't appeal to his mainstream readers.

The novel, as Grant wrote, "begged for" illustrations, and both Grant and King agreed that Michael Whelan was their first choice. Michael had previously illustrated the wraparound cover for the Phantasia Press edition of *Firestarter*. As Grant explained to me, "We both thought that Michael was at the top of the game." And King "certainly liked Michael's work, so we were in accord there." "King was very pleased" with the finished artwork, Grant recalled.

The book went into preproduction, and the early word among fans was that no true fan of fantasy and horror could afford to pass up this book.

The Magazine of Fantasy and Science Fiction *(November 1981), containing King's "The Gunslinger and the Dark Man."*

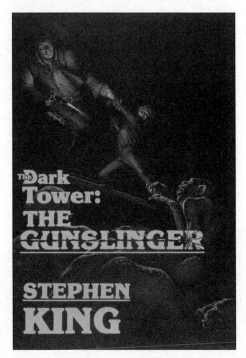

*The first edition, from Donald M. Grant, Publisher, of* The Dark Tower: The Gunslinger, *with art by Michael Whelan.*

Grant sent out a full-color brochure to people on his mailing list, telling them about King's new novel:

> Written over a period of twelve years, *The Dark Tower: The Gunslinger* is the first cycle of stories in a remarkable epic, the strangest and most frightening work that Stephen King has ever written. It is the book of Roland, the last gunslinger, and his quest for the Dark Tower in a world in which time has no bearing.
>
> Against the weird background of a devastated and dying planet—with curious ties to our own world—the last gunslinger pursued the man in black. It is a time when man's thirst for knowledge has been lost, and the haunted, chilling land harbors strange beings: the Slow Mutants, less-than-human troglodytes dwelling in the darkness; a Speaking Demon, laired beneath a forgotten way station; and a nameless vampiric presence, held captive in an ancient circle of altar stones.
>
> Herein lies a tale of science-fantasy that is unlike anything bestselling author Stephen King has ever written; indeed, it is unlike anything anyone else has ever written.

King fans rushed to place orders for the book.

The editor and publisher of the semiprozine *Whispers, Stuart David Schiff,* wrote in the August 1982 issue about Grant's latest offering. He noted,

I am not a partner with Donald Grant, although I would certainly like the opportunity to join up! Still, my never-ending praise for his publications might make it appear I have a financial interest in his press. The reality of the situation is that Don does great work and as such deserves praise. He has just produced what might possibly be the most important book ever from a specialty press. It is Stephen King's *The Dark Tower: The Gunslinger* (HC, $20; *signed* by author and artist, 500 copies, $60) as illustrated by Hugo-award winner, Michael Whelan. The book is an epic tale, weird and unlike anything else King has written. The Whelan artwork is superb. The trade hardcover has "only" a 10,000 copy run. No sarcasm is intended by my quotation marks. King's hardcovers normally sell *many* times that number, so the book may sell out quickly. Regarding the materials, Don has spared no expense. The paper is special, there are colored pictorial endpapers, five color plates, and the usual other expertise the field has come to expect from Grant. Do not miss this book.

The first printing of 10,500 copies (10,000 plus 500 signed/numbered) were immediately snatched up by fans.

"To issue such a book, of course, is one of the few ways I have of saying that I am not entirely for sale," wrote King in an essay for *Castle Rock* in 1985, "that I'm still in the business for the joy of it, and that I have not been entirely subsumed by the commercial juggernaut I have cheerfully fueled and set in motion."

The ones who missed out were the King readers at large who bought his trade editions from bookstores, because they were unaware of the specialty presses that catered to fandom.

*The Dark Tower* quietly went out of print.

King was happy, the fantasy fans were happy, and Donald M. Grant, the publisher, was happy as well, but he would have been even happier if King had allowed a larger print run, because he knew the demand far exceeded the supply. The best he could hope for was a second printing, if King agreed. Unlike most of the books Grant had previously issued, with much smaller print runs, which sold slowly over the years, mainly through book dealers in the field, *The Dark Tower* was a bestseller. It was—as is every signed, limited-edition King book—a license to print money.

## The Firestorm

When *Pet Sematary* went out into the world in 1983 with a first printing of a quarter-million copies in hardback, it alerted King's larger readership that he had previously published *The Dark Tower*. Opposite *Pet Sematary*'s title page was the obligatory listing of previously published books written by Stephen King. Broken down by category—novels, collections, nonfiction, and screenplay—one title in particular stood out: "*The Dark Tower* (1982)." There was no mention of the publisher, which added to the mystery. King's Constant Readers were shocked to discover that there had been a King novel that they somehow had missed out on.

The firestorm began: Where can I get *The Dark Tower*?

Readers besieged his publishers (Doubleday, New American Library, Viking), chain bookstores, and also King's office; when they found out Donald Grant was its publisher, they deluged him with letters asking how they could buy copies.

King was adamant that because *The Dark Tower* had limited appeal, it wouldn't please his mainstream readers, who were accustomed to his horror novels. He therefore refused to allow further printings. "I didn't think anybody would want to read it," King explained in *Castle Rock*. "It wasn't like the other books. The first volume didn't have any firm grounding in our world, in reality; it was more like a Tolkien fantasy of some other world. The other reason was that it wasn't done; it wasn't complete."

"I wanted to do something about it," King explained at a public talk in Pasadena, "and Don wanted to do something about it. He was upset. We talked on the phone one night and I said, 'What if you published another 500 or 5,000?' There was a long sigh. And I said, 'That would be like pissing on a forest fire, wouldn't it?' He said, 'Yeah.'"

Courtesy of Greg Preston of Sampsel & Preston Photography.

But as the firestorm spread, King reluctantly allowed Grant to go back to press. Another ten thousand copies were printed, with priority going to people who specifically had written to King to request information on where to buy it.

Like the first, the second printing was immediately snapped up; once again, the demand *far* exceeded the supply, and it quickly went out of print.

King finally changed his mind, and in 1998 New American Library published *The Dark Tower: The Gunslinger* in an inexpensive edition to ensure as many people as possible could afford to buy it. The book featured a new painting by Michael Whelan depicting Roland, with the Dark Tower in the background; the book also reprinted the interior art from the Grant edition.

*Michael Whelan in front of the door to his home studio.*

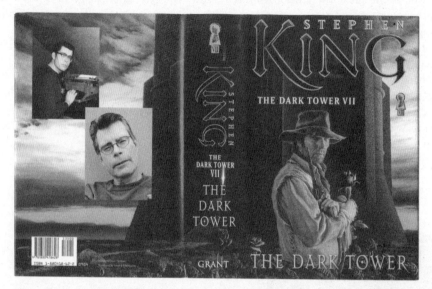

*Wraparound cover art by Whelan for the seventh* Dark Tower *novel, in the Donald M. Grant, Publisher edition.*

*The Donald M. Grant edition of* The Little Sisters of Eluria, *with Michael Whelan art.*

Now the question was no longer *Where can I buy it?* but *When is the next* one coming out?

On his official Web site, King answered:

I am going to continue the *Dark Tower* series, mostly because I have three women who work in my office that answer the fan mail, and a lot of times they don't tell me what's going on with the fan mail, except for the stuff that I pick up myself. But they put every *Dark Tower* letter on my desk. This is like a silent protest saying, *get these people off our backs.*

But my plan this time—if all goes well—is just to continue working until the cycle is done, and then, that way, I can walk away from that.

It's always been my intention to finish. There isn't a day that goes by that I don't think about Roland and Eddie and Detta and all the other people, even Oy, the little animal. But this book has never done what I wanted it to do. I've been living with these guys longer than the readers have, ever since college, actually, and that's a long time ago for me.

I want to finish it. But there are no guarantees in this business. I can walk out of here today and get hit by a bus and that would be the end of that. Unless it came into somebody by Ouija board, which is always a possibility.

But the other thing is, I can try and find out that the words aren't there any more. I don't think that will happen, but you never know 'til you open the cupboard.

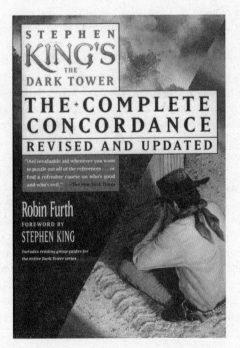

*The Simon & Schuster edition of Robin Firth's encyclopedic Dark Tower concordance, with cover artwork by Michael Whelan.*

MICHAEL COLLINGS ON *THE DARK TOWER: THE GUNSLINGER*

"The man in black fled across the desert, and the gunslinger followed."

These sparse words begin the most atypical and in some ways the most imaginative narrative yet to come from King's pen, the first volume in what promises to be the longest, most complex story from an author whose trademark has become long, complex tales.

As with so many King texts, the basic story of *The Dark Tower: The Gunslinger* is simplicity itself. The gunslinger, Roland of Gilead, has been, is, and (so far as the readers can tell at the beginning) always will be pursuing the dark man, a shadowy, quasi-mythic figure that holds the secrets to Roland's ultimate quest, the Dark Tower, an even more darkly shadowed, more vaguely mythic nexus of worlds, universes, and ultimate possibilities. The quest for the dark man has led Roland from the ruins of his own country—where the world has irrevocably "moved on"—into a vast desert near the far edge of the world. Crossing the desert, he undergoes sore trials and temptations, meeting eventually with Jake, a mysterious young boy from another world, who helps Roland survive and whom Roland in turn grows to love. But he cannot love Jake as much as he loves (or is obsessed with) the Dark Tower. When the brutal choice between Jake's life and his quest forces itself upon him, Roland barely hesitates before sacrificing Jake in order to confront the dark man. At the end of this first installment of the story, Roland has gleaned secret knowledge from the dark man and sits beside the western sea, awaiting dreams of the Dark Tower and the time of the drawing of the three.

The "Afterword" to *The Dark Tower: The Gunslinger* explains that the projected plot outline for the remainder of the story would take nearly three thousand pages to complete . . . and, given the time it took to complete the first volume, King "would have to live approximately three hundred years to complete the tale of the Tower. . . ." It also apologizes for the fact that the *Dark Tower* series is not exactly what King's readers have come to expect from him.

In many ways, however, that is precisely the strength of the series, especially this first volume. Coming from the pen of a writer whose popular image is of a single-minded purveyor of cheap horror and the even cheaper "gross-out," whose style is often condemned as wooden and workmanlike at best, whose books are condemned as overwritten and underedited, *The Dark Tower: The Gunslinger* is a pleasant surprise. There are certainly elements of King's trademark horror; the Slow Mutants, for example, resemble strongly similar characters in *The Talisman* and are described in terms familiar to King's readers, while Roland's first response to them is the equally familiar "atavistic crawl in his intestines and privates" often associated with moments of horror in King's novels. And, of course, there is the sense that this volume is merely the beginning of the longest novel yet, one whose ending is so far distant as to be lost in the mists that obscure the Dark Tower itself.

But as an individual work, *The Dark Tower: The Gunslinger* undercuts many readers' presuppositions about King. It is written in unusually spare diction, ranging from typically coarse colloquialisms to carefully constructed analogues of the refined language of high fantasy. There are few narrative digressions in the novel, and few lines and phrases that do not move the story forward. It is, in fact, the shortest of the *Dark Tower* series thus far, and among King's shorter novels.

Beyond the level of style, however, is the larger issue of genre. While King occasionally blends horror with other genres—with mainstream pseudo documentary fiction in *Carrie*, or with science fiction in *The Long Walk*—in the *Dark Tower* series, he sets himself the ambitious task of combining horror with the Western (Roland is, after all, the last gunslinger), the action-adventure thriller, touches of the romance in both the contemporary and the medieval senses, alternate-universe and multiple-universe extrapolative speculations, philosophical debate, heroic saga, apocalyptic fantasy, and above all, the epic quest. Browning's "Child Roland to the Dark Tower Came" provides a character and a focus for the quest, but King's imagination fills out the spare outlines into a rich tapestry of worlds, some dying, others (ours included) not yet fully aware of an unnamed threat to the Dark Tower itself. Browning also supplies the epic form, but King's imagination again transforms it into prose narrative of a sort rarely attempted.

The epic impulse itself is almost as old as literature, extending at least as far back as *The Epic of Gilgamesh*, inscribed in clay tablets with cuneiform script some four thousand years ago. During much of western history, the epic stood at a pinnacle of human achievement, with works such as Homer's *Iliad* and *Odyssey*, Virgil's *Aeneid*, the Anglo-Saxon *Beowulf*, Ludovico Ariosto's *Orlando Furioso*, Luis de Camoens's *Lusiad*, Edmund Spenser's *The Faerie Queene*, and Sir Philip Sidney's prose *Arcadia* continuously transforming the genre to meet new requirements of new audiences. Until its culmination in John Milton's *Paradise Lost*, the epic reigned virtually unchallenged as the highest literary form, at least for Renaissance audiences; after Milton's superlative achievement, however, verse epic almost disappeared, except for such inverted, mock-epic masterpieces as Alexander Pope's *The Rape of the Lock* and *The Dunciad*, and Lord Byron's *Don Juan*. Serious verse epic simply could not force language, structure, and theme beyond the point to which Milton developed them; to all appearances, verse epic ceased to be a viable literary form.

The need for epic itself did not disappear, however, but reappeared in a startling new eighteenth-century genre, the novel. Until the end of the nineteenth century and the novel's descent into realism, naturalism, and the antiheroic, the quest for a hero found its outlet in long prose narratives; and in the twentieth century that impulse was rapidly transferred from the mainstream novel to the science-fiction / fantasy novel, in works as disparate as J. R. R. Tolkien's *The Lord of the Rings* and Frank Herbert's *Dune*, in which the actions of a single individual could in fact make a difference, could even save the world, the solar system, or the universe itself.

It is this literary heritage that lies behind the *Dark Tower* novels, beginning with *The Gunslinger*. King has created an archetypal epic personage, whose past lies hidden in myth and legend and whose future is wedded completely to the object of his quest. King's fable resonates with epic scope and grandeur, particularly in Roland's dream-vision of the Tower and its casual relation to all things. In good epic fashion, King expands the vision of his tale until it potentially represents an encyclopedia of the culture in which it is written; and in *The Drawing of the Three* and *The Wastelands*, volumes 2 and 3 of the saga, that potential becomes actual as King anatomizes the strengths and weaknesses of American society over the past three decades, thrusting Roland into contact with the 1960s, the 1970s, and the 1980s. Through Roland, King examines our obsessions and our frustrations, our hopes and our dreams, our successes and our failures, all from the perspective of an epic character out of this time and out of this place. Roland's perspectives on our world transform the everyday into the alien, giving readers continuing glimpses into who and what we are.

## THE LONG PUBLICATION PROCESS

As King explained in the introduction to *The Little Sisters of Eluria* (originally published as a separate book in 2009, which included a rewritten version of the first *Dark Tower* novel published in 1982), "I had no idea of how things were going to turn out with the gunslinger and his friends. To know, I have to write."

In other words, the stories would come when they came, and that proved to be an ongoing frustration to readers . . . and to King, too, who was besieged with never-ending queries, until Roland reached the Dark Tower in 2004 and blew his horn.

The publication timetable of the Dark Tower novels from Donald M. Grant, Publisher, stretched over a period of twenty-two years, from *The Dark Tower: The Gunslinger* in 1982 to *The Dark Tower* in 2004. (*The Wind Through the Keyhole*, the eighth Dark Tower novel, which fits into the plot between volume 4 and 5, was published in 2012.)

What accelerated the publication schedule was the accident on June 19, 1999. Struck by a minivan near his home in Center Lovell, Maine, King subsequently endured a slow, painful recovery. That unexpected event emphasized the fragility of life, which hangs on a thread. It gave King the impetus to get the series completed.

The cycle is now complete, at least for the time being. In an interview with *Rolling Stone* (November 6, 2014), King said that he feels impelled to rewrite the books because they feel like "first drafts." It remains to be seen whether he will devote precious time rewriting a previously published saga that readers already feel is complete.

The wild card, though, is that in the same interview King says there's one major book as yet unwritten in the series—depicting the battle of Jericho Hill. My thought is that he will almost certainly write that book. I'm not so sure, though, that he'll rewrite the rest of the books in the series, because the temptation to do so is tempered with the fact that there are new books crying to be written . . . and his time, with each passing year, becomes even more precious.

*The Dark Tower: The Wind Through the Keyhole*

Once again, Dark Tower fans will have to wait and see, which is always a frustrating situation. It's one that fellow fantasist George R. R. Martin fans are currently dealing with, because his saga, Song of Ice and Fire, is a work in progress, which has frustrated fans: Some churlish readers have complained online, adamantly insisting that Martin has an obligation to finish the series before attending to other projects, attending conventions, or giving more interviews. Other readers have speculated about his health, worried that he may die before completing the series. (It happens: the last Gormenghast novel, *Titus Awakes*, was posthumously published as a fragment, owing to Mervyn Peake's death in 1968.)

As Neil Gaiman explained to one impatient fan who had the expectation that Martin should stop everything he's doing, personal and professional, to complete the Fire and Ice story cycle: "George R. R. Martin is not your bitch."

The same holds true for Stephen King.

## YOUR ROAD MAP TO THE DARK TOWER

When it comes to books about the Dark Tower, I am of the firm opinion that such books should only be read *after* the reader has finished the series, just as you should not watch the supplementary material provided on DVDs until after viewing the movie itself.

For instance, if you've yet to read Tolkien's epic fantasy *The Lord of the Rings* (a book that inspired King, influencing not only the Dark Tower series but also *The Stand*), you are best advised to read *The Hobbit* first, since it lays the groundwork for the larger, more ambitious books to follow, and then read, in order, *The Fellowship of the Ring, The Two Towers,* and *The Return of the King*. After that, you're free to round out your reading with the multivolume book series *The Complete History of Middle-earth* or the many nonfiction studies on Tolkien's considerable body of work.

The correct chronology for reading the Dark Tower novels in order:

1. The revised edition of *The Gunslinger,* because of the inclusion of an additional nine thousand words
2. *The Drawing of the Three*
3. *The WasteLands*
4. *Wizard and Glass*
5. *The Wind Through the Keyhole*
6. *The Wolves of the Calla*
7. *The Song of Susannah*
8. *The Dark Tower*

*The Little Sisters of Eluria* is not available as a standalone book in any trade edition; now out of print, the short novel was originally published in *Legends,* edited by Robert Siverberg.

It was subsequently reprinted by Donald M. Grant, Publisher, in a beautiful edition paired with a rewritten version of the first Dark Tower novel, *The Gunslinger,* with new artwork by Michael Whelan.

If you want to read the story itself, it was reprinted in King's anthology, *Everything's*

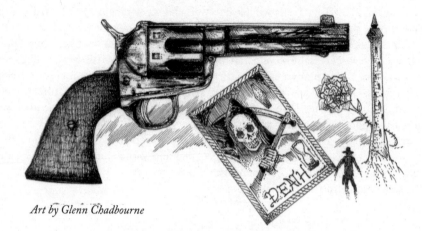

*Art by Glenn Chadbourne*

*Eventual* (Scribner, 2002). In an introductory note to the tale, King eplained, "I had lots of space to move around in—Silverberg wanted short novels, not short stories—but was still hard."

Hard but not impossible, as it turned out. The short novel flowed out of King's word processor. "One thing this story has going for it is that you don't need to have read the Dark Tower novels to enjoy it," King explained in his note.

To guide you to the Dark Tower, I highly recommend Robin Firth's exhaustive and authoritative concordance *Stephen King's The Dark Tower: The Complete Concordance, Revised and Updated* (2012), which incorporates *The Little Sisters of Eluria* and *The Wind Through the Keyhole*.

In his foreword to the book, Stephen King points out that "I needed some sort of exhaustive written summary of *everything* that had gone before, a Dark Tower concordance that would be easy to search when I needed to find a reference in a hurry."

When King asked his mentor and longtime friend Burton Hatlen for a recommendation, Hatlen recommended Robin Firth, "and my wandering gunslinger had found his Boswell," wrote King.

Firth's concordance is an exhaustive work of scholarship and honors the Dark Tower story cycle and King as well. Like carrying an American Express card in the real world, I wouldn't travel through Mid-World without this concordance as my constant companion. And if you need another recommendation, here's King's endorsement from his foreword to Firth's book: "I found this overview of In-World, Mid-World, and End-World both entertaining and invaluable. So, I am convinced, will you."

> I am coming to understand that Roland's world (or worlds)
> actually *contains* all the others of my making; there is a place in
> Mid-World for Randall Flagg, Ralph Roberts, the wandering boys
> from *The Eyes of the Dragon*, even Father Callahan, the damned
> priest from *'Salem's Lot*.

—STEPHEN KING, AFTERWORD, *THE DARK TOWER IV: WIZARD AND GLASS* (1997)

# 38

## MICHAEL WHELAN:

### ILLUSTRATING THE DARK TOWER

As King critic Dr. Tony Magistrale points out, "The Dark Tower reflects King's career-long fascination with culling together diverse genres: the epic, the western, the gothic romance, science fiction, fantasy—all these things into a hybrid text where various elements of literary and cinematic traditions interface and coalesce. And they do so in a way that's totally unexpected."

*The paperback edition of* The Dark Tower: The Gunslinger, *with art by Michael Whelan.*

Clearly, this story presented a formidable challenge for any illustrator, but Michael Whelan was up to the task. I asked him to give me a sense of what it was like to read the first book in manuscript form.

"I found *The Gunslinger* to be an extremely depressing book, despite feeling flattered to have been asked to do it in the first place," Whelan said. "It was January 1981 when I began work on the assignment, a stressful month for me all around. My mother had just died a couple of weeks before, the children of our family's closest friends died in a car crash on I-95, and John Lennon had been killed. The weather was blustery and icy; to tell you the truth, the last thing I wanted to do was illustrate *The Dark Tower: The Gunslinger*. I was just not in the mood."

In addition, Michael and his wife, Audrey, had just become parents for the first time. The birth of their daughter, Alexa, meant that they came to know all about the joys of sleep deprivation and round-the-clock feeding schedules.

Finding himself with back-to-back assignments for specialty presses, Whelan was initially daunted by the demands of illustrating "two dark and disturbing books": Charles Grant's *Tales from the Darkside*, followed by King's *The Dark Tower: The Gunslinger*.

"But in the end I rolled up my sleeves and got into it," Whelan said. "Once I started making sketches, things started going quickly. I prepared some watercolor board panels and started painting, and soon found myself lost in the story. But in retrospect, I don't know why I didn't do some research by watching all the Clint Eastwood movies. Ordinarily, I would have thought that to be part of my homework. I'm really puzzled by this, because they're so obviously an influence on King's *Gunslinger*. But I suppose my thinking was to jump into the project with both feet and complete the commission without delay. I can't go back and do them over again, but I wish I had seen the movies and visited the Southwest before attempting to begin the artwork."

Whelan rendered five paintings and several pen-and-ink pieces for *The Dark Tower: The Gunslinger*, including an iconic image of Roland sitting on a beach, with the nebulous outline of the Dark Tower in the distance, set against a blood-red sun.

The original painting sold for $1,750. "I could easily get up to $35,000 for that today," Whelan shrugs. "Whoever bought it got a good deal."

For the trade paperback edition, published in 1988, Whelan painted the background a "peculiar mustardy color that seemed to express the dusty, oppressive feeling of the book to me," he wrote in *The Art of Michael Whelan*. The portrait depicts Roland in profile with a raven on his shoulder. The resemblance between Roland and King is deliberate. "I had a profile shot of Steve that I used because at that point he was describing the Gunslinger in terms of having similar features of his, so I thought he should look faintly like Steve."

"There's only one scene when you really see Roland well: he and Cuthbert are standing at the foot of the hanged figure of Hax. I deliberately gave him a Stephen King feeling to his face because it felt to me that he had already inserted himself into the story, into Roland's character. Even at that early stage, I had no idea that he would write himself in as an *actual* character in *The Dark Tower* [book 7, 2004]. I just felt that. So you can see King's dark hair and some of his facial planes."

"King's description of Roland evolves through the series. At first he's described as a hard-bitten guy with a face that seems chiseled out of 'obdurate granite.' Then to Susannah he says he looks like he has the 'face of a tired poet,' and so on. I became something of a weathervane in response to King's changing descriptions, responding to different sections as I encountered them. I came to accept that Roland would change over time and become a more sympathetic and complex character. I feel I got a good fix on him now, but it went through a lot of change in the process."

"The way I depicted him on the cover of book seven (*The Dark Tower*) was a pastiche of all the hard guys in the movies that I could think of. There's some of James Coburn in his face, some Lee Marvin, and a little bit of Clint Eastwood. There are different people I think of when I painted the face on the cover of the book, but now I admit I regret having done so. I wish I had thrown his face into shadow. Everyone has a slightly different idea of what the character looks like—even me—and to fix it so solidly was a mistake. Ah, well, live and learn."

"Over time I believe I've settled on how I think Roland should look. You'd think it late in the game to do that, after having illustrated so much of the material, but my conception of a character evolved over time, just as Steve's idea of Roland's appearance evolved considerably over the course of the seven books. I feel I've gotten closer and closer to the mark."

Just as Roland's look proved illustratively elusive, so too did the look of the Dark Tower itself. "That's the other thing," Whelan said. "King doesn't get around to describing what the damned Dark Tower looks like until the end of the last book. He has scenes of different characters throughout the series that 'see' the tower appearing one way or another, as if the tower itself changes its look depending on who is confronting it. Consequently, I tried not to be too specific about it. There's all kinds of room for interpretation, until King definitively portrays it in the last book as a rather plain, squat tower."

What was it like to come full circle and illustrate the seventh Dark Tower novel?

"I was *so* stoked. I must have whooped and hollered for two days. To be asked back to do it again made my year."

Whelan rose to the challenge and turned in more artwork than what the contract called for. In the end, he submitted twenty-five paintings (in color and monochrome), and thirty-four pen-and-ink illustrations.

"Any final thoughts about the Dark Tower?" I asked.

Whelan replied, "Well, the story's not long enough. I'm not sure it ever *can* be!" He laughed. "After his accident, King surely had a flash of his own mortality and didn't want to leave the 'roundness' of the saga incomplete. Like so many other fans, I'm hoping there will be more additions to the whole story, if for no other reason than that the number *nine* is so important to the whole series. I always felt it should have been a nine-book series. Certainly, there's plenty of more room to explore unanswered issues."

"In any case," Whelan concluded, "I love the books and the characters. Some may complain about it being too long, but as King explains in the seventh book, it's not the destination but the journey that is important. The road can be as long as you choose to make it."

## MICHAEL WHELAN: A PORTFOLIO

"And if you are one of those who have never visited the strange
world through which Roland and his friends move, I hope you
will enjoy the marvels you find there. More than anything else, I
wanted to tell a tale of wonder."

—STEPHEN KING ON *THE DARK TOWER* STORY CYCLE,
FROM THE "FOREWORD" TO *THE LITTLE SISTERS OF ELURIA* (2008)

Elsewhere in this book, you'll find a 16-page color insert of artwork drawn by artist Michael Whelan, inspired by Stephen King's Dark Tower series.

Whelan and King go all the way back to 1982 when the first Dark Tower book was published by Donald M. Grant. He mailed his customers a sales flyer, stating that "*The Dark Tower: The Gunslinger* was unlike anything bestselling author Stephen King has ever written; indeed, it is unlike anything anyone has ever written. And it is a volume that begs for illustrations! *The Dark Tower: The Gunslinger* is a joining of the foremost author and artist in the fields of science fiction and fantasy. Complementing Stephen King in this most unusual of books is artist Michael Whelan, recepient of both Howard and Hugo awards as best artist in the genre."

Whelan accepted the commission and threw himself into the project with brio. He eventually rendered five full-color paintings, in acrylic; color endleaves, also in acrylic; and chapter-head illustrations, with complementary end-piece illustrations, in pen-and-ink.

Grant recalled that "King was very pleased" with Whelan's finished work.

Twenty-two years later, Whelan was once again approached by King to illustrate a Dark Tower novel—this time, the final book in the series, *The Dark Tower VII: The Dark Tower* (2004).

In a phone call to Whelan, King explained that because they both started out on a quest to tell Roland's story in the first book, it seemed only fitting that they should end it together as well, with which Whelan concurred.

As with the first Dark Tower novel, Whelan approached the final book commission with unbridled enthusiasm, resulting in a remarkable suite of paintings and drawings.

It's not hyperbole to state that Whelan's work for the final Gunslinger novel towers above all the previously published artwork in the series, including his own. In book seven, Whelan exhibited a mature vision of Roland's world, a technical mastery in all media, and an unsurpassed imagination that firmly cemented his reputation as the preeminent Dark Tower artist.

# 39

## CHRISTINE

### 1983

> This is the story of a lover's triangle, I suppose you'd say—Arnie
> Cunningham, Leigh Cabot, and, of course, Christine. But
> I want you to understand that Christine was there first. . . . I
> think she was his only true love. So I call what happened
> a tragedy.
>
> —STEPHEN KING, PROLOGUE TO *CHRISTINE*

In the afterword to *Different Seasons*, King recounts a conversation with Alan Williams, his editor, who asked him, "Loved *Cujo*. . . . Have you thought about what you're going to do next?"

King suggested a novella collection titled *Different Seasons*, which wasn't what his crestfallen book editor wanted to hear: Collections don't sell as well as novels. King then said, "How about a haunted car?"

*That* was what he wanted to hear: King, who wrote about a haunted hotel, would now write a horror story about a haunted car, which was a first. Haunted houses were plentiful—done to perfection in Shirley Jackson's *The Haunting of Hill House*—but a haunted *car?*

In retrospect, given the milieu he had grown up in during the fifties, a time when cars and rock and roll held sway, King was driven to write about American car culture. In fact, another baby boomer named George Lucas did just that, writing and directing

213

*American Graffiti* (1973), a coming-of-age movie that paid homage to rock and roll, and cruising in cars, as does *Christine*. Cars, a consuming interest of Lucas's, are chariots of fire: In the movie, the teenage boys driving them are contemporary knights driving supercharged cars propelled by powerful engines.

In an interview with Randy Lofficier in 1984, King explained what it was like growing up in the fifties:

> That was my generation. . . . So, there are a lot of us who actually developed our understanding of life, and who grew to be, not adults, but thinking human beings in the fifties. Somebody once said that "Life was the rise of consciousness." For me, rock-and-roll was the rise of consciousness. It was like a big sun bursting over my life. That's when I really started to live, and that was brought on by the music of the fifties. . . . I don't have any bad memories of the fifties. . . . There was stuff going on, there was uneasiness about the [atomic] bomb, but on the whole I'd have to say that people in the fifties were pretty loose.

The car itself, as King explained to Randy Lofficier, "is a symbol for the technological age, or for the end of innocence, when it plays such a part in adolescence and growing up." In short, it's King's horror version of *American Graffiti*.

King sold the book to his publisher for one dollar. As he explained to *Locus* (January 1983), "I wanted not to be taking a lot of cash which I didn't need, and it ties up money other writers could get for advances. . . . On *Christine*, the first time they sell a book, they're in the black, I'm in the black. There are no staggered payments—it's hard to stagger a dollar!"

## MICHAEL COLLINGS ON *CHRISTINE*

*Christine* is a ghost story. Here, however, the Bad Place is not a house like the Marsten House or the Overlook Hotel, and the Bad Thing is embodied not as vampire or werewolf or monster but as a rust-ridden old car that catches the eye and the fancy of a passing teenager. A young novel in the sense that most of the central characters are in their teens, *Christine* explores ghostly possession with King's characteristic energy and verve. If the basic story approaches absurdity on one level—a haunted Plymouth no less!—it at least partially redeems itself by the sheer force of its narrative movement. Christine creates a kaleidoscope of cars, rock music (the copyright page lists credits for over forty-five songs quoted in the text), archetypal teenage rebellion against equally archetypal overbearing parents (mostly Arnie Cunningham's, since Dennis's and Leigh's parents hardly figure in the novel), fast-food joints, incipient sexuality explored in front—and backseats—all overlying the frightening insecurities and frustrations of adolescence.

*Rage* without a classroom held hostage or a teenaged terrorist as narrator, *Carrie* without telekinesis, *The Long Walk* without even the release valve of a socially sanctioned way to kill young people (although drivers licenses come close, as *Christine* ultimately suggests)—*Christine* is an anatomy of the ambivalences of adolescence. Perhaps not one of King's "great" novels, it nevertheless has garnered its own following and performs well enough according to its own standards.

## The King's and Queen's Cars

These days Stephen tools around in a Mercedes. He has one and Tabitha has her own. They also have other cars more suited for harsh Maine winters. Stephen King also has a Harley, which he used to ride down to Boston, to watch his beloved Red Sox play. (I suspect that because of his atrophied right leg, he's less inclined to do so these days.) But in the early days, King's chariots of fire were modest. His first car was a hand-me-down from his brother, a monstrous 1956 Plymouth. (In *Christine,* the haunted car was a 1958 Plymouth Fury.) King drove the aged black Plymouth when he was in college.

The first car he ever bought new, in cash, was a Ford Pinto, which Stephen could drive but Tabitha could not. In an introduction to the Collectors Edition of *Carrie,* Tabitha King wrote about her own horror story with that car: "We bought a better car, a Pinto, but I couldn't drive it because it was a standard shift. I tried, but one day I stalled it on State Street Hill, the steepest one in Bangor. Some flaming asshole behind me pounded his horn and screamed at me."

Currently parked in Bangor: a Toyota Prius, a black Pontiac GTO, a Mercedes coupe, and a Mercedes sedan. And, of course, a Harley-Davidson motorcycle. And when he's in Florida, King tools around in a red Tesla, or a black Chevrolet Volt, which he bought as a birthday present for Tabitha. As Stephen told *The Sarasota Herald-Tribune* in 2011, "I just love it because every time you [recharge it for free at a public, electric-vehicle charging station], it's like saying to the oil cartel, 'Here, stick this in your eye.' . . . It is like a license to steal."

## 40

# ROCK AND ROLL HAVEN:

## STEPHEN KING'S STATION, WKIT 100.3 FM

Well, for me, radio, and in particular, music, made me real as a
kid. It's where I discovered my identity. You reach out and find
something that belongs to you and it's yours. It's difficult to
explain, but it's like a pair of shoes that fit you. My first record
was a 78 rpm version of Elvis Presley's "Hound Dog." From that
moment on I knew it's what I wanted, and I wanted all I could get.

—STEPHEN KING, *RADIO AND RECORDS*, 1984

*The former WZON sign outside of King's radio station
in Bangor.*

*King's radio tower.*

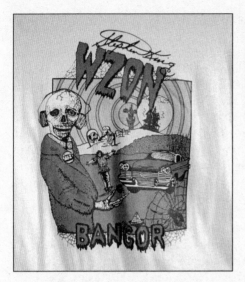

*A disc jockey at a console at WZON (circa 1990).*

*A T-shirt design for WZON.*

On Broadway, not far from Bangor High School, there used to be a large sign that read: z62, WZON, THE ZONE CORPORATION.

That sign has since been replaced with another, more colorful sign, with artwork by Maine artist Glenn Chadbourne, who has illustrated numerous books by King for Cemetery Dance. The art and King's stylized signature is proof that if you're looking for King's rock and roll radio station, WKIT on the FM dial, you've just found it.

Online, it can be found at www.wkitfm.com, and it's billed as "Stephen King's Rock n' Roll Station." It's where the rock jocks get into the groove, playing the platters that matter. From its Web site:

WKIT 100.3 is a radio station located in Bangor, Maine; and is owned by Stephen and Tabitha King, making it one of the few commercial stations in the country that is still locally owned. We have been a classic rock station ever since Bobby Russell became program director in 1990, and the ratings have always been consistently good, launching us to #1.

We can also say we're the only station in the state (and one of the few in the U.S.) that is still LIVE 24-7, meaning we have rock jocks on at all times. If you call, someone is actually here to answer the phone.

Stephen King, who played guitar in a high school band, the Mune Spinners, and later played rhythm guitar as a founding member of the Rock Bottom Remainders, had no intention of ever buying a radio station, but circumstances forced his hand. In "Between Rock and a Soft Place" (*Playboy*, January 1982), he spoke about picking up a rental car at Boston's Logan Airport to drive home to Bangor. The car radio had AM radio stations only, which frustrated him. He "wanted to dial some good rock 'n' roll and turn up the volume until the speakers started to distort" but couldn't do it because there was no hard rock station on the AM band. "That was when I began to worry—to seriously worry—about rock 'n' roll," he concluded.

A year later, King decided to make a sound investment in Bangor: an AM radio station. As he explained in a piece for *Castle Rock* (October 1987), "I did it because the cutting edge of rock and roll has grown dangerously blunt in these latter days." He bought WACZ, which became WZON, on the AM band at 620 kilohertz.

Back in the day, you could rock in the dead zone by tuning in on WZON, but today it broadcasts progressive talk-radio programs. For rock and roll, listeners tune in to WKIT-FM, which is owned by the Zone Corporation. On the Web, you can listen to its programming at: http://streamdb4web.securenetsystems.net/v5/WKIT.

King also owns WZLO (103.1 FM), which is billed as "Maine's Adult Alternative," playing "the very best adult rock music." The station's Web site notes:

> On our station you'll hear everyone from the geniuses who gave birth to the progressive sounds of the 60's and 70's, such as Bob Dylan, Paul Simon, Van Morrison, Jackson Browne & James Taylor, to the musical heirs of those legends, like John Mayer, Dave Matthews Band, Norah Jones, Ryan Adams, Sheryl Crow, David Gray & Mumford & Sons, just to name a few.

WZLO's site also boasts that the station is "locally owned and operated like so many other great Maine institutions. Not a big out-of-state conglomerate with a cookie cutter approach to radio and a boring playlist."

King, clearly, no longer has to worry, seriously worry, about rock and roll.

# 41

## Pet Sematary
### 1983

Death is a mystery, and burial is a secret.

—*Pet Sematary*

*The house the Kings rented when they lived in Orrington, Maine.*

*The stone wall that separates an open field behind the Kings' home in Orrington, beyond which is the original "Pet Sematary."*

## ORRINGTON, MAINE

On a cold day in December 1988, I went to see for myself what was left of the "Pet Sematary" in Orrington, Maine, located south of Bangor. I pulled my rental car into the parking lot of a nearby convenience store and asked a local where it was. He replied, "There's nothing left up there, you know."

I knew that, I told him. I wanted to see the house that the Kings had temporarily rented when Stephen returned to his alma mater for a one-year stint as a writer in residence and the actual site of the pet cemetery.

I soon found myself at a two-story white house with fading paint. It had a used tire hanging on a rope from a tree in the front yard. Past the house lay the site of the "pet sematary."

There was nothing left because souvenir hunters took what they could, including the makeshift wooden gravestone markers. I took a few pictures and left. Coming back down the hill, I watched in fascination as an 18-wheeler came into view, rising taller as it crested a nearby hill. I was near the road, Route 15, and instinctively stepped back when the large truck passed by me, its wind buffeting me. The road was a winding ribbon of death for stray animals, claiming countless cats and dogs.

## SMUCKY

Smucky was Naomi King's tabby. As her father explained about *Pet Sematary* and its connections to real life, in an interview with *The Paris Review* (fall 2006):

> That book was pretty personal. Everything in it—up to the point where the little boy is killed in the road—everything is true. We moved into that house by the road. It was Orrington instead of Ludlow, but the big trucks did go by, and the old guy across the street did say, You just want to watch 'em around the road. We did go out in the field. We flew kites. We did go up and look at the pet cemetery. I did find my daughter's cat, Smucky, dead in the road, run over. We buried him up in the pet cemetery, and I did hear Naomi out in the garage the night after we buried him. I heard all these popping noises—she was jumping up and down on packing material. She was crying and saying, *Give me my cat back! Let God have his own cat!* I just dumped that right into the book.

And the book went into the drawer, because "it was so gruesome by the end of it, and so awful. I mean, there's no hope for anybody at the end of that book," he concluded. He told the *Bangor Daily News* (October 12, 1988):

> In trying to cope with these things, the book ceased being a novel to me, and became instead a gloomy exercise, like an endless marathon run. It never left my mind: it never ceased to trouble me. I was trying to teach school, and the boy was always there, the funeral home was always there, the mortician's room was always there. And when I finished, I put the book in a drawer.

*Pet Sematary* is a grim read and an unremitting horror novel. It's a parent's worst nightmare that becomes reality. It's a cautionary tale of a doctor named Louis Creed, whose credo is to believe in the world of science, until he feels it has abandoned him; lacking hope, he turns to a more primal belief, recalling a classic story, "The Monkey's Paw."

King's wife agreed it was too dark in tone, and he decided that it should remain unpublished; if anything, it was a Richard Bachman book, not a King story, but circumstances eventually forced his hand and its publication.

By then King was feeling pressure from his readers as well, especially in the fantasy/horror field, because King had given interviews explaining that he had just finished a novel too nasty and too terrifying to publish, which set King fans clamoring for it. But King remained firm: *Pet Sematary* was buried deep in a drawer, and, as far as he was concerned, it would never be unearthed.

## RESURRECTION

In *The Writer's Home Companion*, James Charlton and Lisbeth Mark tell the tale of Doubleday and the IRS forcing King's hand. As they explained, *Pet Sematary* was published because of a contractual dispute. The problem began when King agreed to take a fixed amount of $50,000 a year from Doubleday, which was drawn from his accumulated royalties. But when the balance kept growing and it rose to $3 million, it was clear that the inflexible payout schedule would take sixty years for King to recover his royalties, not including any new revenue. But Doubleday refused to simply write him a check for the balance in the account, citing contractual and legal issues.

The IRS decided that if "due consideration" was met, and King gave Doubleday *Pet Sematary*, the unfair contract could be terminated. King acquiesced, and Doubleday was now the publisher of what would prove to be one of King's finest novels, which went to press with 500,000 copies in hardback, and went on to sell 657,000 copies.

Unlike *Christine*, published earlier in the year, *Pet Sematary* was enthusiastically embraced by critics and readers alike. *The Portsmouth Herald* said it was "a work of such skill and quality that it transcends the horror genre to become an unforgettable piece of literature about death and bereavement. At 36, [King] is not only far from running out of steam but becoming a better novelist."

The book industry's trade publication, *Publishers Weekly*, also sang the book's praises, in effect saying King had hit the high notes with his latest tale:

> King's newest novel is a wonderful family portrait that is also the most frightening novel he has ever written. . . . [T]he last 50 pages are so terrifying, one might try to make it through them without a breath—but what is most astonishing here is how much besides horror is here. . . . Witty, wise, observant, King has never been a more humane artist than he is here.

Michael Collings's eerily prescient review of *Pet Sematary*, in the *Stephen King Companion* (1995), explains why it is a work of unspeakable horror:

*Pet Sematary* is King's darkest novel in part because of the underlying theme that there *are* things worse than death, and in part because he has spent so much time in the first half lovingly creating an intense relationship between Louis Creed and his son, Gage. . . . [The novel is] one unrelenting horror following immediately upon, and in fact initiated by, another. Without an emotional or narrative break, the novel penetrates darkness within darkness within darkness, until all that remains is madness or death . . . or both. The result is one of the few King narratives that move unrelievedly into obsessive pessimism. The cautious optimism of *Pet Sematary,* where, in the final moment, midnight darkness reigns as undisputed monarch over all.

Gunslinger '88, Roland

The Gunslinger: On the Beach

The Gunslinger: The Dead Town

"The Gunslinger stood in his dusty boots."

The Dark Tower:
The Gate of Eluria

The Dark Tower: Callahan

The Dark Tower: Algul Siento

"The Gunslinger followed."

Legends: The Gunslinger

# 42

## THINNER

### 1984; ORIGINAL TITLE: *GYPSY PIE*

Richard Bachman is an incredibly talented writer,
and *Thinner* is a riveting novel that gives a new meaning
to the word "horror."

—PROMOTIONAL LETTER, ADVANCE COPY OF *THINNER*

### A "DEAD" GIVEAWAY

It's 1984 and I am at the American Booksellers Association convention in Washington, D.C. There are too many publishers' booths to count, each pushing its fall list—among them, New American Library, which promoted a little-known writer named Richard Bachman. His four previously published novels, issued in mass market editions only, built up his fan base sufficiently to justify publishing what they hoped would be his breakout book, *Thinner*. New American Library spared no expense beating the drums, and drumming up sales for, Bachman. In front of the display, in the aisle, were two square pallets of wood, forty-six inches on each side, stacked four feet high with advance copies of *Thinner*, free for the taking.

Booksellers, though, rush by the stacks, ignoring Bachman's free books in their eagerness to get to the Viking booth, because they were promoting the biggest book of the season, *The Talisman*, a collaboration between Stephen King and Peter Straub.

## BACHMAN—OR KING?

*Thinner* was published in hardback ($12.95 retail) in November 1984. The author's photo depicted a friend of Kirby McCauley. Careful readers smiled when they ran across references in the novel to Stephen King. In one scene, Dr. Houston warns Billy Halleck that his tale of a curse had begun to "sound a little like a Stephen King novel. . . ." Later, this telling line: "[I]f you add Cary Rossington with his alligator skin and William J. Halleck with his case of involuntary anorexia nervosa into the equation, it starts to sound a little like Stephen King again."

It was, in fact, King having a little literary fun with himself.

But a careful reader could have picked up the clues that King was Bachman. As Michael Collings wrote in the *Stephen King Companion* (1995):

> The fifth "Bachman" novel is also closest to what readers have come to expect from Stephen King. The first four contained implicit clues (particularly when we read with the gift of superior hindsight) as to who Richard Bachman really was. Place names connect, as when one notes that Ray Garraty's mailing address is apparently the same as Johnny Smith's father's in *The Dead Zone* (1979)—rural delivery, Pownal, Maine. Brand names connect, especially the Blue Ribbon Laundry in *Roadwork*, in a branch of which Margaret White working in *Carrie*. Dedications to Jim Bishop, Burt Hatlen, and others already familiar to King's readership add to these connections, along with a gritty, tough-talk tone that King had already mastered when *Carrie* appeared, and stories that were consistent with King's recurrent themes.

## THE THREAD UNRAVELS

In January 1985, a Washington, D.C. bookstore clerk who had researched copyright forms filed for Bachman's books discovered that all were registered to "Richard Bachman" except his first book, *Rage*: That one was registered to . . . Stephen King.

Filed by someone at the literary agency owned by King's agent at the time, Kirby McCauley, the error proved to be incontrovertible evidence: further denial was useless.

The bookstore clerk wrote to King, explaining what he had discovered.

By then, the thread was already unraveling fast.

By late January, a major television show, *Entertainment Tonight*, ran a story speculating that King and Bachman were one and the same.

Also, in its second issue, the official King newsletter, *Castle Rock*, announced that it had big news, "a secret revealed at last."

Then in February, Joan H. Smith, of the *Bangor Daily News*, told King that she going to run the King-Bachman story, confirmation or not.

The story, unfortunately, was rushed to print and filled with factual errors. Haste, as the saying goes, makes waste. The story prompted King to write a letter to the editor, which was published, setting the record straight. Here's how it looked to me:

1. King did not try to time the release of the information to benefit two Bachman books optioned for the movies; both had sold on their own *before* the revelation came to light;

2. King had in fact confirmed the pen name to Steve Brown, a bookstore clerk, a month before the newspaper article was published.
3. King felt that there was no point in further denial and opted to confirm Joan Smith's story, since it was scheduled to run anyway.
4. Noting fan criticism about his use of a pen name, King asserted that the fans had confused "enjoyment with ownership." He was not being mean-spirited and deliberately withholding the Bachman books from his Constant Readers.

Before the confirmation, Bachman, unassisted, had sold 28,000 copies of *Thinner*, which had gone into a second printing—a very respectable showing for a midlist author who was slowly building his readership.

The anthology *Fangoria: Masters of the Dark*, published in 1997 and edited by Anthony Timpone, prints an interview with King by Edward Gross ("Stephen King Takes a Vacation") in which King explained that

With the last Bachman novel, *Thinner*, my wife said, "You know, it's your own goddamned fault. You knew it was like the other ones. Somebody was bound to recognize it." If it was Joe Schmoe, nobody would have cared. Instead, you've got this guy who was familiar with the Library of Congress and works at a bookstore. He deliberately tracks down the copyrights, and our tracks were covered except for the first one.

*Thinner* immediately went back to press to meet the increasing demand, and by the time the presses stopped, 280,000 copies were in print.

But the hunger games had just started: Fans also wanted the earlier Bachman books, but only two of them were in print. New American Library then issued an omnibus edition to satisfy the growing demand. *The Bachman Books: Four Early Novels* included *Rage* (1977), *The Long Walk* (1979), *Roadwork* (1981), and *The Running Man* (1982). The book also included an introduction, "Why I Was Bachman."

Though King had put on a brave face in public, in private he seethed. As he told the *Maryland Coast Dispatch*:

I was pissed. It's like you can't have anything. You're not allowed to, because you are a celebrity. What does it matter? Why should anyone care? It's like they can't wait to find stuff out, particularly if it's something you don't want people to know. That's the best, that's the juice. It makes me think about that Don Henley song, "Dirty Laundry." Hell, give it to them.

As for the book itself, Michael Collings pointed out that it "is the first Bachman novel to approach the intensity, complexity, horrific texturing, and wide market appeal that the King books had long since demonstrated" and that King's "private hope was that 'Dicky' might gradually build his own faithful audience, unhindered by the expectations and hoopla that automatically attached to a novel under King's name." King, Collings wrote, "notes that *Misery* might have been Bachman's breakthrough novel."

## The First Bachman Book: *Rage*

*Rage*, the first Bachman book, has a singular distinction among King's published fiction: It is out of print, and deliberately so: Four separate school shootings were linked to the novel. In each case, a connection to *Rage* had been established; in one particularly deadly case, three people were killed by a fourteen-year-old in Kentucky whose school locker contained a copy of—you guessed it—*Rage*.

King told his publisher to take the book out of print immediately. "I pulled it because in my judgment it might be hurting people, and that made it the responsible thing to do," he wrote in *Guns*, an e-book published on Amazon in 2013. The book, King said, was a "possible accelerant."

Tapping into his feelings of alienation as a young student himself, King had written too convincingly of an angry teenage boy who held his class hostage at Placerville High School: "The morning I got it on was nice; a nice May morning. What made it nice was that I'd kept my breakfast down, and the squirrel I spotted in Algebra II. . . . Two years ago. To the best of my recollection, that was about the time I started to lose my mind."

## "H-e-r-e's Johnny!" . . . Er, "Dicky!"

Richard Bachman died of "cancer of the pseudonym," as King said, but two novels were posthumously published. King published *The Regulators* in 1996 and *Blaze* in 2007 under the name Bachman.

Obviously, dead men *do* tell tales.

# 43

## The Talisman

### 1984

As Casey Stengel used to say, you've got to put an asterisk by it.

—Stephen King, quoted in Winter's
*Stephen King: The Art of Darkness*

When you combine Stephen King with Peter Straub, what do you get?
You get a book with a print run so large that it took nine warehouses strategically placed around the country to ensure a national laydown on the same day—October 8, 1984; a major book from two major authors with no book club sales to erode trade bookstore sales; and gleeful critics lined up to take a swing at King and Straub as they ran the proverbial gauntlet.

King, who termed himself a "Bestsellasaurus Rex" and who was used to suffering the slings and arrows that accompanied his outrageously good fortune, found that this time criticisms were more barbed.

"In horror fiction," *People* magazine asserted, "two heads are better than one only if they're on the same body." Ouch.

It began to really hurt, though, when *Esquire* magazine wrote:

King, whose own style is American yahoo—big, brassy, and bodacious—has always expressed admiration for Straub's cooler, less emotional diction, and Straub in turn has praised the grand, "operatic" quality of King's work. Their collaboration is both cool and operatic—and very, very scary. It's a horrific work of art. But is it really art? Probably not. We are talking about mass-market books and popular music here. People consume horror in order to be scared, not *arted*.

Regardless of whether the reading audience was scared or "arted," *The Talisman* quickly racked up sales, totaling an impressive 880,000 copies within two months of publication. An ambitious novel of 653 pages, *The Talisman* was followed by a sequel in 2001, *Black House*. (During a book tour in November 2014 for *Revival*, King announced that he and Straub planned to write in 2015 a third book in the series.)

Perhaps what the critics expected was a horror novel in which the two would collaborate and bring their respective strengths to the table; instead, what *The Talisman* delivers is an ambitious, cross-genre novel in which the two writing styles are seamlessly integrated, to the point where it's not certain who wrote what, which was by design.

As Peter Straub recalled, in an interview for *Tenebres*, for its special double issue on Stephen King, he and King had discussed collaborating on a novel when King was living in England, where Straub also then lived. But because of their respective contractual obligations, the planned collaboration had to be postponed for the next four years. It became logistically possible to collaborate when the Straubs moved back to the United States (as had the Kings). Straub told *Tenebres*:

> Steve drove from Maine to my house in Westport, Connecticut, to start the actual writing. He stayed maybe four days, during which we wrote the first fifteen or twenty pages, taking turns at my word processor. Then he went back to Maine, and I spent ten days writing up a seventy-page, single-spaced outline based on everything we had discussed. After that, he continued from where we had left off, transmitted his pages to me, and I picked up from his last sentence. We went on like this for about a year and a half, each of us firing off hundred-page, hundred-and-fifty-page segments at intervals of a month or so. When we were nearing the end, my wife and I went back to Maine, and Steve and I wrote the last fifty or so pages at his house, taking turns sitting down before his machine.
>
> Not long after submission, our editor joined us at Steve's place, and we went through the book, making whatever cuts and changes seemed necessary.

The final result was a book that was neither in King's voice nor in Straub's but in a third voice that was only possible as a result of careful collaboration. For that reason, the book wasn't exactly what King fans expected, and it wasn't exactly what Straub's fans expected, but it did find a ready audience willing to go along for the ride.

## MICHAEL COLLINGS ON *THE TALISMAN*

[*The Talisman*] was an intricately interlaced combination of horror and fantasy, or real-world terror and alternate-universe science fantasy, in which atomic testing in our world can create vast expanses of the wastelands in the Territories (and perhaps, in the world of Roland of Gilead as well). Instead of allusions to Poe and Lovecraft, *The Talisman* echoes Tolkien

## Anthologist Peter Straub

Readers who know Straub's work only through his two collaborations with Stephen King or through his novels—*Ghost Story, Julia, Floating Dragon, Shadowland,* to name a few— shouldn't be surprised to discover that he is a first-rate anthologist as well. Published as a two-book set, in slipcase, with 1,500 pages, *American Fantastic Tales* spans horror stories from the Edwardian era to the twentieth century. As with any anthology, depending on your taste, some of your favorites are bound to be missing. What is important is that it's a very good representative sampling of horror fiction that offers something for everyone.

Of course, there's Stephen King and Ray Bradbury and Edgar Allan Poe, but there's much more. As Straub told Scott Simon of NPR (October 31, 2009), "I wanted to get a good representation of stories from across the decades, from as early as possible to the present. And otherwise I was looking for really, really good stories. In some cases when I got into the pulps, I was looking for very bizarre stories of the sort that only flourished in pulp fiction." In other words, it didn't matter *where* the stories originally appeared; it only mattered that they were good.

How good?

In a *Washington Post* review (October 31, 2009), Dennis Drabelle wrote:

Inside this double-decker set lurks more spookiness than you can shake a broomstick at: four score and more tales, written by horripilating favorites (H. P. Lovecraft, Stephen King, Poppy Z. Brite); mainstream powerhouses (Nathaniel Hawthorne, Willa Cather, John Cheever); and revenants from the crypt of literary obscurity (Madeline Yale Wynne, W. C. Morrow, Seabury Quinn). Until now, the best and bulkiest anthology of its kind was Herbert A. Wise and Phyllis Fraser's *Great Tales of Terror and the Supernatural* (1944). But these new, paired volumes, edited by novelist Peter Straub of *Ghost Story* fame, almost double the length of *Great Tales* while casting a wider net. Wise and Fraser eschewed authors who published mainly in pulp magazines (with the notable exception of Lovecraft), but Straub embraces pulpiness in the first volume's subtitle. The idea seems to be that, whatever the source, all goose bumps are created equal. I'll shiver to that.

and C. S. Lewis, Mark Twain and *The Wizard of Oz*. Its structure echoes the immensely popular Xanth and Proton/Phase novels of Piers Anthony—both ultimately amalgams of science fiction and fantasy, of "this world" and "others." Instead of King's vividly colloquial prose, or Straub's coolly ironic academic tone, a third, almost wholly unexpected voice emerged, one appropriate not to the ultimate in horror but to an extended narrative that takes on a pacing and movement of its own. And instead of a single-minded quest to destroy (or at least incapacitate) a monster, there is the open-ended epic quest for the Talisman, the mystic nexus of possible worlds—an image as ethereal and powerful as Jake's vision of the Dark Tower itself in *The Wastelands*. Even given the length of *The Talisman*, it would be nearly impossible to do justice to the mythic echoes the Talisman evokes, or to the multiple landscapes in this world and in the Territories that lead to the Black Hotel and the confrontation between light and darkness.

That King and Straub also incorporated critiques of contemporary politicians and writers, of social and economic conditions, of education, of parenting—all of this made *The Talisman* more difficult to approach, and hence seemed to justify the cavils of reviewers and critics.

It did not, however, keep the novel from reaching literally millions of readers. . . .

In the decade that has followed its first appearance, *The Talisman* has emerged to be ranked as one of King's (and Straub's) stronger novels. . . .

*The Talisman* leaves behind the antiheroic naturalism of much modern fiction and returns to the same roots that underlie Tolkien and Lewis and even, in its own way, the Mark Twain of *Tom Sawyer* and *Huckleberry Finn*—to the prose-epic impulse that King has already evoked in *The Stand* and *The Dark Tower*.

## PETER STRAUB ON FICTION

Peter Straub, interviewed by Rick Kelley for the Library of America newsletter online, had the following to say about fiction:

All fiction, literary or genre, seeks to manipulate its readers. Every novel is an effort to present a completely formed and coherent view of the way its particular world works, and every novelist is doing her best to make her case persuasive. As Marilynne Robinson once remarked, novelists are always standing on top of a hill, shouting, "No, you're all wrong, *this* is how the world works." In this regard, there is no essential difference between the writer of a literary novel and the writer of a crime novel. The differences have to do with matters other than manipulation: open-endedness, psychological acuity, formal beauty, the quality of the prose, depth of feeling, alertness to ambiguity, suggestions of the world's depth and richness, supple transitions, and a hundred other things. A writer of the fantastic may or may not possess the kind of writerly authority implied by these considerations, but if she does, her work might as well be called "literary." It won't be, though; the fences are too high. However, to be completely frank, work of this kind is always as good, in a literary sense, as most "literary" efforts, and often better than most.

# 44

# Douglas E. Winter's
## *Stephen King: The Art of Darkness*

Eight years after Stephen King published *Carrie*, two books not *by* but *about* Stephen King were published. The books came out from specialty presses, one from Underwood-Miller, and the other from Starmont House.

The first was *Fear Itself: The Horror Fiction of Stephen King*, edited by Tim Underwood and Chuck Miller, which included essays from eleven contributors, including King's "On Becoming a Brand Name," reprinted from *Adelina* (February 1980). The book featured an introduction by Peter Straub, "Meeting Stevie." (One of the other contributors was Douglas E.

*Douglas E. Winter
in his living room.*

*The vampire from "The Night Flier" illustrated by Glenn Chadbourne.*

Winter, whose essay "The Night Journeys of Stephen King" was reprinted, with revisions, from an issue of *Fantasy Newsletter*.) The second was titled, simply, *Stephen King* and written by Douglas E. Winter. Both publishers—Underwood-Miller and Starmont House—went on to publish additional titles about King, but these two were the first of many to appear in print.

Of the two, *Stephen King* proved to be more influential, paving the way for its extensively revised and updated version: In 1984, Douglas E. Winter's authorized study/appreciation, *Stephen King: The Art of Darkness,* was published in hardback by New American Library Books to critical acclaim.

Then a lawyer by day (now a retired partner) and writer, editor, anthologist, novelist, and rock musician by night, Winter described his book "as a critical appreciation; it is an intermingling of biography, literary analysis, and unabashed enthusiasm, spiced with commentary by Stephen King transcribed from our more than twelve hours of recorded conversations—including the only interview that he intends to give on the subject of his novel *Pet Sematary*."

Following the introduction is a chapter titled "Notes Toward a Biography," which implied that he intended to write an authorized biography of King. Though Winter did go on to write a full-length, authorized biography, it would be on Clive Barker, not Stephen King.

For the 1989 edition of *The Stephen King Companion*, Winter consented to an interview. As expected, his answers were thoughtful, deliberate, and illuminating. I asked, "What kind of reaction have you gotten from people who've read your book on King?" He replied:

It's all been good. I got a ton of letters when the book first came out. I would always get these letters from school kids, from teachers, from librarians, from federal prisoners—all telling me how much they enjoyed the book. . . .

There's obviously a tremendous number of Stephen King fans out there, and I think this was the sort of thing that they were waiting for, that was perfect for them, because it more or less organized the fiction and I think also served as a real companion, and I hope illuminated the books a great deal. That was the intent of it, to say: here's not only some fiction that you're reading for enjoyment, but there are messages, there are themes, there are subtexts here that are important. To me, that's always been key: to consider what fiction is all about and how it affects me and my thinking.

I always hate it when people discount Steve as being just an entertainer, because he's not. The same thing's true about other major writers of horror fiction. And here was my opportunity to make clear some very significant things that were going on.

Winter, an early critic of King fiction, paved the way and showed critics who followed not only that King was a writer to be taken seriously but also that to write about King's work required a serious frame of mind.

Today, thirty years after its initial publication, which was followed by updated editions in trade paperback and mass market paperback, *Stephen King: The Art of Darkness* remains a seminal book about King.

## ANTHOLOGIES

If you have any interest in horror fiction, you should not walk but run to your nearest bookstore, online or brick-and-mortar, and hunt down one of Winter's anthologies. He has three attributes essential to editing an anthology: He has a real talent for titling them (*Prime Evil, Revelations, Millennium*); he has great literary taste; and he's got connections to name-brand writers, notably Stephen King (who wrote an original story, "Night Flier," for *Prime Evil*), Peter Straub, Clive Barker, and others.

Of the three anthologies, I'd recommend *Prime Evil*. I especially liked King's vampire tale, "Night Flier," an original take on what could have been a hoary tale in the wrong hands. But these stories are all first-rate and worth your time.

As Winter writes in his introduction:

Great horror fiction has never really been about monsters, but about mankind. It shows us something important about ourselves, something dark, occasionally monstrous—and usually in bad taste. Its stories proceed from the archetype of Pandora's Box: the tense conflict between pleasure and fear that is latent when we face the forbidden and the unknown. In horror's pages, we open the Box, exposing what is taboo in our ordinary lives, and test the boundaries of acceptable behavior. Its writers literally drag our terrors from the shadows and force us to look upon them with despair—or relief.

# 45

# THE EYES OF THE DRAGON

## PHILTRUM PRESS EDITION, 1984

### ORIGINAL TITLE: *THE NAPKINS*

A real limited edition, far from being an expensive autograph stapled
to a novel, is a treasure. And like all treasures do, it transforms
the responsible owner into a caretaker, and being a caretaker of
something as fragile and easily destroyed as ideas and images is not
a bad thing but a good one . . . and so is the re-evaluation of what
books are and what they do that necessarily follows.

—STEPHEN KING, "THE POLITICS OF LIMITEDS," *CASTLE ROCK,* JULY 1985

A s 1984 drew to a close, people on the Kings' Christmas list looked forward to
getting the third installment of *The Plant* in chapbook form, having received installments in 1982 and 1983. But instead of *The Plant,* they received a new King novel that
wouldn't see trade publication until February 1987. Originally titled *The Napkins, The Eyes
of the Dragon* was published as a signed limited edition from King's own Philtrum Press;
one thousand copies were sold through a lottery, enabling King to give away 250 inscribed
copies. (Twenty-six red-lettered and twenty-six black-lettered copies were also available.)

Printed on heavy stock, the limited edition of *The Eyes of the Dragon* stands as a sterling
example of specialty publishing. Designed by Michael Alpert, who also shepherded *The
Plant* through production, *The Eyes of the Dragon* featured artwork by a Maine artist
named Kenneth R. Linkhaüser (real name: Kenny Ray Linkous).

*The Philtrum Press edition of* The Eyes of the Dragon: *the book and its matching slipcase.*

*The Eyes of the Dragon* remains a rarity among King's fiction in that it is his only children's book. Dedicated to his daughter, Naomi King, and to Peter Straub's son, Ben, *The Eyes of the Dragon* was written because Stephen King wanted to write a book that his daughter would read. Because she liked to read fantasy, not horror, she had not read any of her father's books.

That changed with *The Eyes of the Dragon*.

Michael Alpert said that the book required over 45,000 sheets of paper, made in France, which took four months to produce. The heavy, textured, off-white paper stock does indeed have the "feel" of a linen napkin, which was by intent. Alpert consulted with King throughout the production process. Alpert explained in an August 1985 article for *Castle* Rock that

> We decided that the finished book would be quite large in format, printed from metal type on fine acid-free paper, illustrated with black-and-white line draw-ings, bound attractively in a sturdy binding, and housed in a matching protective

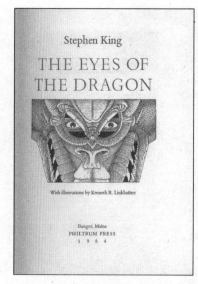

*Interior page spread to* The Eyes of the Dragon.

*The title page to* The Eyes of the Dragon, *with art by Kenneth R. Linkhäuser.*

slipcase. This was the general basis from which I began to work on the details of my design.

From my point of view, a book is very definitely a *private theater,* and the presentation of a book's content is very much like the presentation of a play through creative stage-design. Just as the dimming of lights in a theater lets an audience know that they are about to be invited into a world of fantasy, so the design of a book can give visual and psychological space between the content of the book and the rest of the universe. The primary work of a book-designer is to make sure that nothing interferes with a reader's immersion into the text.

Years later, this oversized edition of *The Eyes of the Dragon* (8.5 by 13 inches) inspired the work of another classic book designer / publisher, Jerad Walters, on a signed, limited edition of *'Salem's Lot.* Trained in classic book illustration and subscribing to the design tenet of "less is more," Jared was impressed with the large format of the Philtrum Press edition of *The Eyes of the Dragon* and decided to make *'Salem's Lot* oversized as well.

In my opinion Alpert's elegant design for *The Eyes of the Dragon* is one that other book designers should emulate. Books should be designed to be *read.* As Alpert pointed out, the priority should always be the "reader's immersion into the text." In plainer terms, the reader should find himself "falling" into the book, unaware that he's reading a book. It's an illusion that's easily shattered, especially with bad or inept design that pulls—often jerks—the reader out of the book.

For good reason, the colophon in the back of the book read, in part, "This first edition was designed and cared for by Michael Alpert."

If you want a copy of the Philtrum Press edition, issued at $120, be prepared to dig deep in your wallet, because its current value hovers around $1,000 a copy.

Though *The Eyes of the Dragon* is clearly a children's book, it's one with teeth. As King explained in the jacket copy of the trade edition, "I respect my daughter enough then— and now—to try and give her my best . . . and that includes a refusal to 'talk down.' Or put another way, I did her the courtesy of writing for myself as well as for her."

When Stephen finished it and gave it to his daughter, she "took hold of the finished manuscript with a marked lack of enthusiasm. That look gradually changed to one of rapt interest as the story kidnapped her. It was good to have her come to me later and give me a hug and tell me the only thing wrong with it was that she didn't want it to end. That, my friends, is a writer's favorite song."

## MICHAEL COLLINGS ON *THE EYES OF THE DRAGON*

Emerging momentarily from his public personas as the King of Horror and the Master of the Macabre, King here offers a fantasy that is unusually restrained in content and in style. Often criticized for his use of rough street language, King demonstrates in *The Eyes of the Dragon* that he can follow the verbal decorum of fantasy as ably as that of contemporary horror. In a narrative voice that suggests the lyricism and deceptively simple-seeming power of folk epic and the oral traditions of storytelling, he weaves a tale originally designed for a listening audience—his own children (the novel is dedicated to his daughter and Peter Straub's son). From the opening sentence, a variation upon the time-honored "Once upon a time," King rapidly settles into the timeless no-time of fantasy, introducing readers to old King Roland, young and beautiful Queen Sasha (like many queens of fabled lands, she dies early and tragically . . . in childbirth), the two princes Peter and Thomas, and the evil magician Flagg (the fact that his name is the same as the Dark Man's in *The Stand* is no coincidence). All of the major characters reflect the centuries-old conventions of fairy tale, both in personality and in actions. The good queen, for example, is almost too good to live; the evil magician, on the other, is almost too evil to live. In many ways, the land of Delain is a land of physical and moral extremes; the climactic storm, we are told, is the worst in the history of Delain. Certainly Flagg is the most maleficent king's adviser in its history. Through it all, the storyteller-narrator mediates among these extremes, weaving order out of chaos and stability out of disruption. . . .

Throughout, King displays his considerable powers as a storyteller, with few episodes that do not relate directly to his primary plot. Each action has repercussions; something as simple as the way the imprisoned Peter's meals are delivered ultimately becomes a key to restoring the true monarch (not coincidentally, King's working title was *The Napkins*, acknowledging the centrality of what at times seems a minor point).

# Illustrator Kenny Ray Linkous

A self-taught artist with no professional contacts, Kenny's first professionally published work was the set of illustrations he did for Stephen King's The Eyes of the Dragon. No artist could want for a better showcase. That King, who could have called on any number of pro artists, had chosen an unknown spoke well of Kenny's art. It also spoke well of King, who has a real eye for artwork.

Kenny's strategy in approaching King directly—to mail him framed artwork—was a long shot; most artists seeking collaborative work with him go through his agent or office staff. The local frame shop he just happened to walk in was Alpert's, who just happened to be the designer of a book for King, and they were looking for a good pen-and-ink artist. In other words, Kenny was in the right place at the right time with the right art folio.

Kenny's work for the book is in my opinion much more pleasing than David Palladini's illustrations for the trade edition, published three years later. Art, though, is a matter of taste: I'm sure there are fans of Palladini who would debate me vigorously on this subject.

In terms of imagination and draftsmanship, Kenny Linkous is a rare talent. I immediately began commissioning him for several projects, and he turned in artwork that delighted everyone.

Kenny's art for King is available only in the limited edition of The Eyes of the Dragon, which is a shame. From cover to cover, it's a first-class presentation of an enchanting King novel that I count among my favorites.

Kenny describes how he got the job:

One night in bed I was thinking that since I was doing a series of drawings called "Lunatics," I would take one of those drawings, have it mounted, and then mail it to him. I'd ask, if you would like to work with a local artist, here's a sample of my work.

I took it down to a frame shop I picked at random. I walked in, showed Michael Alpert the work, and asked if he would mount it. He asked if this was my work, and could I bring in some more? I immediately thought that he wanted to give me a show.

He said that he was a book designer, that he was designing a book as a limited edition for one of Stephen King's projects. Michael was very cautious, saying, "Just bring it in. We'll review it and let you know."

He had no idea that it was my intention of bringing that drawing to Stephen. A day later, I brought him a portfolio, which he took to Stephen, who looked it over. Then he contacted me, said they liked the work, and asked if I would do the illustrations.

On a fluke, I got the opportunity to work with Stephen King.

# 46

# CASTLE ROCK:

## "ALL THE NEWS THAT'S FIT TO PRINT"

If you want the straight stuff about me, subscribe to . . .
*Castle Rock.*

—STEPHEN KING, LETTER TO THE EDITOR
(*BANGOR DAILY NEWS*, MARCH 1985)

*Christopher Spruce and Stephanie Leonard from* Castle Rock.

*Christopher Spruce holds up a copy of* Castle Rock.

In January 1985, Stephen King's sister-in-law, who then doubled as his full-time secretary and part-time staffer for Philtrum Press, published the first issue of *Castle Rock*, inspired by Harlan Ellison's self-published newsletter, *Down the Rabbit Hole*. "*Castle Rock*," she explained in that first issue, "will be a monthly newsletter and we will have, along with all the news, trivia, puzzles, reviews, classifieds, contests, and, we hope, readers' contributions."

The first issue was modest indeed. Six letter-sized pages set in a difficult to read typeface, which made reading a challenge, *Castle Rock* dramatically jumped in circulation when New American Library began running full-page ads for it in their mass market paperback editions of King's books.

By the fourth issue, the newsletter morphed into a tabloid-sized newspaper, professionally designed by Stephanie's brother, Christopher, who was then working full-time as the station director of King's radio station in Bangor, WZON.

At its peak, *Castle Rock*, which never had to beat the bushes for subscriptions, reached a circulation high of 5,500 subscribers who paid twelve dollars for a year's subscription. Issued monthly, *Castle Rock* became the watering hole for King fans long before the popularity of the Internet made such newsletters obsolete.

For fans of *Castle Rock*, named after the fictional Maine city that King put on the map, the principal appeal was that it did in fact publish all the news fit to print. Occasionally, despite his initial assertion that he was fine with its publication as long as he didn't have an active role in it, King contributed text or clarified matters. "Dolan's Cadillac" first saw publication in *Castle Rock*, as did a lengthy, two-part essay, "The Politics of Limiteds," in which King explained from his unique perspective what he liked and disliked about his own limited edition books. (It's an illuminating essay that, unfortunately, has never been reprinted.)

*Castle Rock*, frankly, was only for the hard-core King fan. This was their publication, and if you didn't love Stephen King's work, you would obviously find it too King-centric. So what if the reviews tended to be uncritical and, often, adulatory, even sycophantic? This was the place for fans to gush, without fear of criticism.

There was even a parody of *Castle Rock* published, *Castle Schlock*, which had fans rolling in the aisles. Packed with humor and in-jokes, the late Ray Rexer's *Castle Schlock* poked good-natured fun at its inspiration.

*Castle Rock* finally gave up the ghost in December 1989, when the confluence of King's avowed retirement from publishing and Chris Spruce's desire to get his master's degree made ongoing publication untenable. As Chris explained in an editorial in the last issue:

> Rushing to haul the next issue together begins just about the time the previous issue rolled off the presses. It was always done in between this, that, and the other thing. Sometimes it looked that way, too. For the most part, however, it seemed to come out all right. Your letters and cards over the years confirmed that impression.

*Castle Rock* remains an important part of Stephen King history, much beloved by its subscribers, of whom I count myself. The individual issues are collector's items in their own right. It's now high time for an enterprising print publisher to issue a serious journal about Stephen King and his work.

# 47

## CYCLE OF THE WEREWOLF

### 1983

*The werewolf from* Cycle of the Werewolf, *illustrated by Glenn Chadbourne.*

Glenn Chadbourne

GLENN CHADBOURNE

S tephen King got propositioned in a hotel lobby, but it wasn't by a female groupie. He was at a World Fantasy Convention in Providence, Rhode Island, the stomping grounds of H. P. Lovecraft.

That's how this story starts, but by the time it ends, Bernie Wrightson was also involved, and from there you can draw your own conclusions.

It was 1979 and a specialty publisher, Chris Zavisa of the Land of Enchantment, best known for an art book, *Satan's Tears,* by Alex Nino, and the recently published *A Look Back,* an overview of Bernie Wrightson's career, approached King with the idea of a calendar: King would write the text, and Bernie would illustrate it.

King was amenable to the idea, in part because he felt guilty. As he wrote in the foreword to *Silver Bullet,* at the World Fantasy Convention in 1979, he was in the august presence of writers like Frank Belknap Long, Bob Bloch, and Fritz Leiber, none of whom had done anywhere near as well financially as he had.

Long, a member of the original Lovecraft circle, shared guest-of-honor status with King at the convention. The difference was that Long, now in his elder years, "had come up to the convention from New York on a Greyhound bus because, at the age of eighty-two, he could not afford a train ticket, let alone a plane ticket," wrote King. Bloch and Leiber, King said, were in much better circumstances, but still, the difference between their incomes and his was embarrassing to his fellow writers at the convention because of the great disparity. As King explained in his foreword to *Silver Bullet,* "They had labored long and honorably in the pulp jungles; I came bopping along twenty years after the demise of *Weird Tales,* the most important of them, and simply reaped the bountiful harvest they had sown in that jungle."

King agreed to the project partly because of his guilt. The plan was that he'd write five hundred words per vignette (one for each month), which Bernie would illustrate. But two problems arose. One problem was logistical: King found that five hundred words was a straightjacket. The other problem was legal: New American Library had the rights to publish King calendars and refused to let Zavisa's specialty press go ahead with the planned project, despite King's endorsement. A contract's a contract, and if anybody's going to be publishing a "Year of Fear" calendar with King, it's going to be us, said New American Library.

Both problems were overcome when King decided he'd write a limited edition book instead, which presented no conflict, especially since it'd subsequently be published by New American Library after the limited edition went out of print. The finished book was an oversized (nine-by-eleven-inch) book sumptuously illustrated by Bernie Wrightson. With full-color illustrations and pen-and-ink drawings, the book's large format provided an ample canvas that displayed the art to full effect: every inked line and every subtle shading in the coloring, printed on glossy stock, stood out.

The title illustration, in color, shows a werewolf crashing through a shack door as a Maine railroad worker looks on in horror. It set the tone for what was to come. The color pieces illustrated the main story, and the black-and-white pieces illustrated the change of seasons, from January's snow-covered scene to December's radiant scene of a heavenly light shining down on rural Maine.

The pen-and-ink drawings are among Bernie's best work. Recalling Joseph Clement

Coll's pen-and-ink drawings, Bernie's exquisitely detailed seasonal illustrations depicted them in a way that no mere camera could.

The 114-page book had a trade print run of only 7,500 copies; there were also 250 deluxe copies and 100 copies with original werewolf drawings.

*Cycle of the Werewolf* is a short but memorable tale. The plot: For reasons unknown, just as a winter storm descends on the small Maine town of Tarker's Mills, a werewolf comes to afflict its unsuspecting population. As the dark beast's depredations continue, terrifying the townsfolk, only one person suspects the truth—a young boy confined to a wheelchair named Marty Coslaw, who must take matters into his own hands when the efforts of law enforcement fall short.

As Michael Collings explained in the *Stephen King Companion* (1995):

> Unlike many of King's longer novels, *Cycle* remains morally ambivalent. The werewolf simply appears—there is no logical or rational explanation, no working out of the inevitable consequences of evil choices. As the human vessel for the werewolf says in November of that fatal year, "this—whatever it is—is nothing I asked for. I wasn't bitten by a wolf or cursed by a gypsy. It just . . . happened." The werewolf may be evil; the man beneath the werewolf's flesh is not necessarily so. Yet when the compulsion to kill rises, the good man must give way to the darker, evil impulses. At heart, this seems to be the metaphorical significance of the werewolf in any of its many guises—evil sometimes simply asserts itself, and then its workings must continue until their inevitable and bloody conclusion.

Collings declared, "*Cycle of the Werewolf* does not disappoint. The words are vintage King through and through," concluding that it "lingers in the memory as a fundamentally disquieting, dark, foreboding tale."

*A Stephen King "Year of Fear" calendar.*

# Bernie Wrightson and *Cycle of the Werewolf*

In the 2009 interview I conducted with Bernie Wrightson, he spoke about his work on *Cycle of the Werewolf*:

> This was the first time I met Stephen King. I don't think he remembers it, though.
>
> I pitched this to Chris Zavisa, who was in contact with Steve. My wacky idea was to illustrate a Stephen King calendar. We'd have a story with twelve "chapters," each with a picture and a block of text underneath it for each month. A werewolf story seemed like a logical thing because a full moon is common to every month.
>
> There was a bookseller's convention in Chicago that year. I flew out there from Florida to meet with Chris and Steve. King was going to have dinner with us, but my plane got stuck in bad weather and I couldn't land. I finally got in, but I was three hours late. Steve, though, had to be somewhere else, so we only had time for a slice of pizza and a Coke before he had to run. My recollection was that he was a big fan of mine and knew my stuff from comics. He said, "I'd love to work with you. Let's do this."
>
> When King started writing the story, he found the format of one block of text per calendar page to be too restrictive. He writes from the gut, and at some point his stories and his characters take over; his characters begin telling him the story and take it where it should go. So he was writing something much longer than what Chris and I had been talking about.
>
> Also, at the same time, NAL, King's publisher, told Chris in no uncertain terms that we could not do a calendar because those publishing rights belonged exclusively to them.
>
> We thought, *What are we going to do?* We've got a story that is growing into a book, but we can't do a calendar or a book. But NAL told Chris that he could publish a book, so long as it was a limited edition.

One hundred copies had an original pencil drawing of a werewolf laid in, which Bernie soon found became a Sisyphean task:

> I had to do the same drawing of the werewolf a hundred times. The only way to be fair was to do the same drawing, so everyone got essentially the same thing.
>
> I drew one werewolf face as a template, taped it to the drawing board, and copied it repeatedly. Because I had never done anything like that before, I did not conceive how boring and soul-sucking the experience was going to be. After a dozen drawings, I was thinking, *this is a life sentence and I am in hell*.
>
> I think *Cycle of the Werewolf* got a review in *People* magazine. The review was mostly about King, but there was a little slug about the illustrations that they said looked like Norman Rockwell filtered through EC's *Tales from the Crypt*. I thought that was really cool, that the reviewer had really gotten it.

# 48

## SKELETON CREW

### 1985; ORIGINAL TITLE: *NIGHT MOVES*

[A] short story is like a quick kiss in the dark from a stranger.
That is not, of course, the same thing as an affair or a marriage,
but kisses can be sweet, and their very brevity forms their own
attraction.

—STEPHEN KING, INTRODUCTION TO *SKELETON CREW*

As King's career moves into its fourth decade of published work, its progression clearly shows that any attempt to brand King only as a genre writer is short-sighted. It's best to simply call him a writer, because the scope and breadth of his work defies simple categorization.

*Skeleton Crew,* his third collection of short fiction, is early proof: *Night Shift,* his first collection, published in 1978, can broadly be categorized as horror or suspense.

*Different Seasons* (1982) is further proof that America's best-loved bogeyman doesn't always wear a fright mask. Only one of its four stories, "The Breathing Method," is supernatural horror, and the rest explore life in a realistic vein.

In a review of *Skeleton Crew* for the *Stephen King Companion* (1995), Michael Collings explains that it "contains some of King's best work," which is drawn from nearly eighteen years. The standouts in this large collection are "The Mist," reprinted from *Dark Forces,* and "The Reach," one of King's finest stories.

What impresses is the range of the stories in this collection and the ease with which King writes in various genres. It speaks to his versatility and skill as a writer and his wide-ranging interests as a reader.

Glenn Chadbourne

*Nona from the short story of the same name, illustrated by Glenn Chadbourne.*

### Michael Collings on *Skeleton Crew*

Following ["The Mist"] are other stories that are narrow in ambition but that taken as a series examine a wide range of horror, from psychological to physical, from the internal to the external: "Here There Be Tygers," "The Monkey," "Cain Rose Up," "Mrs. Todd's Shortcut" and "The Jaunt." Almost all the central tales deserve to be discussed individually; certainly "The Raft" and "Word Processor of the Gods" are hallmark stories that remain with the readers as potent images. "Beachworld" shows what happens when King immerses himself in a science-fictional universe; "Nona" owes its power to Lovecraftian horror and the directness of Poe. "The Reaper's Image" similarly suggests Poe, while "Survivor Type" hinges on a grisly (and gristly) pun when the unsympathetic and exploitative survivor of a shipwreck realizes that he now has to depend only upon himself. "Uncle Otto's Truck" tells about a similarly irascible exploiter whose demise has all of the mechanical, symmetrical justice of a classic tragedy. The semiautobiographical "Gramma" returns to Lovecraftian horror in the story of a monstrous woman willing herself to come back from the grave—and on a psychic level, at least, to devour her own grandson as she has figuratively devoured her daughter. "Morning Deliveries (Milkman #1)" and "Big Wheels: A Tale of the Laundry Game (Milkman #2)" are strange tales (even in a volume whose stated purpose is to present strangeness) that depend for their effectiveness more upon a particularly chilling tone than upon complete narratives. Interspersed in the stories are rare but welcome examples of King's poetry: "Paranoid: A Chant" and "For Owen."

In the final story, however, King exceeds all expectations. "The Reach" is nothing less than one of the finest stories King has ever told, regardless of length. First published as "Do the Dead Sing?" and reprinted here under King's original title, this is a ghost story that does not frighten, a story about death that bursts with life, a tale of loss and sorrow that merges seamlessly with joy and restoration. Stella Flanders is the oldest resident of Goat Island. At ninety-five, she has decided to cross the reach (a strip of ocean separating island from mainland) for the first time and visit the mainland. Setting out in a violent snowstorm, she sees the dead of Goat Island coming to greet her. Later, when searchers find her body on a rock on the mainland, they realize that she is wearing her dead husband's hat.

A blunt plot summary is inadequate to the tone, texture, and feeling King gives this tale of life and death and the delicate line that separates them. His landscape functions perfectly on literal and symbolic levels (a technique he will exploit later in *Dolores Claiborne* as well). Island and mainland represent themselves, as well as a wealth of possibilities: life and death, experience and innocence, the physical and the spiritual, the ordinary and the extraordinary. Both as a story and as the capstone to a remarkably consistent collection of strong stories, "The Reach" ties up a number of themes and motifs scattered throughout the book and, along with "The Mist," makes *Skeleton Crew* a standout short story collection.

# 49

# J. K. Potter:

## Illustrating the Limited Edition

### of Skeleton Crew

On the heels of the limited edition of *The Eyes of the Dragon,* the limited edition of *Skeleton Crew* from Scream Press also deserves praise. Elegantly designed in an oversized format and featuring manipulated photographs by J. K. Potter, the book's illustrative material is all the more impressive because the photo manipulations were done in a "wet" darkroom, years before computers equipped with Adobe's powerful software, Photoshop, made such darkrooms obsolete.

Jeffrey Knight Potter recalls the moment when he got the word that he had been selected to illustrate the limited edition of *Skeleton Crew:* "I was elated. Not only would I have top-notch material to illustrate, but I would finally be working on an expensive limited edition with the highest production values. My work would finally be printed as it was meant to be seen."

It's a justifiable concern among artists. Far too often in trade books, the illustrations take a backseat to the text; in many cases, the expense of illustrating the book's interior is bypassed by not hiring an illustrator; and far too often, when illustrations are commissioned, they are severely cropped, often changed in coloration to suit an art director, and manipulated until the published image looks very different from what the artist had submitted.

Cover art, too, often suffers: Festooned with type crowded on a six-by-nine-inch cover, the artwork is buried beneath, barely able to be glimpsed through oversized type demanding attention.

Mindful that the Scream Press edition would be a major showcase for his work, Potter threw himself into the project with enthusiasm. He rushed out to buy a skeleton from a medical-supply company, hired models, and spent countless hours producing black-and-white photographs spanning seventy-five photo sessions, followed by months of messy photographic hand-printing in a darkroom and, as Potter explained to me in an interview for *Knowing Darkness*, "lots of cut and paste photo finishing all done by hand."

Though Potter was disappointed with the book that was printed, saying it was "the most poorly reproduced art of all the Stephen King limited editions," I beg to differ: I thought its reproduction was very good.

Like other artists whose work depends heavily on photo manipulation, Potter now uses Photoshop, a graphics tool of extraordinary versatility. Back in the day, photographers worked in darkrooms to expose photosensitive paper to light from an enlarger and carefully slipped the sheets into trays of developer, stop bath, and fixer; artists and photographers had to be focused and dedicated: It was an arduous process necessary to make nonmanipulated, "straight" prints.

In Potter's case, he made multiple manipulations for *every* print in *Skeleton Crew*. Given the range of King's subject matter, Potter could hardly have had a more difficult book to illustrate. As a black-and-white photographer myself, relying on making prints in a home darkroom, I know full well the challenges he faced to "pull" and manipulate images from the photo paper.

To get his distinctive effects, Potter used specialized techniques like "multiple printing" and "force developing" (longer immersion in the developer tray) to directly manipulate the print; he then cut and pasted images by hand to recombine them in a collage; finally, he airbrushed or hand-colored the photos with watercolors, gouache, and transparent dyes until he got the final print he desired.

In the 1999 introduction to *Neurotica*, Stephen King wrote, "J. K. Potter's best work may sometimes unsettle me, but it never leaves me feeling let down, presumed upon, or demeaned." (I respectfully submit that any artist illustrating horror *should* be unsettling. I have both of Potter's art books, and the word "horripilation" comes to mind when viewing the phantasmagoric images.)

As for his own assessment on the project, Potter admitted that he "went a little crazy and overillustrated the book. The end result was that some of my illustrations were substandard, and there were certainly *way* too many skeletons."

I submit that in a book titled *Skeleton Crew* there cannot be *too* many skeletons . . .

Potter later provided illustrations, as did Edward Miller and Glenn Chadbourne, for Stephen King's *The Colorado Kid*, which was originally published as a paperback in 2005 by Hard Case Crime, and subsequently reissued in 2007 for PS Publishing in multiple states: an unsigned hardback, a signed hardback, and a traycased edition signed by King and all three artists. Using Adobe's Photoshop software, Potter's work in *The Colorado Kid* is a giant leap forward in terms of technical expertise and aesthetic impact when compared to his earlier work in *Skeleton Crew*.

# 50

# OFF THE BEATEN PATH:

## STEPHEN KING'S OFFICE

We can't be on a main road because people would find us. And
it's not people you want to find you. He draws some weird
people.

—ONE OF KING'S OFFICE ASSISTANTS, QUOTED
IN ANDY GREENE'S
"STEPHEN KING: THE *ROLLING STONE* INTERVIEW,"
NOVEMBER 6, 2014

I f you're interested in visiting Stephen King's office in Bangor, Maine, the welcome
mat is laid out for you; the door open. All you have to do is enter . . . by clicking your
computer's track pad or mouse. On the official Stephen King Web site (www.stephen-
king.com/the_office), you can tour his main office, which is as close as most people are
going to get to him and his office assistants.

In recent years, though, according to Andy Greene, who interviewed King at length
for *Rolling Stone,* King rarely makes it to his office. Greene says King's there once a
month, but does anyone really think the Stephen King empire is run by a boss who shows
up only a dozen times a year? It strains credulity.

So where does King spend most of his time? He spends it—according to Greene—
in one of his homes in Center Lovell, Maine. The Kings winter down in Florida, near
Sarasota; and during the spring and summer, they're at the Bangor home on West

Broadway, but again, says Greene, not with great frequency. (Again, I'm skeptical. I think the Kings spend more time in Bangor than Greene thinks.)

But no one can blame King for wanting a little privacy. The West Broadway home is a magnet that draws visitors worldwide. What was intended as a private residence has become Bangor's biggest tourist attraction, which distresses the Kings and their neighbors, who'd prefer a little more privacy.

As Naomi King told the hometown newspaper, "The press is as the press will be. The American public tends to have an appetite for knowing the private lives of people that they adore, to make themselves feel closer to these people. That's as it will be. I can't change that."

Now that King owns two adjacent homes on West Broadway, there's even more reason for fans to show up and take pictures.

A home is a man's castle, but in King's case, it's a castle under siege. The Kings bought the first West Broadway house in 1980, and for a while it did double duty as a private residence and offices for Stephen and Tabitha King. Moreover, while the Kings' three children lived at home, the house was only semiprivate from Monday to Friday because full-time staffers came and went, as did the occasional business visitors. Eventually it became clear that the office space was best moved off-site so that the house could be reclaimed as a private residence for the King family, which was the reason the Kings originally bought it.

King's staffers now work at an office in an undisclosed location near the Bangor airport, where they can screen visitors before entry by closed circuit TV, because we're talking about a man whose fame draws some people who are clearly mentally unstable. It'd be wrong to say those are King fans, because they likely have never read his fiction; they probably haven't even seen movies based on his books. But they know he's famous, and that's enough for them to pay an unwelcome and unsolicited visit.

Such is the price of fame.

At King's office, it's business as usual, and staffers manning the ramparts must do their best to keep a prying public away, so their boss can do what he does best: write stories for his millions of fans worldwide, and also manage the business aspects of the Stephen King universe.

# 51

## Marsha DeFilippo

### An Interview by Hans-Åke Lilja

2004

*We rarely get a peek at the inner workings at King's office. One such peek was given in 1991, when Stephen J. Spignesi interviewed Shirley Sonderegger, King's secretary, and another was given in 2004, when Hans-Åke Lilja interviewed Marsha De-Filippo, who runs King's office, ably assisted by Julie Eugley.*

**Lilja: Do you think that Stephen has more male fans than female fans, and if so, why is that do you think?**

**Marsha DeFilippo:** I haven't noticed a big gender difference in his fans. What I've noticed more is a diversity of his fan base and that it includes such a wide range of ages, gender, ethnicity, etc.

**Lilja: Tell me a bit about yourself. How did you get (what many would consider the dream job) the job of being Stephen's assistant?**

**Marsha DeFilippo:** I first worked for Stephen in 1986 on a temporary assignment to type the manuscript for *The Eyes of the Dragon*. Although it had been published as a limited edition previously, he needed it on computer disks for the Viking publication. It was supposed to take me a month to do, but I was enjoying the story so much that I finished the typing in two weeks. Not very smart for someone on temporary duty! Stephen was impressed with my typing skills, though, so kept me on to type the manuscript for *The*

*Tommyknockers.* Two years later when his assistant, Stephanie Leonard, decided to return to college, I was contacted to see if I would be interested in a part-time position. The timing was right and the job developed into a full-time position.

**Lilja: What [does] the assistant to Stephen King do? Is it a dream job or is it just like all other jobs? Can you describe a typical day at the office?**

**Marsha DeFilippo:** I do a bit of everything as Stephen's personal assistant—answering phones, fan mail, administering and moderating the web site, making travel arrangements, publicist, working with the various publishers and film/television production companies when Stephen is personally involved, interview/appearance requests, etc. It can become routine but overall it's the best job I've ever had. The longest I'd ever worked at another job was three years and I've been here over fifteen (not counting the temp assignment). There's no such thing as a typical day at the office!

**Lilja: What is the most asked question that you have to answer? I guess the questions about *The Dark Tower* are getting fewer and fewer now....**

**Marsha DeFilippo:** You're right, now that the Dark Tower books have been finished, the shift has gone to when will you make a movie of the Dark Tower series. The next most frequently asked question probably is "When will you finish *The Plant*?"

**Lilja: Have the things you do changed over the years? I guess that Stephen has gotten more fans, or at least more fans that contact you since the Internet became [ubiquitous].**

**Marsha DeFilippo:** It does seem that the majority of fan mail is now received through the web site although we do still receive quite a bit at our office. We didn't have computers or fax machines when I first started so the biggest change, as for most people, has been on the technological side. Because of the technology we now have, there is little impact on what we do at the office even though Stephen and Tabitha do not spend as much time in Bangor since their children have grown up and live elsewhere.

**Lilja: I know that there are many fans that contact Stephen by regular mail or e-mail but are there many fans that show up at the office or at his home? How do you handle these incidents?**

**Marsha DeFilippo:** The summer months are when this happens more frequently, as this is the most popular time of year for visitors. It's not a problem at their home as long as fans respect their privacy and remain on the public street or sidewalk. Unfortunately, there are the ones that ignore the PRIVATE PROPERTY, NO TRESPASSING signs and knock on their front door. They are told politely that this is not okay and asked to leave.

**Lilja: Has there ever been any "dangerous" fans showing up? What happened?**

**Marsha DeFilippo:** For the most part, there are no disturbances that require any further intervention but if necessary, the Bangor Police Department can and has been called upon. In at least two instances, arrests have been made.

**Lilja: What is the strangest thing a fan has sent to Stephen?**

**Marsha DeFilippo:** Define strange :-)

**Lilja: I guess I mean something that Stephen (or you) never expected to get in the mail or delivered, something that made you gasp and caused your chin to fall on the floor.**

**Marsha DeFilippo:** It was before I came to work for Stephen so I didn't experience it first-hand, but some very disturbed person sent a box with dead kitten bones.[1]

**Lilja: Do you read all the books so you can answer questions from fans or do you ask Stephen?**

**Marsha DeFilippo:** When I first started working for him I had not read any of them and I still have not read all of Stephen's works. For the most part, I answer the questions either by having read the book or looking in other resources we have to see if I can first find the answer myself and then depending upon his schedule and the question asked, I will sometimes ask Stephen if he can answer it.

**Lilja: There has been a list on which you can get to get a signed book by King. I have heard that it doesn't exist anymore, is that correct? I know that a lot of fans are wondering about it.**

**Marsha DeFilippo:** Stephen recently decided that he will now only sign books at book signings.

---

1 In *The Shape Under the Sheet: Complete Stephen King Encyclopedia* (1991), Spignesi interviewed King's then secretary, Shirley Sonderegger and asked her, "What's the most bizarre thing that's happened to you since you began working for Steve?" She replied, "One of the strangest things that happened occurred . . . one day [when] I went to the post office and picked up a box addressed to Steve. The return address was from someone in the Bangor area. . . . I opened it up and it was filled with hay, and in the hay were the bones and hair of several dead kittens. Apparently these people had cleaned out a barn somewhere and found these bones, and who did they think to send them to but Stephen?"

# Fan Mail

Your mother was right when she told you reading science fiction and fantasy books will make you warped. All fantasy people are warped.

—Stephen King, at the World Fantasy Convention,
October 15, 1979

*King saves all of his fan mail, and it eventually ends up in the special collections at the University of Maine at Orono's Fogler Library. Here's some choice tidbits from King's fan mail.*

**A fan who read *The Shining* and was concerned about reading *Carrie* and *'Salem's Lot*:** "Though I consider myself a strong person, I must think of my own mental health."

**Linda Z., Connecticut:** "While reading, it is almost as if I'm right there when everything is going on."

**Peter C., Maine:** "All I want is for someone to tell me that I'm a lousy writer who should stop wasting his time, or that I have some potential and should keep trying. PS: If there is nothing you can do, send money."

**Lisa B., North Carolina, written pre-Internet:** "Due to the fact that I live in a small town, I have been unable to find enough articles and reviews of *The Shining*. Therefore, I would appreciate it greatly if you would send me your personal analysis and any other articles and reviews you may have."

**Linda N., Iowa:** "My husband, who very rarely reads books, could not put [the King novel] down."

**Paul G., Missouri:** Do you write just as a money-making job, for literary value, or in hopes it will be sold for a television or movie screenplay?"

**Randee T., Michigan:** "It's gotten so that all it takes is the name 'Stephen King' on a book, and I know it will be good."

**Tamara J., California:** "Pardon the phrase, but you scared the shit out of this twenty-year-old."

**Joyce F., a sixteen-year-old aspiring novelist:** "I've been working (and I really mean *working*) on a novel for close to a year, and it is a lot tougher than I thought writing one would be. It's a pretty good little book but there are so many *problems*! I really need help! Sometimes I can be writing a very gory blood-and-guts scene that should make a person want to throw up, but when I take the scene from my mind and try to put it down on paper, it just doesn't seem scary."

**Shelly C., Michigan:** "How did you get started in the writing business? Where do you get the ideas for your books? Do you enjoy writing? Do you have any suggestions to a sprouting writer?"

## 52

## IT

### 1986

*It* isn't really about It, or monsters, or anything; it's about
childhood, and it's about my ideas that you re-experience your
own childhood, and are finally able to put it away and become
an adult with no regrets, by raising your children.

—STEPHEN KING, INTERVIEW WITH FRANK MULLER, FOR RECORDED BOOKS

In a letter to Michael Collings, Stephen King explained the genesis of *It*. "The idea came to me in Colorado, while I was writing *The Stand*." King said that the transmission to his AMC Matador had dropped out on the street, so he had the car towed to the dealership.

When it was ready to be picked up, King decided to walk there. After crossing a small bridge, he saw a field that made him think of "The Three Billy Goats Gruff," "and the whole story" of *It*, he said, "just bounced into my mind on a pogo-stick. Not the characters, but the split time frame, the accelerating bounces that would end with a complete breakdown which might result in a feeling of 'no-time,' all the monsters that were one monster . . . the troll under the bridge, of course."

King explained, in an essay about the book for a book-of-the-month club brochure:

Sometime in the summer of 1981 I realized that I had to write about the troll under the bridge or leave him—It—forever. Part of me cried to let it go. But

258

part of me cried for the chance; did more than cry; it *demanded*. I remember
sitting on the porch, smoking, asking myself if I had really gotten old enough to
be afraid to *try*, to just jump in and drive fast.

I got up off the porch, went into my study, cranked up some rock 'n' roll,
and started to write the book. I knew it would be long, but I didn't know how
long. I found myself remembering that part of *The Hobbit* where Bilbo Baggins
marvels at how you may leave your front door and think you are only strolling
down your front walk, but at the end of your walk is the street, and you may turn
left or you may turn right, but either way there will be another street, another
avenue, and roads, and highways, and a whole world.

When he finished *It*, he said it was a "final summing up of everything I've tried
to say in the last twelve years on the two central subjects of my fiction," monsters and
children. He told *Time* magazine: "Wouldn't it be great to bring on all the monsters one

*Pennywise the Clown from* It, *illustrated by Glenn Chadbourne.*

last time? Bring them all on—Dracula, Frankenstein, Jaws, the Werewolf, the Crawling Eye, Rodan, It Came From Outer Space—and call it It."

The book, when published, ran a boggling 1,138 pages. On the last page, King wrote that he had started it in September 1981 and finished it in December 1985.

In *The Essential Stephen King: The Complete and Uncut Edition,* Stephen J. Spignesi assayed King's canon and ranked *It* in the number one position. What follows is why Spignesi feels *It* deserves the premiere place of honor in his book. This is what he wrote:

Why *It* belongs in the number 1 spot:
*It* is more than just a novel.

I know, I know . . . that sounds like fan hyperbole, but truth be told, *It* is undeniably a contemporary literature event.

I remember finishing reading *It* and feeling the way I did when I turned the last page of Dickens's *Great Expectations:* unabashed awe at the storytelling talents of the author.

*It* is not only one of King's longest works, it is the book I and many other King researchers and fans consider to be his *magnum opus.* It is the greatest manifestation of his many narrative gifts, and the book that may very well be the definitive, quintessential "Stephen King" novel—if we make the questionable leap that such a thing can ever be defined.

Michael Collings, professor emeritus at Pepperdine University and Stephen King authority, feels that *It* and *The Stand* are interchangeable as holders of the number one spot on the list of King's top 100 works. He told me that he considers both novels "contemporary epics" (and, he specified, "in the true, literary sense of the term, not the facile commercial sense") and admitted to now and then surrendering to this belief and stating that both novels are his "top pick."

I decided to grant *It* the hallowed rank of number one, however, because I believe wholeheartedly that the novel is a literary performance of the highest caliber; yes, even more accomplished than *The Stand.*

In his gargantuan epic, King juggles multiple characters, parallel and overlapping timelines, a ghoul's parade of monsters, plus several complex sociological themes. These include childhood and coming of age, child abuse, homophobia, bigotry, the nature of existence, the eternal nature of good and evil, and the power of faith, trust, and love.

Longtime King fans (King calls them his "Constant Readers") can intuitively sense when Stephen King was in "the zone" (and not the Dead Zone!) while writing a specific work. The story seems to emanate a narrative confidence and flow that seems to transcend the mere words with which it is being told. I have often described this experience as being pulled through the book; being dragged through the story at breakneck speed; the tale being absorbed by the brain almost by osmosis, seemingly without actually reading the words. This is a feeble way of describing a transcendent experience, but I think you Constant Readers have an understanding of this phenomenon. It happens with *The Stand*, *The Shining*, *'Salem's Lot*, *Misery*, *The Green Mile*, *Pet Sematary*, and many other works, but never more so than with *It*.

King was in the aforementioned zone when he wrote *It* (as I am sure J. R. R. Tolkien was likewise inspired when he wrote *The Lord of the Rings*) and he has never been better.

The story told in *It* is truly epic. The haunted town of Derry, Maine has a dark soul. In 1958, seven friends—dubbed The Losers Club—fight an apocalyptic battle with It, a monster from "outside" who has been feeding on Derry's children in 27-year cycles for centuries. It is gravely wounded in the 1958 battle and returns to its subterranean pit beneath the town to heal. The Losers promise to return to Derry if It ever resurfaces and, in 1985, they must come together to honor their vow and try to defeat and destroy It for the final time.

King confidently interweaves the dual stories of all seven Losers, plus the stories of an array of secondary characters, using only italic typeface to indicate flashbacks to 1958, all the while managing to keep everyone's story clear in the reader's mind at all times. It—*It*—is truly a virtuoso performance.

I do not recommend *It* to first-time King readers. The novel is daunting and may scare off readers who are not used to novels over 50,000 words, let along 500,000 or so words. It requires effort and concentration, yet it pays off in amazing ways, and thus, *It* should be "prepared for," for lack of a better term. I usually suggest newcomers to King begin with something more accessible like *The Dead Zone* or *'Salem's Lot*; then move on to *The Shining* and *The Stand*; then to the stories in *Skeleton Crew*, and then, finally, to *It*. They can then go back and fill in the holes in their Stephen King reading list, but by that time they will have experienced a healthy, heaping dose of Stephen King's imaginative powers and storytelling genius.

Both scholars and fans alike now perceive *It* as the completion of the "monster" phase of King's career as a novelist. From *It* on, for the most part, King has focused on the "monster within" (as opposed to from the outside), in such works as *Misery*, *The Dark Half*, *Gerald's Game*, *Dolores Claiborne*, *Rose Madder*, and other diverse works; in addition to novels that ponder the existence of God and his involvement (or lack thereof) in human events, as in *Desperation*, *The Green Mile*, and others. The Mummy, the Werewolf, and the other classic denizens of the horror genre are of less interest to King in his post-*It* works. *It* may be his final word on childhood and its mythic hold on the adult. There will be child characters in later works, but *It* marks a turning point in King's treatment of childhood: We get the sense that the underlying message at the conclusion of *It* is that childhood can once again be remembered with nostalgia, rather than fear.

So there you have it: I consider *It* the best thing Stephen King has ever written. So far.

## MICHAEL COLLINGS ON *IT*

*It* presents reviewers and critics with a complication of plot beyond anything King had yet attempted or has attempted to date. Interweaving seven characters at two critical junctures in their lives twenty-seven years apart, moving back and forth from childhood to adulthood for each narrator, controlling the pace at which each remembers key elements of the childhood experience and can relate them to what happens to the fellowship as adults, with frequent forays into earlier, deadly twenty-seven-year cycles that have haunted Derry, Maine, throughout its history—all of this is enough to keep writer and reader constantly at attention. Adding the typographical convention of shifting from italics to roman typeface to indicate a parallel shift from narrator as child to narrator as adult helps control the temporal sequences, but even so, *It* requires intense concentration as it spins its sometimes perplexing tale of a Lovecraftian Great Old One–style monster that emerges periodically to glut itself on the physical and psychic suffering of Derry's children. To be fair, however, both the length and the complexity are justified by what King is attempting in *It*. He has frequently referred to the novel as an act of closure, as the summation of all of his preceding children-under-threat novels.

All of this is to say that *It* does in fact climax a stage in King's development as a novelist. For the first time, he successfully and completely combines children and adults, innocence and experience, naive energy and studied maturity. His monster is as multifaceted as the fears that face all children and all adults. It may be defeated in one form but returns in another. Some monsters are nonhuman, the stuff of myths and legends and stories told at midnight. Others, and often the most dangerous, bear the guises of other children whose disturbed impulses lead to viciousness and violence, especially against the loners, the outsiders—the losers. Or they may appear as fathers of preadolescent girls who "worry a lot" about their daughters. Or as mothers of frail young boys, whose sole purpose in life seems to be to keep those sons frail and dependent. Or otherwise goodhearted parents whose grief over the loss of one son almost causes them to lose another. Repeatedly, *It* moves from one level of fear and horror to another, from the physical to the psychological, from the material to the spiritual, from the external to the emotional.

Throughout all of this complex maneuvering, however, King does not lose sight of his primary objective: storytelling. Complicated as *It* becomes, each of its parts is involving, drawing readers ever deeper into King's imagined world. Small episodes merge to create larger movements of characters and events. Past memories link with present events to create tapestries of understanding. The children who fought and almost defeated a faceless monster deep in the sewers beneath Derry in 1958—and who are inextricably linked during that experience by their initiation into adult sexuality (one of the few times in a King story when teenage sex does not lead inevitably to death)—grow up to be adults, almost without exception capable and willing to risk all a second time to complete what they hoped was finished twenty-seven years before. The fact that all the adults enter the story childless is significant, since only by retracing the paths of their own childhood, and remaking the decisions that brought them to where they are, can they take the final steps into adulthood and become parents themselves.

Monsters—both symbolic and real—have been met and, finally, convincingly defeated.

## "Stephen King, the Master of Pop Dread"

One month after *It* landed in bookstores nationwide, *Time* magazine honored Stephen King with a cover story in its October 6, 1986, issue. Titled "King of Horror," it shows how far he has come since the story ran.

The story stated that with the publication of *It,* "Stephen proves once again that he is the indisputable King of horror, a demon fabulist who raises gooseflesh for fun and profit. At 39, he seems to be the country's best-known writer."

The story goes on to say that "King has become a brand name himself, and his publishers ordered a supernatural first printing of 800,000 copies—and then demanded five additional printings, for a current total of 1,025,000 copies. When an author receives that kind of recognition, two factors are at work: his skills and the vitality of the genre."

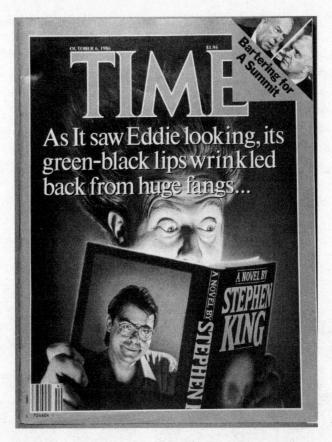

*The* Time *magazine cover story on Stephen King (Oct. 6, 1986).*

## Michael Collings on Stephen King as Storyteller

King has always had the strength of being a storyteller. Whatever else scholars and critics might find lurking in his texts (and subtexts, and probably sub-subtexts), he has always given his readers the sense of a fair payback for the time spent in reading. This has led him into taking real risks: the length and narrative complexity of *It,* for example, or the even greater length and scope of the unexpurgated *Stand.*

When King tells stories—and they are often *important* stories—he simply cannot be touched. When his message shouts louder than his narrative voice, the techniques that make his best works strong seem to act against him, making him seem strident, aggressive, and assertive.

I think some of King's works have a strong chance to last. *'Salem's Lot, The Shining, The Dead Zone* (in spite of its sometimes dated historical setting), *It, The Stand* (unexpurgated version)—all of these are remarkable narratives told with authenticity and truth. All of them lend themselves well to both the classroom and scholarly/academic study. All of them repay the reader/critic with new insights into life, society, literature, and art. And all of them are unique artifacts of the movement of American life in the final quarter of the twentieth century, chronicled by an unblinking and highly perceptive eye. I think that at least these— and probably several others—should have a long, long literary life.

*An aerial shot of downtown Bangor.*

*A cemetery in Bangor.*

# 53

# SK Tours of Maine:

## Stephen King's Maine Haunts

**B**angor is a working-class town. There are no fancy restaurants and no fancy hotels, unless you count the Lucerne Inn, fifteen minutes away by car. It's also not an accidental destination: from Kittery, the first town after crossing the Kittery Bridge from New Hampshire into Maine, Bangor is two and a half hours by car; even by plane, it's an end destination, not a hub. Tourists coming for the Maine experience head to Bar Harbor or, if they want to shop, to Freeport, home of L.L.Bean. They don't usually come to Bangor . . . unless they want to get spooked or, more specifically, to see the sights, and sites, that Stephen King calls home most of the year. A snowbird, he and his wife take off to Florida for the winter, and who can blame him? In January and February, Bangor's one big icebox.

*The Kenduskeag Stream running through a canal in downtown Bangor.*

*An aerial shot of the Standpipe, which figures prominently in* It.

*Stuart Tinker of SK Tours of Maine, LLC.*

*Downtown Bangor.*

*Statues with crucifix in the Bangor-Orono area.*

*Clay bricks mounted on a wall in the Bangor Public Library, each etched with the names of the donors who raised funds for its restoration.*

*Oil storage tanks on the waterfront in Bangor, which inspired the Trashcan Man from* The Stand.

*The Bangor Public Library.*

*The third brick down, on the left hand side, records for posterity two significant donors: the* Bangor Daily News, *and Stephen King.*

But good weather or bad, seven days a week, year-round, fans come.

They come by car and by bus, and they come with digital cameras dangling like necklaces and shoot picture after picture of a red-colored house on West Broadway. They come because it's Stephen King's main home.

The most famous house in Bangor is indisputably a tourist magnet, but then, for Stephen King readers, so is the town itself, which can be found in the pages of one of his longest novels, *It*, which is set fictionally in Derry, Maine, but is based on Bangor. Armed with a copy of *It* with pages marked, die-hard fans make the trek to see how many real-world places they can identify. They also buy a local map to mark it up and use that as a guide to get around town.

But there's an easier and better way: spend forty bucks for a three-hour tour to see thirty sites of major interest to King fans.

So how good is the tour?

In a 2014 article in *Yankee* magazine, "Best Attractions in Maine," an Editors' Choice Award was given to SK Tours of Maine because it's the "best tour of Stephen Kingdom."

Ayuh, it's the way to go: in a van driven by Stuart Tinker, a lifelong resident of Bangor, and best known in Stephen King circles as the previous owner of Betts Books, which specializes in Stephen King books and memorabilia.

In fact, TripAdvisor praised the tour's operator:

> Stuart Tinker is undeniably one of the world's most knowledgeable persons about Stephen King, his books, and King lore. He's also a good storyteller, which is important because not everyone who takes the tour is a King reader: an innocent spouse usually comes along for the ride, but always comes away from the tour with an appreciation of Bangor and King.

And unlike the ill-fated three-hour tour on the S.S. *Minnow* that left tourists stranded on "Gilligan's Island," the three-hour SK Tours journey will pick you up from your hotel, take you to all the King-related sites in Bangor and in nearby towns, and safely deposit you back where you started.

If you are a die-hard King fan and reader, a trip to Bangor is a must. But don't be your own tour guide, because that's not nearly as fun as seeing the sites in the company of other King fans, who will be regaled with facts, fun, and trivia about Bangor and King.

There's also another reason why SK Tours of Maine is far preferable to a DIY tour or monstrous tour bus: On occasion, when Stephen King is out in his yard, especially in the spring and summer months, he'll actually stop what he's doing to greet the van riders or talk to them from his yard. As one rider put it: It's to *die* for.

My only caution is to stay clear of sewer grates because, as little Georgie found out in Derry, it can be a grating experience.

Go to: sk-tours.com for booking information.

**Stuart Tinker, from his Web site, on SK Tours**

"We have been Stephen King fans since 1974 when *Carrie* was first published and have remained so ever since. In 1990 we bought Betts Bookstore and always kept a complete catalog of both Stephen and Tabitha's works in stock in both hardcover and paperback for twenty years. Because of the help that the Kings gave us, we became well known throughout the world as THE place to go for Stephen King items. In the last nine years we owned the store, [our inventory was] 100% King.

"After selling the store, I decided to do Stephen King Tours here in 'Derry,' something we had done ... originally years ago, and it has become a tremendous hit. I've met people from all over the world, all brought together by the love and enjoyment of Steve's stories. But we also have a lot of spouses, partners, and 'tag alongs' that are not fans. That's where the real fun is. The non-fan is truly amazed when they find out that their favorite movie—usually *Shawshank Redemption* or *The Green Mile*—is a Stephen King story!"

# 54

---

# MISERY

## 1987

They didn't see it as a horror novel. They saw it as something
that could really happen. Famous people can fall into the
clutches of their most psychotic fan. You can have the fatal
juxtaposition of somebody like that guy Mark Chapman and
John Lennon.

—STEPHEN KING, ON WHY CRITICS LIKED *MISERY* SO MUCH
(*WALDENBOOKS NEWSWEEKLY* 145, 1987)

### STAYING ALIVE

King, during a period of his life, abused substances, including cocaine. "Cocaine," according to the Foundation for a Drug-Free World, "is one of the most dangerous drugs known to man. Once a person begins taking the drug, it has proven almost impossible to become free of its grip physically and mentally. Physically it stimulates key receptors . . . within the brain that, in turn, create a euphoria to which users quickly develop a tolerance. Only higher dosages and more frequent use can bring about the same effect. . . . Cocaine use can lead to death from respiratory (breathing) failure, stroke, cerebral hemorrhage (bleeding in the brain) or heart attack."

King, who freely admits he was once hooked on cocaine, is lucky to be alive. Getting

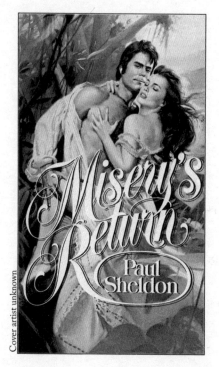

*The "fake" fantasy cover of* Misery's Return *by Paul Sheldon, inserted in the paperback edition of* Misery.

Cover artist unknown

hit by a reckless driver out of control and behind the wheel of a minivan was a matter of being in the wrong place in the wrong time; but he *chose* to start using cocaine. As he revealed in *On Writing*, "In the spring and summer of 1986 I wrote *The Tommyknockers*, often working until midnight with my heart running at a hundred and thirty beats a minute and cotton swabs stuck up my nose to stem the coke-induced bleeding."

Only an intervention, engineered by his wife, saved him. "The point of this intervention," he wrote in *On Writing*, "which was certainly as unpleasant for my wife and kids and friends as it was for me, was that I was dying in front of them."

King has said that *Misery* is about cocaine, to which he was addicted until he finally kicked the habit, just as Annie Wilkes, the antagonist in *Misery*, needed her fix of stories about her favorite heroine, Misery Chastain.

Originally intended to be a Richard Bachman book until King's cover was blown, *Misery* can be read on many different levels: biographically, of course, as being about substance abuse, as well as sociologically, as addressing the one-way relationship that exists between celebrities and those who, drawn to them, intrude in a potentially dangerous way. I wouldn't necessarily call such intruders fans; I would call them celebrity stalkers, disturbed individuals who desperately need help with their mental illnesses. King's stalkers aren't his readers or fans but people who only see his celebrity and are, for that reason, drawn to him.

When the Kings bought their prominent Bangor home in 1980, they wanted it to be accessible; they didn't want to live like Hollywood celebrities imprisoned in their own homes for security. For that reason, the Kings at first had no fence surrounding the property and no electronic surveillance devices on the premises. King may not have even owned a handgun at the time, but he sure as hell does now: three of them.

The Kings felt secure in their Bangor home, until reality shattered that illusion: In 1991 a man came in through the kitchen window when Tabitha King was home alone; Stephen and his two sons were in Boston, at a Red Sox game. Dressed in her nightgown, Tabitha was informed by the intruder that the cigar box in his hand was a bomb. She ran out the front door to a neighbor's house, who called the police.

After that close encounter, things changed because they *had* to: the unscalable fence was supplemented with motion detection devices and surveillance, signage, and closed circuit TV cameras. As King told the media, he hated to harden his property, but he had no choice. If he couldn't stop the celebrity stalkers from coming in, he'd make it more difficult, to buy time as he waited for the police to show up.

"I don't want to live like Michael Jackson or like Elvis Presley did at Graceland. That's gross. It was bad enough when we had to put up a fence. It was worse when we had to put up a gate. I hate to think I have to keep that gate locked," King told the *Bangor Daily News*.

It's the reason why King hates being perceived not as a writer but a celebrity, which was forced on him. Even living in a gated community wouldn't necessarily protect him from intrusions: Because millions of people know King's name, a handful of the disturbed have sought him out.

In *Castle Rock,* Tabitha King's article "Co-miser-a-ting with King" addressed issues raised by fans after reading *Misery,* who felt the book was a slam against them. "*Misery,*" she wrote, "is not the first novel to examine the relationship between writer and reader, or between celebrity and fan, but its exploration of the worst aspects of the celebrity-fan connection is obvious and real."

About *Misery,* Stephen King said, "It's pretty accurate in terms of emotional feeling. I sometimes don't know what people want. . . . People really like what I do . . . but some of them are quite crackers. I have not met Annie Wilkes yet, but I've met all sorts of people who call themselves my 'number-one fan' and, boy, some of these guys don't have six cans in a six-pack."

Until 2013, intruders had always been out-of-towners, but in October of that year a young man from nearby Orono entered the home and was ordered to leave by a caretaker; fortunately, the Kings were not home at the time.

It's the dark side of fame—the unwanted aspect—and it's the reason celebrities have to take commonsense measures to protect themselves in public and at home as well.

## THE NOVEL

*Misery* is a novel of psychological suspense set in one room. It is one of King's most riveting stories because it's firmly grounded in reality: the world of celebrity stalkers is real, and in Paul Sheldon's case, he falls into the wrong hands: a disturbed ex-nurse named Annie Wilkes.

Paul Sheldon's Misery Chastain books have a hold on Annie Wilkes that goes beyond normal. Thus when Sheldon—fearful of being pigeonholed and condemned to write about the same character forever—kills off the fictional character, Annie Wilkes is not a happy camper. She rescues him from a car crash and nurses him back to health, but in exchange she demands that he bring Misery Chastain back to life, which he does involuntarily: He has no other choice. Held prisoner in her remote farmhouse, Sheldon's growing fear is what will she do to him *after* he finishes the book.

The psychological hold that Wilkes exerts over Paul Sheldon, even after he's rid of her, is so tenacious that, as Tabitha King pointed out in her article for *Castle Rock*, he "has not freed himself of Annie Wilkes; she holds him captive still, emotionally and creatively."

The monsters, Stephen King tells us, are real and they are us, an idea that forms the basis of *Misery*'s exploration of horror. It's a familiar theme for King, who wrote about it extensively in his foreword to *Night Shift*. Michael Collings explicated King's theme of human monsters in the *Stephen King Companion* (1995):

> In both novel and film, audiences realize with shudders of horror that the character King has created and Bates has portrayed is a human monster. But in a larger sense, she is terrifyingly *realistic*, in ways that King's earlier vampires or werewolves or shape shifters cannot be. Monstrous as she is, Annie Wilkes merely reflects similar monsters that *really* exist out there. After reading a novel like *'Salem's Lot* or *The Shining* or *Pet Sematary*, one can look out the window and breathe a sign of relief that, difficult as the real world might be, King's fictive world is worse. But with *Misery*, audiences inured to the never-ending horrors of the six o'clock news might feel almost the opposite sense: for once, Stephen King has made no attempt to move beyond the darkest possibilities of the world in which we live.

---

### "Happiness Is a Warm Gun"

I think it's unhealthy for people to live vicariously through others. John Belushi and Elvis Presley were truly victims of their fame—and hence their fans—because a weak character has no defense against sycophancy. . . . Mark Chapman's assassination of John Lennon was the result of celebrity worship in a country where the mentally unbalanced have a de facto right to both lethal weapons and access to famous people. Chapman, by his own admission, was out to kill someone famous; it did not matter to him whether it was John Lennon, or Paul Simon, or Steve [King]—all to whom he made personal approaches. Murder is the ultimate fan possession of the idol. It will happen again, given the American refusal to stop the epidemic of gun murder and the media-enforced insistence that a public person is public property.

—Tabitha King, "Co-miser-a-ting with Stephen King," *Castle Rock,* August 1987

---

## Fans, Celebrity, and Crazy Stuff

As Stephen King told Michael Kilgore of the *Tampa Tribune*, "The occupational hazard of the successful writer in America is that once you begin to be successful, then you have to avoid being gobbled up. America has developed this sort of cannibalistic cult of celebrity, where first you set the guy up, and then you eat him."

*Misery* is dedicated to King's sister-in-law, Stephanie Leonard, and her husband, Jim, "who know why. Boy, do they." Both have witnessed year-round the behavior of King's fans, the more ardent having made pilgrimages to Bangor to see where their favorite author lives.

On four occasions over the years, the Kings have seen the uglier side of fame, from men who clearly live in the world of the weird. One such incident occurred in 2003 when a man drove up to Tabitha King, who was walking her dog, and told her, "I see you just came from the King residence. I need to see him. This is concerning national security." According to the *Bangor Daily News*:

> Tabitha King told police she saw the same man in the same car parked in their driveway around noon Sunday. She told her husband, who went outside and asked [him] what he wanted, according to the report. [He] asked to come inside the house to talk with King. The author refused and told him that if he did not leave, King would call the police.
>
> Stephen King told police he was fearful of this man, "so much so that when he came back into the house he went upstairs and loaded his handgun," wrote Officer Butch Moor.

As Tabitha King explained to *Castle Rock*, "The public is frequently possessive and unforgiving, without seeming to understand that what they are attempting to exercise is a kind of emotional slavery. Money and fame attract the self-seeking, who are willing to do anything . . . even if it hurts or kills you."

## 55

# MAKING WHOOPEE

## STEPHEN KING'S "GIFT OF GOTTA"

*Kathy Bates introduces Stephen King at a fund-raiser, "Harry, Carrie, and Garp" at Radio City Music Hall in NYC (August 2006).*

Radio City Music Hall has, over its sixty-year history, hosted some of the biggest names in show business. Best known for its Rockettes and its annual Christmas show, Radio City Music Hall is a haven for brand-name singers and a heaven for fans, because in terms of its views and acoustics, as its Web site states, "every seat in Radio City Music Hall is a good seat."

On August 1, 2006, at 7:30 P.M., Radio City Music Hall hosted some of the biggest names in entertainment—comedian and film star Whoopi Goldberg, actress Kathy Bates, TV star Andre Braugher, comedian and TV star Jon Stewart, and reporter Soledad O' Brien. These entertainers, however, did not showcase themselves and their talents; instead, they introduced and set the stage for three writers, who read from their works: in order of appearance, Stephen King, John Irving, and J. K. Rowling.

It's a half hour before the show is scheduled to start, and after a six-block walk from my hotel to Radio City Music Hall, I'm tired and hot, and it's no wonder: New York City is in a heat wave, with temperatures hovering near 100 degrees. Everyone is sweating profusely, seeking refuge in air-conditioned retail stores, coffee shops, and any other place that can provide relief from the oppressive heat. Concerned about power outages, New York City's mayor has asked residents to conserve, to turn up their thermostats (yeah, right), as the city officials dim the lights at public attractions like the Statue of Liberty and the Empire State Building. After a prolonged power outage in Queens, the mayor isn't taking any chances.

In the back of my mind, I'm wondering if the power grid will hold this evening. Broadway is lit up to the max—the show, after all, must go on—and store owners, in an effort to entice customers, have left front doors wide open, as air conditioners push themselves to their cooling limits.

Muggles—nonmagical folk in Rowling lingo—rush around the streets of the city, and I wonder how many of them knew that three of the most famous and most successful authors of our time are in their midst, preparing to read tonight to an audience of six thousand fans, some of whom had traveled from Europe to attend the event.

I expected a long line at Radio City Music Hall, but the length of the actual line surprises me. It stretches down only one city block and doubles back on itself. Even though it's early evening, it's unspeakably hot, muggy, and very uncomfortable. But the weather isn't foremost on the minds of those standing patiently in line as it snakes around metal stalls where security guards check bags, purses, and backpacks for contraband: cameras and recording devices.

I immediately think that, no matter how hard security screens the seemingly never-ending line of people, the die-hard fans are not going to leave without a memento: if nothing else, a photograph or possibly an audio recording. They will want, and get, a tangible souvenir from tonight's event.

Additionally, some people—mostly younger readers—have brought books that they hope to get signed. The opportunity is unlikely, but just in case. . . .

After a twenty-minute wait, I make my way from the end of the line through the ticket and security checkpoints and gratefully walk inside, where the air-conditioning is cranked up to the max. With a full house of six thousand people, the air-conditioning needs to be functioning at full capacity.

As I head upstairs, I worry that my balcony ticket, with a face value of a hundred dollars, is not going to afford the best view, which turns out to be a groundless concern. Located in the center section on the first mezzanine, I can see the stage clearly. Unlike a sports stadium where columns often obscure views of the playing field, Radio City Music Hall has no columns to obstruct a view of the stage.

I had expected a sell-out crowd and wall-to-wall people, but entire seat sections are empty. Were these tickets still available, or did people simply not show up?

It was clear, too, that most of the audience was composed of young adults. This isn't a literary crowd—in other words, not a John Irving crowd—and, given the lack of older readers in their thirties and forties, it clearly isn't a Stephen King crowd, either. It is obviously a J. K. Rowling crowd: The number of teenage girls present rivals that of a concert for a boy band.

At 7:35, the lights dim and, to introduce all three writers, a short film montage plays to the accompaniment of rock and roll music.

On four oversized backlit screens, we get a quick visual and audio overview of the careers of King, Irving, and Rowling, who, collectively, have sold over 400 million copies of their books worldwide, in dozens of languages.

In the book industry, this kind of celebration is as big as it gets. In a world-class city on a world-class stage with thousands of fans paying rapt attention, it's a world apart from the one that these writers inhabit when they work and produce the stuff of nightmares . . . and dreams: a small room in which the writer sits alone, dreaming, imagining, creating something out of nothing. It's what a writer does most of the time—it's the day job.

The clip plays and we see King walking through a forest. Rowling in an open, windswept field. Irving walking down a country road. Rowling amidst a large crowd of fans. A close-up of King in Durham, Maine; a black-and-white photo of him taken by his brother, Dave, showing a copy of *Startling Mystery Stories* propped up against the black platen of his manual Underwood typewriter, open to the page featuring his first pro sale, "The Glass Floor." A young Irving looking up at a fan at a book signing. King laughing as he's being strapped down in an electric chair on the set of *The Green Mile*, with director Frank Darabont looking on. Rowling at home, holding up *Harry Potter and the Goblet of Fire*. Irving working out, punching, swaying, boxing. A close-up of Irving's signature book, *The World According to Garp*. A close-up of King's first published novel, *Carrie*, the book and movie that launched his career, like a fighter jet catapulted off an aircraft carrier. Rowling in her home office, holding a British edition of a Harry Potter novel. Irving casually dressed, seated in front of an IBM Selectric II typewriter, pecking away with two fingers. Rowling in an Edinburgh café, writing longhand, with a picture window in the background. King, wearing a Center Lovell sweatshirt, at his summer home, where he's typing on a portable computer. Rowling standing up against a brick pillar as crowds of people rush past her, oblivious that a world-famous author is in their midst. From the first Harry Potter movie, actor Dan Radcliffe, in Quidditch uniform, looking skyward. A close-up of Kathy Bates in her most famous role as Annie Wilkes in King's *Misery*. Tobey Maguire in a car from Irving's *The Cider House Rules*. King walking down a country road in Center Lovell as he's reading a book with his Welsh corgi walking by his side. Rowling coming on stage at the Royal Albert Hall in England. Quick shots of all three authors. John Irving boxing.

The lights come up and the audience bursts into applause and cheers as a casually dressed Whoopi Goldberg heads stage right to a podium fronted with a facade of upright books bearing tonight's authors' names: Stephen King, John Irving, and J. K. Rowling.

It was a night to remember.

Whoopi Goldberg introduces the audience to the three writers, explaining that "these three writers are forces of nature equal to or greater than any of the supernatural events you can find in any of their books. Listen, I have read every book by all three of these writers, and with a book your mind takes you on the adventure, and the writer shows you the path."

After riffing on a plotline involving all three writers and their fictional universes, Whoopi gets serious and tells the collective crowd of six thousand that "this evening is really a tribute to you all. So put your paper-cut fingers and carpal-tunneled hands together and give yourselves a round of loving applause, because in this room are the best readers in the world. And if this evening proves nothing else, it does prove that what this evening really does is communicate to everyone that reading is alive and well. We proved that what happens when great books fall into the hands of great readers, we all want to talk about it."

She then introduces actress Kathy Bates, who gives a surprisingly humorous introduction to Stephen King. As she explains, "It's no wonder at all why I have been asked to introduce the first author. After all, I am his number one fan. I used to be the number two fan up until about fifteen years ago when a woman named Annie Wilkes came off the list and the top spot opened up. I'm very proud to own that title and I'm very proud to have my name so closely associated with his. And I hope that all Stephen King fans will forgive me for being morbid. But I already know that no matter what happens to me in the rest of my life, one day the name Stephen King will appear in my obituary."

She explains that she came to be chosen as the actress in the key role of Annie Wilkes in the film *Misery* after a friend read the novel and told her that "when they do the movie you ought to play Annie Wilkes." Her response: "Yeah, *that'll* happen in a million years." But it happened because "Rob Reiner happened to be dating Elizabeth McGovern who just happened to be acting in a play with me. I was playing the part of a crazed fanatic, so I guess that gave Rob the idea to cast me as Annie," a role that, when played by Bates, deservedly won her an Academy Award.

She closes her introduction with the reason why King's fiction is so compelling: "But most of all, Stephen has the 'gift of gotta.' You know? I *gotta* turn the page. I *gotta* see what happens next. I know I *gotta* get up early tomorrow morning to go to work but I *gotta* keep reading this book."

It is, as Bates knows, the reason why millions of readers worldwide eagerly look forward to his next book.

## Harry, Carrie, and Garp:
## Stephen King at the Press Conference

I feel like I've just been told the Beatles and the Stones are warming up for me.

—J. K. Rowling at the press conference, after both Stephen
King and John Irving said that they were the "warm-up
dance" for her

The morning before the first night's reading, King, Rowling, and Irving sat for a press conference to share their thoughts on book publishing, reading, and the event itself. Below are some of the answers King gave in response to media queries.

### How much money do you expect to raise for your respective charities?
I think we're going to be able to raise at least $250,000 for each charity, which for three people who write books is a lot of money. When we set out to do this, we decided that we would do two nights: one to benefit the charity of my choice, Haven Foundation, to raise money for freelance artists who find themselves after catastrophic accidents and diseases with no resources for themselves, and one designed by Jo [Rowling], Doctors Without Borders; and she can talk very cogently about that.

As I say, all of this came out of the fact that last year I read for John's charity, which was Maple Street School in Vermont, and he said he would read for me. And so while I read for a small school, I dragged him to Radio City Music Hall, and he came along!

### What advice do you have for young people wanting to become writers?
You have to read, and you have to hold out hope, because as a young writer you have to remember that we will all die.

### Fiction is often reflective of a particular community area. Is that true for you?
I think we all have a tendency to write about places that we know best. It's where we feel most comfortable and grounded.

### What are your thoughts on killing off your characters?
I don't plan the books out very clearly.

There are writers who plan, and I think there are people who fire missiles the way that the United States fires missiles. I fire them the way Hezbollah fires missiles. I have a certain idea of where they're going to land, but if they get within twelve miles one way or another, I'm happy.

I wrote a book called *Cujo* and it's about a mother and a son trapped in a car by a rabid dog. I thought I had a pretty good idea of what was going to happen at the end. I thought that the little boy would be okay, but the little boy *wasn't* okay, and that really shook me.

I had a book called *Pet Sematary* that disturbed me so much that I put it in a drawer. I ended up publishing it only because of a contractual issue. . . . Well, things happen. I felt like I had to publish the book, and I did, and with a lot of distress because I felt the audience would think, "Oh, this is the most dreadful thing," but they loved it.

But the thing is, I've written other books where the strangest things happen. I wrote a book called *The Dead Zone,* which begins with a character named Greg Stillson. In the prologue, he kicks a dog to death. I wanted to establish this character as a real awful person in the beginning who covers it with this cheerful, smiling, happy, "Hey, I'm just a good ol' fella" . . . and I got more letters asking "How can you *do* that to that dog?"

You write people back and you want to be nice to them, and you say, "I'm sorry you don't like that." I'm thinking to myself: number one, it was a dog, not a person; and number two, the dog wasn't even real—I made that dog up. That was a fake dog, a fictional dog.

### Do you have advice for Rowling as she comes to the end of her series?

Do I have any advice? I just want the story to be fair—that's what I always want. I want to read the book. I love that series. I want to read the book, and I have total confidence because I read the other books. Man, I'm just up for it, that's all.

### Are you comfortable reading your own work onstage?

I don't mind reading my own work. I know it best. That's fine. The challenge is to find something that can hold a broad audience.

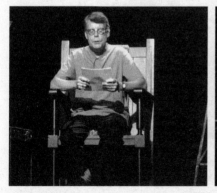

*King reads "The Revenge of Lard Ass Hogan" at "Harry, Carrie, and Garp" at Radio City Music Hall in NYC (August 2006).*

*King, J. K. Rowling, and John Irving applaud at the end "Harry, Carrie, and Garp" at Radio City Hall in NYC.*

After the event, Stephen King left by a side entrance, where a limousine waited for him. But fans immediately congregated around him, thrusting papers to be autographed; he dutifully signed two or three, and then got in the limo and left.

The two-night event sold out every ticket, and King's Haven Foundation benefitted from the generosity of fans who attended and supported it.

What struck me most from all three of their readings was that it reminded us of the oral tradition of storytelling. There's authenticity to the source material when the author reads his or her own work, because you're hearing it the way the author had intended: every inflection, every accent, every word carefully pronounced. It explains why King is so enamored with audiobooks. It also explains why his stories, especially the ones told in first person, sound like campfire stories; it's as if King is there telling you a story himself. The oral tradition of storytelling is intimate and connective; it's one reason why his readers feel he is talking directly to them, one on one, especially in his varied nonfiction.

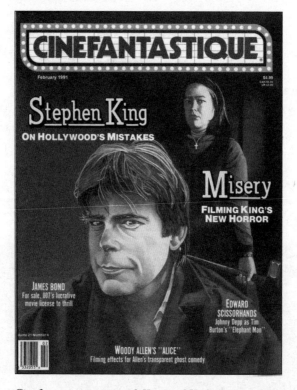

Cinefantastique *cover with King, and Kathy Bates as Annie Wilkes* (Misery), *cover-dated February 1991.*

---

# 56

# WHERE DO YOU GET YOUR IDEAS?

Over the years King has responded to The Question with various responses. Here's a few from his grab bag.

"I really don't know." (*Insomnia* book tour, Manchester, Vermont, October 4, 1994)

"Well, there's a great little bookstore on Forty-second Street in New York called Used Ideas. I go there when I run dry." (University of Massachusetts at Amherst, 1985)

"I get them at 239 Center Street in Bangor, just around the corner from the Frati Brothers Pawnshop." ("On *The Shining* and Other Perpetations," *Whispers* 17–18, 1982)

"The Question boggles most writers of fiction because it is so general. . . . So what writers mean, I think, when they say that they hate The Question is that it's impossible to answer. Twenty different sexual encounters may result in twenty different children, and twenty different ideas may result in twenty different books, brothers and sisters, but each individual in itself. There is no idea-bin, no general case, so the writer is left groping, trying to answer an unanswerable question without looking too dumb." (King, "On *The Shining* and Other Perpetations," *Whispers* 17–18, 1982)

"I do research. I get different ideas from one source or another. You know, a lot of the phenomena, the case histories you read of psychic phenomena, things like telekinesis or telepathy or pyrokinesis. Those things fascinate me. If you read a few case histories you get a kind of feel for it. Then I'll sit down and write the book." ( "An Evening with King," Billerica, Massachusetts, public library, 1983)

"So where do the ideas—the salable ideas—come from? For myself, the answer is simple enough. They come from my nightmares. Not the nighttime variety, as a rule, but the ones that hide just beyond the doorway that separates the conscious from the unconscious." (interview with Joyce Lynch Dewes Moore, 1981)

"Where do you get your inspirations? It comes from nowhere, it comes from every place. Something just hits. For me, writing is like walking through a desert and all at once, poking up through the hardpan, I see the top of a chimney. I know there's a house under there, and I'm pretty sure I can dig it up if I want. That's how I feel. It's like the stories are already there." (*Larry King Live,* April 10, 1986)

"Utica! No, really, I don't know. There is no way to answer that question so I just say the first thing that comes to mind. They come from every place. When people ask, 'Where do you get your ideas?,' the reason that question is so frustrating for a writer is because he knows they do come from some central source, but there's no way to pinpoint that because it is somewhere deep down inside. It is some subconscious thing." (interview with Loukia Louka, *Maryland Coast Dispatch,* August 8, 1986)

## DAVE BARRY'S CLOSE ENCOUNTER WITH STEPHEN KING

*(from "Name of the Chapter, Broadway Chapter," in*
**Mid-Life Confidential** *(1994)*

We also got to know each other better, and got to share our ideas about the craft of writing. For example, on our first lunch break, Stephen King, whom I had never met, walked up to me, leaned down to put his face about an inch from mine, and said, in a booming, maniacal voice, "SO, DAVE BARRY, *WHERE DO YOU GET YOUR IDEAS??"*

Stephen was making a little writer's joke. He *hates* this question. Like most writers, he has been asked this question nine hundred squintillion times.

# 57

## The Tommyknockers

### 1987

As King has readily admitted, *The Tommyknockers* is not one of his best efforts. It is a bloated novel written under trying circumstances when he was struggling with substance abuse issues. As he told *Rolling Stone* (November 2014):

> *The Tommyknockers* is an awful book. That was the last one I wrote before I cleaned up my act. And I've thought about it a lot lately and said to myself, "There's a really good book in there, underneath all the spurious energy that cocaine provides, and I ought to go back." The book is about 700 pages long, and I'm thinking, "There's probably a good 350-page novel in there."

Sold to Putnam for $5 million as part of a two-book deal, the wordy novel ended the year with 1.4 million copies sold, making it third in a listing of bestselling novels for 1987. In other words, it's a remarkable achievement for a lackluster book that reviewers panned with glee.

A *Publishers Weekly* review (October 7, 1987) summarized the feeling of many reviewers, who felt it was the print equivalent of a Rube Goldberg device:

> *The Tommyknockers* is consumed by the rambling prose of its author. Taking a whole town as his canvas, King uses too-broad strokes, adding cartoon-like characters and unlikely catastrophes like so many logs on a fire; ultimately, he loses all semblance of style, carefully structured plot or resonant meaning, the

hallmarks of his best writing. It is clear from this latest work that King has "become" a writing machine.

With the benefit of hindsight, King judged the novel to be one of his less successful efforts. But at the time *The Tommyknockers* was published, in a newsletter from Waldenbooks, King said, "That book's a really good read and a fast read and a monster story. ... In the case of *The Tommyknockers*, what I was writing about were gadgets. I had to write this book to realize that all of these things—the Minuteman [missile], the Skyhawk [fighter jet], the Polaris submarine—are nothing but gadgets. If we kill ourselves, that's what we're going to do it with: a lot of Disney World gadgets of the sort that kids build with chemistry sets."

## MICHAEL COLLINGS ON *THE TOMMYKNOCKERS*

When it appeared, *The Tommyknockers* confirmed the fact that King's perennial concern for children had largely been resolved. Both *Misery* and *The Tommyknockers* are about adults, and it is not coincidental that key adults in both novels are writers at crux points in their respective careers. Or that whatever happens in the narrative challenges their perceptions of themselves and their art. But the central point is that they are adults.

In addition, *The Tommyknockers* refurbishes the dark fantasy of earlier novels with a science-fictional overlay. King almost immediately thrusts his readers into a world where alien spacecraft might lie hidden under tons of soil . . . but still reach out to disrupt hundreds of lives. Equally rapidly, however, it becomes clear that this fundamentally science-fictional premise merely becomes the vehicle for quintessential horror. Aliens may influence humans, but after a while, it is difficult to tell whether the motivation for horrific acts is truly to be blamed on the aliens, or more properly on unacknowledged pools of darkness within us (a theme expanded upon in *Needful Things*). And on a more fundamental level, the novel has more in common with *Cycle of the Werewolf* than with stories about flying saucers and alien technology providing almost unlimited power sources; in *The Tommyknockers*, an unexpected evil simply materializes. As with the abrupt appearance of the werewolf in *Cycle*, there is no reason why Bobbi Anderson should stumble onto an exposed piece of the ship and thus set in motion the destruction of everything she loves.

*The Tommyknockers* not only seems to shift genres, but also incorporates more self-referential allusions than any other of King's major works. The frequent mention of previous novels and previous characters can be read either as part of the summation he intends *The Tommyknockers* to provide, or as merely self-inflating. Critics who see the novel as overly long, underedited, and careless in its particulars are especially savage about the intrusion of Jack Sawyer from *The Talisman*; Pennywise the Clown from *It*, appropriately enough as a hallucination; David Bright, John Smith, and the dead zone itself from *The Dead Zone*; the Shop from *Firestarter*; and more generalized but nevertheless recognizable allusions to *Silver Bullet*, *Thinner*, *Pet Sematary*, *Cujo*, *Roadwork*, and *'Salem's Lot*, as well as echoes of several short stories. At one point, in fact, King even includes himself as an allusion, when one character refers to stories "all full of make-believe monsters and a bunch of dirty words, like the ones that fellow who lived up in Bangor wrote." If *It* suggested an encyclopedia of horror and monsters, *The Tommyknockers* equally suggests an encyclopedia of Things-King.

The charge of self-indulgence these references elicited, coupled with the sense that the novel was wordy even by the standard set by King's other novels, has given *The Tommyknockers* the general reputation of being among his weakest works. Certainly its bleak ending keeps readers from any sort of deep empathy; by the end, only two major characters remain alive, and they are children who have no understanding of what has gone on. As with *'Salem's Lot*, an entire town (and the area for miles around) has been destroyed. There has been more than a full measure of grief and suffering and death (and a living form of death that is even more horrifying, since it is inflicted not by aliens but by humans in the process of transforming).

In spite of this, it is not as unreservedly dark as *Pet Sematary*. Bobbi Anderson and Jim Gardener learn what Louis Creed refuses to acknowledge: that there are things worse than death. While probably not among King's most effective works, *The Tommyknockers* nevertheless repays the five years King spent working through its themes, tying together disparate strands that had accumulated in over fifteen years of storytelling and end-bracketing one segment of his progress as a writer that began with the appearance of *Carrie*.

---

## Stephen King on *The Tommyknockers*

It's science fiction of a type. But the people who write science fiction are going to look down their noses at it and say, "This is crap because it doesn't say how anything works." There's a suggestion that the spaceship in *The Tommyknockers* is propelled by mental power. There are also suggestions made that there are physiological and psychological changes going on with these people called "the becoming." But it's never explained how those things happen. It's not a book like *The Legacy of Heorot* by Larry Niven, Jerry Pournelle, and Steven Barnes, which is about colonists in a faraway world. That book's a really good read and a fast read and a good monster story. But I would say that *The Tommyknockers* is science fiction of a different type.

The science fiction people like to categorize what they do. They even talk about it in the sense of hard science fiction, like Larry Niven does, and soft science fiction, like *The Invasion of the Body Snatchers*. My own philosophy has always been that I don't care how the gadgets work; I care how the people work.

—Stephen King, in the Waldenbooks in-house publication *WB*

# 58

# BAG OF NERVES:

## MEETING STEPHEN KING

### BY KEVIN QUIGLEY

Kevin Quigley gets a King novel signed at a Betts Bookstore signing in Bangor.

Kevin Quigley gives King a book, which he peruses.

*It's 1998, and King's number one fan, Kevin Quigley, has traveled with King's number two fan, Bob Ireland, to Bangor, Maine, to attend a Stephen King book signing at Betts Books. Keyed up with anticipation, after a previous day crowded with sightseeing, Kevin arrives at Betts Books with Bob just as it gets dark. The line outside goes down the street. It's cold, but Stuart Tinker, the proprietor, thoughtfully provided refreshments for people patiently waiting in line.*

*King shows up in a Mercedes and parks it roadside right by the back exit of the store, probably just in case he needs to have a quick get-away.*

*This is a big event for Betts Books. Its best customers have come from all over the United States to attend, including the "super-collectors" who were interviewed by the local media; they are the ones who have virtually every signed King limited edition published and have spent a small fortune building their collections. But for most of the people attending, they're just happy to get a minute or two with King in person and get a book or two signed.*

*It's going to be a long night. Nobody's going to get rushed through the line. It's a hometown book signing, and King doesn't want anyone to go away disappointed. If it means staying a little later than usual, King's game.*

*I'm not there to get a book signed, though; I'm there to photograph the event for Betts Books, and when Kevin had his moment with King, I captured it on film.*

*What follows is Kevin's recollection of his close encounter with the Writing Man who is King.*

S tu Tinker has set up the signing table in the back with a large display of nearly every King book set up behind that. Nervously, some of us take turns posing behind the table, sitting in the seat that King will sit in [in] a few short hours, which is in no way weird. My heart has begun its jittery little jump. The reality of the signing is hitting me. I have been a Stephen King fan my whole life, and I will be one for the rest of my life, but twenty-three is an apex of fan intensity for me. I'd met King once before, but I was a teenager and my *Mom* had been there and I was all dumb about it. This is my chance to be smart. This is my chance to make meeting Stephen King an awesome thing that I don't screw up. God, I hope I don't say anything stupid.

Some of us wait at the tableau between Betts and the Phoenix Inn instead of jumping in line immediately. We know there's a space for King's car beside the building, and we wanted to catch the first glimpse of him. I need to underline that *none* of this is creepy. We're talking some, burning off our nervous energy, the excitement and tension growing in our bellies. Suddenly, shouts like a clarion bell behind me, "There he is!"

There he is. Oh my God, seriously, there he is, just *being* like a person who walks and does stuff and is around people. King turns to us, smiles, and waves. Some of us, stunned, raise our hands in return. Then, he favors us with a thumbs-up. Way to go, kids. Welcome to Bangor. Then he's was gone, into the bookstore and out of sight.

I can't believe it. Stephen King had walked right past me and I. Couldn't. Talk. What's *wrong* with me?

My friend Jay Torreso turns to me and says, "Wow, that was really him."

I grab him by the sleeves of his jacket. "You need to *help* me."

Wide-eyed, he says, "Okay, Kev. Anything you need, buddy."

Here's what I need: Something simple that won't fly out of my mind the second I see King. Something I can say that isn't stupid, and isn't, like, one of those dumb fan questions like, "How are you so scary?" or "When's the next *Dark Tower* book coming?" Then I hit on it: I'd ask about Alan Pangborn and Polly Chalmers from *Needful Things*, two of my favorite characters of all time, folks I really want to see in a book again. Great, that was simple and direct, and absolutely *not* the type of question Stephen King is sick of, despite the fact that much later he said it was exactly the type of question he was sick of and I would be mortified all over again. But I don't know any of that now. Alan and Polly, Alan and Polly. You've got this, Kev. You've *got* this.

We make our way into line then, where we're treated to cookies and cocoa and hot cider. I eat when I'm nervous, so on top of the large meal from Oriental Jade, I stack a few cookies and a cup of cocoa, too. And a few more cookies. And why not some cider? It's all sloshing in my belly like I'm carrying a half-deflated kiddy pool after a rainstorm. My copies of *Misery* and *The Dark Half* are tucked under my arm, ready for the signature. Because *Bag of Bones* is a book about writing, and *these* are books about writing, and Stephen King will surely notice I'm being thematically consistent.

"Hey!" I look around to Bob and Jay, with me in line. "Maybe I can talk to King about writers and writing. You know? Like a whole discussion, and I can pick his brain, and I can learn something about the mysteries of the universe and stuff."

"Kev," Bob says. "You know you're going to be up there a total of, like three minutes, right?"

"Also," Jay adds, "I have literally never seen a human this nervous about anything. Alan and Polly, Kev. Stick with Alan and Polly." Okay, yes, Alan and Polly. Simple. Direct. You can *do* this.

Soon, it's Bob's turn to meet King. I hear him talking with King about the Rock Bottom Remainders concert Bob had seen that Thursday. Mute envy rose in me. Bob, as usual, seems so calm, so collected. Should *I* talk about the Remainders concert I'd seen earlier in the year? King had sung, "Stand By Me" and Warren Zevon had been there and we could talk about Warren Zevon, maybe? I—

Oh my God. It's me. It's me. It's my turn. Oh God.

I move up, lightheaded glee going off in my head like fireworks. I can't blink. My heart is racing. My brain is a heap of images and misfiring synapses. It is quite honestly a miracle of autonomic response that I am able to breathe. Then Stephen King smiles at me.

"Nervous?" he asks, sticking out his hand. Automatically I grip it in my own numb hand, shaking a little.

"Y-yeah." Then I smile. My smile is *ridiculous*. Dammit, I'd promised myself I wouldn't be a total freak here. This is *exactly* what a total freak does. I am a total freak. Oh God. I'm vapor-locking. I'm supposed to be speaking. Where am I? Are these books under my arms? Is this Maine? Am I in Maine?

From somewhere behind me, I hear Jay Torreso's voice, *sotto voce* and saving my sanity. "*Aaaallllan and Poooolllllyyyy.*"

"Oh yeah," I say, thankful for my dry mouth only because it means I'm not drooling. My train of thought isn't derailing, but now I have a direction. "I wanted to ask you about Alan and Polly." King grins.

"Alan and Polly?" he asks. "Those names sound so familiar . . ."

Then—*then*—I decide to *remind Stephen King who they are.* "You know. From *Needful Things.*" What the actual hell are you . . . did you just tell Stephen King which book his characters are from? Did you just do that in a real life that is happening? Are you for *serious* right now?

"Oh yeah," King says casually, grinning. "Yeah, they're doing okay."

"Okay. That's good. I want them to do okay. Okay." Translated: Mr. Stephen King, this is what a full-on fan meltdown sounds like.

With shaky hands, I give him my books, and watch him sign them, trying not to fall over in sensory overload. The line is being ushered out the back door into a little outdoor courtyard back there, and right then, I'm just glad that someone's giving simple directions I can easily follow.

Then I open my copy of *Misery* and I see what he's written on the title page in in blue ink: *Best wishes from your number one fan, Stephen King.*

Oh. Oh, that's. Oh. It's hitting me. It's all too much. *I had met Stephen King, talked with him, and shook his hand.* From *your* number one fan. And now I'm hyperventilating. Oh my God, I'm seriously hyperventilating. This is real. Why are my wrists and my ears tingling? Are my knees suddenly made of water balloons? I'm pretty sure they are. The world is swimming in front of me. Everything's coming in flashes; the world isn't a movie but a series of overexposed snapshots. Blackness is crowding in on me.

Blink. Blink. *Black.*

And then there are arms around me before I can collapse to the cobblestones below, helping me to a nearby bench. The blackness in front of my eyes is dissipating. Had I seriously gone into this thing promising not to be a weirdo fan boy and finished off *fainting* because Stephen King shook my hand and signed my book. Well, Kev, all signs point toward yes.

Then George Beahm is there, and Stu Tinker, and Roy Robbins from Bad Moon Books crowding around and verifying that I'm okay.

"Sure! Yes. Completely okay."

# 59

## THE DARK HALF

### 1989

> I'm indebted to the late Richard Bachman for his help and
> inspiration. This book could not have been written without him.
>
> —STEPHEN KING, "AUTHOR'S NOTE," *THE DARK HALF*

When Richard Bachman died unexpectedly in 1985, no one figured he'd come back from the grave, but he did. You can't keep a good man down. He posthumously published *The Regulators* in 1996 and *Blaze* in 2007. Bachman also "signed" the limited edition of *The Regulators,* but in an unorthodox fashion: faux checks bearing his signature were glued in the book itself.

In *The Dark Half,* King draws on the real-world circumstances surrounding the revelation of the Bachman pen name. He crafts a story that, like *Misery* and *The Tommyknockers,* deals with the nature of creativity and writing and what happens when they violently collide: In *Misery,* Paul Sheldon deliberately kills off a popular fictional character, Misery Chastain, to prevent writing more romance novels about her; and in *The Tommyknockers,* an alien intelligence is at work substantially transforming, through a process known as "becoming," a writer named Bobbi Anderson.

In *The Dark Half,* Thad Beaumont's cover as George Stark is blown by an inquisitive "Creepazoid" named Frederick Clawson, who forces Thad's hand. Clawson—even his name is suggestive—works to unearth the connection between Thad and his pen name; he places invasive phone calls to people in the publishing industry and takes a trip to the post office in Brewer to stake out Thad's mailbox for surveillance purposes, finally getting what he wants: incontrovertible proof that Beaumont and Stark are one and the same. He then contacts Beaumont to request an "assistance package," a blatant, ham-handed attempt at blackmail.

As Thad Beaumont's wife explains, "When a genuine Creepazoid gets his teeth in you, he doesn't let go until he's bitten out a big chunk."

Clawson meets an untimely end at the hands of George Stark himself: Thad's pen name that comes roaring back to life and goes on a murder rampage.

*Publishers Weekly* praised the novel, calling it "so wondrously frightening that mesmerized readers won't be able to fault the master for reusing a premise that puts both *Misery* and *The Dark Half* among the best of his voluminous work."

Collings, in the *Stephen King Companion* (1995), fills in the much-needed details:

> In this marginally autobiographically inspired horror tale, King touches on inner fears that are intimately related to the external horrors his readers have come to expect, if not demand. Almost obscured by the creatures (supernatural, science fictional, and other) populating the pages of *It*, *The Tommyknockers*, and *Misery* is yet another species of "creature" that finally emerges in *The Dark Half* to command full attention.
>
> *The Dark Half* anatomizes the complexity of creative imagination, merging King's experiences with his own pseudonym-run-wild (as witnessed by the continuing collecting mania for Bachman books) with thoughtful discussions of creativity and responsibility, of artistic integrity, of the destructive and regenerative powers of fiction, all without losing the essential sense of *story*.

In *The Bachman Books*, King wrote that *The Dark Half* is "a book my wife has always hated, perhaps because, for Thad Beaumont, the dream of being a writer overwhelms the reality of being a man; for Thad, delusive thinking overtakes rationality completely, with horrible consequences."

# 60

---

## THE STAND

### THE COMPLETE & UNCUT EDITION

### 1990

So here is *The Stand,* Constant Reader, as its author originally
intended for it to roll out of the showroom. All its chrome is
now intact, for better or for worse. And the final reason for
presenting this version is the simplest. Although it has never
been my favorite novel, it is the one people who like my books
seem to like the most.

—STEPHEN KING, PART 2 OF "PREFACE IN TWO PARTS,"
THE STAND: *THE COMPLETE & UNCUT EDITION*

Twelve years before the uncut version was published with illustrations, *The Stand* was
published sans illustrations and significantly truncated in wordage. As with *The Lord
of the Rings,* whose fans complained that it was too short (a view also held by its author, J.
R. R. Tolkien), *The Stand*'s fans also complained that they wanted more, much more, than
what they had been given for a first serving: They wanted what was kept back in the kitchen.

This second serving adds 150,000 words to the original text, updates the time frame
from the eighties to the nineties, adds a new beginning and ending, and is illustrated with
a dozen Bernie Wrightson pen-and-ink illustrations.

Accounts differ as to why the cuts were made. On one hand, King writes in *The Stand: The Complete & Uncut Edition* that "[t]he reason was not an editorial one; if that had been the case, I would be content to let the book live its life and die its eventual death as it was originally published."

Doubleday, however, saw things differently. As stated in the *Science Fiction Chronicle*:

> King's editor at that time, William G. Thompson, who is now a freelance editor, says he edited the manuscript strictly for editorial reasons. "There was no pressure on me to cut it because it was too big," Thompson told *The New York Times*.
>
> However, Thompson was fired by Doubleday before *The Stand* went into production, and according to King, Doubleday's publisher Samuel S. Vaughan told him that the book would have to be cut even more, to keep the retail price down.
>
> Vaughan, now a senior vp and editor at Random House, says, "Steve has always made me the heavy in the story. It's the book that was heavy. By trying to keep the price down so that it was not prohibitive, we were trying to build the career and sales of a young author."

The consensus among King fans, at least, is that his numerous additions to the primary text, the updates, and the other changes deepen an already rich novel. The fans who wanted more text got their wish. In short, *The Complete & Uncut Edition* quickly replaced the original version as the edition of choice among his fans.

Michael Collings enumerated the changes:

> The 1990 version also incorporates far more detail concerning the spread and the devastation of the superflu. The alterations range from single-paragraph vignettes, frightening in their simplicity and in King's ability to sketch plausible characters in a minimum of space, to near chapters designed to enrich the novel's portraits of social dissociation. These restorations establish more plausibly the survivors' reactions to the new world the superflu has created.
>
> Each of the restorations and changes strengthens the novel. King was not satisfied to merely reconstruct the novel as he had originally envisioned it; he also carefully revised the entire manuscript to bring it up to date for the 1990's readers. This often includes changing or adding such details as the names of songs and singing groups, fleeting political and social allusions, and brand-name references more immediately recognizable to later audiences. The fantasy elements intrude into the science-fictional framework much sooner, diminishing the sense that the novel begins as post-apocalypse science fiction and then, about halfway through, abruptly introduces the fantastical elements of dreams and portents, prophets and prophecy. The greater emphasis on the superflu and its consequences makes the transition from extrapolation to mysticism more believable. In this respect, it is significant that most of the changes—especially those relating to characterization, setting, backgrounds, and atmosphere—occur early in the book.

In either of its manifestations, *The Stand* is one of King's strongest novels. It is a consistent, readable, teachable response to life in a frighteningly technology-oriented world; it also reminds us that we may sometimes be forced to find a place for the spiritual and the supernatural within that world. The restored novel confirms King's position as a master storyteller; and at the same time it provides even readers familiar with all of his works to date increasing insight into the growth and transformation over more than a decade of his abilities, his themes, and his narrative power.

# 61

## STEPHEN KING DRAWS ON BERNIE WRIGHTSON TO ILLUSTRATE THE STAND

Significantly, unlike the original version, the revised edition of *The Stand* was illustrated with pen-and-ink artwork commissioned not by the publisher but by Stephen King. Deciding that he wanted Wrightson and no other artist, King paid him out of his own pocket and told him to carefully wrap up the art and pack it away for safekeeping until the time came to publish them.

Wrightson pocketed King's money, drew a dozen striking illustrations, packed up and stored the art, and turned his attention to other projects.

Two years later, King called with the surprising news that Wrightson would have to negotiate a fee with Doubleday for use of his art. Reminding King that he had already been paid, Wrightson was understandably puzzled. But King told him that what he had been previously paid amounted to a finder's fee; the rights, though, to publish the art would exact a separate cost payable by the publisher, who was contractually bound to include the art. King made it clear to Wrightson that Doubleday could *not* publish the book without Wrightson's art, so he should make sure to get paid a fair price.

After a series of back-and-forth negotiations between Wrightson and Doubleday, they finally agreed on a fee. Had Wrightson forced the issue, he could have asked for significantly more money, but he did not, because he is a gentleman. As Wrightson explained to me, he had no interest in taking advantage of the situation and financially holding the publisher hostage; his only interest was in getting adequate compensation for a book that he knew would make its publishers millions of dollars.

Wrightson was thankful for King's largesse. King had gone out of his way to make sure he took care of Wrightson in this matter. Wrightson knew that King was well within his rights to have claimed the art was paid for, to the point where King himself could have resold the rights to the publisher for a large sum and simply pocketed the money for himself. But from the start, King's strategy was to put money in Wrightson's pocket by subsidizing him in a way that the artist would find acceptable: not with an outright gift of money but with an art fee the artist would negotiate with the publisher.

Wrightson's twelve illustrations were rendered in pen and ink. Its first plate was a film noir piece depicting Larry after he put his sick mother to bed; its last plate depicted Randall Flagg, the Dark Man, presenting himself as Russell Faraday as he lords it over a group of "brown, smooth-skinned folk . . . simple folk." With his sharply defined portraits, sweeping landscapes, and "freeze frame" shots of the novel's significant moments, Wrightson's cinematic art lends the right visual touch to King's epic novel: artist and author working together, at the height of their artistic talent, to create a textual and visual work of wonder.

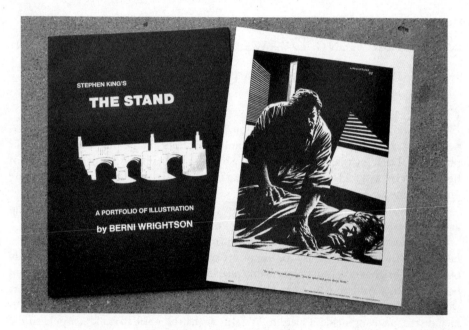

## "I Nearly Jumped Out of My Skin"

I have read every word King's ever published in book form. I love his stories. I love everything he does. He's one of the most accessible writers I've ever read. His voice just runs through every sentence, every paragraph, every page. It's like having him actually tell you a story. I have read a lot of Poe, Lovecraft, and Edgar Rice Burroughs, but I haven't read everything they have done as I have done with King.

The first King book I read was *The Shining*. It had been out for about a year. I knew who Stephen King was because of the movie *Carrie,* but I hadn't read the book. I didn't even know about *'Salem's Lot*. I was in Detroit, working on *A Look Back* when Chris Zavisa asked me, "Have you read any of this stuff by Stephen King?" He loaned me a copy of *The Shining*. I took it back to the hotel and started reading, and I was up reading until four in the morning. I was just exhausted, but I couldn't put it down. I was in a dismal little motel room. The light was out in the bathroom. And when I got to the scene with the woman in room 217, I was scared to death to go into my darkened bathroom.

Then someone in the next room threw something against the wall when I was reading that scene, and I jumped out of my bed; I nearly jumped out of my skin. I've always loved horror stories, but there aren't too many guys whose books have scared me: *The Shining* is one of them.

I always freeze up a bit when I'm illustrating Stephen King. My idea of an illustrator is to be a servant to the story and the writer's vision. I try to be a faithful interpreter. This opens up a lot of doors in my head.

When I read a King story, I realize that everything that's happening in the story is set in the real world, not some fantasy world. I'm not reading a fantasy, a ghost story, or a horror story. King's world is so real I'm afraid that the world I'm creating won't be as real as his. I would ultimately do a disservice to his story if I get something wrong.

—Bernie Wrightson, interview, *Knowing Darkness: Artists Inspired by Stephen King*

# 62

## A Dark Treasure

### The Limited Edition of The Stand

Dedicating the novel to his wife, Tabby, Stephen King called the book "this dark chest of wonders." He also described *The Stand* as a "long tale of dark Christianity," and the limited edition's design plays off both motifs.

The limited edition of 1,250 copies, issued at $325, resembles either a "dark chest" or a red-velvet-lined black casket, depending on your viewpoint. Regardless, the limited edition stands as the most collectible, and most desirable, limited edition of any King book.

Designed by Peter Schneider, who is best known in the specialty-book-publishing field as a cofounder of Hill House, the signed limited edition of *The Stand: The Complete & Uncut Edition* is a stark contrast to the uninspired production values of the previously published Doubleday editions, including *The Stand* in its 1978 edition, which King singled out in interviews as being a fat, ugly brick; in contrast, the limited edition is a bar of gold bullion.

Doubleday spared no expense in publishing this limited edition; in fact, making a profit wasn't an issue, as it always must be for a specialty press. Doubleday's exceptionally high production values meant that the final bill for the book and its custom-made box probably covered costs but didn't generate a big profit. The idea, clearly, was to give fans a limited edition that would be, like the family Bible, an heirloom to be passed down to the next generation. Doubleday, after all, could afford it: the costs of the limited were likely "folded" into the cost of the trade edition, which made millions of dollars for the publisher.

The limited edition book itself is bound in authentic black leather, not leatherette, which is often used for limited editions to keep costs down. There is foil stamping in metallic gold and red on the leather boards. The book is printed on heavy, opaque, off-white interior paper stock. Two-color printing is used throughout, for maximum visual effect: red ink for ornamentation devices, and black for the text. The gilt edges are in gold ink.

The box itself is a work of art. It's a varnished wooden box painted in flat black paint, its case lined with red silk, like that of an expensive coffin. On top of the two-piece box, a brass plate identifies its content. The final touch: a sewn-in silk ribbon to facilitate book extraction.

Not surprisingly, demand for this edition far exceeded supply. It was a feeding frenzy. Anxious fans besieged the publisher, offering up to $1,250 for a copy when it was first announced.

Today, twenty-four years after its publication, the $325 book predictably commands a collector's price on the specialty market. Betts Books recently sold a copy for $1,850; copies online range in price up to $2,500.

If you are adamant about owning just one limited edition Stephen King book, get this one. It's always held its value and will always be in demand because it's the centerpiece of any King collection.

Insofar as limited editions go, fan favorites include *The Eyes of the Dragon*, because it's from King's own press; *'Salem's Lot*, because it's oversized and classically designed; and *Skeleton Crew*, with J. K. Potter's photo illustrations. But towering above them all is *The Stand: The Complete & Uncut Edition*. For die-hard King fans, it's the book of choice in terms of its popularity, its production values, and its investment potential.

## STEPHEN KING ON LIMITED EDITIONS

*(from "The Politics of Limited Editions," Castle Rock, July 1985)*

> A real limited edition, far from being an expensive autograph stapled to a novel, is a treasure. And like all treasures do, it transforms the responsible owner into a caretaker, and being a caretaker of something as fragile and easily destroyed as ideas and images is not a bad thing but a good one ... and so is the re-evaluation of what books are what they do that necessary follows.

# 63

## Michael Collings on
## Four Past Midnight

### 1990

As with *Different Seasons*, which shares the overriding time metaphor both in its title and in the arrangement of its stories, each of the four tales in *Four Past Midnight* is virtually novel-length, each approaches the art of writing from different directions, each seems to belong to slightly different genres, and ultimately each varies in quality and evocative power.

"The Langoliers," for example, shows the quintessential King at his best, spinning a tale of fantasy and horror. In what readers will recognize as vintage *Twilight Zone* fashion, characters discover that *something* has happened . . . and worse, that something unknown and indefinable is coming, threatening the eventual disintegration of everything (perhaps including time itself). King's images of diminishing solidity, of worn-out matter, and of encroaching nothingness that is the Langoliers remain long after the story is over.

"Secret Window, Secret Garden," on the other hand, belongs to a sequence of stories that anatomize the writer's imagination and that includes *Misery*, *The Tommyknockers*, and *The Dark Half*. If Thad Beaumont is haunted by a murderous pseudonym, Morton Rainey is pursued by the specter of plagiarism personified in "his greatest creation—a character so vivid that he actually did become real."

"The Library Policeman," like so many of King's finer shorter works, parallels psychic horrors with the deeper, darker horrors of "real life." And, simply put, any horror story that depends for its climax on combining a variation on Heinleinian puppet masters with a wad of Bull's Eye red licorice squashed on the railroad tracks deserves to be read.

"The Sun Dog" provides a narrative link between *The Dark Half* and *Needful Things*.

In spite of the fact that the "sun" in question is a Polaroid camera—a "needful thing," as it were, for young Kevin Delevan—King quickly connects that common, everyday object with an encroaching supernatural horror. In this story, King's penchant for detail at times overwhelms his storytelling, so several pages, for example, are devoted to the relatively insignificant task of buying a roll of film. Similarly, when the Polaroid begins to develop and show something—the sun dog—moving inexorably closer to the barrier separating its world and ours, the story slows almost to a halt. One of the few tales that seem longer than required, it nevertheless prepared readers for what is to come in *Needful Things*.

Responses to the stories will vary with each reader, of course. Arguments as to which of the stories is the "best" will likely depend as much on the readers as on the stories. Of the four, however, "The Sun Dog" seems the weakest, particularly because it illustrates King's occasional need for careful, stringent editing. "Secret Window, Secret Garden," on the other hand, with its probing of diseased psychological states, resonates well with the earlier novels. Although none of the stories carries the weight and focus of "Rita Hayworth and Shawshank Redemption" in King's earlier quartet of tales (and arguably among his better performances), *Four Past Midnight* nevertheless demonstrates once again King's unusual versatility and range of vision.

# 64

## ROCK BOTTOM REMAINDERS

I love rock 'n' roll. But writing is not like being a rock 'n' roll star. I think a lot of writers in my generation are closet rock and roll freaks. I would guess—I don't think there's ever been a survey done of this—that you would find a lot of closet air guitar players who know all the Eric Clapton solos and that sort of thing.

So when I write, I just crank the music. I inundate myself in rock and roll, and it kind of poisons the atmosphere around me so that people don't approach me, unless they really, really want to get close—you know, 'Steve, the house is burning down.' That kind of thing."

—STEPHEN KING, IN AN INTERVIEW PROMOTING BMG'S VIDEO RECORDING OF THE FIRST RBR CONCERT

As Kathi Kamen Goldmark explained, "In the fine rock & roll tradition, the Rock Bottom Remainders were conceived in a car. As a semi-pro musician with a day job in book publicity, I spent a lot of time driving touring authors around San Francisco . . . I decided to form a band of authors!"

*King and Robert Fulghum face off in a "guitar-fest" at the first Rock Bottom Remainders concert in Anaheim, California, on May 25, 1992.*

*King in concert with the Rock Bottom Remainders in Bangor.*

On May 25, 1992, the Rock Bottom Remainders[1] made their first and second public appearances for booksellers. The first was billed as "The Rock Bottom Remainders Unplugged," in which the band members appeared on stage in the grand ballroom of the Disneyland Hotel, where they sang two songs A cappella at Garrison Keillor's "A Celebration for Free Expression: An Evening of Censored Classics." The second appearance, later that night, was when they kicked out the jams; they plugged in guitars and cranked up the volume on their amps at a nearby club, the Cowboy Boogie.

You had to be there.

I was.

I wanted to be down on the floor, buying the autographed T-shirts, photos, and other memorabilia that raised money for three charities, including the Homeless Writers Coalition of Los Angeles, or dancing like crazy, but instead I was on a raised platform packed with other photographers who tinkered with their *film* cameras, wondering about their camera settings, because the light level was low and constantly changing.

So how was the music?

Not important.

So how much fun did everyone have?

Man, it was a blast, in every sense of the word. That place was rocking with traditionally sedate booksellers who got out on the dance floor and kicked it up: They turned out to be a pretty lively bunch!

What made it all the more remarkable was that the band members weren't trained musicians; they were baby boomers who harbored daydreams of playing rock and roll in a band. They turned off their word processors to turn on the music and the audience—and had fun doing it, too.

## "THE DAY THE MUSIC DIED"

When Kathi Kamen Goldmark passed on in 2012, the band members felt it was time to move on. As Stephen King—one of the original members—noted, things just didn't seem the same afterward. Her death took the wind out of the band's sails. The last concert, two decades after the first one, was for the members of the American Library Association, also in Anaheim.

Playing for fun, the Rock Bottom Remainders raised the roof onstage for two decades and in the process also raised $2 million for charity.

For the band members, it was a rare opportunity to get away from their day jobs, get together to jam with other authors, and have a little fun just hanging out after hours, and in between gigs.

It did take a while for the band to get their act together. As recounted by Dave Barry in *Mid-Life Confidential: The Rock Bottom Remainders Tour America with Three Chords and*

---

1 The original band members, self-termed "The Anaheim Version": Dave Barry, Tad Bartimus, Roy Blount, Jr., Michael Dorris, Robert Fulghum, Kathi Kamen Goldmark, Matt Groening, Stephen King, Barbara Kingsolver, Al Kooper, Greil Marcus, Dave Marsh, Ridley Pearson, Joel Selvin, and Amy Tan.

*an Attitude,* ringer Al Kooper listened to the first rehearsal and offered helpful suggestions like "Don't play so loud," "Don't play at all," and "I don't think we should do this song."

It was all in good fun.

Here's a great moment, recalled by Dave Barry, when they were playing at a concert in Los Angeles:

> I picked up one of the two guitars I'd been using, and just as we were about to start, Stephen King tapped me on the shoulder and said, "We have a special guest." I turned around, and there was Bruce Springsteen. I still don't know how he came to be at this convention; I don't believe he's a bookseller. All I know is, he was picking up the other guitar. *My* guitar. "Bruce," I said to him, "Do you know the guitar part to 'Gloria'?" This is like asking James Michener if he knows how to write his name.

## Yesterday . . .

I was there, as I said, at their first two public appearances. When they toured, and when I had the time and opportunity, I got to a few more of their gigs. At one, in New York City, I remember seeing Neil Gaiman invited onstage by Stephen King to play the harmonica. And there was also a concert in Bangor, Maine, when King broke into a wide grin when he saw Warren Zevon play the guitar behind his head, a moment I was glad I caught on camera. (Sadly, Zevon passed away in 2003.) I remember *that* concert because a good friend of mine, the late Charlie Fried, with whom I had driven up from Connecticut, had paid for tickets for dozens of local teenagers who otherwise couldn't afford to attend. (Charlie had the biggest heart of anyone I've ever known.)

*King and the late Charlie Fried at the Betts Bookstore book signing.*

## ...And Today: The Reunion

You can't keep a good band down, though, and some of the remaining band members still wanted to rock and roll, so at the Tucson Festival of Books (March 14–15, 2015), Amy Tan, Mitch Albom, Dave Barry, Scott Turow, Ridley Pearson, Roy Blount Jr., Alan Zweibel, and Greg Iles plugged in, tuned up, and rocked on. As Barry commented to the local media before the concert: "'Play' is probably a strong term for what we do with our instruments, but we have them with us onstage for sure. I would say a better term is we hold our own instruments."

But it wasn't the same without Stephen (and still the) King there, who has unplugged for good—the day, King fans noted, the music died.

In Stephen King's "The Neighborhood of the Beast," from *Mid-Life Confidential,* King wrote, "Playing music again—playing for an actual audience—after all those years was fun. Well, actually it was a little more than fun; it *had* to have been, or the Three Chords and an Attitude Tour never would have gotten off the ground. It was, in fact, exhilarating."

Now *that's* music to anyone's ears.

*King in concert with the Rock Bottom Remainders in Bangor (1998).*

*A signed Rock Bottom Remainders print for their Miami '93 concert.*

*The late Warren Zevon and King at the Rock Bottom Remainders concert in Bangor (1998).*

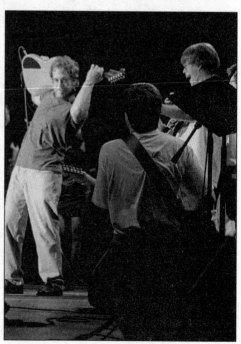

*The late Warren Zevon plays his guitar behind his head, to Kings' surprise, at the Rock Bottom Remainders concert in Bangor (1998).*

# 65

# Quotes by and About the
# Rock Bottom Remainders

## Quotes by the Band

### Solo

- **Dave "His Mind May Be Full of Boogers and Dog Poop, But His Heart Is Full of Love" Barry (guitar and vocals):** "We play music as well as Metallica writes novels."
- **Michael "Whoever Heard of a Man Named" Doris (percussion):** "And so the Remainders played. Played, played, played. It was a sound to hear. And to forget." (essay in *Mid-Life Confidential*, 1994)
- **Robert "But Then I Forgot It All in Grade School" Fulghum (mandocello, guitar, and vocals):** "Anyhow, we're in this hotel and this maid comes in and she keeps looking at me and she smiled and she said, 'I know who you are.' And I said, 'No, you don't. Who am I?' And she said, 'You're Kenny Rogers.' And of course I said, 'No, no, no.' And she said, 'If you were Kenny Rogers you wouldn't say you were Kenny Rogers, would you? So you must be Kenny Rogers.' So that evening I'm walking along with my guitars going to the elevator and she went up like a skyrocket, 'See! I knew you were Kenny Rogers!' So I signed her card, 'Love and kisses, Kenny Rogers.'" (Linda Richards, *January* magazine, date not listed)
- **Kathi "the Queen of the Book Tour" Goldmark (band mother and Remainderette vocals):** "I realized that I had a lineup of band members simply from the folks I was driving around. So one day I asked Dave and Barbara and Amy and a few others if they'd consider doing a rock show to raise money for charity. They said yes. When Stephen King came onboard, things really took off." Hope Katz Gibbs, "Meet the Leader of the Band," beinkandescent.com, April 2011.

- **Matt "Happy Families Are All Alike" Groening (critics' chorus):** "People are throwing panties at you. They certainly never do that at my book-signings." (general attribution)
- **Stephen "and Still the" King (guitar and vocals),** on their final concert after twenty years: "Since I've been on this tour, a lot of people have come up to me and said, 'You guys don't sound too bad, but don't quit the day job yet.' As if I'd quit my fucking day job! I *like* my day job!" (Carlin Romano, philly.com, 1993)

    "I'm looking forward to reuniting with all my band mates. . . . Some of us can remember all of the words; all of us can remember some of the words; but NONE of us can remember all of the music. That's why they call it rock and roll." (marquee.blogs. cnn.com)
- **Barbara "She May Be the Answer to Stephen" Kingsolver (keyboard and vocals):** "We really thought it was a one-time thing. We didn't count on this vampire syndrome. We're kind of thinking about doing something new, like maybe a professional hockey team." (Carlin Romano, philly.com, 1993)
- **Al "He May Be a Mother-You-Know-What, but We All Call Him Dad" Kooper (keyboard and guitar),** on when the band members found their musical "legs": "This time we're so much better because everybody really did their homework. We picked the songs via fax, and everyone really practiced hard, so when we came to rehearsal, it was like—we're actually really playing music this time." (Carlin Romano, philly.com, 1993)
- **Greil "Elvis Is Dead in My Books" Marcus (critics' chorus):** "The idea of a tour—a heroic barnstorm down the East Coast, Massachusetts to Florida, just a happy-go-lucky troupe of crazy scribblers with their repertoire of sock-hop tearjerkers and frat-house drinking songs—struck me as utter lunacy, all but criminal hubris, the indulgence of infantile fantasies of mastery and sexiness by those less wise than I. I figured the jig would be up by the third gig at the latest." (From "The Bosnian Connection," *Mid-Life Confidential,* 1994)
- **Dave "I'll Say 'Fuck the Police' If I Want To" Marsh (critics' corner):** "I never intended to become known for cross-dressing. . . . Yet . . . this is how I will best be recalled: appearing during rock 'n' roll's ultimate teen death fantasy, 'Teen Angel,' while wearing a hideous transvestite getup, stalking Stephen King from beyond the grave into the wilds of imagination, covered in taffeta and fake blood." ("Name of the Chapter—Broadway Chapter," *Mid-Life Confidential,* 1994)
- **Ridley "He Do Know Diddly" Pearson (bass and vocals):** "With the reserve lights on our fuel tanks, we were, by day, too close to empty. But not at curtain time. We became, in our own small way, professionals. . . . We took it on the road, and it worked. Every show was sold out. Every performance earned an enthusiastic encore." ("Cujo Meets the Booger Man: The Rehearsals," *Mid-Life Confidential,* 1994)
- **Joel "If You Rearrange His Name It Spells Nelvis" Selvin (critics' chorus):** "All along the way, our fellow members of the press evidenced zero interest in the Critics' Chorus. Dave Barry, yes. Amy Tan, maybe. But as long as Steve King was available, everybody was happy. 'Stephen King, Others Killed in Crash' went the joke on the tour bus." ("The Critics Chorus," *Mid-Life Confidential,* 1994)
- **Amy "If You Can't Stand the Heat, Get Out of My Kitchen" Tan (Remainderette vocals):** "We've chosen comedic songs for me, so it's part of the act, that I don't re-

member my lyrics. The songs are *These Boots Are Made for Walking* and *Leader of the Pack*. I wear costumes for both. For *Boots* I'm especially gifted. I wield a whip and at the end of the song, I tell the boys to bend over. The audience somehow forgets that I'm not a good singer, and they go wild!" (Noah Charney, *The Daily Beast*, 2013)

## Acoustic Feedback

*Entertainment Tonight* **reporter who couldn't find the Big Name Writers before a Rock Bottom Remainders concert, to Tad Bartimus:** "Where's Dave Barry? Where's King or Tan? Where are the real authors?" ("Chain of Fools," *Mid-Life Confidential*, 1994)

**Metallica (Kirk Hammett):** "Rock Bottom Remainders? Who the hell are they?" (general attribution)

**Bruce Springsteen, after playing in concert in Los Angeles with them:** "Your band's not too bad. It's not too good, either. Don't let it get any better; otherwise, you'll just be another lousy garage band." (general attribution)

**Tabitha King:** "Somebody had to do photographs for the RBR tour. Since I was going along anyway and had been seen working a camera at the rehearsal for the Anaheim ABA show, I was asked to do it. Let's get it right out front. I didn't get paid enough." ("I Didn't Get Paid Enough," *Mid-Life Confidential*)

**Stephen King:** "I usually play chords on a word processor, which is a very private thing. It was great. It was a lot of fun. . . . If nothing else, at least I've improved my guitar skills." (*Bangor Daily News*, 1992)
        **To an interviewer for Waldenbooks, when asked if there's a career he'd like to pursue:** "Yes. I'd like to play rock and roll. I play an adequate rhythm guitar but I'm not very versatile. So I guess I'll stay with writing. I kind of like it."

**Dave Barry:** "Recently I played lead guitar in a rock band, and the rhythm guitarist was—not that I wish to drop names—Stephen King." (from his newspaper article "The Great Literary Band: If You Can't Play It Well, Play It Loud")

**Diane Donovan, on their first concert:** "Were they any good, these rock 'n' roll wannabees who gamely camped their way through a generous sampling of '60s singles? Well, they probably sang better than most rock musicians can write, and with a good deal more enthusiasm. Bolstered by three 'real' musicians, ear-splitting amplification and a wildly supportive crowd of more than a thousand booksellers and publishing types, the Rock Bottoms put on a good show. Stephen King dominated center stage with his almost preternatural sex appeal, matching chords with [Ridley] Pearson and [Dave] Barry, who apparently hasn't changed a bit since 1965." ("Writers Rock at Benefit for Literacy," *Chicago Tribune*, May 27, 1992)

*Leland Gaunt from* Needful Things *illustrated by Glenn Chadbourne.*

# 66

## Needful Things

### (1991)

"I'll never leave Maine behind," King told *Publishers Weekly* (January 24, 1991), "but Castle Rock became more and more real to me. It got to the point where I could draw maps of the place. On the one hand, it was a welcoming place to write about. But there is a downside to that. You become complacent; you begin to accept boundaries; the familiarity of the place discourages risks. So I am burning my bridges and destroying the town. It's all gone—kaput. It's sad but it had to be done."

Taking the name of the town from a child's fortification in William Golding's *The Lord of the Flies,* Castle Rock is now forever linked to King. In interviews over the years, King's said that home is where you know where all the roads go; in King's case, he knows where all the roads go in Castle Rock. He has reiterated, however, that the town had become too familiar, as he did at a press conference at the American Booksellers Association convention in New York City in June 1991:

> It's easy to dig yourself a rut and furnish it. I've done that a little bit in Castle Rock. Going back to Castle Rock for me has been like going home and slipping into an old smoking jacket or an old pair of blue jeans and settling down. After a while, I started to feel excessively comfortable in Castle Rock.
>
> I don't think that's a good state for a novelist to be in, particularly if you're in my situation and you've sold a lot of books. Let's face it: When you become extremely popular and you command extremely big bucks, bloat sets in no matter what you do. I'm just trying to postpone it as long as possible.

*Needful Things* received mixed reviews, leaning toward the positive side. *Publishers Weekly*, enthusing about the book, wrote, "King bids a magnificent farewell to the fictional Maine town where much of his previous work has been set. Of grand proportion, the novel ranks with King's best, in both plot and characterization. . . . King, like Leland Gaunt, knows just what his customers want."

## THE VOICES OF UNREASON

On the negative side, in *The New York Times*, Joe Queenan gleefully took a whiz on the novel:

> Yes, the maestro of the macabre, the czar of the zany, the sultan of shock, the liege of loathsomeness, is back with another of his gruesome novels, this time bidding farewell to Castle Rock, Maine, the site of so much mayhem in his previous books. . . . If [the plot] sounds a tad adolescent, well, it is. *Needful Things* is not the sort of book that one can readily recommend to the dilettante, to the dabbler or anyone with a reasonable-size brain. It is the type of book that can be enjoyed only by longtime aficionados of the genre, people who probably have a lot of black t-shirts in their chest of drawers and either have worn or have dreamed of wearing a baseball cap backward. Big, dumb, plodding and obvious, Mr. King's books are the literary equivalent of heavy metal.

Queenan's purported review, which was in fact a hatchet job, is equally insulting to King's readers, but at this point in the game, such clueless remarks are par for the course, and King never responded. But when Professor Walter Kendrick of Fordham University attacked *Needful Things* in a review for the *Washington Post*, writing that "King has spat in his readers' faces before, and they have lapped it up," King responded and called the review "a combination of academic arrogance, elitism and critical insularity," adding that the critical approach Kendrick took "says more about his shortcomings as a reader than his subject's shortcomings as a writer." King also said:

> At one point in his jeremiad—one cannot quite call it a review—Kendrick states that I have achieved my success as a popular writer over the bleeding bodies of reviewers who have pointed out my lack of moral vision and inability to deal with any concepts larger, say, than my own bank account. That is absolutely not true. I have never stepped over a bleeding reviewer in my life. I have stepped over a few who were bleating, however, as I now intend to do with Kendrick.

## THE VOICE OF REASON

Another academic, Michael Collings, professor emeritus at Pepperdine University, offered a more balanced view. Collings, unlike Kendrick, had approached King with the benefit of having read all of King's published fiction and written several books about King for Starmont House. Collings's "take" on *Needful Things* stands in stark contrast to the book's detractors, for whom attacking and insulting King's readers is standard operating procedure. He wrote:

> What would happen if a twentieth-century reincarnation of Mark Twain's Mysterious Stranger or his equally discomforting Man That Corrupted Hadleyburg decided to open a modest shop called "Needful Things" in the small New England town of Castle Rock, and began selling dreams? Or at least what *seemed* to be the answers to dreams?
>
> In *Needful Things*, the result is a chain of initially superficial pranks that escalate into an unbroken and irrevocable sequence of interlocking horrors. By design, the actions in *Needful Things* culminate in King's starkest, most powerful confrontation to date of the Dark powers and the White. Along the way King touches upon and brings to final resolution the terrors and secrets revealed in earlier Castle Rock stories—*The Dead Zone, Cujo,* "The Body," *The Dark Half* (with echoes of *Christine, The Talisman,* and *The Tommyknockers*)—and opens his reader's imaginations to a place where love, belief, and magic tricks can fight evil to a draw. And by the end of *Needful Things,* he has also destroyed his most recognizable landscape, the haunted city of Castle Rock.
>
> If *Needful Things,* with its destruction of Castle Rock, represents a capstone to one specific segment of King's career, it is an appropriate one. The novel concludes with a sense of farewell, as readers take leave of a familiar landscape through a forceful, complex, and ultimately uplifting parable of good and evil . . . and the triumph of the good.

Nearly a quarter century later, though, Castle Rock was center stage once again, in a harrowing novel titled *Revival,* in which the lives of a young boy and a new young preacher who comes to town become intertwined, with disastrous results.

# 67

## GERALD'S GAME

### 1992

Long before Anastasia Steele, a lip-biting, virginal college coed, meets Mr. Christian Grey in *Fifty Shades of Grey*, the games—that is, the bondage games—received fictional treatment, including Stephen King's 1992 novel, *Gerald's Game*.

It's Gerald's game, though, not his wife's; and she wasn't bound to be pleased: At the last minute, she decided not to have any part in his kinky bondage fantasy, and her well-placed kick below the belt to Gerald prompted his inelegant swan dive off the bed, resulting in his death.

### A CHANGE OF SCENERY

With Castle Rock behind him—burning brightly, like the town in *Carrie*, like 'Salem's Lot, like the Overlook Hotel in *The Shining*, and like Las Vegas in *The Stand*—King turned his attention to exploring characters' interior landscapes in *Gerald's Game* and *Insomnia*. With the spotlight tightly focused on one room, *Gerald's Game* recalls *Misery*. The protagonist of *Gerald's Game*, Jessie Burlingame, is naked and has been handcuffed to a bed's headboard by her husband in their summer home, far from help, as she ponders her dilemma.

Stephen King told Terry Gross of NPR that *Gerald's Game*

> started with the concept of the woman being chained to a bed. . . . And I thought, originally, this was the takeoff point for the book, wouldn't it be interesting to see what would happen if you had one character in a room?

The question then became, what caused this woman to be in this room by herself? And the answer that I came up with was bondage. She's handcuffed to a bed. And that forced me to consider what causes people to do this sort of thing. And so once I'd set up the situation, I knew what it was going to be. I went in and read a little bit about it, and thought a little bit about it, and the whole thing struck me as a little bit Victorian. There was something very Snidely Whiplash about the whole thing, and I tried to get that into the book.

Over the years *Publishers Weekly* has spoken positively of King's books, but this one gave them pause. While admitting that it's "one of the best stories King has ever published," it noted that "[t]he gory stuff . . . is prime King, but this is subsumed in the book's general tastelessness. A lame wrap-up to what might have been a thrilling short story only further compromises the enjoyment readers might have found in this surprisingly exploitative work."

*Publishers Weekly* was not alone in its criticism. Responding to a reviewer's comment that *Gerald's Game* is more mature fare because it avoids the monsters and the supernatural in favor of realism and social relevance, Michael Collings points out that the admiration is misplaced, that the novel was being admired for the wrong reasons:

It is not that the story eschews horror, but that for the first time Stephen King subordinates his story to a specific political or social agenda. Rather than making *Gerald's Game* King's first true masterpiece, however, the decision to do so undercuts his primary strength—that of storyteller who along the way reveals important truths about human nature and social conventions.

The plot of *Gerald's Game* is straightforward, almost blunt. Gerald Burlingame enjoys (if not requires) kinky sex games, including bondage. When he handcuffs his wife, Jessie, to the headboard of their bed in an isolated cabin near an equally isolated lake . . . she decides in a moment of feminist consciousness that she doesn't have to put up with such humiliation any longer. She demands to be released; Gerald assumes that she is responding to the game and comes on anyway; she kicks him in two strategic places; and Gerald dies of a heart attack.

Leaving Jessie handcuffed to the bed.

For almost 250 pages, she tries to get loose. Then for the remaining eighty pages, she tries to adjust to post-Gerald life.

In the end, *Gerald's Game* seems more single-dimensional than one expects from King. Everything is neatly explained away, including Jessie's hallucinatory awareness that someone has been in the house with her. There seems little growth, little change. In important ways, she is still as handcuffed to herself and her past as she was handcuffed to her bed for most of the story.

# 68

## PHILTRUM PRESS

*We are, in other words, a very humble storefront in a world*
*dominated by a few great glassy shopping malls.*

—STEPHEN KING, FORENOTE TO DON ROBERTSON'S *THE IDEAL, GENUINE MAN*
(PHILTRUM PRESS)

In many ways, Philtrum Press shares much in common with other, high-quality small presses: It's small in size, publishes infrequently, operates with a skeleton crew, and takes exquisite care in the manufacture and design of its publications.

What makes Philtrum unique is that, unlike most small presses, funding is not a problem: The publisher, Stephen King, not only has deep pockets, but every publication offered for sale sells out immediately upon announcement. Moreover, the books are mostly his own, so it's self-publishing. (The exception was Don Robertson's novel, *The Ideal, Genuine Man*, about which King said he could not *not* publish it.)

All of their publications to date have been designed by Michael Alpert, who is currently the director of the University of Maine Press. (Alpert was one of the students in Burton Hatlen's writing workshop at the University of Maine at Orono, along with Stephen and Tabitha King.) Also, all Philtrum Press's printed publications are now collector's items and long out of print.

Philtrum Press publishes infrequently and maintains no mailing list.

Its first publication was *The Plant*, in chapbook form. "It's sort of an epistolary novel in progress," King said on *The Larry King Show*. "A couple of years ago, I got to thinking about Christmas cards and how mass-produced they were. It didn't seem like a sincere, personal thing. So I thought, well, I'll do this little book . . . and send it out to friends."

What made all the chapbooks unique was that each was inscribed to its recipient.

The three chapbooks, designed by Alpert, went out to friends and family. The small print run was two hundred copies plus twenty-six lettered copies.

Though *The Plant* was never completed, it's one that King's fans hope to see completed. (Parts 1-6 are currently free in two PDF downloads on King's Web site.)

"*The Plant* is a present," Stephen King explained in *Castle Rock*. "If I gave someone a coffee-maker and they sold it at a yard sale, it wouldn't bother me. If they want to sell *The Plant*, fine. It's theirs. They can tear out the pages and use 'em for toilet paper, if that's what they feel like doing. For the record, I've never seen an inscribed copy for sale. Some that are sold may be printers' overruns." (For the record, inscribed copies have gone up on the marketplace.)

Philtrum's list includes:

*The Plant*, parts 1 to 6, in PDF; parts 1-3 published as an e-book (2000)

*The Eyes of the Dragon* (1984), a limited edition, signed, and numbered hardback book, with slipcase

*The Ideal, Genuine Man* (1997), by Don Robertson

*Six Stories* (1977)

*The New Lieutenant's Rap* (1999), with some copies distributed as keepsakes at a party in New York City, on April 6, 1999, at the Tavern on the Green, to celebrate King's silver anniversary in book publishing

*Guns* (2013), an essay published in Kindle format and as an audiobook

There's room in the Stephen King universe for his books that, like *Doctor Sleep*, sold over 900,000 copies in trade hardback (*Publishers Weekly*), just as there's room for small, elegant self-published books with modest print runs, the kind Philtrum Press excels in publishing.

# 69

## NIGHTMARES AND DREAMSCAPES

### 1993

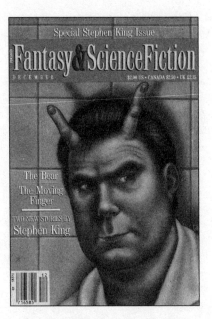

*The cover of the "Special Stephen King Issue" of* The Magazine of Fantasy & Science Fiction *(December 1990).*

I n King's lengthy introduction to this collection totaling 816 pages in the trade hardback edition, he explains that "[t]here are some genuine curiosities" in the volume and concluded that it is "an uneven Aladdin's cave of a book. . . ."

In other words, it's a stew in which King serves up something for everyone's literary tastes; there's even a long nonfiction essay about Little League baseball titled "Head Down" that at first glance seems out of place. "It doesn't really fit in a collection of stories which concern themselves mostly with suspense and the supernatural . . . except somehow it does," wrote King in his introduction.

The value of this miscellany is its breadth. Trying to find the originally published versions of these stories would be time-consuming, expensive, and frustrating. The original sources variously include a newsletter for King fans only, mainstream magazines, original anthologies, specialty magazines, small press releases, and limited edition books.

"Dolan's Cadillac" was serialized in five consecutive issues of *Castle Rock: The Stephen King Newsletter*. Inspired by Poe's "The Cask of Amontillado," King's updated version features a Cadillac. (Note: If you are claustrophobic, you may want to avoid reading this story.) It was then published as an expensive limited edition from Herb Yellin's Lord John Press, best known for its broadsides with handset type, chapbooks, and limited edition books.

"The Night Flier" appeared in an original anthology, *Prime Evil,* edited by Douglas E. Winter, a longtime King friend and author of *Stephen King: The Art of Darkness*.

"Chattery Teeth," in *Cemetery Dance* magazine, was published by the good folks at Cemetery Dance Publications, which issues more books by and about King for the specialty market than any other publisher.

"The Moving Finger" appeared in a special issue of *The Magazine of Fantasy and Science Fiction* honoring King.

"Head Down" came from *The New Yorker* magazine.

"My Pretty Pony" was published by the Whitney Museum of American Art, in what King correctly considered an overpriced and overdesigned edition. The limited edition run was composed of 280 copies, of which 150 were for sale for $2,200. The Knopf trade edition, at $50, was still overpriced for a short story, no matter how elaborate the final package. In King's opinion, "My Pretty Pony" gets the award for being a triumph of form over function: The design is wonky, the book is needlessly oversized considering that it's a short story, and it's heavy. The cover is brushed aluminum, with a liquid crystal display watch embedded on the front cover.

As for the collection as a whole, Michael Collings points out:

If there is a single flaw in *Nightmares & Dreamscapes*, it would be the lack of distinctive strength in the opening and closing selections. "Dolan's Cadillac" is a worthwhile story, but not on the same level, among King's works, as *Skeleton Crew*'s "The Mist." And putting "Head Down," a prose piece on baseball, in the final position only underscores the lack of a powerhouse conclusion such as that provided by "The Woman in the Room" in *Night Shift* and to an even greater extent by "The Reach" in *Skeleton Crew*.

On the whole, *Nightmares & Dreamscapes* offers King's readers a great deal to sample and enjoy; in the last analysis, however, it does not meet, let alone exceed, the remarkable strength of *Skeleton Crew*.

# 70

## DOLORES CLAIBORNE

### 1993

Sometimes being a bitch is all a woman has to hold onto.

—DOLORES CLAIBORNE, FROM THE FILM *DOLORES CLAIBORNE*

King fans can be divided into two camps: those who want only horror fiction, and those who want *everything* he's written.

Those in the former camp may be disappointed with *Dolores Claiborne,* but those in the latter camp are delighted. This one's a cooker.

Following on the heels of *Gerald's Game, Dolores Claiborne* is a poignant story about a woman with a justifiable 'tude honed to a sharp edge by a hardscrabble life. For any reader who wants to see the texture of Maine life from an insider's perspective, this book delivers the goods.

The title character is one of King's most fully realized and carefully drawn portraits. Dolores Claiborne is one of the most memorable in his cast of Maine characters. She's a straight-talking, no-nonsense, lifelong resident of Little Tall Island, and when she's talking, you'll sit up and pay attention.

Longtime King fans will appreciate the map of Maine reproduced in the book, which depicts the locations of all his fictional towns.

The book was also adapted as a major motion picture, released in 1995. Kathy Bates, who brilliantly acted her memorable role as Dolores Claiborne, was nominated for but did not win the following awards: the Chicago Film Critics Association Award, the

Chlotrudis Award, and the Saturn Award. To which I say: There ain't no justice in the universe.

This is a near-flawless novel, one that can stand on its own merits, though some have noted that it has a superfluous supernatural element that ties it to *Gerald's Game*. Besides that minor caveat, the novel is a classic Maine story by King, as Michael Collings explains:

> This remarkable story of an old woman's life, loves, omissions, and sins show-cases King's undeniable storytelling powers—not the least because the entire novel consists of a single, unbroken monologue. There are no chapter divisions, no bits of dialogue from other characters to break Dolores's spell. The entire story is told from a single point of view, through the mouth of Dolores Claiborne, with only momentary pauses as she listens to her questioners (although readers are never allowed to do so) and responds. The result is a work that depends for its overriding success upon an undeviating sense of character . . . and upon a character interesting enough to repay the readers' investment of time.
>
> [As he does in] *Rage, Roadwork,* and *Misery,* King very nearly steps completely out of his "horrormeister" persona to present a compelling portrait of a believable character. His story is bolstered by underlying wells of anger and frustration, not consumed by it. And his point comes through clearly and directly in the character and speech of Dolores Claiborne, without any obscuring layers of overt agenda or political correctness.

# 71

# Michael Collings on Insomnia

## (1994)

*A T-shirt design for King's* Insomnia *tour in 1994.*

*Insomnia* is probably not to every reader's taste. A long novel that threatens an odd kind of stasis in its opening chapters, it has as its hero an old man of seventy, recently widowed, and increasingly suffering from an unnerving kind of insomnia. It is not that he can't *get* to sleep but that he awakens a minute or so earlier every day until eventually he is living on two or three hours of sleep, constantly fatigued, almost hoping for death. This is a relatively long process, and King allows the novel to move slowly over the course of months, detailing the consequences of the affliction on Ralph Roberts's life and on his relationship with old friends and neighbors—some of whom simultaneously begin acting strangely, even threateningly.

Ralph Roberts discovers that he is not the only one who sees mysteriously energizing auras and little bald men carrying odd implements, or even the only one who can look on someone's aura and abruptly know everything there is to know about that person, including whether he or she (or it, in the case of Rosalie the dog) is about to die. With that discovery comes the concomitant discovery that he is *not* insane, that his insomnia has a larger purpose beyond anything he can truly comprehend, and that he and his newfound love, Lois Chasse, have been involved in actions on the cosmic scale approached in *It* and *The Talisman*. Confronting one of the little "docs" (who willingly go by the names Ralph suggests for them—Lachesis, Clotho, and Atropos, after the Greek Fates that spin, measure, and cut the thread of life), Roberts demands an explanation for their intrusion into human affairs.

He gets one.

This moment of true apocalypse is as startling as the equivalent revelation of the vampire in *'Salem's Lot*. After almost three hundred pages of text—interesting and engaging in its own way but not as focused as one usually finds in King—*Insomnia* asserts itself in one short paragraph as a linchpin in King's quest-vision, linking itself with *The Stand*, *The Talisman*, *The Eyes of the Dragon*, and the *Dark Tower* novels as explorations of that mystic nexus of all existence whose own existence is threatened by a single action about to take place in Derry, Maine.

*Insomnia* is slow-paced at the beginning, but the pace has the stolidity, solemnity, and inevitability of something approaching epic, appropriate to the incremental power of revelation and truth. As King makes connection after connection in the second half of this novel to other works and other worlds, the story takes its place as one of King's most ambitious works, attempting with *It*, *The Talisman*, and the *Dark Tower* series to penetrate the underpinnings of reality itself. And with an adroitness that demonstrates the intensity of his vision, King links the novel's earlier (mundane and therefore transitory) social and political concerns with the heightened sense of a cosmic game between the unseen forces of Light and Dark—between the Purpose and the Random. Susan Day's appearance at the Civic Center, as well as the disruption it causes in thousands of lives, also becomes the focus for this episode in the struggle for the Dark Tower and the scene of a key victory for the Purpose in the war that may have no end.

In his final sacrifice, and in its final moments—and Ralph Roberts's—*Insomnia* attains a dignity, grace, and even grandeur that place Death firmly in the pantheon of immutable cosmic forces, along with Life, the Random, and the Purpose.

# 72

## Rose Madder

### 1995

In *Entertainment Weekly*, Mark Harris opined, "When did Stephen King's books stop being so scary?" Citing *The Shining, Pet Sematary,* and *Carrie* as novels in which "the horror . . . springs from the ease with which evil can take hold of (or masquerade as) decent people," he felt that *Rose Madder* offered "no seductive ambiguity" (what does *that* mean?), with an ending that he believed was "a cheat." He gives the following reason:

> She steps through an oil painting of a toga-clad woman warrior into another world, where she has some sort of empowering experience involving a feminist goddess, a maze, a magical stream, and something called the Temple of the Bull. Temple of the Bull, indeed. In the context of a novel that means to explore the psychology of a beaten woman, the random imposition of a supernatural gimmick—especially a wan, fairy-tale-ish conceit that's about as convincing as a CD-ROM game—constitutes a rather stunning cop-out.

Or, alternatively, and more significantly, it suggests an ongoing exploration of what it means to be female in our time: *Gerald's Game* and *Dolores Claiborne* necessarily precede *Rose Madder,* which I admit is not what King's horror readers are looking for: the danse macabre.

To them, Stephen King—as Clive Barker put it—is "the architect of the most popular ghost-train rides in the world." As Barker elaborates in an essay in *Kingdom of Fear: The World of Stephen* King, "Surviving the Ride," King's fiction rockets down the roller-coaster tracks by virtue of "his charm and accessibility of his prose, the persuasiveness of his characters, the ruthless drive of his narratives."

No wonder, then, that when King's horror-hungry fans find themselves staring at a novel like *Rose Madder* in the bookstore, their appetite for such fare is curbed.

The publishers surely recognized this, since they pulled out all the stops, distributing an unprecedented number of advance copies to prime the pump: a reported fifteen thousand copies, bound in rose-colored paper covers, went out to reviewers.

Overtly addressing the theme of domestic violence, which is also at the heart of *Dolores Claiborne*, the discussion is extended into *Rose Madder*, which King said is not one of his more successful books, as he told *The Paris Review* (fall 2006):

> As the science-fiction writer Alfred Bester used to say, The book is the boss. You've got to let the book go where it wants to go, and you just follow along. If it doesn't do that, it's a bad book. And I've had bad books. I think *Rose Madder* fits in that category, because it never really took off. I felt like I had to force that one.

In her review, Laura Wise (examiner.com) noted that *Rose Madder* is what might be termed an "issues novel" given its focus on domestic violence, pointing out that the novel "isn't vampires-and-aliens horror" but "a look at the human monster": Rose's abusive husband, Norman.

W. David Atwood, writing for Book-of-the-Month-Club's monthly newsletter in 1995, summarized the plot:

> King went from high-school English teacher to one of history's best-selling authors for one simple reason: He dared to confront the 20th century's unspoken fears. The dog in *Cujo*, the teenage loser in *Carrie*, the obsessive fan in *Misery*, the fatal disease in *The Stand*, the sexual experimentation of *Gerald's Game*, the crazed dad in *The Shining*, the sleeplessness of *Insomnia*—all aspects of modern life that scare us, of which we rarely speak openly.
>
> Now, in *Rose Madder*, King takes on one of our oldest taboos, one that is very much in today's headlines and, at long last, open for discussion: domestic violence.
>
> Rosie Daniels tries hard to be a good wife, but she keeps messing up in little ways—spilling iced tea or getting caught with a racy novel. And when she does, *he's* always there, every night, to punish her. People around town respect Police Detective Norman Daniels, the handsome, well-built high school sweetheart Rosie married 14 years ago. But they don't know what goes on each night

in his own house: the carefully placed punches, the biting that leaves scars, the pencil-stabbing, or the shameful thing he did with his tennis racket.

Agreeing with Stephen King that *Rose Madder* does matter, but falls short of its goal, *People* magazine concluded, "Though this is an engrossing story of a battered woman, its supernatural elements are neither super nor natural. And that's what's the matter with *Rose Madder.*"

# 73

## CLIVE BARKER:

### DEMON FABULIST

Every body is a book of blood; whenever we're opened, we're red.

—CLIVE BARKER, EPIGRAM IN *BOOKS OF BLOOD* (SCREAM PRESS, 1985)

A s Douglas E. Winter tells the tale, he's in England, visiting Ramsey and Jenny Campbell. Doug tells them that he's currently writing *Stephen King: The Art of Darkness*. He notes that:

> Ramsey disappeared into the shadows of his writing eyrie, only to emerge with a towering stack of manuscripts: the short stories of an unpublished playwright named Clive Barker. "You're about to read the most important new horror writer of this decade," Ramsey told me. After reading only fifty pages, I was convinced that he was right.

In 1984 that towering stack of short stories saw publication by Sphere Books in the United Kingdom. *Books of Blood* did indeed herald the arrival of a new, major talent, one so bright that, as Stephen King, the reigning King of Horror, told *Time* magazine, "You read him with a book in one hand and an airsick bag in the other. That man is not fooling around. He's got a sense of humor, and he's not a dullard. He's better than I am now. He's a lot more energetic."

It appeared that the horror heir apparent had arrived—a British invasion, as it were, consisting of a one-man army. The young Brit, who grew up on Penny Lane, and whose resemblance to former Beatle Paul McCartney was unmistakable, was heralded and anointed by King, who had been given a copy of *Books of Blood* and proclaimed, "I have seen the future of horror fiction, and his name is Clive Barker." (King paraphrased Jon Landau, who said "I saw rock and roll's future and its name is Bruce Springsteen.")

Emblazoned on the back cover of the U.S. editions of *Books of Blood* (1984 and 1985), King's endorsement went a long way toward helping introduce and sell Barker to an American audience out for buckets of blood.

The horror fans rejoiced at the appearance of a new dark prince of horror, but it soon became clear that Barker never intended to write only horror fiction. A man of towering creative ambition and a talented visual artist, Clive Barker wrote books that shifted from horror and began to become increasingly complex texts, notably *Weaveworld*.

As Barker said in *The Dark Fantastic*, "To be continually engaged, to be continually excited about getting up in the morning, I need to feel like I'm pushing onto new ground. . . . My best hope for another thirty years of creation is to continue to surprise myself."

And so it is with Stephen King.

In order for him to be excited about getting up in the morning, it means finding the right story and its storytelling mode, and it's not always going to be a tale of supernatural horror. To King, and to any creative person looking to grow, the challenge is in *not* repeating oneself; the challenge is in finding new worlds to explore, which explains in part the towering edifice known as the Dark Tower with its intersecting worlds.

King's desire is that his readers join him for the ride. Sometimes it's a ride into the dark night, on the hell-bound train, with a skeletal figure as the conductor; sometimes it's immersion in a fantasy world where anything can, and does, happen; and sometimes it's looking in the mirror and seeing a reflection that doesn't look quite right.

Stephen King's canvases are large, and though not all readers will enjoy every picture in his gallery, because many of them only wish to visit his night gallery, he must follow his muse and write the books his way.

As King explained in an interview in *WB* (Nov/Dec 1989):

> The only thing that matters is the story, not the person who writes it. A writer is not a can of peas. Presumably if you buy Birds Eye frozen peas, you're going to get the same block of frozen peas every time you pick one up. But every time you pick up a novel by Stephen King or Tom Clancy or Frederick Forsyth, you are not going to get the same thing. You shouldn't get the same thing. The books shouldn't be standardized to the point where you can say, "If I pick this guy up, I know exactly what I'm going to get." If that were the case, why would anybody bother to pick up a particular book? They'd all be the same.

## Clive Barker on Stephen King

King is not old-fashioned. He is contemporary because he describes a real world. I'd say that old-fashioned horror lacks immediacy. King is a very immediate writer. I aim to be an immediate writer. We want our depictions to appear in the reader's mind with the clarity of a movie—that's part of our modernity. I want my images to be flashing—you know, wham! wham! wham!—whereas Poe and Lovecraft create a distance between the reader and the image. The experience is safer. You're detached.

—Murray Cox, *Omni* magazine, October 1986

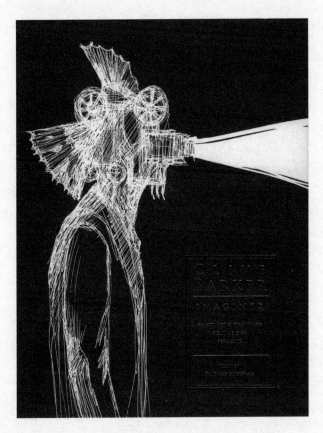

*Cover to* Clive Barker: Imaginer *(Vol. 1, 1993–2012).*

# 74

## DESPERATION AND THE REGULATORS

### (1996)

I had been toying with this idea called *The Regulators* because I
had a sticker on my printer that said that. Then one day I pulled
up in my driveway after going to the market and the Voice said,
"Do *The Regulators* and do it as a Bachman book and use the
characters from *Desperation* but let them be who they're going
to be in this story." Of course, the first thing I say when the
Voice speaks up is "Bachman is dead," but the guy just laughs.

—STEPHEN KING, *PUBLISHERS WEEKLY,* 1997

King's dual books of the 1996 bookselling season were launched with considerable
fanfare and support. New American Library's Dutton shipped 1.75 million copies in hardback of *The Regulators,* by Richard Bachman, and Viking shipped 1.25 million
copies of *Desperation.* Both bore cover art by Mark Ryden; in fact, if both books are
placed side by side, with *The Regulators* on the left and *Desperation* on the right, a contin-
uous picture is formed, visually tying them together.

Originally, when King approached New American Library about issuing the books
simultaneously, the publisher recoiled in horror. "They didn't want to do it," King recalled.

Mark Ryden art

*The combined book covers to* The Regulators *and* Desperation

Then the publisher wanted to make sure everybody knew *The Regulators* was also a Stephen King book, so they wanted to publish Bachman's *The Regulators* with cover credit to King to make the connection clear, but he vetoed that, too, because, as he told Bookwire, "you might as well then just say 'written by Stephen King.'"

King's commonsense viewpoint prevailed.

Faced with the challenge of promoting two major books by King at the same time, the hip-joined publishers pulled out all the stops. The $2 million advertising and promotion campaign included a two-for-one pack, in which both books were shrink-wrapped together, with a "keep-you-up-all-night" book light, limited to two hundred thousand sets; a floor display unit with a revolving top, stocked with a dozen copies; a special toll-free number (1-888-4-Bachman) for recorded information on *The Regulators*; abridged audios read by Kathy Bates (for *Desperation*) and Mary-Louise Parker (for *The Regulators*); thirty-second TV ads to push the paired books; and linked Web sites.

What the publishers termed the "in your face, in your mind" campaign worked as planned: King—and Bachman—fans knew the books were stacked in bookstores awaiting their arrival.

## TEMPEST IN A TEAPOT

King fans were happy to get a free book light when they bought both novels together, but when they found out subsequent customers got a little paperback with the first two chapters of his forthcoming Dark Tower novel, *Wizard and Glass,* some of the aggrieved fans complained loudly online. King's response, posted online on November 21, 1996, follows:

> Gentle Readers: It's reached my attention that there's been a fair degree of pissing and moaning about the *Wizard and Glass* booklet which comes with a dual purchase of *Desperation* and *The Regulators.* I swear to God, some of you guys could die and go to heaven and then complain that you had booked a double occupancy room, and where the hell is the sauna, anyway? The major complaints seem to be coming from people who have already bought both books. Those of you who bought the double-pack got the light, right? A freebie. So whatcha cryin' about? The booklet was my idea, not the publisher's—a little extra for people who wanted to buy both books after supplies of the famous "Keep You Up All Night" light ran out. If you expected to get the booklet in addition to the light, all I can say is sorry, Cholly, but there may not be enough booklets to go around. If you bought the two books separately, because there weren't any gift packs left (they sold faster than expected, which is how this booklet deal came up in the first place), go back to where you bought them, tell the dealer what happened, show him or her your proof of (separate) purchase, and they'll take care of you. If they get wise wicha, tell 'em Steve King said that was the deal. If you're just jacked because you want to read the first two chapters of *Wizard and Glass,* wait until the whole thing comes out. Or put it on your T.S. [tough shit] List and give it to the chaplain. In any case, those of you who are yelling and stamping your feet, please stop. If you're old enough to read, you're old enough to behave.

## *DESPERATION,* BY STEPHEN KING

The idea for the novel came to King in 1991. He had flown out to Reed College in Portland, Oregon, to retrieve his daughter Naomi's car, and driving on the way back through Ruth, Nevada, he noticed its sparse population and thought, "The sheriff killed them all." And thus was born the mining town of Desperation and its deputy named Entragian, who is not what he seems.

As King explained to Gilbert Cruz in *Time* magazine (2009):

> I was raised in a religious household, and I really wanted to give God his due in this book. So often, in novels of the supernatural, God is a sort of kryptonite substance, or like holy water to a vampire. You just bring on God, and you say "in his name," and the evil thing disappears. But God as a real force in human lives is a lot more complex than that. And I wanted to say that in *Desperation.* God doesn't always let the good guys win.

I always wanted to say that you can still reconcile the idea that things are not necessarily going to go well without falling back on platitudes like "God has a plan" and "This is for the greater good." It's possible to be in pain and still believe that there is some force for good in the universe. That certainly doesn't mean to say that everybody should go out and join the First United Church of My God Is Bigger Than Your God. That's half the trouble with the world. Maybe more.

## THE REGULATORS, BY RICHARD BACHMAN

King's unpublished screenplay, "The Shotgunners," written for film director Sam Peckinpah, was the inspiration for *The Regulators*. As King recalled in Ann Lloyd's *Films of Stephen King*, "It was a strange story of vigilante ghosts from the last century appearing in a Western town to avenge a hanging. They came not on horseback but in three, long black Cadillacs with darkened windows. Peckinpah was in preproduction when he died of a heart attack in 1984."

In a review of *The Regulators*, Robert Polito of *The New York Times* (October 20, 1996) wrote:

> *The Regulators* forsakes even the promise of genre play for generic (and interminable) Tak savagery. It transports the same cast to a mirror-image "Nevada of the mind"—suburban Wentworth, Ohio—with countless verbal echoes and many role reversals. David Carver is now father to his parents, the whiny Ralph and Ellen. Collie Entragian is a former police officer—not a satanic killing machine but disgraced, ineffectual and sad. John Marinville writes children's books about a feline detective, Pat the Kitty-Cat. And characters in this "Richard Bachman" fiction occasionally talk about reading Stephen King novels.

---

### A Bulleted Book

In what has to be the most imaginative limited edition book ever conceived for a King novel, *The Regulator*'s fifty-two lettered copies were each placed in an oversized box to make room for its spent bullet casings. Overseen by Peter Schneider and designed by Joe Stefko, of Charnel House, the Western motif is carried literally all the way through the book's design, as Peter explained in its press release:

We used a western theme. The box is basically a wooden tray case, but the book inside is bound in full grain leather, with the name, the title of the book, and the author's name branded on the spine. Protruding from the cover are the heads of four Winchester .30-.30 bullets that stick up approximately a half inch; on the back cover, the ends of the fired cartridges protrude—the little pin marks show on the back of each cartridge, since Joe Stefko actually had them fired.

# 75

## THE GREEN MILE

### MARCH–AUGUST 1996

It's just an appliance.
It's job is not to fry toast or to fry eggs
but to fry human beings' asses.

—STEPHEN KING, ON "OLD SPARKY,"
THE ELECTRIC CHAIR ON THE MOVIE SET OF
*THE GREEN MILE* (*THE GREEN MILE:
WALKING THE MILE*, 2014)

The practice of releasing works in serial form reached its height of popularity in the nineteenth century, when writers—including Arthur Conan Doyle and Charles Dickens—published novels in installments to boost magazine sales.

The practice, however, continues: Even before the renewed interest in serial publication spawned by the Internet, in 1996, Stephen King agreed to serialize a novel published in six installments as mass market paperbacks. The project was a result of a conversation about serialized fiction between Ralph Vicinanza, the literary agent who handled King's foreign rights, and Vicinanza's friend, the British publisher Malcolm Edwards, who suggested the idea. Vicinanza then approached King with the idea, and King, who is always game for a new way of publishing, wholeheartedly embraced the idea. An intuitive novelist who doesn't outline, his experiment would be a challenge, and a matter of faith.

Illustrated by Atlanta artist Mark Geyer, the books were originally published as mass market paperbacks, each priced at $2.99. The publisher cumulatively sold twenty million copies. It was a record year for King, with eight titles on the bestseller list, including the six installments of *The Green Mile, Desperation,* and *The Regulators.*

No one in book publishing history, before or after, had ever accomplished that feat. (As a result of *The Green Mile, The New York Times* changed its rules for their bestseller lists so that episodes of a serialized novel counted only as one book.)

## THE GENESIS

In an introduction that appeared in the trade paperback edition, King confessed that he suffers from cyclical insomnia and thus tries "to keep a story handy for those nights when sleep won't come." On one such night, a story came to him. He describes it as:

> a bedtime story called "What Tricks Your Eye." It was about a man on death row—a huge black man—who develops an interest in sleight-of-hand as the date of his execution draws near. . . . At the end of the story, just before his execution, I wanted the huge prisoner, Luke Coffey, to make himself disappear.
>
> It was a good idea, but the story wouldn't work for me. I tried it a hundred different ways, it seemed, and it still wouldn't work for me.

But as time passed, King thought of a way that would work, and Luke Coffey became John Coffey, whose initials are deliberately suggestive. The completed book is one of his finest works, as is the major motion picture based on a screenplay by Frank Darabont, who also directed it.

Since King doesn't outline, he in effect was driving blind in thick fog. "That is part of the excitement of the whole thing, though," he wrote in an introduction to *The Green Mile.* To an *Entertainment Weekly* interviewer, King explained that the serialization process is "old-fashioned. The opposite of instant gratification—like pushing a button online and getting something off your laser printer. Not this time."

This time, you'd have to wait to read the next installment, just like the American readers in 1841 who stood dockside in New York City to get *Master Humphrey's Clock* serializing *The Old Curiosity Shop.* In other words, no instant gratification. Better yet, from King's perspective, you wouldn't be able to turn to the last few pages to see how it ended, which he hates.

If you are prone to say, "The suspense is killing me," then *The Green Mile,* stretched out over a period of several months, from March to August 1996, was surely a frustrating experience.

As King began publishing the individual installments, it became clear that the high-wire act was going to be a success. As Ralph Vicinanza wrote in an introduction to *The Green Mile,* "The first title in the series, *The Two Dead Girls,* went on sale at the end of March . . . and within days we knew it was a hit. It zoomed to the number one position on the *New York Times* best-seller list. Sales were heavy in all locations."

After the six installments were published, they were collected as one novel of 399 pages, along with an introduction and a foreword by King.

As King frequently says in interviews, he's not interested in plot—he's interested in characters, and in this novel, we understand why: The characters drive the plot, and not the other way around. The novel is centered on a black man standing six feet, eight inches, who dwarfs the prison staff manning death row at Cold Mountain Penitentiary in Georgia.

The supporting cast includes Paul Edgecombe who realizes that there's more to John Coffey than meets the eye; a sadistic guard named Percy Wetmore, who looks down at the world from his short height; a crazed inmate named "Wild Bill" Wharton, who lives up to his name; and a mouse named Mr. Jingles, who figures largely herein.

Burdened by man's woes, by man's inhumanity to his fellow man, their cumulative weight falls squarely on John Coffey's large, broad shoulders, who must bear up under the load—or die trying.

John Coffey's numinous presence is a light that shines, even in the darkest of places: a prison's death row, in cell block E, where the green mile—named after its green-colored linoleum floor—is the end of the road for its inmates.

# PART FIVE

# SCRIBNER: BUILDING BRIDGES

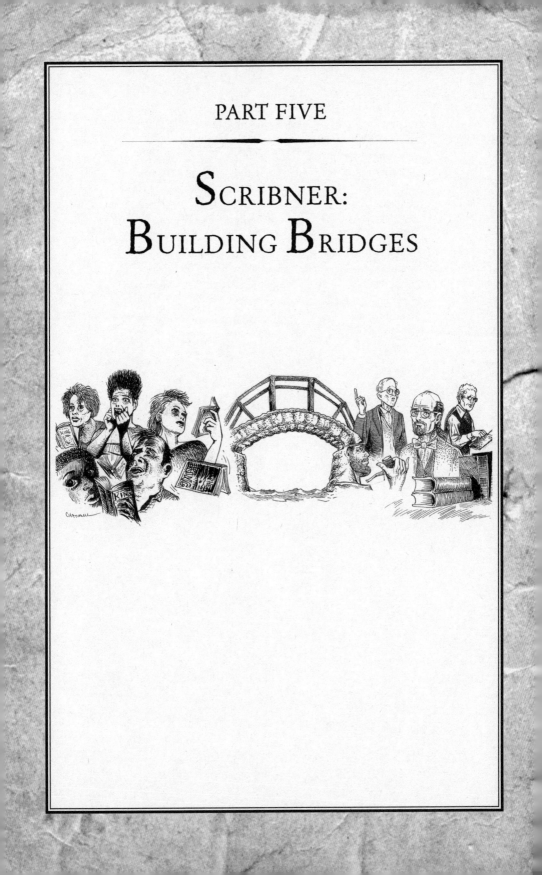

# 76

# THE WINTER OF KING'S DISCONTENT

The only guy he ever cared about was Tom Clancy. They were
both at Penguin once, and it was made clear to King that he
was seen as the second banana to Clancy. He didn't like that,
but he's very content where he is right now [Scribner].

—KING'S LITERARY AGENT, CHUCK VERRILL, *ROLLING STONE*, OCTOBER 2014

## EASY RIDER

### *Angus and Robertson Bookstore, Hurstville, Australia*

It's closing time, late at night, and the store owner is happy to see the day end without seeing any trouble in his new bookstore. Other retailers in the area have suffered robberies, which have all taken place at closing, so when he sees two men in leather jackets, worn jeans, and ass-kicking boots walk in, his heart skips a beat. One of them stands over six feet tall and looks like he could be trouble. A badass. Bad to the bone. The bookseller swallows hard. *Looks like it's my turn*, he thinks. The taller man puts his large hand in a pocket, and the bookseller gulps. *Is he going for a handgun or brass knuckles?* But out comes a fistful of dollars.

"I'd like to see your bestseller list because I probably have a few books on it," the stranger says. The bookseller, visibly relieved, finds it and hands it over to the man, who studies it carefully. "Yeah, I've got a few on here," he says.

It's Stephen King, who drove up on his Harley-Davidson motorcycle, which he arranged to have flown in from Bangor.

## *Meanwhile, in New York City . . .*

Halfway around the world, Arthur B. Greene, King's business manager, who then doubled as literary agent, was hard at work. King was unhappy with New American Library and made no bones about it. The root cause was a recent merger with Putnam, which meant that he was now displaced as king of the hill; he now occupied the number two position in book sales, clobbered by Tom Clancy, about whom King wrote, in *The New York Times* (November 9, 1998), "Clancy sells more copies than I do and [former Penguin Putnam CEO] Phyllis Grann is their rabbi, simple as that." (In her defense, in the same story, an anonymous person "said that Mr. King was nervous that the publishing house had become 'Tom Clancy's company and he had this incredible competition with Clancy.'")

No longer the belle of the ball in his publisher's eyes, King realized that the only thing missing was a bucket of pig blood. King told *The New York Post*, "Putnam brought in a very potent list . . . I'm only speculating here, but I think I was just not that important anymore to them. I got the feeling from them, 'If you want to go, go.'"

Marilyn Ducksworth, a publicity flack for New American Library, vehemently disagreed. "We wanted to continue the relationship and did everything in our power to keep him that was economically viable."

I'm speculating here, but I think that New American Library tendered its best offer and honestly didn't want to lose him but that Scribner was adamant about bagging King no matter what it took.

In terms of representing King to prospective publishers, Greene (an attorney, accountant, and longtime business manager in New York City), handled the deal in an unorthodox manner. King told *The New York Times* that Greene had "done a great job. . . . But he's not primarily a literary agent. It would not have been handled this way by an agent."

As one publisher, who had a bone to pick with Greene's method, explained to *The New York Times*, "A letter was submitted, which seemed very weird, while King was in Australia. You have a Stephen King, you pick up the phone. You don't write a letter; the publisher meets with the author."

The anonymous publisher's comments were echoed by an anonymous literary agent, who said, "You call a publisher and say, 'let's talk.' And by then, you've worked up the numbers. You don't just pull them out of the air. But it's not only about money; it's about editing, publishing philosophy, which psychology works best."

Greene, though, simply sent out letters to prospective publishers and asked for bids, stipulating the size of the next book advance (for *Bag of Bones*) to be $17 million, the royalty rate 27 percent, and a reversion clause that effectively leases the books, instead of selling them outright in perpetuity for the duration of the copyright.

At the Frankfurt Book Fair, the industry's international gathering in October 1997, the talk was about the negotiations as much as it was about *Bag of Bones*. "I know we did it the wrong way," King told *The New York Times* in an article by Martin Arnold published a month later. "Hopefully, in the end, the talk will be about the book and not about the negotiations."

## What's the Big Deal?

Scribner, FSG (Farrar, Straus and Giroux), Random House, Warner, Morrow, and Atlantic Monthly/Grove got Greene's package. They all began crunching numbers, knowing what was at stake: millions of dollars over the long run, and an author who came with a loyal, book-buying fan base. Publishing King, in short, was risk-free publishing if the terms were right.

New American Library had a lot to lose. They had a vested interest and had made a big investment in King over the years. Though New American Library gave it their best shot, their effort fell short, and in the end King made a decision to move to Scribner, whose executives were elated. It would prove to be, as they had hoped, a highly profitable deal.

The Scribner deal went well beyond a traditional author-publisher relationship. From what I understand, in exchange for a smaller advance for each book ($2 million a book), King would be partners with the publisher, not simply a client. For King, it was one hell of a good deal. The guarantee of an equitable split meant that King had a stake in the company, just as the company had a stake in him. In other words, it was symbiotic, and not a traditional publisher-author relationship, the kind that hobbled him at Doubleday in his early years.

Scribner signed his next three books, including *Bag of Bones*, which was already complete, a short story collection (*Hearts in Atlantis*), and a book on writing (*On Writing*).

Years later, in *Time* magazine, King reflected on what had happened:

> I was squeezed out at Viking, because Phyllis Grann came from Putnam, and she brought with her Tom Clancy, who sold more books than I did. There was a feeling at Viking that they couldn't support two big money writers. And I was the one that went. . . . But the people I still deal with at Scribner were people who were interested in the book rather than the reputation of the writer, which was a penny-dreadful reputation at that point. I give them a lot of credit. To some degree, they rehabilitated my reputation.

## "Bag of Treasures"

The company's executives were dancing in the streets, and for good reason: If *Bag of Bones* was any indication, King was at the top of his game. Susan Moldow, the publisher at Scribner, was quoted in a company news release:

> *Bag of Bones* is the work of a writer at the peak of his powers. It combines a story of a child in jeopardy with familiar elements from King's other works such as a haunted house, an insular and isolated community, and forces no one can control. Its story of the numbing effect of grief, the endless manifestations of the creative process and the emotional richness of an April romance, introduce a host of issues and themes of interest to a very broad readership. The book offers an emotional resonance that does not take a back seat to special effects. *Bag of Bones* is a bag of treasures for a publisher's promotional effort.

Gina Centrello, president of Pocket Books, said:

> With *Bag of Bones*, Stephen King has proven he can still delight and surprise readers. It is exciting to launch King's career with Pocket with this novel. King was one of the first writers to experiment with categories and formats—as seen recently in the widely imitated serial publication of *The Green Mile*—and has a history of making deals with publishers that emphasize growth.

Carolyn Reidy, president of the Simon and Schuster trade division, said:

> From the appearance of *Carrie* in 1974, Stephen King has demonstrated not just an ability to capture an audience of unprecedented size with more than 225 million copies of 38 books in print, but has always demonstrated a unique sensitivity to the dynamics of the publishing industry. His career has been marked by experimentation and collaboration with his various publishers.

And Simon and Schuster's Consumer Group president Jack Romanos said:

> Stephen King has proven to be as creative with his deal-making as his writing. Our partnership is based on the value of the works. The actual performance of each title will determine the profit participation. The deal structure puts priority on growing the Stephen King readership to even greater levels.

As for the author himself, King concluded: "I'm happy that the search for a new publisher has ended so successfully. *Bag of Bones* contains everything I now know about marriage, lust, and ghosts, and it was essential to me that I find the right partner to publish it."

It was a smart move for both King and Scribner, and this third time may prove to be the charm: It's a relationship that shows every sign of continuing for the foreseeable future.

# 77

# Michael Collings on Bag of Bones

## 1998

*B*ag *of Bones* was one of the strongest tales Stephen King had published in some time. Eschewing overt social criticism while simultaneously examining a number of such social issues as integral parts of the story, this new novel harkened back to the Stephen King who wrote such memorable novels as *The Shining* and *It*, yet it also suggested that he was looking forward to new possibilities.

That initial compliment delivered, it needs to also be noted that in some important ways, *Bag of Bones* resembles earlier successes perhaps only too strongly. The tone at times seems derivative—derivative of King at his best. As occurred in *The Shining, It, The Dark Half,* and elsewhere, this story focuses on the problems of a best-selling novelist confronting writer's block. Now, while writer's problems might certainly present persistent threats for a writer of King's stature (although no one has even suggested that he himself has suffered from writer's block—if anything, he is criticized more frequently for the opposite issue), their recurrence in novel after novel, story after story, makes it increasingly difficult for readers to empathize with the characters—especially, as in this case, when the writer in question, Michael Noonan, is worth over five million dollars. King does seem aware of the implicit complications involved in writing novels about novels, since he takes pains to shift his narrator-writer's chosen genre from horror to quasi-erotic romance, and then pits him against an antagonist whose half-billion fortune makes Noonan's five million seem paltry. But still, readers may have difficulty squaring precisely with the travails of a man with an abundance of ready cash, homes, and seemingly much going for him.

At heart, then, *Bag of Bones* is about humanity, about the bag of flesh and bones that encompasses each of us and links us with past and future. It is a *generational* story in several senses. Noonan's ability to generate, whether it be novels or children, remains much in doubt; William Devore, on the other hand, has generated too much—too much wealth, too much power, too much greed and ambition, and, ironically, too many children. One of his sons is gay and will never generate children; another is dead and yet has given life to Ki. Not content with exploring his role as grandparent, Devore wants to possess—metaphorically devour—Ki; and, we discover eventually, there are several senses in which his compulsion to devour ceases being purely metaphorical. Other local families face similar problems in generating lasting progeny—and we are reminded again and again of the childless adults of *It* and of that novel's close identification of adult responsibility with adult generation.

But it would not be surprising if *Bag of Bones* pointed to a shift in direction for King, as it does for his fictional author. The monsters—both human and supernatural—are sublimated to story, and in this way, King asserts triumphantly that whatever monsters may lie in the past, whatever loss and grief and death and sorrow colors the past, the future lies in human ties, human relationships, and human love.

# Storm of the Century

## An Original Screenplay

### 1999

Some folks in New England still shudder when they recall major storms of two different centuries: one in 1978 and another in 2011. I remember the 1978 storm. I was working in the Boston area and saw the city paralyzed, when the then governor Michael Dukakis shut down traffic coming in and out of the city. Out in the 'burbs where I lived, a goodly number of people, who couldn't get around by car because the roads were unplowed and impassible, took to their skis. I, on the other hand, was housebound; a transplanted Virginian, I couldn't ski. The storm in 1978 was "a classic Nor'easter. It moved up the coast, it stalled in the waters over Nantucket and it didn't go anywhere," recalled meteorologist "Dr. Mel" Goldstein of WTNH-TV, in *The New Haven Register*.

The mother of all storms, though, was the blizzard of 1888, when a record fifty inches of snow fell. History repeated itself in 2011, when a storm dumped thirty inches of snow the first day and, over three days, fifty inches total. As Goldstein remarked, "I was so amazed that, yes, I was living through a period of time that was duplicating the Blizzard of 1888!"

There's nothing like a major meteorological event to make everything in life grind to a complete halt, as depicted in the made-for-TV movie *Storm of the Century* (air date: February 14–18, 1999), based on King's screenplay of the same title, which was published in book form with his introduction.

## TRAPPED!

Stephen King has frequently used the device of being trapped in place for several novels and short stories: a town (*Under the Dome*), a supermarket ("The Mist"), a hotel (*The Shining*), a car (*Cujo*), a bedroom (*Gerald's Game, Misery*), an interrogation room ("In the Deathroom") . . . even a toilet stall and a port-a-potty (no shit).

In *Storm of the Century*, the location of entrapment is once again a town, but this time the entrapper is a snowstorm, not a massive dome that descends on the hapless townsfolk. King's screenplay is a contemporary revisiting of a time-honored literary device, "the stranger who comes to town," which recalls Richard Straker and his master, a vampire named Kurt Barlow in *'Salem's Lot* and Leland Gaunt in *Needful Things*. As King writes in the introduction to the screenplay, published in book form, Andre Linoge in *Storm*, is "an extremely evil man. Maybe not a man at all"—an entity so terrifying that Mike Anderson's wife has no compunctions about asking her husband, the constable on Little Tall Island, to ensure Andre Linoge has an "accident." In other words, she's asking her husband to kill Linoge for the good of the community; she feels murder, in this case, is justified . . . and she's right.

What makes *Storm of the Century* unique among King's publications is that it is a screenplay, though it could just as easily have been written as a novel. The $33 million production, which began shooting in late February 1998 and ended eighty days later, airing on ABC, is quintessential King. It exposes the dark heart of an insular community isolated from the mainland and left to its own devices. What's at stake: whether the townsfolk will unanimously agree to Linoge's unthinkable demand.

"Give me what I want," Linoge says, "and I'll go away."

But it's too high a price to pay. As Mike Anderson, the town constable, tells us on the first page of the screenplay, "I know one thing: in this world, you have to pay as you go. Usually a lot. Sometimes all you have. That's a lesson I thought I learned nine years ago, during what folks in these parts call the Storm of the Century." He should know. . . .

The raging storm mirrors the internal angst, indecision, and roiling turmoil that churns within each member of the community; they are forced by Linoge to literally choose between the devil and the deep blue sea.

In his introduction, King takes a neutral stance on whether a screenplay trumps a novel. "I won't argue, either pro or con, that a novel for television is the equal of a novel in a book; I will just say that, once you subtract the distractions [ads] . . . I myself think that is possible." Perhaps, but I think most people will pass over reading the screenplay and pop the DVD in their player, turn the lights low, snuggle up to their honey-bunny on the couch, and munch on popcorn while viewing it.

King explains that, like *The Green Mile*, "*Storm of the Century* also started with a jailhouse image." He elaborates:

> [T]hat of a man (white, not black) sitting on the bunk in his cell, heels drawn up, arms resting on knees, eyes *unblinking*. This was not a gentle man or a good man, as John Coffey in *The Green Mile* turned out to be; this was an extremely evil man. Maybe not a man at all.

I find it easy enough to read screenplays, and I think you will, too. The Pocket Books edition, published in 1999, I'm happy to say, provides screenshots from the TV movie, so you'll get a visual sense of the movie itself. I'm confident in saying that once you start reading the screenplay or watching the TV movie, you won't want to stop. Because, as Kathy Bates so eloquently explained when she introduced King at a public reading in New York City, Stephen King's got "the gift of gotta." Gotta read, gotta keep reading, gotta finish. *Gotta*.

And on that note, I gotta go . . . to my well-worn copy of *Storm of the Century*, because I want to again read about the mysterious stranger who is wicked bad and comes unbidden to an unsuspecting town to claim what is not his own. As a result, we are properly horrified.

---

## On *Storm of the Century*

This series also makes it clear that Steve knows a lot more about Maine than the people who put together the TV show *Murder, She Wrote*. *Storm of the Century* doesn't offer much aid and comfort to the people who want to promulgate a sentimental vision of quaint, old Downeast folks, for like most Maine natives Steve feels a good deal of ambivalence about his state: He loves AND hates it, and sometimes the love feels like hate . . . or is it plain old fear? Surrounded by all that gorgeous but inhuman nature, we can never forget how fragile are the communities that we create, and this sense of vulnerability creates a certain claustrophobia. "You mean I'm going to live out the rest of my life with *these* people?" At some point these words go through the mind of every one of us, and it is this peculiar combination of dependence and paranoia that defines the Maine character. So, too, what makes Steve King a Maine writer is his persistent, even obsessive exploration of this claustrophobic territory.

—Burton Hatlen, from joshuamaine.com

# 79

## THE GIRL WHO LOVED TOM GORDON

### 1999

The woods themselves are real. If you should visit them on your

vacation, bring a compass, bring good maps . . . and try to stay

on the path.

—STEPHEN KING, "AUTHOR'S POSTSCRIPT,"

*THE GIRL WHO LOVED TOM GORDON*

*The Girl Who Loved Tom Gordon*, King wrote in a letter to book reviewers that accompanied galleys, was Grimm's "Hansel and Gretel" without Hansel. In Grimm's grim tale, it's Gretel who saves the day; and in King's short 219-page novel, it's Trisha McFarland who saves herself. She's on her own, and her Hansel, as it were, is Tom Gordon. A nine-year-old-girl wandering in the great and terrible wilderness for nine days and eight nights, Trisha is far from home and faces possible death.

"The world has teeth and it could bite you with them anytime it wanted," King writes in the first chapter, "Pregame," and, indeed, Trisha's world is filled with predators, with something stalking her . . . and it has teeth.

What helps sustain Trisha through her ordeal is an imagined Tom Gordon (who, of course, in real life, was a Major League baseball pitcher for the Red Sox from 1996 to 1999). Listening to the Red Sox games on her Sony Walkman sustains her; and in her fevered imaginings, Tom Gordon appears to come alive.

Distracted, perhaps, by the werewolves and the vampires, the monsters within and without, readers may not necessarily notice a running thread that binds all King's fiction together: an ongoing exploration, and examination, of God. Raised in the Methodist faith, Stephen King "walked away," as the saying goes, at an early age. Life is a mystery, as King postulates in this novel, and God is even more of a mystery—the ultimate one, because it requires faith; and without faith, we, too, like Trisha McFarland, are lost in the wilderness.

But this is a story, and like the revised version of the "Hansel and Gretel" story, this one also ends well. (I don't think anyone would be surprised by that revelation.) But as King continues to ponder the nature of existence, in this world and in whatever world beyond when one "crosses over," his vision has gotten darker: King's *Revival*, for example, is not so much an exploration of God but of His absence.

Novelists write books as a form of internal dialogue, to think aloud, to make sense of the world, and to grapple with the mysterious on a regular basis.

In the end, *The Girl Who Loved Tom Gordon* is an optimistic tale.

There's room in the Stephen King universe for stories about the ghosts and the ghoulies, and the werewolves and the vampires, just as there's room for courageous little girls—the Gretels of the world—who rise to the occasion and find solace by discovering the strength in themselves to persevere and overcome obstacles, no matter how seemingly insurmountable.

Christopher Lehmann-Haupt (*New York Times*, April 15, 1999) wrote:

[R]eading the novel produces several satisfying moments of feverish terror where you can picture Trisha's bones bleaching in a sunlit landscape utterly indifferent to her being.

As the narrator puts it: "The world had teeth and it could bite you with them anytime it wanted. She knew that now. She was only 9, but she knew it, and she thought she could accept it."

Thanks to King's gruesome imagination, you as a reader feel the sharpness of those teeth.

# 80

## THE DAY THAT CHANGED KING'S LIFE
### THE ACCIDENT—JUNE 19, 1999

*The imaginative person has a clearer fix on the fact of his/her fragility; the imaginative person realizes that anything can go disastrously wrong, at any time.*

—STEPHEN KING, "A FORENOTE TO THE 2010 EDITION," *DANSE MACABRE*

The phone call came in late in the evening from Stephen Spignesi, a good friend and pop culture writer.

"Did you hear Stephen King just died?" he asked.

I thought he was kidding, but he was not. Further conversation revealed that cyberspace was abuzz with speculation about Stephen King's current condition, after the media reported that he had been hit by a careless driver in Maine near his summer home. As is always the case with breaking news, the rush to report supersedes accuracy.

The fact was that King *had* been involved in an accident in which he was seriously injured. He was struck by a van driven by Bryan Smith, or Mr. B.S., whose driving record was blemished. Put differently, he should have had his driving license revoked years before, because he was an accident waiting to happen. But the courts in Maine saw differently and continued to let him drive, even after the evidence suggested he was a danger. His list of moving violations incontestably proved that the state of Maine is reluctant to "pull" licenses from their drivers, no matter how justified.

Smith had gone out on the road because he wanted to go to the store and get a Mars bar. Smith was driving on the highway near Center Lovell, where the Kings maintain a summer home, and Stephen King was walking on the shoulder of the road when he saw Smith's minivan come over the hill, rapidly bearing down on him at forty-five miles per hour.

Because King has brilliantly told his harrowing tale—a real-life horror story—in "On Living: a Postscript," I won't repeat what he said. Instead, you should read it for yourself. But what's important here is that he realized it was a turning point in his life; depending on what happened afterward, it would either be very bad or passably good: He could die, or he would survive after rounds of operations and physical therapy. It was a throw of the dice.

"I don't want to die," he wrote in his essay, "and as I lie in the helicopter looking out at the bright summer sky, I realize that I am actually lying in death's doorway. Someone is going to pull me one way or the other pretty soon; it's mostly out of my hands." In point of fact, it was *entirely* out of his hands.

King survived his harrowing, near-death experience; and like others who have had similar experiences, he came away with four immutable truths: first, life is fragile; second, every new day is a gift, and a new lease on life; third, it's later than you think, so it's time to get your life in high gear and get what you want done; and fourth, you cherish the people in your life because they are your nearest and dearest, and everything else is a distant second.

By the grace of God—if you believe in Him, and King, like most Americans, wants to believe—King miraculously recovered, and in the years since, King has completed numerous books, including the Dark Tower series, putting an end to questions about when he'd *ever* complete it.

His other fiction, too, reflected the growing concerns of his inevitable aging. In a career known—indeed, celebrated—for fear, that old bogeyman has never left the building. What changed was only the *nature* of fear. Back when he was a new dad and a recent college graduate, his fears concerned not being able to provide for his family and his children getting injured.

Now King is a wealthy man, and his kids are adults and have their own kids. His fears are those of his fellow aging baby boomers, including the fear of memory loss from Alzheimer's disease or dementia. That he'd lose the ability to write because of mental incapacitation is King's greatest fear. For him, it'd be the equivalent of a debilitating stroke for an artist, the kind suffered by the late Frank Frazetta, an athletic, healthy man for most of his life, who was forced in his last few years to learn how to draw with his left hand after losing control of his right.

Not surprisingly, King's thoughts of death and the afterlife are increasingly the subjects of his fiction. It's one reason why King is driven to write. He knows that at his age, he doesn't have time to waste. In *On Writing* (Scribner, 2000), he expressed his exasperation of fellow writers who publish infrequently: ". . . I always wonder two things about these folks: how long did it take them to write the books they *did* write, and what did they do the rest of their time? ... If God gives you something you can do, why in God's name wouldn't you do it?"

I am reminded of what King wrote many years ago, in an essay for *Fear Itself,* which still holds true today:

But the writer's job is to write, and there are no brand names in the little room where the typewriter or the pen and notebook sit waiting. There are no stars or brand names in that place; only people who will try to create something out of nothing, and those who succeed and those who fail.

It's not a bad life. It's a writer's life. It's Stephen King's life, and he wouldn't have it any other way.

---

## "The Bonus Round" and Gallows Humor:
### An Interview by Katie Couric, *Dateline,* November 1, 1999

*In the King household, the phrase "the bonus round" is a reference to Stephen's life after the accident. (It was inspired by the TV show* Wheel of Fortune *and its "bonus round" puzzle.)*

**Stephen King:** I never shut up. I was thinking, I'd like to have an open-viewing coffin with a pull ring, so I could actually prerecord things like, "Aren't I looking natural? Isn't it nice that I didn't suffer." You know, things like that.

**Tabitha King:** And I tell him, "Don't get too excited; you're getting a coffee can. A nice, old Maxwell House coffee can."

**Katie Couric:** You are all sick.

**Stephen King:** We joke about it because we had a close one. Nobody makes you any promises. They're saying you have a good chance to walk again. Look, I'm really delighted not to be a quadriplegic. It's great to be alive, and they don't have to promise anything.

*The minivan that struck him was bought by the Kings for $1,500 through his attorney, to prevent it from being sold to fans who might try to sell pieces of it as a macabre souvenir on eBay; the minivan was taken to a junkyard, crushed into a square, and likely sold for junk metal. As for Mr. B.S., he died a year later on September 21 . . . Stephen King's birthday.*

# 81

# Hearts in Atlantis

## 1999

S tephen King was a BMOC, a big man on campus, at the University of Maine at Orono. A baby boomer who graduated in 1970, three years before the United States formally ended its involvement in Vietnam, King was an imposing figure at college. A tall man with long black hair and a beard, King manned the ramparts at student rallies and protested the ill-conceived and futile American involvement in the Vietnam War. In one yearbook photo, he's captured in an angry pose: an arm upraised as he rallies students to get involved and denounce the war.

As every military veteran says about their experiences during wartime: You had to have been there to know what it was like. But if you were fortunate enough *not* to have an all-expenses-paid trip to the rice paddies of South Vietnam, count yourself lucky. (There's been a lot of books written about the war, but if you read only one, which captured its true essence, read *Dispatches,* by Michael Herr.)

Stephen King never saw South Vietnam because he flunked his army physical. He had high blood pressure, flat feet, and burst eardrums, but even if he hadn't, he would have qualified for a student deferment. Counting his lucky stars, King sat out the war, but he sure as hell let the establishment know how he felt: He and his fellow college students supported the troops, but not the freaking war.

### The Lottery

Back then, all males eighteen and older had to register for the draft. It was a lottery, pure and simple, a spin of the wheel of fortune that, if you were lucky, kept you stateside.

The U.S. involvement in South Vietnam ended on March 29, 1973, but the war itself dragged on for another two years, and on April 30, 1975, South Vietnam was easily overrun by the North Vietnamese. We knew then that the bitter and bloody war was lost . . . and it had all been for nothing.

Not counting the MIAs, which we're still trying to account for forty years after the fact, 58,282 body bags came back, and another 303,644 troops came back wounded, their lives forever changed, and not for the better: Back then, we didn't know enough about post-traumatic stress disorder to effectively treat it.

"We blew it."

That line, from *Easy Rider*, spoken by Captain America (played by Peter Fonda) to Billy (played by Dennis Hopper), encapsulated our involvement in the Vietnam War. Tragically, it was damn true, and for that reason it became the epigraph to *Hearts in Atlantis*.

## SURVIVOR GUILT

In "There but for Fortune," a book review of *Hearts in Atlantis* in *The New York Times*, Caleb Crain writes:

> We now know what Stephen King, the master of horror, is afraid of. In *Hearts of Atlantis*, King takes up the Vietnam War, and it scares him so bad he won't let his hero act imprudently. Only the book's minor characters enlist and serve. At the last minute, and with a touch of regret, the book's central figure thinks better of flunking out of college in 1966. He stays enrolled, and he stays civilian. This time, instead of horror, King has written something with an emotional strategy much slower and much more diffuse. *Hearts in Atlantis* is a book about survivor guilt.

## TEACH YOUR CHILDREN WELL

King's dedication for *Hearts in Atlantis*: "This is for Joseph and Leanora and Ethan: I told you all that to tell you this."

Joseph (Joe Hill) is his firstborn son; Leanora is Hill's ex-wife; and Ethan is their son. In telling the stories—two novellas, two short stories, and an epilogue—that compose this book, Stephen King has written a cautionary tale for them and other young people everywhere.

Crain, in his lengthy review, calls the book "messy." Perhaps, but if it is, it certainly mirrors the nature of the Vietnam War itself, which stands at the dark heart of this lengthy 522-page book. It ends with a brief author's note that includes this illuminating observation: "Although it is difficult to believe, the sixties are not fictional; they actually happened."

These stories are not so much filtered through the war as they are permeated with it; thus the stories serve as much more than cautionary tales. They deserve to be read, and they do what fiction does best: They make us feel human.

## Coda: "Squad D"

The stories in *Hearts in Atlantis*, as far as most of King's readers know, comprise the bulk of his meditations on the Vietnam War and its aftermath, but there's another story, which serves as a coda, that remains unpublished: "Squad D," written for Harlan Ellison's unpublished anthology titled *Last Dangerous Visions*, which was originally scheduled for publication in 1973. "Squad D" is a short story that needs work, according to Harlan, who asked Stephen King for a rewrite because he thought there's more in the story than what King delivered.

As to when we will see King's story, no one—not even its editor, Harlan Ellison—knows: *Last Dangerous Visions* remains unpublished.

# 82

# On Writing: A Memoir of the Craft and Secret Windows:

## Essays and Fiction on the Craft of Writing

### 2000; ORIGINAL TITLE OF *ON WRITING: ON FICTION*

> Most of what writers write about their work is
> ill-informed bullshit.
>
> —Stephen King, foreword,
> *The Little Sisters of Eluria*

### Writer's Block

"After the accident, I was totally incapable of writing," King told Katie Couric on *Dateline*, in an interview that aired on November 1, 1999, adding:

> At first it was as if I'd never done this in my life. It was like starting over again from square one; I mean, from like being twelve, thirteen years old. There was this one awful minute when I sat there and I thought, "I can't do this. I don't know how to do this anymore."
>
> I don't know whether it was a confidence thing or whether it was a memory thing. It took about four days to actually look at the sentences and see that they still made sense. But I thought if I didn't go back to work, maybe I wouldn't go back to work.

Even before *Carrie* was published in 1974, Stephen King was fielding questions about how to get professionally published: several of his English students at Hampden Academy asked for his advice, which he gladly gave.

In interviews, at public speeches, and in profile pieces, King has generously provided detailed information on the art and craft of writing fiction, but it wasn't until 2000 that he published two books codifying his thoughts on the subject.

In the wake of the near-fatal minivan accident, King found himself suffering from writer's block, for the first time in many years. At the time of his accident, he was working on *On Writing*. In that book, he wrote, "Writing is not life, but I think that sometimes it can be a way back to life. That was something I found out in the summer of 1999, when a man driving a blue van almost killed me."

*On Writing*'s subtitle is "A Memoir of the Craft." It is organized in four sections: The first, "C.V." (curriculum vitae), is an autobiographical overview, with an emphasis on his writing efforts; the second, "On Writing," explains the nuts and bolts of how to write; the third, "On Living: A Postscript," brilliantly recounts in detail his near-fatal accident; and, last, "And Furthermore," shows King's editing process at work, using "The Hotel Story" as an example. The book ends with a detailed reading list.

I've read countless books about editing, writing, and publishing, and if I had to pick just two, I'd recommend, as does King, *The Elements of Style,* by William Strunk Jr. and E. B. White; and for a how-to manual, I'd recommend *On Writing,* for several reasons:

1. It's compulsively readable and entertaining.
2. It gives you a very good sense of what a writer's life is like.
3. The practical section is filled with time-tested advice.
4. The nonfiction essay about King's accident is a brilliant example of *how* to write. (In other words, he first tells you what to do in this book, and then shows you how to do it.)
5. He provides an example of his own editing, to show you how to tighten and improve the work.
6. He provides a useful reading list—consider it enjoyable homework.

Boiled down to its essence, King's advice is "read a lot and write a lot," which is easy to say but a lot harder to implement. Remember, King started writing in his early teens, and even then took his craft very seriously: He learned, at age twelve, how to write a professional cover letter, how to properly format a manuscript, and how to deal with editors.

King's cinematic style of storytelling developed early, but he honed it to a sharp edge over the years. By the time he submitted *Carrie,* he was an unpublished novelist but no novice: Six books had preceded *Carrie,* including two trunk novels, one of which was eventually published (*Blaze,* 2007), and four Richard Bachman books that were also subsequently published, attesting to his early mastery of storytelling skills.

If you are interested in publishing fiction professionally or want to give a young, aspiring writer a book on the subject as a starting point, *On Writing* is right on the mark.

## SECRET WINDOWS: ESSAYS AND FICTION ON THE CRAFT OF WRITING

Taking its title from a King story ("Secret Window, Secret Garden," in *Four Past Midnight*), this 431-page book from Book-of-the-Month Club is, unfortunately, out of print. BOMC has been absorbed by the Literary Guild, which has not reissued this companion book to *On Writing*.

The book's introduction, by Peter Straub, was done especially for this book, and properly sets the stage for what follows.

The book, though, needed a good editor to serve up this collection of fiction and nonfiction pieces, which are haphazardly arranged, with no contextual notes.

In anthologies, the rule is that you start and end with a big bang, so with this book, I'd put "On Becoming a Brand Name" as the lead-in piece instead of King's juvenilia and end with "An Evening with Stephen King" instead of a piece of fiction, "In the Deathroom," which is an odd choice for this collection, and especially odd for its placement as the final piece. Moreover, it's a weak story: King could have written a horrific piece but instead wrote one that reads more like a badly told joke, with stereotyped characters and an implausible plot hole through which one could drive a Mack truck.

Most of the pieces are readily available in King's other books, which makes you wonder why they appear here: the lengthy introduction to *Night Shift*; the short story, "The Ballad of the Flexible Bullet," from *Skeleton Crew*; and the introduction to "Secret Window, Secret Garden," from *Four Past Midnight*. The space would have been better utilized to reprint unpublished pieces or interviews on King talking about writing.

Perhaps the next time around—and there's plenty of pieces yet to be reprinted—King will find a capable editor who can do a better job.

Am I saying you *shouldn't* buy the book? No, I'm not. Buy it because it does have some pieces that are otherwise difficult to find, but skim the outdated pieces and give your full attention to the set pieces: "On Becoming a Brand Name" (reprinted from *Fear Itself*) and the two talks he gave to library groups, including a long one for his Virginia Beach fans.

I recommend the book but wish it had been more rigorously edited; as is, it seems rushed and thrown together in a hurry to meet a deadline; its contents are not carefully culled to serve up King's choicest tidbits of writing wisdom.

———◆———

# 83

# Dreamcatcher

## 2001; original title: *Cancer*

In the "Afternote" to *Dreamcatcher,* Stephen King wrote that Tabitha used to call this novel "the one about the shit-weasels." It's certainly an unappealing subject, but as King told *Time* magazine:

> I'd never really read a story about something terrible happening revolving around bathroom functions, eliminatory functions. And I wanted to do that because it just occurred to me that so much of the really terrible news we get in our lives, we get in the bathroom. Either because we discover a lump or because there's blood in our stool or even when you look in the mirror and all at once you say, "Shit, man, I'm going bald!" All those things happen in the bathroom. Half of really scaring people is getting them in a place that's undefended. Nobody's as defenseless as they are in the bathroom, with their pants down.

Putting all that aside, what's left in the end is, as *The Guardian* pointed out, a novel that's "slightly heavy going, but by no means a disappointment. King retains his crown."

But it's not a favorite of King's, who in 2014 told *Rolling Stone,* "I don't like *Dreamcatcher* very much." Written while under the influence of the painkiller Oxycontin, *Dreamcatcher* was the first novel he wrote after The Accident. Finding it difficult to sit up and type on his portable Mac, he wrote in longhand with a Waterman fountain pen; the ink, as well as the story, flowed out.

Recalling *It,* as four buddies from Derry, Maine, come together for their annual hunting trip in the Maine woods, *Dreamcatcher* quickly moves from the mundane to the bizarre straight out of Ripley's "Believe It or Not." But the four lifelong friends are forced to believe the impossible when things go south in a hurry, and the hunters become the hunted.

*The Guardian* said:

*Dreamcatcher* falls squarely into the baroque category, and will probably be most enjoyed by fans of *The X-Files*. . . . The first surprise is that King makes explicit reference to his accident; one of his characters is hit by a car within the first few pages. In his afterword, King explains that several elements of his physical discomfort during the time of writing followed him into the narrative, and there is a painful, nightmarish quality to much of the action.

It is a familiar device in King's fiction to have groups of characters united by a stand they have taken together in the past. Here it was a stand for good, when they stopped a gang from bullying a child with mental difficulties. It is not until much later in the novel that the men realize exactly how this good deed has changed their lives.

In short, *Dreamcatcher* is a midrange book for King. It's fun, entertaining reading, but it does show the debilitating effects of writing while taking painkillers, as well as how King persevered to pull a novel out of his imagination despite his physical and medicinal handicaps.

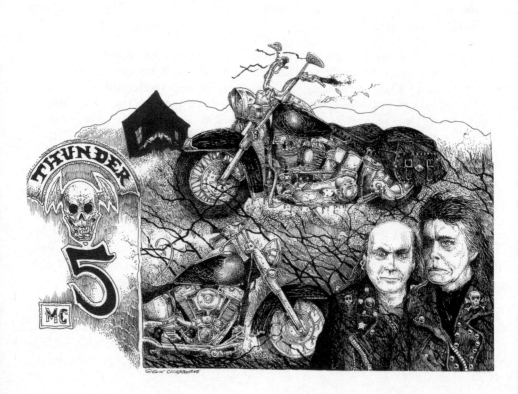

# 84

<hr>

## Black House, with Peter Straub

### (2001)

I remember working on the end of *Black House,* the book I wrote with Peter Straub, and coming to a scene where one of the characters is talking about never being able to go back to this plane of existence—American life in the year 2001 or 2002—because this person would sicken and die if that happened. And I was thinking that it was an elegant way to describe where I was coming from at that time. I was in pain a lot of the time, but when I was writing, I felt fine, because I would be…wherever you go when you're making these things up.

—STEPHEN KING, *PARIS REVIEW,* FALL 2006

When I think about the Dark Tower and all King's fiction publications that tie into it, I don't think of individual, small paintings but one large canvas that remains unfinished, because he's always adding to it. It's a "weaveworld," to borrow the title of a Clive Barker novel, in which numerous threads are intricately interwoven.

*Black House* is another part of the large canvas known as the Dark Tower.

*Black House*—a sequel to *The Talisman*—takes Jack Sawyer on another journey. At first glance, it's a journey set in this world, but that soon proves to be illusory. A former police detective for the LAPD, Jack comes out of retirement at the behest of a small-town police department in Wisconsin beset by a serial killer nicknamed "the Fisherman."

What Jack finds is more than simply the work of a deranged serial killer intent on killing, and cannibalizing, children: He finds his way back into the world of the Dark Tower through the Black House, where he's once again challenged by unimaginable and formidable forces.

Michael Collings, who admired *The Talisman*, puts *The Black House* in proper perspective, explaining that

> It is *not* a commercially-driven sequel. It is in fact a linchpin narrative bringing together—explicitly, undeniably, and utterly—the mythic worlds King and Straub have drawn, pulling them together and knotting them at the core, providing for them, as had the original Talisman itself, a "nexus for all possible worlds." Implicit in *Black House* are Straub's signal accomplishments in novels as diverse as *Ghost Story, Shadowlands, Floating Dragon,* and the Blue Rose Trilogy. *Black House* fits seamlessly into the themes, the structures, and the styles of those books, those worlds, and expands upon them to give us a glimpse of a unity underlying Straub's fictions. Even more explicitly—it links most of King's major work over the past decade and looks directly forward to what may turn out to be the capstone work of his remarkable career: the completion of *The Dark Tower*.

Collings concludes, "For anyone interested in either King or Straub, and particularly for readers caught in the wonder of the Dark Tower, *Black House* is a must."

85

## THE ULTIMATE STEPHEN KING
## HORROR STORY: RETIREMENT?

I'm done . . . done writing books."

—STEPHEN KING, *LOS ANGELES TIMES*

W hen Stephen King speaks, the media listens.
In January 2002, he told the *Los Angeles Times* that he was finally calling it quits after collecting the stories for *Everything's Eventual,* the novel *From a Buick 8,* and completing the Dark Tower series:

> Then, that's it. I'm done. Done writing books. . . . You get to a point where you get to the edges of a room, and you can go back and go where you've been, and basically recycle stuff. I've seen it in my own work. People when they read *Buick Eight* are going to think *Christine*. It's about a car that's not normal, OK? You say, "I've said the things that I have to say, that are new and fresh and interesting to people." Then you have a choice. You can either continue to go on, or say I left when I was still on top of my game. I left when I was still holding the ball, instead of it holding me.

In case people didn't get the message, the cover story for the September 27, 2002, issue of *Entertainment Weekly* shouted it: EXCLUSIVE! STEPHEN KING CALLS IT QUITS: AMERICA'S MOST POPULAR AUTHOR TELLS US WHY HE'S WRITTEN HIS LAST BOOK.
It's the one horror story King fans don't want to read.

But some were properly skeptical, including his publisher at Scribner, Susan Moldow. In a phone interview with King's hometown newspaper, she said:

> That rumor is older than Methuselah, and yet he keeps writing and publishing. I've heard him describe a novel that I know he wants to write that isn't a part of the Dark Tower series, and that doesn't seem to duplicate anything he's done before. And since he's described it to me, it would be harsh and cruel for him to withhold it from me.

Years later, King recanted, explaining:

> When I said to that lady from the *LA Times* I might retire, I was still recovering from the accident that I was in. I was in a lot of pain, and I was under the pressure of finishing The Dark Tower. At that point, retirement looked good. When the pain went away and The Dark Tower finished up, retirement started to look bad.

For King fans, it proved to be a false alarm.
Next time, Mr. King, how about *not* scaring us?

---

*The Onion,* on October 2, 2002, irreverently answered the question: "How does the King of Horror plan to spend his retirement?"

Devote more time to getting rammed by vans.

Trim front-yard hedges under alias of Richard Bachman.

Learn how to build ship in a bottle, make thousands of them.

Finally get around to cleaning out that back room where for years he'd been throwing shopping bags full of cash.

Spend more time terrifying family.

Walk slowly down basement steps, each step creaking ominously as he descends into the darkness, to grab the weed wacker.

Hit his boneless leg over and over with hammer.

Rid flower garden of woodchucks in most disturbing way possible.

Scream "No! No! Never again!" at the typewriter for six hours a day.

# 86

---

## FROM A BUICK 8

### 2002

For just cause, Stephen King hates to fly. Back in the day when he flew commercial, sitting in the first-class section, it meant being hit on for autographs because he's a celebrity. Later, when King leased commercial private jets out of Bangor International, he got the privacy he wanted, but on one Learjet flight, the air turbulence was so bad that King, strapped into the seat, fell to the ground when the seat was torn free; he was sitting sideways on the floor, strapped in, as the multimillion-dollar jet was shaken like a toy plane.

That hair-raising experience goes a long way toward explaining why King has a fear of flying. (In a dedication to *Four Past Midnight*, he wrote: "This is for Joe [King], another white-knuckle flyer.")

He prefers to drive. And when he's not listening to audiobooks on CD, he's woolgathering, mentally mulling over story ideas. It's also an opportunity for King to get off the road and plant himself on a stool at Waffle House to enjoy a cuppa coffee, a plate of waffles, and eggs with cheese. Plain food for plain folks. (He's also known to pull into rest stops and raid the vending machines for "a typical Steve King Health Meal: a soda and a candybar," as he wrote in his afterword to *Full Dark, No Stars*.)

Though King always adds extensive notes to the short fiction collections, he rarely does so for novels, on the assumption that a novel must speak for itself.

I think a lot of his readers are interested in whatever he has to say about his work, be it short or long fiction. It's an opportunity for the author to speak his mind, to share his thoughts on a novel's creation.

In the "Author's Note" to *From a Buick 8,* King explains its genesis: "I had a truckload of furnishings, books, guitars, computer components, clothes, and paper. My second or third day on the road found me in western Pennsylvania. I needed gas and got off the turnpike at a rural exit."

He went to the restroom to take a leak, and afterward, when checking out what was behind the station, he slipped ten feet down its steep grade, checking himself by grabbing onto a random something. Had he continued the downward slide into the creek, how long, he mused, would it have been before the attendants at the gas station noticed he was missing? "How long before they'd have found me if I had drowned?"

The story is set in Pennsylvania, which is where King took his tumble. Its texture can be attributed to the face time he spent with state troopers, who shared their war stories, which gives the novel its verisimilitude.

Drawn from a Bob Dylan song, the story centers on a 1953 Buick Roadmaster stored in a shed near the state troopers' barracks. As with the malevolent car Christine, this Buick is also not what it seems—and on that note, I should say no more, lest I give away too much about the plot.

The point of the novel, though, is really not the mysterious car that came from places unknown. The novel, wrote Andrew O'Hehir for Salon, "is that we don't get any answers to the Big Questions. Strange things happen, and more often than not they can't be explained. Life ends in death, and more often than not it's a horrible, wrenching experience (at least for those of us left behind). Where have the dead gone? We don't know, but from here it looks dark and far away."

The big questions, as O'Hehir said, have come to the forefront in King's fiction. But on those, he can only speculate; like the rest of us, he cannot *know.*

In the end, the book is a fun, fast read and belongs right next to *Christine* on the bookshelf. Christine, after all, is a haunted car; and the Buick 8 in this novel is haunted, but in a different, stranger way.

"The novel," said *Publishers Weekly* in its review, "isn't major King, but it's nearly flawless—and one terrific entertainment."

Fasten your seat belt and enjoy the ride.

## 87

## STEPHEN KING RECEIVES
## THE NATIONAL BOOK AWARD

I'd like to win the National Book Award, the Pulitzer Prize, the Nobel Prize; I'd like to have someone write a *New York Times Book Review* piece that says, "Hey, wait a minute, guys, we made a mistake—this guy is one of the great writers of the 20th century." But it's not going to happen, for two reasons. One is I'm not the greatest writer of the 20th century, and the other is that once you sell a certain number of books, the people who think about "literature" stop thinking about you and assume that any writer who is popular across a wide spectrum has nothing to say. The unspoken postulate is that intelligence is rare. It's clear in the critical stance; I hear it in the voices of people from the literary journals where somebody will start by saying, "I don't lower myself." But the fact is that intelligence is fairly common. What's rare is education—or it used to be.

—STEPHEN KING, *PUBLISHERS WEEKLY*, JANUARY 24, 1991

## NATIONAL BOOK FOUNDATION PRESS RELEASE
## September 15, 2003

The Board of Directors of the National Book Foundation today announced that its 2003 Medal for Distinguished Contribution to American Letters will be conferred upon Stephen King, one of the nation's most popular, imaginative, and well-loved authors.

Mr. King has published more than 200 short stories (including the O. Henry Award-winning "The Man in the Black Suit") and 40 books during a career spanning three decades. He has earned the reputation among readers and book lovers as a genre-defying stylist, vivid storyteller, and master of suspense.

The Medal will be presented to Mr. King on Wednesday evening, November 19, at the 54th National Book Awards Ceremony and Benefit Dinner at the New York Marriott Marquis Hotel in Times Square. Mr. King will deliver a keynote address to an audience of more than 1,000 authors, editors, publishers, friends, and supporters of books and book publishing. The evening benefits the National Book Foundation's many educational outreach programs for readers and writers across the country.

The annual award was created in 1988 by the Foundation's Board of Directors to celebrate an American author who has enriched the literary landscape through a lifetime of service or body of work.

The previous recipients are Jason Epstein, Daniel Boorstin, Saul Bellow, Eudora Welty, James Laughlin, Clifton Fadiman, Gwendolyn Brooks, David McCullough, Toni Morrison, Studs Terkel, John Updike, Ray Bradbury, Arthur Miller, and Philip Roth.

In making the announcement on behalf of the Board of Directors, Neil Baldwin, executive director of the Foundation, said, "Stephen King's writing is securely rooted in the great American tradition that glorifies spirit-of-place and the abiding power of narrative. He crafts stylish, mind-bending page-turners that contain profound moral truths—some beautiful, some harrowing—about our inner lives. This Award commemorates Mr. King's well-earned place of distinction in the wide world of readers and book lovers of all ages."

Mr. King will receive $10,000 along with the Medal.

"This is probably the most exciting thing to happen to me in my career as a writer since the sale of my first book in 1973," Mr. King said. "I'll return the cash award to the National Book Foundation for the support of their many educational and literary outreach programs for children and youth across the country; the Medal I will keep and treasure for the rest of my life."

## 88

# TAKE STEPHEN KING. SERIOUSLY.

I never felt a conflict in my own soul between popular fiction
and so-called literary fiction; when I sit down at the word
processor, I just do what I do. I am always disappointed,
however, when my work or another writer's work is relentlessly
ghettoized by people who would protest vehemently if blacks
were excluded from their local country club.

—STEPHEN KING, "THE BOOK REVIEW," AOL, NOVEMBER 1997

*King teaching at UMO.*

*King driving home a point about censorship at a lecture
in Virginia Beach, Virginia.*

O n one side of the bridge is popular fiction, and on the other, literary fiction, and never the twain will meet. The unbridgeability of the two is an elitist view that Stephen King adamantly rejects. In college, King was frustrated at the faculty members in the English department who had no time for popular culture, until King—an undergraduate—suggested a college course on the topic and offered to teach it. (He did so, with a front man; it was the only time at the University of Maine at Orono that an undergraduate taught a class.) Like Rodney Dangerfield, whose famous line was "I don't get no respect," popular fiction has always been dissed and dismissed.

As King told *Publishers Weekly* in January 1977, "Everyone should study [James M. Cain] in writing class, instead of the marsh gas they put out for us to admire."

What's admired, and celebrated, by the National Book Awards, is literature, the kind written by Shirley Hazzard, who won the award for fiction the same year King got an award for his contribution to American letters.

Hazzard, born in 1931, is clearly a card-carrying member of the literati: She's won several notable literary awards, including a National Book Award for fiction for *The Great Fire*.

When asked if she had ever read a Stephen King novel, she told the Associated Press, "I just haven't had time to get around to one." She further explained that she's too busy reading Shakespeare and Joseph Conrad.

It's not likely she'll ever find time to read a Stephen King novel; moreover, she doesn't endorse King's suggested list of popular culture novels. "I don't think giving us a reading list of those who are most read at this moment is much of a satisfaction," she said.

As Stephen King likes to say: Oh, man, who farted?

The popularity of King and his fellow bestselling writers is a sore point with the literati, who once commanded book advances disproportionately large in contrast to their net sales. In short, the literati saw pop writers as overpaid interlopers hogging the limelight in terms of media attention and book sales; morever, they contended, pop writers were inferior craftspeople when compared to their own work. But the fact remained that the bestselling books subsidized the literary books.

The inevitable sea change came when investors and their corporate bean counters weighed in, took control of the sinking publishing ships, and decided it was time for all authors to fish or cut bait. In the end, it was all about the lucrative catch—the bounty they brought in.

What most people present at the ceremony didn't know was that King had almost killed himself to make an appearance to accept his award. Sick with pneumonia in his right lung, King spent Thanksgiving recovering at a Maine hospital. As Warren Silver, his lawyer and spokesman, explained, "He had been walking around with it, and it got worse and worse."

King was so proud of being the recipient of an award that he had spent $60,000 for five tables for family and friends. This was his moment to shine, and he took advantage of it: He wanted to share the moment with his nearest and dearest.

The full text of King's acceptance speech is free online (nationalbook.org). It's also available as a downloadable audiofile from Amazon (*Building Bridges: Stephen King Live at the National Book Awards*). Not surprisingly, his acceptance speech is a love letter to his wife, whom he credited in large part for her role in supporting him over the years, when encouragement was sparse: Tabitha kept the faith, and kept him going when he was plagued with self-doubt and, at times, writer's block.

Stephen King graciously ended his 2003 acceptance speech:

> I want to salute all the nominees in the four categories that are up for consideration and I do; I hope you'll find something to read that will fill you up as this evening filled me up. Thank you.

## The Literati Strikes Back

Like the stormtroopers in *Star Wars* hastily putting on body armor and digging in to take offensive positions, when the committee for the National Book Awards sent out a press release announcing King as a recipient, the literati began their war of words.

In an article by *Orlando Sentinel* book critic Nancy Pate (November 19, 2003), on the day King accepted his award, critics nationwide chimed in in unison:

> Harold Bloom, quoted in *The New York Times*, said of King that "He is a man who writes what used to be called penny dreadfuls. That they could believe that there is any literary value there or any aesthetic accomplishment or signs of an inventive intelligence is simply a testimony to their own idiocy."

> J. Peder Zane (book review editor of the North Carolina *Raleigh News and Observer*): "There's nothing wrong with being elitist when you're talking about literary standards. Stephen King receiving a literary award is just another sign that we don't take books and culture seriously. We're equating arts and culture with entertainment. I don't think King being honored by the National Book Awards is a good thing."

> Dennis Loy Johnson (of Melville House, a small press): "There appears to be some confusion. No, King's not getting the National Book Award. But there's still a big difference from when Oprah got the award for promoting readership. He's an entertainer. Giving Stephen King the award is not as bad as giving Henry Kissinger the Nobel Peace Prize, but it's right up there. Being literary is not being elitist, it's just being literary. And if anyone is elitist, it's the National Book Awards because they're so expensive."

# 89

EVERYTHING'S EVENTUAL

2002

King says he has always wanted to "build a bridge between
wide popularity and a critical acceptance. But my taste is too
low, there is a broad streak of the *vulgate*, not the 'vulgar,' in my
stuff. But that is the limitation of my background, and one of
my limitations as a writer. I've got a lot of great things out of a
small amount of talent."

—STEPHEN KING, *PUBLISHERS WEEKLY*, JANUARY 24, 1991

By conventional rules, when compiling an anthology, the lead story should be the strongest in the collection, and the final piece the second strongest. In the case of *Everything's Eventual*, the lead story should have been "The Man in the Black Suit," and the final story should have been "The Little Sisters of Eluria," with its thematic suggestion that there are many open roads yet to explore.

This time, though, King used a pack of cards to determine the arrangement of the stories. No matter.

Consider the arrangement, then, like a box of chocolates without the "cheat sheet" telling you what's in each piece: Take a chance, this collection suggests, and you'll find most, if not all, of them tasty. Go ahead: Take a bite.

If you're pressed for time, though, read "The Man in the Black Suit." One of three stories in this book drawn from the pages of *The New Yorker*, "The Man in the Black Suit" won the World Fantasy Award and also the O. Henry Award for Best Short Fiction (*Prize Stories 1996: The O. Henry Awards*, edited by William Abrahams).

What levels the playing field is that all the stories for *Prize Stories* are blind submissions; they are judged on their own merits.

When Stephen King won its top prize, it took a lot of people by surprise. As Megan Harlan of *Entertainment Weekly* (May 10, 1996) wrote, "Stephen King is the inexplicable winner of this year's prestigious O. Henry first prize, for a fair-to-middling psychological horror story. . . . Perhaps this was a dry year for American short-fiction writers? Clearly not, as the nineteen other stories included are . . . overall, rich and eclectic."

She wasn't alone in dissing King's contribution: *Publishers Weekly* called it "one of the weaker stories in this year's collection."

The story had its origin in a conversation with a friend, whose grandfather claims to have had a face-to-face encounter with Satan himself. King took that idea and wrote the story, which he's said in interviews is an homage to a Nathaniel Hawthorne story, "Young Goodman Brown," published in 1835.

The weakest story in *Everything's Eventual* is "In the Deathroom." Meant to be a serious story it unfortunately reads like a parody.

But anthologies aren't graded on their worst stories; they're assessed on their best stories, and along with "The Man in the Black Suit," a short story from King's Dark Tower story cycle is compelling reading: "The Little Sisters of Eluria" strikes all the right notes and can be read as a stand-alone story, though it's obviously part of a much larger work in progress, the tapestry that is the Dark Tower series.

On that note, I strongly urge you to check out eBay and AbeBooks, since no trade edition from Scribner exists of *Little Sisters of Eluria*,[1] which includes the revised first novel in the Dark Tower series, *The Gunslinger*. This gorgeous Donald M. Grant edition also sports illustrations by Michael Whelan, which alone is worth the price of admission.

This collection, as *People* magazine points out, is "an eclectic but finely balanced group. There are some pieces that could even be called uplifting, and one ("1408") . . . that provides an almost perfect glimpse into madness. Anyone who appreciates a good yarn, especially those for whom a little King goes a long way, should give *Everything's Eventual* a turn."

---

1 The story itself is in *Everything's Eventual*.

# 90

## FAITHFUL

### 2004

I'm always bummed out on the day baseball goes back into hibernation.

—STEPHEN KING, TWITTER, OCTOBER 30, 2014

*An aerial view of the Shawn Trevor Mansfield baseball park.*

Directly behind the Kings' home in Bangor is a state-of-the-art ballpark. It was a gift to the city from its most famous residents, who dug deep into their pockets to pay $1.5 million for its construction. No one would have complained if, like other donors, the park had been named in their honor, but that's not the Kings' style.

The ballpark is named the Shawn T. Mansfield Stadium, after the late son of Dave Mansfield, who coached a Little League team that made it all the way to the Maine state championship. (Shawn, who suffered from cerebral palsy, died in 1980. He was only fourteen years old.) A plaque at the entrance to the ballpark states that it's dedicated to "Shawn Trevor Mansfield and all the other kids who never got to play baseball."

The year that the Bangor Little League team went on to win the state championship, Stephen King's son Owen was on the team, and Stephen, who was an assistant coach, was surprised at the poor state of the field; when the season was over, he decided to do something about it.

"I thought to myself, what a shame it is that [children] have to make adjustments on substandard fields with shoddy equipment. . . . It's not on par with world peace or ending hunger here in Bangor, but I was taught that charity begins at home," he told Ryan R. Robbins (bangorinfo.com, 1992).

The baseball park is now one of the most actively used facilities in the Queen City.

King and baseball go back a long way. Before he was drafted to write about sports in high school for a local newspaper, King, who grew up without a father, found that baseball filled a need in him. Even as a nine-year-old child, he watched with rapt attention the 1956 World Series on a black-and-white television.

"Baseball has saved my life," he told Bob Haskell, in *The Complete Handbook of Baseball* (1992). "Every time I needed a lifeline, baseball was it. I grew up alone. My mother worked. I was a latchkey kid before anyone knew what that was. I would watch baseball when I got home from school. I listened to the games on the radio before that."

*A plaque mounted at the entrance of the Shawn Trevor Mansfield baseball park.*

*A coach talks to the players at a game being played at the Shawn Tevor Mansfield baseball park (circa 1989).*

Unlike other small boys who played catch with their fathers in the backyard or sat next to them at baseball games or played Little League baseball with their fathers watching from the bleachers, King missed out because, as the saying went in their small family, "Daddy done gone." But baseball remained, King became a lifelong fan, and the game still plays an integral part in his life.

## CLEARING THE BASES

Life, as King has said, has a funny way of coming around full circle, and so it has with King's writings about baseball. From "Head Down," his insightful diary turned article about Little League baseball published in *The New Yorker* (1990) to a book about the Red Sox titled *Faithful*, cowritten with novelist Stewart O'Nan, King has rounded the bases all the way to home plate.

"Head Down" is the story of how Bangor West, a Little League team, made it all the way to the state championship, and won; *Faithful* is the story of how the Red Sox made it all the way to the World Series in 2004, and won—their first in eighty-six years.

But King, who frequently employs baseball metaphors when explaining his own writing career, usually strikes out with literary critics who summarily dismissed his fiction, the ones who published in such tony magazines as *The New Yorker* and in literary journals where the bona fides often mentioned grant support, which infuriated King when he was a struggling writer who didn't have resources to fall back on.

But when Stephen King published "Head Down" in the April 16, 1990, issue of *The New Yorker*, it signaled a sea change. King was establishing himself on their home turf, and the critics could no longer ignore him.

I can't help imagining some of those hifalutin literary writers sitting down at the breakfast table with scones and coffee and opening up that issue, only to find King's lengthy contribution staring them right in the face. The writer who said his work was the equivalent of a Big Mac and large fries had created literary cordon bleu: He had published in *their* magazine, and the evidence stared them in the face. King can write. In baseball terms, it was a whole new ball game. Make no mistake: Stephen King was clearly in a league of his own; he could write for the masses and for the literary crowd as well. He had, in effect, built a bridge from pop culture to literature, which he had been working toward since his college days. The two, he suggested, could coexist; they were brothers separated at birth, and shared a common heritage—storytelling.

"Head Down" is a fine piece of nonfiction writing. As an assistant coach for the team, Stephen King had a great view from the sidelines. He chronicled the young boys' hopes and dreams as they triumphed over their counterparts: On August 5, 1989, in an 11-8 victory, Bangor West won the Maine State Little League Championship.

In the movie *A League of Their Own*, actor Tom Hanks famously said, "There's no crying in baseball." Well, it may be true of pro baseball, but not so in Little League, where the young boys wear their hearts on their sleeves. As King recounted in "Head Down," at the 1989 Little League championship game, when the pitcher of the team that lost to Bangor West realized in the final moments that they were going to lose, "he begins to weep."

The essay was reprinted as the final piece in King's 816-page anthology, *Nightmares and Dreamscapes*. (The audiobook for "Head Down" was read by Stephen King.)

It's no surprise that baseball metaphors sprinkle King's conversation in interviews, in his nonfiction, and especially in his fiction: a Sandy Koufax baseball card in *Needful Things* that is prominent in the plot, and the key figure of Tom Gordon in *The Girl Who Loved Tom Gordon*. King also published a short book, *Blockade Billy*, about a promising young ball player from the game's old days named William Blakely, whose career crashed and burned. "I love old-school baseball, and I also love the way people who've spent a lifetime in the game talk about the game," said King, talking about the book.

But if you want to talk about King, baseball, and enduring love, you gotta talk about the Boston Red Sox. You *gotta*.

## SEMPER FIDELIS

On December 6, 2014, tickets for the Red Sox's spring training games went on sale. The prices ranged from $5 for a lawn seat to $48 for a home-plate dugout box. There were eighteen home exhibition games played at JetBlue Park's stadium at 11500 Fenway South Drive in Fort Myers, Florida, and my guess is that there was a tall man with square-framed wire glasses wearing a ball cap and a T-shirt, who either was holding a book to read between innings or a notebook in which to write. That man would be Stephen King, who makes his winter home in nearby Sarasota.

Just so you know, he's not there to sign autographs, and he's not there to give you advice on how to get published or how to get an agent. He's there, just like you, to watch his favorite baseball team practice before it moves back north to its real home in Boston, in Fenway Park, where hope springs eternal: The team won the World Series in 2004, and fans want to see a repeat, and a three-peat, and, well, you get the idea.

The weather's always warm in Fort Myers. I've spent my fair share of time there, because my mother-in-law made a permanent move down from Delaware to the City of Palms, as it's called. When Maine's getting hit with massive snowstorms that intimidate snowplows, sitting on a bleacher in sunny Fort Myers and watching your favorite baseball team under a clear blue sky, feeling a light breeze with the temperature in the high seventies, holding a cold brewski in one hand and a juicy hot dog slathered with condiments in the other . . . well, life doesn't get much better than that.

It's a time when the Red Sox are working out the kinks, shaking off the winter doldrums, before things get serious, really serious, when they get back to Fenway, which comes alive every spring with a packed crowd cheering on the home team as they take to the field.

In the bleachers at Fenway, you'll find Stephen King. Sometimes he's alone, and sometimes he's with a friend, but he's always got a book to read and a notebook for the down times during the game. He sometimes fills that notebook with fiction, which will get transcribed by an assistant when he gets back to Bangor, a three-hour, forty-minute drive.

King is a permanent fixture at the games. He's even thrown out the first ball of the season, but that doesn't mean he's public property, which acquisitive fans soon find out.

He absolutely doesn't sign for "graphers"—a term his daughter Naomi employed in an article she wrote for *Castle Rock*—because this is his personal time; he's just a baseball fan who happens to be a guy named Stephen King.

In other words, save yourself some trouble and disappointment and don't play the role of a demanding fan. If you want to show your appreciation, give him what he wants: Let him enjoy the game in peace, just as you'd want to do, too.

King may not mind if people come up and talk baseball—that's what they're all there for, after all—but if you ask his thoughts on how the team is going to do that year, you get his stock answer: "I'm not an expert; I'm just a fan, and I don't know. I'm hoping for the best, just like you are." (He told NPR's Michele Norris that's what he tells everyone who asks.) It's short, it's quick, and it satisfies the fan who wants to be able to go home and tell the wife, "Guess what, honey? I saw Stephen King at the game, and I talked to him for a minute."

How big is Stephen King? And how big a fan is Stephen King? Big enough on both counts that when the Red Sox published a retrospective, *Fenway Park: 100 Years,* they turned to—you guessed it—Stephen King to write an introduction, and he obliged. It's a $75 book, and according to the team's official Web site, in short supply and available nowhere else, so get it while you can.

### ABOUT FAITHFUL: TWO DIEHARD BOSTON RED SOX FANS CHRONICLE THE HISTORIC 2004 SEASON

"As far as writers go, Stewart and I were the two luckiest sons of bitches alive. Events conspired to even make it an uplifting book. . . . Thanks to the Red Sox, it even has a beginning, a middle, and an end!" said Stephen King in an Audiofile interview, on Stewart O'Nan's and his good fortune to write a book about the Red Sox during the season the team won the World Series.

King and O'Nan are buddies, now, but their professional relations got off to a rocky start. If you take a gander at the spine of the first printing of Stewart O'Nan's novel *The Speed Queen,* you'll notice something odd: There's a white bar running down its length, with black text overprinted: "*The Speed Queen,* Stewart O'Nan, Doubleday." What's underneath that white bar is *Dear Stephen King,* the original title, which King hated, spurring his lawyers into action. Obviously, by the time Doubleday got the legal complaint, it was too late to stop the presses. Either the books had already been printed and bound or the cover boards, in black, had already been printed. Regardless, the publisher was forced to go back and overprint.

"I loved the book, hated the title. I felt he was using me," King told Audiofile.

In "Necessary Evil," an original article written for *Phantasmagoria,* a King zine, Stewart O'Nan explained, "*The Speed Queen, Dear Stephen King*—by any name, the book is a hot, funny, sexy, wild ride. It's fast as hell and I think the voice is the best I've done. Go to the work, and you'll see."

The legal entanglements aside, good writers admire good writing, and King saw that O'Nan had the goods. They also shared something else in common: They are both Red Sox fans, and in time became fast friends that collaborated on a nonfiction book titled

*Faithful*, a chronicle of the 2004 season in which the Red Sox won the World Series. In King's essay, in the back part of the book, he paints a word picture:

It may still be March in the Northeast, with air as raw as hamburger and snow up to David Ortiz's belt buckle, but as the Boston Red Sox take the field against the St. Louis Cardinals here on the afternoon of March 16 for a World Series rematch, it feels like midsummer in Florida; the sunshine is hazy, the temperature is a humid 80 degrees, and the clouds over the Gulf of Mexico promise thunderstorms later.

King's piece largely discusses his thoughts on "The Question" posed to him from a Rhode Island newspaper reporter, in response to which, he says, "I cunningly answer I don't know, because I want to answer it here and get paid for it."

If you want to find out what "The Question" is and pay King for it, buy the book: I ain't gonna tell ya. But what I *will* tell you is that *Faithful* is a 445-page love letter to King's favorite baseball team, and as such it's worth reading.

Think about it: In *Faithful*, we read how the Red Sox went on to win the World Series, even though they hadn't won one in nearly nine decades. You can't ask for a better ending to a book.

That's life, that's baseball, and *this* time, in the big leagues, there was no need for crying . . . unless you're a Cardinals fan.

---

## "Not in My Lifetime. Not in Yours, Either"

In *The Shawshank Redemption,* Andy Dufresne says, "Remember, Red, hope is a good thing, maybe the best of things, and no good thing ever dies."

The same can be said of the Red Sox's legion of fans who are true believers at the start of every season, hoping to see their team get to the World Series and, once again, win.

Michele Norris of NPR interviewed King for "Stephen King on Baseball's Spring Training." It aired on March 16, 2005. In the piece, King explains that, before the miraculous 2004 season, he despaired of ever seeing his team win a World championship, hence the words he figured would be engraved on his tombstone: "Not in my lifetime. Not in yours, either."

King now has to pick different words for his tombstone.

As Norris explains, for Stephen King, the Red Sox are "an addiction," not merely a passion. "I generally find a way to finagle tickets, although I have to tell you this year has been an extremely tough 'get' as far as Red Sox tickets go," said King. "The feeling is one of possibility, endless possibility, anything can happen at that point in the season; everybody is tied for first place."

# 91

# STEWART O'NAN: AN INTERVIEW

## BY HANS-ÅKE LILJA
### NOVEMBER 18, 2004

**Lilja: How is *Faithful* going? I'm guessing that you had a lot of work to do recently since it'll be out in about a week, right? Was it your or the publisher's choice to put it out so soon after the Red Sox won the World Series?**

**Stewart O'Nan:** *Faithful* is done, or at least it's at the printer. We had expected all along to have the book in stores by early December, no matter how the team did. The fact that they played all the way until October 27th made us work a little harder, but it was definitely worth it. And the publishers, realizing they now had an even more special book, decided to move the publication date up to November 22nd. But Steve and I both work quickly and cleanly, and they counted on that.

**Lilja: How happy were you and Stephen when they won? It's almost too good to be true that they won the same year you decide to write a book about them, right?**

**Stewart O'Nan:** It's still a bit of a dreamy feeling. Remember, the Red Sox hadn't won the World Series for eighty-six years. Whole generations of Sox fans never got to see them win it all. Steve thought he'd never see it in his lifetime. So now, when I'm just sitting somewhere doing something, I'll remember: "Oh yeah, the Red Sox won the World Series," and I can't help but smile.

**Lilja: How did you and Stephen decide to write the book?**

**Stewart O'Nan:** Steve and I have been going to games together for years. We e-mail and talk about the team all the time, and last year in August when the team got hot, Steve decided we should keep a log of our reactions to their games. This spring, when the season was about to start, my agent asked if I wanted to write a book about the Red Sox (every year he asks me this, but this year I'd just finished a novel and finally had the time). I said I'd write it only if Steve could be my coauthor. Steve was busy, but said he'd try to contribute as much as he could. And once the season got going, his natural love for the game kicked in and he couldn't stay away.

**Lilja: How was the book written? Was it hard to write with someone else compared to writing alone?**

**Stewart O'Nan:** The book is in a double-diary format. For each game or Sox-related issue that we found interesting, we'd write separate entries. There are also e-mail exchanges on hot topics. Essentially, the book is a season-long conversation between two supremely interested fans. Working with another writer, in this case, was easy, since as fans we basically agree about what's important. In drafting pieces about players or the games, there was some overlap, but in those cases I'd just edit out any redundancies.

**Lilja: Is this your first collaboration?**

**Stewart O'Nan:** No, I once wrote a screenplay about the life of Clara Schumann with novelist A. Manette Ansay. That was much more difficult, as we didn't quite agree on the role of Brahms or her many children in her life.

**Lilja: On the first two covers for the book it said "Stewart O'Nan with Stephen King" and not "Stewart O'Nan and Stephen King." Now, on the final cover, it only lists both your names. Can you explain why? Did you write the majority of the book?**

**Stewart O'Nan:** I'm not quite sure why they have our names that way, other than that's what the publisher wanted for stocking purposes (that is, how it's listed in bookstores' computers). I'm not sure what the word count or page count is, but I can safely say I wrote a majority of the text.

**Lilja: I remember that you wrote a book you wanted to call *Dear Stephen King* (later renamed *Speed Queen*) some years ago. I then heard (don't know if it's true) that Stephen wouldn't let you use his name in the title. Is that correct, and if so, did he give you a reason? And now you're writing a book with Stephen King. Are there any hard feelings about the *Dear Stephen King* title?**

**Stewart O'Nan:** Yes, the whole *Speed Queen* flap was over using Steve's name, and now that I've spent time with him, I see why. Everyone wants a piece of him. So no, there are no hard feelings. He's a prince of a guy, very giving.

**Lilja: Why did you use Stephen's name when you wrote *Speed Queen* and not just some fictional name? Were/are you a fan of his books?**

**Stewart O'Nan:** I used the name because it made sense to me that, to my character, Stephen King would be the only person who would understand her. He's a confessor-judge figure for her, and for all of America. He understands our deepest hopes and fears (or so she hopes!). And yes, I'm a huge fan of his work, always have been. Without his work—and Ray Bradbury's—I would have never become the reader and writer (the person) I am.

**Lilja: I heard some time ago that Christina Ricci was going to star in and direct a movie version of *Speed Queen*. What happened to that project?**

**Stewart O'Nan:** Christina Ricci was supposed to direct and star in the movie version of *Speed Queen,* but could never make time in her schedule to make that happen. As it turned out, she ended up playing a similar role in *Monster,* so I sometimes wonder if she was just blocking our project to make sure it didn't get in the way of that one. *Speed Queen* apparently will get done, as the option was just exercised.[1]

**Lilja: Do you think there is any chance Stephen will play himself in the movie if it's ever done?**

**Stewart O'Nan:** The screenplays that I've seen don't even deal with that aspect of the book. I think the flap over the title scared the producers.

**Lilja: You have written quite a few books yourself, such as *The Good Wife: A Novel* coming in April 2005. What kind of books would you say you write? Horror? Drama? Fiction? All of the above? And which one would you recommend to someone who hasn't read any of your books before?**

**Stewart O'Nan:** *Speed Queen*'s a wild satire of American appetites, and a great departure from my usual stuff. I tend to write two kinds of novels—pastorals and gothics—and sometimes combine the two, as in *A Prayer for the Dying* or *The Night Country.* Even my first novel, *Snow Angels,* has that mix of stillness and foreboding in it. In my best work I'm trying not just for surface effects, but something more real and heartfelt. Those are my favorite kinds of books and movies, so it makes sense. For someone who's never read my work, I'd recommend *Snow Angels* first.

---

1 The movie has yet to appear.

# 92

# THE COLORADO KID

2005

*Cover to* The Colorado Kid *by Stephen King from Hard Case Crime books.*

*A lobster design on an outside wall at a York, Maine restaurant.*

A s Chris Chesley pointed out, Stephen King always had his nose in a book; most often, a paperback book, because in those days neither Chris nor Stephen could afford hardbacks. (It wasn't until King struck it rich with the paperback sale of *Carrie* that he could afford to buy hardbacks on a regular basis.)

King has written before about how there's always time to read, if you take advantage of those moments in life when there's nothing else to do to pass the time. Take small sips, he wrote in *On Writing*; not everything has to be consumed in a big gulp.

Sipping books works for King. In his underground library located beneath his garage at his main Bangor home, there are seventeen thousand books on its shelves, which represent the books the family has read: The Kings consume books like most people consume peanuts.

If you had to pick one representative photo of King, it's a *Bangor Daily News* staff photo showing King with a book in hand, leaning up against a brick wall in downtown Bangor.

King's first love was paperback books, and publishing *The Colorado Kid* as a mass market paperback was his way of paying homage to the mass market paperback book format he remembered seeing as a kid on spinner racks at the drugstore in Durham, Maine. Published by Hard Case Crime, whose book covers often feature nubile girls in various states of undress, the cover for *The Colorado Kid* is a visual come-on: The buxom brunette in a black dress, shapely legs crossed, is holding up a microphone; her bemused expression invites self-confession.

But readers thinking it's going to be a salacious book are in for a rude surprise: The cover is misleading, as *USA Today*'s Carol Memmott noted: "The real question may be the identity of the sultry brunette on the book's cover. There's no one like her in the story."

You can't always judge a book by its cover.

At the end of the book, there's a big surprise, and it's a doozy. Sometimes seeing is believing, and nothing else can substitute. You'll know what I mean when you read this book.

## THE PUBLISHER'S BACKSTORY

The original book, in mass market paperback, lacks an introduction. The U.K. hardback edition, though, sports "Birth of the Colorado Kid," written by Hard Case Crime publisher Charles Ardai, who explains

> I was minding my own business when a call came in from Steve's agent and long-time editor, Chuck Verrill. "Steve asked me to give you a call," he said. "He wanted me to let you know that he does not want to write you a blurb—"
>
> "Of course," I said. "I understand completely. That's completely understandable."
>
> "—because," Chuck went on, "he wants to write you a book."
>
> I sat on the other end of the phone while this sank in and tried to sound cool, like this was the sort of phone call I get every day and twice on Fridays. But inside I was turning cartwheels.

The submitted book, though, wasn't *quite* like any of the other books published in the Hard Case Crime lineup, which may have disappointed some of the publisher's hardcore readers. But I submit that any book publisher blessed with a new King novel should stay calm and publish well, even if it's not a perfect fit.

*The Colorado Kid,* as Charles Ardai wrote in his piece, "is an unusual and ambitious book, a tale about frustration that some readers have found frustrating—to which I answer *Yes, exactly, that's the whole point!*"

In this instance, King's afterword proves illuminating because he explains the why and wherefores, and though it may be small comfort for the frustrated readers who wanted a definitive resolution to the story, King still delivers a well-told tale: I liked the interplay between two old salts, journalists who share a small office at the *Weekly Islander* at Moose-Lookit Island, and their avuncular relationship with the pretty, young college graduate who is their intern. I liked the leisurely telling of the story, which mirrors the relaxed pace of life on the small island. I especially liked its element of mystery, which as King stated in his afterword is not insoluble.

King explains in his afterword that life itself is an unfathomable mystery:

> Where do we come from? Where were we before we were here? Don't know.
> Where are we going? Don't know. A lot of churches have what they assure us are
> the answers, but most of us have a sneaking suspicion all that might be a con-job
> laid down to fill the collection plates.

This really isn't a Hard Case Crime book in the traditional sense; in fact, the only crime associated with the book was when an advance copy went missing and showed up on eBay, where it was auctioned off for $1,623.

If you're a King fan who passes this one up because it's not horror, I'd say that's not a crime—a misdemeanor, maybe.

Read the book and see what you think. Better yet, read it carefully and see if you can figure out the mystery. But don't be surprised if it flies over your head; some things, after all, can be found only with hard evidence, and others things only with faith.

Glenn Chadbourne

*A Maine seascape*

# 93

---

## How to Speak Like a "Mainah"

In a short piece at goneengland.about.com, "Speak Like a Mainer," Debby Fowles, who returned to her native Maine after seeking her fortune elsewhere, gave some good advice on how to "speak like a Mainah."

I suspect Steffie, in *The Colorado Kid*, would have appreciated this advice because it would have been easier for her to fit in with the old-timers at the paper.

Here's Fowles's advice:

The key is to relax your jaw. Say "Mainer." Notice the tension in your jaw and how it opens only slightly. Now say "Mainah," letting your lower jaw drop on the "ah" paht (er, I mean "part"). Practice saying it in an exaggerated manner to get the feel. Now you're ready for the rules of Mainespeak.

1. Words that end in "er" are pronounced "ah." Mainer = Mainah. Car = Cah. Mother and Father = Muthah and Fathah. Water = Watah. You get the drift.

2. Conversely, words that end in "a" are sometimes, but not always, pronounced "er." California becomes Californier. Idea becomes idear. Yoga becomes Yoger.

3. Drop the "g" in "ing." Stopping and starting = stoppin' and startin', or more correctly, stoppin' and stahtin'.

4. Broaden *a* and *e* sounds. Calf becomes cahf. Bath becomes bahth. Can't becomes cahn't.

5. Drag out some one-syllable words into two syllables. There becomes they-uh. Here becomes hee-ah.

Fowles also recommended the humorist Tim Sample's Web site (timsample.com), and helpfully provides her favorite Maine words or phrases, of which I'm listing only a few, to give you a taste:

**Ayuh**: Yup. Sure. Okay. That's right. You bet.

**Cah**: A four wheel vehicle, not a truck.

**Cunnin'**: Cute.

**From Away**: Not from Maine.

**Numb**: Dumb. Stupid.

**Wicked**: Very. To a high degree, such as wicked good, wicked bad, wicked exciting.

---

## A Mainer on Actors' Maine Accents

### *Dave Lowell*

Although the dialogue and Maine accents ring true in King's fiction, Hollywood seems to have a difficult time getting it right on film.

Not only are Mainers usually portrayed in a stereotypical fashion (missing teeth, poor hygiene, uneducated and trapped in poverty), but the accents are often so far off the mark that Mainers are embarrassed.

Only a handful of Hollywood actors have gotten it correct, but most butcher the accent completely, sounding more like a Scotsman than a true Mainer.

Among those who have succeeded are Kathy Bates and David Strathairn in *Dolores Claiborne*. Strathairn who portrays Joe St. George is right on the money. Practically flawless. Ed Lauter's accent is okay as Joe Camber in *Cujo*. Fred Gwynne's is fairly convincing as Jud Crandall in *Pet Sematary*, and although purposely comical, Stephen King did a great job as Jordy Verrill in *Creepshow*, but the truth is, most actors simply fail when trying to tackle a true Maine accent. They are often so far over-the-top that the situation turns into a parody.

# 94

## Cell

### 2006

It was an instant concept. Then I read a lot about the cell-
phone business and started to look at the cell-phone towers. So
it's a very current book, but it came out of a concern about the
way we talk to each other today.

—Stephen King, *Paris Review*, fall 2006

Here's a question for King fans: How much would it be worth to you to be fictionalized as a character in a Stephen King novel?

For Pam Huizenga Alexander of Fort Lauderdale, Florida, that would be $25,100.
But it wasn't for her; it was for her father, who owns the Miami Dolphins. He appears
in the novel *Cell* as one of the good guys, a construction worker whose specialty is
explosives. But, of course, it being a King novel, he meets an untimely end, which is why
King cautioned prospective bidders:

> One (and only one) character name in a novel called *Cell*, which is now in
> work. . . . Buyer should be aware that *Cell* is a violent piece of work, which
> comes complete with zombies set in motion by bad cell phone signals that de-
> stroy the brain. Like cheap whiskey, it's very nasty and extremely satisfying. . . .

In any case, I'll require physical description of auction winner, including any nickname (can be made up, I don't give a rip).

The rest of us sprung for the book at its retail price of $26.95.

A cautionary tale about technology gone amok—think *The Tommyknockers*—inspired by George Romero's *Dawn of the Dead* zombie movie, *Cell* is the story of an impoverished Maine artist named Clayton Riddell who is in Boston when the Pulse hits, turning cell phone users into zombies.

If only . . .

"Stripped of social constraints, the Pulse people create a Hieronymus Bosch tableau of hellish depravity," wrote Janet Maslin of *The New York Times*. "They can be found reeling, staggering, biting their own mothers or fighting over Twinkies." (Truth is stranger than fiction: As I was writing this, a story on a local television station, WAVY 10, told about an arrest after a man in Newport News, who bit his mother in a fight, was charged with malicious wounding.) Maslin continued:

> The cell-from-hell premise gives this story an instantly powerful book. But there are times when the book threatens to become all hook and no fish. Though *Cell* is not unduly long, it moves slowly and somewhat repetitively along its highway of horrors. And Mr. King is in no hurry to build upon the Pulse idea after he has deployed its initial shock value.

As King told *The Paris Review*:

> I came out of a hotel in New York and I saw this woman talking on her cell phone. And I thought to myself, What if she got a message over the cell phone that she couldn't resist, and she had to kill people until somebody killed her? All the possible ramifications started bouncing around in my head like pinballs. If everybody got the same message, then everybody who had a cell phone would go crazy.

Eli Roth, who was set to direct it for Dimensions Films but in the end did not, had a great take on how he'd handle it, in a story reposted on a Stephen King fan Web site, Lilja's Library:

> I love that book. Such a smart take on the zombie movie. I am so psyched to do it. I think you can really do almost a cross between the *Dawn of the Dead* remake with a "Roland Emmerich" approach (for lack of a better reference) where you show it happening all over the world. When the pulse hits, I wanna see it hit EVERYWHERE. In restaurants, in movie theaters, at sports events, all the places that people drive you crazy when they're talking on their cell phones. I see total Armageddon. People going crazy killing each other—everyone at once— all over the world. Cars smashing into each other, people getting stabbed, throats getting ripped out. The one thing I always wanted to see in zombie movies is

the actual moment the plague hits, and not just in one spot, but everywhere. You usually get flashes of it happening around the world on news broadcasts, but you never actually get to experience it happening everywhere. Then as the phone crazies start to change and mutate, the story gets pared down to a story about human survival in the post-apocalyptic world ruled by phone crazies. I'm so excited, I wish the script was ready right now so I could start production. But it'll get written (or at least a draft will) while I'm doing *Hostel 2*, and then I can go right into it. It should feel like an ultra-violent event movie.

The movie, which at the time of writing is in postproduction, is set to come out in 2015, directed by Tod Williams. (Roth explained that he told Dimension Films' Bob and Harvey Weinstein, "I'm not really interested in doing the film [your] way. You guys go ahead and I'm going to make my own films.")

Given the book's zombie apocalypse, *Cell* was bound to take a few knocks. Dave Itzkoff, reviewing it for *The New York Times* (February 5, 2006), confuses King himself with King as writer. "They say it pays to steer clear of one's heroes, and after reading *Cell*, I can honestly admit I am scared as hell about the prospect of ever crossing paths with Stephen King. Because if King regards actual human beings the same way he thinks about the characters in his latest novel, his passion for enforcing rules of etiquette would most likely place him somewhere on the spectrum between Emily Post and Vlad the Impaler."

Just so you get the point—or in this case, the shaft—Itzkoff adds, "In *Cell*, the author's latest work of sadistic wish fulfillment, his wrath is largely directed at those little Lucifers who have cast God's natural order into disarray by talking constantly on their cellphones ('the devil's intercoms,' as one character calls them)."

Well, you can't win them all.

Bookslut's Ned Vizzini, though, sees things differently. While admitting it's "not a hopeful book," he explains that "[t]his is less a horror novel than one of extreme pessimism. Whatever cell phones are a stand-in for . . . it is here, now, and it can bite us at any time. The apocalypse takes away a lot of responsibility, and our fascination with it is in part due to our desire to escape through it; once the bombs go off, we won't have to pay our cell phone bills anymore. King is here to remind us that when we pick an apocalypse, we had better take seriously what we're talking about."

Now that's a message we can all understand and appreciate. In other words, *Cell* is, like *The Stand*, a cautionary tale for our times. Trust me, Dave Itzkoff, *Cell* is not about King sublimating his anger; it's about King sounding an alarm, if only we'll listen.

# 95

## LISEY'S STORY

### 2006; ORIGINAL TITLE: *LISEY LANDON*

That one felt like an important book to me because it was about
marriage, and I'd never written about that. I wanted to talk
about two things: One is the secret world that people build
inside a marriage, and the other was that even in that intimate
world, there's still things that we don't know about each other.

—STEPHEN KING, *ROLLING STONE*, NOVEMBER 6, 2014

### STEPHEN KING WAS A "BAG OF BONES"

At "Dialogue with Stephen King," a public talk on November 3, 2006, in Beverly Hills, King recounted the inspiration for *Lisey's Story*: Recuperating from the run-in with a careless driver on June 19, 1999, Stephen King, in an ICU room at Central Maine Medical Center in Lewiston, was, as he put it, "a bag of bones." He had dropped thirty-five pounds and now weighed 145 pounds, and it showed. His wife, Tabitha, told him, "I'm going to take this opportunity to redo your study." (Stephen's writing room is on the second floor of his main Bangor home.)

When he was finally released from the hospital and sent home, he noticed the door to his study was shut.

"I wouldn't go in there," Tabitha said. "It's disturbing."

He refrained, but because of his insomnia, he was up at two A.M. and decided to take a look at his study.

"I did go in there and it was disturbing because all the books were off the shelves and in cartons. The rugs had been rolled up, and the furniture taken away for reupholstering. I thought, this is what it would look like if I died. I feel like a ghost in my own study; I feel like a ghost in my own place. This is what it WILL look like when I die, because I will, and somebody will have to clean this place out, and have to go through all the papers and inventory them, and see what I've left behind, what's worth keeping, and what needs to be taken to the library collection [at the University of Maine at Orono]. A light went on in my head. What if someone wanted to steal those papers, and they came in and started to bother Tabby about it? That became *Lisey's Story*."

King cites *Lisey's Story* as his personal favorite among all his works and cautions readers, despite the obvious similarities to his real life, that it shouldn't be taken as a portrait of his marriage.

Sam Leith of *The Guardian* wrote that the book "also has serious and moving things to say about the private language of marriage and the workings of grief, about relationships between siblings, about where fiction comes from and how it works. . . . I think *Lisey's Story* stands among the best things this formidable writer has done."

Ron Charles of the *Washington Post* proclaimed:

With *Lisey's Story*, King has crashed the exclusive party of literary fiction, and he'll be no easier to ignore than Carrie at the prom. His new novel is an audacious meditation on the creative process and a remarkable intersection of the different strains of his talent: the sensitivity of his autobiographical essays, the insight of his critical commentary, the suspense of his short stories, and the psychological terror of his novels. . . .

But what works beautifully throughout *Lisey's Story* is the rich portrait of a marriage and the complicated affection that outlives death. Who would have thought that a man who's spent the last 30 years scaring the hell out of us would produce a novel about the kind of love that carries us through grief?

Bestselling novelist Nora Roberts, who wrote that King had "hooked me about three decades ago" wrote that

With *Lisey's Story*, King has accomplished one more feat. He broke my heart.

*Lisey's Story* is, at its core, a love story—heart-wrenching, passionate, terrifying, and tender. It is the multi-layered and expertly crafted tale of a twenty-five year marriage, and a widow's journey through grief, through discovery and—this is King, after all—through a nightmare scape of the ordinary and extraordinary. Through Lisey's mind and heart, the reader is pulled into the intimacies of her marriage to bestselling novelist Scott Landon, and through her we come to know this complicated, troubled and heroic man.

*Lisey's Story* is bright and brilliant. It's dark and desperate. While I'll always consider *The Shining*, my first ride on King's wild Tilt-A-Whirl, a gorgeous, bloody jewel, I found, on this latest ride, a treasure box heaped with dazzling gems.

# 96

## BLAZE

### 2007

*B*laze is likely the last Richard Bachman book to be unearthed from King's fabled trunk. Its publication history goes back to early 1974, when William G. Thompson had gotten two manuscripts, *Blaze* and *Second Coming* (a preliminary title for *'Salem's Lot*), for consideration as a follow-up to *Carrie*.

Thompson wisely chose *Second Coming*, and King was well on his way to becoming a brand-name horror writer.

As King wrote in the afterword to *Different Seasons*, *Blaze* "was a melodrama about a huge, almost retarded criminal who kidnaps a baby, planning to ransom it to the child's rich parents . . . and then falls in love with the child instead." King explained that it was something of a literary imitation of John Steinbeck's short novel *Of Mice and Men*.

Blaze (born Clayton Blaisdell Jr.) recalls John Coffey of *The Green Mile*; both are outsiders, large men with dreams that are doomed to fail. Failure is a central theme in both works, just as it is in *Of Mice and Men*, through its depiction of Lenny.

In an introduction to *The Short Novels of John Steinbeck*, Joseph Henry Jackson wrote that in *Of Mice and Men* Steinbeck is championing

the man-without, the dispossessed, who nevertheless cherished The Dream. But something else should be noted. Because he was the artist, Steinbeck also saw that the reasons The Dreams failed, would always fail, lay with Man himself. It would have been simpler to declare that Man's frustrations might all be laid at the door of an evil social system.

So it is with both Blaze and Coffey, who are tragic figures doomed to fail.

In the summer of 1974, Stephen King and Eric Flower, then the special collections librarian at the Fogler Library at the University of Maine at Orono, discussed the possibility of Stephen King depositing his papers at his alma mater. In November 1975, Flower followed up. King, as it turned out, had gathered a large quantity of manuscripts for the collection. In 1980, King added three unpublished novels, including *Blaze*.

The library's collection is a treasure trove for King researchers that contains unpublished material, which used to include *Blaze*, which had gone undisturbed until 1988, when I spent a week reading it and the other two unpublished manuscripts, "The Aftermath" (a science fiction work of juvenilia) and "Sword in the Darkness" (a lengthy novel about a race riot).

*Blaze* recalls the famous 1932 kidnapping of Charles Lindbergh's son and also *Of Mice and Men*. King's fusion of the two yielded a rich novel, a tragic story about Blaze, who we know will come to a bad end.

In an interview with Hans-Åke Lilja (posted on Lilja's Library), Stephen King explained his thoughts about *Blaze*:

> I have been thinking about [*Blaze*] off and on for a while . . . I did the early books as Richard Bachman books, and this is going to be a Bachman because it came from the same time. It was written right before *Carrie* . . . the reason I've never done it was because it was a tearjerker of a book.

The original dedication to *Blaze*, which was submitted for publication in 1973, read: "This book is for my mother, Ruth Pillsbury King."

The book was published in 2007, with a new foreword to explain its history. It's an atypical novel, certainly for a King book, but even for a Bachman book. Nonetheless, the short novel enjoyed generally positive reviews. David J. Montgomery of the *Chicago Sun-Times* wrote, "By showing us the tortured life that [Blaze] has suffered since childhood, *Blaze* makes us feel for this poor, damaged man. We don't excuse his crimes—it's unlikely that anything could make us do that—but in the end, we do at least understand."

Once again, it's helpful to go back to Steinbeck for context.

In Jackson's introduction to *The Short Novels of John Steinbeck*, he quotes a letter from Steinbeck to his publisher: "My whole work drive has been aimed at making people understand each other." Stephen King shares this impulse, which is evident in much of his work, including *Blaze*. "Steinbeck is always aware of mankind's weaknesses, frustrations, failures, grotesqueries," writes Jackson. And so is Stephen King.

# 97

# THE HAVEN FOUNDATION:

## A PLACE FOR FREELANCE ARTISTS

Among King's books, *Blaze* is unique in one regard: All the income from the book goes to fund the Haven Foundation, which exists to provide money to freelance artists who have suffered a catastrophe, especially health-related, resulting in financial ruin.

King, who had health insurance when he was struck by a minivan near Center Lovell, sued Commercial Union York Insurance Company for $10 million, "claiming it didn't provide full coverage for the injuries he received," according to the *Bangor Daily News* (February 13, 2001).

ABC News reported that "Attorney Warren Silver said the $10 million insurance policy will not cover all of his client's losses from the accident. He estimated that medical bills, future surgeries, and lost writing income as a result of the accident would add up to between $65 million and $75 million."

OneBeacon, which took over coverage from Commercial Union, settled for $750,000, which King donated to the hospital that treated him, Central Maine Medical Center in Lewiston. Both parties agreed it was best to avoid prolonged and costly litigation.

But King, unlike most freelancers, is wealthy, and he can weather almost any financial storm. As he told *Rolling Stone* in an October 2014 interview, he's debt-free, which can't be said for most people in the country.

It certainly wasn't true of the late Frank Muller, a classically trained actor who turned to voice narration to make a living; he read numerous books in unabridged form for Recorded Books. On November 5, 2001, Muller was riding his motorcycle when he had a near-fatal accident, sustaining severe head trauma that required seven expensive and painful surgeries. Unlike King, though, Muller had no health insurance and wasn't wealthy. From his Web site:

Frank lost control of his motorcycle on the freeway when he accidentally clipped a construction barrel and was sent skidding into a median barrier at about 65 miles per hour. Frank flew off the bike, landing on his head on the concrete. He sustained multiple fractures, lacerations and abrasions, and went into cardiac arrest three times. He suffered severe head trauma, which was subsequently diagnosed as Diffuse Axonal Injury.

His career as a reader for Recorded Books ended abruptly that day, and he never worked again. Muller, though, was fortunate to have a good friend in Stephen King, who held a benefit in 2002 to raise money to fully cover Muller's medical bills. King, recognizing that Muller wasn't alone, later set up the Haven Foundation: Many freelance artists are pursuing their craft on a wing and a prayer, hoping they'll stay healthy, but when sudden illness strikes and they're faced with debilitating medical injuries that even insurance (if indeed they have any) won't cover in full, life becomes a matter of not only physical but financial survival.

Frank Muller, though, passed away in June 2008 as a result of complications from the injuries he sustained. As King wrote on the Haven Foundation's Web site (www. thehavenfdn.org),

My luck was infinitely better than Muller's, but the two events set me thinking about the uniquely perilous situation of many freelance artists. The majority of mid-list writers, audio readers, and freelancers in the book and publishing industry have little or no financial cushion in the event of a sudden catastrophic accident such as that suffered by Muller and myself.

The foundation accepts donations. For more information about the foundation and how to donate, contact it through www.thehavenfdn.org/contact-us.

# 98

## DUMA KEY

### 2008

There's a charm-bracelet of keys lying off the west coast of
Florida. If you had your seven-league boots on, you could step
from Longboat to Lido to Siesta, from Siesta to Casey. The
next step takes you to Duma Key, nine miles long and half a
mile wide at its widest, between Casey Key and Don Pedro
Island. Most of it's uninhabited, a tangle of banyans, palms and
Australian pines with an uneven, dune-rumpled beach running
along the Gulf edge. The beach is guarded by a waist-high band
of sea oats. . . . I know nothing about the history of Duma Key.
I only knew one reached it by crossing a WPA-era drawbridge
from Casey Key.

—STEPHEN KING, *DUMA KEY*

King is fond of saying that home is where you know where all the roads go. Lifelong Mainers, the Kings know where all the roads go in "Vacationland" (Maine's
state motto on its license plates), but the *real* Vacationland is Florida, where the climate
is hospitable year-round, the pace of life relaxed, the locals are friendly, and the seafood
is always fresh.

Annually, during the heart of winter, Stephen and Tabitha drive down to Florida, leaving the Bangor homes with caretakers; King returns by car in the spring, followed a month later by Tabitha, who flies back.

Having lived in Florida for over a decade, the Kings know where all the roads down there go, too. Now, as sure as the sun rises over the palm trees on the Keys, King can find horror lurking even in the "Sunshine State."

King told Gilbert Cruz of *Time*:

If *Desperation* is a book that's full of pain and unhappiness, *Duma Key* is a book where there actually is hope, because I was feeling in a more hopeful place. The two books are really the polarities of my recovery from my accident. I was feeling a lot better by the time that I wrote *Duma Key,* and I think it shows in the book.

This time, the main character is not a writer or teacher—both occupations he knows well—but an artist, which is a departure from his norm, as King readily admits he's no artist.[1] Set on the west coast of Florida, on Duma Key, a Minnesota contractor named Edgar Freemantle barely survives an on-site accident after a crane crushes his truck. He survives, but with significant injuries: He loses his right arm and also suffers from mental maladies—memory, vision, and speech problems. Filled with rage, he contemplates suicide. His wife also divorces him, after he attacks her.

Because life is falling apart around Freemantle, he seeks help from his psychologist, Dr. Kamen, who asks him what he enjoys doing. Freemantle tells the shrink that he used to enjoy drawing, and Kamen suggests he take that up again, and so he does. Freemantle also moves to Florida, to Duma Key, to recover; he takes up brush and paint and slowly recuperates.

In King's fiction, there are several characters with paranormal powers: Carrie is telekinetic, Johnny Smith is precognitive, and Charlie McGee is pyrokinetic. Enter Edgar Freemantle, whose power is the ability to manipulate people, places, and events through his paintings; and he does so, with devastating effect.

Janet Maslin of *The New York Times* starts out her review of the book noting that, given the author and the setting, Dire Things Will Happen:

Stephen King's *Duma Key* ventures to an all-but-uninhabited Florida island where the shells groan at high tide, tennis balls appear unexpectedly, foliage grows ominously quickly, and at least one heron flies upside-down. Given this combination of author and setting, it's inevitable that something terribly un-dead will show up before the book is over.

And it does.

---

1 King, though, did draw a cartoon for auction to benefit the Back Alley Theatre, which sold for $225 in 1987. It showed a sun setting behind a tombstone bearing the words: "Planet Earth / Someone Hit the Wrong Button / July 11, 1992 / RIP."

In Alison Flood's review for *The Guardian*, she too remains close-lipped; after all, loose lips sink ships. . . .

I'm not going to explain what the horror is, because I don't want to spoil it for you. But rest assured, if you've been burned by not-all-that-scary-when-the-evil-is-revealed Stephen King novels in the past—*The Tommyknockers, Dreamcatcher*, I'm looking at you—the horror "inbound on rotted sails" in *Duma Key* is properly terrifying. Built up too slowly as Edgar makes friends with Wireman, who looks after an old lady with secrets of her own living down the beach, it's given me no end of the jitters. Just what I was after. . . . For me, it was his best book in ages and the ending, although admittedly a little drawn out, more than justifies the slow build-up.

Flood explains that King, once again, has delivered the goods as the book reaches its climax:

[I]n these scenes toward the end, King not only thickened the shadows and made things move in my peripheral vision, he kept me awake for hours afterwards while every image he'd drawn came at me out of the dark. I didn't go to sleep til it was light outside.

So there you go: horror for the beach, and even set on a beach, just to make it even more perfect.

# 99

## THE KINGS' MAIN HOME IN FLORIDA

In Bangor, tourists and fans make privacy impossible for the city's most famous couple, but Florida hasn't quite been a haven, either. The Internet makes it impossible to have privacy: On YouTube, for example, there's a fan-shot video of a leisurely drive up the main road that terminates in a roadside view of the Kings' home near Sarasota, Florida.

I recall that even before King showed up in Sarasota, a newspaper reported the impending move and quoted one man who said that when King arrived, he'd inquire about possibly putting on a "Stephen King Film Festival" to honor King. (It never came to fruition.)

The plain facts, according to a story in the *Chicago Tribune*: King, in 1999, rented a condo on Longboat Key, and in 1987, he had toured the Florida house he eventually bought in 2001 for $8.9 million, a record sum for a house in that area.

The house has three bedrooms, four bathrooms, and an outdoor swimming pool. As Neil Gaiman described it, in a profile piece for *The Sunday Times* magazine in the United Kingdom:

> Stephen King's house, on a key in Florida near Sarasota, a strand of land on the edge of the sea lined with houses, is ugly. And not even endearingly ugly. It's a long block of concrete and glass, like an enormous shoebox. It was built, explains Tabby, by a man who built shopping malls, out of the materials of a shopping mall. It's like an Apple store's idea of a McMansion, and not pretty. But once you are inside, the glass window-walls have a perfect view over the sand and the sea, and there's a gargantuan blue metal doorway that dissolves into nothingness and stars in one corner of the garden, and inside the building there are paintings and sculptures, and, most important, there's King's office. It has two desks in it. A nice desk, with a view, and an unimpressive desk with a computer on it, with a battered, much sat-upon chair facing away from the window.
>
> That's the desk that King sits at every day, and it's where he writes.

According to the local paper, *The Sarasota Herald-Tribune,* King sightings are common:

> He has been spotted at the movies, at his beloved Boston Red Sox spring training game both here and in Fort Myers, at concerts, at Publix and browsing at Barnes & Noble.

He even drops by independent bookstores to sign book stock.

Back in Bangor, King tools around in several vehicles, including a Mercedes. Down in Florida, though, he gets a real charge driving the family's electric cars, including a Chevrolet Volt. And although Bangor is his main Maine haunt, Sarasota's environs are now his home away from home, where the streets are lined with palm trees, the roads are lined with sand, the weather is perfect year-round, the breezes are always welcome, and the palm trees throw dark shadows across an idyllic landscape, because King has come to town.

---

## Touring "Duma Key"

On the visitflorida.com Web site, we're told that "there's nothing more thrilling than spending a day tracking down . . . many of the colorful, tropical sites and settings [King] mentions" in *Duma Key,* which are "actual shops, restaurants and galleries located in Sarasota and on the nearby keys."

The Web site cites several examples:

> Your self-guided tour will take you from reading on the beach to reading in the Selby Library, where Freemantle [the story's protagonist] gives a lecture in the story. Nearby, stylish Palm Avenue beckons with its high-end art galleries—though the Scoto Gallery, where Freemantle shows his work, is a King invention—and Main Street's boutiques and restaurants.

> If you're especially interested in gourmet rations, you can follow Freemantle's path as he forks his way through Ophelia's on the Bay on Siesta Key and Verona, the beautiful dining room at the Ritz-Carlton (though he masks the latter with a different name). And if you're incredibly thorough, you can cover even the must mundane mentions, such as Dan's Fan City.

> But readers of all stripes enjoy two sites for sure: the John and Mable Ringling Museum, and the out-of-the-way establishment that King mentions by way of clothing and construction: Casey Key Fish House, where the conch fritters are crunchy and the vibe ultra-casual. After supping on almond-crusted snapper, like King's protagonist you can don a tank top emblazoned with the eatery's logo before you can challenge the one-lane drawbridge.

---

---

# Just After Sunset

## 2008

Look, let's be frank with each other:
When all of us are forgotten, people will still be remembering
Stephen King.

—CRITIC LESLIE FIEDLER,
TO A GROUP OF POSTMODERN WRITERS

In 1978, when King published *Night Shift*, his first collection of short fiction, one story, "The Last Rung on the Ladder," was singled out by John D. MacDonald because it stood in sharp contrast to the others, which are all horror stories.

In 2008, when King published *Just After Sunset*, we find the opposite: Only one story is a traditional horror story: "The Cat from Hell," originally published in *Cavalier* magazine (March 1977). The remaining stories in *Just After Sunset* are more mainstream, the kind of fiction to be found in *Playboy*, *The New Yorker*, *The Paris Review*, and *McSweeney's*, which in fact is where some of the stories in this collection originally appeared.

From horror fiction to mainstream fiction, King has indeed built a bridge from pop culture to literature.

What's interesting is that although "The Cat from Hell" is in fact a bona fide supernatural horror story, there's another tale that recalls King's dictum from *Danse Macabre*, in which he wrote, "I recognize terror as the finest emotion. So I try to terrorize the reader. . . . But if I find I cannot terrify, I will try to horrify. And if I cannot horrify, I'll go for the gross-out. I'm not proud."

In "A Very Tight Place," King does just that: he goes for the gross-out. It's about a man who is trapped in a portable outdoor potty and has to plumb its depths. King, as a writer, likes to break new ground; he likes to go where no man has gone before, just as the protagonist does in this story, which is a harrowing reading experience for claustrophobes, germophobes, and especially coprophobes. It's a crappy story, if you get my drift, though you'll have to read the story for yourself to see what I mean.

The other stories in this collection, though, are thankfully devoid of fecal matter.

Not surprisingly, two deal with death. (There's a reason why the book's epigraph quotes from Arthur Machen's classic story "The Great God Pan." King has cited it several times in his books, most significantly in *Revival,* because of its impact on him.)

In the hardback edition published in the U.S., one will find a DVD sealed and bound in a paper sleeve. The DVD contains a visual version in comic book format of a story intriguingly titled "N." In the liner notes, King writes: "When the idea was pitched to me, I said okay at once, not because I was sure it would work but because new delivery systems interest me and turn my engines . . . although not as much as the core story, which remains the basis for everything."

Charles Taylor, in his review for *The New York Times,* says the collection is "uneven . . . in both tone and execution, and it often reminds you of how King's writing has moved beyond its genre roots."

Had King stayed exclusively within the genre, his career would have suffered the same fate as the others who were rooted in place: He would have seen his readership move on when their taste for horror abated. But King broke new ground, and his faithful readers followed.

I could name scores of horror writers who rushed to fill the void when *The Shining* came out. Hoping to score sales off of King, their book titles sounded similar, as he noted: "I won't mention any by name. But I see a lot of books that must have been inspired by some of the stuff I'm doing. For one thing, those 'horror' novels that have gerund endings are just everywhere: *The Piercing, The Burning, The Searing*—the *this*-ing and the *that*-ing."

Even when King was twenty-five years old and writing short fiction for *Cavalier,* he gave a good bang for the buck; he never cheated the reader, never took the easy way out, never pandered. In *Night Shift,* with the exception of one story told in epistolary form, *all* the stories were optioned for motion pictures and several were made, from the sublime (a "dollar baby" by Frank Darabont, *The Woman in the Room*) to the ridiculous (*Children of the Corn* and *Lawnmower Man*).

This collection, though admittedly uneven, is still impressive. As Taylor pointed out in his review:

> So let's be clear. King isn't good because he's popular. But any critic who puts King's popularity down to the dreadful taste of the masses (cue Harold Bloom) has failed to do the basic work of a critic, which is to understand and probe and not simply to judge. King gets to readers because he renders everyday life so exactly and because he understands it is always ready to rupture.

Taylor falls short of saying King is a literary writer, but NPR's Lizzie Skurnick makes no bones about her assessment of King's work: "After years of advocacy from fans and critics, several appearances in the *New Yorker*, and the 2000 publication of his marvelous *On Writing*, it is now generally agreed that Stephen King is as 'literary' as any moody Whiting-award nominee."

In his review of *Just After Sunset*, Matt Thorne of *The Independent* sees only two clunkers in the collection, arguing that "the other 11 stories in this collection are all brilliant and, taken as a whole, this is King's finest book of short fiction since 1985's *Skeleton Crew*."

## The Story Behind "The Cat from Hell"

Glenn Chadbourne

GLENN CHADBOURNE

I came across this marvelous photo of a cat's face (from UPI, I believe) and half of it was black and the other half white. And it looked very intriguing. I thought up the idea of a short story contest to be based just on that photo. Then I thought how much more interesting it would be if Stephen would write just a short beginning to the story to kick off the contest and writers would then expand on it. So, I sent the photo off to Stephen and he wrote back shortly after, enclosing a complete short story titled "The Cat from Hell."

"I can't write part of a story," he explained. "That would be like having half a baby. So, take part of the story for your contest and then perhaps you'd like to publish my story in its entirety later on as a comparison with your contest winners, or do whatever you wish with it." Which is what happened: We published the winning story, which was very good, and then the next month we published "The Cat from Hell" in its entirety.

—Nye Willden

# IOI

## Under the Dome

### 2009

> The dome is a microcosm of life. We all live under the dome.
> We live on this little blue planet and so far as we know that's
> all we've got. The resources that we've got are the resources that
> we've got; they're finite.
>
> —Stephen King, *The Telegraph*, 19 August 2013

The genesis of this 1,072-page novel goes back to 1976. King tells us in his "Author's Note" that he wrote seventy-five pages before abandoning it. In a Simon and Schuster video interview, King explains that in 1979 it was *The Cannibals*. "It was great to work on a big canvas again," he explained. As he told *The Telegraph*:

> It was a time around when gas prices started to shoot up and OPEC decided they were the tail that wags the dog. Then came Chernobyl and concerns about pollution and global warming. For the first time, people started to ask: "What are we doing to our planet?" I thought, why not put all these people under a glass dome and see what happens to them?

As King told *The Telegraph*, he thought about it more, which prompted more questions. "What if you have someone in power who is making bad decisions and you can't get out? What if you have diminishing resources, diminishing propane, diminishing gasoline, diminishing food, water, medicine?"

He revisited the story on November 22, 2007, and completed it on March 14, 2009, as noted in the book.

Like the residents of Little Tall Island, who are held hostage by a freak blizzard, the residents of Chester's Mill are imprisoned—this time, by a translucent dome that encapsulates the town, sealing it off from the rest of the world. The inversion of normality brings out the best in some people, and in others, like Chester's Mill's James "Big Jim" Rennie, the worst.

When its police chief is killed, Big Jim, who runs a used-car lot, steps up to assume command as the town's second selectman. One of his first tasks is to appoint a new police chief, Peter Randolph, who is clearly incompetent. He then deputizes others, including his son, as he lays down the law, and the situation soon becomes—as Big Jim would say—a "clustermug." (It's a polite variation of a popular, albeit obscene, military expression.)

As Stephen King explained to *The New York Times*:

> I was angry about incompetency. . . . Sometimes the sublimely wrong people can be in power at a time when you really need the *right* people. . . . I want to use the Bush-Cheney dynamic for the people who are the leaders of this town. As a result, you have Big Jim Rennie, the villain of the piece. I got to like the other guy, Andy Sanders. He wasn't actively evil, he was just incompetent—which is how I always felt about George W. Bush.

The good guys are led by a former army lieutenant, who is recalled to active duty and received a "jump-step" promotion to full colonel. Major, maybe, but full bird? No. But the authorities feel that law and order under the Dome, which is quickly descending into lawlessness and disorder, is best restored by a military veteran who needs the gravitas of high rank, because they feel Big Jim is simply rank.

Just as Mrs. Carmody and her disciples unite against David Drayton and his followers in "The Mist," the warring factions in *Under the Dome* split between Big Jim and Dale "Barbie" Barbara.

As the drama unfolds, the body count escalates. A town of more than a thousand people suddenly dwindles dramatically as life grows progressively worse.

## ECOLOGICAL DISASTER

As I am writing this, California is enduring a severe and long-term drought. It's gotten so bad that farmers are being forced to drill to deeper depths, tapping into the groundwater, which, among other side effects, is causing land above the water table to collapse as its water is depleted.

*Under the Dome* sounds an ecological alarm. We live, as King cautions us, in a world of dwindling natural resources that we're exploiting at an unsustainable rate, as he told James Lileks of *The Minneapolis Star Tribune*:

From the very beginning, I saw it was a chance to write about the serious eco-logical problems we face in the world today. The fact is, we all live under the dome. We have this little blue world that we've all seen from outer space, and it appears like that's about all there is. It's a natural allegorical situation, without whamming the reader over the head with it. . . . We're a blue planet in a corner of the galaxy, and for all the satellites and probes and Hubble pictures, we haven't seen evidence of anyone else. There's nothing like ours. We have to conclude we're on our own, and we have to deal with it. We're under the dome. All of us.

As one character opines in the novel, "Who in their right mind would ever have expected this sudden contraction of all resources? You planned for *more than enough*. It was the American way. *Not nearly enough* was an insult to the mind and spirit."

But the novel wouldn't hold water if it was simply King on his soapbox. What makes it work is the Dickensian cast of characters reacting to the anomalous event and interacting with the others as their plight becomes more problematic and life-threatening.

*Under the Dome* is also King's take on the Peter Principle—a person is promoted to his level of incompetency—as seen through a political lens: Big Jim is a thinly disguised Dick Cheney, and the clueless, newly installed sheriff is a thinly disguised George W. Bush. (One more character, a thinly disguised warmongering Donald Rumsfeld, would have rounded it out.)

As King joked on his Web site, there's no place like dome, which is true: Under it is where the townsfolk live, calling it home, where they make their stand.

---

## The TV Adaptation of *Under the Dome*

We're all in this together.

—Big Jim Rennie, in the TV miniseries

---

King fans are used to seeing his books freely adapted for film and TV, with some direc-tors taking a lot of artistic license. But fans were surprised when the television version of *Under the Dome*'s story line significantly diverged from the book, which prompted King to explain that he had no problem with it, taking to his Web site to explain himself:

Many of the changes wrought by Brian K. Vaughan and his team of writers have been of necessity, and I approved of them wholeheartedly. Some have been occasioned by their plan to keep the Dome in place over Chester's Mill for months instead of little more than a week, as is the case in the book. Other story modifications are slotting into place because the writers have completely re-imagined the *source* of the Dome.

The changes are a wise move on Vaughan's part, since King's imagining is out of this world. In 2015, the third season of *Under the Dome* aired on ABC-TV. Tune in and find out what life is like under the dome.

# 102

# BLOCKADE BILLY

## 2010

I love old-school baseball, and I also love the way people
who've spent a lifetime in the game talk about the game. I tried
to combine those things in a story of suspense. People have
asked me for years when I was going to write a baseball story.
Ask no more; this is it.

—STEPHEN KING, IN A PRESS RELEASE FROM CEMETERY DANCE,
BLOCKADE BILLY'S ORIGINAL PUBLISHER

*B*lockade Billy is a short book—so short, in fact, that flensed of the appropriately
haunting artwork by Alex McVey, the Scribner trade edition beefed it up by adding a short story, "Morality," originally published in *Esquire* magazine (July 2009).

As with "The Man in the Black Suit" and *The Green Mile,* the first person narrator
is an old man who looks back to recount his story; this time, he's telling it to Stephen
King himself.

At the heart of this story is a mystery: Who exactly *is* William "Blockade Billy" Blakely?
Recruited as a catcher, "He may have been the greatest player the game has ever seen,"
according to the book-jacket copy, "but today no one remembers his name. He was the
first—and only—player to have his existence completely removed from the record books."

As is often the case, people in a King story—in this case, Blockade Billy—aren't
what they seem. (Are they ever?)

As David Ulin wrote in his review for the *Los Angeles Times*:

Of course, *Blockade Billy* being a Stephen King story, there are bound to be complications, and indeed, these eventually lead to the downfall of both the player and the team. It's not giving anything away to say that: King gleefully telegraphs this from the start. "We contended for a while, partly thanks to Blockade Billy," the aging coach who narrates the story tells us, "but you know how *that* turned out."

## The Skeleton Crew at Cemetery Dance

Anyone who picks up the first edition of *Blockade Billy,* published by a specialty press, Cemetery Dance, might be pleasantly surprised: Though it's a specialty press, a *small* press with a small handful of full-time employees, their books' production values exceed those of bigger publishing houses.

It's one of the endearing aspects of specialty publishing in the horror/fantasy field, and it's possible only through the largesse of Stephen King, whose generosity to specialty presses has enabled many to keep their doors open, to publish short-run books for aficionados of fantasy, science fiction, and horror fiction.

*Blockade Billy*'s original hardback publication features artwork by Alex McVey. It was published in a run of ten thousand copies, a drop in the bucket compared to a print run by Scribner for their trade editions of King's books. The first edition of the Cemetery Dance hardback had a little bonus laid in: a baseball card of William Blakely. And for the signed limited edition, a baseball card of Stephen King wearing a period baseball uniform was laid in. Not surprisingly, King wears it well.

Publisher Richard Chizmar, who has published numerous King titles, is quick to praise the big man from Bangor, who makes it all possible. In an interview for *The Baltimore Sun,* Rich told Andrea K. Walker:

[King] is as smart as can be. . . . He's very gracious. And the biggest compliment I can give him beyond that is that he still does his work for all the right reasons. He loves it. He's passionate about it. He is the last person in the world you could say it's all about the paycheck. He could have taken a book like this and made a whole lot more money from someone other than us. But that's not what he's about.

Arkham House, the granddaddy of small presses in the horror field, is still alive and well, publishing under the auspices of the founder's grandchildren, though the publishing schedule is not as robust as it was back in the day. These days, if you want to talk about robust publishing schedules, look no further than Chizmar's fine small press, which continues to delight and amaze with its high-quality hardbacks and limited editions published for a discerning audience that appreciates the craftsmanship of a well-made book containing a well-told tale.

Well, at that point in the story, we don't, but we're surely about to find out. Erik Spanberg, in his review for *The Christian Science Monitor,* concluded:

All in all, *Blockade Billy* merits a curtain call for the endlessly prolific, and inventive, King. His novella makes a perfect companion for scanning the summer box scores and, most impressive of all, even conjures a momentary twinge of empathy for that most scorned baseball species: the umpire.

Courtesy Cemetery Dance Publications

*Steve King, the catcher for the New Jersey "Titans."*

# 103

---

# FULL DARK, NO STARS

## 2010

Who knows what evil lurks in the hearts of men?
The Shadow knows.

—OPENING LINE OF *THE SHADOW*,
A 1930S RADIO SHOW FEATURING A CRIME FIGHTER

In an afterword to *Full Dark, No Stars,* a novella collection, King states his writing philosophy:

> I felt that the best fiction was both propulsive and assaultive. It gets in your face. Sometimes it shouts in your face. . . . I want to provoke an emotional, even visceral, reaction in my readers.

Three of the four stories in this collection certainly qualify as "propulsive and assaultive." They include "1922," "Big Driver," and "A Good Marriage."

"1922" certainly justifies the lead position in this collection. It's an unremittingly dark and harrowing tale well told, in first person, from an old farmer's perspective. He plotted to kill his wife and dump her down a well (sound familiar?). Set in 1922, the story's protagonist, Wilfred James, foreshadows what will follow in the fourth story in this book, when he says: "I believe that there is another man inside of every man, a stranger, a 'Conniving Man' who does the dirty deeds."

"Big Driver" recalls a 1978 cult film, *I Spit on Your Grave,* in which local yokels chase a young female writer through the woods; she is stalked and gang-raped by four men, who leave her for dead. Seeking and wreaking revenge, she systematically kills them off one by one.

The best story in the book is the last one, a harrowing study in psychological horror. "A Good Marriage" is a title deliberately tinged with irony and shows King at his best. Though the character in his story is imaginary, it's based on a real-world murderer, Dennis Rader, known as the BTK killer, now serving ten consecutive life sentences for a total of 175 years, with no possibility of parole. In an online photo, Rader looks like the churchgoer and Cub Scouts leader that he was. He is also, however, a remorseless murderer whose principal method of executing his victims was strangulation. He is known to have killed one man, one young boy aged nine, one young girl aged eleven, and seven women. (At his interrogation, he confessed that he was planning to kill again, on October 2004, and had already begun stalking his next intended victim.)

In other words, Mr. Rader is a human monster.

In a curious twist of fate, when Dennis Rader's daughter, Kerri Rawson, heard about the movie version of *A Good Marriage* (2014, Screen Media), based on her father's secret life, she was distraught and wrote an open letter to Stephen King through the media:

> My family is done, we are tired. We are not news, we are not a story to be exploited & profited on, to be twisted & retold to your liking whenever you want. Leave us, the families & the community out of it.
>
> My dad is not a monster, that's elevating him. He's just a man, who chose to do some of the most horrible things a person can do. Not a monster, a man. A man who took 10 precious lives & tried to destroy countless others. He's not worth the attention.
>
> My mom is the strongest & bravest woman I know. She doesn't need her life re-spun in a story or on the big screen. Her life is a true testament of all that is good & right in this world.
>
> My family has tried hard to fight the good fight, to stand on our faith & live out a peaceful life. So let us live that life & please, leave us out of it. Out of the noise & chaos & the ugly & the awful.

King responded, sending a copy of the text to *The Wichita Eagle* that ran Ms. Rawson's original letter:

> I don't think Mr. Rader's daughter has to worry about her father getting a big head; there's nothing glamorous about the portrayal of Bob Anderson in "A Good Marriage." He's depicted as a banal little man, and none of the murders are shown. As for making millions from the project . . . not going to happen. AGM is a very small, independently financed feature that is opening in less than two dozen venues. How it does as a video on demand feature film (VOD) is hard to predict, but we don't expect huge returns. The story isn't really about the killer husband at all, but about a brave and determined woman. And while I un-

derstand Ms. Rawson's distress, the BTK crimes have already been chronicled in no less than 4 feature films, and there may be more in the future. I grant there is a morbid interest in such crimes and such criminals—there have been at least a hundred films about Jack the Ripper, who claimed far fewer victims—but there's also a need to understand why they happen. That drive to understand is the basis of art, and that's what I strove for in "A Good Marriage." I maintain that the theme of both the novella and the movie—how some men are able to keep secrets from even their closest loved ones—is valid and deserves exploration.

In other words, King isn't an apologist for writing his "propulsive and assaultive" fiction.

The irony is that Mr. Rader is now taking a page from King's playbook. In a four-page, handwritten letter to *The Wichita Eagle,* Dennis Rader, who has read King's story, is now collaborating with Dr. Katherine Ramsland on a book, with a portion of the proceeds going to the victimized families. Citing King's visit to Wichita as a stop on his book tour for *Revival,* Dennis Rader ungrammatically wrote:

The main reason for the book idea, is to help the VF's (Victims Fund) monetarily wise; something I had hoped for years, to help them and in a way to pay my debt to them. I mean to burn no bridges, and hope some day to open up. People like me, need to be under stood, so the criminal professional field, can better under stand, the criminal mind. That would be my way of helping debt to society. . . . Mr. King, in his book *Full Dark, No Stars,* the last chapter "Good Marriage," the character (Fiction), also kept his secret, until his wife found his main "hidey hole." I'm sure other people have "dark secrets," that love ones don't know about, and live normal Family lives. . . . I figure with Mr. King coming to Wichita, once more "BTK" will be in the spotlight. . . . I hold no bad feelings with the Wichita Police Department.

# 104

## 11/22/63

### 2011

> Save Kennedy, save his brother. Save Martin Luther King.
> Stop the race riots. Stop Vietnam, maybe. . . . Get rid of one
> wretched waif . . . and you could save millions of lives.
>
> —Al Templeton to Jake Amberson,
> whom he recruits to stop Lee Harvey Oswald
> from killing Kennedy, in *11/22/63*

B ang. Bang. Bang.

Three shootings that irrevocably changed the course of history: John F. Kennedy, Martin Luther King Jr., and Robert Kennedy, killed by assassins.

History was changed forever, but what if you could go back in time to change history? Prevent JFK from getting shot, and perhaps prevent, or shorten, the Vietnam War and the assassinations of King and yet another Kennedy?

That's the basic premise for King's *11/22/63*, a date that baby boomers can't forget, just as World War Two veterans can't forget "a day that will live in infamy," and just as we, in more recent times, can't forget 9/11/01, the day the Twin Towers fell in New York City.

King, a baby boomer, was sixteen years old when he got the news that Kennedy had been assassinated. He was getting into a hearse; the driver, Mike, had the radio on.[1]

Ten years later, when King was teaching English at Hampden Academy, he had written fourteen single-spaced pages of a novel about Kennedy's assassination, *Split Track*, but abandoned it. "The research," he said in an interview published in a paperback edition of *11/22/63*, "was daunting for someone who was working full-time at another job. Also, I understood I wasn't ready—the scope was too big for me at the time."

What King mostly needed was time to distance himself from the event, to get a fresh perspective, and look at those times and that dark day in particular with clarity.

## GENESIS

In *Marvel Spotlight*, issue 14 (January 27, 2007), King provided the details about the novel in "An Open Letter from Stephen King." He wrote:

> I'd like to tell a time-travel story where this guy finds a diner that connects to 1958 . . . you always go back to the same day. So one day he goes back and just stays. Leaves his 2007 life behind. His goal? To get up to November 22, 1963, and stop Lee Harvey Oswald. He does, and he's convinced he's just FIXED THE WORLD. But when he goes back to '07, the world's a nuclear slag-heap. Not good to fool with Father Time. So then he has to go back again and stop himself . . . only he's taken on a fatal dose of radiation, so it's a race against time.

King felt his new book, because it's historical fiction, had mainstream possibilities. "This might be a book," King mused, "where we really have a chance to get an audience who's not my ordinary audience. Instead of people who read horror stories, people who read *The Help* or *People of the Book* might like this book," he told Alexandra Alter of *The Wall Street Journal*.

The book was a major departure for King, especially since it required a tremendous amount of research, which is unusual for him; he usually starts with a premise, sets up the characters, and starts writing the story, trusting his instincts to carry the day, and the story as well. But this book had to be historically accurate, which meant he had to have a researcher assist him. He recruited Russ Dorr, a longtime friend who helped on *Under the Dome*, among other books.

King also sought the input of the renowned historian Doris Kearns Goodwin and her husband, Dick Goodwin (a former advisor and speechwriter for Presidents Kennedy and Johnson and Senator Robert F. Kennedy), who speculated that the worst-case scenario was that former Alabama governor George Wallace would become president. (Perish the thought!)

Told in split tracks—one track running through the time period from the late fifties to the early sixties, the other running through contemporary times—the lengthy 849-page novel features Jacob "Jake" Epping, who lives in Lisbon Falls, Maine. Through one

---

1 When commuting to high school in nearby Lisbon Falls, Maine, King and the other kids in Durham were ferried by a converted hearse, and not a school bus. In his case, it seems apropo.

of his students, who becomes a friend, he's introduced to Al Templeton, who owns and operates Al's Diner. Al harbors an astonishing secret: He's got a portal to the past, a doorway that opens up at 11:58 A.M., on September 9, 1958, no matter how many trips are taken in the past. It answers the question Al's patrons can't figure out: How can he sell his burgers so cheap? (It's because he buys beef at 1958 prices, brings them back to the present, and passes on the savings to his customers.)

But everything's not jake. Dying of lung cancer, Al lets Jake in on his big secret and enlists him in his lifelong quest: to go back in time to prevent the assassination of John F. Kennedy on November 22, 1963. As Al tells Jake: "You can change history, Jake. Do you understand that? *John Kennedy can live.*"

History is changed, but not the way Al and Jake had foreseen: He discovers the road to hell *is* paved with good intentions. Father Time, who is dead set in his ways, doesn't like to see his timeline manipulated.

What binds this braided novel together is a love story that remains intact despite time's passage. It's Jake's love for Sadie Dunhill that motivates him to go back in the past to change history and save her from an untimely fate.

Early on, when he first meets her, he's torn between accomplishing his mission or abandoning it for her, so they can live out the remainder of their lives together. It recalls the classic setup posed by Harlan Ellison in the *Star Trek* television episode he wrote, "The City on the Edge of Forever," in which Captain Kirk must choose between letting history run its course and letting the woman he loves die . . . or rescuing her and, in doing so, irrevocably altering the future, clearly not for the better.

Errol Morris, in the *The New York Times Book Review*, called King's novel "a meditation on memory, love, loss, free will and necessity. . . . It all adds up to one of the best time-travel stories since H. G. Wells."

In Janet Maslin's review, also in *The New York Times,* she wrote:

> The pages of *11/22/63* fly by, filled with immediacy, pathos and suspense. It takes great brazenness to go anywhere near this subject matter. But it takes great skill to make this story even remotely credible. Mr. King makes it all look easy, which is surely his book's fanciest trick.

Don Oldenburg, in *USA Today,* enthusiastically wrote, "It is not typical Stephen King. It is extraordinary Stephen King."

Notably, Jeff Greenfield (*Washington Post*) reiterates in his review and echoes Leslie Fiedler's prescient comment that "his work suggests that if a time traveler found a portal to the 22nd century and looked for authors of today still being read tomorrow, Stephen King would be one of them."

*11/22/63* is the work of a mature writer at the height of his powers. As Mark Lawson of the British newspaper *The Guardian* wrote, "In these books, the reader feels the benefit of 40 years of narrative craftsmanship and reflection on his nation's history. Going backwards proves to be another step forward for the most remarkable storyteller in modern American literature."

## "Q&A: Russell Dorr, Stephen King's Researcher"

*Interviewed by Stephanie Klose*

Library Journal *(December 4, 2013)*

*Library Journal:* **How did you start working with Stephen King?**

**Russell Dorr:** Thirty-five years ago, I was in practice in Maine, and Steve came in with food poisoning. He'd listed "author" as his occupation on the form, so I asked him what he wrote.

He said he wrote a book called *Carrie*, and I asked him what it was about. He said it's about a young girl who sets things and people on fire. And I said, oh, that's nice. Have you written anything else? And he said he had a book called *'Salem's Lot* coming out the next week that was about vampires invading a small Maine town.

We were both young, and we'd run into each other around town and got to be friendly. I was working on a master's degree and asked him to come talk to my class, then he asked me to help him. He was working on a book about a virus that was going to kill off 98 percent of the world's population—would I read it? I was taking three courses and it was 1,500 pages long! I didn't have time, but I told him I'd sit down and help him craft the virus and figure out how it would morph over time.

Then I started reading whole books. Back then, he'd hand me a typewritten manuscript. I'd read it and put in changes for the medical stuff. I can't even remember all the books. I didn't touch every book, but I did work on most of them.

I've morphed from being a medical consultant to being his research associate. For *Under the Dome,* he approached me ahead of time with an idea for a story—a small Maine town that would be sealed off for months—and asked me to think of all the ramifications… food sources, energy, medical issues. He'd send me 50 pages at a time as he wrote, I'd give notes, then he'd send the rewrites to me. And he'd have questions on the fly: How do you build a nuclear warhead? What's the most corrosive acid?

With *11/22/63,* he had this idea about going back in time, so I started doing research six months before he started writing. I had a huge three-ring binder that was as big as the book. Since it was historical fiction, I had time lines for [Lee Harvey] Oswald's locations and so on. It was a lot of work but also a lot of fun.

*Library Journal:* **What research methods do you use?**

**Russell Door:** A bunch of sources. I use reference books at the library. The Internet is very good, but like in *All the President's Men,* I make sure I have three independent sources. Not everything is true out there.

And I have people I can contact. In *Under the Dome,* there's a scene where a cruise missile [is] aimed at the Dome. It's going to be released from a B-52. So I called a retired air force colonel who had flown B-52s to find out where they keep the planes, how long it would take to get one, that sort of thing.

**Library Journal: What is the most difficult research question King has asked you?**
He wanted to know where this fellow General Walker had lived in the Dallas area. He was the first person Oswald had tried to assassinate. I spent three or four days researching. I couldn't sleep at night. I just could not find him. It wasn't essential to the story. If I couldn't find the address, it would be okay, but I really wanted to get it.

Luckily, my partner, who's in real estate, has access to websites with old tax records. I finally found the address on a tax receipt from 1963.

**Library Journal: What's the most disgusting thing he's ever asked you to research?**
The most disgusting thing was how to make [methamphetamine]. It's a side story in *Under the Dome.* There's a character who was cooking crystal meth. I told him I had a problem with it, but he said we weren't going to make it a cookbook, he just wanted to make sure we got the ingredients right, that kind of thing. I'm just not into drugs. That really turned me off.

Also, I thought *Pet Sematary* was just a horrible story about child death. I told him he shouldn't publish it. He laughed when I said it, but that was a really tough story.

**Library Journal: What can you tell us about *Doctor Sleep*? [note: his answer contains spoilers]**
**Russell Dorr:** His books are sort of like a seven-layer dip. There's plenty there for the fanatic who likes his scary stuff and gore. But you also have a story about a struggling recovering alcoholic. The main character [Danny Torrance, who was a little boy in *The Shining*] works in a hospice. There are these creatures, the Tribe, who kill children who have "shining" powers. They capture the dying breath and store it in a sort of steam. They live for centuries by breathing the steam. One of the children they kill is sick with the measles, and it's the measles that ends up killing the Tribe.

It's pretty well known how the measles virus affects the body, but we had to figure out how it would affect these creature-people and morph inside their bodies and how to make it plausible. He weaves this stuff into a tapestry that people will believe and care about.

*Library Journal:* **You have such an intimate look at his upcoming releases. Do you have to sign nondisclosure agreements for the books you work on?**

**Russell Dorr:** No, of course not! This is Maine, not New York City.

*Library Journal:* **Is there anything you'd like people to know about Stephen King?**

He's a very regular guy. We've been buddies for years. His wife called the day after his accident [in 1999, King was hit by a van while taking a walk and suffered extensive injuries to his legs and hips] and we spent three weeks together. He was a huge help to me when my wife was dying of cancer. He's a very nice guy.

# 105

# THE DARK MAN

## 2013

Glenn Chadbourne

*The* Dark Man *portfolio*

Randall Flagg came to me when I wrote a poem called "The Dark Man" when I was a junior or senior in college. It came to me out of nowhere, this guy in cowboy boots who moved around on the roads, mostly hitchhiking at night, always wore jeans and a denim jacket. I wrote the poem in the college restaurant on the back of a placemat, but that guy never left my mind.

—STEPHEN KING, *THE DARK MAN* BOOK JACKET

If there's one dark figure whom King readers know well, it's the Dark Man, who goes by several nicknames: the Walkin' Dude, the Hard Case, the Ageless Stranger, the Man in Black. No matter what you call him, he's the ultimate badass, who, as King noted, "came to me out of nowhere." He made his first appearance in a 1969 poem published in the University of Maine at Orono's literary magazine, *Moth*. He's also shown up, significantly, in *The Stand, The Eyes of the Dragon* (as the King's trusted advisor), and the Dark Tower story cycle.

The poem, which appears in book form for the first time in the Cemetery Dance edition (2013), shows a side of King most people are unaware of: he studied and wrote poetry during college.

But the Dark Man's omnipresence visually in this Cemetery Dance book is special because Maine artist Glenn Chadbourne parsed every line of King's original poem to extract every possible image, resulting in a book in which the poem serves the art, with one illustration per page. (Glenn followed it up with a phone-book-sized portfolio crammed with even more art.)

The 88-page book is among my favorites of the ones Glenn has illustrated, because it's obvious that he poured his heart and soul into it. The color art for the dust jacket features a moonlit night with a dark man in the foreground, walking to a ramshackle house.

So, who's Glenn Chadbourne?

For starters, he's a lifelong Mainer. "I live in Damariscotta, which is an hour north of Portland. It's one of those little picture-postcard kind of towns, with lighthouses, the ocean, rocky coast, etc."

He's also a full-time artist, best known for his connection to Stephen King through numerous Cemetery Dance projects, including two anthologies (*The Secretary of Dreams* and *Full Dark, No Stars,* in two volumes). He also provided the logo for the Kings' Haven Foundation and the PS Publishing edition of *Carrie*.

His favorite assignment, though, was illustrating *The Dark Man*, which he described as

an absolute dream gig. It's probably my favorite Stephen King gig to date, because they gave me carte blanche to go wild on it. I had this short, creepy poem to go by and we figured eighty or so pages to play with, so I got to use every drop of imagination to build this eerie nasty atmosphere that creeps along to a climax. I loved every second of dreaming up a real desolate feel. I kept thinking of Rust Belt towns on the fringes of things . . . and a sort of sultry lonely southern gothic thing at the same time. Hopefully I pulled off a decent job; if I did, it was channeled from the Dark Man himself.

## Glenn Chadbourne: An Interview by George Beahm

**George Beahm: As someone who has lived in Maine his entire life ("not yet," I can hear you say), do you feel a special affinity toward King's work because he's a Maine writer, and because he writes horror/suspense fiction?**

**Glenn Chadbourne:** Well, I'd have to say yes to both reasons. Maine is a unique place with a unique atmosphere, especially once you get off the beaten picture-postcard-touristy track. Though if Steve had lived in Ohio and set his backdrops in Cleveland, I'd still love the stories equally as much. It's fun to live around here and read books that take place in fictitious settings while being surrounded by real towns that exist. There's a cool creepy factor to that for [those of us] who live a stone's throw from *'Salem's Lot*! I often tell PFA (people from away) who ask about Stephen's stories that he's put us on the map as the Transylvania of America.

**GB: What are some of your favorite King books or stories?**

**Glenn Chadbourne:** They all speak to me on some level, because you're inside the character's heads and worlds and you can relate more often than not to situations in the books. You feel for the characters. It goes back to the "Maine" thing for me. My old gramma could have been cast in either *Dolores Claiborne* or the great short story "The Reach."

*Glenn Chadbourne*

Courtesy Suzi Thayer

But I guess I'd have to say *'Salem's Lot* because it creeped the bejesus out of me and still holds up. I recently listened to it on my Kindle, not having read it in eons. I also just chewed through *Revival,* and that left me speechless with dread. It's a bleak book that jolted me and shows Steve has plenty of dark mojo left for the gut-wrenching stuff. I could go on and on, but as far as favorites, I think of them more along the lines of a yummy buffet featuring any amount of tasty dishes to munch on, each with its own special flavor.

**GB: What would be your dream Stephen King project? That is, what would you absolutely love to illustrate, if the opportunity came up?**

**Glenn Chadbourne:** "The Mist." I love to draw creepy crawlers!

**GB: Have you ever met King?**

**Glenn Chadbourne:** In all the years I've been lucky enough to illustrate different things for him, I've yet to meet him. I know and deal with his personal assistant, Marsha DeFilippo, with different gigs when they arise, and she's a real sweetheart. I've received e-mail kudos from him over the years, and that's always nice, and I go up to the office from time to time, but he's never been around on any visits I've made.

**GB: How much work have you done for Cemetery Dance?**

**Glenn Chadbourne:** Oodles. The CD staff are among my favorite people on the planet, and I owe them a lot!

# 106

---

# JOYLAND

## (2013)

The major job is still to entertain people. *Joyland* really took
off for me when the old guy who owns the place says, "Never
forget, we sell fun." That's what we're supposed to do—
writers, filmmakers, all of us. That's why they let us stay in the
playground.

—STEPHEN KING, INTERVIEW, *PARADE* MAGAZINE, 2013

Sometimes the best thing about falling *in* love is falling *out* of love, because it means
you can get on with your life, no matter how long it takes. Sometimes, though, even
a lifetime isn't enough.

In *Joyland*, a sixty-one-year-old man looks back at a time when he was twenty-one
and reflects on life's sweet and sour notes. The sweet: growing closer to a girl named
Wendy Keegan, whom he loves. And the sour: growing apart from her, when she no
longer loves him.

*Joyland*, as book reviewers have pointed out, is more a coming-of-age story than it
is a crime/suspense novel, which no doubt surprised some readers who were expecting
the latter. Published by Hard Case Crime, a line of hard-boiled crime fiction, *Joyland*'s
ad copy suggests that its crime/suspense and supernatural elements overshadow the
story's personal and poignant aspects, but that's not the case: If you can enjoy a simple
story of a young man in love, you'll find much to like in this short novel. But if you're

the U.K. edition from PS Publishing

*Cover to* Joyland

looking for spookier fare, you may be crestfallen: "The mystery," wrote Darren Franich for *Entertainment Weekly,* "isn't too mysterious. The ghost hardly appears. Not that much happens, really."

From the book: "That fall was the most beautiful of my life," Devin Jones recalls. "And I was never so unhappy. I can say that, too."

Devin's situation recalls King's relationship with a college girlfriend that also soured. As he told Winter in *Stephen King: The Art of Darkness,* "I had lost my girlfriend of four years, and [*Sword in the Darkness*] seemed to be constantly, ceaselessly pawing over that relationship and trying to make some sense of it. And that doesn't make for good fiction."

In *Joyland,* King perhaps went back for one last time to achieve closure. "I'm in my sixties now," says Devin Jones, "my hair is gray and I'm a prostate cancer survivor, but I still want to know why I wasn't good enough for Wendy Keegan."

Unlike Stephen King, who met Tabitha Spruce in his senior year of college and wound up marrying her—a relationship that has stood the test of time—Devin, a lost boy turned old man, is forever haunted by Wendy—a long-lost love. "I'm not sure anybody ever gets completely over their first love, and that still rankles," recalls Devin.

## THE STORY'S ORIGIN

In an interview with Terry Gross on NPR's *Fresh Air* (May 28, 2013), Stephen King explained that the story's origin began with an image of a wheelchair-bound boy flying a kite on a beach. "It wanted to be a story, but it wasn't a story," he told her.

But the story grew, as it often does with King, and centers on an amusement park called *Joyland,* based on a real park in New Hampshire. And on its fringes is a mother named Annie, whose son, Mike, suffers from muscular dystrophy. Wheelchair-bound, Mike's simple wish is to fly a kite on the beach near Joyland.

## THE PUBLISHER

King chose to go, once again, to Hard Case Crime because it brought back old memories of when he was a kid growing up in rural Maine. "We lived way out in the country," he told Gross, "and my mother would go shopping once a week . . . to the Red and White or the A&P to pick up her groceries. And I would immediately beat feet to Robert's Drugstore, where they had a couple of those wire [spinner] racks with the hard-boiled paperbacks that usually featured a girl with scanty clothing on the front."

That was back in the fifties and sixties, and then the world moved on; the cheap paperbacks with the lurid covers became a part of book publishing history, until Charles Ardai and Max Phillips revived their provocative "in your face" cover art and hard-hitting prose for their line of books.

Their Web site: "Hard Case Crime is dedicated to reviving the vigor and excitement, the suspense and thrills—the sheer entertainment—of the golden age of paperback crime novels. . . . Determined detectives and dangerous women . . . fortune hunters and vengeance seekers . . . ingenious criminals and men on the run."

So *Joyland* doesn't *quite* fit in that mold, which is why I agree with Bill Sheehan, who wrote in *The Washington Post,* that, like *The Colorado Kid, Joyland* "depends on King's typically unerring sense of character for its deepest effects. . . . King has created a moving, immensely appealing coming-of-age tale that encompasses restless ghosts, serial murder, psychic phenomena and sexual initiation."

And though there's joy in Joyland, there's none for wheelchair-bound Mike, who gets to fly the kite on the beach, but not in the way he imagined.

# 107

DOCTOR SLEEP

(2013)

[A] return to balls-to-the-wall, keeping-the-lights-on horror.

—STEPHEN KING ON *DOCTOR SLEEP*,
FROM HIS OFFICIAL WEB SITE

In *Fear Itself*, a collection of essays about Stephen King, Peter Straub wrote "Meeting Stevie," which concerns King's third novel, *The Shining* (1977). "It was obviously a masterpiece, probably the best supernatural novel in a hundred years. He . . . was now quite clearly one of the best writers of any kind in the United States." Thirty-six years later, King wrote a sequel—his only one to date—to *The Shining*.

King told *The Guardian* that it was about

> a cat in a hospice that knows when people are going to die. He would go into that patient's room and curl up next to them. And I thought, that's a good advertisement for death, for the emissary of death. I thought, "I can make Dan the human equivalent of that cat, and call him Doctor Sleep." There was the book.

Titled *Doctor Sleep*, Danny Torrance is middle-aged, and, like his father, he bounces around from job to job; he winds up working at a hospice in Frazier, a small town in New Hampshire. Also like his father, Danny's a recovering alcoholic. It's time, he realizes, to get his life back on track. Haunted by the past and by the Overlook Hotel and its ghosts,

429

who still bedevil his thoughts, Danny once again relies on his old friend and mentor, Dick Hallorann, to help him cope.

Similarly, Danny's role at the hospice, aided by his psychic abilities, is to put people at ease and help them cross over when they realize the end is near; his unusual talent is then put to good use.

## FOREVER YOUNG

Abra Stone, a young girl whose "shining" talent is greater than Danny's, makes contact telepathically with him. After psychically experiencing the murder of a young boy by a group called the True Knot (psychic vampires who feed on their victims' life energy, called "steam," when they die), they are now aware of and hunger for her because their diminishing stock of "steam," stored in canisters, is nearly depleted; without it, they will eventually die.

Rose the Hat, the leader of the True Knot, realizes that Abra's "steam" will replenish their diminished stock for many years to come, because she's a psychic gusher: Her "steam," procured through her torture, means they will have plenty for years to come.

The True Knot heads east in a caravan of RVs to capture and kill Abra Stone.

Understandably, King was concerned about his Constant Readers' perception of the new book: Comparisons with *The Shining* were inevitable, as he told the BBC:

> You are faced with that comparison and that has got to make you nervous be-cause there is a lot of water under the bridge. I'm a different man. . . . What a lot of people are saying is, "Well okay, I will probably read this book but it cannot be as good as *The Shining*." But I am obviously an optimist and I want them to say when they get done with it, that it was as good. But what I really want them to say is that it is better than *The Shining*.

In truth, the issue isn't whether one book is better than the other, because they are very different books. *The Shining* is a recognized classic, the work of King's most cited by college professors for its significance and teachability; it has stood the test of time for nearly four decades. *Doctor Sleep* is a newcomer, and, though it has generally been reviewed well, a distinction between the two must be made, as a reviewer for *The Telegraph* pointed out:

> It's . . . quite a different order from *The Shining*: there isn't the same claus-trophobic, elemental terror that has caused so many people over the years to develop a phobia of hotel lifts. The members of the True Knot are a memorably loathsome bunch, but having brought them vividly to life, King cannot make them as frightening as the more nebulous beings that terrorized Jack Torrance.
>
> *The Shining* was a yell of despair from the darkest of places. *Doctor Sleep* is a warm, entertaining novel by a man who is no longer the prisoner of his demons, but knows where to look when he needs to call on them.

A seasoned writer who has spent a lifetime in New England, King's roots run deep. "King," wrote Margaret Atwood, in a review of the book for *The New York Times*, "is right at the center of an American literary taproot that goes all the way down: to the Puritans and their belief in witches, to Hawthorne, to Poe, to Melville, to Henry James of 'The Turn of the Screw,' and then to later exemplars like Ray Bradbury."

King draws on that taproot for *Doctor Sleep*, just as he did for *The Shining* and countless other tales; though fans aren't likely to favor the former over the latter, the fact remains that *Doctor Sleep* is a worthy addition to King's literary canon: It's the perfect book on a cold night when the wind-driven rain patters against the window and the moon is bright and full. In other words, it's a well-told tale, but not in the same league as *The Shining*, an acknowledged masterpiece.

## Closure

For King, and for Danny Torrance as well, *Doctor Sleep* finally brings much needed, and long postponed, closure. King has now said everything he wanted to say about Danny, who, by novel's end, celebrates fifteen years of sobriety: Just as Danny turned to Dick Hallorann for succor and received it, he in turn provides assistance to Abra Stone, to make sure she doesn't follow his self-destructive path.

In the last chapter, Danny has a heart-to-heart talk with her: She's not like her contemporaries—she has the Power—and she has to learn how to handle her frustrations, her anger, and not give in to it: "I'll try," she says. "I'll try real hard."

Danny hopes that will be enough. So, too, do we.

Abra is fifteen, and she has miles to go before she sleeps—a lifetime ahead that, with sound choices, may be one of fulfilled dreams and not nightmares.

As for the elderly people at the hospice where Danny works, the years of their lives are largely spent, and, unlike her, they don't have miles to go before they sleep: They face the long sleep soon. But Danny, as Doctor Sleep, is there to ease their passage into the next world, in whatever form it takes—if indeed there *is* such a thing as an afterlife.

## Oscar the Cat

His name is Oscar, and he's a handsome little fella with tortoiseshell markings and white fur. Adopted as a kitten, Oscar has no time to spend with healthy people; he prefers the company of the nearly departed, the elderly people who will soon pass on. At the Steere House Nursing and Rehabilitation Center in Providence, Rhode Island, Oscar makes the rounds.

In fifty documented cases, Oscar, according to a story in *The Guardian* newspaper:

> spends . . . days pacing from room to room, rarely spending any time with patients except those with just hours to live. If kept outside the room of a dying patient, Oscar will scratch on the door trying to get in. . . . Dr. Dosa and other staff are so confident in Oscar's accuracy that they will alert family members when the cat jumps on to a bed and stretches out beside its occupant.

To date there has been no scientific inquiry to investigate the phenomenon, though there is a lot of speculation. In any event, Oscar's presence presages the imminent end of a person's life and provides a measure of comfort to the dying by simply being there, especially when the elderly person's family is far away: he serves as their feline friend.

Oscar is one of life's real-world mysteries.

Dr. David Dosa has written a book about the facility's prescient cat, *Making the Rounds with Oscar: The Extraordinary Gift of an Ordinary Cat*. Dosa's Q&A in the book explains Oscar's backstory. He explains that he was originally a skeptic but soon became a convert:

> I became convinced of Oscar's abilities, though, when there were two patients on the floor dying simultaneously. All of the staff thought that one of the patients was closer to death, but Oscar remained attached to the other patient. At one point, a nurse's aide became concerned that Oscar's streak of predicting death would end, and brought the angry cat to the bedside of the more seriously ill patient. Oscar looked at everyone like they were crazy and sprinted out of the room, returning to his vigil at the bedside of the first patient. Oscar's charge died a few hours later, but the other patient rallied for a couple more days. Four hours before the second patient died, Oscar came to his bedside.

# 108

## MR. MERCEDES

### 2014

At a public talk on December 7, 2012, at the University of Massachusetts at Lowell, Stephen King spoke about the genesis of *Mr. Mercedes*.

He explained that, when driving back from Florida to Maine, he stopped in South Carolina and checked into an inexpensive motel. There was, he said, nothing to do but watch TV, and so he turned on the tube and watched with fascination a news story about a woman who drove her car over job seekers who had lined up at a McDonald's restaurant where applications were being handed out.

After attacking a woman in line, whom she "pasted" with "a couple of good ones," she "got back into her car, threw it into reverse, and backed over two more people on the way out . . . and I thought to myself: I want to write about this."

King can't recollect where the incident took place, but it may have been in Cleveland, Ohio, at a "national hiring event" hosted by McDonald's, during a nationwide push to hire fifty thousand new workers.

A witness named Joseph Shores explained, "I was filling out my application when I saw two girls fighting. I don't know their names, but they were fighting over drama, hood stuff," as reported by Philip Caulfield in the *New York Daily News* (April 20, 2011). Caulfield added that "[t]he fight briefly breaks up, and the person on the ground can be seen getting in the car while a shouting mob gathers outside the driver's open door. Suddenly, the car lurches forward with the door still open, and then—as the crowd screams in horror—speeds into reverse, sending four people flying."

*Mr. Mercedes* begins with a similar scene of carnage: A stolen Mercedes sedan is driven into a crowd of job seekers, and in the confusion the killer gets away. He's named

Mr. Mercedes by the media, for obvious reasons, and remains at large. The only significant piece of evidence is a clown's mask, cleaned with bleach. In other words, there's no trace of the killer . . . until he reappears, taunting his old nemesis, a retired police detective named Bill Hodges.

Like others who feel useless in retirement after a very active life in the working world, Bill is profoundly depressed, and clinically so: He's contemplated suicide. But when Mr. Mercedes taunts him online, Bill finds a renewed purpose in life: to close the book on the killer, once and for all, by finding and capturing him.

Of course, since Bill's retired, it's not his responsibility, but he figures that since it's an old case he had previously worked on, he's got a dog in the fight.

The killer turns out to be—as they often are—a disaffected, angry young man who blames society for all his problems. Also, as these killers often turn out to be, he's aspirational: It's not enough to kill innocent victims waiting in line at the First Annual City Job Fair; he wants to up the ante by killing hundreds of people, and plans to do so at a concert. But Bill, who put his service revolver away, is back on the case, albeit unofficially, and this hard-boiled detective novel gets under way: Bill teams up with Janey (the sister of Olivia Trelawney, whose Mercedes was stolen) and a computer-savvy seventeen-year-old boy who helps him with odd jobs around the house.

A stand-alone novel, *Mr. Mercedes* is the first part of a trilogy. A mystery/suspense novel, it won "Best Novel" in 2015 from the Mystery Writers of America, prompting George R.R. Martin to observe, on his Web site,

> I was very pleased to see Stephen King take home the "Best Novel" award for *Mr. Mercedes*. You want to talk about writings who have been shamefully over-looked by the Hugos? (And by the Nebulas and the World Fantasy Award too). Start with King. ... The world thinks of him as a master of horror, and he is...but horror is also sometimes known as "dark fantasy," and King has written plenty of SF [science fiction] and even some high fantasy (*Eyes of the Dragon*, anyone? *The Dark Tower*) too. He's won the National Book Award, but he's never taken home a rocket [Hugo award] or a rock [Nebula award]. So it goes, I guess. But at least now he has the head of Edgar Allan Poe [MWA award]. Bravo!

Coming on the heels of *Doctor Sleep*, a horror/supernatural novel, this one will likely throw some of his newer readers for a loop. But longtime readers know that King will never abandon the horror field, though he embraces other genres because that's just how he rocks and rolls.

As Michael M. Smith of *The Guardian* points out, "Notwithstanding his reputation as the Master of the Dark Side, King is always far more interested in how we get by in life, how we manage to care for one another and walk together toward the light, despite the darkness lurking within us all."

*Mr. Mercedes* is, on the face of it, a "stock" book, as Stephanie Merritt wrote in a review of the book for *The Guardian*: "the maverick detective who must operate outside the confines of the law; the killer with a personal vendetta and an unhealthy relationship with his mother; the band of misfits who cooperate to stop him before he can carry out his murderous plan."

In less capable hands, *Mr. Mercedes* would be mere pulp fiction, but as Merritt observed, there's always more at work in King's fiction, which gives his books staying power:

> Stephen King may be the acknowledged grand master of horror fiction, but he has always known that the everyday demons hiding behind the screen doors of small-town streets can chime with our deepest terrors just as effectively as the evil creature in the sewer. Mental illness, addiction, poverty, childhood trauma, alienation—these are the real monsters that crouch beneath the surfaces of our lives, and they stalk the pages of most of his fiction in one form or another, even in stories that appear to be concerned with more obviously supernatural forces of evil.

# 109

## WORLD FANTASY AND WORLD HORROR CONVENTIONS

I'm still a fan at heart and one of the things which is real rough is not being able to go to a convention and go into the hucksters' room and look around, maybe pick up some copies of *Weird Tales* or other pulps without having people come up for autographs, or talk about something they've written, or you've written. They're hitting on you all the time and you try to be polite and you try to talk to them but often you are just thinking to yourself, "Why can't I be like these other people and just be allowed to browse?" You've become the browsee instead of the browser, kind of like a walking, talking book.

—STEPHEN KING, INTERVIEWED BY HIGH SCHOOL STUDENT
ELAINE LANDA, 1986

E very year professionals in the horror field meet at the World Fantasy Convention (worldfantasy.org). In 2014, the convention was held in Washington, D.C. From its Web site: It's "an annual gathering (almost a reunion) of professionals, collectors, and others interested in the field of Light and Dark Fantasy art and literature."

Attendance in 2014 was strictly capped at 850. The convention's roster of attendees boasted many of the big-name writers in the field, but not its biggest draw, Stephen King, whose success precludes his attendance: His presence is too great a distraction.

Conventions for fans began informally in the thirties. In 1936, seven science fiction fans met at one of their houses in Philadelphia and formally dubbed it the first "science fiction convention."

Since then, conventions catering to fantasy, science fiction, and fantasy fans are held year-round, drawing massive crowds: Comic-Con International, in San Diego, which started out as a comic book convention, is now a major media convention, drawing more than 130,000, with tickets selling out in a matter of minutes online. (The New York Comic Con, which uses a bigger convention center, draws 151,000.)

But for horror fans, the venues are smaller and more intimate by design.

Stephen King was a guest of honor at the fifth World Fantasy Convention in 1979. The guest artist was Michael Whelan, who illustrated the *Firestarter* and *Dark Tower* novels. That convention was held in Providence, Rhode Island, from whence hailed H. P. Lovecraft, who once famously declared, "I am Providence!"

## WORLD HORROR CONVENTION (WORLDHORRORCONVENTION.COM)

The other convention choice for horror fans is the World Horror Convention, which was started in 1991 as an alternative to the World Fantasy Convention. Unlike the WFC, WHC focuses entirely on the dark side: "The World Horror Convention is an annual gathering of professionals in the horror industry: publishers, authors, artists, musicians, filmmakers, dealers, and of course, horror fans. WHC serves as both an industry insider's networking event and a chance for fans of the genre to get together, meet some of the creative talents in the field, and generally spend a weekend celebrating All Things Scary."

# 110

---

## REVIVAL

### 2014

The inspiration was Arthur Machen's "The Great God Pan,"
which is a terrifying story about the world that might exist
beyond this one. Other influences were Lovecraft, Mary
Shelley's *Frankenstein*, and my own religious upbringing. And
I've been wanting to write about tent show healings for a
long time!

I wanted to write a balls-to-the-wall supernatural horror story,
something I haven't done in a long time. I also wanted to use
Lovecraft's Cthulhu mythos, but in a new fashion, if I could,
stripping away Lovecraft's high-flown language.

—STEPHEN KING, INTERVIEW, GOODREADS.COM

I live for rock and roll!

—STEPHEN KING, "LIVE AT POLITICS AND PROSE,"
GEORGE WASHINGTON UNIVERSITY, NOVEMBER 12, 2014

T he roots, the *real* roots, to *Revival* go back to King's life in rural Maine, as King explained in a joint interview with Jerry Jenkins for *Writer's Digest*: "While I'm not a big believer in the Biblical apocalypse and end-times, I was raised in a Christian home, went to church a lot, attended MYF (Methodist Youth Fellowship—lots of Bible drills, which every writer could use, Christian or not)."

Here are some of the most obvious parallels:

King grew up in Durham. In *Revival*, Jamie Morton grows up in rural Maine (in Harlow, near Castle Rock).

King grew up in the Methodist faith. As Stephen King's brother, David, explained to Spignesi in *The Complete Stephen King Encyclopedia*, "[W]hen Stevie turned twelve, we were in Durham by then, and we both joined the West Durham Methodist Church. So basically, we had a traditional Protestant upbringing." In *Revival*, the minister is also of that faith.

By the time he was in high school, King became disenchanted with religion and walked away, after concluding that aspects of the Methodist faith simply made no sense. In *Revival*, it's the preacher who walks away, after he feels God has abandoned him, selling him a bill of goods.

David King recalled that just before Easter one year, Charles Huff, a local Methodist preacher who wasn't an ordained minister, "set up his own version of the Last Supper. We'd all go over to the parish hall where we'd sit around with candles, and we would have Za-Rex.[1] I remember that specifically. Even when he used to take us down to picnics down at Bradbury Mountain, it was always Za-Rex." In *Revival*, the young boys go often to the parsonage to partake of cookies and the preacher's name is Charles Jacobs.

At a relative's attic over the barn in Durham, King discovered his great interest to be horror fiction. Rummaging through books, he found a battered, worn paperback with H. P. Lovecraft fiction. In *Revival*, Lovecraft's fiction is central to the book's conclusion, as is Arthur Machen's classic tale, "The Great God Pan," which King considers to be an influence on his work in general and this novel in particular; so, too, is Mary Wollstonecraft Shelley's *Frankenstein; or, The Modern Prometheus*, a novel about which he wrote about at length in *Danse Macabre*.

For King readers who wanted a horror fix but didn't get it with *Mr. Mercedes*, King's latest, *Revival*, is his return to familiar stomping grounds, recalling *Pet Sematary*.

The novel opens with Jamie Morton playing with toy soldiers when a shadows falls over him, cast by the new preacher in town, Charles Jacobs. It is Jacobs who, for the rest

---

1  A syrup concentrate popular in New England used to mix fruit-flavored drinks.

of Jamie's life, will continue to cast a long shadow over him, and many others. When he's not preaching and teaching the gospel, Jacobs is tinkering with a "secret electricity" that he hopes will open "doorways to the infinite." He is consumed by a single, driving question: What lies in store for us after death? "I want to know what the universe has in store for all of us once this life is over," says Jacob. It is his Moby Dick, a quest that drives him relentlessly on, driving him a little mad in the process.

After suffering a personal disaster that shatters his faith in God, the preacher is forced to leave the small congregation he serves in Harlow, Maine, but Jacobs's life becomes inextricably braided with Jamie's. As a result of an electrical shock treatment that Jacobs administers to Jamie, to cure him of his heroin addiction, he realizes he's changed: "Something, something, something. Happened. Happened. Something happened. Something happened, happened, something happened. Happened. Something."

That shocking encounter sets up a final encounter in *Revival* that goes far beyond what the minister imagined: He gets his dark heart's desire—a glimpse of what is in store for all of us after we die.

As with *Pet Sematary*, which King found too dark and put away in his fabled writer's trunk, he felt even more so with *Revival*. "It's too scary," he told Buzzfeed. "I don't even want to think about that book anymore. It's a nasty dark piece of work. That's all I can tell you."

Here's what I can tell you: The skeleton key to *Revival* can be found in "The Great God Pan," which King says "has haunted me all my life." It can also be found in the following H. P. Lovecraft quote from "The Nameless City":

> *That is not dead which can eternal lie,*
> *And with strange aeons, even death may die.*

As Lovecraft wrote in his story "The Call of Cthulhu," "The most merciful thing in the world, I think, is the inability of the human mind to correlate all its contents. We live on a placid island of ignorance in the midst of black seas of the infinity, and it was not meant that we should voyage far."

Charles Jacob would have been wise to heed Lovecraft's words.

Novelist Danielle Trussoni, in *The New York Times*, wrote that "[r]eading *Revival* is experiencing a master storyteller having the time of his life. All of his favorite fictional elements are at play—small-town Maine, the supernatural, the evil genius, the obsessive addict, the power of belief to transform a life."

Book editor John Freeman, in *The Boston Globe*, wrote:

> There's a strong moral current crackling through King's fiction, so we know there will be a cost. Nothing good in King's world comes for free. . . . *Revival* is a brave book because it dares to look closely at the way that religion is fiction, but perhaps a necessary one. It is a moving novel because it shows how religion's assurances are just that, hardly guarantees of outcome. On that score, there is only one we can count on, and it's that none of us know what's coming in the beyond, not even this marvelous novelist.

Our body knows things, and our brain knows things that don't have anything to do with conscious thought. And I think that it's possible, when you die, that there is a final exit program that goes into effect. And that's what people are seeing when they see their relatives or a white light or whatever it is. In that sense, there may really be a heaven if you believe there's a heaven, and a hell if you believe there is one. But there's some kind of transitional moment. That idea that your whole life flashes before your eyes.

—Stephen King, interview, *The Guardian,* April 28, 2012

# III

## Stephen King's Revival Book Tour

In early 2014, on the message board of King's official Web site, the moderator wrote that King was taking a break and wouldn't be doing any on-road promotion for *Revival*. You could almost hear a collective groan of disappointment from his fans, who hoped to see him in person to promote his latest book. But as fall leaves fell and Halloween approached, King had a change of heart and revived his book tour, to his fans' delight.

Clearly, King doesn't need to go out and tour to promote his books. He sells up to a million copies in hardback of each new novel in the U.S. without touring, so why even bother?

Because it's a way to directly connect with his readership, his die-hard fans. It gets him out of his self-contained, cocooned existence as a writer in a room and into the larger world, from which he draws his inspiration.

In the early years, King didn't set up protocols for book signings or talks, with the result that fans giddy with anticipation, standing in long lines, went home disappointed when it was impossible for him to sign books, after his writing hand cramped up. That's what happened at a mall in Maine, after two hours of straight signing. Aware that there was a long line of fans in line with books who'd be disappointed, he asked if he could go out the back entrance, to avoid confronting them. The bookstore refused, and he had to walk out the front entrance, passing hundreds of unhappy fans who had waited hours to see him; they glared, and some made comments, as he kept his head down and kept walking. Afterward, King no longer left the logistics of book signings to chance: sensible protocols were instituted.

For the *Revival* whirlwind tour in November 2014, King limited it to six cities. In chronological order of appearance: New York City (the eleventh), Washington, D.C. (the twelfth), Kansas City (the thirteenth), Wichita (the fourteenth), Austin (the fifteenth), and, finally, home to South Portland, Maine (the seventeenth).

Of the six events, three were book signings, designed to accommodate as many people as possible. But attendance was strictly limited to what could reasonably be signed in the time period allotted, to ensure that no one went away empty-handed and disappointed. There were no personal inscriptions, and no time for personal chats or selfies.

The remaining three visits were composed of readings or improvisational talks:

> Okay. I'm going to talk for a while. . . . I can't really lecture—I'm not good at that—and I can't speak with any sense from prepared notes. About the most I can do is *chautauqua,* a fine old word that means you babble on for a little while about the thing that you do, and then you sit down.

At his three talks, attendees got a hardback copy of *Revival*; the lucky ones got signed copies, which were randomly placed on seats or handed out when one left the auditorium. But everyone went home with an experience to remember.

King, over the years, has dutifully signed copies of his books, as well as napkins and other pieces of paper thrust at him in public, to the point where there are hundreds of thousands of his signatures floating around. Until a few years ago, King even accepted books mailed to him—one per person, please—to his office, which he would sign and send back; but it's a practice he's stopped for obvious reasons.

These days, King signs sheets of paper from specialty publishers for insertion in their limited editions, which cost $450 and up. He also signs at special events for charity or fund-raising purposes, and occasionally at bookstores.

At a talk King gave with J. K. Rowling and John Irving, I saw King leave the building as soon as possible out of a side entrance, but even then fans saw him, congregated around him, and thrust program books at him for his signature. He signed a few and then begged off, leaving in a waiting limo.

If his fans had their druthers, they would have stayed and gotten more signatures, and the small crowd would have grown to a large one, and pretty soon the situation would have become untenable.

The whole notion of getting a signature on a book is one that befuddles writer Harlan Ellison, who can't understand why the book itself isn't enough. After all, isn't that what the reader is paying for? Why does he need the author's signature on the book at all?

Well, eBay aside, the fact remains that a signature transforms a book into a personal treasure. It's a keepsake and a collectible that can be passed down to the next generation: Out of an estimated one million copies of *Revival* that shipped, it is likely that fewer than five or six hundred were signed at the three signing events on his tour. (It explains why signed copies have sold for up to $400 on eBay.)

Of King's talks, only one was recorded, at George Washington University's Lisner Auditorium in D.C., under the auspices of Politics and Prose bookstore; the talk is available online.

As for the book signings, at the Books-a-Million in Portland, Maine, some fans grumbled that after standing in line in the cold, they didn't have a chance to talk with King at all; they were moved through the line quickly and felt he could have just signed the books and left them on the table for pickup. Well, to be fair to King, by moving the crowd rapidly along, it allowed over a hundred more people to get a signed book who otherwise wouldn't. I think *those* readers had no complaints whatsoever.

---

### Stephen King on Death

Death is it. The one thing we all have to face. Two hundred years from now there won't be any of us walking around and taking nourishment. That's it. Sooner or later, God points at you and says, "It's time to hang up your jock, the game is over, it's time to take a shower. It's the end." But the point is, this is something that every creature on the face of the earth goes through, but so far as we know, we're the only creatures that have an extended sense of futurity. We are the only ones who can look ahead and say, "Yes, that's right, it's going to happen. And how am I going to deal with the idea of my own conclusion?"

Well, if you stop and think about it, and you stop to realize how clearly we grasp the concept, the answer should be: "We can't cope with it. It'll drive us crazy." For me, the fact that it doesn't is one of the really marvelous things in human existence, and probably also one of the true signs of God's grace on the face of this earth.

—Stephen King, public speech, in Truth or Consequences,
New Mexico, on November 19, 1983

# 112

# Are You There, God? It's Me, Stevie

My view is that organized religion is a very dangerous tool
that's been misused by a lot of people. I grew up in a Methodist
church, and we went to services every Sunday and to Bible
school in the summer. We didn't have a choice. We just did it.
So all that stuff about childhood religion in *Revival* is basically
autobiographical. But as a kid, I had doubts. When I went to
Methodist youth fellowship, we were taught that the Catholics
were all going to go to hell because they worship idols. So right
there, I'm saying to myself, "Catholics are going to go to hell,
but my aunt Molly married a Catholic and she converted and
she's got 11 kids and they're all pretty nice and one of them's
my good friend—they're all going to go to hell?" I'm thinking
to myself, "This is bullshit." And if that's bullshit, how much of
the rest of it is bullshit?

—Stephen King, interview, *Rolling Stone*, October 31, 2014

At an early age, King learned to think for himself. Religion, particularly, struck him
as being largely a matter of faith but misplaced: It just didn't make sense. There
was heaven and there was hell, and you could go to hell just for believing in a different
Christian faith.

*Statue in the Bangor-Orono area.*

By high school, as he told *Rolling Stone*, "that was it for me."

Today he's "totally agnostic" on the idea of heaven, but he wants to believe in God for the same reason that we all do: We want to believe that when our mortal lives end, our immortal lives begin, because it's comforting. We want to go to heaven in whatever form it takes and reconnect with our loved ones who have preceded us into death. We want the afterlife to be better than what we have on earth.

The alternative, postulated by theoretical physicist Stephen Hawking, is rational and cold comfort. As he told *The Guardian,* "I regard the brain as a computer which will stop working when its components fail. There is no heaven or afterlife for broken down computers; that is a fairy story for people afraid of the dark."

What logically follows, says Hawking, is that we should make the best use of our limited time in this world. "We should see the greatest value of our action," he says.

King, whatever he says, seeks the greatest value of his actions: He writes as if demon-driven.

King's ongoing exploration of Christianity began with *Carrie* but clearly won't end with his most current novel, *Revival*. From Margaret White, who locks her daughter Carrie into her "prayer closet," to a fallen minister who repudiates his faith and seeks forbidden knowledge, religion is a recurring theme that bears frequent visitation in King's fiction. There will likely be more books from King speculating on the afterlife.

In the end, as he told *Rolling Stone,* "I would like to believe that there is some sort of an afterlife." To which I say: Don't we all?

What we don't want to believe is what cartoonist Gahan Wilson depicted in a 1980 cartoon for *The New Yorker* magazine: Two monks, in robes, are seated and discussing life. One has a serene expression, and the other, who does not, says, "Nothing happens next. This is it."

---

We each owe a death, there are no exceptions.

—Stephen King, *The Green Mile*

---

# 113

# "I Hear Time's Winged Chariot Drawing Near"

I t's always later than you think.

Stephen King, who is painfully aware of time's passage, feels strongly that he wants to get as much written as possible, which means he doesn't waste time. He's structured his life around writing to maximize his literary output. He has no patience with writers whose books are published decades apart. What, he asks, are they *doing* with their time?

Critics often point out how prolific King is, to which he responds: I just work steadily, that's all. That's the King writing formula: Year in and year out, he writes every day of the year except Christmas, and the words pile up: a sentence, a paragraph, a chapter, a completed book. Then rinse and repeat.

When asked by *Rolling Stone* if he expects to still be writing in his eighties, he replied:

> Yeah. What else am I going to do? I mean, shit, you've got to do something to fill up your day. And I can only play so much guitar and watch so many TV shows. [Writing] fulfills me. There are two things about it I like: It makes me happy, and it makes other people happy.

He doesn't worry about his legacy. As he told *Rolling Stone*, "[I]t's out of my control. Only two things happen to writers when they die: Either their work survives, or it becomes forgotten."

If the unthinkable happens—King, for whatever reasons, retires—it'll be a sad day for his readers, but he has created a large body of work, and there's always pleasure in rereading old favorites. It's taken a lifetime for King to write the stories; and it'd take a good part of one's lifetime to read, reread, and appreciate them.

For King it means shutting out the outside world to go into his world of imagination to explore its many dimensions.

He's told *Cosmopolitan* that he'd like to be remembered as a "good storyteller" and that he prefers to deflect attention from him and onto his work. As he said in a *Playboy* interview about "The Breathing Method" (*Different Seasons*):

> I created a mysterious private club in an old brownstone on East 35th Street in Manhattan, in which an oddly matched group of men gathers periodically to trade tales of the uncanny. And there are many rooms upstairs, and when a new guest asks the exact number, the strange old butler tells him, "I don't know, sir, but you could get lost up there." That men's club really is a metaphor for the entire storytelling process. There are as many stories in me as there are rooms in that house, and I can easily lose myself in them. And at the club, whenever a tale is about to be told, a toast is raised first, echoing the words engraved on the keystone of the massive fireplace in the library: IT IS THE TALE, NOT HE WHO TELLS IT.
>
> That's been a good guide to me in life, and I think it would make a good epitaph for my tombstone. Just that and no name.

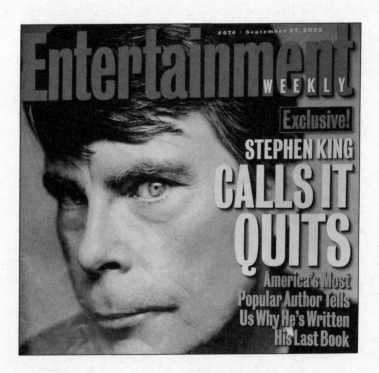

# 114

---

## FINDERS KEEPERS

### 2015

"I love mysteries and suspense most of all ... The most difficult
by far (at least for me [to write]) is the novel of mystery. *Mr.
Mercedes, Finders Keepers,* and the forthcoming *The Suicide
Prince*[1]—the Hodges trilogy—were extremely difficult. I just
can't fathom how people like Agatha Christie, Dorothy Sayers,
Peter Robinson, and Ruth Rendell are able to do this in book
after book."

—STEPHEN KING, "STEPHEN KING: BY THE BOOK,"
INTERVIEW, *NEW YORK TIMES,* JUNE 4, 2015

When the publication of *Joyland* (2013) was announced by Hard Case Crime,
King chimed in: "I love crime. I love mysteries, and I love ghosts. That combo
made Hard Case Crime the perfect venue for this book, which is one of my favorites. I
also loved the paperbacks I grew up with as a kid. ..."

*Joyland,* as it turned out, was a tad lighter on all three counts than some readers,

---

1  Now retitled *End of Watch.*

including myself, had wished for—it was mostly a coming-of-age novel about a high school graduate who had loved and lost, and spent a summer working at an amusement park named Joyland—but the Hodges trilogy that followed would have fit perfectly at Titan Books' imprint, Hard Case Crime.

*Mr. Mercedes,* the first book in the trilogy, published in 2014, introduced us to an engaging trio: a retired cop named Bill Hodges, aided by Holly Gibney and Jerome Robinson.

The linkage between *Mr. Mercedes* and *Finders Keepers* is Tom Saubers, who was in the wrong place at the wrong time—in line at a job fair—and as a result was crippled by a man dubbed Mr. Mercedes, who drove a stolen car into a line of job-seekers. (The incident recalls King's own encounter with a wayward minivan in June 1999.)

The novel literally begins with a bang. As other reviewers have pointed out—spoiler alert!—novelist John Rothstein, lauded by *Time* magazine in a cover story as "America's Reclusive Genius," is shot and killed during a robbery at his home five miles from the nearest town. Rothstein, modeled after J. D. Salinger, had published a series of books (*The Runner, The Runner Sees Action,* and *The Runner Slows Down*) that firmly cemented his literary reputation, and allowed him the luxury of writing without the need to publish to make money.[2]

Though the heist yields envelopes of cash with $400 in each, the real find are holographic manuscripts by Rothstein, including sequels to *The Runner* series. The thief/ murderer Morris Bellamy is an outraged, and unbalanced, reader who practically foams at the mouth when confronting Rothstein:

> "I'm not saying you should have stopped with *The Runner,*" Morrie said. "*The Runner Sees Action* was just as good, maybe even better. They were *true*. It was the last one. Man, what a crap carnival. Advertising? I mean, *advertising*?"

Bellamy is pissed and blames Rothstein for Jimmy Gold having sold out, which turns out to be ironic because, among those unpublished manuscripts recorded in Moleskin notebooks, Rothstein continues the series and writes of Gold's redemption. In other words, had Bellamy known of their existence, he perhaps would not have been so vitriolic in his criticism about Rothstein's depiction of Gold—a moot point, since Rothstein's anger flares, and his verbal attacks against Bellamy push him over the edge: Bellamy simply kills his literary idol, Rothstein.

That would normally be the end of any story, but in *Finders Keepers,* it's just its beginning. And when Bellamy is jailed—again, ironically, not for the murders of his two accomplices in the robbery and Rothstein but for a rape of which he has no recollection—and life goes on outside the prison, Bellamy's cache of cash and manuscripts are

---

2 The titles recall another famous American author—John Updike, with a nod to his Rabbit Angstrom novels. By the way, in numerous interviews, King has talked about some of the publishing myths surrounding Salinger, including one that states he stopped publishing but never stopped writing, because he was known to deposit manuscript-sized boxes at his bank, secured in safe deposit boxes.

discovered by Peter Saubers, a young reader, who realizes it's a life-changing find. But when Rothstein finally gets paroled, it could be a life-*ending* find. Rothstein discovers his ill-gotten gains purloined, but where? And by whom? And how will he recover the goods?

Conceived as a trilogy, the third and final part in the series is titled *End of Watch*, but that won't be the last we see of the winsome team of Hodges, Gibney, and Robinson, because the trilogy has been optioned for television as a miniseries.

A meditation on how fiction can exert a malign hold on an unbalanced reader, *Finders Keepers* is on the beam. It's a tightly focused crime novel that showcases King's considerable storytelling powers, recalling *Misery*, in which another reader also becomes too enamored with the storytelling, at the ultimate expense of the storyteller: The writer is held hostage by Annie Wilkes, a deranged ex-nurse who forces him to bring a beloved character back to life. She considers it quid pro quo: She nurses the writer back to health, and in payment she demands a novel written just for her, his self-proclaimed number-one fan.

Though *End of Watch* will be the end of this series, I doubt that it will be the end of King's exploration of the power of fiction, and the hold it has over the writer and the reader as well.

# 115

## THE BAZAAR OF BAD DREAMS

### (2015)

"I would suggest you start by reading these stories. . . . They
show how vital short stories can be when they are done with
heart, mind, and soul by people who care about them and think
they still matter. They *do* still matter, and here they are, liberated
from the bottom shelf."

—STEPHEN KING, "INTRODUCTION," *THE BEST AMERICAN SHORT STORIES* (2007),
EDITED BY STEPHEN KING

In his introduction to *Skeleton Crew*, King makes his case for the appeal of the short story, a literary form that, in terms of book sales appeal, runs a distant second to novels.

Readers, as publishers know, prefer long stories over short ones, which is why collections of short fiction are tough sells from writer to agent, from agent to publisher, and from publisher to bookseller. Case in point: When Stephen King pitched *Different Seasons* (a novella collection) to his then-editor Alan Williams at Viking Press, he got a lukewarm reception. But when King offered a novel about a haunted car, Williams perked up with unrestrained enthusiasm. "My man!" he cried.

Let's face it: A novel pulls the fiction reading train, and a collection of short fiction is its caboose.

But a good short story—as King knows, and as he's explained in introductions to his own fiction, in interviews, and in his introduction to *The Best American Short Stories*—is not written for money but for love. (Literary magazines often "pay" in contributor's copies, not folding money, as does *Playboy*.)

In *The Bazaar of Bad Dreams*, almost five hundred pages in length, and comparable in length to *Everything's Eventual* (2002), there's something for everyone: Unlike all of King's other book collections, the twenty pieces in this one sports individual introductions giving the reader behind-the-curtain peeks at the writing process. Consider it, if you will, as codas to King's *On Writing* (2000).[1]

In the introduction to *The Bazaar of Bad Dreams*, King extols the virtues of the short form. He explains that "there's something to be said for a shorter, more intense experience. It can be invigorating, sometimes even shocking, like a waltz with a stranger you will never see again, or a kiss in the dark, or a beautiful curio for sale laid out on a cheap blanket at a street bazaar. . . . Feel free to examine them, but please be careful. The best of them have teeth."

The title and King's admonition are reflective of the overall tone of the stories herein.

Here's the breakdown as to where the stories[2] were published: two as e-books only, eight from periodicals (general interest magazines and literary magazines), one in an anthology, one as an audiobook only, two from specialty publishers in book form, one as bonus story to a previously published novel, and three that make their first appearance herein.

It's an eclectic collection that amply demonstrates King's range and—at this late date—his mastery of the short story, where his decision toward concision pays dividends. Unlike a typical King novel that weighs in with hefty wordage requiring a substantial time investment to read, these short stories are quick reads.

Not surprisingly, many of the stories are literary in nature, as implied by the publications in which they appear: *The New Yorker*, *Harpers*, *Esquire*, *The Atlantic*, and literary journals *Tin House* and *Granta*. These are clearly the work of a mature, and older, writer who can see his road ahead on life's path is shorter than the one behind. For that reason, the stories tend to be steeped in realism, with a certain grim tone, and clearly aren't fairy tales. "Afterlife" finds a man who dies and relives his life time and again; "Morality," like "A Good Marriage" (*Full Dark, No Stars*), amply shows how life's circumstances can force an unraveling of a marriage; and "Summer Thunder" is a story of a man and his dog, set in a post-apocalyptic world, that will riven your heart.

Taken collectively, this set of stories is more nightmare than dreamscape. Life itself, as King shows us in these cautionary tales, is sometimes terrifying enough indeed.

---

1 The Cleveland *Plain Dealer* called it "The best book on writing. Ever."
2 There's also two poems.

# PART SIX

# MOVIES: SCREAMPLAYS

I don't write books with movies in mind, although some reviewers say that I do. If Dickens were around today, he'd probably be faced with the same charge, because some of his books have been made into movies.

—Stephen King, *New York Times,* September 27, 1981

The film versions never live up to the original vision, because when you sit down to write a book, you don't need a special effects department to make people catch on fire or levitate, to make people appear and disappear, or even come back from the dead. That all goes on—the special effects factory is built-in. There are no wires, no cords. There's nothing like that—it just happens.

So in that sense, they never live up to my expectations. And only on rare occasions do they live up to the audience's expectations.

My idea of the perfect horror film would be one where you'd have to have nurses and doctors on duty with crash wagons because people would have heart attacks. People would crawl out with large wet spots on their trousers. It would be that kind of experience.

—Stephen King on his film adaptations
(source unknown)

Because of the numerous adaptations, film and television, that have been made from King's work, it'd require a separate, lengthy volume with hundreds of stills to do justice to all of them: the good, the bad, and the fugly.

Stephen Jones's *Creepshows* is the best general interest book on King's visual adaptations to date, but it needs updating because it was published in 2001. A comprehensive critical assessment, though, has yet to be published.

As King will tell you, his movies have been a mixed bag, but the good ones stand out, and those are the ones that bear discussion here. I've focused on eleven films that I feel are representative. I've also reprinted an illuminating interview by one director who has much to say about King's films: screenwriter and director Frank Darabont.

# 116

# STEPHEN: A BOX OFFICE KING

The real superheroes of the industry right now? These writers—
ranked in order of influence—whose books are source material for
more than 300 movie and TV projects, have helped rake in billions
in box office and revenue, and prove every day that originality,
above all else, still matters.

—"HOLLYWOOD'S 25 MOST POWERFUL AUTHORS," *HOLLYWOOD REPORTER,* NOVEMBER 23, 2014
(STEPHEN KING, AT NUMBER 2, IS LISTED AFTER J. K. ROWLING)

King at the press conference for at the world
premiere of Graveyard Shift *in Bangor, at a local
theater.*

*A movie poster for Stanley Kubrick's* The Shining.

Stephen King was ten years old when he went with his mother to see the Walt Disney animated movie *Bambi*. He recalled it was "the first time I got scared . . . when the woods caught on fire. . . . The Disney pictures are scary as shit!" It was the beginning of King's loss of innocence, and his initiation experience; sitting in the dark, watching light passing through flickering still frames of a movie, it was the illusion of life on a large screen. For an impressionable young boy, it was dark and scary magic.

King's early exposure to movies helps explain why his writing style is visual. He paints word pictures that lends themselves to visual adaptation.

Authors are concerned about fidelity to their work, but Hollywood has other priorities. Hollywood treats the original source material as clay, to be twisted and shaped as necessary to enhance sales. With costs running into the millions of dollars, a studio's concern is to recoup the money as quickly as possible and make a big profit by slicing and dicing the "property" to mine multiple revenue streams: foreign film release, multiple DVD / Blu-Ray editions, streaming video, and repeated showings on TV.

Printing up to a million hardbacks is serious business, but it pales in comparison to a major movie release from a big studio that costs tens of millions of dollars, which must reach many millions worldwide to justify its cost; in other words, if just everyone who bought a King book bought a movie ticket, that movie would fail at the box office.

King became a household name not necessarily through his books but through his movies. People who have never picked up a King book will likely have seen at least one of them. It also explains why King's fiction is so often adapted to the visual medium: Stephen King is a brand name, and that reduces Hollywood's risk. Name brand recognition is a deciding factor in choosing to see a King flick over one without any branding.

As King told Tony Magistrale in an interview, he's a "bankable writer" in Hollywood, someone whose movies will almost certainly make a profit, so long as the production and creative talent costs are in line.

Box office is all about filling as many seats as possible, which means keeping films under two hours: It explains why long books like *The Stand* are best suited for television, which allows for more time to let the story naturally unfold. (*The Stand*, released in 1994, aired in four installments with a total running time of over six hours [366 minutes]. But plans are under way to reshoot it, again as a four-parter, this time for the big screen.)

Hollywood loves Stephen King. The real horror story is losing money on a grand scale, which means studio heads roll and jobs are lost at the studio. That's what happened when New Line Cinema's ambitious adaptation of Philip Pullman's *The Golden Compass* tanked. But King's film audience is intensely loyal. They love and support the brand, and a major King movie—when you count all the income streams—almost always adds up to a profit. So King films are a safe bet, which means Stephen's the king of the box office. His films have raked in over two billion dollars, according to boxofficemojo.com, and that counts just thirty-nine of King's movies, adjusted for inflation.

## In the Pipeline

From the Web site denofgeek.us, we learn that King's got a lot of films in various stages of completion in the pipeline—twenty-two and counting: *11/22/63* (2011), a novel about a man who goes back in time to 1963 in an attempt to stop the assassination of President John F. Kennedy, for Hulu; *Ayana*, from the same-named short story (*Just After Sunset*, 2008), for NBC TV; a novella, *The Breathing Method*, from the same-named short story (*Different Seasons*, 1982); a novel, *Cell* (2006), based on a screenplay by Stephen King and Adam Alleca; "Children of the Corn" (*Night Shift*, 1978), from Warner Bros., which makes it the tenth in the series; *Creepshow 4*, rumored to be a Warner Bros. release; *The Dark Tower* (1982), a project still in flux; *Firestarter* (1994) from Universal and Dino De Laurentiis Company; *Gerald's Game* (1992), from Intrepid Pictures; *Grand Central*, based on "*The New York Times* at Special Bargain Rates" (*Just After Sunset*, 2008); *It* (1986), from New Line Cinema; *Joyland* (2013), Woylah Films; *Lisey's Story* (2006); *The Long Walk* (1979), to be directed by Frank Darabont; *Mercy* (based on "Gramma," from *Skeleton Crew*, 1985), based on a Stephen King screenplay; *The Overlook Hotel*, inspired by *The Shining* (1977), a prequel from Warner Bros. and Mythology Entertainment; *Pet Sematary* (1983), Paramount; *Rose Madder* (1995), with a screenplay by Naomi Sheridan; *The Shop* (inspired by *Firestarter*, 1980) for television's TNT, written by Robbie Thompson and produced by James Middleton; *The Stand* as a four-parter (1978 and 1990), written and directed by Josh Boone; *The Talisman* (1984), with Frank Marshall attached; and *The Ten O'Clock People* (*Nightmares and Dreamscapes*, 1993), directed by Tom Holland, based on his screenplay.

## "Dollar Babies"

King's official Web site lists short stories available for "film students who want to try their hands at a Stephen King story." Because the list constantly changes, I won't list them here but instead refer you to the source. (Stories not listed are not available for a student film.)

King asks for your name, e-mail address, and the story selected (via drop-down menu), plus a message with additional details. The deal, laid out in the FAQ section of his Web site, lists four requirements:

1. Dollar Babies can only be adapted from pre-approved short stories; novels are not available.
2. They cannot be "for profit."
3. They can only be exhibited at film festivals, as student projects, or for demo reels.
4. A contract must be completed before a film can be produced.

It's an unprecedented deal, one that's at odds with other writers, notably Harlan Ellison, who responded to a fan online who asked for permission to adapt one of his short stories, "Anywhere but Here, with Anybody but You." Harlan's polite but firm reply was posted on his Web site on October 3, 2014:

Sorry, Matt, permission denied.

It ain't quite that easy.

First, you have to get some money. Not a lot, but at least SOME.

Then we schmooze a little, I vet your previous attempts at screenwriting, and if you got even minimal chops, we arrive at a term of option for the story, in exchange for a palmful of that money. We sign a contract of a page or two, which is called an "option," and we go our separate ways for a period of time—as indicated—during which you do a first adaptation. Thereafter, if the work you've done has some worth, and you get MoneyPeople in the Movie Business in love with your treatment, you renew the option or we move on to an actual contract for pre-production.

Other than that route, kiddo, the story (and all my others) is sacrosanct, and you cannot even idly scrawl a Schaffer-version on chalkboard for your bling-gang to savor.

I cannot be bought . . . but I can be rented.

Hope this lays everything out professionally for you.

## KING'S INVOLVEMENT

One of my editors, Bill Thompson, once said that "Stephen King has a movie projector in his head." He could be right. Whenever I write a scene, I always know left from right, what the depth of perception is. I very rarely give much description of my major characters because I am looking out from inside their eyes. . . . I am interested in the kinetics of the world, which is why so many of my books . . . have been adapted to the screen.

—*Stephen King, quoted by Bob Thomas,* Gainesville Sun, *July 23, 1986*

King's involvement with movies depends on the contract he signed for the book or short story. Since all his novels are reserved for movie/TV options, they are not available for "dollar baby" usage.

King's principal interest are his books. But on behalf of movie projects, he has variously worn several hats: as screenwriter, cameo actor, director (once, for *Maximum Overdrive*), assistant director (*The Shining* TV miniseries), and executive producer (for *The Stand* TV miniseries). Of course, he's most often credited as a screenwriter, for which he's best suited.

By far the most contentious film-related project was King's battle with New Line Cinema, whose 1992 film, *The Lawnmower Man,* struck me as being so tenuously connected to the original story that its major appeal as a film project lay in the box office value of King's name.

In a story reprinted in the *Daily Press* (March 1992), King complained, "I hate it that New Line's got my name plastered all over the place. It's the biggest rip-off that you could imagine because there's nothing of me in there. It just makes me furious. . . . There's also nothing about computers and virtual reality in my story, which seems to be all that the movie is about."

As *Entertainment Weekly* (April 1994) pointed out, "[T]he author charged that the virtual-reality pic bore little resemblance to his tale and demanded that his name be removed from the film and its advertising."

But New Line didn't comply, and the matter went to court, which was eventually decided in King's favor: When the video was released with his name clearly on the product box, it cost New Line big bucks: $10,000 in daily fines, until King's name was removed, and all the profits from the home video, which went directly to King. (His lawyer, Peter Herbert, said, "Stephen is thrilled and feels he's been vindicated.")

On the other hand, when things go well, they go very well indeed. A sleeper that made only $18 million at the box office, *Shawshank Redemption* found its audience on its second run, on home video, and television reruns. As Russell Adams (*Wall Street Journal*, May 2014) pointed out, *Shawshank* actors are getting hefty residuals with no end in sight; licensing fees, home video, and electronic delivery have raked in millions for Warner Bros. long after the film's initial release in 1994.

The rights were bought from King for $5,000, back when Frank Darabont was a relative unknown. Darabont even got the original check back, uncashed, framed, and inscribed with a note from King: "In case you ever need bail money. Love, Steve."

King's principal involvement in two films—*Maximum Overdrive*, as director and *The Shining*, as assistant director—proved instrumental. King bore 100 percent responsibility for *Maximum Overdrive*, a critically panned 1986 release based on "Trucks," a short story collected in *Night Shift*. Budgeted at $9 million, it brought in $7.4 million at the box office. Rotten Tomatoes, a film Web site, gave it an approval rating of only 17 percent. And even King was frank in admitting it was his worst film adaptation.

At a July 1986 press conference in Beverly Hills to promote *Maximum Overdrive*, King defended it by saying, "This is a moron movie, like *Splash*! You can check your brains at the box office and you come out 96 minutes later and pick them up again."

To *New Times*, King explained, "Listen, this movie is all about having a good time at the movies, and that's *all* it's about. Believe me, it's not *My Dinner with Andre*. And little Stevie is not rehearsing his Academy Award speech for *this* baby. . . . When you write a novel, you are the cinematographer, the star, the special-effects crew, everything. You are in total control. Making a film, you have eighty people standing around, waiting for the sun to come out. . . . Now *that* is a primitive way to create. For the record, I don't think the picture is going to review badly."

He finally concluded: "I think most of you know the movie was a critical and financial flop," he wrote in *Castle Rock*. "The curse of expectation wasn't the only reason . . . but it was certainly one of them."

Since the release of *Carrie* in 1976 as a major motion picture, fans have chimed in on what they consider their favorite King films. I've picked what I feel is representative. Your mileage will vary.

King's own list over the years has been pretty consistent. In a *Rolling Stone* interview (November 2014), he cited several. The best, he said, was *Stand by Me*. He added, "But *Stand by Me, Shawshank Redemption, Green Mile* are all really great ones. *Misery* is a great film. *Dolores Claiborne* is a really, really good film. *Cujo* is terrific."

Building on King's list, I'm adding the other films that I think are well worth your attention, in chronological order of their release dates. These are the ones I've most often seen cited as favorites and bests. Also, to give a sense of scale, I've cited each film's "Tomatometer" rating from the Web site Rotten Tomatoes.

# 117

# Ten Notable Films in Chronological Order

I.

*Carrie: High School Hell*

Release date[1]: November 3, 1976; Tomatometer: 92%; audience score; 76%. (Rotten Tomatoes rates it as number 45 out of the top 75 horror films of all time.) Screenplay by Lawrence D. Cohen, directed by Brian De Palma. Budget: $1.8 million; U.S. box office receipts: $33.8 million.

In any list of noteworthy King films, *Carrie* cannot be overlooked, not because it's the first but because of its staying power. In addition to its original 1976 appearance, it was remade for TV in 2002, and in 2013 it was remade as a major motion picture with Chloë Grace Moretz as Carrie and Julianne Moore as her mother. Also, it became a musical on Broadway, where the critics dumped buckets of pig's blood on it.

The novel and the film draw their power from the depiction of high school as a caste system, the perfect setting for a movie aimed for teenagers, which is an important demographic for the film industry. Drawing on his own experiences in grade and high school, and observing high schoolers from the vantage point of a teacher, King saw it all: the good, the bad, and the ugly.

As Tabitha King wrote in an introduction to the New American Library Collectors Edition, "*Carrie*'s readers also respond to the portrait of high school as a zoo, a horror show, as blackly funny, awkward, and cruel as a Punch and Judy show."

---

1 The date a movie opens simultaneously nationwide in U.S. theaters.

King transmuted his own experiences to make *Carrie* come alive on the page, and we empathize and identify with her: Haven't we all felt like an outsider at one point in our lives?

One of his teachers told NPR (May 10, 2003) that

[h]e was taunted by older boys on his way home from school when he was in grade school. The older boys would hide in a hollow, and they would jump out at him or scare him. So I think he was the butt of a lot of pranks. His first book [*Carrie*] was heavily based on Lisbon High, down to several faculty members. We had a bumbling assistant principal who's portrayed in *Carrie* as the guy who closed the file drawer door and slams his thumb.

Keep in mind the time frame: The novel *Carrie* was published in hardback in 1974, and *'Salem's Lot* was published in hardback in 1975. King wasn't a brand-name horror writer at the time; he was unknown to moviegoers, and in the book industry his reputation was growing: He was pegged as an upcoming writer to watch.

A low-budget movie ($1.8 million) directed by Brian de Palma, a relative unknown at the time, *Carrie* was released on November 3, 1976, and the box office receipts exceeded all expectations.

The movie itself is riveting. A timely tale—school bullying still makes the news on a regular basis, almost four decades later—and also a timeless tale (high school is still hell for outsiders), the movie was not only hugely profitable but also served as a vehicle for its two principal actors: Sissy Spacek, who had previously appeared in *Badlands* (1973), and was suddenly thrust into stardom, and Piper Laurie, who had not been in a major film in fifteen years, since *The Hustler,* and who commanded critical attention in her role as a fundamentalist Christian. Both Spacek and Laurie received Oscar nominations in 1977 for their respective roles as actress and supporting actress in what was a low-budget horror film for which no one held high expectations. (The movie also starred Amy Irving, William Katt, John Travolta, and Nancy Allen.)

Spacek, who had been a high school prom queen in real life, didn't win the Oscar for her role, and neither did Laurie, who also received a Golden Globe nomination. In my opinion, they were robbed, but their riveting performances underscored what readers already knew: that Stephen King is one hell of a storyteller, and *Carrie* is one hell of a movie.

As King observed, speaking about the book and the subsequent film adaptation, "I made *Carrie,* and *Carrie* made me."

## Multiple Takes

**Stephen King**: "Brian De Palma's *Carrie* was terrific. He handled the material deftly and artistically, and got a fine performance out of Sissy Spacek. In many ways the film is far more stylish than my book, which I still think is a gripping read but is impeded by a certain heaviness . . . a quality that's absent from the film" (*Playboy*, interviewed by Eric Norden, June 1983).

**Brian de Palma**: "I read the book. It was suggested to me by a writer friend of mine. A writer friend of his, Stephen King, had written it. I guess this was [circa 1975]. I liked it a lot and proceeded to call my agent to find out who owned it. I found out that nobody had bought it yet. A lot of studios were considering it, so I called around to some of the people I knew and said it was a terrific book and I'm very interested in doing it" (Mike Childs and Alan Jones, in *Cinefantastique*).

**Sissy Spacek,** on the pivotal scene: "It wasn't hard for me to get into this scene, because I'd been to a few proms in my time. I'd even been homecoming queen my senior year at Quitman High School. The lights and music were so familiar to me, and I could easily imagine how Carrie would have been dazzled by the attention. Of course, anyone who has seen the movie knows that Carrie's moment of glory is destroyed when her enemies drop a bucket of pig's blood on her head and all hell breaks loose—literally.

"They filled the bucket with Karo syrup and red food dye. Of course we had to film that scene twice, from every angle. At first the 'blood' felt like a warm blanket, but it quickly got sticky and disgusting. I had to wear that stuff for days. And when they lit the fires behind me to burn down the gym, I started to feel like a candy apple" (Spacek, with Maryanne Vollers, *My Extraordinary Ordinary Life*).

## *The Critics' Take*

**Richard Schickel** (*Time*): "An exercise in high style that even the most unredeemably rational among moviegoers should find enormously enjoyable."

**Tom Huddleston** (timeout.com): "This is a truly throat-grabbing horror movie, sporting a handful of pitch-perfect set pieces. . . . Sissy Spacek's performance in the title role is close to flawless: she was 27 when the film was shot, but looks barely half that, and this otherworldly combination of maturity and innocence adds to the film's unsettling tone."

**Roger Ebert** (rogerebert.com): It's "an absolutely spellbinding horror movie, with a shock at the end that's the best thing along those lines since the shark leaped aboard in *Jaws*. It's also (and this is what makes it so good) an observant human portrait. This girl Carrie isn't another stereotyped product of the horror production line; she's a shy, pretty, and complicated high school senior who's a lot like the kids we once knew."

Note: In 2013 the movie was remade on a $35.3 million budget and released by Sony. It starred Chloë Grace Moretz in the title role. It did not, however, please the critics or fans, who respectively gave it ratings of 49% and 46% on the Tomatometer.

2.

## *The Shining: Redrum, Redrum*

I admire Kubrick for the sheer variety in his films. I'm sure *The Shining* will be the best haunted-house movie ever put on film.

—*Steven Spielberg, interview with Chris Hodenfeld*, Rolling Stone, *1980*

Release date: May 23, 1980); Tomatometer: 92%; audience score: 93%. Screenplay by Stanley Kubrick and Diane Johnson; directed by Kubrick. Budget: $19 million; U.S. domestic gross receipts: $44 million. Key cast: Jack Nicholson, as Jack Torrance; Shelley Duvall, as Wendy Torrance; Danny Lloyd, as Danny Torrance; and Scatman Crothers, as Dick Hallorann.

As King told *Playboy* (June 1983):

I'd admired Kubrick for a long time and had great expectations for the project, but I was deeply disappointed in the end result. Parts of the film are chilling, charged with a relentlessly claustrophobic terror, but others fall flat. I think there are two basic problems with the movie. First, Kubrick is a very cold man—pragmatic and rational—and he had great difficulty conceiving, even academically, of a supernatural world . . . a visual skeptic such as Kubrick just couldn't grasp the sheer inhuman evil of the Overlook Hotel. So he looked, instead, for evil in the characters, and made the film into a domestic tragedy with only vaguely supernatural overtones. That was the basic flaw: Because he couldn't believe, he couldn't make the film believable to others.

The second problem was in characterization and casting. Jack Nicholson, though a fine actor, was all wrong for the part. His last big role had been in *One Flew Over the Cuckoo's Nest,* and between that and his manic grin, the audience automatically identified him as a loony from the first scene . . . if the guy is nuts to begin with, then the entire tragedy of his downfall is wasted. For that reason, the film has no center and no heart . . . it's a film by a man who thinks too much and feels too little, and that's why, for all its virtuoso effects, it never gets you by the throat and hangs on the way real horror should.

Because King counts *The Shining* as one of his favorite books, it was King's misfortune (as he sees it) to have had Kubrick at the helm, because the end result was a movie that pleased Kubrick and his fans, but not King and all of his fans, who are right in saying that it's a cold film. (So, too, is Kubrick's *2001: A Space Odyssey,* in which dialogue is minimized, and the most compelling character is Hal, a sentient computer on board a spaceship.)

But because of Kubrick's reputation as a great film director, his version of *The Shining* has gotten an extraordinary amount of coverage in the media, and from critics as well. Had it been directed by a lesser-known director, or a first-time director, it's not likely the coverage would have been so extensive.

King's perceived faults with Kubrick's *The Shining* are encapsulated in the *Playboy* quote above; I see no need to belabor King's point. Kubrick, on the other hand, has said very little about the film, but in an interview with Michael Ciment (visual-memory. co.uk), it's clear that there's a serious disconnect between what King wrote in his novel, and how Kubrick interpreted it, as Kubrick made clear in his wrong assessment of Jack and his family: "Jack comes to the hotel psychologically prepared to do its murderous bidding. He doesn't have very much further to go for his anger and frustration to become completely uncontrollable. He is bitter about his failure as a writer. He is married to a woman for whom he has only contempt. He hates his son."

It proves that Kubrick set out to impose his vision over King's to such an extent that the film is best described as "Stanley Kubrick's *The Shining*," to avoid confusion with King's own remake that aired on ABC-TV in 1997. It's also clear, in retrospect, that Kubrick fumed at King's never-ending barrage of complaints. It seems that Kubrick had grown tired of reading King's interviews about *The Shining*, in which he and his movie were treated as punching bags.

Kubrick kept silent as King, over the years, repeatedly voiced his objections.

All of that said, judging from its Rotten Tomatoes rating, critics and moviegoers liked Kubrick's version, placing it among the highest-rated King films to date. Even among loyal King fans, there's a begrudging admiration for Kubrick's "haunted house" movie, as Spielberg termed it. It may not have been faithful to the book, but it sure as hell was scary—terrifying, even.

The fact remains that, like *The Exorcist*, there's a deeply unsettling—indeed, disquieting— quality to Kubrick's film that invokes terror. From the appropriately eerie music that opens the movie to specific scenes that get under the skin the way a good horror movie does, *The Shining* is simply disturbing, serving Kubrick's vision well: the two little girls inviting Danny to play, the discomfiting scene with the man dressed as a dog, the sense of increased dread as the walls close in on the Torrance family, the obvious mental disintegration of Jack Torrance as he slowly loses his grip on reality—all of these elements work in unison, and powerfully so. After viewing it at the theater, I left with a sense of dislocation. Immersed in the movie and its haunting elements, I appreciated what Kubrick set out to do, and what he accomplished, though I knew Stephen King would come away displeased.

King, after all, is mostly interested in characters, in making an emotional connection with the reader/viewer, and he does so by carefully drawing portraits of sympathetic characters so that, when they are in danger, we feel their fear. But Kubrick's vision for *The Shining* wasn't about the family at all; it was about the Overlook itself. The people, to him, were of secondary concern.

So, in the end, Spielberg is right: It's the ultimate haunted *house* movie, though it should have been the ultimate haunted *person/family* movie, in the form of Jack Torrance.

This explains why King wanted to redo the movie: He wanted to restore the family as its center. *The Shining* is, after all, a haunted movie about a dysfunctional family.

When King decided to do a remake, he contractually needed Kubrick's permission. Kubrick gave it, but with a nonnegotiable requirement: Stephen King had to stop complaining to the media about Kubrick's film, and King agreed. He no longer speaks out against the film, preferring to talk about his own version.

As for the remake, it was directed by Mick Garris, with a script by King, who also served as executive producer. *Stephen King's The Shining,* a three-part miniseries for television, aired in 1997. This second time around, and based on King's own screenplay, it was partially shot at the Stanley Hotel, and the casting reflected King's choices: Steven Weber played Jack Torrance, Rebecca De Mornay played Wendy Torrance, and Courtland Mead played Danny Torrance; they all were relatable in a way that Jack Nicholson, Shelley Duvall, and Danny Lloyd were not. Moreover, the luxury of shooting for television gave King's version more room to breathe: 273 minutes broken up in three 91-minute episodes.

Speaking about his own movie at a press conference (the Ritz-Carlton Huntington Hotel in Pasadena, January 9, 1997), King was joined by director Mick Garris, Steven Weber, and Rebecca De Mornay. King explained:

> What I did was to try to write the truest, most wrenching story. . . . *The Shining* is a story about a haunted hotel, but it's also a story about a haunted marriage. And the two should work together. The reality of that abusive relationship should enhance and make the ghost story even more frightening.
>
> But let's face it: I tried to write a scary book. And I didn't see any sense in taking it and prettying it up for TV, so I went to ABC and said, "Do you have a problem with this, if we do this, this and this?" And they said, "No, we can do that for TV." . . . I think people who've read the book know what they're in for. And I think people who tune in . . . well, hopefully I think that story succeeds on its own terms. That if a story is good and if the characters are believable, and if the acting is good, and if the direction works—if all those things work—people get into the story, and they want to live in that world for a while; they're willing to go into that car of the roller-coaster and go up the slope.
>
> We're promising them a scary ride, but one that they'll come back from alive.

Given that King's 1997 remake succeeds in correcting what he perceives as egregious in Kubrick's film, the TV miniseries is in essence a different take based on the same source: We see Kubrick's version and also King's, and as to what the viewer prefers, it's a matter of taste that depends largely on where one's sympathies lie.

Note: King has steadfastly refused to write sequels, but he felt impelled to tell the story of what happened to Danny Torrance, who escaped with his mother from the Overlook Hotel. The sequel, *Doctor Sleep,* will surely see a major motion picture release. In the meantime, though, Hollywood is going back to *The Shining,* with a prequel: *The Overlook Hotel,* to be directed by Mark Romanek, with a script by Glen Mazzara. No date has been announced, and it's worth noting that Stephen King is not involved, but this prequel should tap into "Before the Play," a reworked version of the *The Shining*'s original prologue, told in five scenes, that his publisher unwisely jettisoned because of length issues: The prologue properly sets the stage for what is to follow and is required reading to fully enjoy the novel.

But if "Before the Play" is not a starting point for the prequel, then I for one am not optimistic. I'd rather not see another King film that trades more on his name than on a faithful adaptation of his work, because it's not about fidelity; it's about infidelity, and screwing everybody over at their expense in pursuit of profits for the studio and its shareholders, and the writer be damned.

## Multiple Takes

**Stephen King**: "I'm not a cold guy. I think one of the things people relate to in my books is this warmth; there's a reaching out and saying to the reader, 'I want you to be a part of this.' With Kubrick's *The Shining* I felt that it was very cold, very 'We're looking at these people, but they're like ants in an anthill; aren't they doing interesting things, these little insects'" (BBC, interview with Will Gompertz, September 19, 2013).

**Diane Johnson** (screenwriter): "I'm not a big Stephen King fan. I'm not a big horror story fan. But I thought when I was reading it that it had a sort of surprising scariness, considering its flaws—how kind of pretentious and predictable it is. But at the same time it was scary. So I admired it in that sense. . . . I know that King didn't really like [the film]. And I can sympathize with that because we did come out with a completely different thing. His book is very baroque and you can't really do that in film. It had to be radically simplified" (Mark Steensland, terrortrap.com, May 2011).

**Shelley Duvall**: "So here was my chance to work with Kubrick. . . . Going through day after day of excruciating work. Almost unbearable. Jack Nicholson's character had to be crazy and angry all the time. And in my character I had to cry 12 hours a day, all day long, the last nine months straight, five or six days a week. . . . After I made *The Shining*, all that work, hardly anyone even criticized my performance in it, even to mention it, it seemed like. The reviews were all about Kubrick, like I wasn't there. . . . Perhaps with a star director such as Kubrick, I said, critics get mesmerized by his name and forget the actors" (interviewed by Roger Ebert, December 14, 1980; rogerebert.com).

## The Critics' Take

**Alexandre Aja** (director of *Horns*): "I was fully mesmerized. I watched maybe a half an hour but it was enough time to present the twin sisters and a vision of the elevator with all the blood floating out. I talk a lot about the immersive experience as the ultimate quest in making all my movies, but I think my desire to be INTO a movie, living it and not just watching it, came from that first experience of being sucked into that flow of images that Stanley Kubrick put together, where each element, from the music to the sound design to the choice of focal length, everything created an experience from which there was no escape. It was way beyond my expectations" ("Hero Complex," *Los Angeles Times*, October 29, 2014).

**Laura Miller** (salon.com): "*The Shining*, in my opinion, is a terrific film. But I suspect that even if King accepted the brilliance and the talent (and for all I know he does) they would not make up for what he feels the movie lacks in humanity. Humanity is what matters most to him, and all the browbeating of all the fan boys in the world is not going to change his mind on that. Kubrick can be the bigger genius; King would rather be the bigger man."

**Josh Larsen** (larsenonfilm.com): "*The Shining* is terrifying for what it *doesn't* do. . . . We're left to fill in the blanks with our own active imaginations. And of course we fill them with pure dread. . . . What I didn't know how to handle were murdered twins fixing me with their blank stares; decomposing bodies rotting in tubs; whatever was going on in that room with the well-dressed man and the person dressed as a rabbit (bear?). For all the fast edits and ugly insert shots that have come to dominate contemporary horror, Kubrick is the only one who truly perfected what those poseurs are after: sheer, subliminal terror."

3.

## Cujo: He Was a Good Dog . . .

Release date: August 12, 1983; Tomatometer: 59%; audience score: 45%. Screenplay by Don Carlos Dunaway and Lauren Currier; directed by Lewis Teague. Budget: $8 million; U.S. box office receipts: $21 million. Key Cast: Dee Wallace, as Donna Trenton; and Danny Pintauro, as Tad Trenton.

This ranks high on King's list of films, but not so much with critics or fans. Even still, it's a compelling film because, unlike the horror films he's known and celebrated for, the horror hits closer to home in this flick: a dog is bit by a rabid bat and changes into a crazed, relentless beast who, after killing his abusive owner and an innocent neighbor, attacks a woman and her son, who are trapped in a Ford Pinto.

Stephen King's recollection, in a 2006 *Paris Review* interview, was that "[i]t was the first new car we ever owned. . . . We had problems with it right away because there was something wrong with the needle valve in the carburetor. It would stick, the carburetor would flood, and the car wouldn't start. I was worried about my wife getting stuck in that Pinto, and I thought, What if she took that car to get fixed like I did my motorcycle and the needle valve stuck and she couldn't get it going—but instead of the dog just being a mean dog, what if the dog was really crazy?"

It's not a flashy movie, but it's relentless, just like Cujo. The movie just keeps coming and coming, and never lets up.

### Multiple Takes

**Stephen King**: "It's one of the scariest things you'll ever see. It's terrifying!" (*Stephen King from A to Z*).

**Dee Wallace**: "The minute I read *Cujo*, I knew that mother. I am the quintessential mother-caretaker. I so understood before I ever had a child that I would give myself up entirely for a child if I had to. Now that I have a child I understood that even more. For me it was 'My God, I'm blessed with the opportunity to bring this alive!'

"And I was very active in getting [the ending of *Cujo*] changed. Actually, Stephen King wrote us and said 'Thank God you changed the end. I never got more hate mail than when I killed the boy at the end of *Cujo*.' . . . You cannot ask a theatre audience to go through and invest all this love and then pulling for this little boy to be saved and then rip that away from them. . . . And obviously it doesn't work in the book" (denofgeek.us).

## The Critics' Take

**Rob Vaux** (mania.com, August 2013): "King's knack for characterization made the dog as sympathetic as the hapless humans it menaced . . . and proved more than a dedicated animal lover like me could bear.

"The movie adaptation gets half of that equation right, thanks to an impressive performance from Dee Wallace as the mother. Fresh off of her standout performance in *E.T.*, she embraced the grindhouse grit of the material here, and cemented her status as a grade-A scream queen in the process. *Cujo* works almost solely because of her, though King's basic scenario doesn't hurt the equation either."

**Jason Thompson** (bullz-eye.com): "*Cujo* is definitely a Stephen King adaptation that doesn't suck. The pacing is well-balanced, the tension is palpable, and the fears are based on things all too frighteningly real. . . . Suffice it to say that Lewis Teague knew what the hell he was doing when directing this picture."

4.

## The Dead Zone: Life as a Wheel of Fortune

Release date: October 21, 1983; Tomatometer: 90%; audience score: 76%. Screenplay by Jeffrey Boam; directed by David Cronenberg. Budget: $7 million; U.S. box office domestic total gross: $20.7 million. Key cast: Christopher Walken, as Johnny Smith; Brooke Adams, as Sarah Bracknell; and Martin Sheen, as Greg Stillson.

The hardest King movies to adapt are the straight horror movies, because they either brilliantly succeed—or fail, relying heavily on special effects to induce the willing suspension of disbelief. The easiest King movies to adapt are those without any supernatural elements, like *Stand by Me* and *The Shawshank Redemption*. In between are the ones like *Carrie* and *The Dead Zone*, in which the supernatural plays an important element, but not overwhelmingly so. In other words, by focusing on characters, which is always King's main interest, the movies hew closer to the heart of King's fiction and are therefore easier to film.

By 1983, with *Carrie*, *'Salem's Lot*, *The Shining*, and *Creepshow* establishing King as a horror writer, and with director Cronenberg identified with horror films (the Internet Movie Database says his nicknames are "the King of venereal horror" and "Baron of Blood"), the release of a nonhorror movie like *The Dead Zone* broke new ground for both of them.

King's departure from Doubleday to New American Library was marked with his first novel that didn't rely on traditional elements of horror, *The Dead Zone*, and the movie version reflected it. As with *Cujo*, the evil was not external but internal. As Douglas E. Winter explained in *The Art of Darkness*, "The evil within is a traditional horror theme, often expressed in the form of a logical insistence that unpleasant consequences await those who meddle in matters best left undisturbed."

In *Creepshows*, Stephen Jones explains that *The Dead Zone* "was Cronenberg's biggest hit—both critically and commercially—up to that date. 'Cronenberg did one of the great jobs of his life,' King later said. 'He got tremendous performances out of people, but the movie was not able to break through.'"

For Christopher Walken, who at that time was best known for his small but memorable role as Duane Hall in Woody Allen's *Annie Hall* (1977) and as a tortured, imprisoned soldier named Nick in *The Deer Hunter* (1978), *The Dead Zone* put him on center stage with the role of Johnny Smith.

Film magazine *Cinefantastique* (December 1983–January 1984) stated it was "not only the finest work to date by director David Cronenberg and the best adaptation of a Stephen King novel, but a splendid film by any standard. . . . In almost every way and on many levels, *The Dead Zone* is a glowing success."

## Multiple Takes

**Stephen King**: "It went through a number of hands and ended up with Dino De Laurentiis, and directed by David Cronenberg. I'm gonna see a rough cut on Monday when I'm back in New York. But I saw twenty minutes of it cut together and I thought it was gorgeous" (Martin Anderson, 1983, shadowlocked.com).

**Roger Ebert**: "*The Dead Zone* does what only a good supernatural thriller can do: It makes us forget it is supernatural. . . . Walken does such a good job portraying Johnny Smith, the man with the strange gift, that we forget this is science fiction or fantasy or whatever and just accept it as this guy's story" (October 26, 1983; posted on rogerebert.com).

**David Cronenberg**: "I loved working with Christopher Walken, I thought I'd work with him again, but there was never quite the role. . . . I had a pretty good time with all of my leading men and women really, so I could imagine a movie which they were all in. The way Fellini in *8½* had everybody in his life, all his actors in a dance with him" (Tim Lewis, September 13, 2014, theguardian.com).

5.

## *Stand by Me: Stephen King's Childhood Journey*

For a long time I thought I would love to be able to find a string to put on the childhood experiences that I remember. A lot of them are funny, and some of them are kind of sad . . . the people that I've known and some of the guys I hung out with that really weren't headed anywhere but down blind alleys.

And nothing came, and what you do when nothing comes is, you don't push, you just put it aside.

And there came a day when I thought to myself, *if these guys go somewhere, if there's a reason for them to go somewhere and do something, what could it be?*

I came up with the idea of going down the train tracks to look for the body of a kid that I made up, a situation whereby they would know the body was there and they could go and find it. And everything else follows from that.

Most stories, good stories about boys, are about journeys.

— *Stephen King, "The Tracks: The Summer of* Stand by Me*,"*
*from the DVD edition of* Stand By Me

Release date: August 22, 1986; Tomatometer, 91%; audience score: 95%. Screenplay by Raynold Gideon and Bruce A. Evans; directed by Rob Reiner. Budget: $8 million; domestic total gross: $52.2 million.

*A railroad track in Durham, Maine.*

Stephen King cites this movie as his favorite among all the adaptations to date, and it's easy to understand why. A classic film based on King's most autobiographical story, "The Body" (*Different Seasons*, 1982), this elegiac film plumbs the depths of King's childhood, a time he vividly recalled, and one that he brought to life with remarkable fidelity, as did Reiner for the film version.

Consider the similarities to King himself. The story and film are set in 1959, when King was twelve years old; the backdrop is small-town Maine, recalling Lisbon Falls, where he attended high school. And his best friend is Chris, who (as in the story) goes on to the University of Maine at Orono, as King did. King, who worked at the Worumbo Mill in Lisbon Falls during high school and college, feared being trapped in that small town.

In the movie, we meet four young teens. The narrator is a twelve-year-old boy named Gordie Lachance, who is the smart one; he goes on to become a bestselling writer. All the others—his best friend, Chris Chambers; Teddy Duchamp; and Vern Tessio—die, never seeing their dreams come to fruition because, as John Lennon once remarked, "Life is what happens when you're making other plans."

Chris, who realized his dream of being accepted to the university, intervenes in a knife fight in a fast food restaurant and gets killed; Teddy, a real wet end, dies ingloriously in a car crash, taking others with him; and Vern, everybody's good buddy, dies in an accidental house fire.

At the end of the movie, we see Gordon Lachance watching Ace Merrill, who terrorized him when he was twelve. Ace, now overweight and resigned to his humdrum life at the mill, heads for a bar where he'll seat his butt on a barstool and bitch about life.

A coming-of-age story, a journey from innocence to experience, the boys' journey doesn't end when they find the dead body in the woods and attempt to claim it. The journey ends further down the road when Gordon becomes an adult, successful by anyone's standards.

In 1986, when Reiner screened the film for Stephen King, Reiner recalled seeing King visibly moved. "I have to go away," King said, and he did. When he returned, he told Reiner some of the personal details that made the viewing such an emotional event for him: It brought King's past back to life, on the big screen, and he was overwhelmed.

But even without knowing the backstory—the connective tissue to King's life—it stands on its own. It's a time machine that takes us back to our past, to a time when we too were twelve and life seemed simple, until we realized our lives are infinite in possibilities, waiting for us to make life's big choices.

## Multiple Takes

**Rob Reiner**: "In the book it was about four boys, but after about five days of driving around I realized this was really Gordie's story. In the book, Gordie was kind of a dispassionate observer, but once I made Gordie the central focus of the piece then it made sense to me: this movie was all about a kid who didn't feel good about himself and whose father didn't love him.

"And through the experience of going to find the dead body and his friendship with these boys, he began to feel empowered and went on to become a very successful writer. He basically became Stephen King" (*The Telegraph*, June 12, 2011).

"King is a good writer. He pens wonderfully complex characters and great dialogue. Yet when people adapt his books into movies, they tend to . . . just concentrate on the horror and the supernatural—all the things that seem to be the most overtly commercial. It's a grave mistake because they lose many levels of his work by doing the obvious" (Alan Jones, *Starburst* magazine, 1991).

**Wil Wheaton** (Gordie Lachance), on River Phoenix, during a reunion with Reiner and cast members: "I spent much of the next few days remembering all the things we did together during production, thinking about how much I looked up to him and how much I loved his entire family. I don't know what would have happened to us if he hadn't overdosed, if he ever would have come back from the edge, or if we would even have had anything in common . . . but when he was fifteen and I was thirteen, he was my friend. That's the person I knew, and that's the person I miss. . . . As I drove home from the theater I was overwhelmed by conflicting emotions. It was wonderful to see those guys again, and especially to reconnect with Jerry, but it was also tremendously sad to truly feel River's loss for the first time. That turbulent mix of joy and sorrow stayed with me for several days. . . . Most actors will go their entire careers without doing a movie like *Stand By Me,* or working with a director like Rob Reiner. I got to do both when I was 12. For a long, long time, I felt like I needed to top or equal that, and it wasn't until I was in my early thirties that I accepted it's unlikely to happen— movies like *Stand By Me* come along once in a generation" (WWdn: In Exile, wilwheaton.typepad.com, March 21, 2011).

*Cinefantastique* **magazine**: "Those who've sworn off Stephen King movie adaptations take heart. King's novella, 'The Body,' hardly his most typical or flashy, makes the best screen transfer since *Carrie*. . . . [T]he 'Master of Macabre' should ditch the killer trucks and direct audiences to this little gem" (January 1987).

**Stephen King**: I think they like the voice. The voice can't be filmed, but at the same time, it can be. Rob Reiner's proved that twice, particularly with *Stand by Me.* You would freak—or maybe you wouldn't—if you knew how many people walk up to me on the street and say, 'Steve, I love your movies.' These people have no idea I do anything *but* movies, so for every person who read 'The Body,' probably fifteen people saw *Stand by Me.* I still get royalty checks on that film, big ones! The voice is there, but the only people who are really tapping into the voice are people who read, and they're a small part of the overall population" (Bill Warren, *Fangoria*).

6.

*The house the Kings rented in Orrington, Maine, when Stephen was teaching at UMO.*

## *Pet Sematary: Sometimes Dead Is Better*

Release date: April 21, 1989; Tomatometer: 43%; audience score: 60%. Screenplay by Stephen King; directed by Mary Lambert. Budget: $11.5 million; domestic total gross: $57.4 million.

"I got the idea," King told Abe Peck of *Rolling Stone* in 1980, "when my daughter's cat died. It got run over. . . . So, anyway, we buried our cat and I started to think about burials." (The movie pays homage to Smucky, as did the book, with a grave marker that reads, "Smucky, he was obedient.")

In terms of critical reviews and audience popularity, this movie is not in the first rank, but it deserves a place in any discussion of King's movies because it's so Maine in many ways.

To begin with, its real-world setting is Orrington, Maine, where a real pet "sematary" (original child's spelling) once existed, behind the house that King rented, when he commuted to Orono to teach a class at the University of Maine at Orono as its writer in residence. In front of the house is a winding road used by truckers that predictably results in roadkill.

King, mindful of W. W. Jacobs's story "The Monkey's Paw," took it one step further and imagined that the road claimed not only felines and canines but also people—specifically, Gage Creed, the son of Dr. Louis Creed.

*Pet Sematary* was the first King movie to bear his name over the title. It was also the first screenplay he wrote for one of his own movies. And it was the first film he insisted be shot entirely in Maine, in Ellsworth, about an hour away from Bangor, which allowed King to stop by weekly. It also allowed him to fit in a cameo appearance as a preacher, filmed at Bangor's Mount Hope cemetery. These reasons were important enough to King so that he turned down a $1 million offer, which would have meant ceding control, so that the film's producer, Rich Rubenstein, could afford to secure the rights for just $1,000.

Though none of the principal actors are from Maine, Fred Gwynne (best known for his roles in the TV shows *Car 54, Where Are You?* and *The Munsters*), in the role of longtime Mainer Jud Crandall, gives a good performance with a spot-on accent, according to a lifelong Mainer, Dave Lowell, who said most actors fall way short of the accent mark, so to speak.

At its dark heart, *Pet Sematary* is about the most horrific nightmare a parent can experience: the loss of a child. For that reason, King was reluctant to allow the book to be published, but that's why the transgressive film comes to life to become a *real* horror show.

## Multiple Takes

**Stephen King**: "Because *Pet Sematary* of all my novels was the one I thought would be the most difficult to film, I just simply made it an unbreakable part of the deal that whoever was going to do it, would have to do it in Maine. And Laurel came along, and Bill Dunn came along and said, 'Yeah, OK, we'll make it in Maine.'

"And again, why not? You've got production facilities, lab facilities, and an acting pool to draw on here in New England. And if you need to go to Boston and New York, they're 600 miles down the road, and they're closer than, say, San Francisco is to Los Angeles.

"We've got stuff up here that nobody's seen. Maine's supposed to be Vacationland. And, ideally, what should happen is that people should look at the movies and say, 'We'd like to go there.' And they should come and say, 'Gee, this is as great as we saw it.' In other words, a movie like *Pet Sematary . . .* should serve as a commercial for the state, as much as all the movies made in California, Los Angeles, and New York have served as commercials for those places" (press conference for *Stephen King's Graveyard Shift*, 1990).

"I think Dale Midkiff is *stiff* in places. I think Denise Crosby comes across cold in places. I don't feel that the couple that's at the center of the story has the kind of warmth that would set them off perfectly against the supernatural element that surrounds them. I like that contrast better. I think it does what horror movies are supposed to do. . . . [Mary Lambert] did a good job. She went in and she didn't flinch. In a way, that's a pretty good compliment to the way that I work. Because I've always wanted to go straight at things and not try to offer a lot of nuance. . . . My idea is to let go in there and hit as hard as you can. Mary understood that" (Gary Wood, *Cinefantastique*, February 1991).

**Mary Lambert**: "*Pet Sematary* is about a love of a father for his child that is obsessive to the point of breaking certain taboos, passing certain boundaries that shouldn't be passed. I think I brought a sense of mystery and mysticism to the story that they were looking for. There are certain aspects of this story that take it beyond just another horror movie" (Frederick C. Szebin, *Cinefantastique*, March 1989).

**Denise Crosby**: "I can't imagine not shooting that film in Maine. You needed to be in that place, and we were blessed that we were there and not some Hollywood sound stage" (*Bangor Daily News*, 1989).

"I think the fact that he wrote the script made a big difference. He can really tell a story. That's his genius" (Gary Wood, *Cinefantastique*, February 1991).

**Fred Gywnne**: "I see it as a frightening fable rather than a horror film, which I think makes it doubly strong. I'd read the book as soon as it came out. I'm a Stephen King nut. I saw it more as a fable for our times. . . . But it will be interesting to see how the powers that be, where they slot it" (*New York Times*, May 20, 1989).

## Unearthed and Untold: The Path to *Pet Sematary*

### (production company, Oceans Light Productions)

At the fifteenth annual Rhode Island International Horror Film Festival, out of thirty documentaries, Oceans Light Productions' *Unearthed and Untold* (estimated release date, 2015) took home a grand prize.

Just so you know: This is a documentary that requires your attention. With luck, once it passes muster with the powers that be, we'll see it released on DVD, so you can see the work of a two-man team so taken by the novel and film adaptation that they went to Orrington to dig deep into the making of *Pet Sematary*.

"What we're doing," said John Campopiano and Justin White, "is taking a deeper look into the making of the film from two different angles: the perspectives of the Maine locals and the perspectives of the cast & crew. What stories and memories do local Maine residents have of the production? How was the production documented in local television, magazine, and newspaper stories? What did the production do for the county of Hancock and the greater Maine communities? These are just a few of the questions we are exploring in our documentary.

"This documentary began when my cameraman and I traveled to Maine over a year ago to see the filming locations. During that weekend, we were overwhelmed by locals who remembered the production and who had home videos, photographs, and a plethora of stories to share. Everyone was so eager and happy to share their memories that I felt we should somehow document them all. This is when our documentary was born."

7.

*Misery: Staying Alive*

> He writes stories that cut through the shower of blood. That makes it human.
> Sharp insights that dig into our innermost secrets.
>
> —*Kathy Bates, introducing Stephen King, at Radio City Music Hall, August 1, 2006*

Release date: November 30, 1990; Tomatometer: 89%; audience score: 89%. Screenplay by William Goldman; directed by Rob Reiner. Budget: $20 million; total domestic gross: $62 million.

*Misery,* explained King to *Cinefantastique*'s Charles Leayman, illustrates "the powerful hold fiction can achieve over the reader. What *Misery* turned out to be about was the life-saving quality of writing stories, how it takes you away and how it heals: both the people who do it and the people who consume it."

It's a theme that King has explored before, in "The Woman in the Room" and also *On Writing.*

In the movie *Misery,* writing is also a way back to life for romance novelist Paul Sheldon, portrayed by veteran actor James Caan. In fact, it is his only ticket, which Annie Wilkes holds. His novels about Misery Chastain hold an unhealthy influence over Annie Wilkes, and she in turn holds Sheldon as her captive. Distraught that he killed off her favorite fictional character, she demands that Misery be brought back to life by him. She sees it as quid pro quo: She's saved his life, and in return he saves Misery's life.

Mindful of Rob Reiner's masterful job as director of *Stand by Me,* King insisted that if he sold the film rights to Reiner's production company, Castle Rock Entertainment, Reiner had to be its producer or, King hoped, its director. Reiner signed on as director and delivered a work of film art. In any list of top ten King film adaptations, *Misery* deserves a place of high honor.

Throwing out a broad net, according to Stephen Jones writing in *Creepshows,* Reiner's choices for the key role of writer Paul Sheldon included "William Hurt, Kevin Kline, Michael Douglas, Harrison Ford, Dustin Hoffman, Robert De Niro, Al Pacino, Richard Dreyfuss, Gene Hackman and Robert Redford, all of whom turned it down." Beatty, noted Jones, was interested but was forced to turn it down because of a prior commitment to *Dick Tracy.* The list narrowed, and Reiner approached James Caan, who was cast in the role.

For the other key role of Annie Wilkes, noted Jones, Bette Midler was considered, but Kathy Bates got the role; in fact, when William Goldman wrote the screenplay, he had written it specifically with Bates in mind.

Since the movie is essentially claustrophobic, taking place in Annie's isolated farmhouse, the performances of both Caan and Bates had to be riveting, and both were. Caan won no awards for his performance, incurring the wrath of Caan, but Kathy Bates's stellar performance did not go unnoticed; in fact, it earned her an Academy Award, a Golden Globe, a Chicago Film Critics Association Award, a Dallas-Fort Worth Film Critics Award, and third place in the New York Film Critics Circle Award.

In other words, Kathy Bates *nailed* it. Like a high-flying acrobat, she soared, she flew, she spun in the air—and landed perfectly. Kathy Bates *was* Annie Wilkes, in all her implacable horror.

It's now difficult, if not impossible, to read the book and not see Annie Wilkes in the image of Kathy Bates because of her riveting film performance.

The movie did differ from the book in two critical ways: the role of the sheriff was expanded to open up the claustrophobic movie, which is essentially a one-room play, and, instead of giving Paul Sheldon the ax, Annie Wilkes hobbles him instead.

## Multiple Takes

**Stephen King**: "Every now and then something strange will happen. Some years ago I went to Philadelphia with my son to see a basketball game. Tabby was here, and she heard the window break and there was this guy there and he claimed he had a bomb (in fact it was a bunch of pencils and erasers and stuff and paperclips). He was an escapee from a mental institution and he had this rant about how I'd stolen *Misery* from him. Tabby fled in her bathrobe and the police came. . . . And every now and then there'll be a letter from someone who is obviously out there in the ozone, people who are convinced I've stolen their ideas. One lady wrote to explain how I had overflown her house in a U2 plane and stolen her thoughts for *The Shining*. But no one has ever actually threatened to kill me, knock on wood. Though there's a guy out in California, Steven Lightfoot, who believes that Ronald Reagan and I conspired to kill John Lennon" (Tim Adams, September 14, 2000, theguardian.com).

**Rob Reiner**: "You're trying to just get the performances you want. . . . I hire people who can do what they're supposed to do. I even told Kathy Bates when we were doing *Misery*, 'You can't take this character home. This is too crazy.' She had started doing that. I said, 'You let it go. You have your talent, your craft, and you have to trust that when you come to work that it will be there for you.' And it was; it was fine. I've heard people like Daniel Day Lewis never let go of a character. Everyone works differently, but to me you have your work and you have your home life. You have to be able to separate the two" (Lauren Bradshaw, July 22, 2014, clotureclub.com).

"Kathy kept saying, 'Jimmy's not relating to me, he's not listening to me.' I said, 'That's true. He isn't. His character doesn't care one iota about yours.' And I said, 'You can use that to fuel your rage'" (David Sacks, *New York Times*, January 27, 1991).

**James Caan**: "The less I feel I act, the better job I feel I do. I try to keep myself open to possibilities on camera. So Kathy and I work a little different" (David Sacks, *New York Times*, January 27, 1991).

**Kathy Bates**: "I have always had a problem with my weight. I'm not a stunning woman. I never was an ingénue; I've always just been a character actor. When

I was younger it was a real problem, because I was never pretty enough for the roles that other young women were being cast in. The roles I was lucky enough to get were real stretches for me: usually a character who was older, or a little weird, or whatever. And it was hard, not just for the lack of work but because you have to face up to how people are looking at you. And you think, 'Well, y'know, I'm a real person'" (David Sacks, *New York Times*, January 27, 1991).

"I've admired King's work over the years, but I'm not a horror devotee. I read metaphysics and Jung and, occasionally, Clive Barker. I'm an eclectic reader. . . . After this film, it'll start again. More Norman Bates references, and *People* magazine will refer to me as Kathy 'Misery' Bates. Everybody wants to type you. There's a human urge to pigeonhole. It's just rampant in Hollywood" (Glenn Lowell, *Daily Press*, December 8, 1990).

8.

## *The Shawshank Redemption: Redeeming Stephen King's Film Reputation*

I never in a million years thought he would get the film made.

—*Stephen King, introduction to* The Shawshank Redemption: The Shooting Script, *1995*

Release date: October 14, 1994; Tomatometer: 91%; audience score: 98%. Directed by and screenplay by Frank Darabont. Budget: $25 million; total domestic gross: $28.3 million.

Frank Darabont is your typical "overnight" success. In his case, the "overnight" success took him thirteen years, from the time he worked as a lowly production assistant on a 1981 film called *Hell Night*, starring Linda Blair, a film described by the Internet Movie Database thus:

Four college pledges are forced to spend the night in a deserted old mansion where they get killed off one by one by the monstrous surviving members of a family massacre years earlier for trespassing on their living grounds.

In 1994, Darabont wrote and directed *The Shawshank Redemption*, which changed his life. His path to Shawshank Prison came by way of a "dollar baby" film, when Darabont received permission from King to film "The Woman in the Room," which King said, in an introduction to *The Green Mile: The Screenplay*, was a "beautiful and moving version" that he counts as the first, and best, "dollar baby" short film.

Darabont, a gentleman, followed up by sending the award citation for his film to King, who had sized him up correctly: "Nice guy."

The nice guy went back a second time, with a request for a major motion picture, for which he paid $5,000 for the rights. Given a green light by King, Darabont wrote a full-length script for *The Shawshank Redemption* and sent it to King, who wrote in an introduction to *The Green Mile: The Screenplay*:

> I gave Frank permission to show the script around—he could shop it until he dropped, as far as I was concerned—but only in my wildest dreams did I expect it would be made. It was too long, too faithful to the source story . . . and a little too kind. Not even in those wild dreams did I expect it would end up being the screen adaptation of my work that people say they like the best—no mean accomplishment, considering there have been over thirty of them.

What King and Darabont didn't expect was that the movie with the awkward title would go on to become a film classic, and launch Darabont's film career into high orbit.

What's telling about Darabont's character is that when Castle Rock Entertainment got the screenplay, which was written on spec (i.e., with no money upfront for Darabont), the company wanted Reiner to be at the helm as director and dangled "shit loads of money" as an inducement. But Darabont remained steadfast and decided being rich overnight wasn't his goal; his goal was to make a world-class film of a story he absolutely loved, and he wanted to bring it to the screen his way.

Remember when I said Darabont was a gentleman? He is. And he's a man of integrity who can't be bought.

But, ironically, *The Shawshank Redemption* wasn't a box office hit when initially released, for several reasons. First, because it was at such variance with the films for which King is known—horror films—the studio heads decided *not* to use King's name for fear that it might alienate mainstream viewers who would dismiss the film outright and refuse to give it a fair viewing. Second, it's a quiet little story about the relationship between two prison inmates; it's not sexy or action-packed, and it lacks women characters, which they felt would make it less appealing to a general audience. And, third, the unrevealing title made it difficult to figure out just what the film was about. What, exactly, is a shawshank? (A "shank," by the way, is prison slang for a homemade knife, so that helped, but not nearly enough.) No wonder Tim Robbins's fans came up to him and asked, "What was that *Shinkshonk Reduction* thing?"

Titles aside, the content is what's most important, and in this film there are two standout performances: Morgan Freeman, playing Ellis Boyd "Red" Redding, and Tim Robbins playing Andy Dufresne. Freeman was nominated for an Oscar and a Golden Globe, and Robbins was nominated for a Screen Actors Guild Award and a Chlotrudis Award; unfortunately, in what can only be perceived as a gross miscarriage of justice, both came away empty-handed.

The movie, though, had "legs." Sturdy legs, as it turned out. It went on to become a critical success and a fan favorite as well. In fact, when the American Film Institute ranked the top one hundred greatest movies of all time, *The Shawshank Redemption* was 72; the readers of *Empire* magazine voted it the best film of the nineties and the fourth best film of all time; and Internet Movie Database subscribers ranked it right up there with *The Godfather* and *Star Wars*.

As Frank Darabont explained to *Empire* magazine: "It was crash and burn. As I discovered, there's a difference between the audience enjoying a movie and being convinced to show up in the first place. . . . Thank God for video."

It went on to become the number one top video rental of 1995, with 320,000 rental copies in the United States alone. It also went on to become a TV favorite, which brought the actors residuals that continue to this day, as Bob Gunton (the prison warden) explained to *The Wall Street Journal*: "I suspect my daughter, years from now, will still be getting checks." (By the film's tenth anniversary, in 2004, Gunton has gotten close to "six figures," noted *The Wall Street Journal*.)

"Castle Rock Pictures has more or less rescued my film-associated reputation from the scrap-heap, and no picture had more to do with that than the one which eventually became known as *The Shawshank Redemption*," King wrote in his introduction to the script used for shooting, published in book form.

King, in fact, loves to recount an encounter he had with a woman who couldn't reconcile the fact that he was the author whose story from *Different Seasons*, "Rita Hayworth and Shawshank Redemption," was the basis for *The Shawshank Redemption*. Neil Gaiman quoted him in an interview for *The Sunday Times*:

> I was down here in the supermarket, and this old woman comes around the corner . . . obviously one of the kind of women who says whatever is on her brain. She said, "I know who you are; you are the horror writer. I don't read anything that you do, but I respect your right to do it. I just like things more genuine, like that *Shawshank Redemption*."
>
> And I said, "I wrote that." And she said, "No, you didn't." And she walked off and went on her way.

That woman's reaction, mirroring that of many others, explains the film's enduring appeal. As Tim Robbins recounted to Mark Kermode, "All I know is that there isn't a day when I'm not approached about that film, approached by people who say how important that film is to them, who tell me that they've seen it 20, 30, 40 times and who are just so . . . thankful."

## Multiple Takes

**Stephen King**: "And Frank will say, 'I have the world's smallest specialty. I only do prison movies written by Stephen King.' And he's been going on about how proud he is that he made *The Mist* and broke out of that mold. But I told him, 'Frank, it's still a story about people in prison. They're just in a prison in a supermarket!'" (Gilbert Cruz, *Time*, November 23, 2007).

**Frank Darabont**: "More than cinematic or visual, I first responded to the emotional content of it. The really wonderful characters, the wonderful relationships, the obstacles they face and overcome. Secondarily, there was the visual element of it which always boiled down to, 'Gee, if we could find a really cool-looking prison to shoot, this is going to be a really cool-looking movie.' And luckily, that happened. We found the Ohio State Reformatory in Mansfield,

Ohio, which they had just shut down two years prior. It was an incredible, gothic place. Mostly though, it was the emotional content. It's the little things that make a movie good, the little emotional moments. The rest of it is all candy" (Daniel Argent and Erik Bauer, *Creative Screenwriting*, Volume 4, #2, Summer 1997).

**Morgan Freeman**: "I don't know what happened when it first came out. . . . In fact I remember someone asking me on the night of the Academy Awards why I thought *Shawshank* had done so poorly at box-office when films like *Dumb and Dumber*, which opened the same season, had done so well. After all, *Shawshank* had gotten pretty good reviews, whereas *Dumb and Dumber* had been thoroughly and relentlessly trashed by critics" (Mark Kermode, August 21, 2004, theguardian.com).

**Tim Robbins**: "It's a film about people being in jail, and having the hope to get out. Why is that universal? Because although not everybody has been in jail, on a deeper, more metaphysical level, many people feel enslaved by their environment, their jobs, their relationships—by whatever it is in the course of their lives that puts walls and bars around them. And *Shawshank* is a story about enduring and ultimately escaping from that imprisonment" (Mark Kermode, August 21, 2004, theguardian.com).

9.

## *Dolores Claiborne: A Happy Accident*

Release date: March 24, 1995; Tomatometer: 82%; audience score: 81%. Screenplay by Tony Gilroy; directed by Taylor Hackford. Budget: not stated; total domestic gross: $24.3 million.

As any actor knows, your looks can work for or against you in Hollywood casting, as in real life. In Kathy Bates's case, after winning an Oscar for her performance in *Misery*, her name would assuredly come up in casting lists for the demanding role of Dolores Claiborne, in which she would have to carry the film on her able-bodied shoulders.

But it wouldn't be a glamorous role; there'd be no place for an actress like Nicole Kidman or Cameron Diaz. It needed an actress who, as Bates saw it, "doesn't take any guff off anybody and she becomes hard and crusty to do it." Dolores Claiborne is a plain-talking, unvarnished woman who speaks her mind, and one line from the movie gives us a sense of who she is:

Now, you listen to me, Mr. Grand High Poobah of Upper Buttcrack, I'm just about half-past give a shit with your fun and games.

Dolores has seen life upfront and personal and has had it with her husband Joe St. George, who is described in the book as a goddamned millstone I wore around my neck. Worse, really, because a mill-stone don't get drunk and then come home smellin of beer and wantin to throw a fuck into you at one in the morning. Wasn't none of that the reason why I killed the sonofawhore, but I guess it's as good a place as any to start.

"All of us would just like to be real people," Kathy Bates told David Sacks of *The New York Times* in 1991. "But for women especially, somehow movies have gotten to be about glamour; either you're gorgeous or you're a dog. And I guess I'll find out more about this as I continue working in films, but I have heard a lot, 'Well, we had something different in mind visually.' And no actor likes to hear that."

Bates got the coveted role for *Dolores Claiborne* and delivered an outstanding performance. Filmed off the coast of Nova Scotia, Canada, the movie gives us a sense of Maine divested from any supernatural trappings. Set on Little Tall Island, off the Maine coast, the movie is a microcosm of insular Maine life as seen through the eyes of an islander who has had more than her full share of sorrow and hardship at the hands of her no-account, shiftless husband, who, in the novel, "didn't leave me a pot to piss in and hardly a window to throw it out of."

Joe St. George, who is no saint, left his mark on his wife, and also on their daughter, Selena; and in this memorable film, a psychological thriller, Dolores must not only clear her own name but build a bridge to reach and reconcile with her daughter, played by Jennifer Jason Leigh, who lives in New York.

Unlike other King novels that lend themselves to big box office potential, *Dolores Claiborne*, bereft of any supernatural component, is one of domestic horror: A woman endures an abusive marriage at the hands of her husband, who also feels their daughter, then underage, is fair game.

Kathy Bates's nuanced performance, performed against a gray-brown canvas of an isolated small island off the Maine coast, garnered attention. Screenwriter William Goldman wrote, "No one gave a better performance than Kathy Bates in *Dolores Claiborne*." And in "The Ten Most Underrated Movies," Elizabeth MacDonald, writing for *Forbes* (2003), wrote, "Not just the movie but both actresses [Kathy Bates and Judy Parfitt] should have won Oscars for their searing performances and catty humor."

Kathy Bates garnered three nominations for her role as Dolores Claiborne: a Saturn Award for best actress, from the Academy of Science Fiction, Fantasy, and Horror Films; a Chicago Film Critics Association Award; and a Chlotrudis Award (as did Jennifer Jason Leigh, for best supporting actress).

Kathy Bates came away empty-handed on the awards front, but the critics and the fans loved her, and isn't that what really counts?

### Multiple Takes

**Roger Ebert**: "Stephen King fans hoping for ghouls and Satanic subplots and bizarre visitations may be disappointed by *Dolores Claiborne*. I was surprised how affecting the movie was, mostly because Bates and Leigh formed such a well-matched and convincing pair. Does this movie creep up on you? Oh, my gravy" (*Chicago Sun-Times*, March 24, 1995).

**Janet Maslin**: "Written as a book-length harangue from its heroine's point of view, and directed efficiently by Taylor Hackford, *Dolores Claiborne* has become a vivid film that revolves around Ms. Bates' powerhouse of a performance. . . . The role of Dolores may be rough around the edges, but it's a windfall for Ms. Bates, who does a walloping good job. She's the perfect no-nonsense actress to bring this woman to life" (*New York Times*, March 24, 1995).


10.

## The Green Mile: A Leap of Faith: Do You Believe in Miracles?

Release date: December 10, 1999; Tomatometer: 80%; audience score: 94%. Directed and screenplay by Frank Darabont. Budget: $65 million; total domestic gross: $136.8 million.

Frank Darabont knows a good story when he reads one, and when he read the first of six installments of *The Green Mile*, he was hooked again. In his introduction to *The Green Mile: The Shooting Script*, he explains that he didn't pick up the phone; instead, he took a plane from Los Angeles to Denver, got a rental car and drove up to Estes Park, and walked in on the TV remake of *The Shining*, where he saw Stephen King dressed in a white tux and "leading" a big band. As Darabont recounts:

> In between takes, Steve saw me, blinked, and came over to ask what I was doing there. I grabbed him by the lapels, ready to start shaking, and said, "I've come for *The Green Mile*."
> Steve shrugged and replied, "Oh, okay, sure. Hey, you wanna be an extra in this scene?"

Darabont, who knows that making a full-length feature film is the most demanding and difficult challenge in the creative arts, picks and chooses them carefully. He's driven by passion and commitment and responds to a well-told tale. So when he picked up *The Two Dead Girls*, as he recounted in his *Shooting Script* introduction, "What I did know was that I was in the hands of a master storyteller, that I was spellbound, that this was King firing on all pistons. In other words, I decided to proceed purely on a leap of faith, convinced Steve would not let me down."

With public expectations high, on the heels of *The Shawshank Redemption*, and a budget big enough to do the film right—including a $20 million paycheck for Tom Hanks as the "E Block" supervisor at Louisiana's Cold Mountain Penitentiary in 1935—the movie's success would stand or fall on the performance of the actor chosen to play John Coffey, whose initials, J.C., are symbolic. The challenging role required an actor with broad shoulders, and the actor who was finally selected was indeed a big man with broad shoulders, and a bigger heart.

As Michael Clarke Duncan recounted in an interview with Matthew Kinne in 2000, for *The John Ankerberg Show*:

> The role came about by Bruce Willis. He told me about *The Green Mile,* and he said, "This will definitely change your career. I'm going to call Frank Darabont when we get back to LA," and he said, "Mike, go buy the novel now, so that when this audition comes up, you'll have a little bit of a better edge than the rest." We got back to LA; four days later, Frank Darabont calls me. He says he wants me to come in for an audition. I went in. . . . I bring the emotion up. He says, "Can you come back?" I said, "O.K." I didn't hear from him for about three weeks. He then said I want you to come in for a screen test. That is the big Hollywood thing. They hired me an acting coach, but the role means a lifetime achievement for me. *Armageddon* put me on the map and let people see me, but . . . this role is my first breakout role.

Standing six feet, five inches tall, and weighing 315 pounds, Duncan seems better suited to be a bouncer or bodyguard, both of which he had done before getting in the film business, but he found his real talent in acting: Duncan, a gentle giant of a man, brought John Coffey to life on screen in a way that touched millions. As a result, Duncan was showered with accolades and nominated for numerous awards that showed he had acting chops.

"Like *Shawshank,* this story is uplifting," said Darabont in *Film Review.* "But this has a much more complex tone. It's also got a sort of lovely melancholy thing going on. I'm looking for something that is hopeful, and that's what I find attractive in these stories. I want something my heart can believe in."

What Darabont responded to was John Coffey's numinous quality, which required a nuanced performance from Duncan. If audiences took him to heart and were convinced by his performance, the movie would almost assuredly be a success.

Not to make too fine a point here, but Duncan delivered the goods. He just nailed it. Put it on the wall, hammered it in, stood back, and said, in effect, go ahead and take a *good* look: That's *me* playing John Coffey.

Running a little over three hours, the movie weaves its narrative through several smaller stories that come together in the end and reveal to us what we knew from the beginning: that the world is filled with mystery and wonder, and the miracles of life reveal God's grace and compassion. To say anything more is to give away too much of the story line, and so I won't: It's King's tale, and Darabont's retelling, and I merely want to point you in the right direction. For the love of God, read the book and see the movie.

The film went on to become a critical and financial success, reaffirming Frank Darabont's prodigious talent. As King wrote in his introduction to The Green Mile: *The Shooting Script,* "In a decade where too many movies are cold and glossy and have all the emotional gradient of a customized muscle-car, Frank makes openhearted audience-pleasers that beg us to go with the belly laughs and turn on the old waterworks . . . to *respond.*"

Life, King reminds us, is fragile; we are at the mercy of powers beyond us and the randomness of the universe, as Johnny Smith, in *The Dead Zone*, finds out when his life is forever changed after a random skating accident.

In a perfect world, we'd see many more performances by the Big Man, Michael Clarke Duncan, but it was not to be. We live in an imperfect world that, at times, seems devoid of justice and sense: On September 3, 2012, at age fifty-two, Michael Clarke Duncan died.

Tom Hanks said, "He was the treasure we all discovered on the set of *The Green Mile*. He was magic. He was a big love of [a] man and his passing leaves us stunned."

Frank Darabont echoed Hanks's words. "Michael was the gentlest of souls—an exemplar of decency, integrity and kindness. The sadness I feel is inexpressible."

And Stephen King said, "No one has ever done a character I wrote more justice."

In this world in which there's not enough justice to go around, which always seems in short supply, I hope heaven booms with the sound of Duncan's expansive voice; his larger-than-life, infectious laugh; and his broad smile that lit up our world . . . and surely, heaven, too.

## Multiple Takes

**Frank Darabont**: "Steve, to me, is like Dickens. He is a storyteller, an old-fashioned storyteller in the best sense of the word. Both Stephen and Dickens were accused by the literary snobs of their day of being horribly populist, pandering writers because, God forbid, there should be a plot. It's not just about plot with Steve" (Daniel Argent and Erik Bauer, *Film Review*, 1997/1999).

"He's got such a spark of humanity, real humanism, in his work, even in the more obviously horror pieces. That's what I found most compelling about this story. It was a hell of an emotional journey" (Donna Freydkin, CNN Interactive, 2001).

**Bruce Willis**, to Darabont: "I found John Coffey" (Donna Freydkin, CNN Interactive, 2001).

**Tom Hanks**: "I've never had the ensemble experience that I had on *The Green Mile*. . . . There was a bona fide affection for one another" (AMC blog).

**Michael Clarke Duncan**: "I think John Coffey is an angel. That is the best way I can describe it. Any time you give of yourself and don't ask for anything in return, I think that is very angelic. And, to want to see the simple things, I think that says a lot about his spirit. And, you have this man if he could, if he had the heart of a villain, there would be no cell in that town that could hold him. It is very humble, and nice and sweet" (Matthew Kinne, *John Ankerberg Show*, 2000).

"It was a wonderful thing to have him. He was like a Zen master. He uses, I call it 'mental capabilities,' on you. No matter how many scenes you're going through, Frank can get you to do more, even when you're tired. . . . But each one,

I wanted to do good for him, cause he makes you feel like you have it in you. You want to achieve for him" (Cynthia Fuchs, July 9, 2009, popmatters.com).

## Critics' Take

**Hollywood.com**: "The amazing Clarke Duncan both physically menacing and radiantly warm also completely inhabits his role. Clarke Duncan is so mesmerizing as the gentle giant you'll be convinced that he was created just for this part. (Though I hope this is just the start of a long career.)" (April 24, 2001).

*Variety*: "[T]he ensemble acting is of a high order. Hanks excels as the prison guard who is well balanced enough to nearly always handle his many troubles in proper, imaginative fashion" (Todd McCarthy, November 28, 1999).

# 118

# FRANK DARABONT: AN INTERVIEW

## by Hans-Åke Lilja

### February 6, 2007

*I wanted to publish an interview with one film director, and though many such interviews are available, I felt that Darabont could speak for his fellow directors.*

*I was privileged to work with Frank on an art book called* Knowing Darkness: Artists Inspired by Stephen King. *He proofread and corrected my interviews with Drew Struzan and Bernie Wrightson, for which I am thankful: His insights improved both pieces. He also contributed the introduction to the book, which set the tone for what followed—a gallery of art that is a visual testimony to the illustrative riches of King's fiction.*

*This interview, conducted by Hans-Åke Lilja, a superfan who has run the best Stephen King fan Web site on the planet since 1996, sheds much light on Frank's thoughts about King, King's books and movies, and Frank himself. Published online on Lilja's Web site and reprinted in* Lilja's Library: The World of Stephen King. *the interview will probably be new to you, and well worth your time and attention.*

*Like many of his contemporaries, Frank's early years in the film business were challenging, mirroring King's early years as a writer; in both cases, their talent and dedication took them from obscurity to worldwide fame. Obviously, both directing and writing are demanding occupations that require one's very best.*

*H-e-r-e's Frank Darabont!*

**Lilja: In 1983 you did *The Woman in the Room*. Can you tell me how that happened? As I understand it it's one of the first "Dollar Babies," right?**

**Frank Darabont:** In 1980, I was 20 years old, working many miserable low-paid jobs just to survive, and dreaming of a career in films someday. During that time I was a theater usher, telephone operator. . . . Man, I can't even remember all the awful jobs I had back then. I even ran a forklift and did a lot of heavy lifting for an auction company that liquidated industrial machine shops. That was the year I approached Stephen King about *The Woman in the Room*, and I hadn't even had my first job in movies yet! But I nonetheless decided I wanted to make a short film from his story, which I thought was lovely and deeply moving, so I wrote him a letter asking for his permission. I was shocked that he said yes. (I found out later about his "dollar baby" policy, which shows what a generous man he is. I doubt *The Woman in the Room* was the first "dollar baby," but I'm certain it must be among the first wave of those films.)

Let me digress to say that my very first real job in films happened later that same year, after I'd gotten Steve's permission to do *The Woman in the Room*. Chuck Russell hired me as a P.A. on a shitty no-budget film called *Hell Night*, starring Linda Blair. If you haven't seen it, I don't really recommend it. Quentin Tarantino keeps telling me he really likes *Hell Night*, but I keep telling him he's the only one. It was one of the cheesier entries in the "slasher movie" cycle. But if you ever do see it, you can check out my name in the end credits—my very first movie job! "P.A.," by the way, stands for "production assistant," although I've always felt it could also stand for "pissant." It is the lowest job in movies, a gofer who runs around doing every crappy job they hand you and never getting any sleep. I made 150 dollars a week, which was horrible pay even back then. But it was my entry into the film business, and began my association with Chuck Russell. Chuck was a line producer on low budget films at that time, just making a living, which is how he hired me. We later became dear friends and wound up collaborating as writers on a number of screenplays, including *A Nightmare on Elm Street 3: Dream Warriors*. That was Chuck's first directing job and my first professional writing credit, in 1986.

Anyway, back to 1980. I wrote Steve King my letter, he said yes, and it took me three years to make *The Woman in the Room*. It took a while to raise enough money (from some kindly investors in Iowa) to shoot the movie and get it in the can. But then I had to personally earn the rest of the money needed to put the film through post-production: editing the film, doing the sound, paying for the lab work, etc. By 1983 I was working as a prop assistant on TV commercials—not great money, but it was enough to get my movie finished. I earned $11,000 that year and spent $7,000 of it finishing my movie—how I survived on $4,000 that year is something I still can't explain; to this day I have no idea how I did it. (The IRS was also quite curious: that was the only year I've ever gotten audited for taxes, because they couldn't believe anybody could survive on $4,000 a year.) All I can say is, my rent was cheap and I lived very frugally. I spent that entire year with a borrowed Moviola in my bedroom, editing the film. I had heaps of 16mm film piled all over the place. At night, I had to move all the piles of film off my bed onto the floor so I could go to sleep. In the morning, I'd have to move the piles of film from the floor back onto my bed so I could walk to the bathroom. Very glamorous!

But eventually the movie did get done, and we entered it for Oscar consideration in the short film category. There are two things we should correct: 1) It wasn't the 1986 Academy Awards, but earlier—either '83 or '84, I forget the exact year. 2) More significantly, *The Woman in the Room* was not nominated; it was named in the top nine out of the ninety short films submitted that year, but we failed to make the final cut of four nominated films. (For some strange reason, the common belief has arisen through the years that the film was nominated, but that is incorrect.)

**Lilja: Did King comment on what he thought about it?** *The Woman in the Room* **is a rather personal story to him. . . .**

**Darabont:** He liked it. In fact, we used his quote "Clearly the best of the short films made from my stuff" on the video box. He did feel the character I added, The Prisoner (played by Brian Libby, who later played Floyd in *The Shawshank Redemption*), was a bit clichéd, and I can't disagree. Steve's favorite bit was the dream sequence where the mom turns into a rotted corpse—he loved that! Hey, give Steve a rotted corpse and he's your pal for life. Here's some trivia: That corpse originally appeared in *Hell Night*. (If I remember correctly, Linda Blair stumbles into a room at one point where a bunch of corpses are propped around a table—it was a male corpse, but in my short I passed him off as a woman. Corpse in drag!)

Some two years after *Hell Night*, I borrowed the corpse to use in *The Woman in the Room* from the makeup FX guys who built it. He wound up sitting in my living room for a few months. Sometimes I'd wake up in the middle of the night and forget he was there. I'd wander half-asleep out to the kitchen to get a glass of water and he'd scare the shit out of me, this big human shape sitting in the dark in my living room.

That dream sequence was something I also added to the story. Looking back on it, I guess I took a lot of liberties with Steve's material. I'm kind of surprised he liked it as much as he did. But he liked it well enough that when I approached him again in 1986 to ask for the rights to *The Shawshank Redemption*, he said yes. So spending three years busting my ass to make that short did pay off in a very nice way: It gave Steve a certain amount of confidence in me.

As for me, I look at *The Woman in the Room* now and wonder what Steve saw in it. The movie actually makes me cringe a little, as I suppose any work you did as a kid will make you cringe (unless you're Mozart). Honestly, it looks like an earnest but very young filmmaker at work to me. The result strikes me as pretty creaky and overly careful in its approach. I think I was really afraid of making any mistakes, so my approach to shooting and editing was cautious, to say the least. And it's slow! Yikes!

**Lilja: He later gave the OK to put it out on video. Whose idea was that? Yours? King's? Most "Dollar Babies" never get out to the big public, so it must have felt good.**

**Darabont:** That was always my intention, even when I first approached him for the rights. So, yes, I was a "dollar baby" in a sense, but I had worked out a deal with his agent that paid Steve some more money if I got video distribution. So he eventually made more than a buck, though it was still a very generous deal for us. Unfortunately, the video distributor we originally got into business with totally fucked us. The guy's name was

Gary Gray (not the director, I hasten to add!), this bottom-feeder with no integrity who made a shitload of money on the video but never paid us a dime of it, even though we had signed contracts. Jeff Shiro, who made *The Boogeyman* (which was paired with *The Woman in the Room* on the video), got equally screwed. Of course I didn't have a dime to my name back then, so hiring a lawyer was out of the question. I don't know if Gray is still out there somewhere, but I bet he is. Any young filmmakers thinking of getting into business with him should run in the opposite direction. And Gary, if you're reading this: shame on you. I may track you down and come after you someday with a tribe of high-priced Hollywood lawyers shrieking like crazed Apaches in an old Western, just to see the look on your face.

At some point along the way, the video got bought by Spelling's video releasing company. I'm not even sure how that happened. I imagine it was that original distributor trying to squeeze a few more bucks out of it. Happily, Spelling did have integrity; they do business in a straightforward manner, so money started trickling in for a few years. It was a pleasure all those years later to track down my Iowa investors and send them checks. That's all I ever wanted, to see them paid back. It took a while, but at least they got their money. I think I might have kicked in a few bucks of my own, since I was making a good living by then.

**Lilja: Then eleven years later you did *The Shawshank Redemption*, which became a big success and nominated for seven Academy Awards. It's also one of the most popular adaptations from a King story. Why do you think that is?**

**Darabont:** Well, it's the power of the story, for sure. Steve wrote a humdinger there; he hit that ball right over the fence. It has a tremendous humanity to it, which makes for the best kind of storytelling. I recognized it the moment I read it. And it works gorgeously as metaphor—everybody who sees it can project their own trials and tribulations, and hopes for triumph, into it. I've often referred to it as the "Rorschach Test" of movies. People see what they want to see in it, even if they've never been to prison. It's a very potent experience that way, and that's all credit to Steve King. The man writes deep, and with that story he was writing deeper than usual. All I had to do was translate it to the screen and not screw it up. I'm probably making that sound easier than it was, but the task was made a lot easier by the fact that I had Castle Rock's complete trust and support. That's an amazing group of people at that company. Bless their hearts, because the level of trust a filmmaker experiences there is almost unique in this business. If I'd had standard studio interference and meddling on that movie, if I'd spent my time battling to defend my film against executives who wanted everything different, Lord knows how that movie would have turned out. Probably not so well. It would have been some crappy prison movie long forgotten by now. But I had Castle Rock, and they were just the best.

**Lilja: How happy are you with that movie yourself? Is it fair to say that *The Shawshank Redemption* was your big break?**

**Darabont:** I'd certainly qualify *The Shawshank Redemption* as a big break. You can't get seven Academy Award nominations including Best Picture and not suddenly be taken very seriously as a director. And that movie led directly to *The Green Mile*. Hanks, one of my favorite people in the world, saw *The Shawshank Redemption* and rang me up and said: "Hey, love your work, we should find something to do together. If you ever have a script you think I'd be right for, send it to me." That's quite a nice door to have opened.

And, yes, I'm delighted with the movie. I watched it again when we had our Ten Year Anniversary screening and DVD re-release. And with all that time and distance, I was knocked out by how well the movie holds up. (I'm glad I didn't get the same feeling I got watching *The Woman in the Room* again!) You know, after a decade goes by, you (the filmmaker) don't really feel like you had anything to do with it, you just kind of sit there and watch the movie on its own terms. It's almost like somebody else's movie by then; you just get caught up in the story like any audience member. And I was very pleased with what I saw. It's that Steve King tale, man, it works a treat. But the thing that really jumped out at me was how great Tim Robbins was. I'd somewhat forgotten that. Everybody talks about Morgan Freeman, and of course he's just superb—I always hear how much everybody loves his narration—but Tim really carries equal weight on his shoulders for the movie working so well. Don't tell him I said that; he'll get a swelled head.

**Lilja: Then five years later you have another success based on a King book. This time it's *The Green Mile*, which was nominated for four Academy Awards. Why do you think your King adaptations are so successful?**

**Darabont:** Because when I recognize that a story is great, I try not to mess with it too much. I promise you, that's not a glib answer. That's why *The Green Mile* wound up being three hours long. I'm the first to admit that's not an optimal length for a movie. It's a lot to ask of an audience to sit for three hours, but if I'd made that movie two hours, it would have cut the heart out of Steve's story. It would have given us a mangled version.

# 119

# The Real Thing: Drew Struzan

## A Profile by George Beahm

### 2009

*The best thing that came out of writing* Knowing Darkness: Artists Inspired by Stephen King *(Centipede Press, 2009) was meeting some of the artists I'd never met before, including Drew Struzan. A mild-mannered and soft-spoken man, Struzan counts Frank Darabont as a dear friend, and in a lengthy introduction written especially for* Knowing Darkness, *Struzan rendered a portrait of Darabont standing between actors Morgan Freeman (who played Ellis Boyd "Red" Redding) and Tim Robbins (who played Andy Dufresne), both wearing prison uniforms. It's a heartwarming portrait, and on the right side Struzan wrote, "Happy Anniversary."*

*Frank Darabont reviewed and edited my piece on Struzan. I am indebted to Darabont for his eagle eye, which considerably improved the piece. (I've rewritten it for its appearance in this book.)*

*I am also indebted to Struzan for an act of generosity that stunned me and caught me totally by surprise: I had rendered what I considered a small favor to Struzan, and he never forgot it. I considered it a minor intervention on his behalf, and I was glad to be of service. I put it out of my mind, but he kept it in his, and when I visited him at his California studio, he gave me two priceless gifts, which I will keep private. I was overcome by his generosity. At a loss for words, I mumbled my thanks.*

*The gifts I cherish, but the friendship I cherish even more.*

*Struzan, who is perhaps best known for his movie posters for George Lucas's* Star

*Wars movies, is also celebrated for his fine work for Frank Darabont, notably* The Shawshank Redemption, The Green Mile, *and* The Mist.

*I've always thought he has the perfect first name for an artist—Drew—and I treasure his art books, which grace my shelves. Check out* Drew Struzan: Oeuvre *(Titan Books, 2011]);* Star Wars: Posters *(Harry N. Abrams, 2014); and* Drew: The Man Behind the Poster *(2013, a documentary about his life and work).*

Like many artists, Drew simply loves to paint. "I love the texture of paint made of colored earth, of oil from the trees and of canvas and paper. I love the expression of paint from a brush or a hand smearing charcoal, the dripping of paint and moisture of water, the smell of the materials. I delight in the changeable nature of a painting with new morning light or in the afternoon when the sun turns a painting orange or by firelight at night. I love to see it, hold it, touch it, smell it, and create it. My gift is to share my life by allowing others to see into my heart and spirit through such tangible, comprehensible and familiar means. The paint is part of the expression," he explained.

It is an important distinction because the film industry traditionally had relied on hand-drawn art for movie posters but now relies exclusively on photography, an expedient and cost-effective but clearly inferior substitute. What has been lost in the process is the magic, the romance, the *uniqueness* of an art form that had its origins in the silent films.

The 1933 poster for *King Kong* serves as a metaphor for the eventual downfall of hand-drawn movie poster art: Like King Kong, who stood like a colossus astride a New York City skyscraper to defiantly fight off buzzing biplanes, hand-drawn movie poster art held its own for decades against the relentless assault of photography, but in the end, it fell from its pinnacle, like the mighty King Kong himself.

It was a battle of the titans: the expressive vision of a sole artist up against an army of computer technicians, the beauty of original art pitted against the beastly abomination of computer-manipulated photos.

In the end, it was the beast that killed the beauty.

Bob Peak, Frank McCarthy, Howard Terpning, Richard Amsel, and Robert McGinnis—if you're a fan of movie-poster art, these names shine bright because, for decades, they gave us memorable, colorful images that drew us into the theater, where we sat in the dark and watched still frames sprocket like a rocket through a film projector at twenty-four frames per second, a visual experience enhanced by an integrated sound system that enveloped us.

Add to that list of artists one more name: Drew Struzan.

Now happily retired from the movie-poster business, though he does an occasional poster—for illustrative, not financial, considerations—he now heads to his custom-made studio to pick up a brush and work at his own pace on subjects of personal interest: mostly figure studies and portraits of his grandchildren.

Drew's statement upon his retirement made his position clear:

Having been working at not working has produced a guy who could never return to illustration again. It took a lot to attempt the idea of retiring from my 40 years of effort and sacrifice, but now that I have, I am delighting in life as never before. I had forgotten how to rest, to smell the proverbial roses and to see the future as opportunity. I am grateful and honored to have had the opportunity to do all the work I did. I am well pleased to have been able to give a gift of beauty and peace through my artwork to so many throughout the world. Now I have laid down the burden and have peace and happiness as the reward for my day's labor.

In an introduction to *Oeuvre,* one of Struzan's two oversized collections of art, George Lucas explained that "Drew has the talent not only to capture the characters faithfully, but to enrich them with something a little grander, a little more glorious and more romantic than a photograph could ever convey."

What, one wonders, would Drew do if he were asked for a new commission from his old friend George Lucas? Would he accept it? He *might,* but only because of their long-standing friendship based on mutual respect.

Drew, who acknowledges that the nature of the movie business is essentially one of compromise and endless frustration, has spent a good part of his working life dealing with the whimsical demands of studio executives in Hollyweird—er, Hollywood. Happily, he no longer endures the aggravation of creating art by committee, a frustrating process that is the norm.

Moreover, on too many occasions, Drew was the "go to" guy when, on short notice, a studio executive panicked because there was no approved art on hand for distribution, and the studio head was clamoring for it—or someone's head on a platter.

Drew would then get a frantic, pleading phone call, because everyone in Hollywood knows that he *always* delivers the goods. In one instance, for a remake of John Carpenter's *The Thing* (1982), Drew took on the assignment to produce a painting within twenty-four hours.

In *Oeuvre,* Drew explained, "A certain amount of insanity is part of my job. I can't really explain why, but after spending millions of dollars and months of planning in order to launch a major motion picture, I routinely get calls from frantic producers who have two days to ship before a release and no poster."

Drew has invested four decades of his life into his illustrative career. His impressive body of work includes album covers, magazine covers, limited edition prints, book covers, comics, postage stamps, and collectibles of every kind.

The movie art, though, is what draws in the film crowd: a single, arresting image that catches one's eye in a print publication, billboard, or outside a movie theater. It's a promise, a visual invitation to leave your troubles behind and escape to another world as seen through the lens of a film director.

Frank Darabont is messianic about the essential difference between hand-drawn movie-poster art and those cobbled together by computer technicians using Photoshop. Citing Drew's work, Darabont illustrates the wide gap in perceived quality between two Harry Potter movie posters. "Drew's art for *The Sorcerer's Stone* makes me weep. It is so gorgeous, so evocative, so romantic, so beautiful. It says: 'Come see the movie.'" But *The Half-Blood Prince* is "an abomination of movie poster art. It's the hip, young cast just standing there. What is that—a Gap ad? There's no *art* in it."

In a *Time* magazine interview, Drew gave us a glimpse of what happened behind the scenes. "A lot of people think I did all the *Harry Potter* posters, but I only did the first one," he said. "The studio came to me and said, 'This is going to be seven movies. So just like you did with *Indiana Jones,* design the look for it, and then we'll repeat that look for the other films.' I did the first one, and when they hit the theaters, people just clamored for it. But when the second movie came out, they decided to just use photography."

It's an important distinction that speaks to the heart of the matter. As Darabont points out, "I find contemporary movie posters to be soulless and sterile. There's no romance to them at all. No individuality, no love of film as an art form."

Put simply, Drew's art is *all* about heart.

There's a story Drew likes to tell that underscores his point and reinforces Darabont's: He and John Alvin were called upon to submit comps for *Bladerunner.* "The other comp was about the architecture and the modernness, and mine was all about the people. The director, Ridley Scott, loved mine but they went with the other one because the studio wanted to emphasize how much money they spent on the special effects. So for years, that's what they used. But mine was always Ridley's favorite, so when the studio came out with its twenty-fifth anniversary edition, Ridley said, 'Now's my chance to finally use the art that I think is appropriate for that movie.' Ridley's reason was [that] it's about connecting, because it's the human experience we value, not the architecture."

Which brings me, finally, to Stephen King.

It seems altogether fitting that of the numerous movies and teleplays adapted from Stephen King's work, Frank and Drew teamed up to give us their visual interpretations of three of King's most memorable stories: "Rita Hayworth and Shawshank Redemption," from *Different Seasons*; *The Green Mile,* a serialized novel; and *The Mist,* a cautionary tale of "the technology of fright," as Dr. Tony Magistrale writes in his book, *Hollywood's Stephen King.*

## THE SHAWSHANK REDEMPTION

*The Shawshank Redemption* is often called a "prison movie," but it's more accurate to characterize it as a *prisoner's* movie. The prison itself is merely the backdrop, the setting. The interaction among the characters, notably the relationship between Andy Dufresne (played by Tim Robbins) and Ellis Boyd "Red" Redding (played by Morgan Freeman), is the essential story.

With its unusual, and awkward, title—one that King himself doesn't care for—and its nonhorror story line, the film is one that catches many moviegoers by surprise when they are told it's by Stephen King. Because they associate him exclusively with horror films, they're surprised when he doesn't fit in their preconceived notions—clearly, theirs is a failure of imagination.

Typically, a movie-poster artist will draw several comps, each a different approach, to give the studio as many choices as possible. The comp finally chosen will then be used as the basis for rendering the final art, the nucleus of the studio's marketing campaign for a movie.

Take a good look at the movie poster for the tenth-anniversary release of *The*

*Shawshank Redemption.* It doesn't feature the original poster's photo; instead, it's an illustration by Drew, drawn from one of the comps.

In lieu of the art, here's descriptive text of the comps:

One captures Red and Andy behind barbed wire, illuminated by a full moon. It is simple and stark, but there's more story elements that can be conveyed.

Another one arranges "snapshots" of the characters. It draws one's eye from the upper left of the image to its lower right: Behind bars, Red has a wistful expression, and Andy a determined one; a small picture of Rita Hayworth in lingerie, the wet dream of convicts barred from sexual congress; the implacable warden, his face symbolically deep in shadow; a prison guard, his arms crossed, his gimlet eyes fixed straight ahead; the weathered face of Brooks Hatlen (named after King's mentor, Burton Hatlen), bearing a wistful, resigned expression; and finally, Red and Andy sharing a private conversation in the prison yard.

Yet another comp incorporates elements of both: Set against a black background, Red's hopeful expression contrasts sharply with Andy's determined one. On its left side, tight close-ups of an unyielding prison guard named Byron Hadley and his hardened boss, Warden Norton—their faces, appropriately, are in shadow; counterbalanced on the right, the face of a young man named Tommy, whom Andy takes under his wing, and the world-weary face of Brooks Hatlen.

The faces—from Red's to Norton's—combine to frame the climactic scene of the movie: Andy Dufresne, his arms outstretched, bathed in light and showered by rain, symbolizing his freedom.

Looking back at his art for *The Shawshank Redemption,* Drew observed, "When you think of the movie, do you *really* think of the setting? That's not what it's about. It's about good old-fashioned storytelling. It's gritty, it's harsh, it's mean, yet the two main people, Red and Andy, are very quiet and not angry."

Long after the prison itself recedes from one's mind, the characters remain, haunting us to linger forever.


## THE GREEN MILE

When Darabont took the helm for a second King film project, it would be, ironically, another movie set in a prison—*The Green Mile,* based on King's serialized novel. As King explained in "Foreword: A Letter" (*The Green Mile,* Scribner, 2000), it would be "a story that could be written the same way it would be read—in installments. And I liked the high-wire aspect of it, too: fall down on the job, fail to carry through, and all at once about a million readers are howling for your blood."

It would prove to be a King story ideally matched to Darabont's deeply held storytelling values—one with heart that could translate to a film worth the two years of his life and the commitment necessary to bring it to the screen with fidelity. As Darabont told Patrick Lee, film directing is punishing work to meet a demanding schedule. "It's too hard. . . . So I was waiting. And wading through lots of *Die Hard* rip-offs that were being sent my way."

*The Green Mile* shares much in common with the film version of *The Shawshank Redemption*. Both focus on a first-person recounting of the story to highlight the principal characters; both significantly and symbolically use a prison as a backdrop; and both are about character, not plot.

What happens to the characters is what makes all the difference. It's a shared perception among Stephen King, Frank Darabont, and Drew Struzan. It also speaks to why each excels at his chosen craft.

The painting that was used for the DVD release of *The Green Mile* is suffused with green light. We see actor Tom Hanks as prison-ward superintendent Paul Edgecombe, stern but obviously humane. We see two guards: a giant of a man with the ironic nickname "Brutal," who, in fact, is anything but a brute, and a small man (in every sense of the word) who flanks Edgecombe and inmate Eduard Delacroix. Significantly, at the center of the picture is John Coffey (played by the late Michael Clarke Duncan), whose palms-up hands emanate an otherworldly light. On the right, we see an electric chair, "Old Sparky," and Delacroix's pet, a mouse miraculously brought back to life by John Coffey—note his initials: J.C.—who is clearly much more than what he appears to be: a giant-sized, uneducated black man with murder in his heart.

Drew Struzan, once again, encapsulates the story of *The Green Mile* in a single, poignant image. Though *The Shawshank Redemption* celebrates the triumph of hope over fear, *The Green Mile* is not so celebratory: Man's "justice" is done, but Edgecombe's faith is shaken to its very core at the cosmic injustice of how God could countenance the destruction of one of His divine creations at the lesser hands of mortal man. John Coffey, clearly, is a divine power in mortal form.

Struzan captures the telling moments through the character's expressions: the expression of doubt and wonder on Edgecombe's face, the kind and gentle look on Brutus "Brutal" Howell's face, the backward and dismissive glance of prison guard Percy Wetmore, the animated face of Eduard Delacroix, and the ethereal beauty of John Coffey's face shining in wonderment.

The combined arts of the writer, the filmmaker, and artist come together to show us the enduring power of the human heart.

## *The Mist*

This archetypal King story, with ordinary people in a pressure-cooker environment, is one in which the depiction of monsters is best left to the imagination, which is the approach Struzan wisely employed in his movie poster and DVD cover for *The Mist*. He knows our imaginations can conjure up monsters aplenty. Struzan's job, simply, is to convey the story's claustrophobic atmosphere and sense of dread: A strange mist rolls in and blankets Maine, bringing with it hellish creatures presumed to be the unforeseen result of the Arrowhead Project, government experiments conducted at a local army post near Bridgton, Maine. Its nearby residents take refuge in a Federal Foods supermarket, where they make a stand: Some stay, and some venture out, and all share the certain knowledge that the world has suddenly gone mad.

Struzan's art shows us the palpable fear in the eyes of the beleaguered, terrified townsfolk. Empty, darkened cars sit abandoned in the parking lot, outlined against the supermarket, a magnet for monsters who seek easy prey.

A man's face, partially obscured by his hand, tells its own story: He doesn't *want* to look but is compelled to do so. But whatever is out there in the mist is being drawn in by the lights of the supermarket, where the monsters seek food. The man's solitary eye harbors a look of bewilderment and unmistakable fear.

The rules of order, of civilization, no longer apply. The distraught man can offer no answer, no explanation, nor can he find sanctuary from the unremitting horror of his situation. He is, simply, prey.

Struzan's work is seen not only on the DVD packaging but in the movie itself. The central figure in *The Mist* is David Drayton, an artist. Using Struzan's Pasadena, California, studio as a model for Drayton's studio ensured authenticity. Darabont also included "prop" paintings by Struzan, drawn from his own movie work: art for *The Thing*, *The Shawshank Redemption*, *Pan's Labyrinth*, and *The Green Mile*.

Keen-eyed King fans also saw in the studio sequence a painting depicting Roland the gunslinger, flanked by the Dark Tower and a single rose; Roland's image deliberately suggests Clint Eastwood, whom King had in mind when he wrote the series. The painting, measuring thirty-by-forty inches, prompted Dark Tower fans to write and inquire about prints for sale. Struzan explained that it was intended as a prop painting only, and not as a basis for prints. (The original now resides in King's collection.)

"I was the last dinosaur to paint for movies," Struzan says. "Nobody does it anymore." Talking about the current crop of Hollywood film executives who have grown up in a wired computerized environment, Drew laments, "They don't understand it. They haven't grown up with it. They don't appreciate it. And they don't think it translates."

In point of fact, it "translates" very well indeed—if only one has a smidgen of imagination. The rich, illustrative heritage that suffuses Struzan's visual storytelling heralds from multiple sources: turn-of-the-century illustrated books, full-color Sunday funnies in newspapers, eye-popping color comic books, and most especially oversized movie posters dating all the way back to the thirties.

Drawing on all of these enchanting sources of visual inspiration, Struzan creates unique images of movie magic, posters imbued with life and animation.

As I sat in his studio, Struzan drew my attention to a 27-by-40-inch acrylic painting used as the DVD cover art for *Bladerunner*. It is, simply, gorgeous. It's a work of art. "You can see the artist in this work," he says. "An original piece of art is about the person who made it, and that's what becomes part of its value and importance. It's the real thing."

And so, too, is Drew, whose work not only touches but, more significantly, illuminates the human heart.

# PART SEVEN

## THE CRITICS' CORNER

In the early eighties, when books about King first began appearing, the earliest were critical books published by a specialty press, Ted Dikty's Starmont House, which issued a series of themed books by Michael Collings, then an English professor at Pepperdine University, and an issue of *Starmont Reader's Guide* (number 16), *Stephen King* (1982), by

Douglas E. Winter, a prefatory exploration to the more ambitious and mainstream study, *Stephen King: The Art of Darkness*.

Since then there's been a veritable explosion of books about every facet of King's universe, especially academic books, the best of which have been written by Collings and his colleague at the University of Vermont, Tony Magistrale; their books are careful, loving works of scholarship.

And then there's Maine's one-man book factory, Sanford Phippen, a friend of the Kings, and a professor in the English department at UMO, whose books are also highly regarded.

On the pop culture side, Stephen Spignesi and Rocky Wood have written reference books that aid students and scholars when researching King's fiction.

Spignesi's concordance in *The Stephen King Encyclopedia* and his ranking of King's works in *The Essential Stephen King* come to mind, as does Wood's bibliographies on King's fiction and non-fiction.

Taken as a whole, their periodical essays and books contribute much to our understanding and appreciation of King's impressive literary output, which will serve as the catalyst for more books in the years to come.

# 120

# STEPHEN SPIGNESI: AN INTERVIEW

## BY GEORGE BEAHM

A king-sized book about Stephen King was published by Popular Culture Ink in 1991. Titled *The Shape Under the Sheet: The Complete Stephen King Encyclopedia*, Spignesi's book is 780 pages and mostly a concordance (80 percent); the remainder is companion-style material, with exclusive interviews, including those with David King (the only one he's ever given), Shirley Sonderegger (a former King secretary), and Chris Chesley (one of only two interviews he ever gave). Authorized by Stephen King, who allowed access to his staff, family, and friends, Spignesi's timing for King's assistance was on the beam.

*Entertainment Weekly,* in its review of his tombstone-sized book, proclaimed Spignesi to be *the* Stephen King expert, and he went on to publish several more books about King's work, including two quiz books (from New American Library), *The Lost Work of Stephen King* and *The Essential Stephen King.*

A prolific author who has written on numerous pop culture subjects, from the sinking of the *Titanic* to the Beatles and Woody Allen, Spignesi is a careful, thoughtful writer, a baby boomer whose love for pop culture is second to none. He's also a New Englander who's as reclusive as H. P. Lovecraft.

**GB: You are known for writing pop culture, and your King encyclopedia was the first of several books you've written about him. Given the level of detail in your encyclopedia, it's obviously a labor of love. What was the first King book you read, and was it the**

**impetus to write your encyclopedia? Or did the idea of doing the encyclopedia come to you after reading several of his books?**

**Spignesi:** The first King book I read was *The Shining*, but that wasn't the catalyst for my decision to chronicle (*obsessively* chronicle, some may say) the people, places, and things in King's work. After *The Shining*, I went back and read *Carrie* and *'Salem's Lot* and, within a couple of years, *Night Shift*, *The Stand*, and *The Dead Zone* came along. I realized that Stephen King's narrative power and meticulously created characters and worlds were something incredible, and I felt a desire to do something with his work. I then got the idea to do with King's work what I had already done with *The Andy Griffith Show*. My first book, which had just sold but wasn't out yet, was *Mayberry, My Hometown*, and in that, I chronicled the people, places, and things of the Mayberry universe. It wasn't too big a leap to extend that idea to King's work. Little did I realize what doing that would entail and that it would take me five years—with an assistant—to complete the encyclopedia.

**GB: King is not the same writer he was when he published *Carrie* in 1974. It's been, as you've pointed out, forty years down the road. A lifetime as a writer. What do you see as the essential difference between who he was in the *Carrie* days, and who he is now as the author of *Revival*, which is admittedly one of his darkest novels?**

**Spignesi:** The truth is, in my opinion, he's still there. The Stephen King narrative voice, philosophical concerns, and extraordinary accessibility are present in everything he's ever written, including *Revival*. As a writer and an artist, I never *judge* any other artist's body of work. I don't like that word. I discuss, describe, assess, and offer informed opinion, but I am not in the school of those who say, "Oh, early King was *better* than post-accident King" or "After *It*, King went downhill," et cetera. It's like saying one Beatles album is better than another Beatles album. They're different, yes, but "*better*"? I love the Beatles. This means I love everything the artists who are the Beatles do. I want their artistic interpretation of the world. I may not enjoy some stuff as much as others, but art is a subjective experience for everyone.

It's the same with King. I love his work. This means I welcome everything that the artist who is Stephen King creates. Again, I may not enjoy some stuff as much as others, but I have found an artist who I relate to and appreciate, so I am eager for more of what he has to say. Can we say late Picasso isn't "as good" as early Picasso? If you're a pompous, arrogant, "art know-it-all," you can. But it's a futile exercise and, I feel, ultimately irrelevant. Analysis is one thing; negative criticism based on personal taste is quite another. And the twain shouldn't meet.

Mike Lewis and I discussed this in depth when writing our book on the top hundred Beatles songs. And we made it very clear in the introduction that we weren't ranking the songs based on our personal taste. We used criteria: songwriting, musicianship, production, and lyrics, all of which have measurable criteria, standards established and agreed upon by experts in each field. And as fans who have studied the Beatles' work, we could offer informed opinion.

It's the same with Stephen King. Just because someone didn't enjoy *It*, for example, does not negate its brilliance as a novel. (Some people cannot read two lines of Shakespeare without recoiling in horror. Does this mean Shakespeare sucks? How dumb is that question?) There are assessable standards we can look to in order to appraise art in a way that is relevant and educational. That's why we have English and music teachers. Simply liking or disliking something is not an intelligent use of our skills. And being able to answer "why" *It* is brilliant is a sign of cognizance of the art, the artist, and their work.

I don't think King is a different writer now. I think his focus has changed, and it changed because he and his life changed. And that's what artists do: they respond to their world. This kind of relates to something Richard Christian Matheson told me when I interviewed him for the *Complete Stephen King Encyclopedia*. I asked him what he thought about writer's block. He said he thought writer's block was simply a change of mood. Makes sense.

**GB: Why do you think King will stand the test of time as a writer?**

**Spignesi:** King's legacy will be epic. He changed horror and dark fiction in ways no one had previously done. That's why I call my Stephen King course at the University of New Haven "The New Gothic Horror of Stephen King." His influences are the greats, from Stoker and Poe to Dickens and Bradbury. His writing voice is one of the most accessible and engaging to ever grace the landscape of American letters. In my *Essential Stephen King*, Michael Collings said, "William Shakespeare was the Stephen King of his time." Think about that. That speaks an encyclopedia of insight and import in one simple declarative sentence. And it speaks directly to your question: Yes, I think Stephen King will stand the test of time as a writer. I think it's a given. After all, H. P. Lovecraft—who didn't have half the talent of King—is still being read, studied, and adapted a century later.

**GB: You're a big movie watcher. I'd be interested in knowing what you think are his top three films, and why.**

**Spignesi:** Although most would probably answer *The Shawshank Redemption* as number one to this question, I wouldn't. I loved the movie when I first saw it, but it is not a perennial favorite for me. And that fact alone eliminates it from my highest spot (and even the top three, truth be told). I think his top three films are *The Green Mile*, *Misery*, and *The Dead Zone*. Those three are flawless adaptations of the novels. I always remember what King said about adapting novels to the screen: It's like shoving a book through a funnel, he said. This is why I sometimes cringe when I hear about movie deals for the big books: sometimes miniseries can do the job, but most of the time they do not. I am not a serious fan of King film adaptation in general. Maybe there are ten in the whole bunch that I can tolerate. The short films are fun, though, and I always recommend to people Jay Holben's *Paranoid* as an example of a genuinely unique adaptation of King. The script is the hundred-line poem "Paranoid: A Chant." And the visuals are amazing. Ultimately, I'm a bit of a Stephen King purist. He's a writer. Thus, I want his writing, not some screenwriter's interpretation of how to show onscreen what King put so perfectly on the page.

**GB: Is there anything, or any subject matter, that you feel King hasn't written about, that you'd like to see him tackle? In other words, are there any new grounds he should be breaking? I'm thinking of how he wrote *The Eyes of the Dragon* and never again went back to write a children's fantasy.**

**Spignesi:** I'd like to see him revisit the death penalty. *Green Mile* was about it, sort of, but not really. And assisted suicide. And I'd be really thrilled if he did more science fiction. I'd also like him to do an updated edition of *Danse Macabre,* as well as more commentary on the literary greats. King reviewed a Raymond Carver biography and a Carver short story collection for *The New York Times,* and they were extraordinarily insightful assessments of Carver and his genius. King reads widely. *Very* widely. I'd love more nonfiction from him about writers like Updike, Cheever, Bellow, Oates . . . even David Foster Wallace, Jonathan Franzen, Donna Tartt, and so forth. He thinks Hemingway sucks. Fine. But please tell us why. There's no doubt that I enjoy King's "teacher-mode" writing.

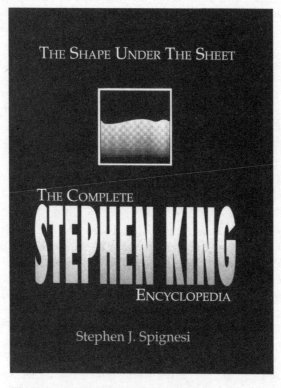

*The tombstone-sized Popular Culture Ink edition of Spignesi's* The Shape Under the Sheet: The Complete Stephen King Encyclopedia.

# 121

# STEPHEN KING AND THE CRITICS:
## A PERSONAL PERSPECTIVE

### BY MICHAEL COLLINGS

*The writings of Michael Collings can be found throughout this book, especially in the write-ups on King's books, for which I excerpted select paragraphs from his full-length reviews, originally published in the second edition of this book (1995).*

*I wanted to add a critical piece by him about Stephen King and academia and thought of this one, which also ran in my 1995 edition. In it, Collings uses as a springboard for his discussion an anecdote relayed to him by his son, then in high school.*

*Collings is now retired from full-time teaching and has moved from California to Idaho, where he continues to write literary criticism with unflagging enthusiasm and perception.*

*Times have changed, but attitudes about King's value as a writer, as judged by those in academia and by "real" writers, are still slow to change. Michael Collings was one of the first whose professional credentials as an English professor lent credibility to King's fiction by taking it seriously.*

*Years later, Joyce Carol Oates, among others, praised King's fiction. She introduced him at a public talk on April 16, 1997, at Princeton University, and said:*

Like all great writers of Gothic horror, Stephen King is both a storyteller and an inventor of startling images and metaphors, which linger long in the memory and would seem to spring from a collective, unconscious and thorough domestic-American soil. His fellow writers admire him for his commitment to the craft of fiction and the generosity of his involvement in the literary community. And he has written with insight and eloquence and a rare sort of humility about his craft.

Several weeks ago, my teenage son came home from high school chuckling—itself an odd enough circumstance to merit remembering. But the reason for his laughter was even more intriguing than the fact of it, particularly as it bore directly on my own efforts in science fiction, fantasy, and horror criticism.

His junior English class is preparing to face the great unmentionable, the horror of the year—the dreaded TERM PAPER. His teacher had handed out a long list of possible topics, all American authors, and the students were required to submit proposals for a paper that would discuss at least three works by a single author, or one work by three authors, combining the students' perceptions with relevant outside sources.

During the discussion, one student noted that Stephen King, his favorite author, was not included on the list. No, the teacher answered solemnly, King was not included. Another student noted that several other contemporary popular authors were also missing from the list and asked why.

In response the teacher said that such writers were only of interest to readers unable to handle the sophisticated expression of the "classics."

"In other words," the second student shot back, defending himself and his friends who read King and others, "we read them because we're too stupid to understand the classics?"

"Uh, no," the teacher answered, obviously backpedaling. She continued to talk in generalities about the lack of sophistication in contemporary popular writers, noting in passing that most students hadn't even considered using King as a topic for the paper until a few years before, when a professor from Pepperdine began publishing books about him.

At this point, my son sat up and began paying more attention.

Then, the teacher continued, the professor made things worse by holding discussion groups at the local library, actually talking with groups of high school students about King and his works, as if they had literary merit. Now my son was really paying attention, wondering if he should raise his hand and say "That's my father," or wait it out and see what else the teacher would say.

He decided to wait it out.

And discovered that in spite of such odd behavior (fortunately isolated) in a college professor, there really wasn't enough criticism on Stephen King or writers like him to merit including them on the list of possibilities for the TERM PAPER.

End of discussion.

When my son reported this experience—grinning the whole while and (I'm sure) wondering how I would take this implied slur on my reputation (such as it is)—I was struck again by the short-sightedness of academic establishments that continue to exclude King, Koontz, and others like them from the lists of "approved" materials.

While Hawthorne and *The Scarlet Letter*, Melville and *Moby-Dick*, and Dickens and *A Tale of Two Cities* are certainly central literary achievements in our culture, even fascinating topics for further research and discussion by adult readers, I am even less convinced now than I was as a high school student that they are necessarily appropriate for freshmen, sophomores, and juniors in high school, many of whom are barely beyond being functionally literate, many of whom lack even the barest backgrounds or historical perspectives for assessing such novels, and many of whom are explicitly more interested in Poe, Bradbury, and King. Yet instructors are forced in turn to force high school students to read works that probably even most teachers would be unlikely to read for pleasure.

On the other hand, the opposite approach seems to be requiring texts that are themselves less literary than exercises in political correctness, sociological conditioning, and artificially induced diversity. Either way, the established programs often simply ignore the fact that kids like to read (and watch) things by Stephen King.

There are, of course, strong arguments against allowing King into curriculums, even as tangentially as letting students use his work for an out-of-class term paper.

His writing is often violent. It is often gross and explicit, both sexually and linguistically. It is often fantastic. It is often highly critical of accepted institutions, including home, family, politics, and education.

But the kids read him. Based on my experiences leading discussion groups about his books, high-school-age readers often devour his books, memorize his books, know more about what he has written than I do. And then they are told by teachers that he is too unsophisticated, too peripheral to what is really important in the universe, too common for students to waste their time on, when it would seem that teachers would welcome the opportunity to confront a writer who perhaps more than any other is molding the imaginations and minds of contemporary adolescents. After all, if so many students read him, and he is so awful, so damaging to the social fabric, so utterly without redeeming social value, it would seem even more important to discover what it is that draws young readers to him. To refer back to my son's experience, the teacher stated to the class that anyone who read more than two or three King novels had to be warped, perverted, highly disturbed. At that point my son couldn't help laughing out loud—and was tempted to put the teacher even more on the spot by noting that he had read about thirty King novels and that his father had read everything that King had published. If two or three relegated a reader to warp-dom, where would thirty, forty, or fifty books put someone? Perhaps wisely, my son restrained his impulse, and the teacher was free to continue her defense of the status quo reading list.

No, King is not sufficiently elevated, not sufficiently elegant, not sufficiently a part of the teachers' own university backgrounds—implying that they might actually have to read him and study him themselves in order to lecture to classes—that he is simply inappropriate as the subject for a research project. And to prove their point, they pound the final nail into the coffin of any would-be term paperist: There's just not enough criticism written about him to make the effort worthwhile.

Again and again I have heard this comment and am stunned by the ignorance it betrays. Certainly for many science-fiction, fantasy, and horror writers, the claim is accurate. Even some of the finest writers in the genres have been ignored by traditional critics and scholars, to the point that accurate bibliographies are not even available for many, if not most. In spite of the valiant efforts of publishers like the late Ted Dikty of Starmont House and his series editor, Roger Schlobin, who between them saw the publication of several dozen introductory monographs, or Rob Reginald at Borgo Press, with his continuing series of definitive bibliographies—in spite of the work of dozens of scholars and critics approaching such monumental tasks as the lifeworks of Isaac Asimov and Robert A. Heinlein and others almost as prolific and as central to our reading heritage—in spite of all this effort, it is still too easy for teachers to issue lists of term-paper topics that ignore some of the most popular and influential writers of our times.

But to make that claim for Stephen King?

I glance at the bookshelf and see the three-inch-thick manuscript that represents my work on a Stephen King bibliography, and I wonder.[1] Woefully out of date since its completion in 1991, the manuscript nevertheless includes over three thousand items, both primary and secondary, including titles of several dozen books exclusively about King (a number of them from prestigious university presses), more dozens of articles in scholarly and popular journals and magazines, and hundreds of reviews ranging from the *New York Times Book Review* to localized fan presses—but this is not enough to allow students sufficient exercise in the fine and ancient art of literary research.

Granted, not all of the criticism and scholarship available on King is first class. I think of one article that discovers Vietnam allegories in a King story, when King himself has stated publicly that he sees (or intended) no such sub-text himself. Or another critic who, after publishing three very expensive specialty editions of interviews and criticism, notes that he considers King little more than a literary hack (although presumably a source of no little income).

Nevertheless, it seems important to recognize that much of the criticism is solid and, more important yet, that horror writers are an intrinsic and essential part of understanding late-twentieth-century American culture. Writers like Stephen King, Dean Koontz, Robert McCammon, Dan Simmons, and others have written works that transcend narrow genre classifications, that have grappled with the fundamental social problems we face today, and have explored them through the metaphor of the monstrous and the horrific—as if AIDS, molestation, homelessness, and -isms of various sorts were not already monstrous and horrific enough. These writers have described us in the clearest and broadest of terms—not pessimistically or nihilistically but often with an undercurrent of true hope. On the surface, their images may be frightening, but then so is our world. The "premillennial cotillion" that Koontz depicts graphically in *Dragon Tears* is not just a figment of his imagination. The worldwide plague that wipes out most of humanity in King's *The Stand* is only a few degrees beyond the plagues—diseases, social unrest, political threats—that we presently face. The fictional disintegration of society in McCammon's *Swan Song* or *Mine* or *Stinger* reflects the real disintegrations we see around us. Their unique visions of what it is to live here, to live now, is captured in these and other novels and stories in ways that no alternative form can legitimately duplicate.

And our children read those novels and stories.

Our children see the world in terms of the visions these novels and stories create.

Our children need to understand more completely what it is that these writers are struggling to achieve.

---

1 Published as *Horror Plum'd: International Stephen King Bibliography and Guide, 1960–2000.*

# 122

# Steve's Take:

## An Interview with Stephen King

### by Tony Magistrale
### May 21, 2002

*Tony Magistrale, who has written extensively about Stephen King's works, teaches in the English department at the University of Vermont, in Burlington. He's also a friend of King's and was the university's liaison when King came to lecture and refused to accept Magistrale's proffered check, stating that the university should use the money to buy books instead.*

 *Interviewed by the media extensively, King's hundreds of profile pieces and interviews vary widely in terms of quality. To my mind, three interviews stand out, for various reasons: Eric Norden's, in* Playboy *(June 1983), which covers his early years in detail, which I reprinted in* The Stephen King Companion *(Andrews and McMeel, 1989); Christopher Lehmann-Haupt and Nathaniel Rich's, in* The Paris Review *(fall 2006), which is readily available online; and this interview, conducted by Dr. Magistrale, which was originally published in his book,* Hollywood's Stephen King *(Palgrave Macmillan).*

 *Of the three, Magistrale's is unique because the questions are not posed by a journalist but, instead, by an academic who has also read King's large body of work and viewed the films adapted from that work. Consequently, he asks probing questions that elicit thoughtful responses from King, who typically answers the same questions from journalists who haven't done their homework: Is horror all you write? Was there a childhood incident that scared you so badly you started writing horror fiction? What scares you?*

*Oh, please, give me a break.*

*Magistrale's interview, which follows, is insightful. His questions, and King's answers, reveal two keen minds, sometimes sparring but more often agreeing on major points. The discussion is organic; the conversation interactive and, for the reader, thought-provoking.*

*Though conducted in 2002, a time when King published* From a Buick 8, Black House, *and* Everything's Eventual: Fourteen Dark Tales, *Magistrale's interview more than holds its own, and it offers much food for thought to King's readers, who want (to use a metaphor from* The Wizard of Oz*) to see the man behind the curtain.*

*Kevin Quigley in front of the Kings' main house in Bangor.*

*A "No Trepassing" sign on the King property.*

*A bat guards the front gate to the Kings' main house.*

*Penney and Stuart Tinker of SK Tours of Maine.*

*Built in 1871–1873 and bought by the Kings in 2007, the Charles P. Brown house is next door to their main home in Bangor.*

New England's northern tier consists of scattered towns, rolling meadows, impenetrable woods and bogs. This is Stephen King's country. Lancaster, New Hampshire, or Skowhegan, Maine, could seamlessly be transformed into the sets for movie remakes of *'Salem's Lot, It,* or *Stand by Me.*

Fewer cars pass me now, mostly trucks, many of them hauling loads of timber and heating oil. This is a land where winter never really loosens its hold on the imagination, even late in May. There are also fewer radio stations, especially as I ascend into the mountains. Long stretches of static are occasionally punctuated by country music and heavy metal. I have lost all contact with classical music.

The first road sign that points the way to Bangor, Maine, appears incongruously at the Vermont–New Hampshire state border. Immediately following it is another sign welcoming travelers to New Hampshire and the Great North Woods, and then, one more sign, as if as an afterthought, "Brake for Moose—It Could Save Your Life." About this point it occurs to me that *Dracula*'s Jonathan Harker and I share some things in common: We are both traveling east through rugged mountains on a strange journey that may prove to be as terrifying as it is beautiful.

Bangor is a small town. Like most New England places, it is difficult to know; it keeps its secrets to itself. On one hand, there is the Bangor of charming downtown boutiques and quaint canals cut through solid blocks of granite. The Bangor Opera House on Main Street is the epicenter of town. But there is also Bangor the blue-collar city. A downtown that—except for the teenagers assembled in the parking lot of a Dunkin' Donuts—is completely deserted at ten o'clock on a Friday night. A place of abandoned factories and concrete oil storage tanks that appears to have more in common with Baltimore or Buffalo than with its upscale coastal cousins, Kennebunkport and Portland. At dinner my first night in town, the waiter, a Bangor native, informs me that the population of his city is 35,000 "and shrinking. We're at the end of the line here."

Stephen King lives on unequivocally the most elegant street in Bangor, composed of large, rambling houses that once belonged to nineteenth-century timber barons. King's house is the largest and most rambling one on the block, a restored Victorian mansion that is ten times as long as it is wide. Yellow surveillance cameras hang from underneath the wide eaves of the structure's first floor, like the suspended nests of giant bees. Lovely landscaping that is now in full bloom graces the front yard. A high black iron gate, similar to what might be found along the perimeters of a cemetery, demarcates King's property lines. The message is clear: This is a well-tended, lovely place, but don't bother ringing the doorbell unless you have an invite.

Stephen King's business office is located on the other side of Bangor, behind an airport runway of the Bangor International Airport and next door to a towering blue General Electric power plant. In a one-floor nondescript, prefabricated concrete building—resembling more a barracks than an office—off to the right of a dead-end street overgrown with weeds pushing through cracked asphalt, America's Storyteller conducts his daily affairs.

The contrast between King's office and home is stunning, but also instructively symbolic. The Victorian mansion is heir to King's own Horatio Alger–like achievement of the American dream. It is a monument to his enormous literary, cinematic, and

*The Thomas Hill Standpipe in Bangor.*

*Road signs outside Bangor, pointing to Bar Harbor,
Brewer, and downtown Bangor.*

financial success. His unassuming office, however, speaks to King's working-class origins and ethics. It is a comfortable but unpretentious space where the humble heroes and heroines who populate his narratives—the Dolores Claibornes and Stu Redmans and Johnny Smiths—would likely feel very much at home.

**Magistrale: I spent most of this morning in downtown Bangor, just walking around. There were a couple of moments down there when I could have sworn I saw a clown, but I might have imagined that. Can you tell me something about the role Bangor has played over the years in helping you to visualize settings for novels and screenplays?**

**Stephen King:** We moved here in 1979. At that time, when we decided the kids would be needing more contact with other kids rather than just the woods—we had been living down in Lovell—we had two choices: There was Portland and there was Bangor. Tabby wanted to go to Portland, and I wanted to go to Bangor because I thought that Bangor was a hard-ass, working-class town—there's no such thing as nouvelle cuisine once you are north of Freeport—and I thought that the story, the big story that I wanted to write, was here. I had something fixed in my mind about bringing together all my thoughts on monsters and the children's tale, "Three Billy Goats Gruff," and I didn't want it to be in Portland because Portland is a kind of yuppie town. There had been a story in the newspaper about the time we decided to move up here about a young man who came out of the Jaguar Tavern during the Bangor Fair. He was gay and some guys got to joking with him. Then the joking got out of hand, and they threw him over the bridge and killed him. And I thought, that's what I want to write about. Tabby did not really want to come here, but eventually we did.

Before I started writing *It*, I did just what you did today: I walked all over town, I asked everybody for stories about places that caught my attention. I knew that a lot of the stories weren't true, but I didn't care. The ones that really sparked my imagination were the myths. Somebody told me something that I still don't know if it is true or not. Apparently, you can put a canoe down into the sewers just over across from here at the Westgate Mall and you can come out by the Mount Hope cemetery at the other end of town. It's one of the stories that you say to yourself, if it isn't true, it ought to be. I like very much the idea of a Plutonian canoe race. This same guy told me that the Bangor sewer system was built during the WPA and they lost track of what they were building under there. They had money from the federal government for sewers, so they built like crazy. A lot of the blueprints have now been lost, and it's easy to get lost down there. I decided I wanted to put all that into a book and eventually I did. But there was one image that remained with me through all this. Whenever I would walk through the two beautifully kept cemeteries that are on this side of town, where the ground slopes down into the woods I would notice these four-foot-deep drifts of dead flowers. This is stuff that came off the individual graves and washed down into the gully, and I thought to myself, This is the truth of the dead, this is where the dead end up. This is what we don't see aboveground.

Eventually, at least in the geography of my mind, Bangor became Derry. There is a Bangor in Ireland, located in the county of Derry, so I changed the name of the fictional town to Derry. There is a one-to-one correlation between Bangor and Derry. It's a place that I keep coming back to, even as recently as the novel *Insomnia*. And the same is true of Castle Rock. There was a piece that appeared last week in the *Sunday Telegram* called "Stephen King's Maine." The writers said that Castle Rock was really Lisbon Falls, which is where I went to high school, but it's not. Castle Rock is a lot more fictionalized than Derry. Derry is Bangor.

**Magistrale: There are also the civic landmarks that you have appropriated, such as the Paul Bunyan statue and the Standpipe water tower.**

**Stephen King:** And don't forget the Bangor Auditorium, which is called the Derry Auditorium in the books. It figures very large in *Insomnia*, where a guy turns a plane into a missile and tries to kill everybody inside.

**Magistrale: Before we get much further into this interview, I'd like to tell you something about the scope of the book I am writing.[1] It's divided into chapters that contain close readings of three to five films that share much in common thematically. But I'm not trying to cover all the films that have been made from your work. Ultimately, perhaps about half.**

**Stephen King:** I hope that in the course of your study you intend to pay some attention to the films that haven't been "done to death." You might find some worthwhile things in these movies that will encourage others to have another look [at these films].

**Magistrale: To be honest, with the notable exception of Kubrick's *The Shining*, which carries with it a critical bibliography as large as all the other interpretative work done on your films combined—and I think this is primarily because Kubrick directed it—I can't think of any other King movie that has been analyzed sufficiently, much less "done to death."**

1  Published as *Holywood's Stephen King* (2003)

Michael Collings wrote an excellent introduction to Hollywood's earliest films adapted from your novels, up to and including *Silver Bullet*, but his book was published back in 1986 and is long out of print. After that, you can find the occasional critical essay on a single film in an academic journal, a chapter in a scholarly book dealing with the particular King adaptation that belongs to the canon of a specific director (e.g., David Cronenberg or Stanley Kubrick) or is associated with a topical issue. Then there are the oversized "fanzine" magazine-books that try to say something about everything that has appeared on celluloid associated with your name. Unfortunately, these magazine-books are big on glossy stills and production history, which are interesting and sometimes helpful to know, but short on serious film analysis. In addition to the seven-paragraph reviews published in newspapers and popular periodicals shortly after a film is released, that's what is out there in the libraries right now.

**Stephen King:** I wonder why this is. Why haven't these movies received more extensive and serious critical attention? Do you know why? I hope you will address this issue somewhere in your book because, quite frankly, I don't have a clue to answering this question and I would be very curious to understand it.

**Magistrale: From the eighteenth century to our own era, the horror genre has always maintained a wide popular interest. Do you feel that the reasons for the genre's popularity changed over time, or has horror sustained a consistently constructed audience?**

**Stephen King:** I think that the appeal of horror has always been consistent. People like to slow down and look at the accident. That's the bottom line. I went out this past week and picked up a copy of *The National Enquirer* because I wasn't supposed to. They featured a story about Dylan Klebold and Eric Harris, the Columbine shooters. This issue of the newspaper, which was censored in some places, had death photos of these two boys. There were also several sidebars that accompanied these photos explaining, no, justifying why *The National Enquirer* was doing the country a real service in running these photographs. Well, that's bullshit. It was all just an attempt on the part of the publishers to justify running the pictures of those two boys lying in a pool of blood. And of course I picked up a copy because that's what I wanted see: I wanted to see the photographs of those two boys lying in a pool of blood.

Now, over the years I have had to answer a lot of questions regarding the scrapbook that I kept about Charles Starkweather when I was a kid. I would argue that there was a constructive purpose behind my scrapbook: It was proof, at least to myself, that the bogeyman is dead. But there is something else at work here as well. There is always the urge to see somebody dead that isn't you. That was certainly the central premise behind the journey those kids take in *Stand by Me*. And that urge doesn't change just because civilization or society does. It's hard-wired into the human psyche. It's a sign of low taste, perhaps, but it's a perfectly valid human need to say "I'm okay," and the way I can judge that—the yardstick, if you will—is that these people are not.

**Magistrale: In *Danse Macabre*, you say that the horror genre has often been able to exploit "national phobic pressure points. . . . Such fears, which are often political,**

economic, and psychological rather than supernatural, give the best work of horror a pleasing allegorical feel—and it's the sort of allegory that most filmmakers seem at home with." When you look back at how Hollywood has treated your own work, which films have been most successful at capturing and allegorizing "national phobic pressure points"?

Stephen King: *Carrie*. It is a film that covers everything that we are afraid of in high school. Also, it explores the feelings we all had in high school: that everybody is laughing at us. The bottom line is Piper Laurie's warning, "They're all going to laugh at you." We're all afraid of that, in high school, and even after we graduate from high school.

Magistrale: Margaret White's (Piper Laurie) vision of the world thoroughly warps Carrie's once the bucket of blood comes crashing down. Mother's intrusive voice becomes a dominating presence in the cataclysmic scene when Carrie burns down the gym. However, Mrs. White is wrong; not everyone is laughing at Carrie. [Director Brian] De Palma makes that very clear. The gym teacher feels great compassion toward Carrie's humiliation—you can read this in her face—and so do the majority of Carrie's other classmates, except, of course, that wretched Norma. I've always thought that one of the most unnerving moments in the film is that everyone gets punished, the empathetic as well as the evil pranksters.

Stephen King: Well, in the book they all do laugh at her, but it's a reaction brought on by hysterical horror. To return to your question, I would say that in addition to *Carrie*, Cronenberg's *The Dead Zone* manages to present strongly developed elements of political allegory, and *'Salem's Lot: The Movie* talks about small-town life as vampiric culture. *Dreamcatcher*,[2] a film that has not yet been released but I have seen it, has a scene in it where there is a group of bewildered Americans who are locked behind barbed wire in a detainment camp. I sometimes think I wrote this entire novel just to be able to have this one woman in the group identified by her Blockbuster video card. There is a terrifying fear of the government that runs throughout *Dreamcatcher*, and that's something that runs through many of the films—*Firestarter*, *The Stand*—the idea that they would rather kill all of us than tell us the truth. This is something we should all remain afraid of.

Magistrale: Could you make some comments from the perspective of a novelist about the production process that takes place in the transformation of a literary text into a film? How much do you get to work with the directors and screenwriters?

Stephen King: Pretty much as much as I want to. I've had a deal for years with Castle Rock Entertainment that goes back to *Stand by Me*. I have told them that you can have my work for a buck. What I want from you is script approval, director approval, cast approval, and I want to have the authority to push the stop button at any point regardless

---

2 *Dreamcatcher*, released on March 21, 2003, was directed by Lawrence Kasdan, who also cowrote the screenplay with William Goldman. It starred Morgan Freeman (*The Shawshank Redemption*) and Thomas Jane (*The Mist*).

of how much money you [the production company] have invested, because none of the money you have put in has gone into my pocket.

What I get on the back end, if things work out, is 5 percent from dollar one. This means that for every dollar that is spent at the box office, I get five cents of it. In most cases, that hasn't amounted to a whole hell of a lot, because most movies made from my work haven't made tremendous amounts of money. But still, even on a movie such as *Needful Things*, which didn't succeed very well, I do okay. Its domestic gross was only twenty million dollars, and out of that sum I got half a million dollars. Now, that doesn't sound like much, especially if I had decided to sell the rights outright, but then, sometimes a picture comes along like *The Green Mile*, and I make twenty-five million dollars, and that makes up for all the rest.

**Magistrale: And you also have an investment regarding your reputation. To this end, I can see why you would want approval over a film's cast and director. Perhaps at this point in your career this issue may be more important to you than the money?**

**Stephen King:** That's right. But I think I have developed a reputation in Hollywood as a "bankable writer." Castle Rock has had better luck than anyone in decoding what it is that I do. That is, with the exception of *Needful Things*.[3] That movie was a special case. The first cut was shown on TNT. I have a copy of it, and the length of this film was four hours long. As a four-hour miniseries, it works. When edited down to "movie length," it is almost indecipherable because it doesn't have time to tell all the stories and do all the setups. It's a complicated book.

**Magistrale: The same thing happened to *'Salem's Lot*. As a miniseries in 1979, it held together pretty nicely. But when it was cut apart and re-released as *'Salem's Lot: The Movie*, it was pale reflection of its former self (no vampire pun intended).**

**Stephen King:** And none taken. When Tobe Hopper finished *'Salem's Lot*, there was a lot of serious talk about buying it back from CBS and releasing it as a feature-length motion picture instead of a miniseries. The reason this never happened is that they couldn't cut it in a way to make it decipherable.

The opposite thing happened with a Danish miniseries called *Kingdom Hospital*, directed by the Danish filmmaker Lars von Trier. I saw this when we were in Colorado remaking *The Shining*, and it scared the hell out of me. I thought, This is a wonderful thing; we have to get it and show it on American television. As soon as *The Shining* came out and did well in the Nielsen ratings, I went to ABC and told them I wanted to adapt *Kingdom Hospital* as a miniseries. Well, by then Columbia Pictures had it, and they didn't want to give it up. Their intention was to make a feature film out of it. They paid for four different scripts, and every one of them had the same problem. It's what I call the hotel towel problem: You steal all the towels in the hotel room and you try to get them into a

---

3 *Needful Things* (August 27, 1993) ran 120 minutes; directed by Fraser C. Heston and produced by Jack Cummins, the screenplay was by W. D. Richter; the cast included Max von Sydow, Ed Harris, Bonnie Bedelia, J. T. Walsh, and Amanda Plummer.

single suitcase. You sit on it and move the towels around, and it still won't shut because you are working with too much material. It's a problem that all moviemakers have when they buy novels. In a way, film producers are like the sharks you see in horror movies. They are eating machines that buy and option titles, and then these projects sit on their desks while they wonder what the fuck to do with them. Columbia tried to make a motion picture out of *Kingdom Hospital*, while I was praying, Please let it all fall through. I mean, if they get it made, it will be just another piece of garbage that will be out for two weeks, put on video release, and then forgotten. And we could really do something with it.

Finally, Columbia Pictures came back to me and asked if I would trade something of mine for theatrical release if they gave me *Kingdom Hospital*. Ultimately, this is the way a lot of what goes on in the movie business gets done. It's the barter system; it's just beads. So I traded them "Secret Window, Secret Garden" from *Four Past Midnight*. Nothing was happening to it. Now Anthony Minghella, who directed *The English Patient* and *The Talented Mr. Ripley*, is going to make it into a movie.[4] My novella is the right length— it's small, and it's in one place. Columbia now has the chance to make a great feature. Castle Rock made a great feature out of *Misery* because it's short and all in one place. The same thing is true of *Gerald's Game*, which is a property that I have decided to hold on to. We've had a lot of offers on *Gerald's Game*, but I have refused. I'm thinking eventually, if I get a chance in my retirement, I want to write the screenplay for *Gerald's Game*.[5]

Now that I have the rights to *Kingdom Hospital*, ABC wants it to be a television series. I think that might work. I want to divide it up into a fifteen-hour series, and that would give ABC two or three seasons of airtime. You see, what everybody wants when they do a TV series is something similar to *CSI* or *Seinfeld*. The magic moment occurs at the end of the fifth season, when a program gets somewhere in the neighborhood of a hundred and fifty episodes. Then the show gets syndicated and everybody gets really, really wealthy all at once. My idea is to take *Kingdom Hospital* and expand it. If you have a short story you can always expand it, whereas if you are working with a novel, you are always thinking of taking stuff out. This is not to say, however, that filming a novel can't be done.[6]

Getting back to your original question, because I knew as soon as you asked it that this is where we would be spending most of our time. I love the movies. I have always loved the movies. And one of the reasons that my work gets bought in the first place is that I write cinemagraphically. Producers pick up my stories because they are cinematic. They are able to take my stories around to directors, and sooner or later a director says, This really pushes my buttons. I really want to do that. This is what happened with the novel *Dreamcatcher*. The first-draft screenplay that Bill Goldman did of it was good, but probably not good enough to justify an eight-million-dollar budget. Lawrence Kasden

---

4 Directed by David Koepp, who also wrote the screenplay, it starred Johnny Depp as Mort Rainey. *Secret Window* was released in 2004.
5 As it turned out, King did not write the script for the movie. The script, written by Mike Flanagan and his writing partner Jeff Howard, is the basis of the film *Gerald's Game*, directed by Flanagan, produced by Intrepid Pictures.
6 A miniseries, *Stephen King's Kingdom Hospital*, originally aired in thirteen episodes on ABC (March 3–July 15, 2004).

[the film's director] broke it open because he understood what Castle Rock has for years, that this is not a novel about spaceships, or interstellar war, or the end of the world. It's a story about four guys who go up to a cabin every year and make "guy food." The definition of "guy food" is that you can't use the oven; everything you eat has to be done on the stove burner. You have a hunk of butter, and you have shit in cans. Maybe you use a little ground beef, but you are talking really basic cooking.

In the first half of the screenplay for *Dreamcatcher*, nothing much happens. But you need to remember that the best fears, the ones that really work in horror stories and movies, are the ones that have not been articulated, that are still looking for some manner of expression. One of the things that I discovered after my accident was that I was having a lot of problems with narcotic drugs and their effect upon my body. Your whole system gets clobbered into the middle of next week, and everything falls out of sync. Things that I had taken for granted, especially about going to the bathroom, changed radically. And I got to thinking about these things. In 1956, in *Peyton Place*, we finally got to see beyond the bedroom door. Since then, graphic sex is just something we take for granted in the movies. I don't know if you have seen *Unfaithful* yet, but it's a terrific film. It is a sexually candid movie and it operates on a number of interesting levels. But I thought to myself that no one in novels, let alone in movies, talks about one of the primal fears that we have: that one day we will stand up from taking a shit only to discover that the toilet bowl is full of blood. This event could signal many things: It could just be a hemorrhoid, or it could be colon cancer. We don't talk about this because it is a function that we are raised not to discuss in polite society. But I thought, If we have gone behind the bedroom door, let's go behind the bathroom door and talk about what is there. In Bill Goldman's script of *Dreamcatcher*, these guys find blood in the woods that leads up to the bathroom door of the cabin where they are staying. This is all very effectively rendered in the rough cut of the film that I have seen. You see the trail of blood going from the bedroom, which is empty—and that's symbolic in a way, because in my story the bedroom stays empty, as I don't care what goes on in the bedroom, only the bathroom—and these guys are standing in front of the bathroom door wondering what to do. All this time, the audience is getting more and more nervous about what is happening behind that bathroom door. And then one of the guys says, "I don't think I want to see this." For me, that's the point where the horror story begins to do its work. The audience is in the dark, particularly if it's a theatrical situation, the suspense has been building steadily, and we are faced with exactly the same issue: Do we want to see what is behind that closed door? The audience is perfectly suspended over this point: the desire to look, the repulsion against looking.

When it comes to films, I want people to try to go beyond what we have seen already. I'm willing to let a director try anything, including Tobe Hooper with *The Mangler*.[7] I knew it wasn't a good idea. The screenwriter that he selected looked like a college sophomore, but he was awfully eager for the chance, and you never know what someone like Tobe Hooper is going to do. *Texas Chainsaw* is still one of the scariest movies ever

---

7 *The Mangler* (March 3, 1995) was directed by Tobe Hooper; the screenplay was written by Hooper, Stephen David Brooks, and Harry Alan Towers (as Peter Welbeck). It starred Robert Englund, Ted Levine, and Daniel Matmor.

made. Now, there's a film that did wonderful things with the hidden terror that lurks behind closed doors. So, my idea is always to give a director the chance, because I am not very personally invested in these things once they are out of my word processor and downloaded from my head and onto the page. Once you move from a single artisan working in his hut to the Hollywood film, the writer is no longer the one in control, and you discover a situation where complications arise exponentially. In the making of a film, you are suddenly dealing with four hundred artists in the studio. Then it becomes a lottery. All you can do is try to pick the best people possible; sometimes it works, sometimes it doesn't.

**Magistrale: In *On Writing* you say, "What I cared about most between 1958 and 1966 was movies." You go on to recall that your favorites were "the string of American International films, most directed by Roger Corman, with titles cribbed from Edgar Allan Poe." You even had a name for these movies—Poepictures. To what extent did these movies influence your writing? Were you influenced more by Poe's written work or by movies based on his work?**

**Stephen King:** Poe influenced me plenty, but not so much through the Poepictures. The best of the Poepictures was the last one, *The Masque of the Red Death*. It was choreographed beautifully, like a Kabuki play. The big scare moments of these films I still treasure. I remember when they discovered Vincent Price's wife in the iron maiden in *The Pit and the Pendulum*. All you see are the horrified eyes of Barbara Steele gazing out through a small opening in the contraption that encases her. She can't talk because she is sealed up to her eyes in the device. She has this horrified, frozen expression that she conveys directly to the audience. And then the picture ends. Brilliant. I've been trying to do something like that ever since.

**Magistrale: The merging of horror and humor characterizes some of the most memorable cinematic adaptations of your work. I'm thinking of films such as *Carrie*, *Misery*, *Stand by Me*. Why do these apparently oppositional elements appear to work so harmoniously with each other in these films?**

**Stephen King:** We can only speculate here. I think that what happens is that you get your emotional wires crossed. The viewer gets confused as to what reaction is appropriate, how to respond. When the human intellect reaches a blank wall, sometimes the only thing left is laughter. It is a release mechanism, a way to get beyond that impasse. Peter Straub says that horror pushes us into the realm of the surreal, and whenever we enter that surreal world, we laugh. Think of the scene with the leeches in *Stand by Me*. It's really funny watching those kids splash around in the swamp, and even when they try to get the leeches off, but then things get plenty serious when Gordie finds one attached to his balls. Everything happens too fast for us to process. We all laugh at Annie Wilkes because she is so obviously crazy. But at the same time, you had better not forget to take her seriously. She's got Paul in a situation that is filled with comedy, and then she hobbles his ankle. Like Paul Sheldon himself, the viewer doesn't know what to do. Is this still funny, or not? This is a totally new place, and it's not a very comfortable place. That's the kind of thing that engages us when we go to the movies. We want to be surprised, to turn a corner and find something in the plot that we didn't expect to be there.

What Billy Nolan and Christine Hargensen do to *Carrie* is both cruel and terrifying, but the two of them are also hilarious in the process. [Actor John] Travolta in particular is very funny. His role as a punk who is manipulated by his girlfriend's blowjobs suggests that he's not very bright. But a lot of guys can appreciate Billy Nolan's predicament: He's got a hot girlfriend who wants to call all the shots. He's the one character in De Palma's film that I wish could have had a more expanded role. He's a comic character who behaves in an absolutely horrific manner.

The character of Roland LeBay in *Christine* starts off to be a funny character, almost a caricature, but if you watch him carefully through his time on the screen, you'll note that he grows ever more horrific, getting uglier and uglier all the time. When I wrote *Christine* I wanted LeBay to be funny in a twisted sort of way. He's the same blend of horror and humor that you find in the car itself. Christine is a vampire machine; as it feeds on more and more victims, the car becomes more vital, younger. It's like watching a film running backwards. The whole concept is supposed to be amusing but scary at the same time.

**Magistrale: In the "Walking the Tracks" section of the DVD edition of *Stand by Me*, you indicate that [director Rob] Reiner's film was the "first completely successful adaptation" of one of your books. Have there been other films that have satisfied you to the same degree?**

**Stephen King:** *Shawshank* did. I thought *Shawshank* was a terrific piece of work, and it is not a one-to-one adaptation. There are a lot of things in that film that are not in my book. The scene where Andy is playing the opera music in the yard is a good example. It's a film about human beings—and human beings are not secondary to the theme of horror. That's an important thing to remember: You cannot scare anyone unless you first get the audience to care about these make-believe characters. They have to become people with whom you identify. After all, they are only as thick as the screen, which means about as thick as your thumbnail. We go to the movies with the understanding that we are watching people who are not real. But if we come to like them, and we recognize that the things they are doing are also part of our own lives, if they are reacting the way in which we would react under similar circumstances, then we become emotionally invested. Once this happens, it is possible to frighten the audience by putting the character in frightening situations.

When Sissy Spacek was cast as Carrie, people wondered how she could play the role of ugly duckling convincingly. I really didn't give a shit what she looked like before the prom, as long as she could appear transformed into a beauty when she got to the dance. It never really mattered to me exactly what she looked like, because I never had a clear picture of her. But I always had a clear picture of her heart. That's what remains important to me. I want to know what my characters feel and think, and I want the reader to know these things, too. De Palma did such a good job in this film because he was interested in these things as well.

I would have to say that I was delighted with *The Green Mile*. The film is a little "soft" in some ways. I like to joke with [director] Frank [Darabont] that his movie was really the first R-rated Hallmark Hall of Fame production. For a story that is set on death row, it has a really feel-good, praise-the-human-condition sentiment to it. I certainly don't have any problem with that because I am a sentimentalist at heart.

**Magistrale: This is a good place for me to ask you this next question. Spike Lee, among other commentators, has been critical of John Coffey's character in *The Green Mile*, arguing that his portrayal is insulting to blacks because his role is essentially to suffer for the sins of white people. According to Lee: "You have this super Negro who has these powers, but these powers are used only for the white star of the film. He can't use them on himself or his family to improve his situation." How accurate is this criticism?**

**Stephen King:** It's complete bullshit. Coffey was black for one reason only: It was the one sure thing about his character that was going to make certain that he was going to burn. That was the situation I was trying to set up. It was completely plot driven and had nothing to do with black or white. I've heard this same argument advanced by Toni Morrison about the so-called "magic Negro." If you want to get me on this, then you should talk about Mother Abigail in *The Stand*. The reason I made Mother Abigail black is because I wanted a character that was old enough to remember slavery. And I wanted to write a song to celebrate their moment of emancipation while Randall Flagg lurked behind the drapes. All this got cut out of the original published version of *The Stand* and then got reinstated in the uncut edition. But in the case of Coffey, who is obviously a Christ figure, he's black because his color makes certain that he will fry. As far as using his powers to help his race, he has no family; he's a total loner. Whatever past he has is completely lost, and that's crucial to the story. And the other thing that is crucial to the story is that he is a Christ figure. Christ figures are supposed to do good to them that revile you, to turn the other cheek to those who strike you. By doing good for white people—and particularly the wife of the warden, the man who is going to put Coffey to death—he is basically exhibiting his saintliness. You ask most people what was Christ's race, and they'll say white, god damn it.

I am not surprised that this is Spike's reaction. It's a knee-jerk reaction of a man who sees everything in terms of his race. And for an artist of his stature, it's a hobbling factor in his creative life. If I took my pants down right now in front of you, you would see that my right leg is withered where there used to be muscle. This is a result of my accident. But the muscles in my left leg are bigger than ever because that leg has had to do all the work. This is the way it is with Spike. He sees things exclusively in racial terms. It has made him a spectacular artist, but the idea of Coffey being a superman is just plain wrong.

**Magistrale: Does John Coffey have to be black? What happens to the film's meaning if he is a white character?**

**Stephen King:** In most cases you can cast a character in either race. Morgan Freeman in *Shawshank* could have been cast as a white man. But in the case of John Coffey, he's supposed to be black because that puts him in a situation where the minute he gets caught with those two little blond girls in his arms, he's a doomed man.

**Magistrale: But isn't that at least part of what Spike Lee is trying to argue? What chance does Coffey, a black man in Depression-era Louisiana weeping over the dead bodies of two little blond girls, have to save himself in spite of his redemptive powers? In one sequence the warden's wife asks Coffey, "Who hurt you?" Why does he have so many wounds, and where did they come from? Much of this seems suggestive, at least to me, of the legacy of being a black man in America.**

Stephen King: I am going to ask you a question now. Can you visualize a giant of a white man in that same situation? A dimwitted white man living in the South, knocking around low-paying jobs, a gentle giant riding the rails that is not able to hurt anybody? But a white man who bears the same scars as Coffey—can you visualize this person?

**Magistrale: Maybe bearing the same physical scars, but not the same psychological scars as Coffey. The internal wounds he carries are particular to his race. If John Coffey is a Christ figure, he's also a black Christ; his suffering, it seems to me, becomes all the more profound because he is black and a victim of wounds that are particular to his racial history.**

Stephen King: I think your answer represents an imaginative failing on your part. Remember Steinbeck's Lenny in *Of Mice and Men*. He's white and he bears similar scars of suffering.

**Magistrale: Have you been satisfied with the televised miniseries that have been done of your work? Do you feel that your novels are better suited for the miniseries genre? What are the limitations of the televised miniseries? Do you have a favorite Stephen King miniseries?**

Stephen King: I think my novels are much better suited for miniseries presentations. I didn't care very much for *The Tommyknockers* because it just didn't seem that the people doing it got behind the project sufficiently and felt the story. As with a feature-length film, again it's a crapshoot to have all the different parts to fall into place. My favorite made-for-television production is *Storm of the Century*. I love that as a piece of work, and I am still very proud of it. In my mind, it is as good as the best of the novels. Everything worked the way it was supposed to: the setting of the harbor town, the convincing sense of snow piling up, and Colm Feore was terrific in the role of Andre Linoge. ABC's Standards and Practices was so obsessed with whether they would see blood on the faces of the some of these children that they totally ignored the fact that the bad guy wins and takes the sheriff's son away with him. *The Storm of the Century* is fairly hard-edged for television. It's not like any other miniseries that you'll see on any of the other networks— you know, the happy-time, everything-works-out-happily-in-the-end program. It's very realistic. And everyone who was involved with that show—from my screenplay, to the director, to the set designer, to the producer—we all did *Rose Red* (2002), and *Rose Red* is just not as good.

**Magistrale: This is a good place to ask about the group decision in *Storm of the Century***

to sacrifice the child, Ralph Anderson. Besides the destruction of Molly and Mike Anderson's marriage, what are the other consequences—especially to the town of Little Tall Island itself—that occur as a result of this sacrifice?

**Stephen King:** Everybody that takes part in that decision is a worse person, a smaller person as a result. Whatever flaws they have are worse afterward. The sheriff's wife is in therapy; she remarries, but she is not very happy in her new marriage. One of the guys commits suicide. The sheriff ends up on the other side of the country, and he is the one person who has a chance at rebuilding his life. He knows that he was the one person who stood up for what was right. Everybody else pays a price for the town's collective lapse in moral judgment.

**Magistrale: Why did the citizens make this choice? Why was the sheriff the only one who stood up for what was right? I keep thinking of Shirley Jackson's short story "The Lottery," and how much you admire it.**

**Stephen King:** Let's put it this way: In all of our lives we are faced with situations in which we are tested. Generally, it isn't until years later that we find out that we actually failed the test. We come to understand that our morals gave out a little here, or our sense of right and wrong slipped, or our misplaced sense of expediency got the better of our morality. I've always been fascinated with the story of Job. The sheriff tells a version of the story of Job in *Storm of the Century*. He faces God and says, You took my kid, you wrecked my crops, and you ruined my marriage and left me alone to wander the earth. And God says, I guess there's just something about you that pisses me off.

We all have a duty to look at our lives. What do we see? Children falling down wells to die, we send our loved ones off to work and crazy people hit their office towers and we never see them again. I was in New York for a screening of *Hearts in Atlantis* at Columbia University the week after the twin towers were destroyed. My taxi driver wanted to show me something. He took me down about four blocks from Ground Zero. He said, "Do you see all those cars in that parking lot?" There were several hundred parked cars all covered with white dust. He told me that the city doesn't know what to do with those cars. They belong to the people who drove in from New Jersey to work at the twin towers the day of the attack. They are never going to come back and claim their cars. The people who escaped the tragedy, who are still alive, came and drove their cars away. You could see by the empty spaces in the parking lot that God had decided to let that one live, but that other poor bastard who parked in the spot next to him is never coming back. God had moved His finger and decided who would get to live a while longer. And you could look inside these remaining cars and see the toys that belonged to their children, the McDonald's coffee that was maybe half drunk the morning of the last morning of their lives.

**Magistrale: The September 11 event challenged many of our assumptions and added to our neuroses as a society and as individuals. How will the post-September 11 climate change the shape of horror? Is there anything on the page or screen that can equal in terror what we witnessed on our living room televisions?**

**Stephen King:** Why should it? Think of how many references you have heard to this event over the past several months. You'll be watching a talking head on television discussing the *Star Wars* movie and somebody will begin a question to George Lucas, "In light of September 11, do you feel. . . ." The event has totally pervaded the American consciousness. I read a lot of new fiction in galleys, and I have noticed the first ripples of awareness in the artistic consciousness—not conscience, it's too early for conscience, that comes much later—that represent the first droplets of a rainstorm that will continue for years.

**Magistrale: On several levels, the terrorist bombing of the World Trade Center was very much a "cinematic event." The planes were timed to hit at least twenty minutes apart from one another so that after the first plane plowed into the first tower cameras would be already in place to record—from a variety of angles and perspectives— the second plane's explosive arrival. And of course, the world learned of the tragedy through its graphic visualization on film. I suppose that is the goal of any terrorist action: to make it as visual and as personal as possible.**

**Stephen King:** And don't forget the desire to traumatize as many people as possible, which occurs when singular events in time are recorded on film and then televised to millions. In *The Stand,* my own rendering of cataclysmic proportions is always brought down to the individual, personal level. Franny Goldsmith trying to bury her father, and saying to Harold Lauder when he shows up in a car, "I'm just so tired." To me, one of the great scenes in the television miniseries is when Harold and Franny are sitting around listening to records. These two people sitting at the end of the world, drinking warm lemonade, and listening to records for what may be the last time in their lives. As an artist, I can show you the end of the world on a microcosmic level, but no one can deal with it the way it actually comes down from the sky.

**Magistrale: Your cameo appearances in your films have become something that fans enjoy and anticipate with each new film. Is this something you inherited from Hitchcock? How much control do you have over your cameo? The most original and humorous may have been your role as a weatherman on the broken TV in *Storm of the Century.* Was this your decision?**

**Stephen King:** I generally pick the cameo. I picked, for example, the pizza guy in *Rose Red,* the weatherman in *Storm of the Century.* I gave myself a bigger role in *The Stand.* It's fun. And yes, I'm playing Hitchcock here; I'm just a frustrated actor.

**Magistrale: I'd like to spend a few minutes with you talking about the eclipse scene in *Dolores Claiborne.* You told me once that you labored hard to get that scene written right for the novel. Do you feel that the film did it justice?**

**Stephen King:** I loved the way they did that; it's probably my favorite scene in the film. I didn't notice this the first time I saw the movie, but the filmmakers of *Dolores Claiborne* actually flip-flop our ordinary perceptions of the world. That is to say, we generally view what is going on right now as bright and colorful, crisp and clear. The past has a tendency to be a little bit misty, even as there are certain things that stand out among all the other things that are faded and fading, just as the color red is the last thing to fade in a photograph. This is how the human mind and its capacity for recollection work. But Taylor Hackford shoots his movie so that everything in the present is dull and monochrome, even the clothes are dull. In contrast, every moment in the past is bright and the colors really jump. It's the best color photography I've seen since the *Godfather* films, particularly *Godfather II,* which is filmed like no other movie before it. It's the difference between a color photograph and one that has been hand-tinted. I think *Dolores Claiborne* is a remarkably beautiful film to watch, if simply as an exercise in cinematography and the technical possibilities of using a camera and colors as active vehicles in the presentation of a story.

**Magistrale: As horrible and as violent as the moments leading to the eclipse are, the actual scene of Dolores gazing down into the well where she has just committed murder with the eclipse at her back is actually almost transcendent, beatific. Is this right?**

**Stephen King:** Yes. If there is anything wrong with *Dolores Claiborne,* it was the decision on the part of the filmmakers to try to tack on this artificial reconciliation between Dolores and her daughter. It's a very human desire, and it's understandable that producers would want to cater to it.

When you go to the movies and put down your cash to see a film, I don't think it out of line to ask for people up on the screen to behave a little bit better than they do in ordinary life; certainly we expect people to look a little bit better than in ordinary life. This urge to make things a little bit nicer than in real life has a tendency to carry over into other aspects of the movie. I have always been interested in emotions. And the difference between books and movies is that when I have you in one of my books I want to move you emotionally, to establish some kind of intense emotional reaction—terror or laughter or serious involvement. But because I am one person and I do everything myself, the creative instrument I use is like a scalpel, it cuts deftly and deep. With films, every time you add another layer of production, the surface gets blunted more and widens. So that when you consider a big Hollywood production such as *Pearl Harbor,* you get a beautifully produced, eye-popping spectacle that does absolutely nothing to you emotionally or spiritually because what should be a hypodermic point has become blunted into a sledgehammer. All you can do is to swing it as hard as you can.

Unfortunately, *Dolores Claiborne* is a film, like Kubrick's *The Shining,* that is nearly overwhelming because of its beautiful photography, but the story that surrounds the photography is flawed.

**Magistrale: I think I have a good spot for us to end. Your film *Maximum Overdrive* has a lot in common with *The Terminator* and *Blade Runner* insofar as these are films about the general paranoia our culture has about our overreliance on technology and machines. Were these conscious considerations as you were writing and directing *Maximum Overdrive?***

**Stephen King:** I had a very clear image of technology having totally overrun our ability to control it. You know, when Bram Stoker wrote *Dracula,* all the men who were part of the Crew of Light were technological men. Seward compiled his medical records on a phonograph; Van Helsing was one of the first doctors to pioneer the use of transfusions. All this fascinated Stoker; these men were his heroes, and their technologies were used to help defeat the evil of a supernatural past embodied in Dracula himself. But look at what has become of technology now. Think of the situation right now between India and Pakistan. These are two countries that do not have very highly developed skills and attitudes about problem solving. They may have a long religious history, which I would argue is in itself very dangerous to the modern world, but they also possess nuclear weapons. That's really what I was thinking about when I did *Maximum Overdrive.* Technology may be its own dead end.

The problem with that film is that I was coked out of my mind all through its production, and I really didn't know what I was doing [as the director of the film]. I learned a lot from the experience, however, and I would like to try directing again sometime. Maybe I'll direct *Gerald's Game.*[8]

**Magistrale: *Gerald's Game* remains one of my favorite books. I have always presented it to students as an appropriate bookend to *Misery*: its limited setting, the gender conflicts, and the bedroom as a battlefield.**

**Stephen King:** I had all these things in mind when constructing both these books, and I've always thought to myself that *Misery* was a kind of trick. You have two people fighting it out in a cabin. That's all it is. *Gerald's Game* is kind of a trick on the trick: one person in a room fighting it out with herself. I've been telling people that the third book in the trilogy will be called *Sofa,* and it's just going to be a sofa in a room.

---

8 It was not to be. *Gerald's Game,* currently in production, is being directed by Mike Flanagan, who also cowrote the script.

123

# THE KING AND I:

## FURTHER ADVENTURES WITH STEPHEN KING

### BY SANFORD PHIPPEN

*King and Sanford Phippen.*

In 1975, I was reviewing books for the now-defunct alternative newspaper, *Tuesday Weekly,* in Ellsworth, Maine, when I heard about this novel *Carrie* written by someone named Stephen King. I'll never forget the face of the young woman clerk in the local bookstore when I asked her if she knew of the book or writer. She left her post to go and get the book for me and handed it to me as if it were the Bible. I knew from her enthusiastic reaction that this guy must be someone very special. I went home and read the book right away. I enjoyed it and I loved the way King wrote about the dark side of Maine.

I first met the Master of Horror in 1978 at a book signing for *The Shining* in the Bangor Mall, but it wasn't until 1979 when I met him at a bar at the Marriott Hotel (now the Sheraton) in Bangor that we had our first talk and drink together. "Hi, I'm Stephen King," he said, and I said, "Yes, I know who you are." I had my copy of *The Dead Zone* with me, and he borrowed my Bic pen to sign autographs that night. He was the featured speaker at that occasion, which was a meeting of the Maine Council of English Language Arts, for which he was serving as either secretary or treasurer. He had been an English teacher for two years at Hampden Academy, a local high school, and was in 1979 teaching at the University of Maine English department. Since we both had been students in Orono, we had several of the same teachers, most notably Edward M. "Ted" Holmes, for creative writing, and Carroll F. Terrell, for literature. I had later taught in the department and so worked with the same colleagues.

A few months after our Bangor encounter, I attended the annual NEATE (New England Association of Teachers of English) convention in Providence, Rhode Island, where, once again, Steve was the featured speaker. I met him in the hotel lobby, and he told me he was essentially going to give the same speech he had in Bangor but that he'd try and add some new stuff. I told him I could listen to the same speech again, and I introduced him to my good friend and former college roommate, David Wiggin.

Dave and I sat in the back of the dining room with some snooty English teachers from Greenwich, Connecticut, who were making fun of Steve and putting him down. He wasn't a very good speaker then, and, sensitive to my own Downeast background, I tried to tell them that they didn't appreciate where Steve was coming from, what he had to overcome. I had a copy of his latest book, *Firestarter*, which I let the ladies examine with their noses in the air.

Back at Orono, there was a party at English professor Nancy MacKnight's house and Steve and Tabby were there. We were all imbibing when at one point, I said to Steve, "Steve, you've got to beat Poe!" And he said, "Shut up!" Later I told him that I had learned that in the nineteenth century Edgar Allan Poe's literary executor had married a girl from Bangor and had stored Poe's manuscripts in an old mansion on Broadway across from what is now John Bapst Memorial High School. Part of the fun of knowing Steve is finding one's name in his books. In *Misery*, for instance, he has two cops with the surnames of MacKnight and Wicks, the latter being Ulrich Wicks, one of Steve's colleagues in the University of Maine at Orono English department.

One day I was walking in the Bangor Mall and ran into Steve with his two sons, Joe and Owen, when they were small, and all three were eating ice cream cones from Baskin-Robbins. When Steve spotted me, he yelled, "Look, boys! It's Sanford Phippen, the famous Maine author!" And he grabbed me and bounced me up and down. Steve was much bigger than he is now, and I was much thinner.

In the summer of 1982, I invited both Steve and Tabby down to the Hancock Point Library, which is on the coast, and where I was the librarian, for a fund-raiser to fix the library's roof. Tabby read from her novel *Caretakers* and Steve premiered his short story "Uncle Otto's Truck." When I asked Steve if he wanted a pitcher of water for his reading, he said he preferred Molson, so I found a white opaque pitcher in the library's kitchen and filled it full of beer. Because the reading was to be in the Hancock Point Chapel, I thought some might object to his drinking beer in a church, especially a beloved institution where Booker T. Washington had spoken in 1905.

When they arrived in their fancy van in the afternoon, Steve came in the library, and when we were talking, I told him I knew that he had written some early novels under the pseudonym Richard Bachman. He said, "How did you know that?" I said, "Ted Holmes." I also had the Signet paperback of *The Long Walk*, by Bachman, which was dedicated to Steve's favorite University of Maine teachers: Jim Bishop, Burt Hatlen, and Ted Holmes. Later in 1984, when *Thinner* came out, how I laughed at the photo of "Richard Bachman" and at the dedication "to My Wife Claudia Inez Bachman"! The movie version was made in Camden, and my late cousin Delmont Clarke, of Brooks, bought the bullet-riddled Cadillac used in the film to display on his lawn.

Before the readings that night, I took Steve and Tabby around Hancock Point, originally an old Bangor summer resort, in my friend Alice Janick's Pontiac, to show them the summer cottages of famous people, like the late Frederick Jackson Turner, the Harvard historian whose famous essay "The Significance of the Frontier in American History" advanced what became known as the "frontier thesis." We also visited the once-secluded Sunset Beach area, where in 1944 two Nazi spies landed from a German U-boat, intent on making it to Bangor and then New York City, where they were to commit terrorist acts; they were, however, apprehended before they had a chance.

Following the tour, we went for cocktails on the western shore of the Point and then had supper on the eastern shore at the Stanleys' cottage, which was built by Dr. Daniel Robinson, of Bangor, in the nineteenth century. Ben Stanley was the president of the library, and his wife, Joanne, made a delicious crabmeat casserole, and Tabby asked her for the recipe.

When we arrived at the chapel, the place was packed with standing room only. My niece Julie Clark was taking tickets. I introduced the Kings and the readings went very well. Steve stayed until every book had been signed. It was quite late when they left for Bangor. I gave Steve twenty dollars for gas and a copy of my first book, *The Police Know Everything*. He said, "Probably Tabby will read this before I get to it, but I will."

We made several hundred dollars that night, enough to patch up the roof. Back in Orono, I was invited by Burt Hatlen, Steve's beloved teacher and friend, to take part in a panel discussion on writing sponsored by the English department. Both Steve and Tabby were there, too, along with this other young visiting writer, whose name escapes me. But what was most memorable, especially perhaps for the students, was our talk about the difficulty of writing about sex, and Steve's outburst at the visitor when he said, "You are great! I'm going to vote for you for president!"

In 1985, I was editing *The Best Maine Stories*, and I wanted one of Steve's stories for the collection. I was told he was an early riser, so I called him in the morning, and I woke him up! (About the same time I did the same thing with E. B. White. I assume I'm the only person who has awakened both our finest essayist and our bestselling horror writer.)

Steve refused to give me a story because he said he didn't believe in Maine literature. I asked him if he believed in French literature? Our argument didn't go anywhere, but in 1989 he did consent to having his haunting story "The Reach" published in *Maine Speaks*, another anthology on which I worked.

In 1986, Steve agreed to an interview with Elaine Landa, one of my journalism students who worked on *Inside*, the Orono High School newspaper. Elaine, accompanied by her mother, did the interview at the Kings' "bat mansion" in Bangor. That interview was later published in *Feast of Fear: Conversations with Stephen King*, edited by Tim Underwood and Chuck Miller.

Throughout the '80s, I worked with Shirley Sonderegger, Steve's former secretary, who told me that he would sign books if I brought them to his office and picked them up later. I did this quite a lot, and I especially remember when Orono High School hosted fourteen Spanish exchange students, all of whom brought Spanish editions of King books to have signed. Both Steve and Tabby were gracious enough to visit my high school classes, as well as other teachers' classes in the Bangor area. When King's movies *Storm of the Century*, *Graveyard Shift*, and *The Langoliers* were being filmed in Maine, a number of my students visited the sets and even got jobs as extras or some kind of assistants. My Orono students were always telling me stories about spying Steve on the city bus and at sports events.

In 1987–88, *Pet Sematary* was filmed in my hometown of Hancock, Maine; it was fun to visit the set, especially the gray cats that were used in the movie. Steve visited the set from time to time. In a local TV news story about the making of the movie, they interviewed me as the town librarian, and the piece was edited so that my head suddenly turned into Steve's.

In the early '90s at Bangor's best independent bookstore, BookMarcs, I ran into Steve one day, and he told me how much he liked my books of short stories, but he also told me I had to write a novel if I wanted to get published in New York. I did write one, *Kitchen Boy*, and Steve offered to send it to his editor. A few weeks later, he called me when I was teaching at Orono High School. I went into the teachers' room to answer the phone, and this man's voice said, "You are about to receive a call from Stephen King!" Then Steve came on to tell me the bad news. His New York editor said that if they were to publish my book, it would only sell around three thousand copies out of ten thousand for a first printing. Steve said he'd give me a blurb to use, which was "Sanford Phippen is a New England treasure, and *Kitchen Boy* is his most impressive work to date. If you love Maine, you will love this book." I'm pleased to note that my novel has by now sold well over thirty thousand copies.

In 1998, Steve and Tabby both showed up at my talk about my new book, *The Messiah in the Memorial Gym*, at the Orono Public Library. Steve wanted to buy three copies at discount! I thought he was kidding, but he wasn't.

Then there was the time with the late poet Leo Connellan, who was a Maine native but who was then the poet laureate of Connecticut. He was always having financial troubles, and he called me about trying to get a new car to replace his old one that had died. I called Steve, because in those days, you could, and he and Tabby were wonderfully generous to everyone. Leo had told me he could get a good used car for $1,500, and I told Steve that. Steve sent a check for $2,000, saying, "He's got to register it, hasn't he?"

With the publication of his last book, *The Maine Poems,* Leo returned to Maine for readings and sales. I drove him to Steve's Bangor office without knowing if Steve would be there or not, but he was. When he saw it was Leo getting out of my car, Steve hollered out the window, "Leo, you old bastard! Get in here!"

Sitting across from both Steve and Leo, who were on the couch in the office, I wished I had had a camera. Two Maine legends, two of the best writers this state has produced. It was a great visit, but in the car afterward, Leo said, "He probably thought I was going to ask him for money." I said, "Yes, that probably did cross his mind."

That night Leo was reading at BookMarcs and Steve and his son Owen showed up. There was a good crowd, and I think for about five minutes Leo was enjoying himself. In 2000, I interviewed Leo for *A Good Read,* my TV series for the Maine Public Broadcasting Network. He died in 2001.

When the film *Desperation* was about to debut on ABC-TV, the Tampa, Florida, TV station sent a crew to the University of Maine to interview Burt Hatlen and others. Burt was not feeling well, so he asked me to talk with them and take them on a tour of the campus. Besides Neville Hall, where the English department is, I took them to Gannett Hall, where Steve had lived his freshman year in room 203 and where I lived for my last two college years in room 201. I showed them, too, around the Fogler Library, where both Steve and I had worked as undergraduates on scholarships. I asked the interviewer if I could get a copy of her story. She said yes, but I never received it.

In 2007, Lisa Rogak, a prolific biographer of famous people, called me from Hanover, New Hampshire, to see if she could meet with me when she came to Bangor to possibly interview Stephen King. I did meet her, and I drove her to Steve's office, where Marsha DeFilippo, Steve's current secretary, agreed to meet with her. As it turned out, Steve was there sneaking around (I saw him in the hall), but he didn't want to talk with Lisa. Her biography is called *Haunted Heart: The Life and Times of Stephen King.*

To be honest, it has been frustrating at times trying to have something of a literary career all these years under the monstrous cloud of Stephen King. When I got to have a reading at the Yale University bookstore a few years ago as part of a series of lesser-known New England writers, I was irked at this woman in the first row who kept asking me, because I was from Maine, if I knew Stephen King. When I said yes, she kept asking me about Steve and his books. It used to be when I first started going out of state, people would ask about lobsters, Bar Harbor, and L.L.Bean, but now it's inevitably about Steve. I did say once, "You know, his wife writes books, too!"

A few years ago, I attended an afternoon luncheon on the University of Maine at Orono campus in honor of Tabitha King, and I was amused, and so were a lot of other people, when she said, "You know, some people think I'm a better writer than he is." Tabby got some well-deserved applause for that.

Probably the most entertaining time I've had while celebrating the achievements of Stephen King was in 1996 when the College of Education at the University of Maine held a worldwide conference, Reading Stephen King: Issues of Censorship, Student Choice, and Popular Literature. It was great fun to meet and observe so many of Steve's groupies from all over, many of them dressed as his characters. I enjoyed a number of the programs offered throughout the day, the evening dinner, and the show held at the Hauck Auditorium with Steve himself.

Over the past few years, Steve and I seem to meet mostly at memorial services and funerals. The first was for Winthrop Libby, who had been president of the University of Maine when Steve was a student. In his retirement, Libby wrote a popular column for my local newspaper, the *Ellsworth American,* called "Thoughts While Shaving," in which he reviewed some of my books most favorably. He also used to visit me at the Hancock Point Library, where we shared lovely talks about Maine, the university, and our common heritage.

When our teacher Carroll F. Terrell was dying in Orono, his nurse, Pam Peddie, told me how he talked all the time about Stephen King and me. "He seemed obsessed by the two of you," she said, "and kept reminding me: 'I taught both Steve and Sandy, you know.'"

In 1990, Terrell even published a book called *Stephen King: Man and Artist,* a critical, philosophical, and intellectual treatise on the importance of Steve's work.

Burt Hatlen died in 2008, and both Steve and I spoke at his memorial service in Orono, along with a number of others. Burt had hired me to teach in the English department, and our last project together was planning the literary-history maps of Maine, one of which was devoted to Steve's work. It was one of the joys of my professional life to work with Burt on those maps.

After Burt's death, Steve had English classroom 416 in Neville Hall refurbished with air-conditioning and plush appointments and named The Burt Hatlen Room (complete with a handsome portrait of Bert) to be used as a seminar room for English majors and grad students.

In 2010, our writing teacher, Edward M. "Ted" Holmes, died at ninety-nine. Both Steve and I were mentioned in his obituary, and I spoke at his funeral.

For the past three and a half years, I have worked with two wonderful young filmmakers who are also great Stephen King fans, John Campopiano and Justin White. They have just premiered their documentary film *Unearthed and Untold: The Path to Pet Sematary,* and which is now making the rounds at film festivals.

In my latest book, *Sturge: A Memoir,* my late friend Sturgis Haskins, the subject of the work, wrote about this encounter with Stephen King:

> After my expensive spree at Staples, in Bangor, I wandered into Borders bookstore. This might have been my first visit in a year and things were considerably re-arranged. I could not find the gay book section (if, indeed, there is one now). For an interim I sat at coffee musing at the assortment of very odd people—rather reminded me of a day care center for eccentrics. . . . Stephen King wandered in. I recognized him at once. Someone near me said, "There is Stephen King." He disappeared for an interim, returning into view at the coffee counter. Here he ordered a bag of sweets. As the two leather chairs adjacent to me were unoccupied, I imagined him soon seated next to me. An engaged conversation would surely follow. A long friendship would be certain. But, alas, sweets in hand, he left. Rather pale-faced for someone who winters in Florida.

Back in 2003, Steve agreed to have me interview him for my old TV series *A Good Read*. The program wasn't aired, though, until 2004, when it was used as a fund-raiser for the Maine Public Broadcasting Network. It was a hot August day and the TV lights in his office were hot, too, but we talked for over an hour. We talked about writing, of course, and especially about his wonderful *On Writing* book, which I've used with my students. We talked about Maine, music, and many of his books. He mentioned starting work with John Mellencamp on this musical, *Ghost Brothers of Darkland County*, which now in 2014 is touring the country. At the opening of the program, I talked about Steve's brilliance, intensity, and his down-to-earth Maineness. I got him to read his first published poem "The Dark Man," from *Moth*, a special University of Maine literary magazine edited by George MacLeod, who was a college roommate of King's. In my closing remarks, I said:

> One of the reasons Stephen King's writings will last is because he understands small towns. He grew up poor in Maine and he has a good sense of community that is innate. Many big city critics don't seem to understand, or fully appreciate, this and how the fragile balance in a small town can be easily upset by any intrusion from away. King, a gifted writer with a good heart, does understand deeply and it's this sense of community that runs throughout his work.

I still agree with that statement.

One final note: In the recent science fiction film *Interstellar*, in which humanity is doomed on earth, the camera sweeps through a library of books, and there, prominently displayed, is a copy of *The Stand*, Stephen King's apocalyptic novel.

# PART EIGHT

# STEPHEN KING IN CYBERSPACE

# 124

# Top Web Sites for King Fans

*King talking at a fundraiser in Bangor to support the Bangor Public Library.*

StephenKing.com should be your first stop on the Web. King has constructed a detailed Web site that serves his Constant Readers well. The site is especially useful for students writing papers because of the resources it hosts.

Under the "Miscellaneous" tab, there are links to affiliated sites, for the Haven

Foundation, the Barking Foundation, the Stephen and Tabitha King Foundation, Joe Hill, Owen King, the Rock Bottom Remainders, WZON and WKIT radio stations, and Café Press (where you can get authorized nonbook product printed on demand).

King fans, though, are principally interested in buying books, and, as does King, I recommend the online bookstore Betts Books (bettsbooks.com).

There are also several small presses who have issued "gift" editions and limited editions of his books, which are listed on King's site; the key ones are Subterranean Press (subterraneanpress.com), Donald M. Grant, Publisher (grantbooks.com), and Cemetery Dance (cemeterydance.com). I would also add Centipede Press (centipedepress.com) and PS Publishing (pspublishing.co.uk).

King also lists several artists, including Bernie Wrightson (berniewrightson.com), Michael Whelan (michaelwhelan.com), Mark Geyer (markedwardgeyer.com), and Mike Perkins (mikeperkinsart.com). I'd also add Glenn Chadbourne (glennchadbourne.com) and Drew Struzan (drewstruzan.com) to the list.

If you have any interest in fantasy art and wish to contact artists directly by e-mail, the best way to do so is to consult the most current edition of the fantasy / horror / SF art anthology, *Spectrum,* from Flesk Publications (fleskpublications.com). It's published annually in November, and its showcased artists have provided their e-mail addresses in the back of the book.

## FAN WEB SITES

The longest-running fan Web site (since 1996) is published by Swedish superfan Hans-Åke Lilja. It called Lilja's Library (liljas-library.com) and subtitled "The World of Stephen King." I go there almost every day, and you will, too, if you have more than a casual interest in King. (He's also on Facebook under the name Lilja's Library.)

For collectors, TheDarkTower.org is the place to go. As its title suggests, its principal interest is the Dark Tower series.

Also, on Facebook you will find the group Fans of Stephen King, which is run by one of his publishers, Doubleday/Anchor Books.

# Glass Onion Graphics: Michael Whelan's Dark Tower Prints

Named after the Beatles' song "Glass Onion," penned by McCartney-Lennon, Glass Onion Graphics is your one-stop shop for high-quality, full-color reproductions, and occasionally original works of art, drawn from Michael Whelan's Dark Tower artwork for King's various publishers.

The mail order company is the brainchild of Michael's wife, Audrey Price, who taught herself everything she needed to know to print, publish, and sell his work to a growing body of fans who appreciate imaginative fantasy illustration.

Though Donald M. Grant, Publisher, Inc., took special pains to insure Whelan's artwork was reproduced with fidelity, as can plainly be seen in *The Little Sisters of Eluria* and *The Dark Tower: The Dark Tower VII*, the fact remains that to truly appreciate the artwork, one must see it on display the way the artist intended: in its original state as original art. But because most of the Dark Tower art is now in private collections worldwide, that's not an option. (On occasion, detailed "rough" compositions from Dark Tower paintings are occasionally sold, as was the case at the World Fantasy Convention in 2014, when Whelan had an exhibit of original art.)

For those who cannot afford original oil paintings or comps but want the image itself in as pristine a form as possible, the solution is to buy a museum-quality print manufactured under the watchful eyes of Michael and Audrey.

The Dark Tower lithographs and giclees are available at reasonable prices, and available unframed or framed.

My favorite reproduction currently on their Web site is "Legends: The Gunslinger" ($195 unframed, $495 framed; image size, 30 x 20 inches; framed size, 38.5 x 28 inches), which originally appeared as the frontispiece for an anthology of original prequels, *Legends*, edited by Robert Silverberg. Depicting the Gunslinger who stands with one foot in our world, and having stepped through a wooden door frame suspended in the air, one foot in another world, the painting resonates with symbolism, both as a metaphor on the art of storytelling and a metaphor of Roland's transformative journey.

Note: This painting is reproduced as the last page of the color insert found elsewhere in this book.

The web address for the Dark Tower artwork is:
http://www.michaelwhelan.com/shop/reproductions/dark-tower/

# 125

# LILJA'S LIBRARY:

## AN INTERVIEW WITH HANS-ÅKE LILJA

### BY GEORGE BEAHM

Published online in 1996, Lilja's Library was a modest effort, but over time it grew to become the premiere Web site for Stephen King fans. (Lilja's also on Facebook and Twitter.)

Over the years, Lilja's made numerous, important connections to people in the King community, including King himself (whom he's met and interviewed twice), King's publishers, and professionals who have worked with King in various capacities. The contacts have given his Web site depth.

In 2011, Cemetery Dance published *Lilja's Library: The World of Stephen King*, which I recommend if you want to read a selection from Lilja's Web site in print.

In the meantime, get acquainted with Lilja's wonderful Web site.

**GB: King is very clearly an American writer, with his stories set in the United States, steeped in American pop culture. In other words, he's very American-centric. That said, why does he appeal to a Swedish reader? Does his "American-ness" present any reading problems for you? Can you explain why he's so popular in Europe?**

**Lilja:** Well, King's stories are definitely based on the American pop culture, but at the same time I don't think the stories are dependent on readers knowing all about American pop culture. In Europe that isn't a big problem, though, since much of American pop culture finds its way here as well and we can relate to it. I imagine that it would be a bigger challenge for readers in a country that isn't as influenced by the United States as we are in Europe, but even so I think they would be able to follow the story anyway. *Faithful* is an exception, though, since it deals with baseball, and that isn't something we play here in Sweden, so that book is a challenge. But other than that there isn't a huge problem for me.

I think King is popular in Europe for the same reason he is popular in the United States or anywhere else on earth: He tells good stories. I really think it's as simple as that if you boil it down, but then there is fandom. A lot of people would read anything King writes without hesitation (me included), and many fans probably started reading King because he is such a big name with all the movies and so on, but I don't think they would have stuck around if they didn't like what he wrote.

**GB: You've met King. What were your impressions of him?**

**Lilja:** I met him once in London and once in Hamburg, and what struck me the most both times is how relaxed he is with people. No matter if he's onstage, signing books, or walking around in a crowded room, he always feels very relaxed and natural. He gives everyone a piece of his time and jokes and talks and poses for photos with those who want that.

**GB: What would you consider his best book, and why would you consider it so? Do you have a favorite King work (novel, short story, novella)?**

**Lilja:** I often get this question: *Which is his best book? I have never read King, which book should I read?* And it's also one of the hardest questions to answer. Let me explain why: King has written many good books. Some are very good right after you have read them, but then if you reread them later they might not be as good as the first time; others might be even better. Some are good horror books and others are good nonhorror books, so there are a lot of books that are good in their own way. It's a little like comparing apples and oranges. But if someone put a gun to my head and said "pick one or I'll pull the trigger," I would say *The Long Walk*. The reason for this is that it's a very simple story. It's "just" about a group of boys out walking. But then King gets his hands dirty and tells us a story about great characters that you care a lot about. He tells a cruel story that you believe in, and this simple story about a group of boys out walking turns into something else, something brilliant.

**GB: You've interviewed King twice, by phone. It's been a few years, though, since the interviews. Are there any questions you'd want to ask him today, if you had the opportunity?**

**Lilja:** Definitely. I interviewed him in 2007 and 2008, and I would have loved to turn that into a yearly tradition. If I got the chance to talk to him today, I would love to follow up on some of the questions I asked him [then]. What are his thoughts on fan sites and the Internet today? What does he think about limited editions of his books today? What about the retirement he talked about back then—is that still something he considers? How would he like to be remembered? How does he think he will be remembered? And so on. I would also like to ask him about all that has happened since the last interviews, all the books and stories he has written, the books and stories he hasn't written yet, and so on. I have no doubt that I could spend at least one hour on the phone with him.

What I wouldn't ask is all those standard questions we get each time something new is released, because most of that stuff those of us who follow the news online already know about.

**GB: What was your first exposure to King? That is, what was your first King book? And what were your impressions of it?**

**Lilja:** When I was little, the Christmas tradition at our home was that I got to open one gift in the morning of the twenty-fourth. In Sweden we open our gifts on the eve of the twenty-fourth, and as I have grown older, I have understood that the one gift in the morning was my parents' way of giving them a break from all my nagging about when we could open the rest of the gifts. When I was thirteen, back in 1983, I got *Carrie* for the morning gift, even though I wasn't a really big reader then. I mostly read comics, but I started this book by this author I didn't know all that much about . . . then, and I was hooked. *Carrie* is a great book, and I have reread it many times after that.

**GB: Have you read any of the books by King's sons?**

**Lilja:** I have. I have read all of Joe Hill's books, and I really love them. He is very similar to his father but still has his own style. I will definitely continue reading his books as he releases them. I also read Owen's book *Double Feature,* and, even though it was well written, it's not really my type of book, so I'm not so sure I'll pick up his next one. I might, but I don't feel as eager as I would for a new Joe Hill book.

# 126

# An Interview with David A. Williamson of Betts Books

## by George Beahm

*David A. Williamson as*
*Fr. Callahan, by Michael Whelan*

If there's one good reason to buy your King collectibles from Betts Books (www .bettsbooks.com) instead of from an online auction site that shares a similar name to a character in King's novel *Christine* named LeBay, it's this: Signed memorabilia offered online is suspect because it is difficult to evaluate any screening process that might be in place and to assess the qualifications of alleged experts who claim to validate authenticity. The Web site simply cannot provide guarantees or even a reasonable assurance that what is said through them is authentic.

Case in point: In December 2014, I saw a copy of a trade edition of book 7 of the Dark Tower novels selling online for $325. The problem, though, is that both Stephen King's and Michael Whelan's signatures are forged. (I confirmed that Michael's signature was fake, through his wife, Audrey. King's signature was blatantly fake, and embarrassingly so.) Unfortunately, it was sold to a King fan who's going to be very upset when he tries to resell it and discovers he was robbed—a real horror story.

Stuart Tinker, who owned and operated Betts Books before David A. Williamson bought it, told me that on a popular online auction site, he routinely saw numerous forged King signatures for sale. It happens all the time, and for that reason I never buy signed memorabilia online, unless I am confident I'm dealing with authentic items.

So your best bet, always, is to buy from a reputable dealer, like David at Betts Bookstore.

There's also the matter of packing and shipping: If you order from online sites the sellers are usually nonspecialists who can't properly identify books and can't pack them properly, either. I've gotten book club editions that the sellers thought were first editions; I've gotten books mailed in plastic bags that arrived so damaged that you'd swear the post office has custom-made machinery designed to fold, spindle, and mutilate packages.

I'd run a photo of David with this interview, but Michael Whelan beat me to it, with a great portrait of him as Father Callahan (see the color insert titled "The Dark Tower: Callahan").

David, who purchased Betts Books on December 1, 2009, runs it as a part-time venture, so if you e-mail him and don't hear back immediately, he'll get back to you as soon as he can.

## GB: Why did you buy Betts Bookstore?

**David:** I purchased Betts Books for a couple of reasons. First, Stuart Tinker (former owner) announced that he was selling the business, and if a buyer could not be found he would close the store. I had, at that time, been a pretty serious King collector for nearly fifteen years and knew personally many of the largest collectors, so I thought I'd be a "natural" as a new owner. Second, financially, I was in a position to step up and purchase Betts; and finally, as a collector myself, I totally "get" the joy/rush/pleasure of filling a hole in my own King collection, and I wanted to be able to help others experience that same feeling. I just knew I would be good at this task.

## GB: What are the books that your customers most often ask for, and want?

**David:** There clearly are fan favorites in the Stephen King collectibles world. *The Stand* signed/numbered edition, lovingly known as the "Coffin" or "Bible" limited, definitely ranks in the top-five demanded books. Those sell out as quickly as I can find copies. Similarly, [editions of] *It*, both the signed original Viking 1986 hardcover and the twenty-fifth-anniversary editions (gift, numbered, lettered) published a couple years ago by Cemetery Dance, are highly sought after collectibles. I do a very brisk business in the Dark Tower series, both signed and numbered editions as well as the first edition trade hardcovers from Donald Grant. . . . Among collectors, early King titles such as *'Salem's Lot*, *The Shining*, *The Stand*, and *Night Shift* all are hard to keep in stock.

**GB: What's the most expensive King collectible you've sold?**

**David:** The single most expensive item, and perhaps the "coolest" King collectible I've ever sold, was a set of three issues of *Comics Review* in which King wrote the story "I Was a Teenage Grave Robber." It was the first appearance of the story and, if I am not mistaken, the first publication of any King story except for the self-published stuff he did with his brother. According to the publisher, this was the *only* surviving complete copy of the full story in those three issues. Let's just say that the three issues sold for north of $10,000.[1]

**GB: Do you have any personal favorites regarding editions of King's limited edition books?**

**David:** Yes, I most certainly do! In terms of sheer brilliance in design and production, I have to give the nod to the lettered *Regulators* produced by Charnel House. The design is nothing short of breathtaking with the leather-bound book appearing to have been shot with Winchester bullets, housed in a wood tray case. But the limitation page is really a stroke of genius. *Regulators* was written under King's pseudonym, Richard Bachman, and at first people involved in the project producing the signed/numbered and lettered states were stymied because Richard Bachman was fictitious. They settled on using checks from Richard Bachman's estate. The check number became the limitation number and the "pay to the order of" for each check is written out to various characters that appear in King's novels and/or entities that are part of Stephen King's "circle." I happen to personally own the Letter "RR" with a check made out to "Betts Bookstore" in the amount of $325 for a limited edition of *The Regulators*.

But the series of books that are near and dear to my heart are the Donald M. Grant Publisher, signed, numbered copies of the Dark Tower series. I own three complete same-number sets, but what is extraordinarily unique about my sets is that my friend, artist Michael Whelan, did original sketches in each of my three *Gunslinger* signed, numbered copies as well as my lettered *Gunslinger* copy. Moreover, Michael cast me as the new image of Father Callahan for Stephen King's *Discordia* online game.

**GB: How much does King's signature in a recently published book (say, *Revival*) add to the book? (On eBay, it's $300 to $400, but is that fair market value?)**

**David:** King's signature in a recently published book like *Revival* is about $275, but generally, the value of the signature rises as one goes back in time to earlier editions. Obviously, King's signature is worth the most in his early Doubleday novels like *Carrie* and *'Salem's Lot,* well over $1,000.

**GB: What are some of the odd collectibles you carry that are King-related?**

**David:** At Betts, I sell almost exclusively special editions or signed copies of Steve's novels. My predecessor at Betts Books, Stuart Tinker, sold more unusual collectibles such as items from movie adaptations of King stories, promotional items given away by booksellers, etcetera. As caretaker of Betts Books, I deal mainly in books and book-related artwork.

---

1 A full set also exists in the special collections at Duke University, courtesy of Edwin and Terry Murray, who are completists in both the comics and science fiction field.

# 127

# Making the Grade

## Assessing Book Condition

The *primary* consideration of a book's value on the secondary market is its condition: the book itself, and (if present) the dust jacket.

In *Book Collecting: A Comprehensive Guide,* Allen and Patricia Ahearn use the term "mint" to describe a pristine copy, which is often used in the comic book industry. *AB Bookman's Weekly* (known as *AB* in the book trade), a weekly buy-and-sell publication for book collectors that is no longer being published, listed its criteria on book grading in every issue. The reason is simple: "These terms may be arbitrary, but whatever terms are employed, they may be useless or misleading unless buyer and seller both agree on what they mean to actually describe a book." *AB* preferred "as new" to "mint." *AB* notes that "as new" is to be used only when the book is in the same immaculate condition in which it was published. This is a very important distinction, specifying that the book in question should be indistinguishable from a copy purchased at the time of publication. *AB*'s definitions are useful:[1]

**Very Good** can describe a used book that does show some small signs of wears—but no tears—on either binding or paper.

**Good** describes the average used and worn book. . . .

**Fair** is a worn book. . . . Binding, jacket (if any), etc., may also be worn.

**Poor** describes a book that is sufficiently worn that its only merit is as a Reading Copy.

---

1 For a detailed listing of book criteria, go to http://www.modernlib.com/General/AB%20Bookman%20content.htm

In addition, *AB* points out that former library copies and book-club copies must be noted, as must all defects, and the presumption is that the book is intact and whole, with dust jacket (if issued).

## ON DEFECTS

It's important to remember that "as new" means just that: The book would be indistinguishable from a copy available on publication date. "As new" implies that there are no defects. This also means there's no bookplate, no owner's signature, no pencil markings—*nothing* added to the book by the owner.

## ON WHERE TO BUY

Superadhesive stickers and plastic antitheft devices permanently attached to the dust jacket are fine for most retail products but not books. "Big box" retailers often use these, and when they can't sell them, they return them to the publisher who recycles them to other sales channels. So be sure to inspect your copy as soon as possible for these unwanted gremlins.

"Churn"—the recycling of books between bookstores and the publisher's or distributor's warehouse—is also a collector's concern: Spend some time in any bookstore and you'll see the wear and tear involved in handling books, because customers pick up, browse, and then put down a copy of a book.

After several such pass-arounds, the book is no longer "as new" because the mere handling of the book introduces oil from fingers on the jacket itself, produces bent pages, or introduces other flaws.

For instance, I've seen a customer in a bookstore moisten a fingertip, putting saliva on the corner of every turned page, and then put the book back on the shelf! (A pity that the free-range rude, as Hannibal Lecter termed them, can walk freely among us.)

Another problem concerns online booksellers: They don't care whether they ship you a first edition or a subsequent printing. Even though a book may have a large printing of the first edition, its publisher may also go back to press with a second printing. Adding to the confusion: The book industry has not standardized how it identifies first editions (or subsequent printings) on copyright pages, so the burden of identifying a book's edition falls on the bookseller or customer, who must know the publishing house's protocols in listing the printings on the legal page.

The problem: If you can't decipher the correct printing, you may not get a coveted first printing but a less valuable second (or later) printing. To minimize the problem, preorder the book as soon as it's announced, which puts you in the queue before the customers who buy later. Presumably, you'll get one of the first copies and not a reprint, but do carefully check the "legal page."

## SINS OF OMISSION AND COMMISSION

On the assumption that there are a few readers out there who are new to book collecting and don't know where to begin, here's some time-tested advice:

- Do *not* discard the dust jacket! It is an integral part of the book.
- Do *not* clip the price—a practice common to copies given as gifts, since the giver doesn't want the recipient to know what they spent on the book.
- Do *not* paste in a bookplate or use a rubber stamp with your name on it.
- Do *not* sign your name in the book, unless you're the author or artist, in which case it becomes an associational copy.
- Do *not* store the book in a place with high humidity. (An unventilated storage unit's heat will warp the cover boards and the pages and prematurely age the book. Store books only in climate-controlled environments.)
- Do *not* buy book club editions. You will save a few bucks up front, but on the resale market, these have no value whatsoever. (The first edition of *The Girl Who Loved Tom Gordon,* for instance, appears to have been published in one printing for both the trade first and the book club edition. But the discerning collection will know that the only difference is its dust jacket—the book club edition has no price listed on the front flap.)
- Do *not* buy former library copies. They're only good as reading copies, because they are often shopworn and underlined or marked with pencil or ink! (If you order used books from Amazon, most booksellers are shipping book club or former library copies, almost always shipped in a plastic bag to save money on postage.)

## ON WRAPPING BOOKS IN PLASTIC

I am not an advocate of keeping books in the original shrink-wrap, for a few reasons. First, the shrink-wrap process itself is designed to shrink plastic with a heat gun from a loose to a tight state, which may eventually warp a book cover if left permanently on the book.

Second, the plastic is chemically harmful to the book because it "breathes"; the only plastic that doesn't "breathe" is a chemically inert brand called Mylar. (A good source for Mylar bags: Bags Unlimited, 7 Canal Street, Rochester, NY 14608; www.bagsunlimited. com.)

Third, keep in mind that shrink-wrapping is used by the publisher as a *short-term method* of protecting the book until it is delivered to the customer, an expedient way to prevent wear and tear in transit to the bookstore.

Novice sellers like to state their copies are "still in the original shrink-wrap!" But buyer beware: Shrink-wrapping is very common and you cannot distinguish between the publisher's shrink-wrapping or one shrink-wrapped with a home machine. Sometimes, the seller shrink-wraps a damaged book or one that's not what was advertised and hopes it's not opened for inspection. In other words, it's important to inspect the book in question, for which the shrink-wrap must be removed.

Case in point: When I received copies, direct from the publisher, of *Stephen King Country,* one copy had loose pages separated from the binding! Had the book been shrink-wrapped and sold thus, the buyer would never have known about it unless he visually examined the book. Yes, the bindery can screw up, as can the printer. These things happen. But it's better to find out when you can still return the book for replacement or credit than when you sell it and the buyer complains, "Hey, it's missing pages!" By then, the publisher may have no replacement copies—a real concern, especially with small presses who don't keep a lot of spare copies on hand for books damaged during the manufacturing or shipping stages.

Case in point: When I ordered the signed limited edition of *The Talisman* from Donald M. Grant, Publisher, it arrived via the U.S. Postal Service by media mail. Upon opening the box, the first book was so badly damaged that the first signature fell out on my lap. The publisher replaced the book, and it wasn't his fault, because it was clearly damaged in transit, but had I waited later to open and inspect it, I might not have been able to get a replacement copy from the publisher.

## Dust Jackets

They are fragile and very susceptible to damage. Even keeping them stored with the book in an acid-free plastic bag is problematic because handling the dust jacket directly leaves oil residue from fingers and other potential damage.

Without exception *every* dust jacket should be covered with an acetate plastic cover. Two companies, who cater to the library trade, sell them: demco.com and shopbrodart.com. They are available in a variety of sizes. I've found you need at least five different sizes to cover books from trade paperbacks to large art books.

As many a collector looking to resell books has discovered, even slightly damaged dust jackets significantly affect their resale value. (Publishers usually don't keep replacement jackets on hand, so make sure yours is in good condition or return/replace it immediately.)

## Caveat Emptor

I am very wary of online auctions because of the imprecision in the seller's description, the obvious lack of proper knowledge in identifying the first editions, and the dubious bookselling credentials of the prospective seller.

I am *very* wary of eBay offerings—sellers aren't as careful about noting defects as you'd wish. I do buy limiteds from eBay, but only after e-mailing the seller for specifics to reassure myself that what I'm buying is exactly what I'm looking for and accurately described.

Direct sellers like Amazon are even worse: I only buy reading copies from them; they deal in volume, with generic listings, and the listings themselves are often inadequate in describing the book.

## Further Reading

The two best sources online are bettsbooks.com and abebooks.com. (The latter is the online source for antiquarian booksellers, who generally do know how to properly grade books. Be sure to read the listing carefully, though.) Of the two, bettsbooks.com is preferred because it specializes in King books and nothing else.

Now, with all of that in mind, here are two horror stories regarding book misidentification.

A woman wanted to sell a bookseller I know a copy of *Cujo* that she insisted was the limited edition; because she was unable to properly describe the book over the phone, the bookseller urged her to come in with the book, and she did. She had brought in a trade edition of *Cujo* but insisted that it was a limited edition because the copyright page stated, "A special limited first edition of 750 numbered and signed copies of this book has been published by The Mysterious Press, New York." (One look at her copy clearly shows that it was published by Viking, not Mysterious Press.) She was upset, and even after explaining that the limited was published by another company, she was not convinced.

In another instance, Waldenbooks got copies of the Donald M. Grant edition of *The Dark Tower II: The Drawing of the Three*, which unfortunately bore two prices on the dust jacket: the trade-edition price ($38, issued in a print run of thirty thousand copies) and the price of the limited edition, in slipcase ($100, issued in a print run of 850 signed and numbered copies, of which 800 were for sale). The retail stores were misinformed by Waldenbooks's corporate office that they were all getting limited editions, so the store clerks marked the higher price on the shrink-wrapped books and sold them to unsuspecting customers, who in turn thought they were buying the limited edition.

I argued with a local clerk, who was adamant in his ignorance. He'd been selling the trade edition to customers for the limited edition price! Imagine the shock the buyer will get when, down the road, somebody who knows what he's talking about explains that he paid $100 for a $38 book that won't have the investment potential of the limited edition.

Bottom line: Caveat emptor (buyer beware). Carefully inspect every book you buy, especially one purported to be signed.

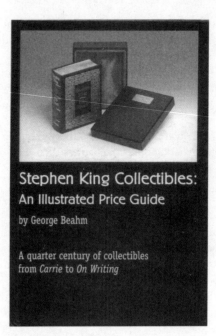

Stephen King Collectibles:
An Illustrated Price Guide
by George Beahm

A quarter century of collectibles
from *Carrie* to *On Writing*

# A Chronology of Stephen King's Life:

## Personal and Professional, 1947–2015

*King giving a public talk.*

King's print and film bibliographies are so extensive that a detailed listing is beyond the scope of this overview, which is limited to personal data, novels, movies and TV adaptations, awards, and significant first books by King critics. A complete listing of short fiction is available on King's Web site; I've noted the most significant works.

For more information, I'd recommend *Stephen King: A Primary Bibliography of the World's Most Popular Author,* by Justin Brooks (2008; e-book, Kindle); *Stephen King: The Non-Fiction,* by Rocky Wood and Justin Brooks (2008; e-book, Kindle), and *Stephen King: Uncollected, Unpublished,* by Rocky Wood (2012; hardback, paperback, and Kindle; Wood also published an update in 2014). Michael Collings also published a bibliography of fiction and nonfiction, *Horror Plum'd* (2002; out of print).

Unfortunately, there is no current bibliography of King's work available.

I am indebted in constructing this chronology to King's official Web site for information, especially about awards, and also Justin Brooks's useful *Stephen King: A Primary Bibliography of the World's Most Popular Author.*

Note: Stephen King's name is abbreviated below as SK.

## 1939

Donald Edwin King, a merchant mariner, marries Nellie Ruth Pillsbury.

## 1945

The Kings adopt a newborn baby, David Victor King, after they were erroneously told that Ruth couldn't conceive.

## 1947

Stephen Edwin King is born at Maine General Hospital (now Maine Medical Center) in Portland (September 21).

## 1949–58

Ruth scrambles to make a living, and the family is geographically fractured; sometimes, they are together, and at other times, they stay temporarily with relatives. As Dave King recalled in an interview in *The Complete Stephen King Encyclopedia,* the boys stayed with relatives on both sides of the family tree until, finally, they settled down in Stratford, Connecticut, where their mother rented a house on West Broad Street, and worked at the Stratford Laundry. (SK would, years later, buy a house on West Broad Street in Bangor and also worked at a commercial laundry.)

## 1949

Donald King abandons family, who never hears from him again, and lights out for the territories.

## 1953

SK hears Ray Bradbury's "Mars Is Heaven" on radio (Dimension X radio program) through Dave's bedroom door and is captivated. Theirs is the last generation of baby boomers to remember radio dramatizations as a mass market form of entertainment.

## 1953 OR 1954

SK spends a year in bed due to health issues and misses a year of school; he's surrounded by comic books and begins writing imitative stories based on the comics on hand, including *Combat Casey.*

## 1957

SK is at the Stratford Theater watching *Earth vs. the Flying Saucers,* which is interrupted when the manager stops the film, raises the house lights, and tells the audience of young boys that the Russians just put *Sputnik* in orbit around earth.

## 1958

The Kings move from Stratford, Connecticut, and permanently settle down in Durham, Maine. They move into a small house near Methodist Corner, down the street from Ruth's sister, Ethelyn, and her husband, Oren Flaws. Ruth becomes a paid caregiver for her elderly parents, who are in declining health. The family gets their first television, a black-and-white model. Their mailing address: Route 1, Pownal, Maine.

SK meets and becomes friends with Chris Chesley, his first literary collaborator, and his movie buddy for Saturday matinees at the Ritz in nearby Lewiston. (He and Chesley hitchhike every Saturday to see the movies for eight years, until SK gets a driver's license in 1966.)

## 1959

Ruth buys a used Underwood typewriter for $35 for Stephen; he starts submitting professionally to digest-sized science fiction magazines.

David King publishes a community newspaper, *Dave's Rag* (January); it's cover-priced five cents. At first, copies are individually hand-typed, then reproduced by hectograph, and finally by mimeograph. David King is the editor in chief and illustrator, Donald P. Flaws is the sports editor, and SK is a general reporter.

### Self-Published
*Thirty-one of the Classics,* mimeographed, an abridgment and retelling by SK of thirty-one classic novels. (Announced but possibly not published.)

"Jumper," a short story serialized in *Dave's Rag.* (One installment of "Jumper" is reprinted in *Secret Windows* in 2000.)

"Land of 1,000,000 Years Ago," a mimeographed short story.

## 1960

SK discovers a box of paperback books, science fiction, and horror, belonging to his father, an aspiring writer who submitted short fiction but never got published. As Ruth told SK, his father lacked persistence.

### Self-Published
*People, Places, and Things—Volume I,* with nine stories by Chris Chesley and eight by SK (19 pages, mimeographed, from Triad Publishing Company). SK's include "The Hotel at the End of the Road," "I've Got to Get Away!," "The Dimension Warp," "The Thing at the Bottom of the Well," "The Stranger," "I'm Falling," "The Cursed Expedition," "The Other Side of the Fog," and "Never Look Behind You" (a collaboration with Chesley).

"Rush Call," published in *Dave's Rag.*

## 1961

### Self-Published
*The Pit and the Pendulum* (a V.I.B. Book), a novelization, printed by mimeograph in a run of forty copies, for twenty-five cents each.

A short story in which the students take over a grammar school. It sold for a quarter a copy to SK's classmates. (Title and publication date unknown.)

SK sends a short story to Forrest J. Ackerman's magazine *Spacemen*, but it's rejected. He tells Forry in a cover letter, "I am 14 years of age, and have been writing as far back as I can remember, and submitting manuscripts for the last couple of years." (It is eventually published by "FSJ" in *Famous Monsters of Filmland* 202, spring 1994.)

## 1962

SK graduates from a one-room grammar school near his home (June).

SK begins his first year at Lisbon Falls High School (September), eight miles away from West Durham; he commutes via Mike's Taxi of Lisbon. (The taxi itself is a converted hearse. As Jeff Pert, in his profile of Brian Hall wrote, "Mike had an old limousine, and he'd haul the handful of Durham kids to school in that. Hall says one of the regular riders was one of the two girls on whom King based the protagonist of Carrie. When the limo arrived, there was a rush to get the best seats. You didn't want to ride all the way to Lisbon with Carrie on your lap." SK, over six feet tall, plays tight end / left tackle on the varsity football team.)

## 1963

SK edits the school newspaper, *The Drum*, as a sophomore. Only one issue is published under his editorship, but it's monster-sized.

SK self-publishes a parody of the school newspaper titled *The Village Vomit*, earning him a three-day suspension; school officials divert his writing talent to more productive use and get him a part-time job as a sports reporter for the Lisbon *Weekly Enterprise*, under the watchful eye of its editor, John Gould.

SK completes "The Aftermath," a seventy-six-page, single-spaced, science fiction story (approx. 45,000 words, his longest fiction to date, on February 15).

**Self-Published**
"The Invasion of the Star-Creatures" (Triad, Inc. and Gaslight Books, June 1964).

## 1965

**Published**
SK publishes "I Was a Teenage Grave Robber" in *Comics Review*, edited by Mike Garrett, a zine for comics fans, printed by Ditto machine, 1965. (It is reprinted as "In a Half-World of Terror," in *Stories of Suspense*, a fanzine published by Marvin Wolfman, in 1966.)

SK publishes "Codename: Mousetrap," a short story (Lisbon High School newspaper, *The Drum*, volume 3, number 1, October 27, 1965).

## 1966

SK plays the rhythm guitar with the Mune Spinners in his senior year at the high school prom.

SK gets a driver's license.

SK gets a job at Worumbo Mill and Weaving in Lisbon Falls, which inspires the story "Graveyard Shift" after he's told about a holiday cleanup basement crew, where rats were purportedly dog-sized.

Dave King graduates cum laude from the University of Maine at Orono (May).

SK is accepted to Drew University but turns it down, despite a partial scholarship offer. He elects to attend the University of Maine at Orono (September).

**Published**

"The 43rd Dream," a short story, in the Lisbon Falls High School newspaper, *The Drum,* January 29, 1966.

## 1967

SK submits *The Long Walk* to a Bennett Cerf first novel competition, but it's rejected. (It is published in 1979 by New American Library.)

**Published**

"The Glass Floor," *Startling Mystery Stories* (fall), SK's first professionally published story, for which he was paid $35. Quoting a line from Dickey's *Deliverance,* SK's assessment, as he wrote in *Weird Tales* 298, is, "Naw—it ain't as bad's I thought."

## 1969

SK is in a work-study job program to pay for tuition and books. SK meets Tabitha Spruce; they both work part-time at the university library.

**Published**

"The Garbage Truck," a column for the University of Maine at Orono newspaper, *The Maine Campus* (February 20).

A short poem titled "The Dark Man," in *Ubris* (University of Maine at Orono literary magazine, fall issue), published as *The Dark Man* by Cemetery Dance (July 2013) and profusely illustrated by Glenn Chadbourne. The poem marks the first appearance of Randall Flagg.

"Night Surf," in *Ubris* (spring, 1969), a trial cut foreshadowing *The Stand.*

## 1970

SK graduates from the University of Maine at Orono with a teaching certificate and a B.S. degree in English (June). Because no teaching positions are available in the local area, SK takes a job pumping gas for $1.25 an hour but quits to work at the New Franklin Laundry because of a pay increase, to $1.60 an hour ($60 a week); Tabitha works the second shift at a Dunkin' Donuts in downtown Bangor.

Naomi Rachel is born (June 1).

The Kings live in an inexpensive rented apartment in Orono.

**Published**

SK makes his first sale to *Cavalier* magazine, which publishes "Graveyard Shift" in its October 1970 issue. He earns $200 for the story—his largest check to date.

SK completes a 485-page, double-spaced manuscript, "Sword in the Darkness" (April 30). An excerpt was published in Rocky Wood's *Stephen King: Uncollected, Unpublished* (2005).

## 1971

SK marries Tabitha Jane Spruce in Old Town (January 2).

SK signs a contract to teach high school English at Hampden Academy at an annual salary of $6,400 (Hampden, Maine).

Tabitha King graduates from the University of Maine at Orono with a B.A. degree in history (May).

SK completes *Getting It On* (published as *Rage* by New American Library under the Bachman pen name in 1977). SK sends a query letter to Doubleday addressed to "The Editor of *The Parallax View,*" which is rerouted to William "Bill" G. Thompson, who reads and rejects it but encourages SK to submit more manuscripts.

## 1972

Joe Hillstrom King is born (June 4).

Stephen begins writing a short story, "Carrie," intended for *Cavalier*. Discouraged, he crumples and throws three pages in the trash, rescued by Tabitha. She gently encourages him to continue, and he does. It grows in length until it becomes a short novel of fifty thousand words, after adding bogus documentation.

SK submits *The Running Man*, which is rejected by Doubleday, and also Ace Books, whose publisher, Donald A. Wollheim, told him they didn't publish dystopian novels. (It is published by New American Library in May 1982 under the Bachman pen name.)

**Published**

A short story, "The Fifth Quarter," (*Cavalier*, April 1972) as John Swithen, a pen name (the only other one ever used).

## 1973

The Kings live in a rented trailer on Klatt Road in Hermon, Maine. To save money, the phone is removed. After they are evicted, they move to a blue-collar neighborhood in Bangor. SK submits and sells *Carrie* to Doubleday for $2,500 (March/April). The paperback rights sell to New American Library (NAL) for $400,000, earning him $200,000 (May).

They rent four rooms on the upstairs floor in a house at 14 Sanford Street (rent is $90 a month). The $200,000 allows him to quit teaching to write full-time; he finishes the school year in June, fulfilling his contract.

SK completes *Blaze*.

The King family moves to Sebago Lake in North Windham, Maine, to be closer to Stephen's mother, who is in failing health. He borrows money against the expected $200,000 check and tells her to quit her blue-collar job at the Pineland Training Center in New Gloucester, Maine. She quits and spends the last few remaining months of her life with her son David in Mexico, Maine.

SK begins writing a novel, *Second Coming*, later retitled *'Salem's Lot*.

Ruth King dies of cancer surrounded by her two sons and their immediate families. Being too ill to read, one of her sisters had read her *Carrie* from the advance galley of the book, which SK lovingly inscribed (December 18).

**Published**

"Trucks," in *Cavalier* (June 1973), the basis for the film *Maximum Overdrive*, with screenplay by SK, who also directed it.

## 1974

The Kings temporarily move to Boulder, Colorado, where he begins work on a novel that would become *The Stand*, the number one fan favorite of all his books.

Stephen and Tabitha take a vacation to the Stanley Hotel in Estes Park, Colorado, where he is inspired to write *The Shining*.

**Published**

*Carrie* (Doubleday, trade hardback, April) is his first published novel. Its cover price is $5.95.

## 1975

The Kings return to Maine, and buy their first home, in Bridgton, the setting for one of his most quintessential stories, "The Mist."

**Published**

'Salem's Lot (Doubleday, trade hardback, October), originally titled *Second Coming*.

"The Lawnmower Man," in *Cavalier* (May 1975), the basis for a movie adaptation that prompted a lawsuit from King because of its tangential story line and excessive use of SK's name for marketing purposes to hype the video release.

"The Revenge of Lard Ass Hogan," in *The Maine Review* (July 1975), revised for its inclusion in "The Body" (from *Different Seasons*).

## 1976

SK meets literary agent Kirby McCauley at a party in New York City. (In 1977 he becomes SK's literary agent.)

Mass market paperback editions of *Carrie* and *'Salem's Lot*, goosed by the movie release of *Carrie*, sell 3.5 million copies. SK is well on his way to becoming the Modern Master of Horror, a title that, over the years, chafes.

SK suffers writer's block and goes through a difficult time with false starts on *Welcome to Clearwater*, *The Corner*, *The Dead Zone*, and *Firestarter*; he's concerned about self-imitation because of *Firestarter*'s similarities to *Carrie*.

**Published**

"Weeds," in *Cavalier* (May 1976), the basis for "The Lonesome Death of Jordy Verrill," in the movie *Creepshow*.

**Visual Adaptation**

*Carrie* is released (November 3). Directed by Brian de Palma, it stars Sissy Spacek in the title role and Piper Laurie as her mother, Margaret White; both were nominated but did not win Academy Awards for their performances.

## 1977

SK's fame and popularity is such that, as Mel Allen for *Writer's Digest* wrote in a profile, "[He's] had his phone number changed, and the local operator tells countless people every day, 'No, I'm sorry, we are not permitted to disclose that number,' because strangers call from all parts of the country to ask for money, interviews, help in finding a publisher for the 800-page novel they've written about werewolves, or advice on how to do away with the demonic neighbor who has caused the vegetables to succumb to root rot."

The Kings' second son, Owen Phillip King, is born (February 21).

The Kings move to England for a one-year stay but return after only three months. While there, SK meets novelist Peter Straub, with whom he will later collaborate on two novels, *The Talisman* (1984) and *The Black House* (2001), with a third projected to be written in 2015.

**Published**

*The Shining* (Doubleday, trade hardback, January 28), originally titled *The Shine*, is published.

"The Cat from Hell," in *Cavalier* (1977). In March, a partial story is published; in June, the completed version of the story is published; and in September, with King's beginning, the second half written by Phil Bowie, who won the story competition, is published in *Cavalier*.

"Children of the Corn," in *Penthouse* (March 1977), which inspired nine movies.

"Weeds," in *Cavalier* (May 1976), the basis for the film segment, "The Lonesome Death of Jordy Verrill," in *Creepshow*, the title role of which is played by SK.

*Rage* (as Richard Bachman), from New American Library (mass market paperback, September

13), originally titled *Getting It On*. (In 1999, SK told his publisher to put the book out of print, citing it as a possible accelerant to school shootings.) It was the first Bachman novel published.

## 1978

The Kings move to Orrington, Maine, with its "pet sematary" (a child's spelling) on the hill behind the house.

SK serves a one-year stint as writer in residence at the University of Maine at Orono (he's asked to stay for a second year but turns down the offer to pursue full-time writing); he teaches Introduction to Creative Writing and gothic fiction.

SK leaves Doubleday after irreconcilable contractual conflicts, significantly a 50/50 split of income on paperback sales, which he feels is unwarranted. SK's editor, Bill Thompson, suffers collateral damage. SK recalled, "When I left Doubleday, they canned him. It was almost like a taunt: we'll kill the messenger that brought the bad news" (Bhob Stewart, *Heavy Metal*, February/March 1980).

### Recognition
*'Salem's Lot* wins an American Library Association Award.

### Published
*Night Shift* (Doubleday, trade hardback, February), new stories: "Jerusalem's Lot," "The Last Rung on the Ladder," "Quitters, Inc.," and "The Woman in the Room."

SK's first sale to *F&SF* with a short story, "The Night of the Tiger" (February).

*The Stand* (Doubleday, trade hardback, September).

SK's first Dark Tower tale, "The Gunslinger," in *F&SF* (October).

## 1979

The Kings move to their home in Center Lovell, Maine.

Donald Edwin King dies, in Wind Gap, Pennsylvania (November).

### Recognition
SK is, along with Frank Belknap Long, a guest of honor at the fifth World Fantasy Convention (Providence, Rhode Island, October 12–13); SK receives a World Fantasy Award for contributions to the field.

### Published
*The Long Walk,* by Richard Bachman (New American Library, trade edition, mass market paperback, July), currently under option by Frank Darabont for a film adaptation.

"The Crate," in *Gallery*, the basis for an episode in the film *Creepshow*.

*The Dead Zone* (Viking Press, trade hardback, August). SK's first novel for Viking.

### Visual Adaptation
*'Salem's Lot,* directed by Tobe Hooper, is broadcast (November 17)

## 1980

The Kings buy a house on West Broadway for $135,000.

### Recognition
Stephen receives an Alumni Career Award from the University of Maine.

*Night Shift* wins a Balrog Award.

SK receives the Convention Award from the World Fantasy Convention.

## Published

*Firestarter* (Phantasia Press, limited edition; Viking Press, trade hardback edition, September). The cover painting by Michael Whelan was used only for the Phantasia Press edition. This was also SK's first novel to be published in a signed and limited edition.

"The Mist," in an original anthology, *Dark Forces,* edited by Kirby McCauley. It is considered one of SK's finest stories and becomes the basis of a major film, directed by Frank Darabont.

## Visual Adaptation

*The Shining,* directed by Stanley Kubrick, is released as a film. SK is its biggest critic, and in the years to come takes to the media to complain about it. (SK's remake was aired on May 23, 1997.)

## 1981

## Recognition

SK receives the Career Alumni Award from the University of Maine.
SK receives a special British Fantasy Award for "outstanding contribution to the genre."
*Firestarter* wins an American Library Association Award.

## Published

*Stephen King's Danse Macabre* (Everest House, limited and trade hardback edition, April 20). SK's first published nonfiction book, a study of the horror field.

*Cujo* (Mysterious Press, limited edition; Viking Press, trade hardback edition, September).

*Roadwork,* by Richard Bachman (New American Library, trade edition, mass market paperback, March).

"Do the Dead Sing?," *Yankee* magazine (November), published as "The Reach" in *Skeleton Crew* (1985). Generally acknowledged as his finest short story.

Tabitha King publishes her first novel, *Small World,* (Macmillan Publishing, April.)

## Visual Adaptation

As screenwriter and an actor ("The Lonesome Death of Jordy Verrill"), SK is hands-on with *Creepshow,* also adapted as a comic book with a cover by EC artist Jack Kamen, with interior art by Bernie Wrightson.

## 1982

## Recognition

At Necon II, Stephen King is the roastee.
"Do the Dead Sing?" wins a World Fantasy Award (tied).
*Danse Macabre* wins a Hugo Award.
SK wins Best Fiction Writer of the Year Award from *Us* magazine.
*Firestarter* wins an award from the New York Public Library Books for the Teen Age.

## Published

*The Running Man,* by Richard Bachman (New American Library, mass market paperback, May).

*The Dark Tower [1]: The Gunslinger* (Donald M. Grant, Publisher, limited and trade hardback edition, June 10). This edition launched Grant's small press into the limelight. Both Grant and King agree Michael Whelan was their primary choice for illustrator, who accepted the commission.

Stephen King's *Creepshow* (with Bernie Wrightson, July), SK's first graphic album (i.e., comic book format).

*Different Seasons* (Viking Press, trade hardcover edition August), SK's strongest novella collection; includes three stories adapted for major movies: "The Body" (the basis for Rob Reiner's film *Stand by Me*) "Rita Hayworth and Shawshank Redemption" (the basis for Frank Darabont's film *The Shawshank Redemption*), and "Apt Pupil."

*The Plant* [1] (Philtrum Press, limited edition, December). The first Philtrum Press publication sent out as a Christmas gift to family and friends in lieu of an impersonal Christmas card.

"Before the Play," in a double issue of *Whispers* 17/18, cut from *The Shining*; its epilogue was rewritten and incorporated in the last chapter, 58, "Epilogue/Summer."

### Published on King
*Fear Itself: The Horror Fiction of Stephen King*, an anthology of nonfiction, the first of several SK-related books published by a specialty press, Underwood-Miller.

*Stephen King*, by Douglas E. Winter, the first single-author, SK-related book from a specialty press, Starmont House; a trial cut for his groundbreaking book, *Stephen King: The Art of Darkness* (1984).

### Visual Adaptation
*Creepshow* (November 10)

### 1983
SK buys WZON radio in Bangor under the auspices of the Zone Corporation (April).

### Published
*Christine* (Donald M. Grant, Publisher, limited edition; Viking Press, trade hardback edition, April).

*Pet Sematary* (Doubleday, trade hardback edition, April), which went into King's trunk because it was too bleak to publish. SK tells Douglas E. Winter in an interview, "Tabby had finished reading it in tears, and I thought it was a nasty book. Maybe I don't have the guts for that end of the business of horror fiction—for the final truths." (A contractual matter forced King's hand and, eventually, its publication in 1983.)

*Cycle of the Werewolf*, illustrated by Bernie Wrightson (Land of Enchantment, limited edition, November), originally intended as a calendar with text by King and art by Wrightson, who originated the idea.

*The Plant* [2] (Philtrum Press, limited edition, December).

### Visual Adaptations
*Cujo*, directed by Lewis Teague (August 12)
*The Dead Zone*, directed by David Cronenberg (October 21)
*Christine*, directed by John Carpenter (December 9)

### 1984
SK approaches American Express's ad agency, Ogilvy & Mather, with the idea of appearing in a commercial. "It's just such a compliment," he told *People* magazine (August 27). "Certainly it's not going to do much for my literary reputation, although many would say that I don't have a literary reputation to worry about." The tagline: "Do you know me?" SK later rues his decision because, more than anything else, it made him a celebrity, instantly recognizable by name and on sight by the man on the street. (SK was paid $10,000 plus residuals to appear in the ad.)

### Published
*The Talisman*, with Peter Straub (Donald M. Grant, Publisher, limited edition; Viking, G. P. Putnam, trade hardback edition, November 8). King's first professional collaboration. (It would be

followed by *The Black House,* again with Straub, in 2001. A third and final book is scheduled to be written in 2015.)

*Thinner* (original title: *Gypsy Pie*), by Richard Bachman (New American Library, trade hardback, November). It was heavily promoted by its publisher in an attempt to "break through" Bachman in the book trade: His previous four books were published as mass market paperbacks.

*The Eyes of the Dragon* (Philtrum Press, limited edition, December), written to please King's daughter, Naomi, who didn't read horror. It was illustrated by Kenneth R. Linkhaüser (pen name for Kenny Ray Linkous). (The 1987 trade hardback edition from Viking reflected requested editorial changes.)

**Published on King**

*Stephen King: The Art of Darkness* (New American Library, trade hardback, November), by Douglas E. Winter. The first major study about SK.

**Visual Adaptations**

*Children of the Corn,* directed by Fritz Kirsch (March 9)

*Firestarter,* directed by Mark Lester (May 11)


## 1985

Stephen's substance abuse includes drugs. Tabitha stages an intervention at their house and delivers an ultimatum: Quit taking drugs or leave the house, because family and friends didn't want to see him slowly kill himself in front of them. He chooses . . . wisely.

SK temporarily moves to Wilmington, North Carolina, to direct *Maximum Overdrive,* based on his screenplay, which in turn is based on his short story.

The hometown newspaper (the *Bangor Daily News*) runs a story by Joan H. Smith revealing SK's pen name of Richard Bachman (February 9).

SK admits he is Richard Bachman, after denials became useless when a reader discovered a copyright form for *Rage* with King's name on it—a clerical error by his literary agent. (The other three novels were registered to his literary agent, Kirby McCauley.)

**Recognition**

*Starlog* magazine lists SK as one of the "100 most important people in science fiction/fantasy."

**Published**

*Castle Rock,* an official SK publication, publishes its first issue (January).

*Cycle of the Werewolf* (Signet trade paperback, April), later published in a movie tie-in edition titled *Silver Bullet* (October).

*Skeleton Crew* (Scream Press limited edition; G. P. Putnam, trade hardback edition, June), SK's strongest story collection to date. Originally titled after the Bob Seger song, "Night Moves," it was changed at Rick Hautala's urging. The lead story is "The Mist."

*The Bachman Books: Four Early Novels,* by Richard Bachman (New American Library, trade hardback, October), an omnibus that collects the first four Bachman novels: *Rage, The Long Walk, Roadwork,* and *The Running Man.* (King's original introduction, "Why I Was Bachman," was revised for the trade paperback and mass market paperback editions.)

*The Plant* [3] (Philtrum Press, limited edition, December).

"Dolan's Cadillac" begins serialization in *Castle Rock* (February to June; in May, *Castle Rock* goes to a tabloid format).

"Heroes for Hope: Starring the X-Men," in a comic book from Marvel Comics Group (December 1); King's story is illustrated by Bernie Wrightson.

**Published on King**
*Stephen King as Richard Bachman,* by Michael R. Collings. From Starmont House, this was Collings's first of many excellent books on King.

**Visual Adaptations**
   *Cat's Eye,* directed by Lewis Teague (April 12)
   *Silver Bullet,* directed by Daniel Attias (October 11)
   *Two Mini-Features from . . . Stephen King's Night Shift Collection* (a VHS compilation): "The Bogeyman," and "The Woman in the Room," directed by Frank Darabont, who went on to helm several King films
   "The Word Processor of the Gods" (TV)

## 1986

SK moves the office staff out of his home on West Broadway and into a former Maine National Guard building near the Bangor International Airport.

**Recognition**
*Skeleton Crew* wins a Locus Award.
   SK is the subject of a *Time* magazine cover story (October 6), which terms him the "Downeast Disney."

**Published**
*It* (Viking Press, trade hardback, September), originally titled *Derry.*

**Visual Adaptations**
   *Stand by Me,* directed by Rob Reiner (August 8)
   *Maximum Overdrive,* directed by Stephen King (July 25)

## 1987

Stephanie Leonard, in *Castle Rock,* writes that SK is going to take a sabbatical. "We've heard him say he'll take five years." Fans are stunned, and the reaction is immediate: It makes the news, and SK quickly recants. Leonard later publishes an update: "Stephen is not really retiring. He is hoping to cut back on work so he can spend more time with his family. There will not be any more five-book years anytime soon. He plans to continue writing but publishing less."

**Recognition**
*It* wins a British Fantasy Society Award.
   *Misery* wins a Bram Stoker Award from the Horror Writers Association.
   SK gives a commencement address to the 169th graduating class at the University of Maine at Orono (May 9), noting that, including this one, he's only given six such addresses (out of the 134 invitations, as of 1998).

**Published**
*The Eyes of the Dragon* (Viking Press, trade edition, February), illustrated by David Palladini. Editor Deborah Brodie asked SK for a textual addition to have Ben, Peter's best friend, appear earlier in the book instead of halfway through; SK obliges and writes a new scene involving a three-legged sack race to establish their relationship.
   *The Dark Tower [2]: The Drawing of the Three* (Donald M. Grant, Publisher, limited edition and trade edition, May). Original title, *The Dark Tower [2]: Roland Draws Three.*

*Misery* (Viking Press, trade hardback edition, June). Originally planned as a Richard Bachman novella titled "The Annie Wilkes Edition."

*The Tommyknockers* (G. P. Putnam, trade hardback edition, November), considered by SK as one of his lesser novels.

**Visual Adaptations**

*Creepshow 2,* directed by Michael Gornick (May 1)

"Sorry, Right Number," directed by Brian Berkowitz, based on a Stephen King teleplay (TV, May 1)

*Return to 'Salem's Lot,* directed by Larry Cohen (September 11)

*The Running Man,* directed by George Pan Cosmos (November 13)

## 1988

*Carrie,* the Broadway play, opens—and closes—to bad reviews. (The 2012 off-Broadway remake fares somewhat better, though it doesn't carry the day, either.)

**Published**

*Nightmares in the Sky: Gargoyles and Grotesques,* by f-stop Fitzgerald, with a short essay by SK (Viking Press, October 7). This is more the photographer's book than SK's, since it's principally a book of his photos. Thinking SK's name would sell the book, the publisher printed far too many, which backfired because there simply wasn't enough original SK content.

*My Pretty Pony* (Library Fellows of the Whitney Museum, limited edition, September 26). Illustrated by Barbara Kruger, this was sixth in its Artists and Writers Series.

"Letters from Hell" (Lord John Press, limited edition broadside).

**Published on King**

*Landscape of Fear: Stephen King's American Gothic* (Bowling Green State University), by Tony Magistrale, professor at the University of Vermont. This is the first of many excellent books on SK by Magistrale.

## 1989

Acts as assistant coach of West Bangor's Little League team, on which his son Owen is playing. (They win the Maine State Tournament in 1989.) ("Head Down," SK's reportage, appeared in *The New Yorker* on April 16, 1990.)

Horrorfest, the first convention celebrating King, is held at the Stanley Hotel in Estes Park, Colorado (May 12–14).

**Published**

*Dolan's Cadillac* (Lord John Press, limited edition). This was the first SK book published by Lord John Press.

*The Dark Half* (Viking Press, trade edition, November). Its original title is *Machine's Way,* and it was originally conceived as a collaboration between King and Bachman.

*My Pretty Pony* (Alfred A. Knopf, trade hardback edition, $50; 15,000 copies, September).

**Published on King**

*The Stephen King Companion* (Andrews and McMeel, 1989), by George Beahm. The second edition of this book was published in 1995. This is the first major pop culture companion book on SK.

**Visual Adaptation**

*Pet Sematary,* directed by Mary Lambert (April)

## 1990

SK receives an estimated five hundred letters a week, 80 percent requesting a response.

### Recognition
*Four Past Midnight* wins a Bram Stoker Award from the Horror Writers Association.

*The Magazine of Fantasy & Science Fiction* publishes a special Stephen King issue (limited edition and trade edition, December) with a fantasy portrait of him on the cover, a bibliography, an appreciation by A. J. Budrys, and two stories: "A Moving Finger" and "The Bear" (from *The Dark Tower [3]: The Waste Lands*).

### Published
SK's first publication in *The New Yorker,* a non-fiction piece titled "Head Down" (April 16). A magazine celebrated for its literary excellence, SK's appearance herein surprises some readers.

*The Stand: The Complete and Uncut Edition* (Doubleday, limited edition and trade hardback edition, May). An additional 150,000 words were added to the text; the timeline was also updated, from the eighties to the nineties.

*Four Past Midnight* (Viking Press, trade hardback edition, September).

### Visual Adaptations
*Tales from the Darkside: The Movie,* directed by John Harrison (May 4)
*Stephen King's Graveyard Shift,* directed by Ralph S. Singleton (October 26)
*It* (TV miniseries), directed by Tommy Lee Wallace (November 18)
*Misery,* directed by Rob Reiner (November 30)

## 1991

A disturbed man keen on breaking into the Kings' home in Bangor comes in through the kitchen window at 6:00 a.m., confronting Tabitha, who is home alone, in her nightclothes. He's holding a wired cigar box, says it's a bomb, and claims Stephen stole the idea of *Misery* from his aunt. Tabitha gets to a neighbor's house, and the police are called. He's found in the attic. The bomb is a fake. In the wake of his intrusion, the Kings take normal security precautions afterward, realizing that their illusion of normalcy as just another family on West Broadway is irrevocably shattered.

### Published
*The Dark Tower [3]: The Waste Lands* (Donald M. Grant, Publisher, limited edition and trade hardback edition, August).

*Needful Things: The Last Castle Rock Story* (Viking Press, trade hardback edition, October).

### Published on King
*The Shape Under the Sheet: The Complete Stephen King Encyclopedia* (Popular Culture Ink, 1991), by Stephen J. Spignesi, a prolific pop culture writer. A concordance (80 percent) with interviews, profiles, articles, and other features, this was the first major reference book on SK.

### Visual Adaptations
*The Dark Half,* directed by George A. Romero (April 23)
*Sometimes They Come Back* (TV), directed by Tom McLoughlin (May 7)
*The Golden Years* (TV miniseries), various directors (July 16)

## 1992

The Kings finance the Shawn Trevor Mansfield Complex in Bangor as a gift to the city, at a cost of $1.5 million. It's dubbed the Field of Screams after the famous Kevin Costner baseball movie

*Fields of Dreams.*

SK performs with fellow band members at the first Rock Bottom Remainders concert in Anaheim, California, for booksellers attending their annual convention (American Booksellers Association).

**Recognition**
*Cujo* wins a British Fantasy Society Award.
SK receives World Horror Grandmaster Award from the World Horror Convention.

**Published**
*Gerald's Game* (Viking Press, trade edition, May). Originally planned as a trilogy, "The Path of the Eclipse," with this as book 1, *Dolores Claiborne* as book 2, and an untitled and unwritten novel as book 3.

**Visual Adaptations**
*Sleepwalkers,* directed by Mick Garris (April 10)
BMG video releases VHS cassette of the first Rock Bottom Remainders concert in Anaheim, California.

**1993**

The Kings, through the Stephen and Tabitha King Foundation, donate $2 million to worthy charities.

**Published**
*Nightmares and Dreamscapes* (Viking Press, trade hardback, October).
  *Dolores Claiborne* (Viking Press, trade hardback, November).

**Film Adaptations**
  *The Dark Half,* directed by George A. Romero (April 23)
  *The Tommyknockers* (TV), directed by John Power (May 9)
  *Needful Things,* directed by Fraser Clarke Heston (August 27)

**1994**

**Recognition**
*Insomnia* wins a Bram Stoker Award from the Horror Writers Association.

**Published**
*Mid-Life Confidential: The Rock Bottom Remainders Tour America with Three Chords and an Attitude* (one chapter by SK; Viking Press, trade hardback).
  *Insomnia: A Novel* (Mark V. Ziesing Books, limited edition and trade hardback edition; Viking Press, trade hardback edition, September 15).
  "The Man in the Black Suit," *The New Yorker* (October 31). The short story is later published in *Prize Stories 1996: The O. Henry Awards* (March 1, 1996). The literati, upright and sniffing the air, note the wind is changing.

**Visual Adaptations**
  *The Stand* (TV), directed by Mick Garris (May 8)
  *The Shawshank Redemption,* directed by Frank Darabont (September 23)

**1995**

**Recognition**

"Lunch at the Gotham Café" wins a Bram Stoker Award from the Horror Writers Association.
"The Man in the Black Suit" wins a World Fantasy Award.

**Published**
*Rose Madder* (Hodder and Stoughton, United Kingdom, limited edition; Viking Press, trade hardback edition, June).

**Visual Adaptations**
*The Mangler*, directed by Tobe Hooper (March 3)
*Dolores Claiborne*, directed by Taylor Hackford (March 24)
*The Langoliers*, directed by Tom Holland (TV, May 14)

## 1996
**Recognition**
*The Green Mile* wins a Bram Stoker Award from the Horror Writers Association.
University of Maine at Orono holds a conference, Reading Stephen King (October 11–12).
"The Man in the Black Suit" wins the coveted O. Henry Award.

**Publications**
*The Green Mile* (Signet, mass market paperback), King's first serialized novel, is issued in mass market paperback editions:
*The Green Mile [1]: The Two Dead Girls* (March)
*The Green Mile [2]: The Mouse on the Mile* (April)
*The Green Mile [3]: Coffey's Hands* (May)
*The Green Mile [4]: The Bad Death of Eduard Delacroix* (June)
*The Green Mile [5]: The Night Journey* (July)
*The Green Mile [6]: Coffey on the Mile* (Signet, August)
The six installments were subsequently published in 1997 as *The Green Mile: The Complete Serial Novel*.
*Desperation* (Donald M. Grant, Publisher, limited edition and trade edition; Viking Press, trade hardback edition, September 24). A "twinner" novel with *The Regulators*, released simultaneously in a well-synchronized national one-day rollout.
*The Regulators*, by Richard Bachman (Dutton, limited edition and trade hardback edition, September 24).
*Desperation / The Regulators* box set (Hodder and Stoughton, United Kingdom, limited edition).

**Visual Adaptation**
*Thinner*, directed by Tom Holland, is released (October 25).

## 1997
SK starts looking around for a new publisher; his business manager, Arthur B. Greene, becomes actively involved and lays the groundwork. SK's ambitious new novel, *Bag of Bones*, is the inducement.
A high school shooting (in West Paducah, Kentucky) reveals a copy of *Rage* in the boy's locker. SK immediately contacts his publisher and tells them to pull the book. He said, "It's almost a blueprint in terms of saying, 'This is how it could be done.' And when it started to happen, I said, 'That's it for me, that book's off the market'" (BBC, December 19, 1999).

**Recognition**
*Desperation* wins a Horror Guild Award and a Hugo Award.

**Published**

*The Green Mile: The Complete Serial Novel* (Plume, trade paperback, May).

   *Six Stories* (Philtrum Press, limited edition, trade paperback).

   *The Dark Tower [4]: Wizard and Glass* (Donald M. Grant, Publisher, limited edition and trade hardback edition, November 4; Hodder and Stoughton, United Kingdom, limited edition).

**Visual Adaptations**

   *The Shining* (TV), directed by Mick Garris (April 27)

   *The Quicksilver Highway* (TV), directed by Mick Garris (May 13)

   *The Night Flier,* directed by Mark Pavia (November 15)

## 1998

New Englanders stoically endure an ice storm that hits Maine hard. The Kings decide it's time to consider spending winters down south in Florida and begin visiting Sarasota, on the west coast of Florida.

**Recognition**

*Bag of Bones* wins a Bram Stoker Award from the Horror Writers Association.

**Published**

*Bag of Bones: A Novel* (Scribner, trade edition, September). It is the first book published by Scribner after King left Doubleday.

**Visual Adaptation**

*Apt Pupil,* directed by Brian Singer, is released (October 23).

## 1999

SK, while on a daily walk in Bridgton, is hit by a minivan and severely injured (4:30 p.m., on June 19). He's taken to North Cumberland Memorial Hospital (Bridgton) and stabilized for a helicopter flight to Central Maine Medical Center (Lewiston). Bryan Smith, the reckless driver, remarked, "Here it is my bad luck to hit the bestselling writer in the world" (NPR, interview with Stephen King, "The Craft of Writing 'Horror' Stories," July 2, 2010). Smith's driving record proves to be execrable. SK returns home, having lost forty pounds.

**Recognition**

*Bag of Bones* wins a British Fantasy Society Award and a Hugo Award.

**Published**

*Storm of the Century* (Pocket Books, trade paperback edition. February), an illustrated screenplay.

   *The New Lieutenant's Rap* (Philtrum Press, limited edition chapbook, April), a heavily revised version of a short story, "Why We're in Vietnam." Not for sale, it was given out as a keepsake at a publishing party on April 6, 1999, in New York City at Tavern on the Green, to celebrate twenty-five years of King in print.

   *The Girl Who Loved Tom Gordon: A Novel* (Scribner, trade hardback edition, April 6).

   *Hearts in Atlantis: New Fiction* (Scribner, trade hardback edition, September). Two alternate titles considered but not used included *Why We Were . . .* , and *Why We're in Vietnam.* ("Squad D," a short story about a haunted veteran, was solicited by Harlan Ellison for *The Last Dangerous Visions,* which remains unpublished. Ellison has asked King for a rewrite.)

**Visual Adaptations**

   *Storm of the Century* (TV miniseries), directed by Craig R. Baxley (February 14–18)

   *The Green Mile,* directed by Frank Darabont (December 10)

## 2000

### Recognition
*Hearts in Atlantis* wins a Deutscher Phantastik Preis Award.

*On Writing: A Memoir of the Craft* wins a Bram Stoker Award from the Horror Writers Association.

### Published
The Green Mile*: The Complete Serial Novel* (Scribner, trade hardback).

*The Plant: Zenith Rising* (Philtrum Press).

*On Writing: A Memoir of the Craft* (Scribner, trade hardback edition, October).

*Secret Windows: Essays and Fiction on the Craft of Writing* (Book-of-the-Month Club, October).

*Riding the Bullet* (Scribner/Philtrum Press), simultaneously offered for free and for sale online at $2.50, is downloaded four hundred thousand times in a twenty-four-hour period, attesting to SK's brand name appeal. (It is currently available on Amazon for the Kindle.)

*The Plant,* parts 1–6, available from Philtrum Press directly from the King Web site, downloadable for free as two PDF files (parts 1-3, 4-6); it's an unfinished epistolary novel.

### Visual Adaptation
*Trucks* (TV) is released (December 26).

## 2001

SK files a lawsuit against Commercial Union York Insurance that paid his medical claims under his policy, saying they refused to honor the $10 million umbrella policy; he sues for $10 million. It's settled out of court for $750,000, which SK donates to Central Maine Medical Center, where he was taken after the accident.

The Kings pay $8.9 million for a large estate home at Casey Key, Florida, near Sarasota. The house is 7,500 square feet, on the waterfront, and accessible only by a residential road that terminates at its north end.

### Recognition
"Riding the Bullet" wins a Horror Guild award.

*On Writing: A Memoir of the Craft* wins a Horror Guild Award and a Hugo Award.

### Published
*Dreamcatcher: A Novel* (Scribner, trade edition, March). Original title: *Cancer.*

*The Black House: A Novel,* cowritten with Peter Straub (Random House, trade edition, September 15), a sequel to *The Talisman* (1984).

### Visual Adaptation
*Hearts in Atlantis* is released (September 28).

## 2002

SK establishes the Wavedancer Foundation in the wake of audiobook reader Frank Muller's motorcycle accident, which leaves Muller financially devastated and physically wrecked. The foundation exists to help freelance artists of all disciplines who suffer unexpected financial catastrophe, typically in the wake of a health-related issue.

### Recognition
*Black House* wins a Horror Guild award.

SK receives a Lifetime Achievement Award from the Horror Writers Association.

**Published**
*Black House* (Donald M. Grant, Publisher, limited edition and a trade hardback edition boxed in a slipcase with a trade hardback edition of *The Talisman*).

*Everything's Eventual: 14 Dark Tales* (Simon and Schuster, trade hardback edition, March). Original title: *One Headlight*.

*From a Buick 8: A Novel* (Cemetery Dance, limited edition, trade hardback edition; Scribner, trade hardback edition, September 24).

**Visual Adaptation**
*Rose Red* is released (January 27).

### 2003

SK begins writing a pop culture column for *Entertainment Weekly*, "The Pop of King" (July). The column runs for eight years, ending in January 2011. King reflected in the last column, "It's time for Uncle Stevie to grab his walking cane, put on his traveling shoes, and head on down the road."

SK is stricken with double pneumonia, a complication from The Accident, in which a collapsed lung caused an infection, and stays in the hospital for nearly a month (November 23). He undergoes a thoracotomy, and when he returns home, he's down to 160 pounds. Returning home, his office, undergoing renovation, looks abandoned, left behind, as if its owner had passed on. It inspires a novel, *Lisey's Story* (October 24).

**Recognition**
Stephen receives the Medal for Distinguished Contribution to American Letters from the National Book Foundation (November 19).

*Black House* wins a Deutscher Phantastik Preis Award.

*From A Buick 8* wins a Horror Guild Award.

*Everything's Eventual* wins a Horror Guild Award.

SK receives a Living Legends Award from the International Horror Guild.

**Published:**
*The Dark Tower [1]: The Gunslinger* (Viking Press, trade hardback edition, June).

*The Dark Tower [2]: The Drawing of the Three* (Viking Press, trade hardback edition, June).

*The Dark Tower [3]: The Waste Lands* (Viking Press, trade hardback edition, June).

*The Dark Tower [4]: Wizard and Glass* (Viking Press, trade hardback edition, June).

*The Dark Tower [5]: Wolves of the Calla* (Donald M. Grant, Publisher, limited edition and trade hardback edition; Viking Press, trade hardback edition, November). Original title: *The Dark Tower: The Crawling Shadow*.

**Visual Adaptations**
*Dreamcatcher*, directed by Lawrence Kasdan (March 6)

*The Diary of Ellen Rimbauer* (TV), directed by Craig R. Baxley (May 12)

### 2004

The Red Sox win the World Series. The Curse of the Bambino is lifted. SK and Stewart O'Nan are gobsmacked (October 27).

**Recognition**
SK wins a Lifetime Achievement Award from the World Fantasy Convention.

SK is selected as the International Author of the Year and also wins for Best International Web site, from Deutscher Phantastik Preis.

**Published**

*The Girl Who Loved Tom Gordon* (abridged text, a paper-engineered pop-up book for children, from Little Simon Publishing, limited edition, and trade hardback edition, January 1).

*The Dark Tower [6]: Song of Susannah* (Donald M. Grant, Publisher, limited edition and trade hardback edition; Viking Press, trade hardback edition, June).

*The Dark Tower [7]: The Dark Tower* (Donald M. Grant, Publisher, limited edition, and trade hardback edition; Viking Press, trade hardback edition, September).

*'Salem's Lot* (Centipede Press, limited edition, trade edition, October), with fifty additional pages of text from the novel.

*Faithful: Two Diehard Boston Red Sox Fans Chronicle the 2004 Season*, cowritten with Stewart O'Nan (Scribner, December 2).

**Visual Adaptations**

*Kingdom Hospital* (TV), directed by Craig R. Baxley (March 3)

*Secret Window,* directed by David Koepp (March 12)

*'Salem's Lot* (TV), directed by Mikael Salamon (June 2)

*Riding the Bullet,* directed by Mick Garris (October 15)

## 2005

Owen King publishes his first book, *We're All in This Together* (Bloomsbury, June).

Joe Hill King publishes his first book, *20th Century Ghosts* (PS Publishing, October).

**Recognition**

*Faithful,* written with Stewart O'Nan, wins a Quill Award.

*The Dark Tower [7]: The Dark Tower* wins a British Fantasy Society Award and a Deutscher Phantastik Preis Award.

**Published**

*The Colorado Kid* (Dorchester Publishing and Winterfall, Hard Case Crime imprint, mass market paperback edition, October).

*'Salem's Lot: Illustrated Edition* (Doubleday, trade hardback edition, November).

**Published about King**

*Stephen King: Uncollected, Unpublished* (Cemetery Dance, 2005), by Rocky Wood, with David Rawsthorne and Norma Blackburn. This was Rocky Wood's first book on SK.

## 2006

**Recognition**

*Lisey's Story* wins a Bram Stoker Award from the Horror Writers Association.

**Published**

*Cell* (Scribner, trade hardback edition, January).

*Nightmares and Dreamscapes* (Viking Press, trade hardback edition, July 12), an anthology. The stand-out piece is the nonfiction essay, "Head Down" (from the *New Yorker*); "Dolan's Cadillac" makes its first appearance in a trade edition.

The publication of "The Man in the Black Suit" for the Halloween issue of *The New Yorker* (October 31) irks SK: "I don't want to bite the hand that feeds me, and I'm grateful for the exposure, but it's still a little bit like being a prostitute and being put at the head of a float on National Whore's Day" (*Fangoria* magazine).

*Lisey's Story* (Scribner, trade hardback edition, October; 1.1 million first printing). Original title: *Lisey Landon.*

*Secretary of Dreams, Volume 1* (Cemetery Dance, signed limited edition, December), illustrated by Maine artist Glenn Chadbourne.

**Visual Adaptation**
*Desperation,* directed by Mick Garris, is released (May 23).

## 2007

Joe Hill's first novel, *Heart-Shaped Box,* named after a Nirvana song, is published (February 13); he comes out of the shadows and admits he's Stephen King's son. Like his father's admission to being Bachman, Joe Hill found further denials useless: The family resemblance—physically and in his fiction—is undeniable.

SK's mother-in-law, Sarah Jane White Spruce, dies (April 14); she was SK's Red Sox buddy in the family.

The Kings buy a second house on Casey Key for $2.2 million, for visiting family and friends.

In Bangor, the Kings buy the house next door for $750,000, historically known as the Charles P. Brown House.

SK is the guest editor for *Best American Short Stories 2007,* aided by editor Heidi Pitlor.

**Recognition**
SK receives a Lifetime Achievement Award from the Canadian Booksellers Association.
SK receives a Grand Master Award from the Mystery Writers of America.

**Published**
*Blaze,* by Richard Bachman (Scribner, trade hardback edition, June 12).
*The Colorado Kid* (PS Publishing, limited editions with art, variously, by Glenn Chadbourne, J. K. Potter, or Edward Miller; trade hardback edition).
*The Green Mile* (Subterranean Press, limited edition and trade hardback edition).
*Best American Short Stories 2007,* edited by SK (trade hardback edition, October).

**Visual Adaptations**
*1408* directed by Mikael Håfström (June 12)
*The Mist,* directed by Frank Darabont (November 21)

## 2008

**Published**
*Duma Key* (Scribner, trade hardback edition, January).
*Just After Sunset* (Scribner, trade hardback edition, November).
"Stephen King's N." (twenty-five installments serialized online; subsequently issued as a bound-in CD in the "Collector's Set" of *Just After Sunset,* 2008).

## 2009

**Recognition**
"Just After Sunset" wins an Alex Award.
*Duma Key* wins a Black Quill Award and a Bram Stoker Award from the Horror Writers Association.
*Just After Sunset* wins a Bram Stoker Award from the Horror Writers Association.

**Published**
*Stephen King Goes to the Movies* (Plume, trade edition in mass market paperback, January; Subterranean Press, a limited edition but not signed or numbered, April), a collection.

*The Little Sisters of Eluria* (Donald M. Grant, Publisher, limited edition and trade hardback edition).
*Under the Dome* (Scribner, trade hardback edition, November).

**Published on King**
*Stephen King's The Dark Tower: The Complete Concordance* (Cemetery Dance Publications, limited edition of 2000 copies, 2009), by Robin Furth. The first concordance to the Dark Tower series; rigorously researched and definitive.

**2010**

Joe Hill publishes *Horns* (William Morrow, trade hardback, February 16).

**Published**
*Blockade Billy* (Cemetery Dance, limited edition and trade hardback edition; Scribner, trade hardback edition, May).
 *The Secretary of Dreams, Volume 2*, illustrated by Glenn Chadbourne (Cemetery Dance, limited edition and trade edition, October).
 *Full Dark, No Stars* (Scribner, trade hardback edition, November), a collection.

**2011**

**Published**
*Mile 81* (e-book, Simon and Schuster Digital, September 1), an excerpt from *11/22/63*.
 *11/22/63* (Scribner, trade hardback edition, November).

**Visual Adaptation**
*Bag of Bones* (TV), directed by Mick Garris, is released (December 11).

**2012**

**Published**
*The Dark Tower [4.5]: The Wind Through the Keyhole*, illustrated by Jae Lee (Donald M. Grant, Publisher, limited edition and trade hardback edition, February 21; Scribner, trade hardback edition, April 24).
 *A Face in the Crowd*, written with Stewart O'Nan (e-book, Simon and Schuster Digital, August 21).

**Visual Adaptation**
*Mercy*, a film based on the short story "Gramma," is released (December 14).

**Live Performance**
*Ghost Brothers of Darkland County* (theater production), with John Mellencamp, and music directed by T Bone Burnett. (CD and DVD edition, with liner notes, from Concord Music Group.)

**2013**
Owen King publishes *Double Feature* (Scribner, trade hardback, March 19).
 Joe Hill King publishes *NOS4A2* (William Morrow, trade hardback, April 30).

**Published**
*Guns* (Amazon, for Kindle, January).
 *Joyland* (Dorchester Publishing, Hard Case Crime imprint, limited edition and trade hardback edition for the United Kingdom, June; U.S. edition from Hard Case Crime was originally published in paperback only).
 *Ghost Brothers of Darkland County* (Concord Music Group, June 4), packaged with 2 CDs, 1 DVD, and a trade paperback of the libretto (theater production dialogue).
 *The Dark Man* (Cemetery Dance, limited edition and trade hardback edition, July).

*Doctor Sleep* (Cemetery Dance, limited edition and trade edition; Scribner, trade hardback edition, September).

*The Shining* (Subterranean Press, limited edition and trade hardback edition).

**Visual Adaptation**

The first episode of the TV series *Under the Dome* aired on June 24; the third season is to air in 2015.

## 2014

**Published**

*Mr. Mercedes* (Scribner, trade hardback edition, June).

*Revival* (Scribner, trade hardback edition, November).

*Carrie* (Cemetery Dance, artist edition and trade edition, December 23).

**Visual Adaptation**

The film *A Good Marriage* was released (October 3).

## 2015

**Published**

*Finders Keepers*, the second in a trilogy featuring former Detective Bill Hodges (Scribner, trade edition, June 2). The first book in the series is *Mr. Mercedes*, which won an Edgar for "Best Novel" from the Mystery Writers of America.

*Joyland: Illustrated Edition* (a reissue, September 8, from Titan Books/Hardcase Crime).

*The Bazaar of Bad Dreams,* a collection (Scribner, trade hardback edition, November 30).

# ACKNOWLEDGMENTS

Writing may be a solitary act, but publishing is a team effort, and on this book, I am especially grateful for the small army of people who signed up to work on this project and turn an idea into a manuscript, and then into a finished book.

They are listed below in alphabetical order.

I'd first like to thank my friends at St. Martin's Press, who believed in this project, put their shoulders to the wheel, and worked as a synchronized team to take my lengthy manuscript and stack of photos and artwork, and create a beautiful book. Those deserving special mention:

My editor, *Peter Joseph*, this book's first reader who helped shape the final manuscript, and shared my vision for a king-sized book, even as it grew in length and grew... Also in Editorial, *Melanie Fried*, my main contact whose constant stream of emails kept the flow of work moving efficiently. *Angela Gibson*, who carefully and diligently went through this tombstone-sized book and thereby significantly improved it. *Eric Gladstone* and *Susannah Noel* who proofread the book with eagle's eyes to catch errors and omissions I missed.

The production team that gave the book its final shape and look, transforming a pile of manuscript into a handsome book. On a truncated timetable, they pulled everything together in record time: *Elizabeth Curione* (Production Editor), *Cheryl Mamaril* (Production Manager), *Nancy Singer* (Interior Designer), *Ervin Serrano* (Jacket Designer), and *Paul Hochman* (Team Leader).

Finally, with a book on hand, ready to bring into the world, *Justin Velella* (Publicist) got the word out, and *Kelsey Lawrence* (Marketing Manager) got the sales in.

I could not ask for a better task force, which assembled on short notice to take on a king-sized book that proved to be so challenging.

I felt strongly that although my voice is the book's narrative thread, its tapestry was enhanced by the contribution of other hands who have given the book its richness and depth. The contributors—artists, writers, and photographers—reflect multiple perspectives that give the book its scope: Indeed, in an overview that covers forty years of King's life, such a book demands diversity.

The following people deserve special thanks:

*Michael Collings,* who was teaching at Pepperdine University when we first began corresponding about King in the eighties, was instrumental in helping King criticism take root in the academic community. His Starmont Press books lent legitimacy and a tone of seriousness to King criticism that, back then, was sorely lacking.

*Glenn Chadbourne,* a Maine artist who's worked on numerous King projects with Cemetery Dance, cheerfully provided much-needed illustrations, working in real-time as I worked my way through the manuscript. No matter what I threw at him in terms of art requests, Glenn delivered.

*Chris Chesley* spent a full day with me, showing me Durham, and sharing details of his time with King when they both were teens and serious about writing, which resulted in their collaborating. No overview book on King is complete without Chris's voice: He was there from the beginning, and is a talented writer in his own right.

I am grateful to the late *Burton Hatlen,* a pivotal figure and mentor at UMO when King was then an undergraduate, and who, in the post-grad years, become his invaluable friend. I am similarly grateful to his wife, *Virginia Nees-Hatlen,* who gave permission for me to reprint his insightful review of *Carrie,* which took King and his work seriously, and helped shape the tone of King criticism in academia.

Thanks, too, to *Frank Darabont,* whose insightful comments about King and the art of making films bring much to this book.

The late *Rick Hautala,* who attended UMO at the same time King did. Rick gave me an interview, which appears here for the first time, and also shared many anecdotes about King during dinners and get-togethers he and I enjoyed, in the company of Dave Lowell and Glenn Chadbourne. Rick is sorely missed.

The late *Edward M. "Ted" Holmes,* who spent an afternoon sharing his thoughts about Stephen King with me.

*Tim Kirk,* who has worked with me on many projects, allowed me to reprint some previously published art, which was tailor-made for the text. Few artists have the range he has, from horror to fantasy and, especially, whimsy.

*Stephanie Kloss,* a *Library Journal* staffer, kindly let me reprint her illuminating interview with Stephen King's researcher, Russell Dorr.

*Hans-Åke Lilja* gave me carte blanche to reprint anything I wished from his Web site and book, *Lilja's Library: The World of Stephen King.* The interviews I chose, which he conducted, gave the book a depth that otherwise would be sorely missed.

*Dave Lowell,* a Maine writer and my drinking buddy, took innumerable phone calls during the course of this project to provide details about Maine, Maine life, and of course King, whose career he's followed since *Carrie.*

*Tony Magistrale,* who is the chair of the English department at the University of Vermont, gave me carte blanche to reprint anything I wished from his body of work on King. I chose a long interview between the two gentlemen, which distinguishes itself by being the most thoughtful and thought-provoking King interview published to date.

*Rob Montana,* managing editor of the *Times Record,* kindly gave me permission to reprint Don Hansen's article about the Kings' home-brewed newspaper.

*Sanford Phippen* (writer, author, and UMO professor) was, as always, an invaluable resource; he revised and updated his classic non-fiction piece about King's years at UMO, and to my delight and surprise, wrote a long piece reminiscing about his friendship with King over the years.

*J. K. Potter,* a magician working in Photoshop, who gave me an interview for *Knowing Darkness* that shed light on his work with Scream Press for *Skeleton Crew.*

Photographer *Greg Preston,* whose portrait of Michael Whalen graces this book.

*Kevin Quigley,* perhaps the most enthusiastic King fan on the planet, began as a fan writer and became a pro with his fine chapbooks about King from Cemetery Dance. He contributed a fine piece recalling the first time he met King. (Kev, you can be my wingman anytime.)

Photo editor *Anthony Ronzio* of the *Bangor Daily News,* who allowed me to reprint the Carroll Hall photo of King that graced the cover of the 1989 edition of *The Stephen King Companion.*

*Stephen Spignesi,* who has been with me in writing about King every step of the way, provided an introduction on short notice, which perfectly set the stage for the main text that followed.

*Terry Steel,* who designed the Kings' gate for their Bangor home, kindly gave me an interview about his work for them, and also gave me permission to reprint what he wrote about the commission from Taunton Press. I am indebted to both for allowing me to use his material in the first, and now third, edition of this book.

*Drew Struzan,* who warmly welcomed me into his studio to give me an interview about his work for his longtime friend, Frank Darabont, and share his insights on illustrating King's work.

The late *Carroll Terrell,* who gave me an interview that shed light on King as an undergraduate and bestselling writer. I was privileged to work with Carroll in helping him behind the scenes on his book, *Stephen King: Man and Artist.*

*Suzi Thayer,* a photographer/writer for the *Boothbay Register,* responded quickly to my request to reprint her portrait of Glenn Chadbourne, and shared a heartwarming anecdote about King that I published as a sidebar.

*Stuart Tinker*, a longtime Bangorite, who knows more about collecting King's books than anyone on the planet, who provided behind-the-scenes information on all things Bangor.

*Michael Whelan* (one of the busiest artists on the planet) and his wife, *Audrey Price*, aided by their webmaster Mike Jackson, stopped everything they were doing to insure a portfolio of Michael's art would be included herein: sixteen pages in full color that amply showcase his talent. Working as a team, they also edited all the text I needed reviewed on short notice, and promptly returned it, including an interview I conducted with him on the Dark Tower for an art book, *Knowing Darkness*. All I can say is: Wow. And thankee-sai.

*Nye Willden*, King's contact at *Cavalier* magazine, who kindly wrote an article about his reminiscences about those early years with a fledgling writer from Bangor whom he deeply respected.

*David A. Williamson* of Betts Bookstore, who gave me an interview and assisted in other matters, large and small.

*Bernie Wrightson*, whom I met through the late Jeffrey Jones and Vaughn Bodé, who opened his apartment to me and Tim Kirk, and gave us an interview about his collaborations with Stephen King over the years. (Thanks, Bernie, for the coffee and donuts as well.)

On a personal note, I owe thanks, more than I can say, to my longtime friend and literary agent, Scott Mendel of Mendel Media LLC. Scott, who has been with me every step of the way, found the perfect home for this book—St. Martin's Press.

And, finally, my wife, Mary, who has heard me talk about King more than any person should ever have to. A sounding board for the contents of this book in all three editions—1989, 1995, and 2015—Mary, a former English teacher, helped me immeasurably on this book from start to finish.

To anyone whom I have inadvertently overlooked, or whose contribution I haven't properly acknowledged, I extend my sincere apologies.

Thank you, one and all.

# ABOUT THE WRITERS

**George Beahm** is a *New York Times* bestselling author whose books on popular culture and business have been translated into over twenty languages worldwide.

A leading authority on Stephen King, Beahm has published extensively about the writer and his work, including *The Stephen King Companion* (first and second edition), *The Stephen King Story; Stephen King: America's Best-Loved Boogeyman; Stephen King Country; Stephen King Collectibles; Stephen King from A to Z;* and *Knowing Darkness: Artists Inspired by Stephen King.*

He has published books on pop culture figures, including Vaughn Bodé, Tim Kirk, Michael Jordan, Anne Rice, Patricia Cornwell, J. R. R. Tolkien, J. K. Rowling, C. S. Lewis, Philip Pullman, Stephenie Meyer, Caribbean pirates, Indiana Jones, the television show *The Big Bang Theory,* and Lee Child.

His Web site is at www.georgebeahm.com.

**Michael R. Collings** is an educator, literary scholar and critic, poet, novelist, essayist, columnist, reviewer, and editor whose work over the past three decades has concentrated on science fiction, fantasy, and horror, with emphasis on the works of Stephen King and related writers. He has served as Guest, Special Guest, and Guest of Honor at a number of cons, professional as well as fan-oriented, including two-time Academic GoH at the World HorrorCon. He has been twice nominated for the Bram Stoker Award® from the Horror Writers Association, once for non-fiction and once for poetry. Now retired after nearly thirty years as an English professor at Pepperdine University, he lives in Idaho with his wife and number-one fan, Judi, and writes and writes and writes. His Web site is http://michaelcollings.blogspot.com.

**Burton N. Hatlen** (1936–2008) was a Professor of English at the University of Maine for more than forty years. As a young assistant professor in the late '60s, he and colleague Jim Bishop were faculty members of an extracurricular writers' workshop group that lasted for years. Stephen and Tabitha (nee Spruce) King were members. Later, he served as Chair of the English Department and Dean of the College of Arts and Humanities. The recently published *Historical Atlas of Maine* (eds. S. Hornsby and R. Judd) is dedicated to him in recognition of the role he played at the inception of the project when he was Dean by calling together a committee of key scholars, spearheading a critical NEH grant, and working with the Dean of Engineering to hire a master cartographer. Reviewers have called it the best historical atlas in the U.S.

His most sustained service to the profession was achieved as director of the National Poetry Foundation founded by Carroll Terrell, and as editor of *Sagetrieb*, a journal of modern poetry in the tradition of Ezra Pound, William Carlos Williams, Hilda Doolittle, and Charles Olsen.

His scholarly and teaching interests were broad: over the years, he edited a number of scholarly collections for NPF and published elsewhere more than 100 articles, reviews, and enyclopedia entries on such figures as Stephen King, Shakespeare, Mary Shelley, George Oppen, Kay Boyle, Milton, Henry Adams, Zukovsky, Robert Creeley, Ezra Pound, Hilda Doolittle, Charles Olsen, and the Language poets; and on such topics as the teaching of rhetoric and composition and the nexus of politics and poetry in the 20th century.

His first book of selected poems, *I Wanted to Tell You*, was published in 1988 by the NPF, and a second selection, *Late Poems and Valedictions*, will be published by the same press.

**Stephanie Klose** is the media editor for *Library Journal* and the audiobooks editor for *School Library Journal*.

**Hans-Åke Lilja** is the webmaster for Lilja's Library: the World of Stephen King, and author of the books *Lilja's Library: The World of Stephen King* and *The Illustrated Stephen King Movie Trivia Book*. Lilja is one of the leading voices on the Internet covering and reporting on Stephen King's books and news, which he's covered for two decades. His website is an international watering hole for fans wanting more information. Lilja's reviews of King's books and interviews with notable figures in the King community, including King himself, have proven to be invaluable for King students and scholars. Lilja's Web address is www.Liljas-Library.com.

**Dave Lowell** is a Maine writer whose non-fiction first appeared in the official Stephen King newsletter, *Castle Rock*. His novels for adults include *Ghost Trap*, *Say Uncle*, and *Blackbird*. His novels for younger readers include *Shadow Point* and *School-Bots*. His Web site is www.DaveLowell.com.

**Tony Magistrale** is Professor of English at the University of Vermont. He is the author of several books about Stephen King, his novels and films adapted from his work. He is currently writing a new book on *The Shawshank Redemption* entitled *The Shawshank Experience*.

**Kevin Quigley** got hooked on King when he was nine years old and read *Creepshow*, and became a lifelong King fan. In 1997 he began one of the best fan Web sites on King, Charnel House (charnelhouse.tripod.com). He's published several chapbooks about King for Cemetery Dance, including *Blood In Your Ears*, *Chart of Darkness*, *Ink in the Veins*, and *Wetware*.

**Stephen Spignesi** is a university professor and bestselling author whose more than 60 published works include books about Stephen King, the Beatles, American and world history, the *Titanic*, George Washington and the American Presidents, John F. Kennedy Jr., world disasters, Robin Williams, the work of Woody Allen, as well as books on TV, popular culture, Native American history, the lost books of the Bible, and even real estate, jewelry and a cookbook. He is also the author of *Dialogues* (Bantam Dell), a novel praised for "reinventing the psychological thriller." Spignesi blogs and occasionally publishes short stories and essays on his Web site, www.stephenspignesi.weebly.com.

**Sanford Phippen** grew up on the coast of Maine and received his B.A. in English from the University of Maine and his M.A. from Syracuse University. He has been a teacher for 51 years at both the high school and college levels in Maine and New York. He has published 13 books and for six years he was the editor of the *Puckerbrush Review* literary journal. He has written for the *New York Times*, *Maine Times*, *Down East* magazine, *Portland* magazine, *Maine Life*, the Bangor *Daily News*, and other periodicals. His email is: SanPhip@AOL.com.

# About the Artists and Photographers

**Glenn Chadbourne** is a freelance artist specializing in the horror/dark fantasy genres. His work has appeared in numerous books and magazines and has accompanied many of today's top authors, notably Stephen King, for whom he illustrated the two volume set, *The Secretary Of Dreams* (Cemetery Dance Publications). Other King projects include the collector's edition of *Colorado Kid* (PS publishing), *The Dark Man*, an illustrated poem by King, as a book and art portfolio (Cemetery Dance Publications), and an anniversary edition of *Carrie* (PS Publishing). Chadbourne lives in Newcastle, Maine, with his wife Sheila and their Boston terrier Evan. His Web site is www.glennchadbourne.com.

The late **Carroll Hall,** who took the iconic photo of King standing in front of his Bangor home, was a staff photographer for the *Bangor Daily News*.

**Tim Kirk** is a designer and illustrator with wide experience in a broad media spectrum, from greeting cards and book and magazine illustration to theme park and museum exhibit design. Tim's paintings based on J.R.R. Tolkien's epic fantasy *The Lord of the Rings* appeared in the 1975 *Tolkien Calendar* published by Ballantine Books. Tim was employed as an imagineer by the Walt Disney Company for 22 years, and still consults with them for the Disney theme parks worldwide. He is a five-time winner of the prestigious Hugo Award for science fiction and fantasy illustration. His Tolkien artwork can be found in the Greisinger Museum in Switzerland, and in private collections worldwide. Kirk's works can be found online at his official website, www.timkirkcreative.com.

**Greg Preston** (Sampsen Preston Photography) is the author/photographer of *The Artist Within* (Dark Horse Books, 2007), a collection of portraits depicting comic book artists in their home studios. He is currently working on a follow-up book. An accomplished lensman whose work includes numerous assignments for commercial clients, Greg is married to photographer Sharon

Sampsel, whom he met when they were both students at Art Center in Pasadena. Their Web site is: sampselpreston.com.

**Suzi Thayer** has worked at the *Boothbay Register* for 10 years. After majoring in art education in college, she switched to graphics, and has been designing ads and laying out pages for more years than she cares to count. She began writing for the *Register* in 2012, winning a first place award from Maine Press Association in 2012 for her feature on the footbridge owners. She now divides her time between writing about new businesses and local characters, and her newest endeavor, her very own column: "On Eating (*and loving*) Food."

**Michael Whelan** has for four decades created iconic cover art for legends like Asimov and Bradbury, as well as contemporary bestsellers Stephen King and Brandon Sanderson. A native Californian, he graduated from San Jose State as a President's scholar with a degree in Painting, and briefly attended the Art Center College of Design, but he dropped out in 1974 to move east and accept his first book cover assignment.

Thinking that one should be able to tell a book by its cover, Whelan, whose art dominated the science fiction/ fantasy field throughout the 1980's and 90's, was largely responsible for the realistic style on covers of that era. Since 1995 he has also pursued a fine art career, and his non-commissioned works are in established collections throughout the world.

Michael was the first living artist inducted into the Science Fiction Hall of Fame. He is a Spectrum Grand Master, and among his many awards are an unprecedented 15 Hugos, 3 World Fantasy Awards, and 13 Chesleys. *Locus* magazine has named him Best Professional Artist 30 times in their annual poll (including 2014). One of his most favorite honors is the Solstice Award from the Science Fiction Writers of America.

He has published three art books, numerous limited edition prints, posters, and licensed products, available on his Web site, www.MichaelWhelan.com.

His paintings are rich in symbolism and offer many layers of meaning to be explored, but Michael Whelan's lifelong passion has been to live up to his favorite quote from G.K. Chesterton: "The dignity of the artist lies in his duty of keeping awake the sense of wonder in the world."

It is the tale, not he who tells it.

—Stephen King, "The Breathing Method," *Different Seasons* (1982)

*Photo by Carroll Hall reprinted by permission from the* Bangor Daily News.

# Michael Whelan's Color Portfolio

Plate 1: Illustration © 2004. From *The Dark Tower VII: The Dark Tower*, for Part Two: Blue Heaven, Chapter V: "Seek-Tete" (Grant, Publisher, 2004).

Plate 2: "Firestarter" © 1980. Dust jacket illustration for the limited edition of *Firestarter* (1980) from Phantasia Press.

Plate 3: "Gunslinger '88: Roland" © 1988. *The Dark Tower: The Gunslinger* (NAL: Plume, 1988).

Plate 4: "The Gunslinger: On the Beach" © 1982. Illustration for *The Dark Tower: The Gunslinger* (Donald M. Grant, Publisher, 1982).

Plate 5: "The Gunslinger: The Dead Town" © 1982. Illustration for *The Dark Tower: The Gunslinger* (Grant, Publisher, 1982).

Plate 6: "The Gunslinger stood in his dusty boots" © 2008. Illustration for *Little Sisters of Eluria* (Grant, Publisher, 2008).

Plate 7: "The Dark Tower: The Gate of Eluria." Illustration for *The Little Sisters of Eluria* (Grant, 2008). Original version © 2005, revised version [Roland on horse] © 2014.

Plate 8: Interior illustration for *The Dark Tower VII: The Dark Tower* © 2004, for Part Two: Blue Heaven, Chapter V: "Steek-Tete" (Grant, Publisher, 2005).

Plate 9: "Father Callahan" © 2010, for a Web site game, "Discordia" (Stephen King's official website).

Plate 10: "The Dark Tower: Algul Siento" © 2003. Illustration for *The Dark Tower VII: The Dark Tower* (Grant, Publisher, 2004).

Plate 11: "The Gunslinger followed" © 2005. Illustration for *The Dark Tower: The Gunslinger*, published in *The Little Sisters of Eluria* (Grant, Publisher, 2008).

Plate 12: "*Legends* of the Gunslinger" © 2008. Illustration for *The Dark Tower: The Gunslinger*, published in *The Little Sisters of Eluria* (Grant, Publisher). Original version of art © 1998, revised art © 2000.